Improving Web Application Security

Threats and Countermeasures

D1504765

patterns & practices

J.D. Meier, Microsoft Corporation
Alex Mackman, Content Master
Srinath Vasireddy, Microsoft Corporation
Michael Dunner, Microsoft Corporation
Ray Escamilla, Microsoft Corporation
Anandha Murukan, Satyam Computer Services

Contents

Chapter 3

Threat Modeling   45

Part II
Designing Secure Web Applications   67

Chapter 4
Design Guidelines for Secure Web Applications   69

Chapter 5

Architecture and Design Review for Security   99

Part III

Building Secure Web Applications   127

Chapter 6

.NET Security Overview   129

Chapter 7
Building Secure Assemblies   145

Chapter 8

Code Access Security in Practice   **181**

Chapter 9

Using Code Access Security with ASP.NET   221

Chapter 10
Building Secure ASP.NET Pages and Controls

253

Part IV
Securing Your Network, Host, and Application   401

Chapter 15
Securing Your Network   403

Chapter 16

Securing Your Web Server   **421**

Chapter 18
Securing Your Database Server   501

Chapter 19
Securing Your ASP.NET Application and Web Services   543

Part V
Assessing Your Security

Chapter 21
Code Review

Chapter 22
Deployment Review

643

Index of Checklists   **687**

Checklist:

Architecture and Design Review   **689**

Checklist

Securing ASP.NET   **695**

How To

Secure Your Developer Workstation   765

How To

Use IPSec for Filtering Ports and Authentication   777

How To

Use the Microsoft Baseline Security Analyzer   787

How To

Use IISLockdown.exe   795

Forewords

Foreword by Mark Curphey

When the public talks about the Internet, in most cases they are actually talking about the Web. The reality of the Web today never ceases to amaze me, and the tremendous potential for what we can do on the Web is awe-inspiring. But, at the same time, one of the greatest fears for many who want to embrace the Web—the one thing that is often responsible for holding back the rate of change—is the security of Web technology. With the constant barrage of high profile news stories about hackers exposing credit card databases here and finding cunning ways into secret systems there, it's hardly surprising that in a recent survey almost all users who chose not to use Internet banking cited security as the reason. Putting your business online is no longer optional today, but is an essential part of every business strategy. For this reason alone, it is crucial that users have the confidence to embrace the new era.

As with any new technology, there is a delay from the time it is introduced to the market to the time it is really understood by the industry. The breakneck speed at which Web technologies were adopted has widened that window. The security industry as a whole has not kept pace with these changes and has not developed the necessary skills and thought processes to tackle the problem. To fully understand Web security, you must be a developer, a security person, and a process manager. While many security professionals can examine and evaluate the security of a Windows configuration, far fewer have access to the workings of an Internet bank or an online book store, or can fully understand the level of security that an online business requires.

Until a few years ago, the platform choices for building secure Web applications were somewhat limited. Secure Web application development was the exclusive playground of the highly experienced and highly skilled developer (and they were more than happy to let you know that). The .NET Framework and ASP.NET in particular are an exciting and extremely important evolution in the Web technology world and are of particular interest to the security community. With this flexible and extensible security model and a wealth of security features, almost anything is possible in less time and with less effort than on many other platforms. The .NET Framework and ASP.NET are an excellent choice for building highly secure, feature-rich Web sites.

With that array of feature choices comes a corresponding array of decisions, and with each and every decision in the process of designing, developing, deploying, and maintaining a site can have significant security impact and implications.

Improving Web Applications Security: Threats and Countermeasures provides an excellent and comprehensive approach to building highly secure and feature-rich applications using the .NET Framework. It accurately sets the context—that security considerations and issues must be addressed with application design, development, deployment, and maintenance in view, not during any one of these phases in isolation. It cleverly walks you through a process, prescribing actions and making suggestions along the way. By following the guide from start to finish you will learn how to design a secure application by understanding what's important to you, who will attack you, and what they will likely look for, and build countermeasures to protect yourself. The guide provides frameworks, checklists, and expert tips for threat modeling, design and architecture reviews, and implantation reviews to help you avoid common mistakes and be secure from the start. It then delves into the .NET security technology in painstaking detail, leading you through decisions you will need to make, examining security components and things you should be aware of, and focusing on issues that you cannot ignore.

This is the most comprehensive and well-written guide to building secure Web applications that I have seen, and is a must read for anyone building a secure Web site or considering using ASP.NET to provide security for their online business presence.

Mark Curphey

Mark Curphey has a Masters degree in Information Security and runs the Open Web Application Security Project. He moderates the sister security mailing list to Bugtraq called *webappsec* that specializes in Web application security. He is a former Director of Information Security for Charles Schwab, consulting manager for Internet Security Systems, and veteran of more banks and consulting clients than he cares to remember. He now works for a company called Watchfire. He is also a former Java UNIX bigot now turned C#, ASP.NET fan.

Foreword by Joel Scambray

I have been privileged to contribute to *Improving Web Application Security: Threats and Countermeasures,* and its companion volume, *Building Secure ASP.NET Web Applications.* As someone who encounters many such threats and relies on many of these countermeasures every day at Microsoft's largest Internet-facing online properties, I can say that this guide is a necessary component of any Web-facing business strategy. I'm quite excited to see this knowledge shared widely with Microsoft's customers, and I look forward to applying it in my daily work.

There is an increasing amount of information being published about Internet security, and keeping up with it is a challenge. One of the first questions I ask when a new work like this gets published is: "Does the quality of the information justify my time to read it?" In the case of *Improving Web Application Security: Threats and Countermeasures,* I can answer an unqualified *yes.* J.D. Meier and team have assembled a comprehensive reference on Microsoft Web application security, and put it in a modular framework that makes it readily accessible to Web application architects, developers, testers, technical managers, operations engineers, and yes, even security professionals. The bulk of information contained in this work can be intimidating, but it is well-organized around key milestones in the product lifecycle—design, development, testing, deployment, and maintenance. It also adheres to a security principles-based approach, so that each section is consistent with common security themes.

Perhaps my favorite aspect of this guide is the thorough testing that went into each page. During several discussions with the guide's development team, I always came away impressed with their willingness to actually deploy the technologies discussed herein to ensure that the theory portrayed aligned with practical reality. They also freely sought out expertise internal and external to Microsoft to keep the contents useful and practical.

Some other key features that I found very useful include the concise, well-organized, and comprehensive threat modeling chapter, the abundant tips and guidelines on .NET Framework security (especially code access security), and the hands-on checklists for each topic discussed.

Improving Web Application Security: Threats and Countermeasures will get any organization out ahead of the Internet security curve by showing them how to bake security into applications, rather than bolting it on as an afterthought. I highly recommend this guide to those organizations who have developed or deployed Internet-facing applications and to those organizations who are considering such an endeavor.

Joel Scambray
Senior Director of Security, MSN
Co-Author, *Hacking Exposed Fourth Edition,* *Windows,* and *Web Applications*

Foreword by Erik Olson

For many years, application security has been a craft learned by apprenticeship. Unfortunately, the stakes are high and the lessons hard. Most agree that a better approach is needed: we must understand threats, use these hard lessons to develop sound practices, and use solid research practices to provide layers of defense.

Web applications are the portals to many corporate secrets. Whether they sit on the edge of the lawless Internet frontier or safeguard the corporate payroll, these applications are a popular target for all sorts of mischief. Web application developers cannot afford to be uncertain about the risks to their applications or the remedies that mitigate these risks. The potential for damage and the variety of threats is staggering, both from within and without. However, while many threats exist, the remedies can be crystallized into a tractable set of practices and procedures that can mitigate known threats and help to guard against the next unknown threat.

The .NET Framework and the Common Language Runtime were designed and built with these threats in mind. They provide a powerful platform for writing secure applications and a rich set of tools for validating and securing application assets. Note, however, that even powerful tools must be guided by careful hands.

This guide presents a clear and structured approach to dealing with Web application security. In it, you will find the building blocks that enable you to build and deploy secure Web applications using ASP.NET and the .NET Framework.

The guide begins with a vocabulary for understanding the jargon-rich language of security spoken by programmers and security professionals. It includes a catalog of threats faced by Web applications and a model for identifying threats relevant to a given scenario. A formal model is described for identifying, classifying, and understanding threats so that sound designs and solid business decisions can be made.

The text provides a set of guidelines and recommended design and programming practices. These guidelines are the collective wisdom that comes from a deep analysis of both mistakes that have been made and mistakes that have been successfully avoided.

The tools of the craft provided by ASP.NET and the .NET Framework are introduced, with detailed guidance on how to use them. Proven patterns and practices for writing secure code, using data, and building Web applications and services are all documented.

Sometimes the desired solution is not the easiest path. To make it faster and easier to end up in the right place, the authors have carefully condensed relevant sample code from real-world applications into building blocks.

Finally, techniques for assessing application security are provided. The guide contains a set of detailed checklists that can be used as guidelines for new applications or tools to evaluate existing projects.

Whether you're just starting on your apprenticeship in Web application security or have already mastered many of the techniques, you'll find this guide to be an indispensable aid that will help you build more secure Web applications.

Erik Olson
Program Manager, ASP.NET Product Team
Microsoft Corp.

Foreword by Michael Howard

The notion that security is only as good as the weakest link is as valid today as it was 15 or so years ago, and it is especially true in today's Web-enabled applications. This truism was emphasized during the eWeek OpenHack contest of October 2002, when various software vendors were pitted against each other in the most hostile of environments—the Internet. During the contest, the computer running Oracle 9i Application Server was compromised in a little over two hours. The defect, that of not checking that user input was well formed and correct, was not in the core Oracle software. The error lay in the custom application that rode atop the server software. The same error could easily have occurred in any Web-based application written in, say, ASP.NET, Perl, or PHP.

Based on my experience, I can safely say that many people focus on securing the "core" code and features, and give the security of features that depend on the core short shrift. You simply cannot do this in a hostile environment such as the Web. Building secure systems requires skill, education, and discipline at every stage of development: from design to coding to testing to documentation to deployment, and finally, to management. Each and every step must be as secure as possible. This is why I am excited about *Improving Web Application Security: Threats and Countermeasures*. It's the first book to offer a "soup to nuts" view of building a secure Web-based system using the Microsoft .NET Framework and ASP.NET. The fact that the authors chose to focus on the Web-based product development end-to-end lifecycle—and not just on securing small islands of technology—is a testament to much of the work we are undertaking at Microsoft as part of the Trustworthy Computing initiative. Delivering security and privacy to customers requires the engagement of every person involved in the software process, rather than focusing on single events or a single development discipline.

This book has something of value for everyone involved in software development, deployment, and management, because everyone involved in these efforts has an impact on product security. I would urge you, at a minimum, to read the sections that affect your discipline. You will learn critical skills, and most importantly, you will secure every link in the chain. After all, it takes only one loose thread and the entire garment unravels!

Michael Howard
Senior Program Manager, Secure Windows Initiative
Co-author Writing Secure Code

Introduction

This guide gives you a solid foundation for designing, building, and configuring secure ASP.NET Web applications. Whether you have existing applications or are building new ones, you can apply the guidance to help you make sure that your Web applications are hack-resilient.

The information in this guide is based on proven practices for improving your Web application's security. The guidance is task-based and presented in parts that correspond to product life cycles, tasks, and roles.

- **Part I, "Introduction to Threats and Countermeasures,"** identifies and illustrates the various threats facing the network, host, and application layers. The process of threat modeling helps you to identify those threats that can harm your application. By understanding these threats, you can identify and prioritize effective countermeasures.

- **Part II, "Designing Secure Web Applications,"** gives you the guidance you require to design secure Web applications. Even if you have deployed your application, we recommend that you examine and evaluate the concepts, principles, and techniques outlined in this part.

- **Part III, "Building Secure Web Applications,"** allows you to apply the secure design practices introduced in Part II to create secure implementations. You will learn defensive coding techniques that make your code and application resilient to attack.

- **Part IV, "Securing Your Network, Host, and Application,"** describes how you will apply security configuration settings to secure these three interrelated levels. Instead of applying security randomly, you will learn the rationale behind the security recommendations.

- **Part V, "Assessing Your Security,"** provides the tools you require to evaluate the success of your security efforts. Starting with the application, you'll take an inside-out approach to evaluating your code and design. You'll follow this with an outside-in view of the security risks that challenge your network, host and application.

Why We Wrote This Guide

Traditionally, security has been considered a network issue, where the firewall is the primary defense (the fortress model) or something that system administrators handle by locking down the host computers. Application architects and developers have traditionally treated security as an afterthought or as a feature to be considered as time permits—usually after performance considerations are addressed.

The problem with the firewall, or fortress model, is that attacks can pass through network defenses directly to the application. A typical firewall helps to restrict traffic to HTTP, but the HTTP traffic can contain commands that exploit application vulnerabilities. Relying entirely on locking down your hosts is another unsuccessful approach. While several threats can be effectively countered at the host level, application attacks represent a serious and increasing security issue.

Another area where security problems occur is deployment. A familiar scenario is when an application fails when it is deployed in a locked-down production environment, which forces the administrator to loosen security settings. This often leads to new security vulnerabilities. In addition, a lack of security policy or application requirements that are inconsistent with policy can compromise security. One of the goals of this guide is to help bridge this gap between development and operations.

Random security is not enough. To make your application hack-resilient, you need a holistic and systematic approach to securing your network, host, and application. The responsibility spans phases and roles across the product life cycle. Security is not a destination; it is a journey. This guide will help you on your way.

What Is a Hack-Resilient Application?

This guide helps you build hack-resilient applications. A *hack-resilient application* is one that reduces the likelihood of a successful attack and mitigates the extent of damage if an attack occurs. A hack-resilient application resides on a secure host (server) in a secure network and is developed using secure design and development guidelines.

In 2002, eWeek sponsored its fourth Open Hack challenge, which proved that hack-resilient applications can be built using .NET technologies on servers running the Microsoft® Windows® 2000 operating system. The Open Hack team built an ASP.NET Web application using Microsoft Windows 2000 Advanced Server, Internet Information Services (IIS) 5.0, Microsoft SQL Server™ 2000, and the .NET Framework. It successfully withstood more than 82,500 attempted attacks and emerged from the competition unscathed.

This guide shares the methodology and experience used to secure Web applications including the Open Hack application. In addition, the guide includes proven practices that are used to secure networks and Web servers around the world. These methodologies and best practices are condensed and offered here as practical guidance.

Scope of This Guide

Web application security must be addressed across the tiers and at multiple layers. A weakness in any tier or layer makes your application vulnerable to attack.

Securing the Network, Host, and Application

Figure 1 shows the scope of the guide and the three-layered approach that it uses: securing the network, securing the host, and securing the application. It also shows the process called *threat modeling*, which provides a structure and rationale for the security process and allows you to evaluate security threats and identify appropriate countermeasures. If you do not know your threats, how can you secure your system?

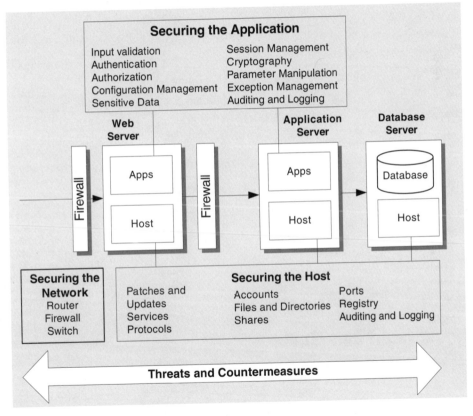

Figure 1
The scope of Improving Web Application Security: Threats and Countermeasures

The guide addresses security across the three physical tiers shown in Figure 1. It covers the Web server, remote application server, and database server. At each tier, security is addressed at the network layer, host layer, and application layer. Figure 1 also shows the configuration categories that the guide uses to organize the various security configuration settings that apply to the host and network, and the application vulnerability categories used to structure application security considerations.

Technologies in Scope

While much of the information in this guide is technology agnostic, the guide focuses on Web applications built with the .NET Framework and deployed on the Windows 2000 Server family of operating systems. The guide also pays special attention to .NET Framework code access security, particularly in relation to the use of code access security with ASP.NET. Where appropriate, new features provided by Windows Server 2003 are highlighted. Table 1 shows the products and technologies that this guidance is based on.

Table 1   Primary Technologies Addressed by This Guide

Area	Product/Technology
Platforms	.NET Framework 1.1
	Windows 2000 Server family
	Windows Server 2003 security features are also highlighted.
Web Server	IIS 5.0 (included with Windows 2000 Server)
Application Server	Windows 2000 Server with .NET Framework 1.1
Database Server	SQL Server 2000
Middleware Technologies	ASP.NET, Enterprise Services, XML Web Services, .NET Remoting
Data Access	ADO.NET

Who Should Read This Guide

This guide is for anyone concerned with planning, building, deploying, or operating Web applications. The guide contains essential information for designers, developers, system administrators, and security analysts.

Designers will learn how to avoid costly security mistakes and how to make appropriate design choices early in the product development life cycle. Developers will learn how to implement defensive coding techniques and build secure code. System administrators will learn how to methodically secure servers and networks, and security analysts will learn how to perform security assessments.

How to Use This Guide

Each chapter in the guide is modular. The guidance is task-based, and is presented in parts which correspond to the various stages of the product development life cycle and to the people and roles involved during the life cycle including architects, developers, system administrators, and security analysts.

Applying the Guidance to Your Role

Each person, regardless of role, who works on the design, development, deployment, or maintenance of Web applications and their underlying infrastructure should read Part I of this guide. Part I, "Introduction to Threats and Countermeasures," highlights and explains the primary threats to Web applications at the network, host, and application layers. It also shows you how to create threat models to help you identify and prioritize those threats that are most relevant to your particular application. A solid understanding of threats and associated countermeasures is essential for anyone who is interested in securing Web applications.

If you are responsible for or are involved in the design of a new or existing Web application, you should read Part II, "Designing Secure Web Applications." Part II helps you identify potential vulnerabilities in your application design.

If you are a developer, you should read Part III, "Building Secure Web Applications." The information in this part helps you to develop secure code and components, including Web pages and controls, Web services, remoting components, and data access code. As a developer, you should also read Part IV, "Securing Your Network, Host, and Application" to gain a better understanding of the type of secure environment that your code is likely to be deployed in. If you understand more about your target environment, the risk of issues and security vulnerabilities appearing at deployment time is reduced significantly.

If you are a system administrator, you should read Part IV, "Securing Your Network, Host, and Application." The information in this part helps you create a secure network and server infrastructure—one that is tuned to support .NET Web applications and Web services.

Anyone who is responsible for reviewing product security should read Part V, "Assessing Your Security". This helps you identify vulnerabilities caused by insecure coding techniques or deployment configurations.

Applying the Guidance to Your Product Life Cycle

Different parts of the guide apply to the different phases of the product development life cycle. The sequence of chapters in the guide mirrors the typical phases of the life cycle. Figure 2 shows how the parts and chapters correspond to the phases of a classic product development life cycle.

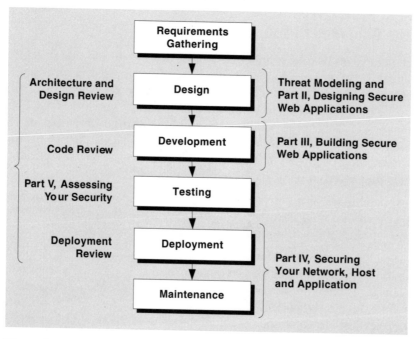

Figure 2

Improving Web Application Security: Threats and Countermeasures as it relates to product lifecycle

Microsoft Solutions Framework

If you use and are more familiar with the Microsoft Solutions Framework (MSF), Figure 3 shows a similar life cycle mapping, this time in relation to the MSF Process Model.

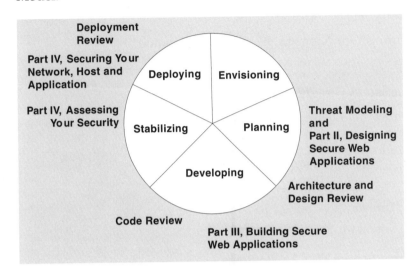

Figure 3
Improving Web Application Security: Threats and Countermeasures as it relates to MSF

Organization of This Guide

You can read this guide from end to end, or you can read the chapters you need for your job. For a quick overview of the guide, refer to the "Fast Track" section.

Solutions at a Glance

The "Solutions at a Glance" section provides a problem index for the guide, highlighting key areas of concern and where to go for more detail.

Fast Track

The "Fast Track" section in the front of the guide helps you implement the recommendations and guidance quickly and easily.

Parts

This guide is divided into five parts:

- Part I, Introduction to Threats and Countermeasures
- Part II, Designing Secure Web Applications
- Part III, Building Secure Web Applications
- Part IV, Securing Your Network, Host, and Application
- Part V, Assessing Your Security

Part I, Introduction to Threats and Countermeasures

This part identifies and illustrates the various threats facing the network, host, and application layers. By using the threat modeling process, you can identify the threats that are relevant to your application. This sets the stage for identifying effective countermeasures. This part includes:

- Chapter 1, "Web Application Security Fundamentals"
- Chapter 2, "Threats and Countermeasures"
- Chapter 3, "Threat Modeling"

Part II, Designing Secure Web Applications

This part provides the guidance you need to design your Web applications securely. Even if you have an existing application, you should review this section and then revisit the concepts, principles, and techniques that you used during your application design. This part includes:

- Chapter 4, "Design Guidelines for Secure Web Applications"
- Chapter 5, "Architecture and Design Review for Security"

Part III, Building Secure Web Applications

This part helps you to apply the secure design practices and principles covered in the previous part to create a solid and secure implementation. You'll learn defensive coding techniques that make your code and application resilient to attack. Chapter 6 presents an overview of the .NET Framework security landscape so that you are aware of the numerous defensive options and tools that are at your disposal. Part III includes:

- Chapter 6, ".NET Security Fundamentals"
- Chapter 7, "Building Secure Assemblies"
- Chapter 8, "Code Access Security in Practice"
- Chapter 9, "Using Code Access Security with ASP.NET"
- Chapter 10, "Building Secure ASP.NET Pages and Controls"
- Chapter 11, "Building Secure Serviced Components"

- Chapter 12, "Building Secure Web Services"
- Chapter 13, "Building Secure Remoted Components"
- Chapter 14, "Building Secure Data Access"

Part IV, Securing Your Network, Host, and Application

This part shows you how to apply security configuration settings to secure the interrelated network, host, and application levels. Rather than applying security randomly, you'll learn the reasons for the security recommendations. Part IV includes:

- Chapter 15, "Securing Your Network"
- Chapter 16, "Securing Your Web Server"
- Chapter 17, "Securing Your Application Server"
- Chapter 18, "Securing Your Database Server"
- Chapter 19, "Securing Your ASP.NET Application and Web Services"
- Chapter 20, "Hosting Multiple Web Applications"

Part V, Assessing Your Security

This part provides you with the tools you need to evaluate the success of your security efforts. It shows you how to evaluate your code and design and also how to review your deployed application, to identify potential vulnerabilities.

- Chapter 21, "Code Review"
- Chapter 22, "Deployment Review"

Checklists

This section contains printable, task-based checklists, which are quick reference sheets to help you turn information into action. This section includes the following checklists:

- Checklist: Architecture and Design Review
- Checklist: Securing ASP.NET
- Checklist: Securing Web Services
- Checklist: Securing Enterprise Services
- Checklist: Securing Remoting
- Checklist: Securing Data Access
- Checklist: Securing Your Network
- Checklist: Securing Your Web Server
- Checklist: Securing Your Database Server
- Checklist: Security Review for Managed Code

"How To" Articles

This section contains "How To" articles, which provide step-by-step procedures for key tasks. This section includes the following articles:

- How To: Implement Patch Management
- How To: Harden the TCP/IP Stack
- How To: Secure Your Developer Workstation
- How To: Use IPSec for Filtering Ports and Authentication
- How To: Use the Microsoft Baseline Security Analyzer
- How To: Use IISLockdown.exe
- How To: Use URLScan
- How To: Create a Custom Encryption Permission
- How To: Use Code Access Security Policy to Constrain an Assembly

Approach Used in This Guide

If your goal is a hack-resilient application, how do you get there? The approach used in this guide is as follows:

- Secure your network, host, and application
- Focus on threats
- Follow a principle-based approach

Secure Your Network, Host, and Application

Security must be addressed at three levels: network, host, and application. A weakness at any layer can be exploited by an attacker. This guide takes a holistic approach to application security and applies it at all three levels. The holistic approach to security is shown in Figure 4.

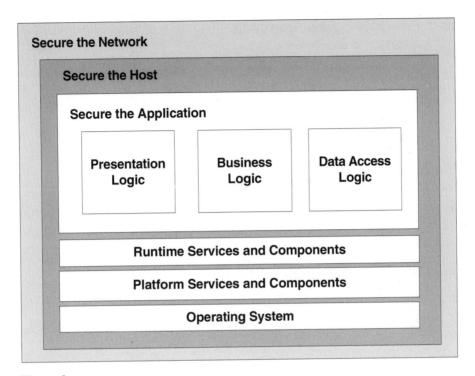

Figure 4
A holistic approach to security

Figure 4 shows the multiple layers covered by the guide, including the network, host, and application. The host layer covers the operating system, platform services and components, and run-time services and components. Platform services and components include SQL Server and Enterprise Services. Run-time services and components include ASP.NET and .NET code access security among others.

Focus on Threats

Your application's security measures can become useless, or even counter productive, if those measures are applied without knowing the threats that the security measures are designed to mitigate.

Threats can be external, such as attacker on the Internet, or internal, for example, a disgruntled employee or administrator. This guide helps you identify threats in two ways:

- It enumerates the top threats that affect Web applications at the network, host, and application levels.
- It helps you to identify which threats are relevant to your application through a process called *threat modeling*.

Follow a Principle-Based Approach

Recommendations used throughout this guide are based on security principles that have proven themselves over time. The analysis and consideration of threats prior to product implementation or deployment lends itself to a principle-based approach where core principles can be applied, regardless of implementation technology or application scenario.

Positioning of This Guide

This is Volume II in a series dedicated to helping customers plan, build, deploy, and operate secure Web applications: Volume I, *Building Secure ASP.NET Applications: Authentication, Authorization, and Secure Communication*, and Volume II, *Improving Web Application Security: Threats and Countermeasures*.

Volume I, Building Secure ASP.NET Applications

Building Secure ASP.NET Applications helps you to build a robust authentication and authorization mechanism for your application. It focuses on identity management through the tiers of a distributed Web application. By developing a solid authentication and authorization strategy early in the design, you can eliminate a high percentage of application security issues. The primary audience for Volume I is architects and lead developers.

Figure 5 shows the scope of Volume I. The guide addresses authentication, authorization, and secure communication across the tiers of a distributed Web application. The technologies that are covered are the same as the current guide and include Windows 2000 Server, IIS, ASP.NET Web applications and Web services, Enterprise Services, .NET Remoting, SQL Server, and ADO.NET.

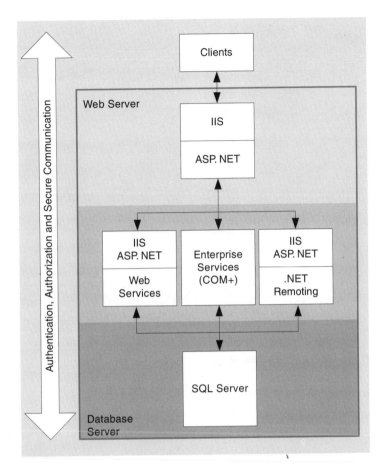

Figure 5
Scope of Volume I, Building Secure ASP.NET Applications

Volume II, Improving Web Application Security

This guide helps you build and maintain hack-resilient applications. It takes a broader look at security across the tiers, focusing on threats and countermeasures at the network, host, and application levels. The intended audience is broader and the guidance can be applied throughout the product life cycle.

For additional related work, see the "Resources" chapter provided at the end of the guide.

Feedback and Support

We have made every effort to ensure the accuracy of this guide and its companion content.

Feedback on the Guide

If you have comments on this guide, send e-mail to *secguide@microsoft.com*. We are particularly interested in feedback regarding the following:

- Technical issues specific to recommendations
- Usefulness and usability issues
- Writing and editing issues

Technical Support

Technical support for the Microsoft products and technologies referenced in this guide is provided by Microsoft Product Support Services (PSS). For product support information, please visit the Microsoft Product Support Web site at *http://support.microsoft.com*.

Community and Newsgroup Support

MSDN Newsgroups: *http://msdn.microsoft.com/newsgroups/default.asp*

Table 2   Newsgroups

Newsgroup	Address
.NET Framework Security	microsoft.public.dotnet.security
ASP.NET Security	microsoft.public.dotnet.framework.aspnet.security
Enterprise Services	microsoft.public.dotnet.framework_component_services
Web Services	microsoft.public.dotnet.framework.aspnet.webservices
Remoting	microsoft.public.dotnet.framework.remoting
ADO.NET	microsoft.public.dotnet.framework.adonet
SQL Server Security	microsoft.public.sqlserver.security
MBSA	microsoft.public.security.baseline_analyzer
Virus	microsoft.public.security.virus
IIS Security	microsoft.public.inetserver.iis.security

The Team Who Brought You This Guide

This guide was produced by the following .NET development specialists:

- **J.D. Meier**, Microsoft, Program Manager, Prescriptive Architecture Guidance (PAG)
- **Alex Mackman**, Content Master Ltd, Founding member and Principal Technologist
- **Srinath Vasireddy**, Microsoft, Developer Support Engineer, PSS
- **Michael Dunner**, Microsoft, Developer Support Engineer, PSS
- **Ray Escamilla**, Microsoft, Developer Support Engineer, PSS
- **Anandha Murukan**, Satyam Computer Services

Contributors and Reviewers

Many thanks to the following contributors and reviewers:

- Thanks to external reviewers: Mark Curphey, Open Web Application Security Project and Watchfire; Andy Eunson (extensive review); Anil John (code access security and hosting scenarios); Paul Hudson and Stuart Bonell, Attenda Ltd. (extensive review of the Securing series); Scott Stanfield and James Walters, Vertigo Software; Lloyd Andrew Hubbard; Matthew Levine; Lakshmi Narasimhan Vyasarajan, Satyam Computer Services; Nick Smith, Senior Security Architect, American Airlines (extensive review of the Securing series); Ron Nelson; Senthil Rajan Alaguvel, Infosys Technologies Limited; Roger Abell, Engineering Technical Services, Arizona State University; and Doug Thews.

- Microsoft Product Group: Michael Howard (Threat Modeling, Code Review, and Deployment Review); Matt Lyons (demystifying code access security); Caesar Samsi; Erik Olson (extensive validation and recommendations on ASP.NET); Andres De Vivanco (securing SQL Server); Riyaz Pishori (Enterprise Services); Alan Shi; Carlos Garcia Jurado Suarez; Raja Krishnaswamy, CLR Development Lead; Christopher Brown; Dennis Angeline; Ivan Medvedev (code access security); Jeffrey Cooperstein (Threat Modeling); Frank Swiderski; Manish Prabhu (.NET Remoting); Michael Edwards, MSDE; Pranish Kumar, (VC++ PM); Richard Waymire (SQL Security); Sebastian Lange; Greg Singleton; Thomas Deml (IIS Lead PM); Wade Hilmo (IIS); Steven Pratschner; Willis Johnson (SQL Server); and Girish Chander (SQL Server).

- Microsoft Consulting Services and Product Support Services (PSS): Ilia Fortunov (Senior Architect) for providing continuous and diligent feedback; Aaron Margosis (extensive review, script injection, and SQL Injection); Jacquelyn Schmidt; Kenny Jones; Wade Mascia (Web Services and Enterprise services); Aaron Barth; Jackie Richards; Aaron Turner; Andy Erlandson (Director of PSS Security); Jayaprakasam Siddian Thirunavukkarasu (SQL Server security); Jeremy Bostron; Jerry Bryant; Mike Leuzinger; Robert Hensing (reviewing the Securing series); Gene Ferioli; David Lawler; Jon Wall (threat modeling); Martin Born; Michael Thomassy; Michael Royster; Phil McMillan; and Steven Ramirez.

- Thanks to Joel Scambray; Rich Benack; Alisson Sol; Tavi Siochi (IT Audit); Don Willits (raising the quality bar); Jay Nanduri (Microsoft.com) for reviewing and sharing real world experience; Devendra Tiwari and Peter Dampier, for extensive review and sharing best IT practices; Denny Dayton; Carlos Lyons; Eric Rachner; Justin Clarke; Shawn Welch (IT Audit); Rick DeJarnette; Kent Sharkey (Hosting scenarios); Andy Oakley; Vijay Rajagopalan (Dev Lead MS Operations); Gordon Ritchie, Content Master Ltd; Chase Carpenter (Threat Modeling); Matt Powell (for Web Services security); Joel Yoker; Juhan Lee [MSN Operations]; Lori Woehler; Mike Sherrill; Mike Kass; Nilesh Bhide; Rebecca Hulse; Rob Oikawa (Architect); Scott Greene; Shawn Nandi; Steve Riley; Mark Mortimore; Matt Priestley; and David Ross.

- Thanks to our editors: Sharon Smith; Kathleen Hartman (S&T OnSite); Tina Burden (Entirenet); Cindy Riskin (S&T OnSite); and Pat Collins (Entirenet) for helping to ensure a quality experience for the reader.

- Finally, thanks to Naveen Yajaman; Philip Teale; Scott Densmore; Ron Jacobs; Jason Hogg; Per Vonge Nielsen; Andrew Mason; Edward Jezierski; Michael Kropp; Sandy Khaund; Shaun Hayes; Mohammad Al-Sabt; Edward Lafferty; Ken Perilman; and Sanjeev Garg (Satyam Computer Services).

Tell Us About Your Success

If this guide helps you, we would like to know. Tell us by writing a short summary of the problems you faced and how this guide helped you out. Submit your summary to:

MyStory@Microsoft.com.

Summary

In this introduction, you were shown the structure of the guide and the basic approach used by the guide to secure Web applications. You were also shown how to apply the guidance to your role or to specific phases of your product development life cycle.

Solutions at a Glance

This document roadmap summarizes the solutions presented in *Improving Web Application Security: Threats and Countermeasures*. It provides links to the appropriate material in the guide so that you can easily locate the information you need and find solutions to specific problems.

Architecture and Design Solutions

For architects, the guide provides the following solutions to help you design secure Web applications:

- **How to identify and evaluate threats**

  Use threat modeling to systematically identify threats rather than applying security in a haphazard manner. Next, rate the threats based on the risk of an attack or occurrence of a security compromise and the potential damage that could result. This allows you to tackle threats in the appropriate order.

  For more information about creating a threat model and evaluating threat risks, see Chapter 3, "Threat Modeling."

- **How to create secure designs**

  Use tried and tested design principles. Focus on the critical areas where the correct approach is essential and where mistakes are often made. This guide refers to these as *application vulnerability categories*. They include input validation, authentication, authorization, configuration management, sensitive data protection, session management, cryptography, parameter manipulation, exception management, and auditing and logging considerations. Pay serious attention to deployment issues including topologies, network infrastructure, security policies, and procedures.

  For more information, see Chapter 4, "Design Guidelines for Secure Web Applications."

- **How to perform an architecture and design review**

  Review your application's design in relation to the target deployment environment and associated security policies. Consider the restrictions imposed by the underlying infrastructure layer security, including perimeter networks, firewalls, remote application servers, and so on. Use application vulnerability categories to help partition your application, and analyze the approach taken for each area.

  For more information, see Chapter 5, "Architecture and Design Review for Security."

Development Solutions

For developers, this guide provides the following solutions:

- **What is .NET Framework security?**

  The .NET Framework provides user and code security models that allow you to restrict what users can do and what code can do. To program role-based security and code access security, use types from the **System.Security** namespace. The .NET Framework also provides the **System.Security.Cryptography** namespace, which exposes symmetric and asymmetric encryption and decryption, hashing, random number generation, support for digital signatures, and more.

  To understand the .NET Framework security landscape, see Chapter 6, ".NET Security Overview."

- **How to write secure managed code**

  Use strong names to digitally sign your assemblies and to make them tamperproof. At the same time you need to be aware of strong name issues when you use strong name assemblies with ASP.NET. Reduce your assembly attack profile by adhering to solid object oriented design principles, and then use code access security to further restrict which code can call your code. Use structured exception handling to prevent sensitive information from propagating beyond your current trust boundary and to develop more robust code. Avoid canonicalization issues, particularly with input file names and URLs.

  For information about how to improve the security of your managed code, see Chapter 7, "Building Secure Assemblies." For more information about how to use code access security effectively to further improve security, see Chapter 8, "Code Access Security in Practice." For information about performing managed code reviews, see Chapter 21, "Code Review."

- **How to handle exceptions securely**

  Do not reveal internal system or application details, such as stack traces, SQL statement fragments, and so on. Ensure that this type of information is not allowed to propagate to the end user or beyond your current trust boundary.

  Fail securely in the event of an exception, and make sure your application denies access and is not left in an insecure state. Do not log sensitive or private data such as passwords, which could be compromised. When you log or report exceptions, if user input is included in exception messages, validate it or sanitize it. For example, if you return an HTML error message, you should encode the output to avoid script injection.

  For more information, see the "Exception Management" sections in Chapter 7, "Building Secure Assemblies," and in Chapter 10, "Building Secure ASP.NET Pages and Controls."

- **How to perform security reviews of managed code**

  Use analysis tools such as FxCop to analyze binary assemblies and to ensure that they conform to the .NET Framework design guidelines. Fix any security vulnerabilities identified by your analysis tools. Use a text search facility to scan your source code base for hard-coded secrets such as passwords. Then, review specific elements of your application including Web pages and controls, data access code, Web services, serviced components, and so on. Pay particular attention to SQL injection and cross-site scripting vulnerabilities.

  Also review the use of sensitive code access security techniques such as link demands and asserts. For more information, see Chapter 21, "Code Review."

- **How to secure a developer workstation**

  You can apply a methodology when securing your workstation. Secure your accounts, protocols, ports, services, shares, files and directories, and registry. Most importantly, keep your workstation current with the latest patches and updates. If you run Internet Information Services (IIS) on Microsoft Windows® XP or Windows 2000, then run IISLockdown. IISLockdown applies secures IIS configurations and installs the URLScan Internet Security Application Programming Interface (ISAPI) filter, which detects and rejects potentially malicious HTTP requests. You may need to modify the default URLScan configuration, for example, so you can debug Web applications during development and testing.

  For more information, see "How To: Secure Your Developer Workstation," in the "How To" section of this guide.

- **How to use code access security with ASP.NET**

  With .NET Framework version 1.1, you can set ASP.NET trust levels either in Machine.config or Web.config. These trust levels use code access security to restrict the resources that ASP.NET applications can access, such as the file system, registry, network, databases, and so on. In addition, they provide application isolation.

  For more information about using code access security from ASP.NET, developing partial trust Web applications, and sandboxing privileged code, see Chapter 9, "Using Code Access Security with ASP.NET."

  For more information about code access security fundamentals, see Chapter 8, "Code Access Security in Practice."

  For more information about the code access security issues that you need to consider when developing managed code, see the "Code Access Security Considerations" sections in Chapter 11, "Building Secure Serviced Components," Chapter 12, "Building Secure Web Services," "Building Secure Remoted Components," and Chapter 14, "Building Secure Data Access."

- **How to write least privileged code**

  You can restrict what code can do regardless of the account used to run the code. You can use code access security to constrain the resources and operations that your code is allowed to access, either by configuring policy or how you write your code. If your code does not need to access a resource or perform a sensitive operation such as calling unmanaged code, you can use declarative security attributes to ensure that your code cannot be granted this permission by an administrator.

  For more information, see Chapter 8, "Code Access Security in Practice."

- **How to constrain file I/O**

  You can use code access security to constrain an assembly's ability to access areas of the file system and perform file I/O. For example, you can constrain a Web application so that it can only perform file I/O beneath its virtual directory hierarchy. You can also constrain file I/O to specific directories. You can do this programmatically or by configuring code access security policy.

  For more information, see "File I/O" in Chapter 8, "Code Access Security in Practice" and "Medium Trust" in Chapter 9, "Using Code Access Security with ASP.NET." For more information about configuring code access security policy, see "How To: Use Code Access Security Policy to Constrain an Assembly" in the "How To" section of this guide.

- **How to prevent SQL injection**

  Use parameterized stored procedures for data access. The use of parameters ensures that input values are checked for type and length. Parameters are also treated as safe literal values and not executable code within the database. If you cannot use stored procedures, use SQL statements with parameters. Do not build SQL statements by concatenating input values with SQL commands. Also, ensure that your application uses a least privileged database login to constrain its capabilities in the database.

  For more information about SQL injection and for further countermeasures, see "SQL Injection" in Chapter 14, "Building Secure Data Access."

- **How to prevent cross-site scripting**

  Validate input for type, length, format, and range, and encode output. Encode output if it includes input, including Web input. For example, encode form fields, query string parameters, cookies and so on, and encode input read from a database (especially a shared database) where you cannot assume the data is safe. For free format input fields that you need to return to the client as HTML, encode the output and then selectively remove the encoding on permitted elements such as the <b> or <i> tags for formatting.

  For more information, see "Cross-Site Scripting" in Chapter 10, "Building ASP.NET Pages and Controls."

- **How to manage secrets**

  Look for alternate approaches to avoid storing secrets in the first place. If you must store them, do not store them in clear text in source code or in configuration files. Encrypt secrets with the Data Protection Application Programming Interface (DPAPI) to avoid key management issues.

  For more information, see "Sensitive Data" in Chapter 10, "Building Secure ASP.NET Pages and Controls," "Cryptography" in Chapter 7, "Building Secure Assemblies," and "Aspnet_setreg.exe and Process, Session, and Identity" in Chapter 19, " Securing Your ASP.NET Application and Web Services."

- **How to call unmanaged code securely**

  Pay particular attention to the parameters passed to and from unmanaged APIs, and guard against potential buffer overflows. Validate the lengths of input and output string parameters, check array bounds, and be particularly careful with file path lengths. Use custom permission demands to protect access to unmanaged resources before asserting the unmanaged code permission. Use caution if you use **SuppressUnmanagedCodeSecurityAttribute** to improve performance.

  For more information, see the "Unmanaged Code" sections in Chapter 7, "Building Secure Assemblies," and Chapter 8, "Code Access Security in Practice."

- **How to perform secure input validation**

  Constrain, reject, and sanitize your input because it is much easier to validate data for known valid types, patterns, and ranges than it is to validate data by looking for known bad characters. Validate data for type, length, format, and range. For string input, use regular expressions. To perform type checks, use the .NET Framework type system. On occasion, you may need to sanitize input. An example is encoding data to make it safe.

  For input validation design strategies, see "Input Validation" in Chapter 4, "Design Guidelines for Secure Web Applications." For implementation details, see the "Input Validation" sections in Chapter 10, "Building Secure ASP.NET Pages and Controls," Chapter 12, "Building Secure Web Services," Chapter 13, "Building Secure Remoted Components," and Chapter 14, "Building Secure Data Access."

- **How to secure Forms authentication**

  Partition your Web site to separate publicly accessible pages available to anonymous users and restricted pages which require authenticated access. Use Secure Sockets Layer (SSL) to protect the forms authentication credentials and the forms authentication cookie. Limit session lifetime and ensure that the authentication cookie is passed over HTTPS only. Encrypt the authentication cookie, do not persist it on the client computer, and do not use it for personalization purposes; use a separate cookie for personalization.

  For more information, see the "Authentication" sections in Chapter 19, "Securing Your ASP.NET Application and Web Services," and Chapter 10, "Building Secure ASP.NET Pages and Controls."

Administration Solutions

For administrators, this guide provides the following solutions:

- **How to implement patch management**

  Use the Microsoft Baseline Security Analyzer (MBSA) to detect the patches and updates that may be missing from your current installation. Run this on a regular basis, and keep your servers current with the latest patches and updates. Back up servers prior to applying patches, and test patches on test servers prior to installing them on a production server. Also, use the security notification services provided by Microsoft, and subscribe to receive security bulletins via e-mail.

  For more information, see "How To: Implement Patch Management" in the "How To" section of this guide.

- **How to make the settings in Machine.config and Web.config more secure**

  Do not store passwords or sensitive data in plaintext. For example, use the Aspnet_setreg.exe utility to encrypt the values for **<processModel>**, **<identity>**, and **<sessionState>**. Do not reveal exception details to the client. For example do not use **mode="Off"** for **<customErrors>** in ASP.NET because it causes detailed error pages that contain system-level information to be returned to the client. Restrict who has access to configuration files and settings. Lock configuration settings if necessary, using the **<location>** tag and the **allowOverride** element.

  For more information on improving the security of Machine.config and Web.config for your scenario, see Chapter 19, "Securing Your ASP.NET Application and Web Services." For more information on the **<location>** tag, see "Machine.Config and Web.Config" explained in Chapter 19, "Securing Your ASP.NET Application and Web Services." For more information on Aspnet_setreg.exe, see "Aspnet_setreg.exe and Process, Session, and Identity" in Chapter 19, "Securing Your ASP.NET Application and Web Services."

- **How to secure a Web server running the .NET Framework**

  Apply a methodology to systematically configure the security of your Web server. Secure your accounts, protocols, ports, services, shares, files and directories, and registry. You can use IISLockdown to help automate some of the security configuration. Use a hardened Machine.config configuration to apply stringent security to all .NET Framework applications installed on the server. Most importantly, keep your server current with the latest patches and updates.

  For more information, see Chapter 16, "Securing Your Web Server."

- **How to secure a database server**

  Apply a common methodology to evaluate accounts, protocols, ports, services, shares, files and directories, and the registry. Also evaluate SQL Server™ security settings such as the authentication mode and auditing configuration. Evaluate your authorization approach and use of SQL Server logins, users, and roles. Make sure you have the latest service pack and regular monitor for operating system and SQL Server patches and updates.

  For more information, see Chapter 18, "Securing Your Database Server."

- **How to secure an application server**

  Evaluate accounts, protocols, ports, services, shares, files and directories, and the registry. Use Internet Protocol Security (IPSec) or SSL to secure the communication channel between the Web server and the application server, and between the application server and the database server. Review the security of your Enterprise Services applications, Web services, and remoting applications. Restrict the range of ports with which clients can connect to the application server, and consider using IPSec restrictions to limit the range of clients.

  For more information, see Chapter 17, "Securing Your Application Server."

- **How to host multiple ASP.NET applications securely**

  Use separate identities to allow you to configure access control lists (ACLs) on secure resources to control which applications have access to them. On the Microsoft Windows Server 2003 operating system, use separate process identities with IIS 6 application pools. On Windows 2000 Server, use multiple anonymous Internet user accounts and enable impersonation. With the .NET Framework version 1.1 on both platforms, you can use partial trust levels and use code access security to provide further application isolation. For example, you can use these methods to prevent applications from accessing each other's virtual directories and critical system resources.

  For more information, see Chapter 20, "Hosting Multiple ASP.NET Applications."

- **How to secure Web services**

  In cross-platform scenarios and where you do not control both endpoints, use the Web Services Enhancements 1.0 for Microsoft .NET (WSE) to implement message level security solutions that conform to the emerging WS-Security standard. Pass authentication tokens in Simple Object Access Protocol (SOAP) headers. Use XML encryption to ensure that sensitive data remains private. Use digital signatures for message integrity. Within the enterprise where you control both endpoints, you can use the authentication, authorization, and secure communication features provided by the operating system and IIS.

  For more information, see Chapter 17, "Securing Your Application Server," Chapter 19, "Securing Your ASP.NET Application and Web Services." For information about developing secure Web services, see Chapter 12, "Building Secure Web Services."

- **How to secure Enterprise Services**

  Configure server applications to run using least privileged accounts. Enable COM+ role-based security, and enforce component-level access checks. At the minimum, use call-level authentication to prevent anonymous access. To secure the traffic passed to remote serviced components, use IPSec encrypted channels or use remote procedure call (RPC) encryption. Restrict the range of ports that Distributed COM (DCOM) dynamically allocates or use static endpoint mapping to limit the port range to specific ports. Regularly monitor for Quick Fix Engineer (QFE) updates to the COM+ runtime.

  For more information, see Chapter 17, "Securing Your Application Server."

- **How to secure Microsoft .NET Remoting**

  Disable remoting on Internet-facing Web servers by mapping .rem and .soap extensions to the ASP.NET **HttpForbiddenHandler** HTTP module in Machine.config. Host in ASP.NET and use the **HttpChannel** type name to benefit from ASP.NET and IIS authentication and authorization services. If you need to use the **TcpChannel** type name, host your remote components in a Windows service and use IPSec to restrict which clients can connect to your server. Use this approach only in a trusted server situation, where the remoting client (for example a Web application) authenticates and authorizes the original callers.

  For more information, see Chapter 17, "Securing Your Application Server."

- **How to secure session state**

  You need to protect session state while in transit across the network and while in the state store. If you use a remote state store, secure the communication channel to the state store using SSL or IPSec. Also encrypt the connection string in Machine.config. If you use a SQL Server state store, use Windows authentication when you connect to the state store, and limit the application login in the database. If you use the ASP.NET state service, use a least privileged account to run the service, and consider changing the default port that the service listens to. If you do not need the state service, disable it.

  For more information, see "Session State" in Chapter 19, "Securing Your ASP.NET Application and Web Services."

- **How to manage application configuration securely**

  Remote administration should be limited or avoided. Strong authentication should be required for administrative interfaces. Restrict access to configuration stores through ACLs and permissions. Make sure you have the granularity of authorization required to support separation of duties.

  For general considerations for secure configuration management, see Chapter 4, "Design Guidelines for Secure Web Applications." To verify the secure defaults and ensure that you apply secure machine-wide settings and secure application specific settings, see Chapter 19, "Securing Your ASP.NET Application and Web Services."

- **How to secure against denial of service attacks**

  Make sure the TCP/IP stack configuration on your server is hardened to protect against attacks such as SYN floods. Configure ASP.NET to limit the size of accepted POST requests and to place limits on request execution times.

  For more information about hardening TCP/IP, see "How To: Harden the TCP/IP Stack" in the "How To" section of this guide. For more information about ASP.NET settings used to help prevent denial of service, see Chapter 19, "Securing Your ASP.NET Application and Web Services."

- **How to constrain file I/O**

  You can configure code access security policy to ensure that individual assemblies or entire Web applications are limited in their ability to access the file system. For example, by configuring a Web application to run at the Medium trust level, you prevent the application from being able to access files outside of its virtual directory hierarchy.

  Also, by granting a restricted file I/O permission to a particular assembly you can control precisely which files it is able to access and how it should be able to access them.

  For more information, see Chapter 9, "Using Code Access Security with ASP.NET" and "How To: Use Code Access Security Policy to Constrain an Assembly" in the "How To" section of this guide.

- **How to perform remote administration**

  Terminal Services provides a proprietary protocol (RDP.) This supports authentication and can provide encryption. If you need a file transfer facility, you can install the File Copy utility from the Windows 2000 Server resource kit. The use of IIS Web administration is not recommended and this option is removed if you run IISLockdown. You should consider providing an encrypted channel of communication and using IPSec to limit the computers that can be used to remotely administer your server. You should also limit the number of administration accounts.

  For more information, see the "Remote Administration" sections in Chapter 16, "Securing Your Web Server" and Chapter 18, "Securing Your Database Server."

Fast Track—How To Implement the Guidance

Goal and Scope

This guide helps you to design, build, and configure hack-resilient Web applications. These applications reduce the likelihood of successful attacks and mitigate the extent of damage should an attack occur. Figure 1 shows the scope of the guide and its three-layered approach: securing the network, securing the host, and securing the application.

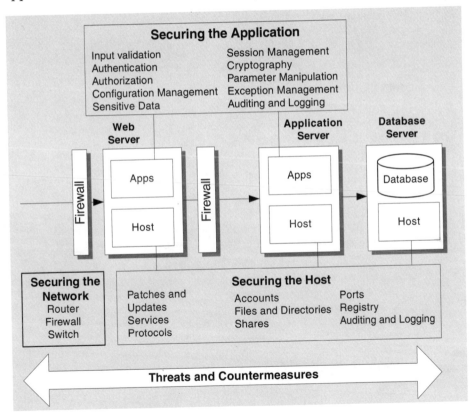

Figure 1
The scope of the guide

The guide addresses security across the three physical tiers shown in Figure 1. It covers the Web server, remote application server, and database server. At each tier, security is addressed at the network layer, host layer, and application layer. Figure 1 also shows the configuration categories that the guide uses to organize the various security configuration settings that apply to the host and network, and the application vulnerability categories, which are used to structure application security considerations.

The Holistic Approach

Web application security must be addressed across application tiers and at multiple layers. An attacker can exploit weaknesses at any layer. For this reason, the guide takes a holistic approach to application security and applies it at all three layers. This holistic approach to security is shown in Figure 2.

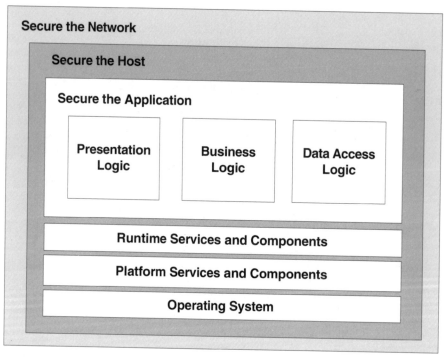

Figure 2
A holistic approach to security

Figure 2 shows the multiple layers covered by the guide, including the network, host, and application. The host layer covers the operating system, platform services and components, and run-time services and components. Platform services and components include Microsoft® SQL Server™ 2000 and Enterprise Services. Run-time services and components include ASP.NET and .NET code access security among others.

Securing Your Network

The three core elements of a secure network are the router, firewall, and switch. The guide covers all three elements. Table 1 provides a brief description of each element.

Table 1   Network Security Elements

Element	Description
Router	Routers are your outermost network ring. They direct packets to the ports and protocols that you have prepared your applications to work with. Insecure TCP/IP protocols are blocked at this ring.
Firewall	The firewall blocks those protocols and ports that the application does not use. Additionally, firewalls enforce secure network traffic by providing application-specific filtering to block malicious communications.
Switch	Switches are used to separate network segments. They are frequently overlooked or over trusted.

Securing Your Host

The host includes the operating system and .NET Framework, together with associated services and components. Whether the host is a Web server running IIS, an application server running Enterprise Services, or a database server running SQL Server, the guide adheres to a general security methodology that is common across the various server roles and types.

The guide organizes the precautions you must take and the settings you must configure into categories. By using these configuration categories, you can systematically walk through the securing process from top to bottom or pick a particular category and complete specific steps.

Figure 3 shows the configuration categories used throughout Part IV of this guide, "Securing Your Network, Host, and Application."

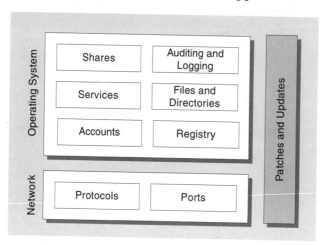

Figure 3
Host security categories

Securing Your Application

The guide defines a set of application vulnerability categories to help you design and build secure Web applications and evaluate the security of existing applications. These are common categories that span multiple technologies and components in a layered architecture. These categories are the focus for discussion through the designing, building, and security assessment chapters in this guide.

Table 2   Application Vulnerability Categories

Category	Description
Input Validation	How do you know that the input your application receives is valid and safe? Input validation refers to how your application filters, scrubs, or rejects input before additional processing.
Authentication	Who are you? Authentication is the process that an entity uses to identify another entity, typically through credentials such as a user name and password.
Authorization	What can you do? Authorization is the process that an application uses to control access to resources and operations.
Configuration Management	Who does your application run as? Which databases does it connect to? How is your application administered? How are these settings secured? Configuration management refers to how your application handles these operational issues.

Table 2   Application Vulnerability Categories *(continued)*

Category	Description
Sensitive Data	Sensitive data is information that must be protected either in memory, over the wire, or in persistent stores. Your application must have a process for handling sensitive data.
Session Management	A session refers to a series of related interactions between a user and your Web application. Session management refers to how your application handles and protects these interactions.
Cryptography	How are you protecting secret information (confidentiality)? How are you tamperproofing your data or libraries (integrity)? How are you providing seeds for random values that must be cryptographically strong? Cryptography refers to how your application enforces confidentiality and integrity.
Parameter Manipulation	Form fields, query string arguments, and cookie values are frequently used as parameters for your application. Parameter manipulation refers to both how your application safeguards tampering of these values and how your application processes input parameters.
Exception Management	When a method call in your application fails, what does your application do? How much does it reveal about the failure condition? Do you return friendly error information to end users? Do you pass valuable exception information back to the caller? Does your application fail gracefully?
Auditing and Logging	Who did what and when? Auditing and logging refer to how your application records security-related events.

Identify Threats

You need to know your threats before you can successfully apply security measures. Threats can be external, such as from an attacker on the Internet, or internal—for example, from a disgruntled employee or administrator. This guide helps you to identify threats in two ways:

- It lists the top threats that affect Web applications at the network, host, and application layers.
- It presents a threat modeling process to help you identify which threats are relevant to your application.

An outline of the threat modeling process covered in the guide is shown in Figure 4.

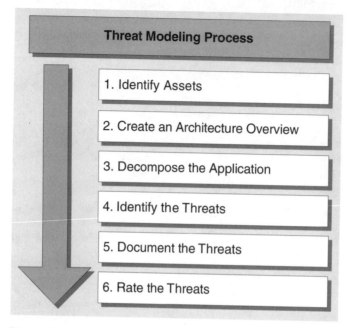

Figure 4
The Threat Modeling Process

The steps shown in Figure 4 are described below:

1. **Identify assets**.

   Identify the assets of value that your systems must protect.

2. **Create an architecture overview**.

   Use simple diagrams and tables to document the architecture of your application, including subsystems, trust boundaries, and data flow.

3. **Decompose the application**.

   Decompose the architecture of your application, including the underlying network and host infrastructure design, to create a security profile for the application. The aim of the security profile is to uncover vulnerabilities in the design, implementation, or deployment configuration of your application.

4. **Identify the threats**.

   Keeping an attacker's goals in mind, and with knowledge of your application's architecture and potential vulnerabilities, you identify the threats that could impact the application.

5. **Document the threats**.

   Document each threat using a common threat template that defines a core set of attributes that you should capture for each threat.

6. **Rate the threats**.

Rate the threats to prioritize and address the most significant threats first. These threats are the ones that present the biggest risk. The rating process weighs the probability of the threat against the damage that could result should an attack occur. It might turn out that certain threats do not warrant any action when you compare the risk posed by the threat with the resulting mitigation costs.

Applying the Guidance to Your Product Life Cycle

Different parts of the guide apply to the different phases of the product development life cycle. The sequence of chapters in the guide mirrors the typical phases of the life cycle. The chapter-to-role relationship is shown in Figure 5.

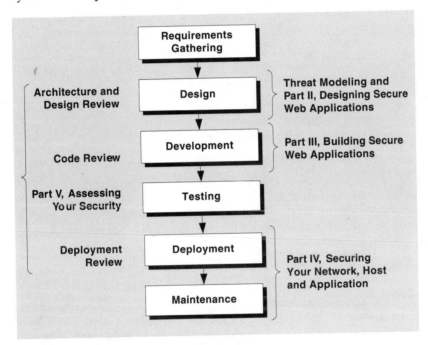

Figure 5
Relationship of chapter to product life cycle

Note   Threat modeling and security assessment (specifically the code review and deployment review chapters) apply when you build new Web applications or when you review existing applications.

Implementing the Guidance

The guidance throughout the guide is task-based and modular, and each chapter relates to the various stages of the product development life cycle and the various roles involved. These roles include architects, developers, system administrators, and security professionals. You can pick specific chapters to perform a particular task or use a series of chapters for a phase of the product development life cycle.

The checklist shown in Table 3 highlights the areas covered by this guide that are required to secure your network, host, and application.

Table 3   Security Checklist

Check	Description
☐	Educate your teams about the threats that affect the network, host, and application layers. Identify common vulnerabilities and attacks, and learn countermeasures. For more information, see Chapter 2, "Threats and Countermeasures."
☐	Create threat models for your Web applications. For more information, see Chapter 3, "Threat Modeling."
☐	Review and implement your company's security policies. If you do not have security policies in place, create them. For more information about creating security policies, see "Security Policy Issues" at the SANS Info Sec Reading Room at http://www.sans.org/rr/catindex.php?cat_id=50.
☐	Review your network security. For more information, see Chapter 15, "Securing Your Network."
☐	Patch and update your servers. Review your server security settings and compare them with the snapshot of a secure server. For more information, see "Snapshot of a Secure Web Server" in Chapter 16, "Securing Your Web Server."
☐	Educate your architects and developers about Web application security design guidelines and principles. For more information, see Chapter 4, "Design Guidelines for Secure Web Applications."
☐	Educate your architects and developers about writing secure managed code. For more information, see Chapter 7, "Building Secure Assemblies" and Chapter 8, "Code Access Security in Practice."
☐	Secure your developer workstations. For more information, see "How To: Secure Your Developer Workstation" in the "How To" section of this guide.
☐	Review the designs of new Web applications and of existing applications. For more information, see Chapter 5, "Architecture and Design Review for Security."
☐	Educate developers about how to perform code reviews. Perform code reviews for applications in development. For more information, see Chapter 21, "Code Review."
☐	Perform deployment reviews of your applications to identify potential security vulnerabilities. For more information, see Chapter 22, "Deployment Review."

Who Does What?

Designing and building secure applications is a collaborative effort involving multiple roles. This guide is structured to address each role and the relevant security factors to be considered by each role. The categorization and the issues addressed are outlined below.

RACI Chart

RACI stands for:

- Responsible (the role responsible for performing the task)
- Accountable (the role with overall responsibility for the task)
- Consulted (people who provide input to help perform the task)
- Keep Informed (people with a vested interest who should be kept informed)

You can use a RACI chart at the beginning of your project to identify the key security related tasks together with the roles that should execute each task.

Table 4 illustrates a simple RACI chart for this guide. (The heading row lists the roles; the first column lists tasks, and the remaining columns delineate levels of accountability for each task according to role.)

Table 4 RACI Chart

Tasks	Architect	System Administrator	Developer	Tester	Security Professional
Security Policies		R		I	A
Threat Modeling	A		I	I	R
Security Design Principles	A	I	I		C
Security Architecture	A	C			R
Architecture and Design Review	R				A
Code Development			A		R
Technology Specific Threats			A		R
Code Review			R	I	A
Security Testing	C		I	A	C
Network Security	C	R			A
Host Security	C	A	I		R
Application Security	C	I	A		R
Deployment Review	C	R	I	I	A

Summary

This fast track has highlighted the basic approach taken by the guide to help you design and develop hack-resilient Web applications, and to evaluate the security of existing applications. It has also shown you how to apply the guidance depending on your specific role in the project life cycle.

Part I

Introduction to Threats and Countermeasures

In This Part:

- Web Application Security Fundamentals
- Threats and Countermeasures
- Threat Modeling

1

Web Application Security Fundamentals

When you hear talk about Web application security, there is a tendency to immediately think about attackers defacing Web sites, stealing credit card numbers, and bombarding Web sites with denial of service attacks. You might also think about viruses, Trojan horses, and worms. These are the types of problems that receive the most press because they represent some of the most significant threats faced by today's Web applications.

These are only some of the problems. Other significant problems are frequently overlooked. Internal threats posed by rogue administrators, disgruntled employees, and the casual user who mistakenly stumbles across sensitive data pose significant risk. The biggest problem of all may be ignorance.

The solution to Web application security is more than technology. It is an ongoing process involving people and practices.

We Are Secure — We Have a Firewall

This is a common misconception; it depends on the threat. For example, a firewall may not detect malicious input sent to your Web application. Also, consider the scenario where a rogue administrator has direct access to your application.

Do firewalls have their place? Of course they do. Firewalls are great at blocking ports. Some firewall applications examine communications and can provide very advanced protection. Firewalls are an integral part of your security, but they are not a complete solution by themselves.

The same holds true for Secure Sockets Layer (SSL). SSL is great at encrypting traffic over the network. However, it does not validate your application's input or protect you from a poorly configured server.

What Do We Mean By Security?

Security is fundamentally about protecting assets. Assets may be tangible items, such as a Web page or your customer database—or they may be less tangible, such as your company's reputation.

Security is a path, not a destination. As you analyze your infrastructure and applications, you identify potential threats and understand that each threat presents a degree of risk. Security is about risk management and implementing effective countermeasures.

The Foundations of Security

Security relies on the following elements:

- **Authentication**

  Authentication addresses the question: who are you? It is the process of uniquely identifying the clients of your applications and services. These might be end users, other services, processes, or computers. In security parlance, authenticated clients are referred to as *principals*.

- **Authorization**

  Authorization addresses the question: what can you do? It is the process that governs the resources and operations that the authenticated client is permitted to access. Resources include files, databases, tables, rows, and so on, together with system-level resources such as registry keys and configuration data. Operations include performing transactions such as purchasing a product, transferring money from one account to another, or increasing a customer's credit rating.

- **Auditing**

  Effective auditing and logging is the key to non-repudiation. Non-repudiation guarantees that a user cannot deny performing an operation or initiating a transaction. For example, in an e-commerce system, non-repudiation mechanisms are required to make sure that a consumer cannot deny ordering 100 copies of a particular book.

- **Confidentiality**

  Confidentiality, also referred to as *privacy*, is the process of making sure that data remains private and confidential, and that it cannot be viewed by unauthorized users or eavesdroppers who monitor the flow of traffic across a network. Encryption is frequently used to enforce confidentiality. Access control lists (ACLs) are another means of enforcing confidentiality.

- **Integrity**

  Integrity is the guarantee that data is protected from accidental or deliberate (malicious) modification. Like privacy, integrity is a key concern, particularly for data passed across networks. Integrity for data in transit is typically provided by using hashing techniques and message authentication codes.

- **Availability**

  From a security perspective, availability means that systems remain available for legitimate users. The goal for many attackers with denial of service attacks is to crash an application or to make sure that it is sufficiently overwhelmed so that other users cannot access the application.

Threats, Vulnerabilities, and Attacks Defined

A threat is any potential occurrence, malicious or otherwise, that could harm an asset. In other words, a threat is any bad thing that can happen to your assets.

A vulnerability is a weakness that makes a threat possible. This may be because of poor design, configuration mistakes, or inappropriate and insecure coding techniques. Weak input validation is an example of an application layer vulnerability, which can result in input attacks.

An attack is an action that exploits a vulnerability or enacts a threat. Examples of attacks include sending malicious input to an application or flooding a network in an attempt to deny service.

To summarize, a threat is a potential event that can adversely affect an asset, whereas a successful attack exploits vulnerabilities in your system.

How Do You Build a Secure Web Application?

It is not possible to design and build a secure Web application until you know your threats. An increasingly important discipline and one that is recommended to form part of your application's design phase is threat modeling. The purpose of threat modeling is to analyze your application's architecture and design and identify potentially vulnerable areas that may allow a user, perhaps mistakenly, or an attacker with malicious intent, to compromise your system's security.

After you know your threats, design with security in mind by applying timeworn and proven security principles. As developers, you must follow secure coding techniques to develop secure, robust, and hack-resilient solutions. The design and development of application layer software must be supported by a secure network, host, and application configuration on the servers where the application software is to be deployed.

Secure Your Network, Host, and Application

"A vulnerability in a network will allow a malicious user to exploit a host or an application. A vulnerability in a host will allow a malicious user to exploit a network or an application. A vulnerability in an application will allow a malicious user to exploit a network or a host."

—Carlos Lyons, Corporate Security, Microsoft

To build secure Web applications, a holistic approach to application security is required and security must be applied at all three layers. This approach is shown in Figure 1.1.

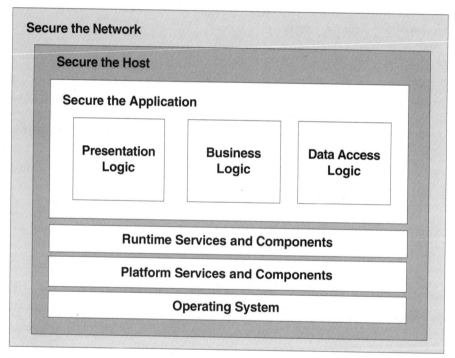

Figure 1.1
A holistic approach to security

Securing Your Network

A secure Web application relies upon a secure network infrastructure. The network infrastructure consists of routers, firewalls, and switches. The role of the secure network is not only to protect itself from TCP/IP-based attacks, but also to implement countermeasures such as secure administrative interfaces and strong passwords. The secure network is also responsible for ensuring the integrity of the traffic that it is forwarding. If you know at the network layer about ports, protocols, or communication that may be harmful, counter those potential threats at that layer.

Network Component Categories

This guide divides network security into separate component categories as shown in Table 1.1.

Table 1.1: Network Component Categories

Component	Description
Router	Routers are your outermost network ring. They channel packets to ports and protocols that your application needs. Common TCP/IP vulnerabilities are blocked at this ring.
Firewall	The firewall blocks those protocols and ports that the application does not use. Additionally, firewalls enforce secure network traffic by providing application-specific filtering to block malicious communications.
Switch	Switches are used to separate network segments. They are frequently overlooked or overtrusted.

Securing Your Host

When you secure a host, whether it is your Web server, application server, or database server, this guide breaks down the various secure configuration settings into separate categories. With this approach, you can focus on a specific category and review security, or apply security settings that relate to that specific category. When you install new software on your servers with this approach, you can evaluate the impact on your security settings. For example, you may address the following questions: Does the software create new accounts? Does the software add any default services? Who are the services running as? Are any new script mappings created?

Host Configuration Categories

Figure 1.2 shows the various categories used in Part IV of this guide, "Securing Your Network, Host, and Application."

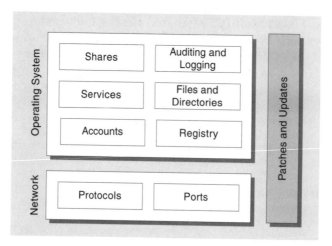

Figure 1.2

Host security categories

With the framework that these categories provide, you can systematically evaluate or secure your server's configuration instead of applying security settings on an ad-hoc basis. The rationale for these particular categories is shown in Table 1.2.

Table 1.2: Rationale for Host Configuration Categories

Category	Description
Patches and Updates	Many top security risks exist because of vulnerabilities that are widely published and well known. When new vulnerabilities are discovered, exploit code is frequently posted on Internet bulletin boards within hours of the first successful attack. Patching and updating your server's software is the first step toward securing the server. If you do not patch and update your server, you are providing more potential opportunities for attackers and malicious code.
Services	The service set is determined by the server role and the applications it hosts. By disabling unnecessary and unused services, you quickly and easily reduce the attack surface area.
Protocols	To reduce the attack surface area and the avenues open to attackers, disable any unnecessary or unused network protocols.
Accounts	The number of accounts accessible from a server should be restricted to the necessary set of service and user accounts. Additionally, you should enforce appropriate account policies, such as mandating strong passwords.

Table 1.2: Rationale for Host Configuration Categories *(continued)*

Category	Description
Files and Directories	Files and directories should be secured with restricted NTFS permissions that allow access only to the necessary Microsoft Windows service and user accounts.
Shares	All unnecessary file shares, including the default administration shares if they are not required, should be removed. Secure the remaining shares with restricted NTFS permissions.
Ports	Services running on a server listen on specific ports to serve incoming requests. Open ports on a server must be known and audited regularly to make sure that an insecure service is not listening and available for communication. In the worst-case scenario, a listening port is detected that was not opened by an administrator.
Auditing and Logging	Auditing is a vital aid in identifying intruders or attacks in progress. Logging proves particularly useful as forensic information when determining how an intrusion or attack was performed.
Registry	Many security related settings are maintained in the registry. Secure the registry itself by applying restricted Windows ACLs and blocking remote registry administration.

Securing Your Application

If you were to review and analyze the top security issues across many Web applications, you would see a pattern of problems. By organizing these problems into categories, you can systematically tackle them. These problem areas are your application's vulnerability categories.

Application Vulnerability Categories

What better way to measure the security of a system than to evaluate its potential weak points? To measure the security resilience of your application, you can evaluate the application vulnerability categories. When you do this, you can create application security profiles, and then use these profiles to determine the security strength of an application.

These categories are used as a framework throughout this guide. Because the categories represent the areas where security mistakes are most frequently made, they are used to illustrate guidance for application developers and architects. The categories are also used as a framework when evaluating the security of a Web application. With these categories, you can focus consistently on the key design and implementation choices that most affect your application's security. Application vulnerability categories are described in Table 1.3.

Table 1.3: Application Vulnerability Categories

Category	Description
Input Validation	How do you know that the input that your application receives is valid and safe? Input validation refers to how your application filters, scrubs, or rejects input before additional processing.
Authentication	"Who are you?" Authentication is the process where an entity proves the identity of another entity, typically through credentials, such as a user name and password.
Authorization	"What can you do?" Authorization is how your application provides access controls for resources and operations.
Configuration Management	Who does your application run as? Which databases does it connect to? How is your application administered? How are these settings secured? Configuration management refers to how your application handles these operational issues.
Sensitive Data	Sensitive data refers to how your application handles any data that must be protected either in memory, over the wire, or in persistent stores.
Session Management	A session refers to a series of related interactions between a user and your Web application. Session management refers to how your application handles and protects these interactions.
Cryptography	How are you keeping secrets, secret (confidentiality)? How are you tamperproofing your data or libraries (integrity)? How are you providing seeds for random values that must be cryptographically strong? Cryptography refers to how your application enforces confidentiality and integrity.
Parameter Manipulation	Form fields, query string arguments, and cookie values are frequently used as parameters for your application. Parameter manipulation refers to both how your application safeguards tampering of these values and how your application processes input parameters.
Exception Management	When a method call in your application fails, what does your application do? How much do you reveal? Do you return friendly error information to end users? Do you pass valuable exception information back to the caller? Does your application fail gracefully?
Auditing and Logging	Who did what and when? Auditing and logging refer to how your application records security-related events.

Security Principles

Recommendations used throughout this guide are based on security principles that have proven themselves over time. Security, like many aspects of software engineering, lends itself to a principle-based approach, where core principles can be applied regardless of implementation technology or application scenario. The major security principles used throughout this guide are summarized in Table 1.4.

Table 1.4: Summary of Core Security Principles

Principle	Concepts
Compartmentalize	Reduce the surface area of attack. Ask yourself how you will contain a problem. If an attacker takes over your application, what resources can he or she access? Can an attacker access network resources? How are you restricting potential damage? Firewalls, least privileged accounts, and least privileged code are examples of compartmentalizing.
Use least privilege	By running processes using accounts with minimal privileges and access rights, you significantly reduce the capabilities of an attacker if the attacker manages to compromise security and run code.
Apply defense in depth	Use multiple gatekeepers to keep attackers at bay. Defense in depth means you do not rely on a single layer of security, or you consider that one of your layers may be bypassed or compromised.
Do not trust user input	Your application's user input is the attacker's primary weapon when targeting your application. Assume all input is malicious until proven otherwise, and apply a defense in depth strategy to input validation, taking particular precautions to make sure that input is validated whenever a trust boundary in your application is crossed.
Check at the gate	Authenticate and authorize callers early—at the first gate.
Fail securely	If an application fails, do not leave sensitive data accessible. Return friendly errors to end users that do not expose internal system details. Do not include details that may help an attacker exploit vulnerabilities in your application.
Secure the weakest link	Is there a vulnerability at the network layer that an attacker can exploit? What about the host? Is your application secure? Any weak link in the chain is an opportunity for breached security.
Create secure defaults	Is the default account set up with least privilege? Is the default account disabled by default and then explicitly enabled when required? Does the configuration use a password in plaintext? When an error occurs, does sensitive information leak back to the client to be used potentially against the system?
Reduce your attack surface	If you do not use it, remove it or disable it. Reduce the surface area of attack by disabling or removing unused services, protocols, and functionality. Does your server need all those services and ports? Does your application need all those features?

Summary

An ever-increasing number of attacks target your application. They pass straight through your environment's front door using HTTP. The conventional fortress model and the reliance on firewall and host defenses are not sufficient when used in isolation. Securing your application involves applying security at three layers: the network layer, host layer, and the application layer. A secure network and host platform infrastructure is a must. Additionally, your applications must be designed and built using secure design and development guidelines following timeworn security principles.

Additional Resources

For more information, see the following resources:

- For more information on the Open Hack Web application, see the MSDN article, "Open Hack: Building and Configuring More Secure Web Sites," at *http://msdn.microsoft.com/library/default.asp?url=/library/en-us/dnnetsec/html /openhack.asp*.

- This is Volume II in a series dedicated to helping customers improve Web application security. For more information on designing and implementing authentication, authorization, and secure communication across the tiers of a distributed Web application, see "Microsoft *patterns & practices* Volume I, *Building Secure ASP.NET Applications: Authentication, Authorization, and Secure Communication*" at *http://msdn.microsoft.com/library/en-us/dnnetsec/html /secnetlpMSDN.asp*.

2

Threats and Countermeasures

In This Chapter

- An explanation of attacker methodology
- Descriptions of common attacks
- How to categorize threats
- How to identify and counter threats at the network, host, and application levels

Overview

When you incorporate security features into your application's design, implementation, and deployment, it helps to have a good understanding of how attackers think. By thinking like attackers and being aware of their likely tactics, you can be more effective when applying countermeasures. This chapter describes the classic attacker methodology and profiles the anatomy of a typical attack.

This chapter analyzes Web application security from the perspectives of threats, countermeasures, vulnerabilities, and attacks. The following set of core terms are defined to avoid confusion and to ensure they are used in the correct context.

- **Asset**. A resource of value such as the data in a database or on the file system, or a system resource
- **Threat**. A potential occurrence—malicious or otherwise—that may harm an asset
- **Vulnerability**. A weakness that makes a threat possible
- **Attack (or exploit)**. An action taken to harm an asset
- **Countermeasure**. A safeguard that addresses a threat and mitigates risk

This chapter also identifies a set of common network, host, and application level threats, and the recommended countermeasures to address each one. The chapter does not contain an exhaustive list of threats, but it does highlight many top threats. With this information and knowledge of how an attacker works, you will be able to identify additional threats. You need to know the threats that are most likely to impact your system to be able to build effective threat models. These threat models are the subject of Chapter 3, "Threat Modeling."

How to Use This Chapter

The following are recommendations on how to use this chapter:

- **Become familiar with specific threats that affect the network host and application**. The threats are unique for the various parts of your system, although the attacker's goals may be the same.
- **Use the threats to identify risk**. Then create a plan to counter those threats.
- **Apply countermeasures to address vulnerabilities**. Countermeasures are summarized in this chapter. Use Part III, "Building Secure Web Applications," and Part IV, "Securing Your Network, Host, and Application," of this guide for countermeasure implementation details.
- **When you design, build, and secure new systems, keep the threats in this chapter in mind**. The threats exist regardless of the platform or technologies that you use.

Anatomy of an Attack

By understanding the basic approach used by attackers to target your Web application, you will be better equipped to take defensive measures because you will know what you are up against. The basic steps in attacker methodology are summarized below and illustrated in Figure 2.1:

- **Survey and assess**
- **Exploit and penetrate**
- **Escalate privileges**
- **Maintain access**
- **Deny service**

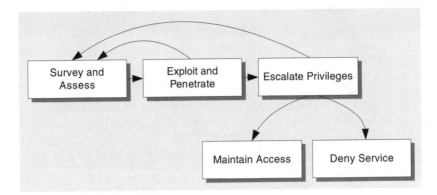

Figure 2.1
Basic steps for attacking methodology

Survey and Assess

Surveying and assessing the potential target are done in tandem. The first step an attacker usually takes is to survey the potential target to identify and assess its characteristics. These characteristics may include its supported services and protocols together with potential vulnerabilities and entry points. The attacker uses the information gathered in the survey and assess phase to plan an initial attack.

For example, an attacker can detect a cross-site scripting (XSS) vulnerability by testing to see if any controls in a Web page echo back output.

Exploit and Penetrate

Having surveyed a potential target, the next step is to exploit and penetrate. If the network and host are fully secured, your application (the front gate) becomes the next channel for attack.

For an attacker, the easiest way into an application is through the same entrance that legitimate users use—for example, through the application's logon page or a page that does not require authentication.

Escalate Privileges

After attackers manage to compromise an application or network, perhaps by injecting code into an application or creating an authenticated session with the Microsoft® Windows® 2000 operating system, they immediately attempt to escalate privileges. Specifically, they look for administration privileges provided by accounts that are members of the Administrators group. They also seek out the high level of privileges offered by the local system account.

Using least privileged service accounts throughout your application is a primary defense against privilege escalation attacks. Also, many network level privilege escalation attacks require an interactive logon session.

Maintain Access

Having gained access to a system, an attacker takes steps to make future access easier and to cover his or her tracks. Common approaches for making future access easier include planting back-door programs or using an existing account that lacks strong protection. Covering tracks typically involves clearing logs and hiding tools. As such, audit logs are a primary target for the attacker.

Log files should be secured, and they should be analyzed on a regular basis. Log file analysis can often uncover the early signs of an attempted break-in before damage is done.

Deny Service

Attackers who cannot gain access often mount a denial of service attack to prevent others from using the application. For other attackers, the denial of service option is their goal from the outset. An example is the SYN flood attack, where the attacker uses a program to send a flood of TCP SYN requests to fill the pending connection queue on the server. This prevents other users from establishing network connections.

Understanding Threat Categories

While there are many variations of specific attacks and attack techniques, it is useful to think about threats in terms of what the attacker is trying to achieve. This changes your focus from the identification of every specific attack—which is really just a means to an end—to focusing on the end results of possible attacks.

STRIDE

Threats faced by the application can be categorized based on the goals and purposes of the attacks. A working knowledge of these categories of threats can help you organize a security strategy so that you have planned responses to threats. STRIDE is the acronym used at Microsoft to categorize different threat types. STRIDE stands for:

- **Spoofing**. *Spoofing* is attempting to gain access to a system by using a false identity. This can be accomplished using stolen user credentials or a false IP address. After the attacker successfully gains access as a legitimate user or host, elevation of privileges or abuse using authorization can begin.

- **Tampering**. *Tampering* is the unauthorized modification of data, for example as it flows over a network between two computers.

- **Repudiation**. *Repudiation* is the ability of users (legitimate or otherwise) to deny that they performed specific actions or transactions. Without adequate auditing, repudiation attacks are difficult to prove.

- **Information disclosure**. *Information disclosure* is the unwanted exposure of private data. For example, a user views the contents of a table or file he or she is not authorized to open, or monitors data passed in plaintext over a network. Some examples of information disclosure vulnerabilities include the use of hidden form fields, comments embedded in Web pages that contain database connection strings and connection details, and weak exception handling that can lead to internal system level details being revealed to the client. Any of this information can be very useful to the attacker.

- **Denial of service**. *Denial of service* is the process of making a system or application unavailable. For example, a denial of service attack might be accomplished by bombarding a server with requests to consume all available system resources or by passing it malformed input data that can crash an application process.

- **Elevation of privilege**. *Elevation of privilege* occurs when a user with limited privileges assumes the identity of a privileged user to gain privileged access to an application. For example, an attacker with limited privileges might elevate his or her privilege level to compromise and take control of a highly privileged and trusted process or account.

STRIDE Threats and Countermeasures

Each threat category described by STRIDE has a corresponding set of countermeasure techniques that should be used to reduce risk. These are summarized in Table 2.1. The appropriate countermeasure depends upon the specific attack. More threats, attacks, and countermeasures that apply at the network, host, and application levels are presented later in this chapter.

Table 2.1 STRIDE Threats and Countermeasures

Threat	Countermeasures
Spoofing user identity	Use strong authentication.
	Do not store secrets (for example, passwords) in plaintext.
	Do not pass credentials in plaintext over the wire.
	Protect authentication cookies with Secure Sockets Layer (SSL).
Tampering with data	Use data hashing and signing.
	Use digital signatures.
	Use strong authorization.
	Use tamper-resistant protocols across communication links.
	Secure communication links with protocols that provide message integrity.

(continued)

Table 2.1 STRIDE Threats and Countermeasures *(continued)*

Threat	Countermeasures
Repudiation	Create secure audit trails. Use digital signatures.
Information disclosure	Use strong authorization. Use strong encryption. Secure communication links with protocols that provide message confidentiality. Do not store secrets (for example, passwords) in plaintext.
Denial of service	Use resource and bandwidth throttling techniques. Validate and filter input.
Elevation of privilege	Follow the principle of least privilege and use least privileged service accounts to run processes and access resources.

Network Threats and Countermeasures

The primary components that make up your network infrastructure are routers, firewalls, and switches. They act as the gatekeepers guarding your servers and applications from attacks and intrusions. An attacker may exploit poorly configured network devices. Common vulnerabilities include weak default installation settings, wide open access controls, and devices lacking the latest security patches. Top network level threats include:

- **Information gathering**
- **Sniffing**
- **Spoofing**
- **Session hijacking**
- **Denial of service**

Information Gathering

Network devices can be discovered and profiled in much the same way as other types of systems. Attackers usually start with port scanning. After they identify open ports, they use banner grabbing and enumeration to detect device types and to determine operating system and application versions. Armed with this information, an attacker can attack known vulnerabilities that may not be updated with security patches.

Countermeasures to prevent information gathering include:

- Configure routers to restrict their responses to footprinting requests.
- Configure operating systems that host network software (for example, software firewalls) to prevent footprinting by disabling unused protocols and unnecessary ports.

Sniffing

Sniffing or *eavesdropping* is the act of monitoring traffic on the network for data such as plaintext passwords or configuration information. With a simple packet sniffer, an attacker can easily read all plaintext traffic. Also, attackers can crack packets encrypted by lightweight hashing algorithms and can decipher the payload that you considered to be safe. The sniffing of packets requires a packet sniffer in the path of the server/client communication.

Countermeasures to help prevent sniffing include:

- Use strong physical security and proper segmenting of the network. This is the first step in preventing traffic from being collected locally.
- Encrypt communication fully, including authentication credentials. This prevents sniffed packets from being usable to an attacker. SSL and IPSec (Internet Protocol Security) are examples of encryption solutions.

Spoofing

Spoofing is a means to hide one's true identity on the network. To create a spoofed identity, an attacker uses a fake source address that does not represent the actual address of the packet. Spoofing may be used to hide the original source of an attack or to work around network access control lists (ACLs) that are in place to limit host access based on source address rules.

Although carefully crafted spoofed packets may never be tracked to the original sender, a combination of filtering rules prevents spoofed packets from originating from your network, allowing you to block obviously spoofed packets.

Countermeasures to prevent spoofing include:

- Filter incoming packets that appear to come from an internal IP address at your perimeter.
- Filter outgoing packets that appear to originate from an invalid local IP address.

Session Hijacking

Also known as man in the middle attacks, session hijacking deceives a server or a client into accepting the upstream host as the actual legitimate host. Instead the upstream host is an attacker's host that is manipulating the network so the attacker's host appears to be the desired destination.

Countermeasures to help prevent session hijacking include:

- Use encrypted session negotiation.
- Use encrypted communication channels.
- Stay informed of platform patches to fix TCP/IP vulnerabilities, such as predictable packet sequences.

Denial of Service

Denial of service denies legitimate users access to a server or services. The SYN flood attack is a common example of a network level denial of service attack. It is easy to launch and difficult to track. The aim of the attack is to send more requests to a server than it can handle. The attack exploits a potential vulnerability in the TCP/IP connection establishment mechanism and floods the server's pending connection queue.

Countermeasures to prevent denial of service include:

- Apply the latest service packs.
- Harden the TCP/IP stack by applying the appropriate registry settings to increase the size of the TCP connection queue, decrease the connection establishment period, and employ dynamic backlog mechanisms to ensure that the connection queue is never exhausted.
- Use a network Intrusion Detection System (IDS) because these can automatically detect and respond to SYN attacks.

Host Threats and Countermeasures

Host threats are directed at the system software upon which your applications are built. This includes Windows 2000, Internet Information Services (IIS), the .NET Framework, and SQL Server 2000, depending upon the specific server role. Top host level threats include:

- **Viruses, Trojan horses, and worms**
- **Footprinting**
- **Profiling**
- **Password cracking**
- **Denial of service**
- **Arbitrary code execution**
- **Unauthorized access**

Viruses, Trojan Horses, and Worms

A virus is a program that is designed to perform malicious acts and cause disruption to your operating system or applications. A Trojan horse resembles a virus except that the malicious code is contained inside what appears to be a harmless data file or executable program. A worm is similar to a Trojan horse except that it self-replicates from one server to another. Worms are difficult to detect because they do not regularly create files that can be seen. They are often noticed only when they begin to consume system resources because the system slows down or the execution of other programs halt. The Code Red Worm is one of the most notorious to afflict IIS; it relied upon a buffer overflow vulnerability in a particular ISAPI filter.

Although these three threats are actually attacks, together they pose a significant threat to Web applications, the hosts these applications live on, and the network used to deliver these applications. The success of these attacks on any system is possible through many vulnerabilities such as weak defaults, software bugs, user error, and inherent vulnerabilities in Internet protocols.

Countermeasures that you can use against viruses, Trojan horses, and worms include:

- Stay current with the latest operating system service packs and software patches.
- Block all unnecessary ports at the firewall and host.
- Disable unused functionality including protocols and services.
- Harden weak, default configuration settings.

Footprinting

Examples of footprinting are port scans, ping sweeps, and NetBIOS enumeration that can be used by attackers to glean valuable system-level information to help prepare for more significant attacks. The type of information potentially revealed by footprinting includes account details, operating system and other software versions, server names, and database schema details.

Countermeasures to help prevent footprinting include:

- Disable unnecessary protocols.
- Lock down ports with the appropriate firewall configuration.
- Use TCP/IP and IPSec filters for defense in depth.
- Configure IIS to prevent information disclosure through banner grabbing.
- Use an IDS that can be configured to pick up footprinting patterns and reject suspicious traffic.

Password Cracking

If the attacker cannot establish an anonymous connection with the server, he or she will try to establish an authenticated connection. For this, the attacker must know a valid username and password combination. If you use default account names, you are giving the attacker a head start. Then the attacker only has to crack the account's password. The use of blank or weak passwords makes the attacker's job even easier.

Countermeasures to help prevent password cracking include:

- Use strong passwords for all account types.
- Apply lockout policies to end-user accounts to limit the number of retry attempts that can be used to guess the password.
- Do not use default account names, and rename standard accounts such as the administrator's account and the anonymous Internet user account used by many Web applications.
- Audit failed logins for patterns of password hacking attempts.

Denial of Service

Denial of service can be attained by many methods aimed at several targets within your infrastructure. At the host, an attacker can disrupt service by brute force against your application, or an attacker may know of a vulnerability that exists in the service your application is hosted in or in the operating system that runs your server.

Countermeasures to help prevent denial of service include:

- Configure your applications, services, and operating system with denial of service in mind.
- Stay current with patches and security updates.
- Harden the TCP/IP stack against denial of service.
- Make sure your account lockout policies cannot be exploited to lock out well known service accounts.
- Make sure your application is capable of handling high volumes of traffic and that thresholds are in place to handle abnormally high loads.
- Review your application's failover functionality.
- Use an IDS that can detect potential denial of service attacks.

Arbitrary Code Execution

If an attacker can execute malicious code on your server, the attacker can either compromise server resources or mount further attacks against downstream systems. The risks posed by arbitrary code execution increase if the server process under which the attacker's code runs is over-privileged. Common vulnerabilities include weak IID configuration and unpatched servers that allow path traversal and buffer overflow attacks, both of which can lead to arbitrary code execution.

Countermeasures to help prevent arbitrary code execution include:

- Configure IIS to reject URLs with "../" to prevent path traversal.
- Lock down system commands and utilities with restricted ACLs.
- Stay current with patches and updates to ensure that newly discovered buffer overflows are speedily patched.

Unauthorized Access

Inadequate access controls could allow an unauthorized user to access restricted information or perform restricted operations. Common vulnerabilities include weak IIS Web access controls, including Web permissions and weak NTFS permissions.

Countermeasures to help prevent unauthorized access include:

- Configure secure Web permissions.
- Lock down files and folders with restricted NTFS permissions.
- Use .NET Framework access control mechanisms within your ASP.NET applications, including URL authorization and principal permission demands.

Application Threats and Countermeasures

A good way to analyze application-level threats is to organize them by application vulnerability category. The various categories used in the subsequent sections of this chapter and throughout the guide, together with the main threats to your application, are summarized in Table 2.2.

Table 2.2   Threats by Application Vulnerability Category

Category	Threats
Input validation	Buffer overflow; cross-site scripting; SQL injection; canonicalization
Authentication	Network eavesdropping; brute force attacks; dictionary attacks; cookie replay; credential theft
Authorization	Elevation of privilege; disclosure of confidential data; data tampering; luring attacks
Configuration management	Unauthorized access to administration interfaces; unauthorized access to configuration stores; retrieval of clear text configuration data; lack of individual accountability; over-privileged process and service accounts
Sensitive data	Access sensitive data in storage; network eavesdropping; data tampering
Session management	Session hijacking; session replay; man in the middle
Cryptography	Poor key generation or key management; weak or custom encryption
Parameter manipulation	Query string manipulation; form field manipulation; cookie manipulation; HTTP header manipulation
Exception management	Information disclosure; denial of service
Auditing and logging	User denies performing an operation; attacker exploits an application without trace; attacker covers his or her tracks

Input Validation

Input validation is a security issue if an attacker discovers that your application makes unfounded assumptions about the type, length, format, or range of input data. The attacker can then supply carefully crafted input that compromises your application.

When network and host level entry points are fully secured; the public interfaces exposed by your application become the only source of attack. The input to your application is a means to both test your system and a way to execute code on an attacker's behalf. Does your application blindly trust input? If it does, your application may be susceptible to the following:

- Buffer overflows
- Cross-site scripting
- SQL injection
- Canonicalization

The following section examines these vulnerabilities in detail, including what makes these vulnerabilities possible.

Buffer Overflows

Buffer overflow vulnerabilities can lead to denial of service attacks or code injection. A denial of service attack causes a process crash;. code injection alters the program execution address to run an attacker's injected code. The following code fragment illustrates a common example of a buffer overflow vulnerability.

```
void SomeFunction( char *pszInput )
{
  char szBuffer[10];
  // Input is copied straight into the buffer when no type checking is performed
  strcpy(szBuffer, pszInput);
  . . .
}
```

Managed .NET code is not susceptible to this problem because array bounds are automatically checked whenever an array is accessed. This makes the threat of buffer overflow attacks on managed code much less of an issue. It is still a concern, however, especially where managed code calls unmanaged APIs or COM objects.

Countermeasures to help prevent buffer overflows include:

- Perform thorough input validation. This is the first line of defense against buffer overflows. Although a bug may exist in your application that permits expected input to reach beyond the bounds of a container, unexpected input will be the primary cause of this vulnerability. Constrain input by validating it for type, length, format and range.

- When possible, limit your application's use of unmanaged code, and thoroughly inspect the unmanaged APIs to ensure that input is properly validated.

- Inspect the managed code that calls the unmanaged API to ensure that only appropriate values can be passed as parameters to the unmanaged API.

- Use the /GS flag to compile code developed with the Microsoft Visual C++® development system. The /GS flag causes the compiler to inject security checks into the compiled code. This is not a fail-proof solution or a replacement for your specific validation code; it does, however, protect your code from commonly known buffer overflow attacks. For more information, see the .NET Framework Product documentation *http://msdn.microsoft.com/library/default.asp?url= /library/en-us/vccore/html/vclrfGSBufferSecurity.asp* and Microsoft Knowledge Base article 325483 "WebCast: Compiler Security Checks: The –GS compiler switch."

Example of Code Injection Through Buffer Overflows

An attacker can exploit a buffer overflow vulnerability to inject code. With this attack, a malicious user exploits an unchecked buffer in a processsby supplying a carefully constructed input value that overwrites the program's stack and alters a function's return address. This causes execution to jump to the attacker's injected code.

The attacker's code usually ends up running under the process security context. This emphasizes the importance of using least privileged process accounts. If the current thread is impersonating, the attacker's code ends up running under the security context defined by the thread impersonation token. The first thing an attacker usually does is call the **RevertToSelf** API to revert to the process level security context that the attacker hopes has higher privileges.

Make sure you validate input for type and length, especially before you call unmanaged code because unmanaged code is particularly susceptible to buffer overflows.

Cross-Site Scripting

An XSS attack can cause arbitrary code to run in a user's browser while the browser is connected to a trusted Web site. The attack targets your application's users and not the application itself, but it uses your application as the vehicle for the attack.

Because the script code is downloaded by the browser from a trusted site, the browser has no way of knowing that the code is not legitimate. Internet Explorer security zones provide no defense. Since the attacker's code has access to the cookies associated with the trusted site and are stored on the user's local computer, a user's authentication cookies are typically the target of attack.

Example of Cross-Site Scripting

To initiate the attack, the attacker must convince the user to click on a carefully crafted hyperlink, for example, by embedding a link in an email sent to the user or by adding a malicious link to a newsgroup posting. The link points to a vulnerable page in your application that echoes the unvalidated input back to the browser in the HTML output stream. For example, consider the following two links.

Here is a legitimate link:

```
www.yourwebapplication.com/logon.aspx?username=bob
```

Here is a malicious link:

```
www.yourwebapplication.com/logon.aspx?username=<script>alert('hacker
code')</script>
```

If the Web application takes the query string, fails to properly validate it, and then returns it to the browser, the script code executes in the browser. The preceding example displays a harmless pop-up message. With the appropriate script, the attacker can easily extract the user's authentication cookie, post it to his site, and subsequently make a request to the target Web site as the authenticated user.

Countermeasures to prevent XSS include:

- Perform thorough input validation. Your applications must ensure that input from query strings, form fields, and cookies are valid for the application. Consider all user input as possibly malicious, and filter or sanitize for the context of the downstream code. Validate all input for known valid values and then reject all other input. Use regular expressions to validate input data received via HTML form fields, cookies, and query strings.

- Use **HTMLEncode** and **URLEncode** functions to encode any output that includes user input. This converts executable script into harmless HTML.

SQL Injection

A SQL injection attack exploits vulnerabilities in input validation to run arbitrary commands in the database. It can occur when your application uses input to construct dynamic SQL statements to access the database. It can also occur if your code uses stored procedures that are passed strings that contain unfiltered user input. Using the SQL injection attack, the attacker can execute arbitrary commands in the database. The issue is magnified if the application uses an over-privileged account to connect to the database. In this instance it is possible to use the database server to run operating system commands and potentially compromise other servers, in addition to being able to retrieve, manipulate, and destroy data.

Example of SQL Injection

Your application may be susceptible to SQL injection attacks when you incorporate unvalidated user input into database queries. Particularly susceptible is code that constructs dynamic SQL statements with unfiltered user input. Consider the following code:

```
SqlDataAdapter myCommand = new SqlDataAdapter(
        "SELECT * FROM Users
        WHERE UserName ='" + txtuid.Text + "'", conn);
```

Attackers can inject SQL by terminating the intended SQL statement with the single quote character followed by a semicolon character to begin a new command, and then executing the command of their choice. Consider the following character string entered into the **txtuid** field.

```
'; DROP TABLE Customers -
```

This results in the following statement being submitted to the database for execution.

```
SELECT * FROM Users WHERE UserName=''; DROP TABLE Customers --'
```

This deletes the Customers table, assuming that the application's login has sufficient permissions in the database (another reason to use a least privileged login in the database). The double dash (--) denotes a SQL comment and is used to comment out any other characters added by the programmer, such as the trailing quote.

Note The semicolon is not actually required. SQL Server will execute two commands separated by spaces.

Other more subtle tricks can be performed. Supplying this input to the **txtuid** field:

```
' OR 1=1 -
```

builds this command:

```
SELECT * FROM Users WHERE UserName='' OR 1=1 -
```

Because 1=1 is always true, the attacker retrieves every row of data from the Users table.

Countermeasures to prevent SQL injection include:

- Perform thorough input validation. Your application should validate its input prior to sending a request to the database.
- Use parameterized stored procedures for database access to ensure that input strings are not treated as executable statements. If you cannot use stored procedures, use SQL parameters when you build SQL commands.
- Use least privileged accounts to connect to the database.

Canonicalization

Different forms of input that resolve to the same standard name (the canonical name), is referred to as *canonicalization*. Code is particularly susceptible to canonicalization issues if it makes security decisions based on the name of a resource that is passed to the program as input. Files, paths, and URLs are resource types that are vulnerable to canonicalization because in each case there are many different ways to represent the same name. File names are also problematic. For example, a single file could be represented as:

```
c:\temp\somefile.dat
somefile.dat
c:\temp\subdir\..\somefile.dat
c:\  temp\  somefile.dat
..\somefile.dat
```

Ideally, your code does not accept input file names. If it does, the name should be converted to its canonical form prior to making security decisions, such as whether access should be granted or denied to the specified file.

Countermeasures to address canonicalization issues include:

- Avoid input file names where possible and instead use absolute file paths that cannot be changed by the end user.
- Make sure that file names are well formed (if you must accept file names as input) and validate them within the context of your application. For example, check that they are within your application's directory hierarchy.
- Ensure that the character encoding is set correctly to limit how input can be represented. Check that your application's Web.config has set the **requestEncoding** and **responseEncoding** attributes on the **<globalization>** element.

Authentication

Depending on your requirements, there are several available authentication mechanisms to choose from. If they are not correctly chosen and implemented, the authentication mechanism can expose vulnerabilities that attackers can exploit to gain access to your system. The top threats that exploit authentication vulnerabilities include:

- **Network eavesdropping**
- **Brute force attacks**
- **Dictionary attacks**
- **Cookie replay attacks**
- **Credential theft**

Network Eavesdropping

If authentication credentials are passed in plaintext from client to server, an attacker armed with rudimentary network monitoring software on a host on the same network can capture traffic and obtain user names and passwords.

Countermeasures to prevent network eavesdropping include:

- Use authentication mechanisms that do not transmit the password over the network such as Kerberos protocol or Windows authentication.
- Make sure passwords are encrypted (if you must transmit passwords over the network) or use an encrypted communication channel, for example with SSL.

Brute Force Attacks

Brute force attacks rely on computational power to crack hashed passwords or other secrets secured with hashing and encryption. To mitigate the risk, use strong passwords.

Dictionary Attacks

This attack is used to obtain passwords. Most password systems do not store plaintext passwords or encrypted passwords. They avoid encrypted passwords because a compromised key leads to the compromise of all passwords in the data store. Lost keys mean that all passwords are invalidated.

Most user store implementations hold password hashes (or digests). Users are authenticated by re-computing the hash based on the user-supplied password value and comparing it against the hash value stored in the database. If an attacker manages to obtain the list of hashed passwords, a brute force attack can be used to crack the password hashes.

With the dictionary attack, an attacker uses a program to iterate through all of the words in a dictionary (or multiple dictionaries in different languages) and computes the hash for each word. The resultant hash is compared with the value in the data store. Weak passwords such as "Yankees" (a favorite team) or "Mustang" (a favorite car) will be cracked quickly. Stronger passwords such as "?You'LlNevaFiNdMeyePasSWerd!", are less likely to be cracked.

Note   Once the attacker has obtained the list of password hashes, the dictionary attack can be performed offline and does not require interaction with the application.

Countermeasures to prevent dictionary attacks include:

- Use strong passwords that are complex, are not regular words, and contain a mixture of upper case, lower case, numeric, and special characters.
- Store non-reversible password hashes in the user store. Also combine a salt value (a cryptographically strong random number) with the password hash.

For more information about storing password hashes with added salt, see Chapter 14, "Building Secure Data Access."

Cookie Replay Attacks

With this type of attack, the attacker captures the user's authentication cookie using monitoring software and replays it to the application to gain access under a false identity.

Countermeasures to prevent cookie replay include:

- Use an encrypted communication channel provided by SSL whenever an authentication cookie is transmitted.
- Use a cookie timeout to a value that forces authentication after a relatively short time interval. Although this doesn't prevent replay attacks, it reduces the time interval in which the attacker can replay a request without being forced to re-authenticate because the session has timed out.

Credential Theft

If your application implements its own user store containing user account names and passwords, compare its security to the credential stores provided by the platform, for example, a Microsoft Active Directory® directory service or Security Accounts Manager (SAM) user store. Browser history and cache also store user login information for future use. If the terminal is accessed by someone other than the user who logged on, and the same page is hit, the saved login will be available.

Countermeasures to help prevent credential theft include:

- Use and enforce strong passwords.
- Store password verifiers in the form of one way hashes with added salt.
- Enforce account lockout for end-user accounts after a set number of retry attempts.
- To counter the possibility of the browser cache allowing login access, create functionality that either allows the user to choose to not save credentials, or force this functionality as a default policy.

Authorization

Based on user identity and role membership, authorization to a particular resource or service is either allowed or denied. Top threats that exploit authorization vulnerabilities include:

- **Elevation of privilege**
- **Disclosure of confidential data**
- **Data tampering**
- **Luring attacks**

Elevation of Privilege

When you design an authorization model, you must consider the threat of an attacker trying to elevate privileges to a powerful account such as a member of the local administrators group or the local system account. By doing this, the attacker is able to take complete control over the application and local machine. For example, with classic ASP programming, calling the **RevertToSelf** API from a component might cause the executing thread to run as the local system account with the most power and privileges on the local machine.

The main countermeasure that you can use to prevent elevation of privilege is to use least privileged process, service, and user accounts.

Disclosure of Confidential Data

The disclosure of confidential data can occur if sensitive data can be viewed by unauthorized users. Confidential data includes application specific data such as credit card numbers, employee details, financial records and so on together with application configuration data such as service account credentials and database connection strings. To prevent the disclosure of confidential data you should secure it in persistent stores such as databases and configuration files, and during transit over the network. Only authenticated and authorized users should be able to access the data that is specific to them. Access to system level configuration data should be restricted to administrators.

Countermeasures to prevent disclosure of confidential data include:

- Perform role checks before allowing access to the operations that could potentially reveal sensitive data.
- Use strong ACLs to secure Windows resources.
- Use standard encryption to store sensitive data in configuration files and databases.

Data Tampering

Data tampering refers to the unauthorized modification of data.

Countermeasures to prevent data tampering include:

- Use strong access controls to protect data in persistent stores to ensure that only authorized users can access and modify the data.
- Use role-based security to differentiate between users who can view data and users who can modify data.

Luring Attacks

A luring attack occurs when an entity with few privileges is able to have an entity with more privileges perform an action on its behalf.

To counter the threat, you must restrict access to trusted code with the appropriate authorization. Using .NET Framework code access security helps in this respect by authorizing calling code whenever a secure resource is accessed or a privileged operation is performed.

Configuration Management

Many applications support configuration management interfaces and functionality to allow operators and administrators to change configuration parameters, update Web site content, and to perform routine maintenance. Top configuration management threats include:

- **Unauthorized access to administration interfaces**
- **Unauthorized access to configuration stores**
- **Retrieval of plaintext configuration secrets**
- **Lack of individual accountability**
- **Over-privileged process and service accounts**

Unauthorized Access to Administration Interfaces

Administration interfaces are often provided through additional Web pages or separate Web applications that allow administrators, operators, and content developers to managed site content and configuration. Administration interfaces such as these should be available only to restricted and authorized users. Malicious users able to access a configuration management function can potentially deface the Web site, access downstream systems and databases, or take the application out of action altogether by corrupting configuration data.

Countermeasures to prevent unauthorized access to administration interfaces include:

- Minimize the number of administration interfaces.
- Use strong authentication, for example, by using certificates.
- Use strong authorization with multiple gatekeepers.
- Consider supporting only local administration. If remote administration is absolutely essential, use encrypted channels, for example, with VPN technology or SSL, because of the sensitive nature of the data passed over administrative interfaces. To further reduce risk, also consider using IPSec policies to limit remote administration to computers on the internal network.

Unauthorized Access to Configuration Stores

Because of the sensitive nature of the data maintained in configuration stores, you should ensure that the stores are adequately secured.

Countermeasures to protect configuration stores include:

- Configure restricted ACLs on text-based configuration files such as Machine.config and Web.config.
- Keep custom configuration stores outside of the Web space. This removes the potential to download Web server configurations to exploit their vulnerabilities.

Retrieval of Plaintext Configuration Secrets

Restricting access to the configuration store is a must. As an important defense in depth mechanism, you should encrypt sensitive data such as passwords and connection strings. This helps prevent external attackers from obtaining sensitive configuration data. It also prevents rogue administrators and internal employees from obtaining sensitive details such as database connection strings and account credentials that might allow them to gain access to other systems.

Lack of Individual Accountability

Lack of auditing and logging of changes made to configuration information threatens the ability to identify when changes were made and who made those changes. When a breaking change is made either by an honest operator error or by a malicious change to grant privileged access, action must first be taken to correct the change. Then apply preventive measures to prevent breaking changes to be introduced in the same manner. Keep in mind that auditing and logging can be circumvented by a shared account; this applies to both administrative and user/application/service accounts. Administrative accounts must not be shared. User/application/service accounts must be assigned at a level that allows the identification of a single source of access using the account, and that contains any damage to the privileges granted that account.

Over-privileged Application and Service Accounts

If application and service accounts are granted access to change configuration information on the system, they may be manipulated to do so by an attacker. The risk of this threat can be mitigated by adopting a policy of using least privileged service and application accounts. Be wary of granting accounts the ability to modify their own configuration information unless explicitly required by design.

Sensitive Data

Sensitive data is subject to a variety of threats. Attacks that attempt to view or modify sensitive data can target persistent data stores and networks. Top threats to sensitive data include:

- **Access to sensitive data in storage**
- **Network eavesdropping**
- **Data tampering**

Access to Sensitive Data in Storage

You must secure sensitive data in storage to prevent a user—malicious or otherwise—from gaining access to and reading the data.

Countermeasures to protect sensitive data in storage include:

- Use restricted ACLs on the persistent data stores that contain sensitive data.
- Store encrypted data.
- Use identity and role-based authorization to ensure that only the user or users with the appropriate level of authority are allowed access to sensitive data. Use role-based security to differentiate between users who can view data and users who can modify data.

Network Eavesdropping

The HTTP data for Web application travels across networks in plaintext and is subject to network eavesdropping attacks, where an attacker uses network monitoring software to capture and potentially modify sensitive data.

Countermeasures to prevent network eavesdropping and to provide privacy include:

- Encrypt the data.
- Use an encrypted communication channel, for example, SSL.

Data Tampering

Data tampering refers to the unauthorized modification of data, often as it is passed over the network.

One countermeasure to prevent data tampering is to protect sensitive data passed across the network with tamper-resistant protocols such as hashed message authentication codes (HMACs).

An HMAC provides message integrity in the following way:

1. The sender uses a shared secret key to create a hash based on the message payload.

2. The sender transmits the hash along with the message payload.

3. The receiver uses the shared key to recalculate the hash based on the received message payload. The receiver then compares the new hash value with the transmitted hash value. If they are the same, the message cannot have been tampered with.

Session Management

Session management for Web applications is an application layer responsibility. Session security is critical to the overall security of the application.

Top session management threats include:

- **Session hijacking**
- **Session replay**
- **Man in the middle**

Session Hijacking

A session hijacking attack occurs when an attacker uses network monitoring software to capture the authentication token (often a cookie) used to represent a user's session with an application. With the captured cookie, the attacker can spoof the user's session and gain access to the application. The attacker has the same level of privileges as the legitimate user.

Countermeasures to prevent session hijacking include:

- Use SSL to create a secure communication channel and only pass the authentication cookie over an HTTPS connection.
- Implement logout functionality to allow a user to end a session that forces authentication if another session is started.
- Make sure you limit the expiration period on the session cookie if you do not use SSL. Although this does not prevent session hijacking, it reduces the time window available to the attacker.

Session Replay

Session replay occurs when a user's session token is intercepted and submitted by an attacker to bypass the authentication mechanism. For example, if the session token is in plaintext in a cookie or URL, an attacker can sniff it. The attacker then posts a request using the hijacked session token.

Countermeasures to help address the threat of session replay include:

- Re-authenticate when performing critical functions. For example, prior to performing a monetary transfer in a banking application, make the user supply the account password again.
- Expire sessions appropriately, including all cookies and session tokens.
- Create a "do not remember me" option to allow no session data to be stored on the client.

Man in the Middle Attacks

A man in the middle attack occurs when the attacker intercepts messages sent between you and your intended recipient. The attacker then changes your message and sends it to the original recipient. The recipient receives the message, sees that it came from you, and acts on it. When the recipient sends a message back to you, the attacker intercepts it, alters it, and returns it to you. You and your recipient never know that you have been attacked.

Any network request involving client-server communication, including Web requests, Distributed Component Object Model (DCOM) requests, and calls to remote components and Web services, are subject to man in the middle attacks.

Countermeasures to prevent man in the middle attacks include:

- Use cryptography. If you encrypt the data before transmitting it, the attacker can still intercept it but cannot read it or alter it. If the attacker cannot read it, he or she cannot know which parts to alter. If the attacker blindly modifies your encrypted message, then the original recipient is unable to successfully decrypt it and, as a result, knows that it has been tampered with.
- Use Hashed Message Authentication Codes (HMACs). If an attacker alters the message, the recalculation of the HMAC at the recipient fails and the data can be rejected as invalid.

Cryptography

Most applications use cryptography to protect data and to ensure it remains private and unaltered. Top threats surrounding your application's use of cryptography include:

- **Poor key generation or key management**
- **Weak or custom encryption**
- **Checksum spoofing**

Poor Key Generation or Key Management

Attackers can decrypt encrypted data if they have access to the encryption key or can derive the encryption key. Attackers can discover a key if keys are managed poorly or if they were generated in a non-random fashion.

Countermeasures to address the threat of poor key generation and key management include:

- Use built-in encryption routines that include secure key management. Data Protection application programming interface (DPAPI) is an example of an encryption service provided on Windows 2000 and later operating systems where the operating system manages the key.
- Use strong random key generation functions and store the key in a restricted location—for example, in a registry key secured with a restricted ACL—if you use an encryption mechanism that requires you to generate or manage the key.
- Encrypt the encryption key using DPAPI for added security.
- Expire keys regularly.

Weak or Custom Encryption

An encryption algorithm provides no security if the encryption is cracked or is vulnerable to brute force cracking. Custom algorithms are particularly vulnerable if they have not been tested. Instead, use published, well-known encryption algorithms that have withstood years of rigorous attacks and scrutiny.

Countermeasures that address the vulnerabilities of weak or custom encryption include:

- Do not develop your own custom algorithms.
- Use the proven cryptographic services provided by the platform.
- Stay informed about cracked algorithms and the techniques used to crack them.

Checksum Spoofing

Do not rely on hashes to provide data integrity for messages sent over networks. Hashes such as Safe Hash Algorithm (SHA1) and Message Digest compression algorithm (MD5) can be intercepted and changed. Consider the following base 64 encoding UTF-8 message with an appended Message Authentication Code (MAC).

```
Plaintext: Place 10 orders.
Hash: TOmUNdEQh13IO9oTcaP4FYDX6pU=
```

If an attacker intercepts the message by monitoring the network, the attacker could update the message and recompute the hash (guessing the algorithm that you used). For example, the message could be changed to:

```
Plaintext: Place 100 orders.
Hash: oEDuJpv/ZtIU7BXDDNv17EAHeAU=
```

When recipients process the message, and they run the plaintext ("Place 100 orders") through the hashing algorithm, and then recompute the hash, the hash they calculate will be equal to whatever the attacker computed.

To counter this attack, use a MAC or HMAC. The Message Authentication Code Triple Data Encryption Standard (MACTripleDES) algorithm computes a MAC, and HMACSHA1 computes an HMAC. Both use a key to produce a checksum. With these algorithms, an attacker needs to know the key to generate a checksum that would compute correctly at the receiver.

Parameter Manipulation

Parameter manipulation attacks are a class of attack that relies on the modification of the parameter data sent between the client and Web application. This includes query strings, form fields, cookies, and HTTP headers. Top parameter manipulation threats include:

- **Query string manipulation**
- **Form field manipulation**
- **Cookie manipulation**
- **HTTP header manipulation**

Query String Manipulation

Users can easily manipulate the query string values passed by HTTP GET from client to server because they are displayed in the browser's URL address bar. If your application relies on query string values to make security decisions, or if the values represent sensitive data such as monetary amounts, the application is vulnerable to attack.

Countermeasures to address the threat of query string manipulation include:

- Avoid using query string parameters that contain sensitive data or data that can influence the security logic on the server. Instead, use a session identifier to identify the client and store sensitive items in the session store on the server.
- Choose HTTP POST instead of GET to submit forms.
- Encrypt query string parameters.

Form Field Manipulation

The values of HTML form fields are sent in plaintext to the server using the HTTP POST protocol. This may include visible and hidden form fields. Form fields of any type can be easily modified and client-side validation routines bypassed. As a result, applications that rely on form field input values to make security decisions on the server are vulnerable to attack.

To counter the threat of form field manipulation, instead of using hidden form fields, use session identifiers to reference state maintained in the state store on the server.

Cookie Manipulation

Cookies are susceptible to modification by the client. This is true of both persistent and memory-resident cookies. A number of tools are available to help an attacker modify the contents of a memory-resident cookie. Cookie manipulation is the attack that refers to the modification of a cookie, usually to gain unauthorized access to a Web site.

While SSL protects cookies over the network, it does not prevent them from being modified on the client computer. To counter the threat of cookie manipulation, encrypt or use an HMAC with the cookie.

HTTP Header Manipulation

HTTP headers pass information between the client and the server. The client constructs request headers while the server constructs response headers. If your application relies on request headers to make a decision, your application is vulnerable to attack.

Do not base your security decisions on HTTP headers. For example, do not trust the HTTP Referer to determine where a client came from because this is easily falsified.

Exception Management

Exceptions that are allowed to propagate to the client can reveal internal implementation details that make no sense to the end user but are useful to attackers. Applications that do not use exception handling or implement it poorly are also subject to denial of service attacks. Top exception handling threats include:

- **Attacker reveals implementation details**
- **Denial of service**

Attacker Reveals Implementation Details

One of the important features of the .NET Framework is that it provides rich exception details that are invaluable to developers. If the same information is allowed to fall into the hands of an attacker, it can greatly help the attacker exploit potential vulnerabilities and plan future attacks. The type of information that could be returned includes platform versions, server names, SQL command strings, and database connection strings.

Countermeasures to help prevent internal implementation details from being revealed to the client include:

- Use exception handling throughout your application's code base.
- Handle and log exceptions that are allowed to propagate to the application boundary.
- Return generic, harmless error messages to the client.

Denial of Service

Attackers will probe a Web application, usually by passing deliberately malformed input. They often have two goals in mind. The first is to cause exceptions that reveal useful information and the second is to crash the Web application process. This can occur if exceptions are not properly caught and handled.

Countermeasures to help prevent application-level denial of service include:

- Thoroughly validate all input data at the server.
- Use exception handling throughout your application's code base.

Auditing and Logging

Auditing and logging should be used to help detect suspicious activity such as footprinting or possible password cracking attempts before an exploit actually occurs. It can also help deal with the threat of repudiation. It is much harder for a user to deny performing an operation if a series of synchronized log entries on multiple servers indicate that the user performed that transaction.

Top auditing and logging related threats include:

- **User denies performing an operation**
- **Attackers exploit an application without leaving a trace**
- **Attackers cover their tracks**

User Denies Performing an Operation

The issue of repudiation is concerned with a user denying that he or she performed an action or initiated a transaction. You need defense mechanisms in place to ensure that all user activity can be tracked and recorded.

Countermeasures to help prevent repudiation threats include:

- Audit and log activity on the Web server and database server, and on the application server as well, if you use one.
- Log key events such as transactions and login and logout events.
- Do not use shared accounts since the original source cannot be determined.

Attackers Exploit an Application Without Leaving a Trace

System and application-level auditing is required to ensure that suspicious activity does not go undetected.

Countermeasures to detect suspicious activity include:

- Log critical application level operations.
- Use platform-level auditing to audit login and logout events, access to the file system, and failed object access attempts.
- Back up log files and regularly analyze them for signs of suspicious activity.

Attackers Cover Their Tracks

Your log files must be well-protected to ensure that attackers are not able to cover their tracks.

Countermeasures to help prevent attackers from covering their tracks include:

- Secure log files by using restricted ACLs.
- Relocate system log files away from their default locations.

Summary

By being aware of the typical approach used by attackers as well as their goals, you can be more effective when applying countermeasures. It also helps to use a goal-based approach when considering and identifying threats, and to use the STRIDE model to categorize threats based on the goals of the attacker, for example, to spoof identity, tamper with data, deny service, elevate privileges, and so on. This allows you to focus more on the general approaches that should be used for risk mitigation, rather than focusing on the identification of every possible attack, which can be a time-consuming and potentially fruitless exercise.

This chapter has shown you the top threats that have the potential to compromise your network, host infrastructure, and applications. Knowledge of these threats, together with the appropriate countermeasures, provides essential information for the threat modeling process It enables you to identify the threats that are specific to your particular scenario and prioritize them based on the degree of risk they pose to your system. This structured process for identifying and prioritizing threats is referred to as *threat modeling*. For more information, see Chapter 3, "Threat Modeling."

Additional Resources

For further related reading, see the following resources:

- For more information about network threats and countermeasures, see Chapter 15, "Securing Your Network."

- For more information about host threats and countermeasures, see Chapter 16, "Securing Your Web Server," Chapter 17, "Securing Your Application Server," Chapter 18, "Securing Your Database Server," and Chapter 19, "Securing Your ASP.NET Application."

- For more information about addressing the application level threats presented in this chapter, see the Building chapters in Part III, "Building Secure Web Applications" of this guide.

- Michael Howard and David LeBlanc, *Writing Secure Code* 2nd Edition. Microsoft Press, Redmond, WA, 2002

- For more information about tracking and fixing buffer overruns, see the MSDN article, "Fix Those Buffer Overruns," at *http://msdn.microsoft.com/library /default.asp?url=/library/en-us/dncode/html/secure05202002.asp*

3

Threat Modeling

In This Chapter

- Steps to decompose an application architecture to discover vulnerabilities
- How to identify and document threats that are relevant to your application

Overview

Threat modeling allows you to systematically identify and rate the threats that are most likely to affect your system. By identifying and rating threats based on a solid understanding of the architecture and implementation of your application, you can address threats with appropriate countermeasures in a logical order, starting with the threats that present the greatest risk.

Threat modeling has a structured approach that is far more cost efficient and effective than applying security features in a haphazard manner without knowing precisely what threats each feature is supposed to address. With a random, "shotgun" approach to security, how do you know when your application is "secure enough," and how do you know the areas where your application is still vulnerable? In short, until you know your threats, you cannot secure your system.

Before You Begin

Before you start the threat modeling process, it is important that you understand the following basic terminology:

- **Asset**. A resource of value, such as the data in a database or on the file system. A system resource.
- **Threat**. A potential occurrence, malicious or otherwise, that might damage or compromise your assets.

- **Vulnerability.** A weakness in some aspect or feature of a system that makes a threat possible. Vulnerabilities might exist at the network, host, or application levels.

- **Attack (or exploit).** An action taken by someone or something that harms an asset. This could be someone following through on a threat or exploiting a vulnerability.

- **Countermeasure.** A safeguard that addresses a threat and mitigates risk.

Consider a simple house analogy: an item of jewelry in a house is an asset and a burglar is an attacker. A door is a feature of the house and an open door represents a vulnerability. The burglar can exploit the open door to gain access to the house and steal the jewelry. In other words, the attacker exploits a vulnerability to gain access to an asset. The appropriate countermeasure in this case is to close and lock the door.

How to Use This Chapter

This chapter outlines a generic process that helps you identify and document threats to your application. The following are recommendations on how to use this chapter:

- **Establish a process for threat modeling.** Use this chapter as a starting point for introducing a threat modeling process in your organization if you do not already have one. If you already have a process, then you can use this as a reference for comparison.

- **Use the other chapters in this guide to familiarize yourself with the most common threats.** Read Chapter 2, "Threats and Countermeasures," for an overview of common threats that occur at the network, host, and application levels.

  - For more specific threats to your network, see "Threats and Countermeasures" in Chapter 15, "Securing Your Network."

  - For more specific threats to your Web server, application server, and database server, see "Threats and Countermeasures" in Chapter 16, "Securing Your Web Server," Chapter 17, "Securing Your Application Server," and Chapter 18, "Securing Your Database Server."

  - For more specific threats to your assemblies, ASP.NET, serviced components, remoted components, Web Services, and data access, see "Threats and Countermeasures" in Chapter 7, "Building Secure Assemblies;" Chapter 10, "Building Secure ASP.NET Pages and Controls;" Chapter 11, "Building Secure Serviced Components;" Chapter 12, "Building Secure Web Services;" Chapter 13, "Building Secure Remoted Components;" and Chapter 14, "Building Secure Data Access."

- **Evolve your threat model.** Build a threat model early and then evolve it as you go. It is a work in progress. Security threats evolve, and so does your application. Having a document that identifies both what the known threats are and how they have been addressed (or not) puts you in control of the security of your application.

Threat Modeling Principles

Threat modeling should not be a one time only process. It should be an iterative process that starts during the early phases of the design of your application and continues throughout the application life cycle. There are two reasons for this. First, it is impossible to identify all of the possible threats in a single pass. Second, because applications are rarely static and need to be enhanced and adapted to suit changing business requirements, the threat modeling process should be repeated as your application evolves.

The Process

Figure 3.1 shows the threat modeling process that you can perform using a six-stage process.

Note The following process outline can be used for applications that are currently in development and for existing applications.

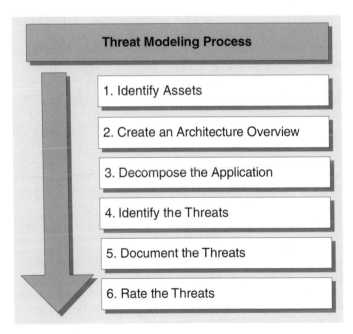

Figure 3.1
An overview of the threat modeling process

1. **Identify assets**.

   Identify the valuable assets that your systems must protect.

2. **Create an architecture overview**.

   Use simple diagrams and tables to document the architecture of your application, including subsystems, trust boundaries, and data flow.

3. **Decompose the application**.

   Decompose the architecture of your application, including the underlying network and host infrastructure design, to create a security profile for the application. The aim of the security profile is to uncover vulnerabilities in the design, implementation, or deployment configuration of your application.

4. **Identify the threats**.

   Keeping the goals of an attacker in mind, and with knowledge of the architecture and potential vulnerabilities of your application, identify the threats that could affect the application.

5. **Document the threats**.

   Document each threat using a common threat template that defines a core set of attributes to capture for each threat.

6. **Rate the threats**.

   Rate the threats to prioritize and address the most significant threats first. These threats present the biggest risk. The rating process weighs the probability of the threat against damage that could result should an attack occur. It might turn out that certain threats do not warrant any action when you compare the risk posed by the threat with the resulting mitigation costs.

The Output

The output from the threat modeling process is a document for the various members of your project team. It allows them to clearly understand the threats that need to be addressed and how to address them. Threat models consist of a definition of the architecture of your application and a list of threats for your application scenario, as Figure 3.2 shows.

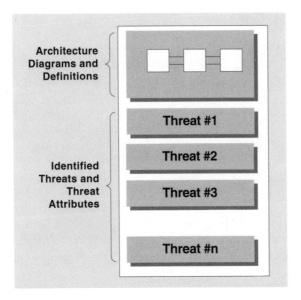

Figure 3.2
Components of the threat model

Step 1. Identify Assets

Identify the assets that you need to protect. This could range from confidential data, such as your customer or orders database, to your Web pages or Web site availability.

Step 2. Create an Architecture Overview

At this stage, the goal is to document the function of your application, its architecture and physical deployment configuration, and the technologies that form part of your solution. You should be looking for potential vulnerabilities in the design or implementation of the application.

During this step, you perform the following tasks:

- **Identify what the application does**.
- **Create an architecture diagram**.
- **Identify the technologies**.

Identify What the Application Does

Identify what the application does and how it uses and accesses assets. Document use cases to help you and others understand how your application is supposed to be used. This also helps you work out how it can be misused. Use cases put application functionality in context.

Here are some sample use cases for a self-service, employee human resources application:

- Employee views financial data.
- Employee updates personal data.
- Manager views employee details.

In the above cases you can look at the implications of the business rules being misused. For example, consider a user trying to modify personal details of another user. He or she should not be authorized to access those details according to the defined application requirements.

Create an Architecture Diagram

Create a high-level architecture diagram that describes the composition and structure of your application and its subsystems as well as its physical deployment characteristics, such as the diagram in Figure 3.3. Depending on the complexity of your system, you might need to create additional diagrams that focus on different areas, for example, a diagram to model the architecture of a middle-tier application server, or one to model the interaction with an external system.

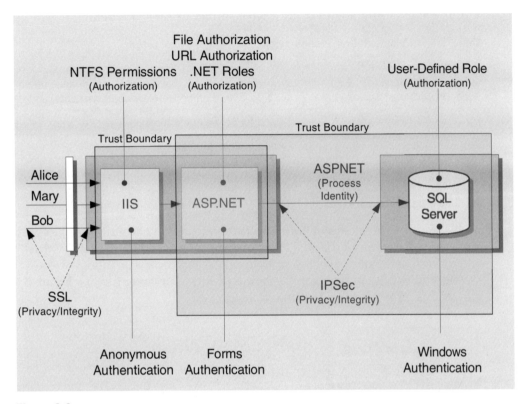

Figure 3.3
Sample application architecture diagram

Start by drawing a rough diagram that conveys the composition and structure of the application and its subsystems together with its deployment characteristics. Then, evolve the diagram by adding details about the trust boundaries, authentication, and authorization mechanisms as and when you discover them (usually during Step 3 when you decompose the application).

Identify the Technologies

Identify the distinct technologies that are used to implement your solution. This helps you focus on technology-specific threats later in the process. It also helps you determine the correct and most appropriate mitigation techniques. The technologies you are most likely to identify include ASP.NET, Web Services, Enterprise Services, Microsoft .NET Remoting, and ADO.NET. Also identify any unmanaged code that your application calls.

Document the technologies using a table similar to Table 3.1, below.

Table 3.1 Implementation Technologies

Technology/Platform	Implementation Details
Microsoft SQL Server on Microsoft Windows Advanced Server 2000	Includes logins, database users, user defined database roles, tables, stored procedures, views, constraints, and triggers.
Microsoft .NET Framework	Used for Forms authentication.
Secure Sockets Layer (SSL)	Used to encrypt HTTP traffic.

Step 3. Decompose the Application

In this step, you break down your application to create a security profile for the application based on traditional areas of vulnerability. You also identify trust boundaries, data flow, entry points, and privileged code. The more you know about the mechanics of your application, the easier it is to uncover threats. Figure 3.4 shows the various targets for the decomposition process.

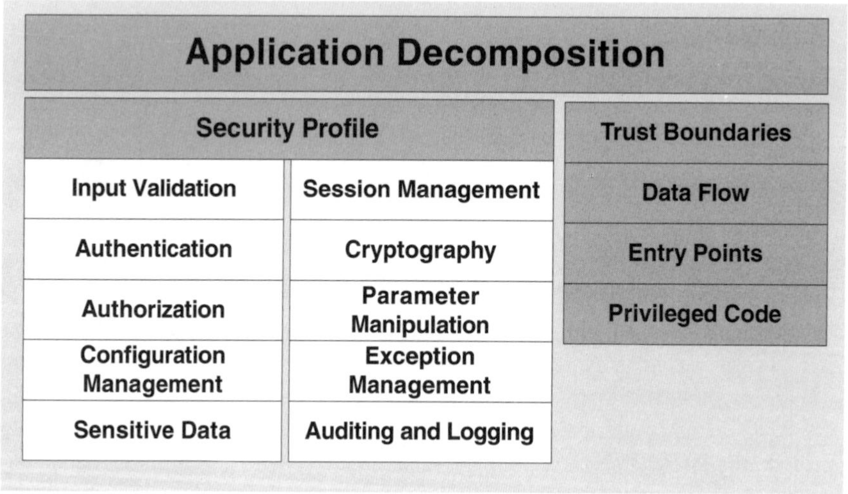

Application Decomposition			
Security Profile		**Trust Boundaries**
Input Validation	Session Management	Data Flow
Authentication	Cryptography	Entry Points
Authorization	Parameter Manipulation	Privileged Code
Configuration Management	Exception Management	
Sensitive Data	Auditing and Logging	

Figure 3.4
Targets for application decomposition

During this step, you perform the following tasks:

- **Identify trust boundaries**.
- **Identify data flow**.
- **Identify entry points**.
- **Identify privileged code**.
- **Document the security profile**.

Identify Trust Boundaries

Identify the trust boundaries that surround each of the tangible assets of your application. These assets are determined by your application design. For each subsystem, consider whether the upstream data flows or user input is trusted, and if not, consider how the data flows and input can be authenticated and authorized. Also consider whether the calling code is trusted, and if it is not, consider how it can be authenticated and authorized. You must be able to ensure that the appropriate gatekeepers guard all entry points into a particular trust boundary and that the recipient entry point fully validates all data passed across a trust boundary.

Start by analyzing trust boundaries from a code perspective. The assembly, which represents one form of trust boundary, is a useful place to start. Which assemblies trust which other assemblies? Does a particular assembly trust the code that calls it, or does it use code access security to authorize the calling code?

Also consider server trust relationships. Does a particular server trust an upstream server to authenticate and authorize the end users, or does the server provide its own gatekeeping services? Also, does a server trust an upstream server to pass it data that is well formed and correct?

For example, in Figure 3.3, the Web application accesses the database server by using a fixed, trusted identity, which in this case is the ASPNET Web application process account. In this scenario, the database server trusts the application to authenticate and authorize callers and forward only valid data request data on behalf of authorized users.

Note In a .NET Framework application, the assembly defines the smallest unit of trust. Whenever data is passed across an assembly boundary—which by definition includes an application domain, process, or machine boundary—the recipient entry point should validate its input data.

Identify Data Flow

A simple approach is to start at the highest level and then iteratively decompose the application by analyzing the data flow between individual subsystems. For example, analyze the data flow between a Web application and an Enterprise Services application and then between individual serviced components.

Data flow across trust boundaries is particularly important because code that is passed data from outside its own trust boundary should assume that the data is malicious and perform thorough validation of the data.

Note Data flow diagrams (DFDs) and sequence diagrams can help with the formal decomposition of a system. A DFD is a graphical representation of data flows, data stores, and relationships between data sources and destinations. A sequence diagram shows how a group of objects collaborate in terms of chronological events.

Identify Entry Points

The entry points of your application also serve as entry points for attacks. Entry points might include the front-end Web application listening for HTTP requests. This entry point is intended to be exposed to clients. Other entry points, such as internal entry points exposed by subcomponents across the tiers of your application, may only exist to support internal communication with other components. However, you should know where these are, and what types of input they receive in case an attacker manages to bypass the front door of the application and directly attack an internal entry point.

For each entry point, you should be able to determine the types of gatekeepers that provide authorization and the degree of validation.

Logical application entry points include user interfaces provide by Web pages, service interfaces provided by Web services, serviced components, and .NET Remoting components and message queues that provide asynchronous entry points. Physical or platform entry points include ports and sockets.

Identify Privileged Code

Privileged code accesses specific types of secure resources and performs other privileged operations. Secure resource types include DNS servers, directory services, environment variables, event logs, file systems, message queues, performance counters, printers, the registry, sockets, and Web services. Secure operations include unmanaged code calls, reflection, serialization, code access security permissions, and manipulation of code access security policy, including evidence.

Privileged code must be granted the appropriate code access security permissions by code access security policy. Privileged code must ensure that the resources and operations that it encapsulates are not exposed to untrusted and potentially malicious code. .NET Framework code access security verifies the permissions granted to calling code by performing stack walks. However, it is sometimes necessary to override this behavior and short-circuit the full stack walk, for example, when you want to restrict privileged code with a sandbox or otherwise isolate privileged code. Doing so opens your code up to luring attacks, where malicious code calls your code through trusted intermediary code.

Whenever you override the default security behavior provided by code access security, do it diligently and with the appropriate safeguards. For more information about reviewing code for security flaws, see Chapter 21, "Code Review." For more information about code access security, see Chapter 8, "Code Access Security in Practice" and Chapter 9, "Using Code Access Security with ASP.NET."

Document the Security Profile

Next, you should identify the design and implementation approaches used for input validation, authentication, authorization, configuration management, and the remaining areas where applications are most susceptible to vulnerabilities. By doing this, you create a security profile for the application.

The following table shows what kinds of questions to ask while analyzing each aspect of the design and implementation of your application. For more information about reviewing application architecture and design, see Chapter 5, "Architecture and Design Review."

Table 3.2   Creating a Security Profile

Category	Considerations
Input validation	Is all input data validated?
	Could an attacker inject commands or malicious data into the application?
	Is data validated as it is passed between separate trust boundaries (by the recipient entry point)?
	Can data in the database be trusted?
Authentication	Are credentials secured if they are passed over the network?
	Are strong account policies used?
	Are strong passwords enforced?
	Are you using certificates?
	Are password verifiers (using one-way hashes) used for user passwords?
Authorization	What gatekeepers are used at the entry points of the application?
	How is authorization enforced at the database?
	Is a defense in depth strategy used?
	Do you fail securely and only allow access upon successful confirmation of credentials?
Configuration management	What administration interfaces does the application support?
	How are they secured?
	How is remote administration secured?
	What configuration stores are used and how are they secured?
Sensitive data	What sensitive data is handled by the application?
	How is it secured over the network and in persistent stores?
	What type of encryption is used and how are encryption keys secured?

(continued)

Table 3.2 Creating a Security Profile *(continued)*

Category	Considerations
Session management	How are session cookies generated?
	How are they secured to prevent session hijacking?
	How is persistent session state secured?
	How is session state secured as it crosses the network?
	How does the application authenticate with the session store?
	Are credentials passed over the wire and are they maintained by the application? If so, how are they secured?
Cryptography	What algorithms and cryptographic techniques are used?
	How long are encryption keys and how are they secured?
	Does the application put its own encryption into action?
	How often are keys recycled?
Parameter manipulation	Does the application detect tampered parameters?
	Does it validate all parameters in form fields, view state, cookie data, and HTTP headers?
Exception management	How does the application handle error conditions?
	Are exceptions ever allowed to propagate back to the client?
	Are generic error messages that do not contain exploitable information used?
Auditing and logging	Does your application audit activity across all tiers on all servers?
	How are log files secured?

Step 4. Identify the Threats

In this step, you identify threats that might affect your system and compromise your assets. To conduct this identification process, bring members of the development and test teams together to conduct an informed brainstorming session in front of a whiteboard. This is a simple yet effective way to identify potential threats. Ideally, the team consists of application architects, security professionals, developers, testers, and system administrators.

You can use two basic approaches:

- **Use STRIDE to identify threats**. Consider the broad categories of threats, such as spoofing, tampering, and denial of service, and use the STRIDE model from Chapter 2, "Threats and Countermeasures" to ask questions in relation to each aspect of the architecture and design of your application. This is a goal-based approach where you consider the goals of an attacker. For example, could an attacker spoof an identity to access your server or Web application? Could someone tamper with data over the network or in a store? Could someone deny service?

- **Use categorized threat lists**. With this approach, you start with a laundry list of common threats grouped by network, host, and application categories. Next, apply the threat list to your own application architecture and any vulnerabilities you have identified earlier in the process. You will be able to rule some threats out immediately because they do not apply to your scenario.

Use the following resources to help you with the threat identification process:

- For a list of threats organized by network, host, and application layers, as well as explanations of the threats and associated countermeasures, see Chapter 2, "Threats and Countermeasures."

- For a list of threats by technology, see "Threats and Countermeasures" at the beginning of each of the "Building" chapters in Part III of this guide.

During this step, you perform the following tasks:

- **Identify network threats**.
- **Identity host threats**.
- **Identify application threats**.

Identify Network Threats

This is a task for network designers and administrators. Analyze the network topology and the flow of data packets, together with router, firewall, and switch configurations, and look for potential vulnerabilities. Also pay attention to virtual private network (VPN) endpoints. Review the network defenses against the most common network layer threats identified in Chapter 2, "Threats and Countermeasures."

Top network threats to consider during the design phase include:

- Using security mechanisms that rely on the IP address of the sender. It is relatively easy to send IP packets with false source IP addresses (IP spoofing).

- Passing session identifiers or cookies over unencrypted network channels. This can lead to IP session hijacking.

- Passing clear text authentication credentials or other sensitive data over unencrypted communication channels. This could allow an attacker to monitor the network, obtain logon credentials, or obtain and possibly tamper with other sensitive data items.

You must also ensure that your network is not vulnerable to threats arising from insecure device and server configuration. For example, are unnecessary ports and protocols closed and disabled? Are routing tables and DNS server secured? Are the TCP network stacks hardened on your servers? For more information about preventing this type of vulnerability, see Chapter 15, "Securing Your Network."

Identify Host Threats

The approach used throughout this guide when configuring host security (that is, Microsoft Windows 2000 and .NET Framework configuration) is to divide the configuration into separate categories to allow you to apply security settings in a structured and logical manner. This approach is also ideally suited for reviewing security, spotting vulnerabilities, and identifying threats. Common configuration categories applicable to all server roles include patches and updates, services, protocols, accounts, files and directories, shares, ports, and auditing and logging. For each category, identify potentially vulnerable configuration settings. From these, identify threats.

Top vulnerabilities to consider include:

- Maintaining unpatched servers, which can be exploited by viruses, Trojan horses, worms, and well-known IIS attacks.
- Using nonessential ports, protocols, and services, which increase the attack profile and enable attackers to gather information about and exploit your environment.
- Allowing unauthenticated anonymous access.
- Using weak passwords and account policies that lead to password cracking, identity spoofing, and denial of service attacks if accounts can be locked out deliberately.

Identify Application Threats

In the previous steps, you defined the architecture, data flow, and trust boundaries of your application. You also created a security profile that describes how the application handles core areas, such as authentication, authorization, configuration management, and other areas.

Now use the broad STRIDE threat categories and predefined threat lists to scrutinize each aspect of the security profile of your application. Focus on application threats, technology-specific threats, and code threats. Key vulnerabilities to consider include:

- Using poor input validation that leads to cross-site scripting (XSS), SQL injection, and buffer overflow attacks.
- Passing authentication credentials or authentication cookies over unencrypted network links, which can lead to credential capture or session hijacking.
- Using weak password and account policies, which can lead to unauthorized access.

- Failing to secure the configuration management aspects of your application, including administration interfaces.
- Storing configuration secrets, such as connection strings and service account credentials, in clear text.
- Using over-privileged process and service accounts.
- Using insecure data access coding techniques, which can increase the threat posed by SQL injection.
- Using weak or custom encryption and failing to adequately secure encryption keys.
- Relying on the integrity of parameters that are passed from the Web browser, for example, form fields, query strings, cookie data, and HTTP headers.
- Using insecure exception handling, which can lead to denial of service attacks and the disclosure of system-level details that are useful to an attacker.
- Doing inadequate auditing and logging, which can lead to repudiation threats.

Using Attack Trees and Attack Patterns

Attack trees and attack patterns are the primary tools that security professionals use. These are not essential components of the threat identification phase but you may find them useful. They allow you to analyze threats in greater depth, going beyond what you already know to identify other possibilities.

Important When you use previously prepared categorized lists of known threats, it only reveals the common, known threats. Additional approaches, such as the use of attack trees and attack patterns, can help you identify other potential threats.

An attack tree is a way of collecting and documenting the potential attacks on your system in a structured and hierarchical manner. The tree structure gives you a descriptive breakdown of various attacks that the attacker uses to compromise the system. By creating attack trees, you create a reusable representation of security issues that helps focus efforts. Your test team can create test plans to validate security design. Developers can make tradeoffs during implementation and architects or developer leads can evaluate the security cost of alternative approaches.

Attack patterns are a formalized approach to capturing attack information in your enterprise. These patterns can help you identify common attack techniques.

Creating Attack Trees

While several approaches can be used in practice, the accepted method is to identify goals and sub-goals of an attack, as well as what must be done so that the attack succeeds. You can use a hierarchical diagram to represent your attack tree, or use a simple outline. What is important in the end is that you have something that portrays the attack profile of your application. You can then evaluate likely security risks, which you can mitigate with the appropriate countermeasures, such as correcting a design approach, hardening a configuration setting, and other solutions.

Start building an attack tree by creating root nodes that represent the goals of the attacker. Then add the leaf nodes, which are the attack methodologies that represent unique attacks. Figure 3.5 shows a simple example.

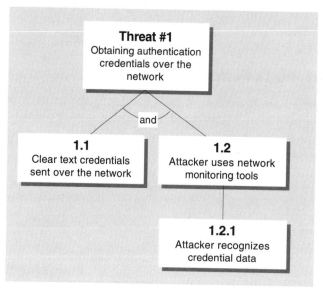

Figure 3.5

Representation of an attack tree

You can label leaf nodes with **AND** and **OR** labels. For example, in Figure 3.5, both 1.1 and 1.2 must occur for the threat to result in an attack.

Attack trees like the one shown above have a tendency to become complex quickly. They are also time-consuming to create. An alternative approach favored by some teams is to structure your attack tree using an outline such as the one shown below.

```
1.  Goal One
      1.1 Sub-goal one
      1.2 Sub-goal two
2.  Goal Two
      2.1 Sub-goal one
      2.2 Sub-goal two
```

Note In addition to goals and sub-goals, attack trees include methodologies and required conditions.

Here is an example of the outline approach in action:

```
Threat #1 Attacker obtains authentication credentials by monitoring the network
    1.1 Clear text credentials sent over the network AND
    1.2 Attacker uses network-monitoring tools
        1.2.1 Attacker recognizes credential data
```

For a complete example, see "Sample Attack Trees" in the "Cheat Sheets" section of this guide.

Attack Patterns

Attack patterns are generic representations of commonly occurring attacks that can occur in a variety of different contexts. The pattern defines the goal of the attack as well as the conditions that must exist for the attack to occur, the steps that are required to perform the attack, and the results of the attack. Attack patterns focus on attack techniques, whereas STRIDE-based approaches focus on the goals of the attacker.

An example of an attack pattern is the code-injection attack pattern that is used to describe code injection attacks in a generic way. Table 3.3 describes the code-injection attack pattern.

Table 3.3   Code Injection Attack Pattern

Pattern	Code injection attacks
Attack goals	Command or code execution
Required conditions	Weak input validation Code from the attacker has sufficient privileges on the server.
Attack technique	1. Identify program on target system with an input validation vulnerability. 2. Create code to inject and run using the security context of the target application. 3. Construct input value to insert code into the address space of the target application and force a stack corruption that causes application execution to jump to the injected code.
Attack results	Code from the attacker runs and performs malicious action.

For more information about attack patterns, see the "Additional References" section at the end of this chapter.

Step 5. Document the Threats

To document the threats of your application, use a template that shows several threat attributes similar to the one below. The threat description and threat target are essential attributes. Leave the risk rating blank at this stage. This is used in the final stage of the threat modeling process when you prioritize the identified threat list. Other attributes you may want to include are the attack techniques, which can also highlight the vulnerabilities exploited, and the countermeasures that are required to address the threat.

Table 3.4   Threat 1

Threat Description	Attacker obtains authentication credentials by monitoring the network
Threat target	Web application user authentication process
Risk	
Attack techniques	Use of network monitoring software
Countermeasures	Use SSL to provide encrypted channel

Table 3.5   Threat 2

Threat Description	Injection of SQL commands
Threat target	Data access component
Risk	
Attack techniques	Attacker appends SQL commands to user name, which is used to form a SQL query
Countermeasures	Use a regular expression to validate the user name, and use a stored procedure that uses parameters to access the database.

Step 6. Rate the Threats

At this stage in the process, you have a list of threats that apply to your particular application scenario. In the final step of the process, you rate threats based on the risks they pose. This allows you to address the threats that present the most risk first, and then resolve the other threats. In fact, it may not be economically viable to address all of the identified threats, and you may decide to ignore some because of the chance of them occurring is small and the damage that would result if they did is minimal.

Risk = Probability * Damage Potential

This formula indicates that the risk posed by a particular threat is equal to the probability of the threat occurring multiplied by the damage potential, which indicates the consequences to your system if an attack were to occur.

You can use a 1–10 scale for probability where 1 represents a threat that is very unlikely to occur and 10 represents a near certainty. Similarly, you can use a 1–10 scale for damage potential where 1 indicates minimal damage and 10 represents a catastrophe. Using this approach, the risk posed by a threat with a low likelihood of occurring but with high damage potential is equal to the risk posed by a threat with limited damage potential but that is extremely likely to occur.

For example, if **Probability**=10 and **Damage Potential**=1, then Risk = 10 * 1 = 10. If **Probability**=1 and **Damage Potential**=10, then Risk = 1 * 10 = 10.

This approach results in a scale of 1–100, and you can divide the scale into three bands to generate a High, Medium, or Low risk rating.

High, Medium, and Low Ratings

You can use a simple High, Medium, or Low scale to prioritize threats. If a threat is rated as High, it poses a significant risk to your application and needs to be addressed as soon as possible. Medium threats need to be addressed, but with less urgency. You may decide to ignore low threats depending upon how much effort and cost is required to address the threat.

DREAD

The problem with a simplistic rating system is that team members usually will not agree on ratings. To help solve this, add new dimensions that help determine what the impact of a security threat really means. At Microsoft, the DREAD model is used to help calculate risk. By using the DREAD model, you arrive at the risk rating for a given threat by asking the following questions:

- **Damage potential:** How great is the damage if the vulnerability is exploited?
- **Reproducibility:** How easy is it to reproduce the attack?
- **Exploitability:** How easy is it to launch an attack?
- **Affected users:** As a rough percentage, how many users are affected?
- **Discoverability:** How easy is it to find the vulnerability?

You can use above items to rate each threat. You can also extend the above questions to meet your needs. For example, you could add a question about potential reputation damage:

Reputation: How high are the stakes? Is there a risk to reputation, which could lead to the loss of customer trust?

Ratings do not have to use a large scale because this makes it difficult to rate threats consistently alongside one another. You can use a simple scheme such as High (1), Medium (2), and Low (3).

When you clearly define what each value represents for your rating system, it helps avoids confusion. Table 3.6 shows a typical example of a rating table that can be used by team members when prioritizing threats.

Table 3.6 Thread Rating Table

	Rating	High (3)	Medium (2)	Low (1)
D	Damage potential	The attacker can subvert the security system; get full trust authorization; run as administrator; upload content.	Leaking sensitive information	Leaking trivial information
R	Reproducibility	The attack can be reproduced every time and does not require a timing window.	The attack can be reproduced, but only with a timing window and a particular race situation.	The attack is very difficult to reproduce, even with knowledge of the security hole.
E	Exploitability	A novice programmer could make the attack in a short time.	A skilled programmer could make the attack, then repeat the steps.	The attack requires an extremely skilled person and in-depth knowledge every time to exploit.
A	Affected users	All users, default configuration, key customers	Some users, non-default configuration	Very small percentage of users, obscure feature; affects anonymous users
D	Discoverability	Published information explains the attack. The vulnerability is found in the most commonly used feature and is very noticeable.	The vulnerability is in a seldom-used part of the product, and only a few users should come across it. It would take some thinking to see malicious use.	The bug is obscure, and it is unlikely that users will work out damage potential.

After you ask the above questions, count the values (1–3) for a given threat. The result can fall in the range of 5–15. Then you can treat threats with overall ratings of 12–15 as High risk, 8–11 as Medium risk, and 5–7 as Low risk.

For example, consider the two threats described earlier:

- Attacker obtains authentication credentials by monitoring the network.
- SQL commands injected into application.

Table 3.7 shows an example DREAD rating for both threats:

Table 3.7   DREAD rating

Threat	D	R	E	A	D	Total	Rating
Attacker obtains authentication credentials by monitoring the network.	3	3	2	2	2	12	High
SQL commands injected into application.	3	3	3	3	2	14	High

Once you have obtained the risk rating, you update the documented threats and add the discovered rating level, which is High for both of the above threats. Table 3.8 shows an example.

Table 3.8   Threat 1

Threat Description	Attacker obtains authentication credentials by monitoring the network
Threat target	Web application user authentication process
Risk rating	High
Attack techniques	Use of network monitoring software
Countermeasures	Use SSL to provide encrypted channel

What Comes After Threat Modeling?

The output of the threat modeling process includes documentation of the security aspects of the architecture of your application and a list of rated threats. The threat model helps you orchestrate development team members and focus on the most potent threats.

Important   Threat modeling is an iterative process. The threat model is a document that evolves and that various team members can work from.

The threat model can be used by the following groups of people:

- Designers can use it to make secure design choices about technologies and functionality.
- Developers who write code can use it to mitigate risks.
- Testers can write test cases to test if the application is vulnerable to the threats identified by the analysis.

Generating a Work Item Report

From the initial threat model, you can create a more formalized work item report that can include additional attributes, such as a Bug ID, which can be used to tie the threat in with your favorite bug tracking system. In fact, you may choose to enter the identified threats in your bug tracking system and use its reporting facilities to generate the report. You can also include a status column to indicate whether or not the bug has been fixed. You should make sure the report includes the original threat number to tie it back to the threat model document.

Organize the threats in the report by network, host, and application categories. This makes the report easier to consume for different team members in different roles. Within each category, present the threats in prioritized order starting with the ones given a high risk rating followed by the threats that present less risk.

Summary

While you can mitigate the risk of an attack, you do not mitigate or eliminate the actual threat. Threats still exist regardless of the security actions you take and the countermeasures you apply. The reality in the security world is that you acknowledge the presence of threats and you manage your risks. Threat modeling can help you manage and communicate security risks across your team.

Treat threat modeling as an iterative process. Your threat model should be a dynamic item that changes over time to cater to new types of threats and attacks as they are discovered. It should also be capable of adapting to follow the natural evolution of your application as it is enhanced and modified to accommodate changing business requirements.

Additional Resources

For additional related reading, see the following resources:

- For information on attack patterns, see "Attack Modeling for Information Security and Survivability," by Andrew P. Moore, Robert J. Ellison, and Richard C. Linger at *http://www.cert.org/archive/pdf/01tn001.pdf*

- For information on evaluating threats, assets and vulnerabilities, see "Operationally Critical Threat, Asset, and Vulnerability Evaluation (OCTAVE) Framework, Version 1.0" on the Carnegie Mellon Software Engineering Institute Web site at *http://www.sei.cmu.edu/publications/documents/99.reports/99tr017 /99tr017figures.html*

- For a walkthrough of threat modeling, see "Architect WebCast: Using Threat Models to Design Secure Solutions" at *http://www.microsoft.com/usa/webcasts /ondemand/1617.asp*

- For more information on creating DFDs, see *Writing Secure Code, Second Edition*, by Michael Howard, David C. LeBlanc.

Part II

Designing Secure Web Applications

In This Part:

- Design Guidelines for Secure Web Applications
- Architecture and Design Review for Security

4

Design Guidelines for Secure Web Applications

In This Chapter

- Designing input validation strategies
- Partitioning Web sites into open and restricted areas
- Implementing effective account management practices
- Developing effective authentication and authorization strategies
- Protecting sensitive data
- Protecting user sessions
- Preventing parameter manipulation
- Handling exceptions securely
- Securing an application's configuration management features
- Listing audit and logging considerations

Overview

Web applications present a complex set of security issues for architects, designers, and developers. The most secure and hack-resilient Web applications are those that have been built from the ground up with security in mind.

In addition to applying sound architectural and design practices, incorporate deployment considerations and corporate security policies during the early design phases. Failure to do so can result in applications that cannot be deployed on an existing infrastructure without compromising security.

This chapter presents a set of secure architecture and design guidelines. They have been organized by common application vulnerability category. These are key areas for Web application security and they are the areas where mistakes are most often made.

How to Use This Chapter

This chapter focuses on the guidelines and principles you should follow when designing an application. The following are recommendations on how to use this chapter:

- **Know the threats to your application so that you can make sure these are addressed by your design**. Read Chapter 2, "Threats and Countermeasures," to gain understanding of the threat types to consider. Chapter 2 lists the threats that may harm your application; keep these threats in mind during the design phase.

- **When designing your application, take a systematic approach to the key areas where your application could be vulnerable to attack**. Focus on deployment considerations; input validation; authentication and authorization; cryptography and data sensitivity; configuration, session, and exception management; and adequate auditing and logging to ensure accountability.

Architecture and Design Issues for Web Applications

Web applications present designers and developers with many challenges. The stateless nature of HTTP means that tracking per-user session state becomes the responsibility of the application. As a precursor to this, the application must be able to identify the user by using some form of authentication. Given that all subsequent authorization decisions are based on the user's identity, it is essential that the authentication process is secure and that the session handling mechanism used to track authenticated users is equally well protected. Designing secure authentication and session management mechanisms are just a couple of the issues facing Web application designers and developers. Other challenges occur because input and output data passes over public networks. Preventing parameter manipulation and the disclosure of sensitive data are other top issues.

Some of the top issues that must be addressed with secure design practices are shown in Figure 4.1.

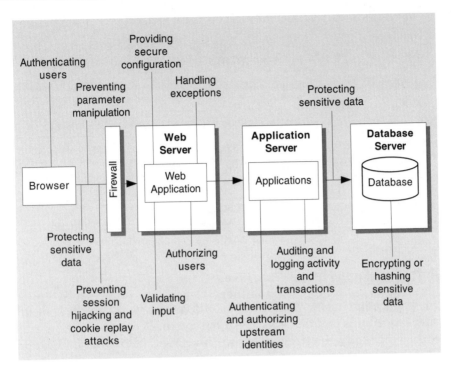

Figure 4.1
Web application design issues

The design guidelines in this chapter are organized by application vulnerability category. Experience shows that poor design in these areas, in particular, leads to security vulnerabilities. Table 4.1 lists the vulnerability categories, and for each one highlights the potential problems that can occur due to bad design.

Table 4.1 Web Application Vulnerabilities and Potential Problem Due to Bad Design

Vulnerability Category	Potential Problem Due to Bad Design
Input Validation	Attacks performed by embedding malicious strings in query strings, form fields, cookies, and HTTP headers. These include command execution, cross-site scripting (XSS), SQL injection, and buffer overflow attacks.
Authentication	Identity spoofing, password cracking, elevation of privileges, and unauthorized access.
Authorization	Access to confidential or restricted data, tampering, and execution of unauthorized operations.
Configuration Management	Unauthorized access to administration interfaces, ability to update configuration data, and unauthorized access to user accounts and account profiles.

(continued)

Table 4.1   Web Application Vulnerabilities and Potential Problem Due to Bad Design *(continued)*

Vulnerability Category	Potential Problem Due to Bad Design
Sensitive Data	Confidential information disclosure and data tampering.
Session Management	Capture of session identifiers resulting in session hijacking and identity spoofing.
Cryptography	Access to confidential data or account credentials, or both.
Parameter Manipulation	Path traversal attacks, command execution, and bypass of access control mechanisms among others, leading to information disclosure, elevation of privileges, and denial of service.
Exception Management	Denial of service and disclosure of sensitive system level details.
Auditing and Logging	Failure to spot the signs of intrusion, inability to prove a user's actions, and difficulties in problem diagnosis.

Deployment Considerations

During the application design phase, you should review your corporate security policies and procedures together with the infrastructure your application is to be deployed on. Frequently, the target environment is rigid, and your application design must reflect the restrictions. Sometimes design tradeoffs are required, for example, because of protocol or port restrictions, or specific deployment topologies. Identify constraints early in the design phase to avoid surprises later and involve members of the network and infrastructure teams to help with this process.

Figure 4.2 shows the various deployment aspects that require design time consideration.

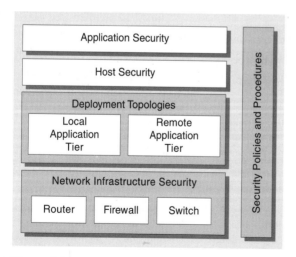

Figure 4.2

Deployment considerations

Security Policies and Procedures

Security policy determines what your applications are allowed to do and what the users of the application are permitted to do. More importantly, they define restrictions to determine what applications and users are not allowed to do. Identify and work within the framework defined by your corporate security policy while designing your applications to make sure you do not breach policy that might prevent the application being deployed.

Network Infrastructure Components

Make sure you understand the network structure provided by your target environment and understand the baseline security requirements of the network in terms of filtering rules, port restrictions, supported protocols, and so on.

Identify how firewalls and firewall policies are likely to affect your application's design and deployment. There may be firewalls to separate the Internet-facing applications from the internal network. There may be additional firewalls in front of the database. These can affect your possible communication ports and, therefore, authentication options from the Web server to remote application and database servers. For example, Windows authentication requires additional ports.

At the design stage, consider what protocols, ports, and services are allowed to access internal resources from the Web servers in the perimeter network. Also identify the protocols and ports that the application design requires and analyze the potential threats that occur from opening new ports or using new protocols.

Communicate and record any assumptions made about network and application layer security and which component will handle what. This prevents security controls from being missed when both development and network teams assume that the other team is addressing the issue. Pay attention to the security defenses that your application relies upon the network to provide. Consider the implications of a change in network configuration. How much security have you lost if you implement a specific network change?

Deployment Topologies

Your application's deployment topology and whether you have a remote application tier is a key consideration that must be incorporated in your design. If you have a remote application tier, you need to consider how to secure the network between servers to address the network eavesdropping threat and to provide privacy and integrity for sensitive data.

Also consider identity flow and identify the accounts that will be used for network authentication when your application connects to remote servers. A common approach is to use a least privileged process account and create a duplicate (mirrored) account on the remote server with the same password. Alternatively, you might use a domain process account, which provides easier administration but is more problematic to secure because of the difficulty of limiting the account's use throughout the network. An intervening firewall or separate domains without trust relationships often makes the local account approach the only viable option.

Intranet, Extranet, and Internet

Intranet, extranet, and Internet application scenarios each present design challenges. Questions that you should consider include: How will you flow caller identity through multiple application tiers to back-end resources? Where will you perform authentication? Can you trust authentication at the frontend and then use a trusted connection to access back-end resources? In extranet scenarios, you also must consider whether you trust partner accounts.

For more information about these and other scenario-specific issues, see the "Intranet Security," "Extranet Security," and "Internet Security" sections in the "Microsoft *patterns & practices* Volume I, *Building Secure ASP.NET Applications: Authentication, Authorization, and Secure Communication*" at *http://msdn.microsoft.com/library/en-us/dnnetsec/html/secnetlpMSDN.asp.*

Input Validation

Input validation is a challenging issue and the primary burden of a solution falls on application developers. However, proper input validation is one of your strongest measures of defense against today's application attacks. Proper input validation is an effective countermeasure that can help prevent XSS, SQL injection, buffer overflows, and other input attacks.

Input validation is challenging because there is not a single answer for what constitutes valid input across applications or even within applications. Likewise, there is no single definition of malicious input. Adding to this difficulty is that what your application does with this input influences the risk of exploit. For example, do you store data for use by other applications or does your application consume input from data sources created by other applications?

The following practices improve your Web application's input validation:

- **Assume all input is malicious**.
- **Centralize your approach.**
- **Do not rely on client-side validation.**
- **Be careful with canonicalization issues.**
- **Constrain, reject, and sanitize your input.**

Assume All Input Is Malicious

Input validation starts with a fundamental supposition that all input is malicious until proven otherwise. Whether input comes from a service, a file share, a user, or a database, validate your input if the source is outside your trust boundary. For example, if you call an external Web service that returns strings, how do you know that malicious commands are not present? Also, if several applications write to a shared database, when you read data, how do you know whether it is safe?

Centralize Your Approach

Make your input validation strategy a core element of your application design. Consider a centralized approach to validation, for example, by using common validation and filtering code in shared libraries. This ensures that validation rules are applied consistently. It also reduces development effort and helps with future maintenance.

In many cases, individual fields require specific validation, for example, with specifically developed regular expressions. However, you can frequently factor out common routines to validate regularly used fields such as e-mail addresses, titles, names, postal addresses including ZIP or postal codes, and so on. This approach is shown in Figure 4.3.

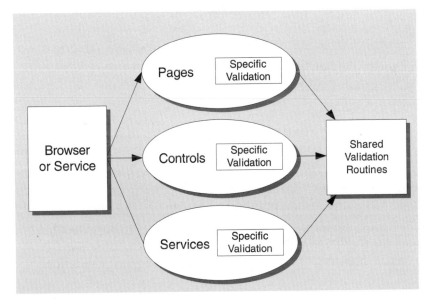

Figure 4.3
A centralized approach to input validation

Do Not Rely on Client-Side Validation

Server-side code should perform its own validation. What if an attacker bypasses your client, or shuts off your client-side script routines, for example, by disabling JavaScript? Use client-side validation to help reduce the number of round trips to the server but do not rely on it for security. This is an example of defense in depth.

Be Careful with Canonicalization Issues

Data in canonical form is in its most standard or simplest form. Canonicalization is the process of converting data to its canonical form. File paths and URLs are particularly prone to canonicalization issues and many well-known exploits are a direct result of canonicalization bugs. For example, consider the following string that contains a file and path in its canonical form.

```
c:\temp\somefile.dat
```

The following strings could also represent the same file.

```
somefile.dat
c:\temp\subdir\..\somefile.dat
c:\  temp\  somefile.dat
..\somefile.dat
c%3A%5Ctemp%5Csubdir%5C%2E%2E%5Csomefile.dat
```

In the last example, characters have been specified in hexadecimal form:

- %3A is the colon character.
- %5C is the backslash character.
- %2E is the dot character.

You should generally try to avoid designing applications that accept input file names from the user to avoid canonicalization issues. Consider alternative designs instead. For example, let the application determine the file name for the user.

If you do need to accept input file names, make sure they are strictly formed before making security decisions such as granting or denying access to the specified file.

For more information about how to handle file names and to perform file I/O in a secure manner, see the "File I/O" sections in Chapter 7, "Building Secure Assemblies," and Chapter 8, "Code Access Security in Practice."

Constrain, Reject, and Sanitize Your Input

The preferred approach to validating input is to constrain what you allow from the beginning. It is much easier to validate data for known valid types, patterns, and ranges than it is to validate data by looking for known bad characters. When you design your application, you know what your application expects. The range of valid data is generally a more finite set than potentially malicious input. However, for defense in depth you may also want to reject known bad input and then sanitize the input. The recommended strategy is shown in Figure 4.4.

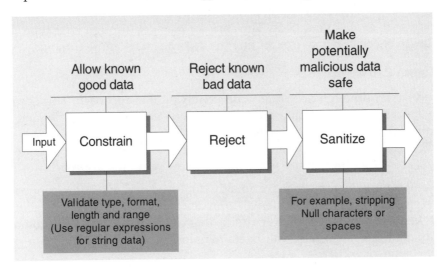

Figure 4.4
Input validation strategy: constrain, reject, and sanitize input

To create an effective input validation strategy, be aware of the following approaches and their tradeoffs:

- **Constrain input.**
- **Validate data for type, length, format, and range.**
- **Reject known bad input.**
- **Sanitize input.**

Constrain Input

Constraining input is about allowing good data. This is the preferred approach. The idea here is to define a filter of acceptable input by using type, length, format, and range. Define what is acceptable input for your application fields and enforce it. Reject everything else as bad data.

Constraining input may involve setting character sets on the server so that you can establish the canonical form of the input in a localized way.

Validate Data for Type, Length, Format, and Range

Use strong type checking on input data wherever possible, for example, in the classes used to manipulate and process the input data and in data access routines. For example, use parameterized stored procedures for data access to benefit from strong type checking of input fields.

String fields should also be length checked and in many cases checked for appropriate format. For example, ZIP codes, personal identification numbers, and so on have well defined formats that can be validated using regular expressions. Thorough checking is not only good programming practice; it makes it more difficult for an attacker to exploit your code. The attacker may get through your type check, but the length check may make executing his favorite attack more difficult.

Reject Known Bad Input

Deny "bad" data; although do not rely completely on this approach. This approach is generally less effective than using the "allow" approach described earlier and it is best used in combination. To deny bad data assumes your application knows all the variations of malicious input. Remember that there are multiple ways to represent characters. This is another reason why "allow" is the preferred approach.

While useful for applications that are already deployed and when you cannot afford to make significant changes, the "deny" approach is not as robust as the "allow" approach because bad data, such as patterns that can be used to identify common attacks, do not remain constant. Valid data remains constant while the range of bad data may change over time.

Sanitize Input

Sanitizing is about making potentially malicious data safe. It can be helpful when the range of input that is allowed cannot guarantee that the input is safe. This includes anything from stripping a null from the end of a user-supplied string to escaping out values so they are treated as literals.

Another common example of sanitizing input in Web applications is using URL encoding or HTML encoding to wrap data and treat it as literal text rather than executable script. **HtmlEncode** methods escape out HTML characters, and **UrlEncode** methods encode a URL so that it is a valid URI request.

In Practice

The following are examples applied to common input fields, using the preceding approaches:

- **Last Name field**. This is a good example where constraining input is appropriate In this case, you might allow string data in the range ASCII A–Z and a–z, and also hyphens and curly apostrophes (curly apostrophes have no significance to SQL) to handle names such as O'Dell. You would also limit the length to your longest expected value.

- **Quantity field**. This is another case where constraining input works well. In this example, you might use a simple type and range restriction. For example, the input data may need to be a positive integer between 0 and 1000.

- **Free-text field**. Examples include comment fields on discussion boards. In this case, you might allow letters and spaces, and also common characters such as apostrophes, commas, and hyphens. The set that is allowed does not include less than and greater than signs, brackets, and braces.

  Some applications might allow users to mark up their text using a finite set of script characters, such as bold "<b>", italic "<i>", or even include a link to their favorite URL. In the case of a URL, your validation should encode the value so that it is treated as a URL.

  For more information about validating free text fields, see "Input Validation" in Chapter 10, "Building Secure ASP.NET Pages and Controls."

- **An existing Web application that does not validate user input**. In an ideal scenario, the application checks for acceptable input for each field or entry point. However, if you have an existing Web application that does not validate user input, you need a stopgap approach to mitigate risk until you can improve your application's input validation strategy. While neither of the following approaches ensures safe handling of input, because that is dependent on where the input comes from and how it is used in your application, they are in practice today as quick fixes for short-term security improvement:

  - **HTML-encoding and URL-encoding user input when writing back to the client**. In this case, the assumption is that no input is treated as HTML and all output is written back in a protected form. This is sanitization in action.

  - **Rejecting malicious script characters**. This is a case of rejecting known bad input. In this case, a configurable set of malicious characters is used to reject the input. As described earlier, the problem with this approach is that bad data is a matter of context.

For more information and examples of input coding, using regular expressions, and ASP.NET validation controls, see "Input Validation" in Chapter 10, "Building Secure ASP.NET Pages and Controls."

Authentication

Authentication is the process of determining caller identity. There are three aspects to consider:

- Identify where authentication is required in your application. It is generally required whenever a trust boundary is crossed. Trust boundaries usually include assemblies, processes, and hosts.

- Validate who the caller is. Users typically authenticate themselves with user names and passwords.

- Identify the user on subsequent requests. This requires some form of authentication token.

Many Web applications use a password mechanism to authenticate users, where the user supplies a user name and password in an HTML form. The issues and questions to consider here include:

- **Are user names and passwords sent in plaintext over an insecure channel?** If so, an attacker can eavesdrop with network monitoring software to capture the credentials. The countermeasure here is to secure the communication channel by using Secure Socket Layer (SSL).

- **How are the credentials stored?** If you are storing user names and passwords in plaintext, either in files or in a database, you are inviting trouble. What if your application directory is improperly configured and an attacker browses to the file and downloads its contents or adds a new privileged logon account? What if a disgruntled administrator takes your database of user names and passwords?

- **How are the credentials verified?** There is no need to store user passwords if the sole purpose is to verify that the user knows the password value. Instead, you can store a verifier in the form of a hash value and re-compute the hash using the user-supplied value during the logon process. To mitigate the threat of dictionary attacks against the credential store, use strong passwords and combine a randomly generated salt value with the password hash.

- **How is the authenticated user identified after the initial logon?** Some form of authentication ticket, for example an authentication cookie, is required. How is the cookie secured? If it is sent across an insecure channel, an attacker can capture the cookie and use it to access the application. A stolen authentication cookie is a stolen logon.

The following practices improve your Web application's authentication:

- **Separate public and restricted areas.**
- **Use account lockout policies for end-user accounts.**
- **Support password expiration periods.**
- **Be able to disable accounts.**
- **Do not store passwords in user stores.**
- **Require strong passwords.**
- **Do not send passwords over the wire in plaintext.**
- **Protect authentication cookies.**

Separate Public and Restricted Areas

A public area of your site can be accessed by any user anonymously. Restricted areas can be accessed only by specific individuals and the users must authenticate with the site. Consider a typical retail Web site. You can browse the product catalog anonymously. When you add items to a shopping cart, the application identifies you with a session identifier. Finally, when you place an order, you perform a secure transaction. This requires you to log in to authenticate your transaction over SSL.

By partitioning your site into public and restricted access areas, you can apply separate authentication and authorization rules across the site and limit the use of SSL. To avoid the unnecessary performance overhead associated with SSL, design your site to limit the use of SSL to the areas that require authenticated access.

Use Account Lockout Policies for End-User Accounts

Disable end-user accounts or write events to a log after a set number of failed logon attempts. If you are using Windows authentication, such as NTLM or the Kerberos protocol, these policies can be configured and applied automatically by the operating system. With Forms authentication, these policies are the responsibility of the application and must be incorporated into the application design.

Be careful that account lockout policies cannot be abused in denial of service attacks. For example, well known default service accounts such as IUSR_MACHINENAME should be replaced by custom account names to prevent an attacker who obtains the Internet Information Services (IIS) Web server name from locking out this critical account.

Support Password Expiration Periods

Passwords should not be static and should be changed as part of routine password maintenance through password expiration periods. Consider providing this type of facility during application design.

Be Able to Disable Accounts

If the system is compromised, being able to deliberately invalidate credentials or disable accounts can prevent additional attacks.

Do Not Store Passwords in User Stores

If you must verify passwords, it is not necessary to actually store the passwords. Instead, store a one way hash value and then re-compute the hash using the user-supplied passwords. To mitigate the threat of dictionary attacks against the user store, use strong passwords and incorporate a random salt value with the password.

Require Strong Passwords

Do not make it easy for attackers to crack passwords. There are many guidelines available, but a general practice is to require a minimum of eight characters and a mixture of uppercase and lowercase characters, numbers, and special characters. Whether you are using the platform to enforce these for you, or you are developing your own validation, this step is necessary to counter brute-force attacks where an attacker tries to crack a password through systematic trial and error. Use regular expressions to help with strong password validation.

For examples of regular expressions to aid password validation, see "Input Validation" in Chapter 10, "Building Secure ASP.NET Pages and Controls."

Do Not Send Passwords Over the Wire in Plaintext

Plaintext passwords sent over a network are vulnerable to eavesdropping. To address this threat, secure the communication channel, for example, by using SSL to encrypt the traffic.

Protect Authentication Cookies

A stolen authentication cookie is a stolen logon. Protect authentication tickets using encryption and secure communication channels. Also limit the time interval in which an authentication ticket remains valid, to counter the spoofing threat that can result from replay attacks, where an attacker captures the cookie and uses it to gain illicit access to your site. Reducing the cookie timeout does not prevent replay attacks but it does limit the amount of time the attacker has to access the site using the stolen cookie.

Authorization

Authorization determines what the authenticated identity can do and the resources that can be accessed. Improper or weak authorization leads to information disclosure and data tampering. Defense in depth is the key security principle to apply to your application's authorization strategy.

The following practices improve your Web application's authorization:

- **Use multiple gatekeepers.**
- **Restrict user access to system-level resources.**
- **Consider authorization granularity.**

Use Multiple Gatekeepers

On the server side, you can use IP Security Protocol (IPSec) policies to provide host restrictions to restrict server-to-server communication. For example, an IPSec policy might restrict any host apart from a nominated Web server from connecting to a database server. IIS provides Web permissions and Internet Protocol/ Domain Name System (IP/DNS) restrictions. IIS Web permissions apply to all resources requested over HTTP regardless of the user. They do not provide protection if an attacker manages to log on to the server. For this, NTFS permissions allow you to specify per user access control lists. Finally, ASP.NET provides URL authorization and File authorization together with principal permission demands. By combining these gatekeepers you can develop an effective authorization strategy.

Restrict User Access to System Level Resources

System level resources include files, folders, registry keys, Active Directory objects, database objects, event logs, and so on. Use Windows Access Control Lists (ACLs) to restrict which users can access what resources and the types of operations that they can perform. Pay particular attention to anonymous Internet user accounts; lock these down with ACLs on resources that explicitly deny access to anonymous users.

For more information about locking down anonymous Internet user accounts with Windows ACLs, see Chapter 16, "Securing Your Web Server."

Consider Authorization Granularity

There are three common authorization models, each with varying degrees of granularity and scalability.

The most granular approach relies on impersonation. Resource access occurs using the security context of the caller. Windows ACLs on the secured resources (typically files or tables, or both) determine whether the caller is allowed to access the resource. If your application provides access primarily to user specific resources, this approach may be valid. It has the added advantage that operating system level auditing can be performed across the tiers of your application, because the original caller's security context flows at the operating system level and is used for resource access. However, the approach suffers from poor application scalability because effective connection pooling for database access is not possible. As a result, this approach is most frequently found in limited scale intranet-based applications. The impersonation model is shown in Figure 4.5.

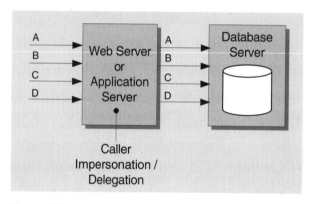

Figure 4.5
Impersonation model providing per end user authorization granularity

The least granular but most scalable approach uses the application's process identity for resource access. This approach supports database connection pooling but it means that the permissions granted to the application's identity in the database are common, irrespective of the identity of the original caller. The primary authorization is performed in the application's logical middle tier using roles, which group together users who share the same privileges in the application. Access to classes and methods is restricted based on the role membership of the caller. To support the retrieval of per user data, a common approach is to include an identity column in the database tables and use query parameters to restrict the retrieved data. For example, you may pass the original caller's identity to the database at the application (not operating system) level through stored procedure parameters, and write queries similar to the following:

```
SELECT field1, field2, field3 FROM Table1 WHERE {some search criteria} AND
UserName = @originalCallerUserName
```

This model is referred to as the trusted subsystem or sometimes as the trusted server model. It is shown in Figure 4.6.

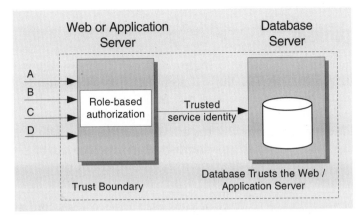

Figure 4.6
Trusted subsystem model that supports database connection pooling

The third option is to use a limited set of identities for resource access based on the role membership of the caller. This is really a hybrid of the two models described earlier. Callers are mapped to roles in the application's logical middle tier, and access to classes and methods is restricted based on role membership. Downstream resource access is performed using a restricted set of identities determined by the current caller's role membership. The advantage of this approach is that permissions can be assigned to separate logins in the database, and connection pooling is still effective with multiple pools of connections. The downside is that creating multiple thread access tokens used to establish different security contexts for downstream resource access using Windows authentication is a privileged operation that requires privileged process accounts. This is counter to the principle of least privilege. The hybrid model using multiple trusted service identities for downstream resource access is shown in Figure 4.7.

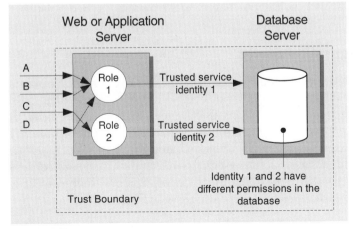

Figure 4.7
Hybrid model

Configuration Management

Carefully consider your Web application's configuration management functionality. Most applications require interfaces that allow content developers, operators, and administrators to configure the application and manage items such as Web page content, user accounts, user profile information, and database connection strings. If remote administration is supported, how are the administration interfaces secured? The consequences of a security breach to an administration interface can be severe, because the attacker frequently ends up running with administrator privileges and has direct access to the entire site.

The following practices improve the security of your Web application's configuration management:

- Secure your administration interfaces.
- Secure your configuration store.
- Maintain separate administration privileges.
- Use least privileged process and service accounts.

Secure Your Administration Interfaces

It is important that configuration management functionality is accessible only by authorized operators and administrators. A key part is to enforce strong authentication over your administration interfaces, for example, by using certificates.

If possible, limit or avoid the use of remote administration and require administrators to log on locally. If you need to support remote administration, use encrypted channels, for example, with SSL or VPN technology, because of the sensitive nature of the data passed over administrative interfaces. Also consider limiting remote administration to computers on the internal network by using IPSec policies, to further reduce risk.

Secure Your Configuration Stores

Text-based configuration files, the registry, and databases are common options for storing application configuration data. If possible, avoid using configuration files in the application's Web space to prevent possible server configuration vulnerabilities resulting in the download of configuration files. Whatever approach you use, secure access to the configuration store, for example, by using Windows ACLs or database permissions. Also avoid storing plaintext secrets such as database connection strings or account credentials. Secure these items using encryption and then restrict access to the registry key, file, or table that contains the encrypted data.

Separate Administration Privileges

If the functionality supported by the features of your application's configuration management varies based on the role of the administrator, consider authorizing each role separately by using role-based authorization. For example, the person responsible for updating a site's static content should not necessarily be allowed to change a customer's credit limit.

Use Least Privileged Process and Service Accounts

An important aspect of your application's configuration is the process accounts used to run the Web server process and the service accounts used to access downstream resources and systems. Make sure these accounts are set up as least privileged. If an attacker manages to take control of a process, the process identity should have very restricted access to the file system and other system resources to limit the damage that can be done.

Sensitive Data

Applications that deal with private user information such as credit card numbers, addresses, medical records, and so on should take special steps to make sure that the data remains private and unaltered. In addition, secrets used by the application's implementation, such as passwords and database connection strings, must be secured. The security of sensitive data is an issue while the data is stored in persistent storage and while it is passed across the network.

Secrets

Secrets include passwords, database connection strings, and credit card numbers. The following practices improve the security of your Web application's handling of secrets:

- **Do not store secrets if you can avoid it.**
- **Do not store secrets in code.**
- **Do not store database connections, passwords, or keys in plaintext.**
- **Avoid storing secrets in the Local Security Authority (LSA).**
- **Use Data Protection API (DPAPI) for encrypting secrets.**

Do Not Store Secrets if You Can Avoid It

Storing secrets in software in a completely secure fashion is not possible. An administrator, who has physical access to the server, can access the data. For example, it is not necessary to store a secret when all you need to do is verify whether a user knows the secret. In this case, you can store a hash value that represents the secret and compute the hash using the user-supplied value to verify whether the user knows the secret.

Do Not Store Secrets in Code

Do not hard code secrets in code. Even if the source code is not exposed on the Web server, it is possible to extract string constants from compiled executable files. A configuration vulnerability may allow an attacker to retrieve the executable.

Do Not Store Database Connections, Passwords, or Keys in Plaintext

Avoid storing secrets such as database connection strings, passwords, and keys in plaintext. Use encryption and store encrypted strings.

Avoid Storing Secrets in the LSA

Avoid the LSA because your application requires administration privileges to access it. This violates the core security principle of running with least privilege. Also, the LSA can store secrets in only a restricted number of slots. A better approach is to use DPAPI, available on Microsoft Windows® 2000 and later operating systems.

Use DPAPI for Encrypting Secrets

To store secrets such as database connection strings or service account credentials, use DPAPI. The main advantage to using DPAPI is that the platform system manages the encryption/decryption key and it is not an issue for the application. The key is either tied to a Windows user account or to a specific computer, depending on flags passed to the DPAPI functions.

DPAPI is best suited for encrypting information that can be manually recreated when the master keys are lost, for example, because a damaged server requires an operating system re-install. Data that cannot be recovered because you do not know the plaintext value, for example, customer credit card details, require an alternate approach that uses traditional symmetric key-based cryptography such as the use of triple-DES.

For more information about using DPAPI from Web applications, see Chapter 10, "Building Secure ASP.NET Web Pages and Controls."

Sensitive Per User Data

Sensitive data such as logon credentials and application level data such as credit card numbers, bank account numbers, and so on, must be protected. Privacy through encryption and integrity through message authentication codes (MAC) are the key elements.

The following practices improve your Web application's security of sensitive per user data:

- **Retrieve sensitive data on demand.**
- **Encrypt the data or secure the communication channel.**
- **Do not store sensitive data in persistent cookies.**
- **Do not pass sensitive data using the HTTP-GET protocol.**

Retrieve Sensitive Data on Demand

The preferred approach is to retrieve sensitive data on demand when it is needed instead of persisting or caching it in memory. For example, retrieve the encrypted secret when it is needed, decrypt it, use it, and then clear the memory (variable) used to hold the plaintext secret. If performance becomes an issue, consider the following options:

- **Cache the encrypted secret.**
- **Cache the plaintext secret.**

Cache the Encrypted Secret

Retrieve the secret when the application loads and then cache the encrypted secret in memory, decrypting it when the application uses it. Clear the plaintext copy when it is no longer needed. This approach avoids accessing the data store on a per request basis.

Cache the Plaintext Secret

Avoid the overhead of decrypting the secret multiple times and store a plaintext copy of the secret in memory. This is the least secure approach but offers the optimum performance. Benchmark the other approaches before guessing that the additional performance gain is worth the added security risk.

Encrypt the Data or Secure the Communication Channel

If you are sending sensitive data over the network to the client, encrypt the data or secure the channel. A common practice is to use SSL between the client and Web server. Between servers, an increasingly common approach is to use IPSec. For securing sensitive data that flows through several intermediaries, for example, Web service Simple Object Access Protocol (SOAP) messages, use message level encryption.

Do Not Store Sensitive Data in Persistent Cookies

Avoid storing sensitive data in persistent cookies. If you store plaintext data, the end user is able to see and modify the data. If you encrypt the data, key management can be a problem. For example, if the key used to encrypt the data in the cookie has expired and been recycled, the new key cannot decrypt the persistent cookie passed by the browser from the client.

Do Not Pass Sensitive Data Using the HTTP-GET Protocol

You should avoid storing sensitive data using the HTTP-GET protocol because the protocol uses query strings to pass data. Sensitive data cannot be secured using query strings and query strings are often logged by the server.

Session Management

Web applications are built on the stateless HTTP protocol, so session management is an application-level responsibility. Session security is critical to the overall security of an application.

The following practices improve the security of your Web application's session management:

- Use SSL to protect session authentication cookies.
- Encrypt the contents of the authentication cookies.
- Limit session lifetime.
- Protect session state from unauthorized access.

Use SSL to Protect Session Authentication Cookies

Do not pass authentication cookies over HTTP connections. Set the secure cookie property within authentication cookies, which instructs browsers to send cookies back to the server only over HTTPS connections. For more information, see Chapter 10, "Building Secure ASP.NET Web Pages and Controls."

Encrypt the Contents of the Authentication Cookies

Encrypt the cookie contents even if you are using SSL. This prevents an attacker viewing or modifying the cookie if he manages to steal it through an XSS attack. In this event, the attacker could still use the cookie to access your application, but only while the cookie remains valid.

Limit Session Lifetime

Reduce the lifetime of sessions to mitigate the risk of session hijacking and replay attacks. The shorter the session, the less time an attacker has to capture a session cookie and use it to access your application.

Protect Session State from Unauthorized Access

Consider how session state is to be stored. For optimum performance, you can store session state in the Web application's process address space. However, this approach has limited scalability and implications in Web farm scenarios, where requests from the same user cannot be guaranteed to be handled by the same server. In this scenario, an out-of-process state store on a dedicated state server or a persistent state store in a shared database is required. ASP.NET supports all three options.

You should secure the network link from the Web application to state store using IPSec or SSL to mitigate the risk of eavesdropping. Also consider how the Web application is to be authenticated by the state store. Use Windows authentication where possible to avoid passing plaintext authentication credentials across the network and to benefit from secure Windows account policies.

Cryptography

Cryptography in its fundamental form provides the following:

- **Privacy** (Confidentiality). This service keeps a secret confidential.
- **Non-Repudiation** (Authenticity). This service makes sure a user cannot deny sending a particular message.
- **Tamperproofing** (Integrity). This service prevents data from being altered.
- **Authentication**. This service confirms the identity of the sender of a message.

Web applications frequently use cryptography to secure data in persistent stores or as it is transmitted across networks. The following practices improve your Web application's security when you use cryptography:

- **Do not develop your own cryptography**.
- **Keep unencrypted data close to the algorithm**.
- **Use the correct algorithm and correct key size**.
- **Secure your encryption keys**.

Do Not Develop Your Own Cryptography

Cryptographic algorithms and routines are notoriously difficult to develop successfully. As a result, you should use the tried and tested cryptographic services provided by the platform. This includes the .NET Framework and the underlying operating system. Do not develop custom implementations because these frequently result in weak protection.

Keep Unencrypted Data Close to the Algorithm

When passing plaintext to an algorithm, do not obtain the data until you are ready to use it, and store it in as few variables as possible.

Use the Correct Algorithm and Correct Key Size

It is important to make sure you choose the right algorithm for the right job and to make sure you use a key size that provides a sufficient degree of security. Larger key sizes generally increase security. The following list summarizes the major algorithms together with the key sizes that each uses:

- Data Encryption Standard (DES) 64-bit key (8 bytes)
- TripleDES 128-bit key or 192-bit key (16 or 24 bytes)
- Rijndael 128–256 bit keys (16–32 bytes)
- RSA 384–16,384 bit keys (48–2,048 bytes)

For large data encryption, use the TripleDES symmetric encryption algorithm. For slower and stronger encryption of large data, use Rijndael. To encrypt data that is to be stored for short periods of time, you can consider using a faster but weaker algorithm such as DES. For digital signatures, use Rivest, Shamir, and Adleman (RSA) or Digital Signature Algorithm (DSA). For hashing, use the Secure Hash Algorithm (SHA)1.0. For keyed hashes, use the Hash-based Message Authentication Code (HMAC) SHA1.0.

Secure Your Encryption Keys

An encryption key is a secret number used as input to the encryption and decryption processes. For encrypted data to remain secure, the key must be protected. If an attacker compromises the decryption key, your encrypted data is no longer secure.

The following practices help secure your encryption keys:

- **Use DPAPI to avoid key management**.
- **Cycle your keys periodically**.

Use DPAPI to Avoid Key Management

As mentioned previously, one of the major advantages of using DPAPI is that the key management issue is handled by the operating system. The key that DPAPI uses is derived from the password that is associated with the process account that calls the DPAPI functions. Use DPAPI to pass the burden of key management to the operating system.

Cycle Your Keys Periodically

Generally, a static secret is more likely to be discovered over time. Questions to keep in mind are: Did you write it down somewhere? Did Bob, the administrator with the secrets, change positions in your company or leave the company? Do not overuse keys.

Parameter Manipulation

With parameter manipulation attacks, the attacker modifies the data sent between the client and Web application. This may be data sent using query strings, form fields, cookies, or in HTTP headers. The following practices help secure your Web application's parameter manipulation:

- **Encrypt sensitive cookie state.**
- **Make sure that users do not bypass your checks.**
- **Validate all values sent from the client.**
- **Do not trust HTTP header information.**

Encrypt Sensitive Cookie State

Cookies may contain sensitive data such as session identifiers or data that is used as part of the server-side authorization process. To protect this type of data from unauthorized manipulation, use cryptography to encrypt the contents of the cookie.

Make Sure that Users Do Not Bypass Your Checks

Make sure that users do not bypass your checks by manipulating parameters. URL parameters can be manipulated by end users through the browser address text box. For example, the URL http://www.<*YourSite*>/<*YourApp*>/sessionId=10 has a value of 10 that can be changed to some random number to receive different output. Make sure that you check this in server-side code, not in client-side JavaScript, which can be disabled in the browser.

Validate All Values Sent from the Client

Restrict the fields that the user can enter and modify and validate all values coming from the client. If you have predefined values in your form fields, users can change them and post them back to receive different results. Permit only known good values wherever possible. For example, if the input field is for a state, only inputs matching a state postal code should be permitted.

Do Not Trust HTTP Header Information

HTTP headers are sent at the start of HTTP requests and HTTP responses. Your Web application should make sure it does not base any security decision on information in the HTTP headers because it is easy for an attacker to manipulate the header. For example, the **referer** field in the header contains the URL of the Web page from where the request originated. Do not make any security decisions based on the value of the referer field, for example, to check whether the request originated from a page generated by the Web application, because the field is easily falsified.

Exception Management

Secure exception handling can help prevent certain application-level denial of service attacks and it can also be used to prevent valuable system-level information useful to attackers from being returned to the client. For example, without proper exception handling, information such as database schema details, operating system versions, stack traces, file names and path information, SQL query strings and other information of value to an attacker can be returned to the client.

A good approach is to design a centralized exception management and logging solution and consider providing hooks into your exception management system to support instrumentation and centralized monitoring to help system administrators.

The following practices help secure your Web application's exception management:

- **Do not leak information to the client**.
- **Log detailed error messages**.
- **Catch exceptions**.

Do Not Leak Information to the Client

In the event of a failure, do not expose information that could lead to information disclosure. For example, do not expose stack trace details that include function names and line numbers in the case of debug builds (which should not be used on production servers). Instead, return generic error messages to the client.

Log Detailed Error Messages

Send detailed error messages to the error log. Send minimal information to the consumer of your service or application, such as a generic error message and custom error log ID that can subsequently be mapped to detailed message in the event logs. Make sure that you do not log passwords or other sensitive data.

Catch Exceptions

Use structured exception handling and catch exception conditions. Doing so avoids leaving your application in an inconsistent state that may lead to information disclosure. It also helps protect your application from denial of service attacks. Decide how to propagate exceptions internally in your application and give special consideration to what occurs at the application boundary.

For more information about designing and implementing an exception management framework for .NET applications, see the MSDN article "Exception Management in .NET," at *http://msdn.microsoft.com/library/en-us/dnbda/html/exceptdotnet.asp*

Auditing and Logging

You should audit and log activity across the tiers of your application. Using logs, you can detect suspicious-looking activity. This frequently provides early indications of a full-blown attack and the logs help address the repudiation threat where users deny their actions. Log files may be required in legal proceedings to prove the wrongdoing of individuals. Generally, auditing is considered most authoritative if the audits are generated at the precise time of resource access and by the same routines that access the resource.

The following practices improve your Web application's security:

- **Audit and log access across application tiers**.
- **Consider identity flow**.
- **Log key events**.
- **Secure log files**.
- **Back up and analyze log files regularly**.

Audit and Log Access Across Application Tiers

Audit and log access across the tiers of your application for non-repudiation. Use a combination of application-level logging and platform auditing features, such as Windows, IIS, and SQL Server auditing.

Consider Identity Flow

Consider how your application will flow caller identity across multiple application tiers. You have two basic choices. You can flow the caller's identity at the operating system level using the Kerberos protocol delegation. This allows you to use operating system level auditing. The drawback with this approach is that it affects scalability because it means there can be no effective database connection pooling at the middle tier. Alternatively, you can flow the caller's identity at the application level and use trusted identities to access back-end resources. With this approach, you have to trust the middle tier and there is a potential repudiation risk. You should generate audit trails in the middle tier that can be correlated with back-end audit trails. For this, you must make sure that the server clocks are synchronized, although Microsoft Windows 2000 and Active Directory do this for you.

Log Key Events

The types of events that should be logged include successful and failed logon attempts, modification of data, retrieval of data, network communications, and administrative functions such as the enabling or disabling of logging. Logs should include the time of the event, the location of the event including the machine name, the identity of the current user, the identity of the process initiating the event, and a detailed description of the event.

Secure Log Files

Secure log files using Windows ACLs and restrict access to the log files. This makes it more difficult for attackers to tamper with log files to cover their tracks. Minimize the number of individuals who can manipulate the log files. Authorize access only to highly trusted accounts such as administrators.

Back Up and Analyze Log Files Regularly

There's no point in logging activity if the log files are never analyzed. Log files should be removed from production servers on a regular basis. The frequency of removal is dependent upon your application's level of activity. Your design should consider the way that log files will be retrieved and moved to offline servers for analysis. Any additional protocols and ports opened on the Web server for this purpose must be securely locked down.

Design Guidelines Summary

Table 4.2 summarizes the design guidelines discussed in this chapter and organizes them by application vulnerability category.

Table 4.2   Design Guidelines for Your Application

Category	Guidelines
Input Validation	Do not trust input; consider centralized input validation. Do not rely on client-side validation. Be careful with canonicalization issues. Constrain, reject, and sanitize input. Validate for type, length, format, and range.
Authentication	Partition site by anonymous, identified, and authenticated area. Use strong passwords. Support password expiration periods and account disablement. Do not store credentials (use one-way hashes with salt). Encrypt communication channels to protect authentication tokens. Pass Forms authentication cookies only over HTTPS connections.
Authorization	Use least privileged accounts. Consider authorization granularity. Enforce separation of privileges. Restrict user access to system-level resources.
Configuration Management	Use least privileged process and service accounts. Do not store credentials in plaintext. Use strong authentication and authorization on administration interfaces. Do not use the LSA. Secure the communication channel for remote administration. Avoid storing sensitive data in the Web space.
Sensitive Data	Avoid storing secrets. Encrypt sensitive data over the wire. Secure the communication channel. Provide strong access controls on sensitive data stores. Do not store sensitive data in persistent cookies. Do not pass sensitive data using the HTTP-GET protocol.
Session Management	Limit the session lifetime. Secure the channel. Encrypt the contents of authentication cookies. Protect session state from unauthorized access.
Cryptography	Do not develop your own. Use tried and tested platform features. Keep unencrypted data close to the algorithm. Use the right algorithm and key size. Avoid key management (use DPAPI). Cycle your keys periodically. Store keys in a restricted location.
Parameter Manipulation	Encrypt sensitive cookie state. Do not trust fields that the client can manipulate (query strings, form fields, cookies, or HTTP headers). Validate all values sent from the client.
Exception Management	Use structured exception handling. Do not reveal sensitive application implementation details. Do not log private data such as passwords. Consider a centralized exception management framework.
Auditing and Logging	Identify malicious behavior. Know what good traffic looks like. Audit and log activity through all of the application tiers. Secure access to log files. Back up and regularly analyze log files.

Summary

Security should permeate every stage of the product development life cycle and it should be a focal point of application design. Pay particular attention to the design of a solid authentication and authorization strategy. Also remember that the majority of application level attacks rely on maliciously formed input data and poor application input validation. The guidance presented in this chapter should help you with these and other challenging aspects of designing and building secure applications.

Additional Resources

For more information, see the following resources:

- The current guide is Volume II in a series dedicated to helping customers improve Web application security. For more information on architecting, designing, building and configuring authentication, authorization, and secure communications across tiers of a distributed Web applications, see "Microsoft *patterns & practices* Volume I, *Building Secure ASP.NET Applications: Authentication, Authorization, and Secure Communication*" at *http://msdn.microsoft.com/library/en-us /dnnetsec/html/secnetlpMSDN.asp*

- The MSDN article "Security Models for ASP.NET Applications" at *http://msdn.microsoft.com/library/default.asp?url=/library/en-us/dnnetsec/html /SecNetch02.asp?frame=true*

- The MSDN article "Designing Authentication and Authorization" at *http://msdn.microsoft.com/library/default.asp?url=/library/en-us/dnnetsec/html /SecNetch03.asp?frame=true*

- "Checklist: Architecture and Design Review" in the "Checklists" section of this guide.

5

Architecture and Design Review for Security

In This Chapter

- Analyzing and reviewing application architecture and design
- Identifying key application deployment and infrastructure security considerations

Overview

To build a secure Web application, you need an appropriate architecture and design. The cost and effort of retrofitting security after development are too high. An architecture and design review helps you validate the security-related design features of your application before you start the development phase. This allows you to identify and fix potential vulnerabilities before they can be exploited and before the fix requires a substantial reengineering effort.

If you have already created your application, you should still review this chapter and then revisit the concepts, principles, and techniques that you used during your application design.

How to Use This Chapter

This chapter gives you the questions to ask when performing a thorough review of your architecture design. The following are recommendations on how to use this chapter:

- **Integrate a security review into your architecture design process**. Start early on, and as your design changes, review those changes with the steps given in this chapter.

- **Evolve your security review**. This chapter provides questions that you can ask to improve the security of your design. To complete the review process, you might also need to add specific questions that are unique to your application.

- **Know the threats you are reviewing against**. Chapter 2, "Threats and Countermeasures," lists the threats that affect the various components and layers that make up your application. Knowing these threats is essential to improving the results of your review process.

Architecture and Design Review Process

The architecture and design review process analyzes the architecture and design from a security perspective. If you have just completed the design, the design documentation can help you with this process. Regardless of how comprehensive your design documentation is, you must be able to decompose your application and be able to identify key items, including trust boundaries, data flow, entry points, and privileged code. You must also know the physical deployment configuration of your application. Pay attention to the design approaches you have adopted for those areas that most commonly exhibit vulnerabilities. This guide refers to these as application vulnerability categories.

Consider the following aspects when you review the architecture and design of your application:

- **Deployment and infrastructure**. You review the design of your application in relation to the target deployment environment and the associated security policies. You also consider the restrictions imposed by the underlying infrastructure-layer security.

- **Application architecture and design**. You review the approach to critical areas in your application, including authentication, authorization, input validation, exception management, and other areas. You can use the application vulnerability categories as a roadmap and to ensure that you do not miss any key areas during the review.

- **Tier-by-tier analysis**. You walk through the logical tiers of your application and examine the security of ASP.NET Web pages and controls, Web services, serviced components, Microsoft .NET Remoting, data access code, and others.

Figure 5.1 shows this three-pronged approach to the review process.

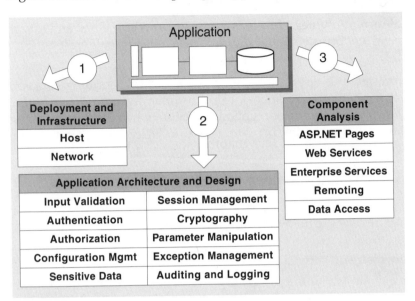

Figure 5.1

Application review

The remainder of this chapter presents the key considerations and questions to ask during the review process for each of these distinct areas.

Deployment and Infrastructure Considerations

Examine the security settings that the underlying network and host infrastructure offer to the application, and examine any restrictions that the target environment might impose. Also consider your deployment topology and the impact of middle-tier application servers, perimeter zones, and internal firewalls on your design.

Review the following questions to identify potential deployment and infrastructure issues:

- **Does the network provide secure communication?**
- **Does your deployment topology include an internal firewall?**
- **Does your deployment topology include a remote application server?**
- **What restrictions does infrastructure security impose?**
- **Have you considered Web farm issues?**
- **What trust levels does the target environment support?**

Does the Network Provide Secure Communication?

Your data is at its most vulnerable while in transit between a client and server, or server to server. How private should the data be? Are you legally responsible for customer data?

While your application is responsible for handling and transforming data securely prior to transit, the network is responsible for the integrity and privacy of the data as it transmits. Use an appropriate encryption algorithm when the data must remain private. Additionally, make sure that your network devices are secured because they maintain network integrity.

Does Your Deployment Topology Include an Internal Firewall?

If an internal firewall separates your Web server from an application server or a database server, review the following questions to ensure that your design accommodates this:

- **How do downstream servers authenticate the Web server?**

  If you use domain accounts and Windows authentication, does the firewall open the necessary ports? If not, or if the Web server and downstream server are in separate domains, you can use mirrored local accounts. For example, you can duplicate the least privileged local ASPNET account that is used to run the Web application on the database server.

- **Do you use distributed transactions?**

  If the Web server initiates distributed transactions using the services of the Microsoft Distributed Transaction Coordinator (DTC), does the internal firewall open the necessary ports for DTC communication?

  For more information about using the DTC through a firewall, see Microsoft Knowledge Base article 250367, "INFO: Configuring Microsoft Distributed Transaction Coordinator (DTC) to Work Through a Firewall."

Does Your Deployment Topology Include a Remote Application Server?

If your deployment topology includes a physically remote middle tier, review the following questions:

- **Do you use Enterprise Services?**

  If so, have you restricted the DCOM port range and does any internal firewall open these ports?

Note In some scenarios, using a middle-tier Web service as a front end to the Enterprise Services application is a superior design choice. With this approach, the Web server can communicate with the application server through port 80 using Simple Object Access Protocol (SOAP).

For more information, see the following Microsoft Knowledge Base articles:

- Article 312960, "Cannot Set Fixed Endpoint for a COM+ Application"
- Article 259011, "SAMPLE: A Simple DCOM Client Server Test Application"
- Article 248809, "PRB: DCOM Does Not Work over NAT-Based Firewall"
- Article 154596, "HOWTO: Configure RPC Dynamic Port Allocation to Work w/Firewall"

- **Do you use .NET Remoting?**

  Remoting is designed to be used in trusted server scenarios. Does the network support an IPSec policy that ensures that your middle-tier Remoting components can only be accessed from the Web server? Does ASP.NET host your remote components to support authentication and authorization?

- **Do you use Web services?**

  If so, how do middle-tier Web services authenticate the Web application? Does the Web application configure credentials on the Web service proxy so that the Web service can authenticate the Web server? If not, how does the Web service identify the caller?

What Restrictions Does Infrastructure Security Impose?

Does your design make any assumptions that the host infrastructure security restrictions will invalidate? For example, the security restrictions may require design tradeoffs based on the availability of required services, protocols, or account privileges. Review the following questions:

- **Do you rely on services or protocols that might not be available?**

  Services and protocols that are available in the development and test environments might not be available in the production environment. Communicate with the team responsible for the infrastructure security to understand the restrictions and requirements.

- **Do you rely on sensitive account privileges?**

  Your design should use least privileged process, service, and user accounts. Do you perform operations that require sensitive privileges that might not be permitted?

  For example, does your application need to create thread-level impersonation tokens to create service identities for resource access? This requires the "Act as part of the operating system" privilege, which should not be granted to Web server processes because of the increased security risk associated with a process compromise. If this feature is required, your design should compartmentalize the higher privileges, for example, in an out-of-process Enterprise Services application.

Have You Considered Web Farm Issues?

If your application is going to be deployed in a Web farm, you can make no assumptions about which server in the farm will process client requests. Successive requests from the same client may be served by separate servers. As a result, you need to consider the following issues:

- **How are you managing session state?**

  In a Web farm, you cannot manage session state on the Web server. Instead, your design must incorporate a remote state store on a server that is accessed by all the Web servers in the farm. For more information, see "Session Management" later in this chapter.

- **Are you using machine-specific encryption keys?**

  If you plan to use encryption to encrypt data in a shared data source, such as a database, the encryption and decryption keys must be the same across all machines in the farm. Check that your design does not require encryption mechanisms that require machine affinity.

- **Are you using Forms authentication or protected view state?**

  If so, you are reliant upon the **<machineKey>** settings. In a Web farm, you must use common key across all servers.

- **Are you using Secure Sockets Layer (SSL)?**

  If you use SSL to encrypt the traffic between browser and Web server, where do you terminate the SSL connection? Your options include the Web server, a Web server with an accelerator card, or a load balancer with an accelerator card. Terminating the SSL session at a load balancer with an accelerator card generally offers the best performance, particularly for sites with large numbers of connections.

  If you terminate SSL at the load balancer, network traffic is not encrypted from the load balancer to the Web server. This means that an attacker can potentially sniff network traffic after the data is decrypted, while it is in transit between the load balancer and Web server. You can address this threat either by ensuring that the Web server environment is physically secured or by using transport-level encryption provided by IPSec policies to protect internal data center links.

What Trust Levels Does the Target Environment Support?

The code access security trust level of the target environment determines the resources your code can access and the privileged operations it can perform. Check the supported trust level of your target environment. If your Web application is allowed to run with Full trust, your code can access any resources, subject to operating system security.

If your Web application must run at a reduced trust level, this limits the types of resources and privileged operations your code can perform. In partial trust scenarios, your design should sandbox your privileged code. You should also use separate assemblies to isolate your privileged code. This is done so that the privileged code can be configured separately from the rest of the application and granted the necessary additional code access permissions.

For more information, see Chapter 9, "Using Code Access Security with ASP.NET."

Note   Trust levels are often an issue if you are planning to deploy your application onto a shared server, or if your application is going to be run by a hosting company. In these cases, check the security policy and find out what trust levels it mandates for Web applications.

Input Validation

Examine how your application validates input because many Web application attacks use deliberately malformed input . SQL injection, cross-site scripting (XSS), buffer overflow, code injection, and numerous other denial of service and elevation of privilege attacks can exploit poor input validation. Table 5.1 highlights the most common input validation vulnerabilities.

Table 5.1   Common Input Validation Vulnerabilities

Vulnerability	Implications
Non-validated input in the Hypertext Markup Language (HTML) output stream	The application is susceptible to XSS attacks.
Non-validated input used to generate SQL queries	The application is susceptible to SQL injection attacks.
Reliance on client-side validation	Client validation is easily bypassed.
Use of input file names, URLs, or user names for security decisions	The application is susceptible to canonicalization bugs, leading to security flaws.
Application-only filters for malicious input	This is almost impossible to do correctly because of the enormous range of potentially malicious input. The application should constrain, reject, and sanitize input.

Review the following questions to help you identify potential input validation security issues:

- **How do you validate input?**
- **What do you do with the input?**

How Do You Validate Input?

What approach to input validation does your design specify? First, your design should lay out the strategy. Your application should constrain, reject, and sanitize all of the input it receives. Constraining input is the best approach because validating data for known valid types, patterns, and ranges is much easier than validating data by looking for known bad characters. With a defense in depth strategy, you should also reject known bad input and sanitize input.

The following questions can help you identify potential vulnerabilities:

- **Do you know your entry points?**

  Make sure the design identifies entry points of the application so that you can track what happens to individual input fields. Consider Web page input, input to components and Web services, and input from databases.

- **Do you know your trust boundaries?**

  Input validation is not always necessary if the input is passed from a trusted source inside your trust boundary, but it should be considered mandatory if the input is passed from sources that are not trusted.

- **Do you validate Web page input?**

  Do not consider the end user as a trusted source of data. Make sure you validate regular and hidden form fields, query strings, and cookies.

- **Do you validate arguments that are passed to your components or Web services?**

  The only case where it might be safe not to do so is where data is received from inside the current trust boundary. However, with a defense in depth strategy, multiple validation layers are recommended.

- **Do you validate data that is retrieved from a database?**

  You should also validate this form of input, especially if other applications write to the database. Make no assumptions about how thorough the input validation of the other application is.

- **Do you centralize your approach?**

  For common types of input fields, examine whether or not you are using common validation and filtering libraries to ensure that validation rules are performed consistently.

- **Do you rely on client-side validation?**

  Do not. Client-side validation can be used to reduce the number of round trips to the server, but do not rely on it for security because it is easy to bypass. Validate all input at the server.

What Do You Do with the Input?

Check what your application does with its input because different types of processing can lead to various types of vulnerabilities. For example, if you use input in SQL queries your application is potentially vulnerable to SQL injection.

Review the following questions to help you identify possible vulnerabilities:

- **Is your application susceptible to canonicalization issues?**

  Check whether your application uses names based on input to make security decisions. For example, does it accept user names, file names, or URLs? These are notorious for canonicalization bugs because of the many ways that the names can be represented. If your application does accept names as input, check that they are validated and converted to their canonical representation before processing.

- **Is your application susceptible to SQL injection attacks?**

  Pay close attention to any input field that you use to form a SQL database query. Check that these fields are suitably validated for type, format, length, and range. Also check how the queries are generated. If you use parameterized stored procedures, input parameters are treated as literals and are not treated as executable code. This is effective risk mitigation.

- **Is your application susceptible to XSS attacks?**

  If you include input fields in the HTML output stream, you might be vulnerable to XSS. Check that input is validated and that output is encoded. Pay close attention to how input fields that accept a range of HTML characters are processed.

Authentication

Examine how your application authenticates its callers, where it uses authentication, and how it ensures that credentials remain secure while in storage and when passed over the network. Vulnerabilities in authentication can make your application susceptible to spoofing attacks, dictionary attacks, session hijacking, and other attacks. Table 5.2 highlights the most common authentication vulnerabilities.

Table 5.2 Common Authentication Vulnerabilities

Vulnerability	Implications
Weak passwords	The risk of password cracking and dictionary attacks increase.
Clear text credentials in configuration files	Insiders who can access the server or attackers who exploit a host vulnerability to download the configuration file have immediate access to credentials.
Passing clear text credentials over the network	Attackers can monitor the network to steal authentication credentials and spoof identity.

(continued)

Table 5.2   Common Authentication Vulnerabilities *(continued)*

Vulnerability	Implications
Over-privileged accounts	The risks associated with a process or account compromise increase.
Long sessions	The risks associated with session hijacking increase.
Mixing personalization with authentication	Personalization data is suited to persistent cookies. Authentication cookies should not be persisted.

Review the following questions to identify potential vulnerabilities in the way your application performs authentication:

- **Do you separate public and restricted access?**
- **Have you identified service account requirements?**
- **How do you authenticate the caller?**
- **How do you authenticate with the database?**
- **Do you enforce strong account management practices?**

Do You Separate Public and Restricted Access?

If your application provides public areas that do not require authentication and restricted areas that do require authentication, examine how your site design distinguishes between the two. You should use separate subfolders for restricted pages and resources and then secure those folders in Internet Information Services (IIS) by configuring them to require SSL. This approach allows you to provide security for sensitive data and authentication cookies using SSL in only those areas of your site that need it. You avoid the added performance hit associated with SSL across the whole site.

Have You Identified Service Account Requirements?

Your design should identify the range of service accounts that is required to connect to different resources, including databases, directory services, and other types of remote network resources. Make sure that the design does not require a single, highly privileged account with sufficient privileges to connect to the range of different resource types.

- **Does the design require least privileged accounts?**

  Have you identified which resources and operations require which privileges? Check that the design identifies precisely which privileges each account requires to perform its specific function and use least privileged accounts in all cases.

- **Does the application need to maintain service account credentials?**

  If so make sure that the credentials are encrypted and held in a restricted location, such as a registry key with a restricted access control list (ACL).

How Do You Authenticate the Caller?

Review the following aspects of authenticating a caller. The aspects you use depend on the type of authentication your design uses.

- **Do you pass clear text credentials over the wire?**

  If you use Forms or Basic authentication, or if you use Web services and pass credentials in SOAP headers, make sure that you use SSL to protect the credentials in transit.

- **Do you implement your own user store?**

  If so, check where and how the user credentials will be stored. A common mistake is to store plaintext or encrypted passwords in the user store. Instead, you should store a password hash for verification.

  If you validate credentials against a SQL Server user store, pay close attention to the input user names and passwords. Check for the malicious injection of SQL characters.

- **Do you use Forms authentication?**

  If so, in addition to using SSL to protect the credentials, you should use SSL to protect the authentication cookie. Also check that your design uses a limited session lifetime to counter the threat of cookie replay attacks and check that the cookie is encrypted.

For more information about Forms authentication, see Chapter 10, "Building Secure ASP.NET Web Pages and Controls" and Chapter 19, "Securing Your ASP.NET Application and Web Services."

How Do You Authenticate with the Database?

When your application connects to the database, examine what authentication mechanism you will use, what account or accounts you plan to use, and how you plan to authorize the application in the database.

The following questions help review your approach to database authentication:

- **Do you use SQL authentication?**

  Ideally, your design uses Windows authentication to connect to SQL Server because this is an inherently more secure approach. If you use SQL authentication, examine how you plan to secure credentials over the network and in database connection strings.

  If your network infrastructure does not provide IPSec encrypted channels, make sure a server certificate is installed on the database to provide automatic SQL credential encryption. Also examine how you plan to secure database connection strings because these strings contain SQL account user names and passwords.

- **Do you use the process account?**

  If you use the process account of the application and connect to SQL Server using Windows authentication, make sure that your design assumes a least privileged account. The local ASPNET account is provided for this purpose, although with local accounts, you need to create a duplicate account on the database server.

  If you plan to use a domain account, make sure that it is a least privileged account and check that all intervening firewalls support Windows authentication by opening the relevant ports.

- **Do you use service accounts?**

  If your design requires multiple identities to support more granular authorization in the database, examine how you plan to store the account credentials (ideally they are encrypted using the Data Protection API (DPAPI) and held in a secured registry key) and how you are going to use the service identity.

  Also examine which process will be used to create the impersonated security context using the service account. This should not be done by the ASP.NET application process on Microsoft Windows 2000 because it forces you to increase the privileges of the process account and grant the "Act as part of the operation system" privilege. This should be avoided because it significantly increases the risk factor.

- **Have you considered using the anonymous Internet user identity?**

  For applications that use Forms or Passport authentication, you can configure a separate anonymous user account for each application. Next, you can enable impersonation and then use the anonymous identity to access the database. This approach accommodates separate authorization and identity tracking for separate applications on the same Web server.

- **Do you use the original user identity?**

  If your design requires impersonation of the original caller, you need to consider whether or not the approach provides sufficient scalability because connection pooling is ineffective. An alternative approach is to flow the identity of the original caller at the application level through trusted query parameters.

- **How do you store database connection strings?**

  If database connection strings are hard coded or stored in clear text in configuration files or the COM+ catalog, it makes them vulnerable. Instead, you should encrypt them and restrict access to the encrypted data.

For more information about the different options for connecting to SQL Server and about storing database connection strings securely, see Chapter 14, "Building Secure Data Access."

Do You Enforce Strong Account Management Practices?

The use of strong passwords, restricted login attempts, and other best practice account management policies can be enforced by Windows security policy if your application uses Windows authentication. Otherwise, the application layer is responsible for this. Review the following aspects of the account management of your application:

- **Does your application enforce strong passwords?**

  For example, do your ASP.NET Web pages use regular expressions to verify password complexity rules?

- **Do you restrict the number of failed login attempts?**

  Doing so can help counter the threat of dictionary attacks.

- **Do you reveal too much information in the event of failure?**

  Make sure you do not display messages such as "Incorrect password" because this tells malicious users that the user name is correct. This allows them to focus their efforts on cracking passwords.

- **Do you enforce a periodic change of passwords?**

  This is recommended because otherwise there is a high probability that a user will not change his or her password, which makes it more vulnerable.

- **Can you quickly disable accounts in the event of compromise?**

  If an account is compromised, can you easily disable the account to prevent the attacker from continuing to use the account?

- **Does your application record login attempts?**

  Recording failed login attempts is an effective way to detect an attacker who is attempting to break in.

Authorization

Examine how your application authorizes its users. Also examine how your application is authorized inside the database and how access to system-level resources is controlled. Authorization vulnerabilities can result in information disclosure, data tampering, and elevation of privileges. A defense in depth strategy is the key security principle that you can apply to the authorization strategy of your application. Table 5.3 highlights the most common authorization vulnerabilities.

Table 5.3   Common Authorization Vulnerabilities

Vulnerability	Implications
Reliance on a single gatekeeper	If the gatekeeper is bypassed or is improperly configured, a user gains unauthorized access.
Failing to lock down system resources against application identities	An attacker can coerce the application into accessing restricted system resources.
Failing to limit database access to specified stored procedures	An attacker mounts a SQL injection attack to retrieve, manipulate, or destroy data.
Inadequate separation of privileges	There is no accountability or ability to perform per user authorization.

Review the following questions to help validate the authorization strategy of your application design:

- **How do you authorize end users?**
- **How do you authorize the application in the database?**
- **How do you restrict access to system-level resources?**

How Do You Authorize End Users?

You should consider authorization from two perspectives at design time. First, consider end-user authorization. Which users can access which resources and perform which operations? Secondly, how do you prevent malicious users from using the application to access system level resources? Review the following questions to validate the authorization strategy of your application:

- **Do you use a defense in depth strategy?**

  Make sure that your design does not rely on a single gatekeeper to enforce access control. Consider what happens if this gatekeeper fails or if an attack manages to bypass it.

- **Which gatekeepers are used?**

  Options include IIS Web permissions, NTFS permissions, ASP.NET file authorization (which applies only with Windows authentication), URL authorization, and principal permission demands. If certain types are not used, make sure you know the reasons why not.

- **Do you use a role-based approach?**

  If so, how are the role lists maintained and how secure are the administration interfaces that are required to do this?

- **Do your roles provide adequate privilege separation?**

  Does your design provide the right degree of granularity so that the privileges that are associated with distinct user roles are adequately separated? Avoid situations where roles are granted elevated privileges just to satisfy the requirements of certain users. Consider adding new roles instead.

How Do You Authorize the Application in the Database?

The accounts that your application uses to connect to the database should have restricted capabilities that are sufficient for the application requirements, but no more.

- **Does the application access the database using stored procedures?**

  This is recommended because the login of the application can only be granted permissions to access the specified stored procedures. The login can be restricted from performing direct create/read/update/delete (CRUD) operations against the database.

  This benefits security, and performance and future maintainability also benefit.

For more information about database authorization approaches, see Chapter 14, "Building Secure Data Access."

How Do You Restrict Access to System-Level Resources?

When you design your application, consider the restrictions that will be placed on the application in terms of which system-level resources it can access. The application should only be granted access to the minimum required resources. This is a risk mitigation strategy that limits damage if an application is compromised. Consider the following issues:

- **Does your design use code access security?**

  Code access security provides a resource constraint model that can prevent code (and Web applications) from accessing specific types of system-level resources. When you use code access security, it inevitably influences your design. Identify whether or not you want to include code access security in your design plans, and then design accordingly by isolating and sandboxing privileged code and placing resource access code in its own separate assemblies.

- **What identities does your application use?**

  Your design should identify all of the identities that the application uses, including the process identity, and any impersonated identities, including anonymous Internet user accounts and service identities. The design should also indicate to which resources these identities require access.

  At deployment time, the appropriate ACLs can be configured on system-level resources to ensure that the identities of the application only have access to the resources they require.

For more information about designing for code access security, see Chapter 9, "Using Code Access Security with ASP.NET."

Configuration Management

If your application provides an administration interface that allows it to be configured, examine how the administration interfaces are secured. Also examine how sensitive configuration data is secured. Table 5.4 shows the most common configuration management vulnerabilities.

Table 5.4   Common Configuration Management Vulnerabilities

Vulnerability	Implications
Insecure administration interfaces	Unauthorized users can reconfigure your application and access sensitive data.
Insecure configuration stores	Unauthorized users can access configuration stores and obtain secrets, such as account names and passwords, and database connection details.
Clear text configuration data	Anyone that can log in to the server can view sensitive configuration data.
Too many administrators	This makes it difficult to audit and vet administrators.
Over-privileged process accounts and service accounts	This can allow privilege escalation attacks.

Use the following questions to help validate the approach of your application design to configuration management:

- **Do you support remote administration?**
- **Do you secure configuration stores?**
- **Do you separate administrator privileges?**

Do You Support Remote Administration?

If your design specifies remote administration, then you must secure the administration interfaces and configuration stores because of the sensitive nature of the operations and the data that is accessible over the administration interface. Review the following aspects of your remote administration design:

- **Do you use strong authentication?**

  All administration interface users should be required to authenticate. Use strong authentication, such as Windows or client-certificate authentication.

- **Do you encrypt the network traffic?**

  Use encrypted communication channels, such as those provided by IPSec or virtual private network (VPN) connections. Do not support remote administration over insecure channels. IPSec allows you to limit the identity and number of client machines that can be used to administer the server.

Do You Secure Configuration Stores?

Identify the configuration stores of your application and then examine your approach to restricting access to the stores and securing the data inside the stores.

- **Is your configuration store in the Web space?**

  Configuration data that is held in files in the Web space is considered less secure than data that is held outside the Web space. Host configuration mistakes or undiscovered bugs could potentially allow an attacker to retrieve and download configuration files over HTTP.

- **Is the data in the configuration store secure?**

  Make sure that key items of configuration data, such as database connection strings, encryption keys, and service account credentials, are encrypted inside the store.

- **How is access to the configuration store restricted?**

  Check that the administration interface provides the necessary authorization to ensure that only authenticated administrators can access and manipulate the data.

Do You Separate Administrator Privileges?

If your administration interfaces support different functionalities—for example, site content updates, service account reconfiguration, and database connection details—verify that your administration interfaces support role-based authorization to differentiate between content developers and operators or system administrators. For example, the person who updates static Web site content should not necessarily be allowed to alter the credit limit of a customer or reconfigure a database connection string.

Sensitive Data

Examine how your application handles sensitive data in store, in application memory, and while in transit across the network. Table 5.5 shows the most common vulnerabilities that are associated with handling sensitive data.

Table 5.5   Common Vulnerabilities with Handling Sensitive Data

Vulnerability	Implications
Storing secrets when you do not need to	This drastically increases the security risk as opposed to not storing the secret in the first place.
Storing secrets in code	If the code is on the server, an attacker might be able to download it. Secrets are visible in binary assemblies.
Storing secrets in clear text	Anyone who can log on to the server can see secret data.
Passing sensitive data in clear text over networks	Eavesdroppers can monitor the network to reveal and tamper with the data.

Use the following questions to help validate the handling of sensitive data by your application:

- **Do you store secrets?**
- **How do you store sensitive data?**
- **Do you pass sensitive data over the network?**
- **Do you log sensitive data?**

Do You Store Secrets?

Secrets include application configuration data, such as account passwords and encryption keys. If possible, identify alternate design approaches that remove any reason to store secrets. If you handle secrets, let the platform handle them so that the burden is lifted from your application wherever possible. If you do store secrets, review the following questions:

- **Can you avoid storing the secret?**

  If you use an alternative implementation technique, it could remove the need to store secrets. For example, if all you need to do is verify that a user knows a password, you do not need to store passwords. Store one-way password hashes instead.

  Also, if you use Windows authentication, you avoid storing connection strings with embedded credentials.

- **How do you store secrets?**

  If you use encryption, how do you secure the encryption keys? Consider using platform-provided DPAPI encryption that takes care of the key management for you.

- **Where do you store secrets?**

  Examine how your application stores its encrypted data. For maximum security, access to the encrypted data should be restricted with Windows ACLs. Check that the application does not store secrets in clear text or in source code.

  If you use the Local Security Authority (LSA), the code that retrieves the secret has to run with administrator privileges, which increases risk. An alternative approach that does not require extended privileges is to use DPAPI.

- **How do you process secrets?**

  Examine how your application accesses the secrets and how long they are retained in memory in clear text form. Secrets should generally be retrieved on demand, used for the smallest amount of time possible, and then discarded.

- **Do you store secrets in cookies?**

  If so, make sure the cookie is encrypted and is not persisted on the client computer.

How Do You Store Sensitive Data?

If you store sensitive application data, such as custom credit card details, examine how you protect the data.

- **What encryption algorithm do you use?** You should encrypt the data using a strong encryption algorithm with a large key size, such as Triple DES.
- **How do you secure the encryption keys?** The data is only as secure as the encryption key, so examine how you secure the key. Ideally, encrypt the key with DPAPI and secure it in a restricted location, for example, a registry key.

Do You Pass Sensitive Data Over the Network?

If you pass sensitive data over the network, check that the data is either encrypted by the application or that the data is only passed over encrypted communication links.

Do You Log Sensitive Data?

Examine whether or not your application (or the host) logs sensitive data such as user account passwords in clear text log files. You should generally avoid this. Make sure the application does not pass sensitive data in query strings because these are logged and are also clearly visible in the client's browser address bar.

Session Management

Because Web applications are built on the stateless HTTP protocol, session management is an application-level responsibility. Examine the approach to session management by your application because it directly affects the overall security of your application. Table 5.6 shows the most common vulnerabilities associated with session management.

Table 5.6   Common Session Management Vulnerabilities

Vulnerability	Implications
Passing session identifiers over unencrypted channels	Attackers can capture session identifiers to spoof identity.
Prolonged session lifetime	This increases the risk of session hijacking and replay attacks.
Insecure session state stores	Attackers can access the private session data of a user.
Session identifiers in query strings	Session identifiers can easily be modified at the client to spoof identity and access the application as another user.

Use the following questions to help validate the handling of sensitive data by your application:

- **How are session identifiers exchanged?**
- **Do you restrict session lifetime?**
- **How is the session state store secured?**

How Are Session Identifiers Exchanged?

Examine the session identifier that your application uses to manage user sessions and how these session identifiers are exchanged. Consider the following:

- **Do you pass session identifiers over unencrypted channels?**

    If you track session state with session identifiers—for example, tokens contained in cookies—examine whether or not the identifier or cookie is only passed over an encrypted channel, such as SSL.

- **Do you encrypt session cookies?**

    If you use Forms authentication, make sure your application encrypts the authentication cookies using the **protection="All"** attribute on the **<forms>** element. This practice is recommended in addition to SSL to mitigate the risk of an XSS attack that manages to steal the authentication cookie of a user.

- **Do you pass session identifiers in query strings?**

    Make sure that your application does not pass session identifiers in query strings. These strings can be easily modified at the client, which would allow a user to access the application as another user, access the private data of other users, and potentially elevate privileges.

Do You Restrict Session Lifetime?

Examine how long your application considers a session identifier valid. The application should limit this time to mitigate the threat of session hijacking and replay attacks.

How Is the Session State Store Secured?

Examine how your application stores session state. Session state can be stored in the Web application process, the ASP.NET session state service, or a SQL Server state store. If you use a remote state store, make sure that the link from the Web server to the remote store is encrypted with IPSec or SSL to protect data over the wire.

For more information about securing ASP.NET session state, see "Session State" in Chapter 19, "Securing Your ASP.NET Application and Web Services."

Cryptography

If your application uses cryptography to provide security, examine what it is used for and the way it is used. Table 5.7 shows the most common vulnerabilities relating to cryptography.

Table 5.7 Common Cryptography Vulnerabilities

Vulnerability	Implications
Using custom cryptography	This is almost certainly less secure than the tried and tested platform-provided cryptography.
Using the wrong algorithm or too small a key size	Newer algorithms increase security. Larger key sizes increase security.
Failing to secure encryption keys	Encrypted data is only as secure as the encryption key.
Using the same key for a prolonged period of time	A static key is more likely to be discovered over time.

Review the following questions to help validate the handling of sensitive data by your application:

- **Why do you use particular algorithms?**
- **How do you secure encryption keys?**

Why Do You Use Particular Algorithms?

Cryptography only provides real security if it is used appropriately and the right algorithms are used for the right job. The strength of the algorithm is also important. Review the following questions to review your use of cryptographic algorithms:

- **Do you develop your own cryptography?**

  Do not. Cryptographic algorithms and routines are notoriously difficult to develop and get right. Custom implementations frequently result in weak protection and are almost always less secure than the proven platform-provided services.

- **Do you use the right algorithm with an adequate key size?**

  Examine what algorithms your application uses and for what purpose. Larger key sizes result in improved security, but performance suffers. Stronger encryption is most important for persisted data that is retained in data stores for prolonged periods of time.

For more information about choosing an appropriate algorithm and key size, see the Cryptography section in Chapter 4, "Design Guidelines for Secure Web Applications."

How Do You Secure Encryption Keys?

The encrypted data is only as secure as the key. To decipher encrypted data, an attacker must be able to retrieve the key and the cipher text. Therefore, examine your design to ensure that the encryption keys and the encrypted data are secured. Consider the following review questions:

- **How do you secure the encryption key?**

  If you use DPAPI, the platform manages the key for you. Otherwise, the application is responsible for key management. Examine how your application secures its encryption keys. A good approach is to use DPAPI to encrypt the encryption keys that are required by other forms of encryption. Then securely store the encrypted key, for example, by placing it in the registry beneath a key configured with a restricted ACL.

- **How often are keys recycled?**

  Do not overuse keys. The longer the same key is used, the more likely it is to be discovered. Does your design consider how and how often you are going to recycle keys and how they are going to be distributed and installed on your servers?

Parameter Manipulation

Examine how your application uses parameters. These parameters include form fields, query strings, cookies, HTTP headers, and view state that are passed between client and server. If you pass sensitive data, such as session identifiers, using parameters such as query strings, a malicious client can easily bypass your server side checks with simple parameter manipulation. Table 5.8 shows the most common parameter manipulation vulnerabilities.

Table 5.8   Common Parameter Manipulation Vulnerabilities

Vulnerability	Implications
Failing to validate all input parameters	Your application is susceptible to denial of service attacks and code injection attacks, including SQL injection and XSS.
Sensitive data in unencrypted cookies	Cookie data can be changed at the client or it can be captured and changed as it is passed over the network.
Sensitive data in query strings and form fields	This is easily changed on the client.
Trusting HTTP header information	This is easily changed on the client.
Unprotected view state	This is easily changed on the client.

Examine the following questions to help ensure that your design is not susceptible to parameter manipulation attacks:

- **Do you validate all input parameters?**
- **Do you pass sensitive data in parameters?**
- **Do you use HTTP header data for security?**

Do You Validate All Input Parameters?

Check that your application validates all input parameters, including regular and hidden form fields, query strings, and cookies.

Do You Pass Sensitive Data in Parameters?

If your application passes sensitive data in parameters such as query strings or form fields, examine why your application favors this approach over the much more secure approach of passing a session identifier (for example, in an encrypted cookie). Use this information to associate the session with the state of a user that is maintained in the state store on the server. Consider the following review points:

- **Do you encrypt cookies with sensitive data?**

  If your application uses a cookie that contains sensitive data, such as a user name or a role list, make sure it is encrypted.

- **Do you pass sensitive data in query strings or Form fields?**

  This is not recommended because there is no easy way to prevent the manipulation of data in query strings or form fields. Instead, consider using encrypted session identifiers and store the sensitive data in the session state store on the server.

- **Do you protect view state?**

  If your Web pages or controls use view state to maintain state across HTTP requests, check that the view state is encrypted and checked for integrity with message authentication codes (MACs). You can configure this at the machine level or on a page-by-page basis.

Do You Use HTTP Header Data for Security?

Make sure that your Web application does not make security decisions based on information in HTTP headers because an attacker can easily manipulate the header. Do not rely on the value of the HTTP referer field to check that the request originated from a page that is generated by your Web application—this creates vulnerabilities. Doing this is inherently insecure because the referer field can easily be changed by the client.

Exception Management

Examine the way that your application handles error conditions. It is recommended that you consistently use structured exception handling. Also, check that your application does not reveal too much information when an exception occurs. Table 5.9 shows the two major exception management vulnerabilities.

Table 5.9   Common Exception Management Vulnerabilities

Vulnerability	Implications
Failing to use structured exception handling	Your application is more susceptible to denial of service attacks and logic flaws, which can expose security vulnerabilities.
Revealing too much information to the client	An attacker can use this information to help plan and tune subsequent attacks.

Review the following questions to help ensure that your design is not susceptible to exception management security vulnerabilities:

- Do you use structured exception handling?
- Do you reveal too much information to the client?

Do You Use Structured Exception Handling?

Examine how your application uses structured exception handling. Your design should mandate that structured exception handling be used consistently throughout the entire application. This creates more robust applications and your application is less likely to be left in inconsistent states that can reveal security vulnerabilities.

Do You Reveal Too Much Information to the Client?

Make sure that a malicious user cannot exploit the overly detailed information that an error message contains. Review the following points:

- **Do you catch, handle, and log exceptions on the server?**

  Make sure that the application does not let internal exception conditions propagate beyond the application boundary. Exceptions should be caught and logged on the server and, if necessary, generic error messages should be returned to the client.

- **Do you use a centralized exception management system?**

  The best way to handle and log exceptions consistently throughout your application is to use a formalized exception management system. You can also tie this system into monitoring systems that can be used by the operations team for health and performance monitoring.

- **Have you defined a set of custom error messages?**

  Your design should define the custom error messages will be used by your application when critical errors occur. Make sure they do not contain any sensitive items of data that could be exploited by a malicious user.

For more information about designing and implementing an exception management framework for .NET applications, see MSDN article, "Exception Management in .NET," at *http://msdn.microsoft.com/library/default.asp?url=/library/en-us/dnbda/html /exceptdotnet.asp.*

Auditing and Logging

Examine how your application uses auditing and logging. Besides preventing repudiation issues, regular log file analysis helps identify signs of intrusion. Table 5.10 shows the most common auditing and logging vulnerabilities.

Table 5.10   Common Auditing and Logging Vulnerabilities

Vulnerability	Implications
Failing to audit failed logons	Attempted break-ins go undetected.
Failing to secure audit files	An attacker can cover his or her tracks.
Failing to audit across application tiers	The threat of repudiation increases.

Review the following questions to help verify the approach to auditing and logging by your application:

- **Have you identified key activities to audit?**
- **Have you considered how to flow original caller identity?**
- **Have you considered secure log file management policies?**

Have You Identified Key Activities to Audit?

Your design should define which activities should be audited. Consider the following:

- **Do you audit failed login attempts?**

  This allows you to detect break-in and password-cracking attempts.

- **Do you audit other key operations?**

  Check that you audit other key events, including data retrieval, network communications, and administrative functions (such as enabling and disabling of logging).

Have You Considered How to Flow Original Caller Identity?

Your design should ensure that activity is audited across multiple application tiers. To do so, the identity of the original caller must be available at each tier.

- **Do you audit across application tiers?**

  Examine whether each tier audits activity as it should.

- **How do you synchronize multiple logs?**

  Log files may be needed in legal proceedings to prove crimes committed by individuals or to settle cases of repudiation. Generally, auditing is considered most authoritative if the audits are generated at the time of resource access and by the same routines that access the resource. Verify that the application design factors in log file synchronization and logs some form of request identifier to ensure that multiple log file entries can be correlated and related back to a single request.

- **How do you flow the original caller identity?**

  If you do not flow the original caller identity at the operating system level, for example, because of the limited scalability that this approach offers, identify how the application flows the original caller identity. This is required for cross-tier auditing (and potentially for authorization).

  Also, if multiple users are mapped to a single application role, check that the application logs the identity of the original caller.

Have You Considered Secure Log File Management Policies?

Check whether your application design factors in how log files are backed up, archived, and analyzed. Log files should be archived regularly to ensure that they do not fill up or start to cycle, and they should be regularly analyzed to detect signs of intrusion. Also ensure that any accounts used to perform the backup are least privileged and that you secure any additional communication channels exposed purely for the purpose of the backup.

Summary

By spending the time and effort up front to analyze and review your application architecture and design, you can improve its overall security by eliminating design-related vulnerabilities. It is much easier and less expensive to fix vulnerabilities at design time than it is later in the development cycle when substantial reengineering might be required.

By considering your design in relation to the target deployment environment and the security policies defined by that environment, you can help ensure a smooth and secure application deployment.

If your application has already been created, the architecture and design review is still an important part of the security assessment process that helps you fix vulnerabilities and improve future designs.

Additional Resources

For more information, see the following resources:

- For more information on designing, building and configuring authentication, authorization and secure communications across the tiers of a distributed Web application, see "Microsoft *patterns & practices* Volume I, *Building Secure ASP.NET Applications: Authentication, Authorization, and Secure Communication*" at *http://msdn.microsoft.com/library/en-us/dnnetsec/html/secnetlpMSDN.asp*.

- For a printable checklist, see "Checklist: Architecture and Design Review for Security," in the "Checklists" section of this guide.

Part III

Building Secure Web Applications

In This Part:

- .NET Security Overview
- Building Secure Assemblies
- Code Access Security in Practice
- Using Code Access Security with ASP.NET
- Building Secure ASP.NET Pages and Controls
- Building Secure Serviced Components
- Building Secure Web Services
- Building Secure Remoted Components
- Building Secure Data Access

6

.NET Security Overview

In This Chapter

- Security benefits of managed code
- Role-based security versus code access security
- Principals and identities
- **PrincipalPermission** objects
- .NET Framework role-based security fundamentals
- .NET Framework security namespaces

Overview

The Microsoft .NET Framework gives numerous techniques and a vast range of types in the security namespaces to help you build secure code and create secure Web applications. This chapter defines the .NET Framework security landscape by briefly introducing the security benefits of managed code development. This chapter also introduces and contrasts the two complimentary forms of security that are available to .NET Framework applications: user security and code security. Finally, the chapter briefly examines the security namespaces that you use to program .NET Framework security.

This chapter emphasizes how .NET Framework security applies to ASP.NET Web applications and Web services.

How to Use This Chapter

This chapter describes the security benefits inherent in using the .NET Framework and explains the complementary features of .NET Framework user (or *role-based*) security and .NET Framework code-based (or *code access*) security. We recommend that you use this chapter as follows:

- **Understand the two-layered defense provided by the .NET Framework**. Role-based security allows you to control user access to application resources and operations, while code access security can control which code can access resources and perform privileged operations.

- **Create applications that use the security concepts in this chapter**. This chapter tells you when you should use user-based security and when you should use code-based security. After reading this chapter, you will be able to identify how any new applications you create can be more secure by using role-based or code-based security.

Managed Code Benefits

Developing .NET Framework applications provides you with some immediate security benefits, although there are still many issues for you to think about. These issues are discussed in the Building chapters in Part III of this guide.

.NET Framework assemblies are built with managed code. Compilers for languages, such as the Microsoft Visual C#® development tool and Microsoft Visual Basic® .NET development system, output Microsoft intermediate language (MSIL) instructions, which are contained in standard Microsoft Windows portable executable (PE) .dll or .exe files. When the assembly is loaded and a method is called, the method's MSIL code is compiled by a just-in-time (JIT) compiler into native machine instructions, which are subsequently executed. Methods that are never called are not JIT-compiled.

The use of an intermediate language coupled with the run-time environment provided by the common language runtime offers assembly developers immediate security advantages.

- **File format and metadata validation**. The common language runtime verifies that the PE file format is valid and that addresses do not point outside of the PE file. This helps provide assembly isolation. The common language runtime also validates the integrity of the metadata that is contained in the assembly.

- **Code verification**. The MSIL code is verified for type safety at JIT compile time. This is a major plus from a security perspective because the verification process can prevent bad pointer manipulation, validate type conversions, check array bounds, and so on. This virtually eliminates buffer overflow vulnerabilities in managed code, although you still need to carefully inspect any code that calls unmanaged application programming interfaces (APIs) for the possibility of buffer overflow.

- **Integrity checking**. The integrity of strong named assemblies is verified using a digital signature to ensure that the assembly has not been altered in any way since it was built and signed. This means that attackers cannot alter your code in any way by directly manipulating the MSIL instructions.

- **Code access security**. The virtual execution environment provided by the common language runtime allows additional security checks to be performed at runtime. Specifically, code access security can make various run-time security decisions based on the identity of the calling code.

User vs. Code Security

User security and code security are two complementary forms of security that are available to .NET Framework applications. User security answers the questions, "Who is the user and what can the user do?" while code security answers the questions "Where is the code from, who wrote the code, and what can the code do?" Code security involves authorizing the application's (not the user's) access to system-level resources, including the file system, registry, network, directory services, and databases. In this case, it does not matter who the end user is, or which user account runs the code, but it does matter what the code is and is not allowed to do.

The .NET Framework user security implementation is called *role-based security*. The code security implementation is called *code access security*.

Role-Based Security

.NET Framework role-based security allows a Web application to make security decisions based on the identity or role membership of the user that interacts with the application. If your application uses Windows authentication, then a role is a Windows group. If your application uses other forms of authentication, then a role is application-defined and user and role details are usually maintained in SQL Server or user stores based on Active Directory.

The identity of the authenticated user and its associated role membership is made available to Web applications through **Principal** objects, which are attached to the current Web request.

Figure 6.1 shows a logical view of how user security is typically used in a Web application to restrict user access to Web pages, business logic, operations, and data access.

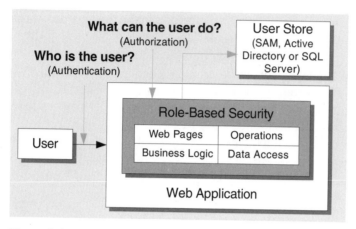

Figure 6.1

A logical view of (user) role-based security

Code Access Security

Code access security authorizes code when it attempts to access secured resources, such as the file system, registry, network, and so on, or when it attempts to perform other privileged operations, such as calling unmanaged code or using reflection.

Code access security is an important additional defense mechanism that you can use to provide constraints on a piece of code. An administrator can configure code access security policy to restrict the resource types that code can access and the other privileged operations it can perform. From a Web application standpoint, this means that in the event of a compromised process where an attacker takes control of a Web application process or injects code to run inside the process, the additional constraints that code access security provides can limit the damage that can be done.

Figure 6.2 shows a logical view of how code access security is used in a Web application to constrain the application's access to system resources, resources owned by other applications, and privileged operations, such as calling unmanaged code.

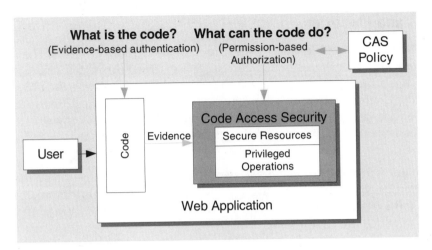

Figure 6.2
Logical view of code-based security

The authentication (identification) of code is based on evidence about the code, for example, its strong name, publisher, or installation directory. Authorization is based on the code access permissions granted to code by security policy. For more information about .NET Framework code access security, see Chapter 8, "Code Access Security in Practice."

.NET Framework Role-Based Security

.NET Framework role-based security is a key technology that is used to authorize a user's actions in an application. Roles are often used to enforce business rules. For example, a financial application might allow only managers to perform monetary transfers that exceed a particular threshold.

Role-based security consists of the following elements:

- **Principals and identities**
- **PrincipalPermission objects**
- **Role-based security checks**
- **URL authorization**

Principals and Identities

Role-based security is implemented with **Principal** and **Identity** objects. The identity and role membership of the authenticated caller is exposed through a **Principal** object, which is attached to the current Web request. You can retrieve the object by using the **HttpContext.Current.User** property. If the caller is not required to authenticate with the application, for example, because the user is browsing a publicly accessible part of the site, the **Principal** object represents the anonymous Internet user.

There are many types of **Principal** objects and the precise type depends on the authentication mechanism used by the application. However, all **Principal** objects implement the **System.Security.Principal.IPrincipal** interface and they all maintain a list of roles of which the user is a member.

Principal objects also contain **Identity** objects, which include the user's name, together with flags that indicate the authentication type and whether or not the user has been authenticated. This allows you to distinguish between authenticated and anonymous users. There are different types of Identity objects, depending on the authentication type, although all implement the **System.Security.Principal.IIdentity** interface.

The following table shows the range of possible authentication types and the different types of **Principal** and **Identity** objects that ASP.NET Web applications use.

Table 6.1   Principal and Identity Objects Per Authentication Type

Authentication Type	Principal and Identity Type	Comments
Windows	**WindowsPrincipal + WindowsIdentity**	Verification of credentials is automatic and uses the Security Accounts Manager (SAM) or Active Directory. Windows groups are used for roles.
Forms	**GenericPrincipal + FormsIdentity**	You must add code to verify credentials and retrieve role membership from a user store.
Passport	**GenericPrincipal + PassportIdentity**	Relies on the Microsoft Passport SDK. **PassportIdentity** provides access to the passport authentication ticket.

PrincipalPermission Objects

The **PrincipalPermission** object represents the identity and role that the current principal must have to execute code. **PrincipalPermission** objects can be used declaratively or imperatively in code.

Declarative Security

You can control precisely which users should be allowed to access a class or a method by adding a **PrincipalPermissionAttribute** to the class or method definition. A class-level attribute automatically applies to all class members unless it is overridden by a member-level attribute. The **PrincipalPermissionAttribute** type is defined within the **System.Security.Permissions** namespace.

Note   You can also use the **PrincipalPermissionAttribute** to restrict access to structures and to other member types, such as properties and delegates.

The following example shows how to restrict access to a particular class to members of a **Managers** group. Note that this example assumes Windows authentication, where the format of the role name is in the format *MachineName\RoleName* or *DomainName\RoleName*. For other authentication types, the format of the role name is application specific and depends on the role-name strings held in the user store.

```
[PrincipalPermissionAttribute(SecurityAction.Demand, Role=@"DOMAINNAME\Managers")]
public sealed class OnlyManagersCanCallMe
{
}
```

Note   The trailing **Attribute** can be omitted from the attribute type names. This makes the attribute type name appear to be the same as the associated permission type name, which in this case is **PrincipalPermission**. They are distinct (but logically related) types.

The next example shows how to restrict access to a particular method on a class. In this example, access is restricted to members of the local administrators group, which is identified by the special **"BUILTIN\Administrators"** identifier.

```
[PrincipalPermissionAttribute(SecurityAction.Demand,
                    Role=@"BUILTIN\Administrators")]
public void SomeMethod()
{
}
```

Other built-in Windows group names can be used by prefixing the group name with **"BUILTIN\"** (for example, **"BUILTIN\Users"** and **"BUILTIN\Power Users"**).

Imperative Security

If method-level security is not granular enough for your security requirements, you can perform imperative security checks in code by using **System.Security.Permissions.PrincipalPermission** objects.

The following example shows imperative security syntax using a
PrincipalPermission object.

```
PrincipalPermission permCheck = new PrincipalPermission(
                                 null, @"DomainName\WindowsGroup");
permCheck.Demand();
```

To avoid a local variable, the code above can also be written as:

```
(new PrincipalPermission(null, @"DomainName\WindowsGroup")).Demand();
```

The code creates a **PrincipalPermission** object with a blank user name and a specified
role name, and then calls the **Demand** method. This causes the common language
runtime to interrogate the current **Principal** object that is attached to the current
thread and check whether the associated identity is a member of the specified role.
Because Windows authentication is used in this example, the role check uses a
Windows group. If the current identity is not a member of the specified role, a
SecurityException is thrown.

The following example shows how to restrict access to an individual user.

```
(new PrincipalPermission(@"DOMAINNAME\James", null)).Demand();
```

Declarative vs. Imperative Security

You can use role-based security (and code access security) either declaratively using
attributes or imperatively in code. Generally, declarative security offers the most
benefits, although sometimes you must use imperative security (for example, when
you need to use variables that are only available at runtime) to help make a security
decision.

Advantages of Declarative Security

The main advantages of declarative security are the following:

- It allows the administrator or assembly consumer to see precisely which security
  permissions that particular classes and methods must run. Tools such as
  permview.exe provide this information. Knowing this information at deployment
  time can help resolve security issues and it helps the administrator configure code
  access security policy.

- It offers increased performance. Declarative demands are evaluated only once at
  load time. Imperative demands inside methods are evaluated each time the
  method that contains the demand is called.

- Security attributes ensure that the permission demand is executed before any other code in the method has a chance to run. This eliminates potential bugs where security checks are performed too late.

- Declarative checks at the class level apply to all class members. Imperative checks apply at the call site.

Advantages of Imperative Security

The main advantages of imperative security and the main reasons that you sometimes must use it are:

- It allows you to dynamically shape the demand by using values only available at runtime.

- It allows you to perform more granular authorization by implementing conditional logic in code.

Role-Based Security Checks

For fine-grained authorization decisions, you can also perform explicit role checks by using the **IPrincipal.IsInRole** method. The following example assumes Windows authentication, although the code would be very similar for Forms authentication, except that you would cast the **User** object to an object of the **GenericPrincipal** type.

```
// Extract the authenticated user from the current HTTP context.
// The User variable is equivalent to HttpContext.Current.User if you are using
// an .aspx or .asmx page
WindowsPrincipal authenticatedUser = User as WindowsPrincipal;
if (null != authenticatedUser)
{
  // Note: If you need to authorize specific users based on their identity
  // and not their role membership, you can retrieve the authenticated user's
  // username with the following line of code (normally though, you should
  // perform role-based authorization).
  // string username = authenticatedUser.Identity.Name;

  // Perform a role check
  if (authenticatedUser.IsInRole(@"DomainName\Manager") )
  {
    // User is authorized to perform manager functionality
  }
}
else
{
  // User is not authorized to perform manager functionality
  // Throw a security exception
}
```

URL Authorization

Administrators can configure role-based security by using the **<authorization>** element in Machine.config or Web.config. This element configures the ASP.NET **UrlAuthorizationModule**, which uses the principal object attached to the current Web request in order to make authorization decisions.

The authorization element contains child **<allow>** and **<deny>** elements, which are used to determine which users or groups are allowed or denied access to specific directories or pages. Unless the **<authorization>** element is contained within a **<location>** element, the **<authorization>** element in Web.config controls access to the directory in which the Web.config file resides. This is normally the Web application's virtual root directory.

The following example from Web.config uses Windows authentication and allows Bob and Mary access but denies everyone else:

```
<authorization>
  <allow users="DomainName\Bob, DomainName\Mary" />
  <deny users="*" />
</authorization>
```

The following syntax and semantics apply to the configuration of the **<authorization>** element:

- "*" refers to all identities.
- "?" refers to unauthenticated identities (that is, the anonymous identity).
- You do not need to impersonate for URL authorization to work.
- Users and roles for URL authorization are determined by your authentication settings:
  - When you have <authentication mode="Windows" />, you are authorizing access to Windows user and group accounts.

    User names take the form *"DomainName\WindowsUserName"*.

    Role names take the form *"DomainName\WindowsGroupName"*.

    Note The local administrators group is referred to as "BUILTIN\Administrators". The local users group is referred to as "BUILTIN\Users".

  - When you have **<authentication mode="Forms" />**, you are authorizing against the user and roles for the **IPrincipal** object that was stored in the current HTTP context. For example, if you used Forms to authenticate users against a database, you will be authorizing against the roles retrieved from the database.

- When you have **<authentication mode="Passport" />**, you authorize against the Passport User ID (PUID) or roles retrieved from a store. For example, you can map a PUID to a particular account and set of roles stored in a Microsoft SQL Server database or Active Directory.

- When you have **<authentication mode="None" />**, you may not be performing authorization. "None" specifies that you do not want to perform any authentication or that you do not want to use any of the ASP.NET authentication modules, but you do want to use your own custom mechanism.

    However, if you use custom authentication, you should create an **IPrincipal** object with roles and store it in the **HttpContext.Current.User** property When you subsequently perform URL authorization, it is performed against the user and roles (no matter how they were retrieved) maintained in the **IPrincipal** object.

Configuring Access to a Specific File

To configure access to a specific file, place the **<authorization>** element inside a **<location>** element as shown below.

```
<location path="somepage.aspx" />
  <authorization>
    <allow users="DomainName\Bob, DomainName\Mary" />
    <deny users="*" />
  </authorization>
</location>
```

You can also point the **path** attribute at a specific folder to apply access control to all the files in that particular folder. For more information about the **<location>** element, see Chapter 19, "Securing Your ASP.NET Application."

.NET Framework Security Namespaces

To program .NET Framework security, you use the types in the .NET Framework security namespaces. This section introduces these namespaces and the types that you are likely to use when you develop secure Web applications. For a full list of types, see the .NET Framework documentation. The security namespaces are listed below and are shown in Figure 6.3.

- **System.Security**
- **System.Web.Security**
- **System.Security.Cryptography**
- **System.Security.Principal**
- **System.Security.Policy**
- **System.Security.Permissions**

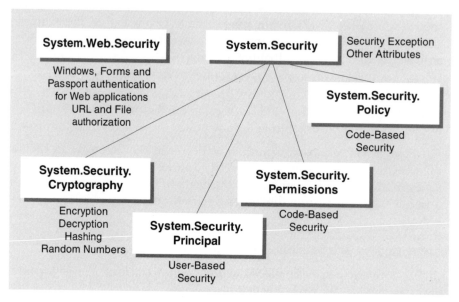

Figure 6.3
.NET Framework security namespaces

System.Security

This namespace contains the **CodeAccessPermission** base class from which all other code access permission types derive. You are unlikely to use the base class directly. You are more likely to use specific permission types that represent the rights of code to access specific resource types or perform other privileged operations. For example, **FileIOPermission** represents the rights to perform file I/O, **EventLogPermission** represents the rights for code to access the event log, and so on. For a full list of code access permission types, see Table 6.2 later in this chapter.

The **System.Security** namespace also contains classes that encapsulate permission sets. These include the **PermissionSet** and **NamedPermissionSet** classes. The types you are most likely to use when building secure Web applications are:

*   **SecurityException**. The exception type used to represent security errors.
*   **AllowPartiallyTrustedCallersAttribute**. An assembly-level attribute used with strong named assemblies that must support partial trust callers. Without this attribute, a strong named assembly can only be called by full trust callers (callers with unrestricted permissions.)

- **SupressUnmanagedSecurityAttribute**. Used to optimize performance and eliminate the demand for the unmanaged code permission issued by the Platform Invocation Services (P/Invoke) and Component Object Model (COM) interoperability layers. This attribute must be used with caution because it exposes a potential security risk. If an attacker gains control of unmanaged code, he is no longer restricted by code access security. For more information about using this attribute safely, see "Unmanaged Code" in Chapter 8, "Code Access Security in Practice."

System.Web.Security

This namespace contains the classes used to manage Web application authentication and authorization. This includes Windows, Forms, and Passport authentication and URL and File authorization, which are controlled by the **UrlAuthorizationModule** and **FileAuthorizationModule** classes, respectively. The types you are most likely to use when you build secure Web applications are:

- **FormsAuthentication**. Provides static methods to help with Forms authentication and authentication ticket manipulation.
- **FormsIdentity**. Used to encapsulate the user identity that is authenticated by Forms authentication.
- **PassportIdentity**. Used to encapsulate the user identity that is authenticated by Passport authentication.

System.Security.Cryptography

This namespace contains types that are used to perform encryption and decryption, hashing, and random number generation. This is a large namespace that contains many types. Many encryption algorithms are implemented in managed code, while others are exposed by types in this namespace that wrap the underlying cryptographic functionality provided by the Microsoft Win32®-based CryptoAPI.

System.Security.Principal

This namespace contains types that are used to support role-based security. They are used to restrict which users can access classes and class members. The namespace includes the **IPrincipal** and **IIdentity** interfaces. The types you are most likely to use when building secure Web applications are:

- **GenericPrincipal** and **GenericIdentity**. Allow you to define your own roles and user identities. These are typically used with custom authentication mechanisms.
- **WindowsPrincipal** and **WindowsIdentity**. Represents a user who is authenticated with Windows authentication together with the user's associated Windows group (role) list.

System.Security.Policy

This namespace contains types that are used to implement the code access security policy system. It includes types to represent code groups, membership conditions, policy levels, and evidence.

System.Security.Permissions

This namespace contains the majority of permission types that are used to encapsulate the rights of code to access resources and perform privileged operations. The following table shows the permission types that are defined in this namespace (in alphabetical order).

Table 6.2   Permission Types Within the System.Security.Permissions Namespace

Permission	Description
DirectoryServicesPermission	Required to access Active Directory.
DNSPermission	Required to access domain name system (DNS) servers on the network.
EndpointPermission	Defines an endpoint that is authorized by a SocketPermission object.
EnvironmentPermission	Controls read and write access to individual environment variables. It can also be used to restrict all access to environment variables.
EventLogPermission	Required to access the event log.
FileDialogPermission	Allows read-only access to files only if the file name is specified by the interactive user through a system-provided file dialog box. It is normally used when FileIOPermission is not granted.
FileIOPermission	Controls read, write, and append access to files and directory trees. It can also be used to restrict all access to the file system.
IsolatedStorageFilePermission	Controls the usage of an application's private virtual file system (provided by isolated storage). Isolated storage creates a unique and private storage area for the sole use by an application or component.
IsolatedStoragePermission	Required to access isolated storage.
MessageQueuePermission	Required to access Microsoft Message Queuing message queues.
OdbcPermission	Required to use the ADO.NET ODBC data provider. (Full trust is also required.)

Table 6.2   Permission Types Within the System.Security.Permissions Namespace *(continued)*

Permission	Description
OleDbPermission	Required to use the ADO.NET OLE DB data provider. (Full trust is also required.)
OraclePermission	Required to use the ADO.NET Oracle data provider. (Full trust is also required.)
PerformanceCounterPermission	Required to access system performance counters.
PrincipalPermission	Used to restrict access to classes and methods based on the identity and role membership of the user.
PrintingPermission	Required to access printers.
ReflectionPermission	Controls access to metadata. Code with the appropriate ReflectionPermission can obtain information about the public, protected, and private members of a type.
RegistryPermission	Controls read, write, and create access to registry keys (including subkeys). It can also be used to restrict all access to the registry.
SecurityPermission	This is a meta-permission that controls the use of the security infrastructure itself.
ServiceControllerPermission	Can be used to restrict access to the Windows Service Control Manager and the ability to start, stop, and pause services.
SocketPermission	Can be used to restrict the ability to make or accept a connection on a transport address.
SqlClientPermission	Can be used to restrict access to SQL Server data sources.
UIPermission	Can be used to restrict access to the clipboard and to restrict the use of windows to "safe" windows in an attempt to avoid attacks that mimic system dialog boxes that prompt for sensitive information such as passwords.
WebPermission	Can be used to control access to HTTP Internet resources.

The **SecurityPermission** class warrants special attention because it represents the rights of code to perform privileged operations, including asserting code access permissions, calling unmanaged code, using reflection, and controlling policy and evidence, among others. The precise right determined by the **SecurityPermission** class is determined by its **Flags** property, which must be set to one of the enumerated values defined by the **SecurityPermissionFlags** enumerated type (for example, **SecurityPermissionFlags.UnmanagedCode**).

Summary

This chapter has introduced you to the .NET Framework security landscape by contrasting user security and code security and by examining the security namespaces. The .NET Framework refers to these two types of security as role-based security and code access security, respectively. Both forms of security are layered on top of Windows security.

Role-based security is concerned with authorizing user access to application-managed resources (such as Web pages) and operations (such as business and data access logic). Code access security is concerned with constraining privileged code and controlling precisely which code can access resources and perform other privileged operations. This is a powerful additional security mechanism for Web applications because it restricts what an attacker is able to do, even if the attacker manages to compromise the Web application process. It is also an extremely powerful feature for providing application isolation. This is particularly true for hosting companies or any organization that hosts multiple Web applications on the same Web server.

Additional Resources

For more information, see the following resources:

- For more information about code access security, see Chapter 8, "Code Access Security in Practice," and Chapter 9, "Using Code Access Security with ASP.NET."
- For information about code access security and role-based security, see the MSDN article, ".NET Framework Security," at *http://msdn.microsoft.com/library /default.asp?url=/library/en-us/cpguide/html/cpconnetframeworksecurity.asp*.

7

Building Secure Assemblies

In This Chapter

- Improving the security of your assemblies with simple, proven coding techniques.
- Reducing the attack surface through well-designed interfaces and solid object oriented programming techniques.
- Using strong names and tamperproofing your assemblies.
- Reducing the risks associated with calling unmanaged code.
- Writing secure resource access code including file I/O, registry, event log, database, and network access.

Overview

Assemblies are the building blocks of .NET Framework applications and are the unit of deployment, version control, and reuse. They are also the unit of trust for code access security (all the code in an assembly is equally trusted). This chapter shows you how to improve the security design and implementation of your assemblies. This includes evaluating deployment considerations, following solid object-oriented programming practices, tamperproofing your code, ensuring that internal system level information is not revealed to the caller, and restricting who can call your code.

Managed code, the .NET Framework, and the common language runtime eliminate several important security related vulnerabilities often found in unmanaged code. Type safe verification of code is a good example where the .NET Framework helps. This makes it virtually impossible for buffer overflows to occur in managed code, which all but eliminates the threat of stack-based code injection. However, if you call unmanaged code, buffer overflows can still occur. In addition, you must also consider many other issues when you write managed code.

How to Use This Chapter

The following are recommendations on how to use this chapter:

- **Use this chapter in conjunction with Chapter 8, "Code Access Security in Practice."** Chapter 8 shows you how to use code access security features to further improve the security of your assemblies.
- **Use the corresponding checklist**. For a summary checklist that summarizes the best practices and recommendations for both chapters, see "Checklist: Security Review for Managed Code" in the Checklists section of this guide.

Threats and Countermeasures

Understanding threats and the common types of attack helps you to identify appropriate countermeasures and allows you to build more secure and robust assemblies. The main threats are:

- **Unauthorized access or privilege elevation, or both**
- **Code injection**
- **Information disclosure**
- **Tampering**

Figure 7.1 illustrates these top threats.

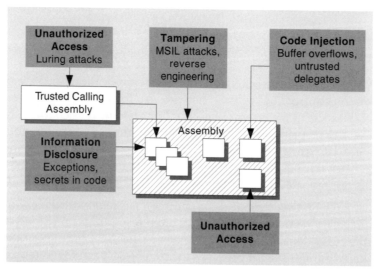

Figure 7.1

Assembly-level threats

Unauthorized Access or Privilege Elevation, or both

The risk with unauthorized access, which can lead to privilege elevation, is that an unauthorized user or unauthorized code can call your assembly and execute privileged operations and access restricted resources.

Vulnerabilities

Vulnerabilities that can lead to unauthorized access and privileged elevation include:

- Weak or missing role-based authorization
- Internal types and type members are inadvertently exposed
- Insecure use of code access security assertions and link demands
- Non-sealed and unrestricted base classes, which allow any code to derive from them

Attacks

Common attacks include:

- A luring attack where malicious code accesses your assembly through a trusted intermediary assembly to bypass authorization mechanisms
- An attack where malicious code bypasses access controls by directly calling classes that do not form part of the assembly's public API

Countermeasures

Countermeasures that you can use to prevent unauthorized access and privilege elevation include:

- Use role-based authorization to provide access controls on all public classes and class members.
- Restrict type and member visibility to limit which code is publicly accessible.
- Sandbox privileged code and ensure that calling code is authorized with the appropriate permission demands.
- Seal non-base classes or restrict inheritance with code access security.

Code Injection

With code injection, an attacker executes arbitrary code using your assembly's process level security context. The risk is increased if your assembly calls unmanaged code and if your assembly runs under a privileged account.

Vulnerabilities

Vulnerabilities that can lead to code injection include:

- Poor input validation, particularly where your assembly calls into unmanaged code
- Accepting delegates from partially trusted code
- Over-privileged process accounts

Attacks

Common code injection attacks include:

- Buffer overflows
- Invoking a delegate from an untrusted source

Countermeasures

Countermeasures that you can use to prevent code injection include:

- Validate input parameters.
- Validate data passed to unmanaged APIs.
- Do not accept delegates from untrusted sources.
- Use strongly typed delegates and deny permissions before calling the delegate.
- To further reduce risk, run assemblies using least privileged accounts.

Information Disclosure

Assemblies can suffer from information disclosure if they leak sensitive data such as exception details and clear text secrets to legitimate and malicious users alike. It is also easier to reverse engineer an assembly's Microsoft Intermediate Language (MSIL) into source code than it is with binary machine code. This presents a threat to intellectual property.

Vulnerabilities

Vulnerabilities that can lead to information disclosure include:

- Weak or no formal exception handling
- Hard-coded secrets in code

Attacks

Common attacks include:

- Attempting to cause errors by passing malformed input to the assembly
- Using ILDASM on an assembly to steal secrets

Countermeasures

Countermeasures that you can use to prevent information disclosure include:

- Solid input validation
- Structured exception handling and returning generic errors to the client
- Not storing secrets in code
- Obfuscation tools to foil decompilers and protect intellectual property

Tampering

The risk with tampering is that your assembly is modified by altering the MSIL instructions in the binary DLL or EXE assembly file.

Vulnerabilities

The primary vulnerability that makes your assembly vulnerable to tampering is the lack of a strong name signature.

Attacks

Common attacks include:

- Direct manipulation of MSIL instructions
- Reverse engineering MSIL instructions

Countermeasures

To counter the tampering threat, use a strong name to sign the assembly with a private key. When a signed assembly is loaded, the common language runtime detects if the assembly has been modified in any way and will not load the assembly if it has been altered.

Privileged Code

When you design and build secure assemblies, be able to identify privileged code. This has important implications for code access security. Privileged code is managed code that accesses secured resources or performs other security sensitive operations such as calling unmanaged code, using serialization, or using reflection. It is referred to as privileged code because it must be granted permission by code access security policy to be able to function. Non-privileged code only requires the permission to execute.

Privileged Resources

The types of resources for which your code requires code access security permissions include the file system, databases, registry, event log, Web services, sockets, DNS databases, directory services, and environment variables.

Privileged Operations

Other privileged operations for which your code requires code access security permissions include calling unmanaged code, using serialization, using reflection, creating and controlling application domains, creating Principal objects, and manipulating security policy.

For more information about the specific types of code access security permissions required for accessing resources and performing privileged operations, see "Privileged Code" in Chapter 8, "Code Access Security in Practice."

Assembly Design Considerations

One of the most significant issues to consider at design time is the trust level of your assembly's target environment, which affects the code access security permissions granted to your code and to the code that calls your code. This is determined by code access security policy defined by the administrator, and it affects the types of resources your code is allowed to access and other privileged operations it can perform.

When designing your assembly, you should:

- **Identify privileged code**
- **Identify the trust level of your target environment**
- **Sandbox highly privileged code**
- **Design your public interface**

Identify Privileged Code

Identify code that accesses secured resources or performs security sensitive operations. This type of code requires specific code access security permissions to function.

Identify Privileged Resources

Identify the types of resources your assembly needs to access; this allows you to identify any potential problems that are likely to occur if the environment your assembly ultimately runs in does not grant the relevant code access security permissions. In this case you are forced either to update code access security policy for your application if the administrator allows this, or you must sandbox your privileged code. For more information about sandboxing, see Chapter 9, "Using Code Access Security with ASP.NET."

Identify Privileged Operations

Also identify any privileged operations that your assembly needs to perform, again so that you know which code access permissions your code requires at runtime.

Identify the Trust Level of Your Target Environment

The target environment that your assembly is installed in is important because code access security policy may constrain what your assembly is allowed to do. If, for example, your assembly depends on the use of OLE DB, it will fail in anything less than a full trust environment.

Full Trust Environments

Full trust means that code has an unrestricted set of code access security permissions, which allows the code to access all resource types and perform privileged operations, subject to operating system security. A full trust environment is the default environment for a Web application and supporting assemblies installed on a Web server, although this can be altered by configuring the **<trust>** element of the application.

Partial Trust Environment

A partial trust environment is anything less than full trust. The .NET Framework has several predefined trust levels that you can use directly or customize to meet your specific security requirements. The trust level may also be diminished by the origin of the code. For example, code on a network share is trusted less than code on the local computer and as a result is limited in its ability to perform privileged operations.

Supporting Partial Trust Callers

The risk of a security compromise increases significantly if your assembly supports partial trust callers (that is, code that you do not fully trust.) Code access security has additional safeguards to help mitigate the risk. For additional guidelines that apply to assemblies that support partial trust callers, see Chapter 8, "Code Access Security in Practice." Without additional programming, your code supports partial trust callers in the following two situations:

- Your assembly does not have a strong name.
- Your assembly has a strong name and includes the **AllowPartiallyTrustedCallersAttribute** (APTCA) assembly level attribute.

Why Worry About the Target Environment?

The trust environment that your assembly runs in is important for the following reasons:

- A partial trust assembly can only gain access to a restricted set of resources and perform a restricted set of operations, depending upon which code access security permissions it is granted by code access security policy.
- A partial trust assembly cannot call a strong named assembly unless it includes **AllowPartiallyTrustedCallersAttribute**.
- Other partial trust assemblies may not be able to call your assembly because they do not have the necessary permissions. The permissions that a calling assembly must be able to call your assembly are determined by:
  - The types of resources your assembly accesses
  - The types of privileged operation your assembly performs

Sandbox Highly Privileged Code

To avoid granting powerful permissions to a whole application just to satisfy the needs of a few methods that perform privileged operations, sandbox privileged code and put it in a separate assembly. This allows an administrator to configure code access security policy to grant the extended permissions to the code in the specific assembly and not to the whole application.

For example, if your application needs to call unmanaged code, sandbox the unmanaged calls in a wrapper assembly, so that an administrator can grant the **UnmanagedCodePermission** to the wrapper assembly and not the whole application.

Note Sandboxing entails using a separate assembly and asserting security permissions to prevent full stack walks.

For more information about sandboxing unmanaged API calls, see "Unmanaged Code" in Chapter 8, "Code Access Security in Practice."

Design Your Public Interface

Think carefully about which types and members form part of your assembly's public interface. Limit the assembly's attack surface by minimizing the number of entry points and using a well designed, minimal public interface.

Class Design Considerations

In addition to using a well defined and minimal public interface, you can further reduce your assembly's attack surface by designing secure classes. Secure classes conform to solid object oriented design principles, prevent inheritance where it is not required, limit who can call them, and which code can call them. The following recommendations help you design secure classes:

- **Restrict class and member visibility**
- **Seal non base classes**
- **Restrict which users can call your code**
- **Expose fields using properties**

Restrict Class and Member Visibility

Use the **public** access modifier only for types and members that form part of the assembly's public interface. This immediately reduces the attack surface because only public types are accessible by code outside the assembly. All other types and members should be as restricted as possible. Use the **private** access modifier wherever possible. Use **protected** only if the member should be accessible to derived classes and use **internal** only if the member should be accessible to other classes in the same assembly.

> **Note**   C# also allows you to combine **protected** and **internal** to create a **protected internal** member to limit access to the current assembly or derived types.

Seal Non-Base Classes

If a class is not designed as a base class, prevent inheritance using the **sealed** keyword as shown in the following code sample.

```
public sealed class NobodyDerivesFromMe
{}
```

For base classes, you can restrict which other code is allowed to derive from your class by using code access security inheritance demands. For more information, see "Authorizing Code" in Chapter 8, "Code Access Security in Practice."

Restrict Which Users Can Call Your Code

Annotate classes and methods with declarative principal permission demands to control which users can call your classes and class members. In the following example, only members of the specified Windows group can access the **Orders** class. A class level attribute like this applies to all class members. Declarative principal permission demands can also be used on individual methods. Method level attributes override class level attributes.

```
[PrincipalPermission(SecurityAction.Demand,
                    Role=@"DomainName\WindowsGroup")]
public sealed class Orders()
{
}
```

Expose Fields Using Properties

Make all fields **private**. To make a field value accessible to external types, use a read only or a read/write property. Properties allow you to add additional constraints, such as input validation or permission demands, as shown in the following code sample.

```
public sealed class MyClass
{
  private string field; // field is private
  // Only members of the specified group are able to
  // access this public property
  [PrincipalPermission(SecurityAction.Demand,
        Role=@"DomainName\WindowsGroup")]
  public string Field
  {
    get {
        return field;
    }
  }
}
```

Strong Names

An assembly strong name consists of a text name, a version number, optionally a culture, a public key (which often represents your development organization), and a digital signature. You can see the various components of the strong name by looking into Machine.config and seeing how a strong named assembly is referenced.

The following example shows how the System.Web assembly is referenced in Machine.config. In this example, the **assembly** attribute shows the text name, version, culture and public key token, which is a shortened form of the public key.

```
<add assembly="System.Web, Version=1.0.5000.0, Culture=neutral,
            PublicKeyToken=b03f5f7f11d50a3a" />
```

Whether or not you should strong name an assembly depends on the way in which you intend it to be used. The main reasons for wanting to add a strong name to an assembly include:

- You want to ensure that partially trusted code is not able to call your assembly.

  The common language runtime prevents partially trusted code from calling a strong named assembly, by adding link demands for the FullTrust permission set. You can override this behavior by using **AllowPartiallyTrustedCallersAttribute** (APTCA) although you should do so with caution.

  For more information about APTCA, see APTCA in Chapter 8, "Code Access Security in Practice."

- The assembly is designed to be shared among multiple applications.

  In this case, the assembly should be installed in the global assembly cache. This requires a strong name. The global assembly cache supports side-by-side versioning which allows different applications to bind to different versions of the same assembly.

- You want to use the strong name as security evidence.

  The public key portion of the strong name gives cryptographically strong evidence for code access security. You can use the strong name to uniquely identify the assembly when you configure code access security policy to grant the assembly specific code access permissions. Other forms of cryptographically strong evidence include the Authenticode signature (if you have used X.509 certificates to sign the assembly) and an assembly's hash.

Note Authenticode evidence is not loaded by the ASP.NET host, which means you cannot use it to establish security policy for ASP.NET Web applications.

For more information about evidence types and code access security, see Chapter 8, "Code Access Security in Practice."

Security Benefits of Strong Names

Strong names provide a number of security advantages in addition to versioning benefits:

- Strong named assemblies are signed with a digital signature. This protects the assembly from modification. Any tampering causes the verification process that occurs at assembly load time to fail. An exception is generated and the assembly is not loaded.

- Strong named assemblies cannot be called by partially trusted code, unless you specifically add **AllowPartiallyTrustedCallersAttribute** (APTCA.)

> **Note**   If you do use APTCA, make sure you read Chapter 8, "Code Access Security in Practice," for additional guidelines to further improve the security of your assemblies.

- Strong names provide cryptographically strong evidence for code access security policy evaluation. This allows administrators to grant permissions to specific assemblies. It also allows developers to use a **StrongNameIdentityPermission** to restrict which code can call a public member or derive from a non-sealed class.

Using Strong Names

The .NET Framework includes the Sn.exe utility to help you strong name assemblies. You do not need an X.509 certificate to add a strong name to an assembly.

▶ **To strong name an assembly**

1. Generate the key file in the assembly's project directory by using the following command.

```
sn.exe -k keypair.snk
```

2. Add an **AssemblyKeyFile** attribute to Assemblyinfo.cs to reference the generated key file, as shown in the following code sample.

```
// The keypair file is usually placed in the project directory
[assembly: AssemblyKeyFile(@"..\..\keypair.snk")]
```

Delay Signing

It is good security practice to delay sign your assemblies during application development. This results in the public key being placed in the assembly, which means that it is available as evidence to code access security policy, but the assembly is not signed, and as a result is not yet tamper proof. From a security perspective, delay signing has two main advantages:

- The private key used to sign the assembly and create its digital signature is held securely in a central location. The key is only accessible by a few trusted personnel. As a result, the chance of the private key being compromised is significantly reduced.

- A single public key, which can be used to represent the development organization or publisher of the software, is used by all members of the development team, instead of each developer using his or her own public, private key pair, typically generated by the **sn –k** command.

▶ To create a public key file for delay signing

This procedure is performed by the signing authority to create a public key file that developers can use to delay sign their assemblies.

1. Create a key pair for your organization.

```
sn.exe -k keypair.snk
```

2. Extract the public key from the key pair file.

```
sn -p keypair.snk publickey.snk
```

3. Secure Keypair.snk, which contains both the private and public keys. For example, put it on a floppy or CD and physically secure it.

4. Make Publickey.snk available to all developers. For example, put it on a network share.

▶ To delay sign an assembly

This procedure is performed by developers.

1. Add an assembly level attribute to reference the key file that contains only the public key.

```
// The keypair file is usually placed in the project directory
[assembly: AssemblyKeyFile(@"..\..\publickey.snk")]
```

2. Add the following attribute to indicate delay signing.

```
[assembly: AssemblyDelaySign(true)]
```

3. The delay signing process and the absence of an assembly signature means that the assembly will fail verification at load time. To work around this, use the following commands on development and test computers.

- To disable verification for a specific assembly, use the following command.

```
sn -Vr assembly.dll
```

- To disable verification for all assemblies with a particular public key, use the following command.

```
sn -Vr *,publickeytoken
```

- To extract the public key and key token (a truncated hash of the public key), use the following command.

```
sn -Tp assembly.dll
```

Note Use a capital **–T** switch.

---

4. To fully complete the signing process and create a digital signature to make the assembly tamper proof, execute the following command. This requires the private key and as a result the operation is normally performed as part of the formal build/release process.

```
sn -r assembly.dll keypair.snk
```

ASP.NET and Strong Names

At the time of this writing, it is not possible to use a strong name for an ASP.NET Web page assembly because of the way it is dynamically compiled. Even if you use a code-behind file to create a precompiled assembly that contains your page class implementation code, ASP.NET dynamically creates and compiles a class that contains your page's visual elements. This class derives from your page class, which again means that you cannot use strong names.

Note You can strong name any other assembly that is called by your Web page code, for example an assembly that contains resource access, data access or business logic code, although the assembly must be placed in the global assembly cache.

Global Assembly Cache Requirements

Any strong named assembly called by an ASP.NET Web application configured for partial trust should be installed in the global assembly cache. This is because the ASP.NET host loads all strong-named assemblies as domain-neutral.

The code of a domain-neutral assembly is shared by all application domains in the ASP.NET process. This creates problems if a single strong named assembly is used by multiple Web applications and each application grants it varying permissions or if the permission grant varies between application domain restarts. In this situation, you may see the following error message: "Assembly <assembly>.dll security permission grant set is incompatible between appdomains."

To avoid this error, you must place strong named assemblies in the global assembly cache and not in the application's private \bin directory.

Authenticode vs. Strong Names

Authenticode and strong names provide two different ways to digitally sign an assembly. Authenticode enables you to sign an assembly using an X.509 certificate. To do so, you use the Signcode.exe utility, which adds the public key part of a full X.509 certificate to the assembly. This ensures trust through certificate chains and certificate authorities. With Authenticode (unlike strong names,) the implementation of publisher trust is complex and involves network communication during the verification of publisher identity.

Authenticode signatures and strong names were developed to solve separate problems and you should not confuse them. Specifically:

- A strong name uniquely identifies an assembly.
- An Authenticode signature uniquely identifies a code publisher.

  Authenticode signatures should be used for mobile code, such as controls and executables downloaded via Internet Explorer, to provide publisher trust and integrity.

You can configure code access security (CAS) policy using both strong names and Authenticode signatures in order to grant permissions to specific assemblies. However, the Publisher evidence object, obtained from an Authenticode signature is only created by the Internet Explorer host and not by the ASP.NET host. Therefore, on the server side, you cannot use an Authenticode signature to identify a specific assembly (through a code group.) Use strong names instead.

For more information about CAS, CAS policy and code groups, see Chapter 8, "Code Access Security in Practice."

Table 7.1 compares the features of strong names and Authenticode signatures.

Table 7.1   A Comparison of Strong Names and Authenticode Signatures

Feature	Strong Name	Authenticode
Unique identification of assembly	Yes	No
Unique identification of publisher	Not necessarily. Depends on assembly developer using a public key to represent the publisher	Yes
The public key of the publisher can be revoked	No	Yes
Versioning	Yes	No
Namespace and type name uniqueness	Yes	No
Integrity (checks assembly has not been tampered with)	Yes	Yes
Evidence used as input to CAS policy	Yes	IE host — Yes ASP.NET host — No
User input required for trust decision	No	Yes (pop-up dialog box)

Authorization

There are two types of authorization that you can use in your assemblies to control access to classes and class members:

- **Role-based authorization to authorize access based on user identity and role-membership**. When you use role-based authorization in assemblies that are part of an ASP.NET Web application or Web service, you authorize the identity that is represented by an **IPrincipal** object attached to the current Web request and available through **Thread.CurrentPrincipal** and **HttpContext.Current.User**. This identity is either the authenticated end user identity or the anonymous Internet user identity. For more information about using principal-based authorization in Web applications, see "Authorization" in Chapter 10, "Building Secure ASP.NET Pages and Controls."

- **Code access security to authorize calling code, based on evidence, such as an assembly's strong name or location**. For more information, see the "Authorization" section in Chapter 8, "Code Access Security in Practice."

Exception Management

Do not reveal implementation details about your application in exception messages returned to the client. This information can help malicious users plan attacks on your application. To provide proper exception management:

- **Use structured exception handling.**
- **Do not log sensitive data.**
- **Do not reveal system or sensitive application information.**
- **Consider exception filter issues.**
- **Consider an exception management framework.**

Use Structured Exception Handling

Microsoft Visual C# and Microsoft Visual Basic .NET provide structured exception handling constructs. C# provides the **try / catch** and **finally** construct. Protect code by placing it inside **try** blocks and implement **catch** blocks to log and process exceptions. Also use the **finally** construct to ensure that critical system resources such as connections are closed irrespective of whether an exception condition occurs.

```
try
{
    // Code that could throw an exception
}
catch (SomeExceptionType ex)
{
    // Code to handle the exception and log details to aid
    // problem diagnosis
}
finally
{
    // This code is always run, regardless of whether or not
    // an exception occurred. Place clean up code in finally
    // blocks to ensure that resources are closed and/or released.
}
```

Use structured exception handling instead of returning error codes from methods because it is easy to forget to check a return code and as a result fail to an insecure mode.

Do Not Log Sensitive Data

The rich exception details included in **Exception** objects are valuable to developers and attackers alike. Log details on the server by writing them to the event log to aid problem diagnosis. Avoid logging sensitive or private data such as user passwords. Also make sure that exception details are not allowed to propagate beyond the application boundary to the client as described in the next topic.

Do Not Reveal Sensitive System or Application Information

Do not reveal too much information to the caller. Exception details can include operating system and .NET Framework version numbers, method names, computer names, SQL command statements, connection strings, and other details that are very useful to attackers. Log detailed error messages at the server and return generic error messages to the end user.

In the context of an ASP.NET Web application or Web service, this can be done with the appropriate configuration of the **<customErrors>** element. For more information, see Chapter 10, "Building Secure ASP.NET Web Pages and Controls."

Consider Exception Filter Issues

If your code uses exception filters, your code is potentially vulnerable to security issues because code in a filter higher up the call stack can run before code in a **finally** block. Make sure you do not rely on state changes in the **finally** block because the state change will not occur before the exception filter executes. For example, consider the following code:

```csharp
// Place this code into a C# class library project
public class SomeClass
{
  public void SomeMethod()
  {
    try
    {
      // (1) Generate an exception
      Console.WriteLine("1> About to encounter an exception condition");
      // Simulate an exception
      throw new Exception("Some Exception");
    }
    // (3) The finally block
    finally
    {
      Console.WriteLine("3> Finally");
    }
  }
}
```

(continued)

```
// Place this code into a Visual Basic.NET console application project and
// reference the above class library code
Sub Main()
    Dim c As New SomeClass
    Try
        c.SomeMethod()
    Catch ex As Exception When Filter()
        ' (4) The exception is handled
        Console.WriteLine("4> Main: Catch ex as Exception")
    End Try
End Sub

' (2) The exception filter
Public Function Filter() As Boolean
    ' Malicious code could do something here if you are relying on a state
    ' change in the Finally block in SomeClass in order to provide security
    Console.WriteLine("2> Filter")
    Return True ' Indicate that the exception is handled
End Function
```

In the above example, Visual Basic .NET is used to call the C# class library code because Visual Basic .NET supports exception filters, unlike C#.

If you create two projects and then run the code, the output produced is shown below:

```
1> About to encounter an exception condition
2> Filter
3> Finally
4> Main: Catch ex as Exception
```

From this output, you can see that the exception filter executes before the code in the **finally** block. If your code sets state that affects a security decision in the **finally** block, malicious code that calls your code could add an exception filter to exploit this vulnerability.

Consider an Exception Management Framework

A formalized exception management system can help improve system supportability and maintainability and ensure that you detect, log, and process exceptions in a consistent manner.

For information about how to create an exception management framework and about best practice exception management for .NET applications, see "Exception Management in .NET" in the MSDN Library at *http://msdn.microsoft.com/library /en-us/dnbda/html/exceptdotnet.asp.*

File I/O

Canonicalization issues are a major concern for code that accesses the file system. If you have the choice, do not base security decisions on input file names because of the many ways that a single file name can be represented. If your code needs to access a file using a user-supplied file name, take steps to ensure your assembly cannot be used by a malicious user to gain access to or overwrite sensitive data.

The following recommendations help you improve the security of your file I/O:

- **Avoid untrusted input for file names**.
- **Do not trust environment variables**.
- **Validate input filenames**.
- **Constrain file I/O within your application's context**.

Avoid Untrusted Input for File Names

Avoid writing code that accepts file or path input from the caller and instead use fixed file names and locations when reading and writing data. This ensures your code cannot be coerced into accessing arbitrary files.

Do Not Trust Environment Variables

Try to use absolute file paths where you can. Do not trust environment variables to construct file paths because you cannot guarantee the value of the environment variable.

Validate Input File Names

If you do need to receive input file names from the caller, make sure that the filename is strictly formed so that you can determine whether it is valid. Specifically, there are two aspects to validating input file paths. You need to:

- Check for valid file system names.
- Check for a valid location, as defined by your application's context. For example, are they within the directory hierarchy of your application?

To validate the path and file name, use the **System.IO.Path.GetFullPath** method as shown in the following code sample. This method also canonicalizes the supplied file name.

```
using System.IO;

public static string ReadFile(string filename)
{
  // Obtain a canonicalized and valid filename
  string name = Path.GetFullPath(filename);
  // Now open the file
}
```

As part of the canonicalization process, **GetFullPath** performs the following checks:

- It checks that the file name does not contain any invalid characters, as defined by **Path.InvalidPathChars**.
- It checks that the file name represents a file and not an another device type such as a physical drive, a named pipe, a mail slot or a DOS device such as LPT1, COM1, AUX, and other devices.
- It checks that the combined path and file name is not too long.
- It removes redundant characters such as trailing dots.
- It rejects file names that use the //?/ format.

Constrain File I/O Within Your Application's Context

After you know you have a valid file system file name, you often need to check that it is valid in your application's context. For example, you may need to check that it is within the directory hierarchy of your application and to make sure your code cannot access arbitrary files on the file system. For more information about how to use code access security to constrain file I/O, see "File I/O" in Chapter 8, "Code Access Security in Practice."

Event Log

When you write event-logging code, consider the threats of tampering and information disclosure. For example, can an attacker retrieve sensitive data by accessing the event logs? Can an attacker cover tracks by deleting the logs or erasing particular records?

Direct access to the event logs using system administration tools such as the Event Viewer is restricted by Windows security. Your main concern should be to ensure that the event logging code you write cannot be used by a malicious user for unauthorizedaccess to the event log.

To prevent the disclosure of sensitive data, do not log it in the first place. For example, do not log account credentials. Also, your code cannot be exploited to read existing records or to delete event logs if all it does is write new records using **EventLog.WriteEvent**. The main threat to address in this instance is how to prevent a malicious caller from calling your code a million or so times in an attempt to force a log file cycle to overwrite previous log entries to cover tracks. The best way of approaching this problem is to use an out-of-band mechanism, for example, by using Windows instrumentation to alert operators as soon as the event log approaches its threshold.

Finally, you can use code access security and the **EventLogPermission** to put specific constraints on what your code can do when it accesses the event log. For example, if you write code that only needs to read records from the event log it should be constrained with an **EventLogPermissin** that only supports browse access. For more information about how to constrain event logging code, see "Event Log" in Chapter 8, "Code Access Security in Practice."

Registry

The registry can provide a secure location for storing sensitive application configuration data, such as encrypted database connection strings. You can store configuration data under the single, local machine key (**HKEY_LOCAL_MACHINE**) or under the current user key (**HKEY_CURRENT_USER**). Either way, make sure you encrypt the data using DPAPI and store the encrypted data, not the clear text.

HKEY_LOCAL_MACHINE

If you store configuration data under **HKEY_LOCAL_MACHINE**, remember that any process on the local computer can potentially access the data. To restrict access, apply a restrictive access control list (ACL) to the specific registry key to limit access to administrators and your specific process or thread token. If you use **HKEY_LOCAL_MACHINE**, it does make it easier at installation time to store configuration data and also to maintain it later on.

HKEY_CURRENT_USER

If your security requirements dictate an even less accessible storage solution, use a key under **HKEY_CURRENT_USER**. This approach means that you do not have to explicitly configure ACLs because access to the current user key is automatically restricted based on process identity.

HKEY_CURRENT_USER allows more restrictive access because a process can only access the current user key, if the user profile associated with the current thread or process token is loaded.

Version 1.1 of the .NET Framework loads the user profile for the ASPNET account on Windows 2000. On Windows Server 2003, the profile for this account is only loaded if the ASP.NET process model is used. It is not loaded explicitly by Internet Information Services (IIS) 6 if the IIS 6 process model is used on Windows Server 2003.

Note   Version 1.0 of the .NET Framework does not load the ASPNET user profile, which makes **HKEY_CURRENT_USER** a less practical option.

Reading from the Registry

The following code fragment shows how to read an encrypted database connection string from under the **HKEY_CURRENT_USER** key using the **Microsoft.Win32.Registry** class.

```
using Microsoft.Win32;
public static string GetEncryptedConnectionString()
{
  return (string)Registry.
                CurrentUser.
                OpenSubKey(@"SOFTWARE\YourApp").
                GetValue("connectionString");
}
```

For more information about how to use the code access security **RegistryPermission** to constrain registry access code for example to limit it to specific keys, see "Registry" in Chapter 8, "Code Access Security in Practice."

Data Access

Two of the most important factors to consider when your code accesses a database are how to manage database connection strings securely and how to construct SQL statements and validate input to prevent SQL injection attacks. Also, when you write data access code, consider the permission requirements of your chosen ADO.NET data provider. For detailed information about these and other data access issues, see Chapter 14, "Building Secure Data Access."

For information about how to use **SqlClientPermission** to constrain data access to SQL Server using the ADO.NET SQL Server data provider, see "Data Access" in Chapter 8, "Code Access Security in Practice."

Unmanaged Code

If you have existing COM components or Win32 DLLs that you want to reuse, use the Platform Invocation Services (P/Invoke) or COM Interop layers. When you call unmanaged code, it is vital that your managed code validates each input parameter passed to the unmanaged API to guard against potential buffer overflows. Also, be careful when handling output parameters passed back from the unmanaged API.

You should isolate calls to unmanaged code in a separate wrapper assembly. This allows you to sandbox the highly privileged code and to isolate the code access security permission requirements to a specific assembly. For more details about sandboxing and about additional code access security related guidelines that you should apply when calling unmanaged code, see "Unmanaged Code" in Chapter 8, "Code Access Security in Practice." The following recommendations help improve the security of your unmanaged API calls, without using explicit code access security coding techniques:

- **Validate input and output string parameters.**
- **Validate array bounds.**
- **Check file path lengths.**
- **Compile unmanaged code with the /GS switch.**
- **Inspect unmanaged code for "dangerous" APIs.**

Validate Input and Output String Parameters

String parameters passed to unmanaged APIs are a prime source of buffer overflows. Check the length of any input string inside your wrapper code to ensure it does not exceed the limit defined by the unmanaged API. If the unmanaged API accepts a character pointer you may not know the maximum permitted string length, unless you have access to the unmanaged source. For example, the following is a common vulnerability.

```
void SomeFunction( char *pszInput )
{
  char szBuffer[10];
  // Look out, no length checks. Input is copied straight into the buffer
  // Check length or use strncpy
  strcpy(szBuffer, pszInput);
  . . .
}
```

If you cannot examine the unmanaged code because you do not own it, make sure that you rigorously test the API by passing in deliberately long input strings.

If your code uses a **StringBuilder** to receive a string passed from an unmanaged API, make sure that it can hold the longest string that the unmanaged API can hand back.

Validate Array Bounds

If you pass input to an unmanaged API using an array, check that the managed wrapper verifies that the capacity of the array is not exceeded.

Check File Path Lengths

If the unmanaged API accepts a file name and path, check that it does not exceed 260 characters. This limit is defined by the Win32 **MAX_PATH** constant. It is very common for unmanaged code to allocate buffers of this length to manipulate file paths.

Note Directory names and registry keys can only be a maximum of 248 characters long.

Compile Unmanaged Code With the /GS Switch

If you own the unmanaged code, compile it using the /GS switch to enable stack probes to help detect buffer overflows. For more information about the /GS switch, see Microsoft Knowledge Base article 325483, "WebCast: Compiler Security Checks: The -GS compiler switch."

Inspect Unmanaged Code for Dangerous APIs

If you have access to the source code for the unmanaged code that you are calling, you should subject it to a thorough code review, paying particular attention to parameter handling to ensure that buffer overflows are not possible and that it does not use potentially dangerous APIs. For more information see Chapter 21, "Code Review."

Delegates

Delegates are the managed equivalent of type safe function pointers and are used by the .NET Framework to support events. The delegate object maintains a reference to a method, which is called when the delegate is invoked. Events allow multiple methods to be registered as event handlers. When the event occurs, all event handlers are called.

Do Not Accept Delegates from Untrusted Sources

If your assembly exposes a delegate or an event, be aware that any code can associate a method with the delegate and you have no advance knowledge of what the code does. The safest policy is not to accept delegates from untrusted callers. If your assembly is strong named and does not include the **AllowPartiallyTrustedCallersAttribute**, only Full Trust callers can pass you a delegate.

If your assembly supports partial trust callers, consider the additional threat of being passed a delegate by malicious code. For risk mitigation techniques to address this threat, see the "Delegates" section in Chapter 8, "Code Access Security in Practice."

Serialization

You may need to add serialization support to a class if you need to be able to marshal it by value across a .NET remoting boundary (that is, across application domains, processes, or computers) or if you want to be able to persist the object state to create a flat data stream, perhaps for storage on the file system.

By default, classes cannot be serialized. A class can be serialized if it is marked with the **SerializableAttribute** or if it derives from **ISerializable**. If you use serialization:

- **Do not serialize sensitive data.**
- **Validate serialized data streams.**

Do Not Serialize Sensitive Data

Ideally, if your class contains sensitive data, do not support serialization. If you must be able to serialize your class and it contains sensitive data, avoid serializing the fields that contain the sensitive data. To do this, either implement **ISerializable** to control the serialization behavior or decorate fields that contain sensitive data with the [**NonSerialized**] attribute. By default, all private and public fields are serialized.

The following example shows how to use the [**NonSerialized**] attribute to ensure a specific field that contains sensitive data cannot be serialized.

```
[Serializable]
public class Employee {
  // OK for name to be serialized
  private string name;
  // Prevent salary being serialized
  [NonSerialized] private double annualSalary;
  . . .
}
```

Alternatively, implement the **ISerializable** interface and explicitly control the serialization process. If you must serialize the sensitive item or items of data, consider encrypting the data first. The code that de-serializes your object must have access to the decryption key.

Validate Serialized Data Streams

When you create an object instance from a serialized data stream, do not assume the stream contains valid data. To avoid potentially damaging data being injected into the object, validate each field as it is reconstituted as shown in the following code sample.

```
public void DeserializationMethod(SerializationInfo info, StreamingContext cntx)
{
  string someData = info.GetString("someName");
  // Use input validation techniques to validate this data.
}
```

For more information about input validation techniques, see "Input Validation" in Chapter 10, "Building Secure ASP.NET Pages and Controls."

Partial Trust Considerations

If your code supports partial trust callers, you need to address additional threats. For example, malicious code might pass a serialized data stream or it might attempt to serialize the data on your object. For risk mitigation techniques to address these threats, see "Serialization" in Chapter 8, "Code Access Security in Practice."

Threading

Bugs caused by race conditions in multithreaded code can result in security vulnerabilities and generally unstable code that is subject to timing-related bugs. If you develop multithreaded assemblies, consider the following recommendations:

- **Do not cache the results of security checks.**
- **Consider impersonation tokens.**
- **Synchronize static class constructors.**
- **Synchronize Dispose methods.**

Do Not Cache the Results of Security Checks

If your multithreaded code caches the results of a security check, perhaps in a static variable, the code is potentially vulnerable as shown in the following code sample.

```
public void AccessSecureResource()
{
  _callerOK = PerformSecurityDemand();
  OpenAndWorkWithResource();
  _callerOK = false;
}
private void OpenAndWorkWithResource()
{
  if (_callerOK)
    PerformTrustedOperation();
  else
  {
    PerformSecurityDemand();
    PerformTrustedOperation();
  }
}
```

If there are other paths to **OpenAndWorkWithResource**, and a separate thread calls the method on the same object, it is possible for the second thread to omit the security demand, because it sees **_callerOK=true**, set by another thread.

Consider Impersonation Tokens

When you create a new thread, it assumes the security context defined by the process level token. If a parent thread is impersonating while it creates a new thread, the impersonation token is not passed to the new thread.

Synchronize Static Class Constructors

If you use static class constructors, make sure they are not vulnerable to race conditions. If, for example, they manipulate static state, add thread synchronization to avoid potential vulnerabilities.

Synchronize Dispose Methods

If you develop non-synchronized **Dispose** implementations, the **Dispose** code may be called more than once on separate threads. The following code sample shows an example of this.

```
void Dispose()
{
  if (null != _theObject)
  {
    ReleaseResources(_theObject);
    _theObject = null;
  }
}
```

In this example, it is possible for two threads to execute the code before the first thread has set **_theObject** reference to null. Depending on the functionality provided by the **ReleaseResources** method, security vulnerabilities may occur.

Reflection

With reflection, you can dynamically load assemblies, discover information about types, and execute code. You can also obtain a reference to an object and get or set its private members. This has a number of security implications:

- If your code uses reflection to reflect on other types, make sure that only trusted code can call you. Use code access security permission demands to authorize calling code. For more information, see Chapter 8, "Code Access Security in Practice."

- If you dynamically load assemblies, for example, by using **System.Reflection.Assembly.Load**, do not use assembly or type names passed to you from untrusted sources.

- If your assemblies dynamically generate code to perform operations for a caller, make sure the caller is in no way able to influence the code that is generated. This issue is more significant if the caller operates at a lower trust level than the assembly that generates code.

- If your code generation relies on input from the caller, be especially vigilant for security vulnerabilities. Validate any input string used as a string literal in your generated code and escape quotation mark characters to make sure the caller cannot break out of the literal and inject code. In general, if there is a way that the caller can influence the code generation such that it fails to compile, there is probable security vulnerability.

For more information, see "Secure Coding Guidelines for the .NET Framework" in the MSDN Library.

Obfuscation

If you are concerned with protecting intellectual property, you can make it extremely difficult for a decompiler to be used on the MSIL code of your assemblies, by using an obfuscation tool. An obfuscation tool confuses human interpretation of the MSIL instructions and helps prevent successful decompilation.

Obfuscation is not foolproof and you should not build security solutions that rely on it. However, obfuscation does address threats that occur because of the ability to reverse engineer code. Obfuscation tools generally provide the following benefits:

- They help protect your intellectual property.

- They obscure code paths. This makes it harder for an attacker to crack security logic.

- They mangle the names of internal member variables. This makes it harder to understand the code.

- They encrypt strings. Attackers often attempt to search for specific strings to locate key sensitive logic. String encryption makes this much harder to do.

A number of third-party obfuscation tools exist for the .NET Framework. One tool, the Community Edition of the Dotfuscator tool by PreEmptive Solutions, is included with the Microsoft Visual Studio® .NET 2003 development system. It is also available from *http://www.preemptive.com/dotfuscator*. For more information, see the list of obfuscator tools listed at *http://www.gotdotnet.com/team/csharp/tools/default.aspx*.

Cryptography

Cryptography is one of the most important tools that you can use to protect data. Encryption can be used to provide data privacy and hash algorithms, which produce a fixed and condensed representation of data, can be used to make data tamperproof. Also, digital signatures can be used for authentication purposes.

You should use encryption when you want data to be secure in transit or in storage. Some encryption algorithms perform better than others while some provide stronger encryption. Typically, larger encryption key sizes increase security.

Two of the most common mistakes made when using cryptography are developing your own encryption algorithms and failing to secure your encryption keys. Encryption keys must be handled with care. An attacker armed with your encryption key can gain access to your encrypted data.

The main issues to consider are:

- **Use platform-provided cryptographic services**
- **Key generation**
- **Key storage**
- **Key exchange**
- **Key maintenance**

Use Platform-provided Cryptographic Services

Do not create your own cryptographic implementations. It is extremely unlikely that these implementations will be as secure as the industry standard algorithms provided by the platform; that is, the operating system and the .NET Framework. Managed code should use the algorithms provided by the **System.Security.Cryptography** namespace for encryption, decryption, hashing, random number generating, and digital signatures.

Many of the types in this namespace wrap the operating system CryptoAPI, while others implement algorithms in managed code.

Key Generation

The following recommendations apply when you create encryption keys:

- **Generate random keys.**
- **Use PasswordDeriveBytes for password-based encryption.**
- **Prefer large keys.**

Generate Random Keys

If you need to generate encryption keys programmatically, use **RNGCryptoServiceProvider** for creating keys and initialization vectors and do not use the **Random** class. Unlike the **Random** class, **RNGCryptoServiceProvider** creates cryptographically strong random numbers which are FIPS-140 compliant. The following code shows how to use this function.

```
using System.Security.Cryptography;
. . .
RNGCryptoServiceProvider rng = new RNGCryptoServiceProvider();
byte[] key = new byte[keySize];
rng.GetBytes(key);
```

Use PasswordDeriveBytes for Password-Based Encryption

The **System.Security.Cryptography.DeriveBytes** namespace provides **PasswordDeriveBytes** for use when encrypting data based on a password the user supplies. To decrypt, the user must supply the same password used to encrypt.

Note that this approach is not for password authentication. Store a password verifier in the form of a hash value with a salt value order to authenticate a user's password. Use **PasswordDeriveBytes** to generate keys for password-based encryption.

PasswordDeriveBytes accepts a password, salt, an encryption algorithm, a hashing algorithm, key size (in bits), and initialization vector data to create a symmetric key to be used for encryption.

After the key is used to encrypt the data, clear it from memory but persist the salt and initialization vector. These values should be protected and are needed to re-generate the key for decryption.

For more information about storing password hashes with salt, see Chapter 14, "Building Secure Data Access."

Prefer Large Keys

When generating an encryption key or key pair, use the largest key size possible for the algorithm. This does not necessarily make the algorithm more secure but dramatically increases the time needed to successfully perform a brute force attack on the key. The following code shows how to find the largest supported key size for a particular algorithm.

```
private int GetLargestSymKeySize(SymmetricAlgorithm symAlg)
{
  KeySizes[] sizes = symAlg.LegalKeySizes;
  return sizes[sizes.Length].MaxSize;
}

private int GetLargestAsymKeySize(AsymmetricAlgorithm asymAlg)
{
  KeySizes[] sizes = asymAlg.LegalKeySizes;
  return sizes[sizes.Length].MaxSize;
}
```

Key Storage

Where possible, you should use a platform-provided encryption solution that enables you to avoid key management in your application. However, at times you need to use encryption solutions that require you to store keys. Using a secure location to store the key is critical. Use the following techniques to help prevent key storage vulnerabilities:

- **Use DPAPI to avoid key management**.
- **Do not store keys in code.**
- **Restrict access to persisted keys.**

Use DPAPI to Avoid Key Management

DPAPI is a native encryption/decryption feature provided by Microsoft Windows 2000. One of the main advantages of using DPAPI is that the encryption key is managed by the operating system, because the key is derived from the password that is associated with the process account (or thread account if the thread is impersonating) that calls the DPAPI functions.

User Key vs. Machine Key

You can perform encryption with DPAPI using either the user key or the machine key. By default, DPAPI uses a user key. This means that only a thread that runs under the security context of the user account that encrypted the data can decrypt the data. You can instruct DPAPI to use the machine key by passing the **CRYPTPROTECT_LOCAL_MACHINE** flag to the **CryptProtectData** API. In this event, any user on the current computer can decrypt the data.

The user key option can be used only if the account used to perform the encryption has a loaded user profile. If you run code in an environment where the user profile is not loaded, you cannot easily use the user store and should opt for the machine store instead.

Version 1.1 of the .NET Framework loads the user profile for the ASPNET account used to run Web applications on Windows 2000. Version 1.0 of the .NET Framework does not load the profile for this account, which makes using DPAPI with the user key more difficult.

If you use the machine key option, you should use an ACL to secure the encrypted data, for example in a registry key, and use this approach to limit which users have access to the encrypted data. For added security, you should also pass an optional entropy value to the DPAPI functions.

Note An entropy value is an additional random value that can be passed to the DPAPI **CryptProtectData** and **CryptUnprotectData** functions. The same value that is used to encrypt the data must be used to decrypt the data. The machine key option means that any user on the computer can decrypt the data. With added entropy, the user must also know the entropy value.

The drawback with using entropy is that you must manage the entropy value as you would manage a key. To avoid entropy management issues, use the machine store without entropy and validate users and code (using code access security) thoroughly before calling the DPAPI code.

For more information about using DPAPI from ASP.NET Web applications, see "How To: Create a DPAPI Library," in the How To section of "Building Secure ASP.NET Applications," at *http://msdn.microsoft.com/library/en-us/dnnetsec/html /SecNetHT07.asp*.

Do Not Store Keys in Code

Do not store keys in code because hard-coded keys in your compiled assembly can be disassembled using tools similar to ILDASM, which will render your key in plaintext.

Restrict Access to Persisted Keys

When storing keys in persistent storage to be used at runtime, use appropriate ACLs and limit access to the key. Access to the key should be granted only to Administrators, SYSTEM, and the identity of the code at runtime, for example the ASPNET or Network Service account.

When backing up a key, do not store it in plain text, encrypt it using DPAPI or a strong password and place it on removable media.

Key Exchange

Some applications require the secure exchange of encryption keys over an insecure network. You may need to verbally communicate the key or send it through secure e-mail. A more secure method to exchange a symmetric key is to use public key encryption. With this approach, you encrypt the symmetric key to be exchanged by using the other party's public key from a certificate that can be validated. A certificate is considered valid when:

- It is being used within the date ranges as specified in the certificate.
- All signatures in the certificate chain can be verified.
- It is of the correct type. For example, an e-mail certificate is not being used as a Web server certificate.
- It can be verified up to a trusted root authority.
- It is not on a Certificate Revocation List (CRL) of the issuer.

Key Maintenance

Security is dependent upon keeping the key secure over a prolonged period of time. Apply the following recommendations for key maintenance:

- **Cycle keys periodically.**
- **Protect exported private keys.**

Cycle Keys Periodically

You should change your encryption keys from time to time because a static secret is more likely to be discovered over time. Did you write it down somewhere? Did Bob the administrator with the secrets change positions in your company or leave the company? Are you using the same session key to encrypt communication for a long time? Do not overuse keys.

Key Compromise

Keys can be compromised in a number of ways. For example, you may lose the key or discover that an attacker has stolen or discovered the key.

If your private key used for asymmetric encryption and key exchange is compromised, do not continue to use it, and notify the users of the public key that the key has been compromised. If you used the key to sign documents, they need to be re-signed.

If the private key of your certificate is compromised, contact the issuing certification authority to have your certificate placed on a certificate revocation list. Also, change the way your keys are stored to avoid a future compromise.

Protect Exported Private Keys

Use **PasswordDeriveBytes** when you export an Rivest, Shamir, and Adleman (RSA) or Digital Signature Algorithm (DSA) private key. The RSA and DSA classes contain a **ToXmlString** method, which allows you to export the public or private key, or both, from the key container. This method exports the private key in plain text. If you export the private key to be installed on multiple servers in a Web farm, a recommended method is to encrypt the key after exporting the private key by using **PasswordDeriveBytes** to generate a symmetric key as shown in the following code sample.

```
PasswordDeriveBytes deriver = new PasswordDeriveBytes(<strong password>, null);
byte[] ivZeros = new byte[8];//This is not actually used but is currently
required.
//Derive key from the password
byte[] pbeKey = deriver.CryptDeriveKey("TripleDES", "SHA1", 192, ivZeros);
```

Summary

This chapter has shown you how to apply various techniques to improve the security of your managed code. The techniques in this chapter can be applied to all types of managed assemblies including Web pages, controls, utility libraries, and others. For specific recommendations that apply to specific types of assemblies, see the other building chapters in Part III of this guide.

To further improve the security of your assemblies, you can use explicit code access security coding techniques, which are particularly important if your assemblies support partial trust callers. For more information about using code access security, see Chapter 8, "Code Access Security in Practice."

Additional Resources

For additional related reading, refer to the following resources:

- For more information about using DPAPI from ASP.NET Web applications, see "How To: Create a DPAPI Library" in the "How To" section of "Microsoft *patterns & practices* Volume I, *Building Secure ASP.NET Applications: Authentication, Authorization, and Secure Communication*" at *http://msdn.microsoft.com/library /en-us/dnnetsec/html/SecNetHT07.asp*.

- For more information about secure coding guidelines for the .NET Framework, see MSDN article, "Secure Coding Guidelines for the .NET Framework," at *http://msdn.microsoft.com/library/default.asp?url=/library/en-us/dnnetsec/html /seccodeguide.asp*.

- Michael Howard discusses techniques for writing secure code and shows you how to add them in your own applications in his MSDN column, "Code Secure," at *http://msdn.microsoft.com/columns/secure.asp*.

8

Code Access Security in Practice

In This Chapter

- Code access security explained
- Using APTCA
- Requesting permissions
- Sandboxing privileged code
- Authorizing code with identity demands
- Serialization, delegates, and threading
- Calling unmanaged code

Overview

Code access security is a resource constraint model designed to restrict the types of system resource that code can access and the types of privileged operation that the code can perform. These restrictions are independent of the user who calls the code or the user account under which the code runs.

Code access security delivers three main benefits. By using code access security, you can:

- **Restrict what your code can do**

  For example, if you develop an assembly that performs file I/O you can use code access security to restrict your code's access to specific files or directories. This reduces the opportunities for an attacker to coerce your code to access arbitrary files.

- **Restrict which code can call your code**

  For example, you may only want your assembly to be called by other code developed by your organization. One way to do this is to use the public key component of an assembly's strong name to apply this kind of restriction. This helps prevent malicious code from calling your code.

- **Identify code**

  To successfully administer code access security policy and restrict what code can do, the code must be identifiable. Code access security uses evidence such as an assembly's strong name or its URL, or its computed hash to identify code (assemblies.)

How to Use This Chapter

This chapter takes up where Chapter 7, "Building Secure Assemblies," left off. It shows how you can use code access security to further improve the security of your managed code. To get the most out of this chapter:

- **Read Chapter 6, ".NET Security Fundamentals"** for an overview and comparison of user (role)-based security versus code access security. Chapter 6 helps set the scene for the current chapter.

- **Read Chapter 7, "Building Secure Assemblies."** Read Chapter 7 before this chapter if you have not already done so.

- **Read Chapter 9, "Using Code Access Security with ASP.NET."** After you read this chapter, read Chapter 9 if you are interested specifically in ASP.NET code access security policy and ASP.NET trust levels.

Code Access Security Explained

To use code access security effectively, you need to know the basics such as the terminology and how policy is evaluated. For further background information about code access security, see the "Additional Resources" section at the end of this chapter. If you are already familiar with code access security, you may want to skip this section and go to the "APTCA" (**AllowPartiallyTrustedCallersAttribute**) section later in this chapter.

Code access security consists of the following elements:

- **Code**
- **Evidence**
- **Permissions**
- **Policy**
- **Code groups**

Code

All managed code is subject to code access security. When an assembly is loaded, it is granted a set of code access permissions that determines what resource types it can access and what types of privileged operations it can perform. The Microsoft .NET Framework security system uses evidence to authenticate (identify) code to grant permissions.

Note An assembly is the unit of configuration and trust for code access security. All code in the same assembly receives the same permission grant and is therefore equally trusted.

Evidence

Evidence is used by the .NET Framework security system to identify assemblies. Code access security policy uses evidence to help grant the right permissions to the right assembly. Location-related evidence includes:

- **URL**. The URL that the assembly was obtained from. This is the codebase URL in its raw form, for example, http://webserver/vdir/bin/assembly.dll or file://C:/directory1/directory2/assembly.dll.
- **Site**. The site the assembly was obtained from, for example, http://webserver. The site is derived from the codebase URL.
- **Application directory**. The base directory for the running application.
- **Zone**. The zone the assembly was obtained from, for example, LocalIntranet or Internet. The zone is also derived from the codebase URL.

Author-related evidence includes:

- **Strong name**. This applies to assemblies with a strong name. Strong names are one way to digitally sign an assembly using a private key.
- **Publisher**. The Authenticode signature; based on the X.509 certificate used to sign code, representing the development organization.

Important Publisher evidence (the Authenticode signature) is ignored by the ASP.NET host and therefore cannot be used to configure code access security policy for server-side Web applications. This evidence is primarily used by the Internet Explorer host.

- **Hash**. The assembly hash is based on the overall content of the assembly and allows you to detect a particular compilation of a piece of code, independent of version number. This is useful for detecting when third party assemblies change (without an updated version number) and you have not tested and authorized their use for your build.

Permissions

Permissions represent the rights for code to access a secured resource or perform a privileged operation. The .NET Framework provides *code access permissions* and *code identity permissions*. Code access permissions encapsulate the ability to access a particular resource or perform a privileged operation. Code identity permissions are used to restrict access to code, based on an aspect of the calling code's identity such as its strong name.

Your code is granted permissions by code access security policy that is configured by the administrator. An assembly can also affect the set of permissions that it is ultimately granted by using permission requests. Together, code access security policy and permission requests determine what your code can do. For example, code must be granted the **FileIOPermission** to access the file system, and code must be granted the **RegistryPermission** to access the registry. For more information about permission requests, see the "Requesting Permissions" section later in this chapter.

Note   Permission sets are used to group permissions together to ease administration.

Restricted and Unrestricted Permissions

Permissions can be *restricted* or *unrestricted*. For example, in its unrestricted state, the **FileIOPermission** allows code to read or write to any part of the file system. In a restricted state, it might allow code to read files only from a specific directory.

Demands

If you use a class from the .NET Framework class library to access a resource or perform another privileged operation, the class issues a permission demand to ensure that your code, and any code that calls your code, is authorized to access the resource. A permission demand causes the runtime to walk back up through the call stack (stack frame by stack frame), examining the permissions of each caller in the stack. If any caller is found not to have the required permission, a **SecurityException** is thrown.

Link Demands

A link demand does not perform a full stack walk and only checks the immediate caller, one stack frame further back in the call stack. As a result, there are additional security risks associated with using link demands. You need to be particularly sensitive to luring attacks.

Note   With a luring attack, malicious code accesses the resources and operations that are exposed by your assembly, by calling your code through a trusted intermediary assembly.

For more information about how to use link demands correctly, see the "Link Demands" section later in this chapter.

Assert, Deny, and PermitOnly Methods

Code access permission classes support the **Assert**, **Deny**, and **PermitOnly** methods. You can use these methods to alter the behavior of a permission demand stack walk. They are referred to as *stack walk modifiers*.

A call to the **Assert** method causes the stack walk for a matching permission to stop at the site of the **Assert** call. This is most often used to sandbox privileged code. For more information, see the "Assert and RevertAssert" section later in this chapter.

A call to the **Deny** method fails any stack walk that reaches it with a matching permission. If you call some non-trusted code, you can use the **Deny** method to constrain the capabilities of the code that you call.

A call to the **PermitOnly** method fails any unmatching stack walk. Like the **Deny** method, it tends to be used infrequently but it can be used to constrain the actions of some non-trusted code that you may call.

Policy

Code access security policy is configured by administrators and it determines the permissions granted to assemblies. Policy can be established at four levels:

- **Enterprise**. Used to apply Enterprise-wide policy.
- **Machine**. Used to apply machine-level policy.
- **User**. Used to apply per user policy.
- **Application Domain**. Used to configure the application domain into which an assembly is loaded.

  ASP.NET implements application domain policy to allow you to configure code access security policy for Web applications and Web services. For more information about ASP.NET application domain policy, see Chapter 9, "Using Code Access Security with ASP.NET."

Policy settings are maintained in XML configuration files. The first three levels of policy (Enterprise, Machine, and User) can be configured by using the .NET Framework Configuration tool, which is located in the Administrative Tools program group or the Caspol.exe command line utility. ASP.NET application domain level policy must currently be edited with a text or XML-based editor.

For more information about policy files and locations, see Chapter 19, "Securing Your ASP.NET Application and Web Services."

Code Groups

Each policy file contains a hierarchical collection of code groups. Code groups are used to assign permissions to assemblies. A code group consists of two elements:

- **A membership condition**. This is based on evidence, for example, an assembly's zone or its strong name.
- **A permission set**. The permissions contained in the permission set are granted to assemblies whose evidence matches the membership condition.

How Does It Work?

Figure 8.1 shows a simplified overview of code access security.

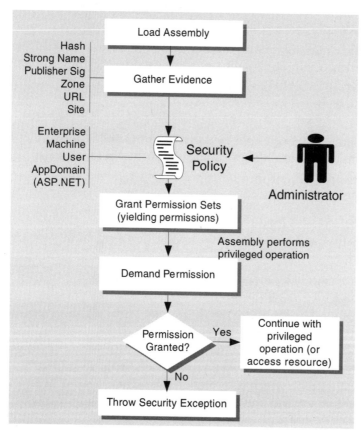

Figure 8.1
Code access security—a simplified view

The steps shown in Figure 8.1 are summarized below.

1. An assembly is loaded.

   This operation is performed by an application domain host. On a Web server loading a Web application assembly, this is the ASP.NET host.

2. Evidence is gathered from the assembly and presented by the host.

3. Evidence is evaluated against the defined security policy.

4. The output from security policy evaluation is one or more named permission sets that define the permission grant for the assembly.

Note An assembly can include permission requests, which can further reduce the permission grant.

---

5. Code within the assembly demands an appropriate permission prior to accessing a restricted resource or performing a privileged operation.

   All of the .NET Framework base classes that access resources or perform privileged operations contain the appropriate permission demands. For example, the **FileStream** class demands the **FileIOPermission**, the **Registry** class demands the **RegistryPermission**, and so on.

6. If the assembly (and its callers) have been granted the demanded permission, the operation is allowed to proceed. Otherwise, a security exception is generated.

How Is Policy Evaluated?

When evidence is run through the policy engine, the output is a permission set that defines the set of permissions granted to an assembly. The policy grant is calculated at each level in the policy hierarchy: Enterprise, Machine, User, and Application Domain. The policy grant resulting from each level is then combined using an intersection operation to yield the final policy grant. An intersection is used to ensure that policy lower down in the hierarchy cannot add permissions that were not granted by a higher level. This prevents an individual user or application domain from granting additional permissions that are not granted by the Enterprise administrator.

Figure 8.2 shows how the intersection operation means that the resulting permission grant is determined by all levels of policy in the policy hierarchy.

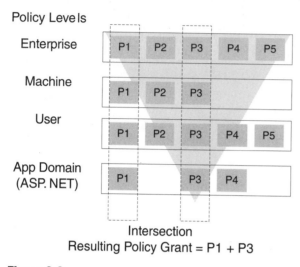

Figure 8.2

Policy intersection across policy levels

In Figure 8.2, you can see that the intersection operation ensures that only those permissions granted by each level form part of the final permission grant.

How Do Permission Requests Affect the Policy Grant?

You can add security attributes to your assembly to specify its permission requirements. You can specify the minimal set of permissions that your assembly must be granted in order to run. These do not affect the permission grant. You can also specify the optional permissions your assembly could make use of but does not absolutely require, and what permissions you want to refuse. Refused permissions are those permissions you want to ensure your assembly never has, even if they are granted by security policy.

If you request optional permissions, the combined optional and minimal permissions are intersected with the policy grant, to further reduce it. Then, any specifically refused permissions are taken away from the policy grant. This is summarized by the following formula where PG is the policy grant from administrator defined security policy and P_{min} , P_{opt} , and $P_{refused}$ are permission requests added to the assembly by the developer.

Resulting Permission Grant = $(PG \cap (P_{min} \cup P_{opt})) - Prefused$

For more information about how to use permission requests, their implications, and when to use them, see the "Requesting Permissions" section later in this chapter.

Policy Evaluation at a Policy Level

An individual policy file at each specific level consists of a hierarchical arrangement of code groups. These code groups include membership conditions that are used to determine which assemblies they apply to, and permission sets that are used to determine the permissions that should be granted to matching assemblies. A hierarchical structure enables multiple permission sets to be assigned to an assembly, and it allows security policy to support simple AND and OR logic. For example, consider the sample security policy shown in Figure 8.3.

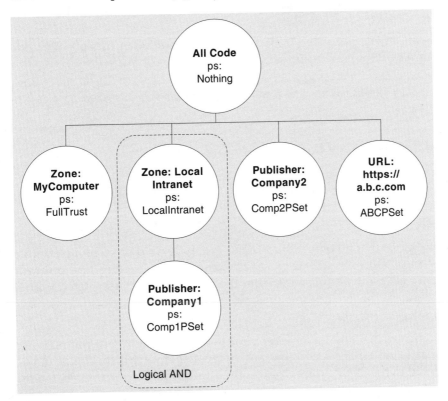

Figure 8.3
Hierarchical code groups at a single policy level

Note   The **All Code** code group is a special code group that matches all assemblies. It forms the root of security policy and in itself grants no permissions, because it is associated with the permission set named **Nothing**.

Consider the granted permissions based on the security policy shown in Figure 8.3.

- Any assembly originating from the **My_Computer_Zone** (any locally installed assembly), is granted the permissions defined by the **FullTrust** permission set. This is a built-in permission set defined when the .NET Framework is installed and represents the unrestricted set of all permissions.

- Assemblies authored by Company1 and originating from the intranet zone are granted the permissions defined by the built-in **LocalIntranet_Zone** permission set and the custom **Comp1PSet** permission set.

- Assemblies authored by Company2 are granted permissions defined by the custom **Comp2PSet** permission set.

- Any assembly downloaded from a.b.c.com is granted permissions defined by the custom **ABCPSet** permission set.

Note If the membership condition for a particular code group is not satisfied, none of its children are evaluated.

Exclusive and Level Final Code Groups

Policy hierarchy processing and traversal can be fine-tuned using a couple of attributes specified at the code group level, both of which can be set through the .NET Framework Configuration Tool. These are:

- **Exclusive**

    This indicates that no other sibling code groups should be combined with this code group. You mark a code group as **exclusive** by selecting **This policy level will only have the permissions from the permission set associated with this code group** in the .NET Framework Configuration Tool.

- **Level Final**

    This indicates that any lower level policies should be ignored. You mark a code group as **Level Final** by selecting **Policy levels below this level will not be evaluated** in the .NET Framework Configuration Tool. For example, if a matching code group in the machine policy is marked **Level Final**, policy settings from the user policy file is ignored.

Note The application domain level policy, for example, ASP.NET policy for server-side Web applications, is always evaluated regardless of the level final setting.

APTCA

An assembly that has a strong name cannot be called by a partial trust assembly (an assembly that is not granted full trust), unless the strong named assembly contains **AllowPartiallyTrustedCallersAttribute** (APTCA) as follows:

```
[assembly: AllowPartiallyTrustedCallersAttribute()]
```

This is a risk mitigation strategy designed to ensure your code cannot inadvertently be exposed to partial trust (potentially malicious) code. The common language runtime silently adds a link demand for the **FullTrust** permission set to all publicly accessible members on types in a strong named assembly. If you include APTCA, you suppress this link demand.

Avoid Using APTCA

If you use APTCA, your code is immediately more vulnerable to attack and, as a result, it is particularly important to review your code for security vulnerabilities. Use APTCA only where it is strictly necessary.

In the context of server-side Web applications, use APTCA whenever your assembly needs to support partial trust callers. This situation can occur in the following circumstances:

- Your assembly is to be called by a partial trust Web application. These are applications for which the **<trust>** level is set to something other than **Full**. For more information about partial trust Web applications and using APTCA in this situation, see Chapter 9, "Using Code Access Security in ASP.NET."

- Your assembly is to be called by another assembly that has been granted limited permissions by the code access security administrator.

- Your assembly is to be called by another assembly that refuses specific permissions by using **SecurityAction.RequestRefuse** or **SecurityAction.RequestOptional**. These make the calling assembly a partial trust assembly.

- Your assembly is to be called by another assembly that uses a stack walk modifier (such as **Deny** or **PermitOnly**) to constrain downstream code.

Diagnosing APTCA Issues

If you attempt to call a strong named assembly that is not marked with APTCA from partial trust code such as a partial trust Web application, you see an exception similar to the one shown in Figure 8.4. Notice that the exception details provide no permission details and simply indicate that the required permissions (in this case, **FullTrust**) cannot be acquired from the calling assembly. In this case, the somewhat confusing description text means that the error occurred because the application's **<trust>** level was set to something other than **Full**.

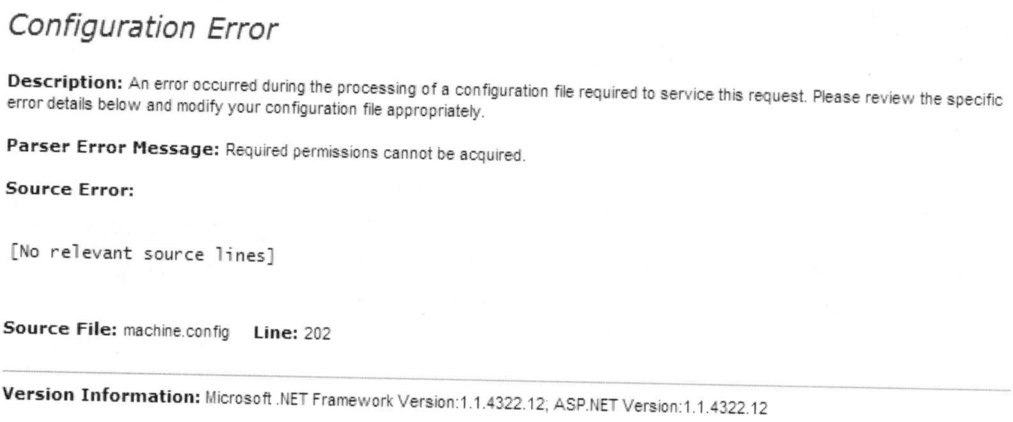

Configuration Error

Description: An error occurred during the processing of a configuration file required to service this request. Please review the specific error details below and modify your configuration file appropriately.

Parser Error Message: Required permissions cannot be acquired.

Source Error:

```
[No relevant source lines]
```

Source File: machine.config   **Line:** 202

Version Information: Microsoft .NET Framework Version:1.1.4322.12; ASP.NET Version:1.1.4322.12

Figure 8.4

The result of partial trust code calling a strong named assembly

To overcome this exception, either the calling code must be granted **FullTrust** or the assembly being called must be annotated with APTCA. Note that individual types within an assembly marked with APTCA might still require full trust callers, because they include an explicit link demand or regular demand for full trust, as shown in the following examples.

```
[PermissionSet(SecurityAction.LinkDemand, Name="FullTrust")]
[PermissionSet(SecurityAction.Demand, Unrestricted=true)]
```

Privileged Code

When you design and build secure assemblies, you must be able to identify privileged code. This has important implications for code access security. Privileged code is managed code that accesses secured resources or performs other security-sensitive operations, such as calling unmanaged code, using serialization, or using reflection. Privileged code is *privileged* because code access security must grant it specific permissions before it can function.

Privileged Resources

Privileged resources for which your code requires specific code access security permissions are shown in the Table 8.1.

Table 8.1   Secure Resources and Associated Permissions

Secure Resource	Requires Permission
Data access	SqlClientPermission OleDbPermission OraclePermission **Note** The ADO.NET OLE DB and Oracle-managed providers currently require full trust.
Directory services	DirectoryServicesPermission
DNS databases	DnsPermission
Event log	EventLogPermission
Environment variables	EnvironmentPermission
File system	FileIOPermission
Isolated storage	IsolatedStoragePermission
Message queues	MessageQueuePermission
Performance counters	PerformanceCounterPermission
Printers	PrinterPermission
Registry	RegistryPermission
Sockets	SocketPermission
Web services (and other HTTP Internet resources)	WebPermission

Privileged Operations

Privileged operations are shown in Table 8.2, together with the associated permissions that calling code requires.

Table 8.2   Privileged Operations and Associated Permissions

Operation	Requires Permission
Creating and controlling application domains	**SecurityPermission** with **SecurityPermissionFlag.ControlAppDomain**
Specifying policy application domains	**SecurityPermission** with **SecurityPermissionFlag.ControlDomainPolicy**
Asserting security permissions	**SecurityPermission** with **SecurityPermissionFlag.Assertion**
Creating and manipulating evidence	**SecurityPermission** with **SecurityPermissionFlag.ControlEvidence**
Creating and manipulating principal objects	**SecurityPermission** with **SecurityPermissionFlag.ControlPrincipal**
Configuring types and channels remoting	**SecurityPermission** with **SecurityPermissionFlag.RemotingConfiguration**
Manipulating security policy	**SecurityPermission** with **SecurityPermissionFlag.ControlPolicy**
Serialization	**SecurityPermission** with **SecurityPermissionFlag.SerializationFormatter**
Threading operations	**SecurityPermission** with **SecurityPermissionFlag.ControlThread**
Reflection	**ReflectionPermission**
Calling unmanaged code	**SecurityPermission** with **SecurityPermissionFlag.UnmanagedCode**

Requesting Permissions

When you design and develop your assemblies, create a list of all the resources that your code accesses, and all the privileged operations that your code performs. At deployment time, the administrator may need this information to appropriately configure code access security policy and to diagnose security related problems.

The best way to communicate the permission requirements of your code is to use assembly level declarative security attributes to specify minimum permission requirements. These are normally placed in Assemblyinfo.cs or Assemblyinfo.vb. This allows the administrator or the consumer of your assembly to check which permissions it requires by using the Permview.exe tool.

RequestMinimum

You can use **SecurityAction.RequestMinimum** method along with declarative permission attributes to specify the minimum set of permissions your assembly needs to run. For example, if your assembly needs to access the registry, but only needs to retrieve configuration data from a specific key, use an attribute similar to the following:

```
[assembly: RegistryPermissionAttribute(
                SecurityAction.RequestMinimum,
                Read=@"HKEY_LOCAL_MACHINE\SOFTWARE\YourApp")]
```

If you know up front that your code will run in a full trust environment and will be granted the full set of unrestricted permissions, using **RequestMinimum** is less important. However, it is good practice to specify your assembly's permission requirements.

Note Permission attributes accept a comma-delimited list of properties and property values after the mandatory constructor arguments. These are used to initialize the underlying permission object. A quick way to find out what property names are supported is to use Ildasm.exe on the assembly that contains the permission attribute type.

RequestOptional

If you use **SecurityAction.RequestOptional** method, no other permissions except those specified with **SecurityAction.RequestMinimum** and **SecurityAction.RequestOptional** will be granted to your assembly, even if your assembly would otherwise have been granted additional permissions by code access security policy.

RequestRefused

SecurityAction.RequestRefuse allows you to make sure that your assembly cannot be granted permissions by code access security policy that it does not require. For example, if your assembly does not call unmanaged code, you could use the following attribute to ensure code access security policy does not grant your assembly the unmanaged code permission.

```
[assembly: SecurityPermissionAttribute(SecurityAction.RequestRefuse,
                                UnmanagedCode=true)]
```

Implications of Using RequestOptional or RequestRefuse

If you use **RequestOptional**, the set of permissions that are specified with **RequestOptional** and **RequestMinimum** are intersected with the permission grant given to your assembly by policy. This means that all other permissions outside of the **RequestOptional** and **RequestMinimum** sets are removed from your assembly's permission grant. Additionally, if you use **RequestRefuse**, the refused permissions are also removed from your assembly's permission grant.

So if you use **RequestOptional** or **RequestRefuse**, your assembly becomes a partial trust assembly, which has implications when you call other assemblies. Use the following considerations to help you decide whether you should use **SecurityAction.RequestOptional** or **SecurityAction.RequestRefuse**:

- Do not use them if you need to directly call a strong named assembly without **AllowPartiallyTrustedCallersAttribute** (APTCA) because this prevents you from being able to call it.

  Many strong named .NET Framework assemblies contain types that do not support partial trust callers and do not include APTCA. For more information, and a list of assemblies that support partial trust callers, see "Developing Partial Trust Web Applications," in Chapter 9, "Using Code Access Security with ASP.NET."

  If you must call strong named assemblies without APTCA, let the administrators who install your code know that your code must be granted full trust by code access security policy to work properly.

- If you do not need to access any APTCA assemblies, then add permission requests to refuse those permissions that you know your assembly does not need. Test your code early to make sure you really do not require those permissions.

- If downstream code needs the permission you have refused, a method between you and the downstream code needs to assert the permission. Otherwise, a **SecurityException** will be generated when the stack walk reaches your code.

Authorizing Code

Code access security allows you to authorize the code that calls your assembly. This reduces the risk of malicious code successfully calling your code. For example, you can use identity permissions to restrict calling code based on identity evidence, such as the public key component of its strong name. You can also use explicit code access permission demands to ensure that the code that calls your assembly has the necessary permissions to access the resource or perform the privileged operation that your assembly exposes.

Usually, you do not explicitly demand code access permissions. The .NET Framework classes do this for you, and a duplicate demand is unnecessary. However, there are occasions when you need to issue explicit demands, for example, if your code exposes a custom resource by using unmanaged code or if your code accesses cached data. You can authorize code in the following ways:

- **Restrict which code can call your code**.
- **Restrict inheritance**.
- **Consider protecting cached data**.
- **Protect custom resources with custom permissions**.

Restrict Which Code Can Call Your Code

A method marked as **public** can be called by any code outside of the current assembly. To further restrict which other code can call your methods, you can use a code access security identity permission demand as shown in the following example.

```
public sealed class Utility
{
  // Although SomeOperation() is a public method, the following
  // permission demand means that it can only be called by assemblies
  // with the specified public key.
  [StrongNameIdentityPermission(SecurityAction.LinkDemand,
                       PublicKey="00240000048...97e85d098615")]
  public static void SomeOperation() {}
}
```

The above code shows a link demand. This results in the authorization of the immediate caller. Therefore, your code is potentially open to luring attacks, where a malicious assembly could potentially access the protected resources or operations provided by your assembly through a trusted intermediary assembly with the specified strong name.

Depending on the nature of the functionality provided by your class, you may need to demand another permission to authorize the calling code in addition to using the identity-based link demand. Alternatively, you can consider using a full demand in conjunction with the **StrongNameIdentityPermission**, although this assumes that all code in the call stack is strong name signed using the same private key.

Note Issuing a full stack walk demand for the **StrongNameIdentityPermission** does not work if your assembly is called by a Web application or Web service. This is because it is not possible to strong name the dynamically compiled classes associated with ASP.NET Web applications or Web services.

▶ **To extract a public key from an assembly**

- Run the following command to obtain a hex representation of a public key from an assembly:

```
secutil -hex -strongname yourassembly.dll
```

▶ **To extract the public key from a key pair file**

1. Generate the key pair file with the following command:

```
sn -k keypairfile
```

2. Extract the public key from the key pair file:

```
sn -p keypairfile publickeyfile
```

3. Obtain a hex representation of the public key:

```
sn -tp publickeyfile > publickeyhex.dat
```

Restrict Inheritance

If your class is designed as base class, you can restrict which other code is allowed to derive from your class by using an inheritance demand coupled with a **StrongNameIdentityPermission** as shown in the following example. This prevents inheritance of your class from any assembly that is not signed with the private key corresponding to the public key in the demand.

```
// The following inheritance demand ensures that only code within the
// assembly with the specified public key (part of the assembly's strong
// name can sub class SomeRestrictedClass
[StrongNameIdentityPermission(SecurityAction.InheritanceDemand,
                         PublicKey="00240000048...97e85d098615")]
public class SomeRestrictedClass
{
}
```

Consider Protecting Cached Data

If you access a resource by using one of the .NET Framework classes, a permission demand appropriate for the resource type in question is issued by the class. If you subsequently cache data for performance reasons, you should consider issuing an explicit code access permission demand prior to accessing the cached data. This ensures the calling code is authorized to access the specific type of resource. For example, if you read data from a file and then cache it, and you want to ensure that calling code is authorized, issue a **FileIOPermission** demand as shown in the following example.

```
// The following demand assumes the cached data was originally retrieved from
// C:\SomeDir\SomeFile.dat
new FileIOPermission(FileIOPermissionAccess.Read,
                     @"C:\SomeDir\SomeFile.dat").Demand();
// Now access the cache and return the data to the caller
```

Protect Custom Resources with Custom Permissions

If you expose a resource or operation by using unmanaged code, you should sandbox your wrapper code and consider demanding a custom permission to authorize the calling code.

Full trust callers are granted the custom permission automatically as long as the permission type implements the **IUnrestrictedPermission** interface. Partial trust callers will not have the permission unless it has been specifically granted by code access security policy. This ensures that non-trusted code cannot call your assembly to access the custom resources that it exposes. Sandboxing also means that you are not forced to grant the powerful **UnmanagedCodePermission** to any code that needs to call your code.

For more information about calling unmanaged code, see the "Unmanaged Code" section later in this chapter. For an example implementation of a custom permission, see "How To: Create a Custom Encryption Permission" in the "How To" section of this guide.

Link Demands

A link demand differs from a regular permission demand in that the run-time demands permissions only from the immediate caller and does not perform a full stack walk. Link demands are performed at JIT compilation time and can only be specified declaratively.

Carefully consider before using a link demand because it is easy to introduce security vulnerabilities if you use them. If you do use link demands, consider the following issues:

- **Luring attacks**
- **Performance and link demands**
- **Calling methods with link demands**
- **Mixing class and method level link demands**
- **Interfaces and link demands**
- **Structures and link demands**
- **Virtual methods and link demands**

Luring Attacks

If you protect code with a link demand, it is vulnerable to luring attacks, where malicious code gains access to the resource or operation exposed by your code through a trusted intermediary as shown in Figure 8.5.

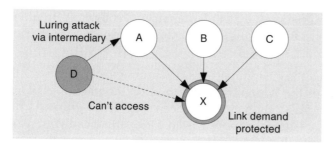

Figure 8.5

An example of a luring attack with link demands

In figure 8.5, methods in assembly X, which access a secure resource, are protected with a link demand for a specific public key (using a **StrongNameIdentityPermission**). Assemblies A, B, and C are signed with the private key that corresponds to the public key that assembly X trusts, and so these assemblies can call assembly X. Assemblies A, B, and C are subject to a luring attack if they do not check their callers for specific evidence before making calls to assembly X. For example, assembly D that is not signed with the same private key cannot call assembly X directly. It could, however, access assembly X through the trusted assembly A, if A does not check its callers, either with another link demand or through a full demand.

Only use link demands in an assembly when you trust the assembly's callers not to expose its functionality further (for example, when the caller is an application, not a library) or when you know it is safe just to verify the immediate caller's identity with an identity permission demand.

Performance and Link Demands

Compared to other Web application performance issues such as network latency and database access, the cost of a stack walk is small. Do not use link demands purely for performance reasons. Full demands provide a much greater degree of security.

Calling Methods with Link Demands

If you call a link demand protected method, only your code will be checked by the link demand. In this situation, you should make sure your code takes adequate measures to authorize its callers, for example, by demanding a permission.

Mixing Class and Method Level Link Demands

Method level link demands override class level link demands. For example, in the following code fragment, the link demand for **FileIOPermission** must be repeated on the method declaration or the **EnvironmentPermission** link demand replaces the class level **FileIOPermission** demand.

```
[FileIOPermission(SecurityAction.LinkDemand, Unrestricted=true)]
public sealed class SomeClass
{
  // The unrestricted FileIOPermission link demand must be restated at the
  // method level, if the method is decorated with another link demand.
  // Failure to do so means that (in this example) that the
  // EnvironmentPermission link demand would override the class level
  // FileIOPermission link demand
  [FileIOPermission(SecurityAction.LinkDemand, Unrestricted=true)]
  [EnvironmentPermission(SecurityAction.LinkDemand, Read="PATH")]
  public void SomeMethod()
  {
  }
}
```

Interfaces and Link Demands

If your class implements an interface and one of the method implementations has a link demand, make sure that the method declaration on the interface definition has the same link demand. Otherwise, the caller simply has to call your method through the interface to bypass the link demand. An example is shown below.

```
public interface IMyInterface
{
  // The link demand shown on the method implementation below
  // should be repeated here
  void Method1();
}

public class MyImplementation : IMyInterface
{
  // The method implementation has a link demand but the interface does not
  [SecurityPermission(SecurityAction.LinkDemand,
           Flags=SecurityPermissionFlag.ControlPrincipal)]
  public void Method1()
  {
  }
}
```

With the following code, the caller is subject to the link demand:

```
MyImplementation t = new MyImplementation();
t.Method1();
```

With the following code, the caller is not subject to the link demand:

```
IMyInterface i = new MyImplementation();
i.Method1();
```

Structures and Link Demands

Link demands do not prevent the construction of structures by untrusted callers. This is because default constructors are not automatically generated for structures. Therefore, the structure level link demand only applies if you use an explicit constructor.

For example:

```
[SecurityPermission(SecurityAction.LinkDemand,
          Flags=SecurityPermissionFlag.ControlPrincipal)]
public struct SomeStruct
{
  // This explicit constructor is protected by the link demand
  public SomeStruct(int i)
  {
    field = i;
  }
  private int field;
}
```

The following two lines of code both result in a new structure with the field initialized to zero. However, only the first line that uses the explicit constructor is subject to a link demand.

```
SomeStruct s = new SomeStruct(0);
SomeStruct s = new SomeStruct();
```

The second line is not subject to a link demand because a default constructor is not generated. If this were a class instead of a structure, the compiler would generate a default constructor annotated with the specified link demand.

Virtual Methods and Link Demands

If you use link demand to protect a method override in a derived class, make sure you also put it on the corresponding virtual base class method. Otherwise, if the JIT compiler sees a reference to the base class type where no link demand is present, no link demand is performed.

Assert and RevertAssert

You can call the **CodeAccessPermission.Assert** method to prevent a demand propagating beyond the current stack frame. By using **Assert**, you vouch for the trustworthiness of your code's callers. Because of the potential for luring attacks, **Assert** needs to be used with caution.

Asserts are most often used to sandbox privileged code. If you develop code that calls **Assert**, you need to ensure that there are alternate security measures in place to authorize the calling code. The following recommendations help you to minimize the risks.

- **Use the demand / assert pattern**
- **Reduce the Assert duration**

Use the Demand / Assert Pattern

Demanding a specific permission before calling **Assert** is an effective way to authorize upstream code. Sometimes you might be able to demand a built-in permission type to authorize calling code.

Often, if your assembly is exposing functionality that is not provided by the .NET Framework class library, such as calling the Data Protection API (DPAPI), you need to develop a custom permission and demand the custom permission to authorize callers. For example, you might develop a custom **Encryption** permission to authorize callers to a managed DPAPI wrapper assembly. Demanding this permission and then asserting the unmanaged code permission is an effective way to authorize calling code.

For more information about this approach and about developing custom permissions, see "How To: Create a Custom Encryption Permission" in the "How To" section of this guide.

Reduce the Assert Duration

If you only need to call **Assert** to satisfy the demands of a single downstream method that your code calls, then place the **Assert** immediately prior to the downstream method call. Then immediately call **RevertAssert** to keep the assertion window as small as possible, and to ensure that any subsequent code your method calls does not inadvertently succeed because the **Assert** is still in effect.

A common practice is to place the call to **RevertAssert** in a **finally** block to ensure that it always gets called even in the event of an exception.

Constraining Code

Constraining code and building least privileged code is analogous to using the principle of least privilege when you configure user or service accounts. By restricting the code access security permissions available to your code, you minimize scope for the malicious use of your code.

There are two ways to constrain code to restrict which resources it can access and restrict which other privileged operations it can perform:

- **Using policy permission grants**
- **Using stack walk modifiers**

Using Policy Permission Grants

You can configure code access security policy to grant a restricted permission set to a specific assembly. This constrains its ability to access resources or perform other privileged operations. For more information, see "How To: Configure Code Access Security Policy to Constrain an Assembly" in the "How To" section of this guide.

Using Stack Walk Modifiers

You can use stack walk modifiers to ensure that only specific permissions are available to the code that you call. For example, you can use **SecurityAction.PermitOnly** to ensure that your method and any methods that are called only have a restricted permission set. The following example applies a very restrictive permission set. The code only has the permission to execute. It cannot access resources or perform other privileged operations.

```
[SecurityPermissionAttribute(SecurityAction.PermitOnly,
                        Flags=SecurityPermissionFlag.Execution)]
public void SomeMethod()
{
  // The current method and downstream can only execute. They cannot access
  // resources or perform other privileged operations.
  SomeOtherMethod();
}
```

The following sections show you how to use code access security to constrain various types of resource access including file I/O, event log, registry, data access, directory services, environment variables, Web services, and sockets.

File I/O

To be able to perform file I/O, your assembly must be granted the **FileIOPermission** by code access security policy. If your code is granted the unrestricted **FileIOPermission**, it can access files anywhere on the file system, subject to Windows security. A restricted **FileIOPermission** can be used to constrain an assembly's ability to perform file I/O, for example, by specifying allowed access rights (read, read/write, and so on.)

Constraining File I/O within your Application's Context

A common requirement is to be able to restrict file I/O to specific directory locations such as your application's directory hierarchy.

Note If your Web application is configured for **Medium trust**, file access is automatically restricted to the application's virtual directory hierarchy. For more information, see Chapter 9, "Using Code Access Security with ASP.NET."

Configuring your application for **Medium trust** is one way to constrain file I/O, although this also constrains your application's ability to access other resource types. There are two other ways you can restrict your code's file I/O capabilities:

- **Using PermitOnly to restrict File I/O**
- **Configuring code access security policy to restrict File I/O**

Using PermitOnly to Restrict File I/O

You can use declarative attributes together with **SecurityAction.PermitOnly** as shown in the following example to constrain file I/O.

```
// Allow the code only to read files from c:\YourAppDir
[FileIOPermission(SecurityAction.PermitOnly, Read=@"c:\YourAppDir\")]
[FileIOPermission(SecurityAction.PermitOnly, PathDiscovery=@"c:\YourAppDir\")]
public static string ReadFile(string filename)
{
  // Use Path.GetFilePath() to canonicalize the file name
  // Use FileStream.OpenRead to open the file
  // Use FileStream.Read to access and return the data
}
```

Note The second attribute that specifies **PathDicovery** access is required by the **Path.GetFilePath** function that is used to canonicalize the input file name.

To avoid hard coding your application's directory hierarchy, you can use imperative security syntax, and use the **HttpContext.Current.Request.MapPath(".")** to retrieve your Web application's directory at runtime. You must reference the **System.Web** assembly and add the corresponding **using** statement as shown in the following example.

```
using System.Web;

public static string ReadFile(string filename)
{
  string appDir = HttpContext.Current.Request.MapPath(".");
  FileIOPermission f = new FileIOPermission(PermissionState.None);
  f.SetPathList(FileIOPermissionAccess.Read, appDir);
  f.SetPathList(FileIOPermissionAccess.PathDiscovery, appDir);
  f.PermitOnly();

  // Use Path.GetFilePath() to canonicalize the file name
  // Use FileStream.OpenRead to open the file
  // Use FileStream.Read to access and return the data
}
```

Note For a Windows application you can replace the call to **MapPath** with a call to **Directory.GetCurrentDirectory** to obtain the application's current directory.

Configuring Code Access Security Policy to Restrict File I/O

An administrator can also configure code access security policy to restrict your code's ability to perform file I/O beyond your application's virtual directory hierarchy.

For example, the administrator can configure Enterprise or Machine level code access security policy to grant a restricted **FileIOPermission** to your assembly. This is most easily done if your assembly contains a strong name, because the administrator can use this cryptographically strong evidence when configuring policy. For assemblies that are not strong named, an alternative form of evidence needs to be used. For more information about how to configure code access security to restrict the file I/O capability of an assembly, see "How To: Configure Code Access Security Policy to Constrain an Assembly, " in the "How To" section of this guide.

If your assembly is called by a Web application, a better approach is to configure ASP.NET (application domain-level) code access security policy because you can use $AppDirUrl$ which represents the application's virtual directory root. For more information about restricting File I/O using ASP.NET code access security policy, see Chapter 9, "Using Code Access Security with ASP.NET."

Requesting FileIOPermission

To help the administrator, if you know your assembly's precise file I/O requirements at build time (for example, you know directory names), declare your assembly's **FileIOPermission** requirements by using a declarative permission request as shown in the following example.

```
[assembly: FileIOPermission(SecurityAction.RequestMinimum, Read=@"C:\YourAppDir")]
```

The administration can see this attribute by using permview.exe. The additional advantage of using **SecurityAction.RequestMinimum** is that the assembly fails to load if it is not granted sufficient permissions. This is preferable to a runtime security exception.

Event Log

To be able to access the event log, your assembly must be granted the **EventLogPermission** by code access security policy. If it is not, for example, because it is running within the context of a medium trust Web application, you need to sandbox your event logging code. For more information about sandboxing access to the event log, see Chapter 9, "Using Code Access Security with ASP.NET."

Constraining Event Logging Code

If you want to constrain the actions of event log wrapper code—perhaps code written by another developer or development organization—you can use declarative attributes together with **SecurityAction.PermitOnly** as shown in the following example.

The following attribute ensures that the **WriteToLog** method and any methods it calls can only access the local computer's event log and cannot delete event logs or event sources. These operations are not permitted by **EventLogPermissionAccess.Instrument**.

```
[EventLogPermission(SecurityAction.PermitOnly,
                    MachineName=".",
                    PermissionAccess=EventLogPermissionAccess.Instrument)]
public static void WriteToLog( string message )
```

To enforce read-only access to existing logs, use **EventLogPermissionAccess.Browse**.

Requesting EventLogPermission

To document the permission requirements of your code, and to ensure that your assembly cannot load if it is granted insufficient event log access by code access security policy, add an assembly level **EventLogPermissionAttribute** with **SecurityAction.RequestMinimum** as shown in the following example.

```
// This attribute indicates that your code requires the ability to access the
// event logs on the local machine only (".") and needs instrumentation access
// which means it can read or write to existing logs and create new event sources
// and event logs
[assembly: EventLogPermissionAttribute(SecurityAction.RequestMinimum,
                            MachineName=".",
                            PermissionAccess=
                            EventLogPermissionAccess.Instrument)]
```

Registry

Code that accesses the registry by using the **Microsoft.Win32.Registry** class must be granted the **RegistryPermission** by code access security policy. This permission type can be used to constrain registry access to specific keys and sub keys, and can also control code's ability to read, write, or create registry keys and named values.

Constraining Registry Access

To constrain code to reading data from specific registry keys, you can use the **RegistryPermissionAttribute** together with **SecurityAction.PermitOnly**. The following attribute ensures that the code can only read from the **YourApp** key (and subkeys) beneath HKEY_LOCAL_MACHINE\SOFTWARE.

```
[RegistryPermissionAttribute(SecurityAction.PermitOnly,
                     Read=@"HKEY_LOCAL_MACHINE\SOFTWARE\YourApp")]
public static string GetConfigurationData( string key, string namedValue )
{
  return (string)Registry.
               LocalMachine.
               OpenSubKey(key).
               GetValue(namedValue);
}
```

Requesting RegistryPermission

To document the permission requirements of your code, and to ensure your assembly cannot load if it is granted insufficient registry access from code access security policy, add an assembly level **RegistryPermissionAttribute** with **SecurityAction.RequestMinimum** as shown in the following example.

```
[assembly: RegistryPermissionAttribute(SecurityAction.RequestMinimum,
                     Read=@"HKEY_LOCAL_MACHINE\SOFTWARE\YourApp")]
```

Data Access

The ADO.NET SQL Server data provider supports partial trust callers. The other data providers including the OLE DB, Oracle, and ODBC providers currently require full trust callers.

If you connect to SQL Server using the SQL Server data provider, your data access code requires the **SqlClientPermission**. You can use **SqlClientPermission** to restrict the allowable range of name/value pairs that can be used on a connection string passed to the **SqlConnection** object. In the following code, the **CheckProductStockLevel** method has been enhanced with an additional security check to ensure that blank passwords cannot be used in the connection string. If the code retrieves a connection string with a blank password, a **SecurityException** is thrown.

```
[SqlClientPermissionAttribute(SecurityAction.PermitOnly,
                              AllowBlankPassword=false)]
public static int CheckProductStockLevel(string productCode)
{
  // Retrieve the connection string from the registry
  string connectionString = GetConnectionString();
  . . .
}
```

For more information about how to sandbox data access code to allow the OLE DB and other data providers to be used from partial trust Web applications, see Chapter 9, "Using Code Access Security with ASP.NET."

Directory Services

Currently, code that uses classes from the **System.DirectoryServices** namespace to access directory services such as Active Directory must be granted full trust. However, you can use the **DirectoryServicesPermission** to constrain the type of access and the particular directory services to which code can connect.

Constraining Directory Service Access

To constrain code, you can use the **DirectoryServicesPermissionAttribute** together with **SecurityAction.PermitOnly**. The following attribute ensures that the code can only connect to a specific LDAP path and can only browse the directory.

```
[DirectoryServicesPermissionAttribute(SecurityAction.PermitOnly,
                    Path="LDAP://rootDSE",
                    PermissionAccess=DirectoryServicesPermissionAccess.Browse)]
public static string GetNamingContext(string ldapPath)
{
  DirectorySearcher dsSearcher = new DirectorySearcher(ldapPath);
  dsSearcher.PropertiesToLoad.Add("defaultNamingContext");
  dsSearcher.Filter = "";
  SearchResult result = dsSearcher.FindOne();
  return (string)result.Properties["adsPath"][0];
}
```

Requesting DirectoryServicesPermission

To document the permission requirements of your code, and to ensure your assembly cannot load if it is granted insufficient directory services access from code access security policy, add an assembly level **DirectoryServicesPermissionAttribute** with **SecurityAction.RequestMinimum** as shown in the following example.

```
[assembly: DirectoryServicesPermissionAttribute(SecurityAction.RequestMinimum,
               Path="LDAP://rootDSE",
               PermissionAccess=DirectoryServicesPermissionAccess.Browse)]
```

Environment Variables

Code that needs to read or write environment variables using the **System.Environment** class must be granted the **EnvironmentPermission** by code access security policy. This permission type can be used to constrain access to specific named environment variables.

Constraining Environment Variable Access

To constrain code so that it can only read specific environment variables, you can use the **EnvironmentPermissionAttribute** together with **SecurityAction.PermitOnly**. The following attributes ensure that the code can only read from the *username*, *userdomain*, and *temp* variables.

```
[EnvironmentPermissionAttribute(SecurityAction.PermitOnly, Read="username")]
[EnvironmentPermissionAttribute(SecurityAction.PermitOnly, Read="userdomain")]
[EnvironmentPermissionAttribute(SecurityAction.PermitOnly, Read="temp")]
public static string GetVariable(string name)
{
   return Environment.GetEnvironmentVariable(name);
}
```

Requesting EnvironmentPermission

To document the permission requirements of your code, and to ensure your assembly cannot load if it is granted insufficient environment variable access from code access security policy, add an assembly level **EnvironmentPermissionAttribute** with **SecurityAction.RequestMinimum** as shown in the following code.

```
[assembly: EnvironmentPermissionAttribute(SecurityAction.RequestMinimum,
                        Read="username"),
           EnvironmentPermissionAttribute(SecurityAction.RequestMinimum,
                        Read="userdomain"),
           EnvironmentPermissionAttribute(SecurityAction.RequestMinimum,
                        Read="temp")]
```

Web Services

Code that calls Web services must be granted the **WebPermission** by code access security policy. The **WebPermission** actually constrains access to any HTTP Internet-based resources.

Constraining Web Service Connections

To restrict the Web services to which your code can access, use the **WebPermissionAttribute** together with **SecurityAction.PermitOnly**. For example, the following code ensures that the **PlaceOrder** method and any methods it calls can only invoke Web services on the http://*somehost* site.

```
[WebPermissionAttribute(SecurityAction.PermitOnly,
                        ConnectPattern=@"http://somehost/.*")]
[EnvironmentPermissionAttribute(SecurityAction.PermitOnly, Read="USERNAME")]
public static void PlaceOrder(XmlDocument order)
{
  PurchaseService.Order svc = new PurchaseService.Order();
  // Web service uses Windows authentication
  svc.Credentials = System.Net.CredentialCache.DefaultCredentials;
  svc.PlaceOrder(order);
}
```

In the prior example, the **ConnectPattern** property of the **WebPermissionAttribute** class is used. This allows you to supply a regular expression that matches the range of addresses to which a connection can be established. The **EnvironmentPermissionAttribute** shown previously is required because the code uses Windows authentication and default credentials.

The following example shows how to use the **Connect** attribute to restrict connections to a specific Web service.

```
[WebPermissionAttribute(SecurityAction.PermitOnly,
                        Connect=@"http://somehost/order.asmx")]
```

Sockets and DNS

Code that uses sockets directly by using the **System.Net.Sockets.Socket** class must be granted the **SocketPermission** by code access security policy. In addition, if your code uses DNS to map host names to IP addresses, it requires the **DnsPermission**.

You can use **SocketPermission** to constrain access to specific ports on specific hosts. You can also restrict whether the socket can be used to accept connections or initiate outbound connections, and you can restrict the transport protocol, for example, Transmission Control Protocol (TCP) or User Datagram Protocol (UDP).

Constraining Socket Access

To constrain code so that it can only use sockets in a restricted way, you can use the **SocketPermissionAttribute** together with **SecurityAction.PermitOnly**. The following attributes ensure that the code can connect only to a specific port on a specific host using the TCP protocol. Because the code also calls **Dns.Resolve** to resolve a host name, the code also requires the **DnsPermission**.

```
[SocketPermissionAttribute(SecurityAction.PermitOnly,
                           Access="Connect",
                           Host="hostname",
                           Port="80",
                           Transport="Tcp")]
[DnsPermissionAttribute(SecurityAction.PermitOnly, Unrestricted=true)]
public string MakeRequest(string hostname, string message)
{
  Socket socket = null;
  IPAddress serverAddress = null;
  IPEndPoint serverEndPoint = null;
  byte[] sendBytes = null, bytesReceived = null;
  int bytesReceivedSize = -1, readSize = 4096;

  serverAddress = Dns.Resolve(hostname).AddressList[0];
  serverEndPoint = new IPEndPoint(serverAddress, 80);
  socket = new Socket(AddressFamily.InterNetwork,
                  SocketType.Stream, ProtocolType.Tcp);
  bytesReceived = new byte[readSize];
  sendBytes = Encoding.ASCII.GetBytes(message);
  socket.Connect(serverEndPoint);
  socket.Send(sendBytes);
  bytesReceivedSize = socket.Receive(bytesReceived, readSize, 0);
  socket.Close();
  if(-1 != bytesReceivedSize)
  {
    return Encoding.ASCII.GetString(bytesReceived, 0, bytesReceivedSize);
  }
  return "";
}
```

Requesting SocketPermission and DnsPermission

To document the permission requirements of your code, and to ensure your assembly cannot load if it is granted insufficient socket or DNS access from code access security policy, add an assembly level **SocketPermissionAttribute** and a **DnsPermissionAttribute** with **SecurityAction.RequestMinimum** as shown in the following example.

```
[assembly: SocketPermissionAttribute(SecurityAction.RequestMinimum,
                                     Access="Connect",
                                     Host="hostname",
                                     Port="80",
                                     Transport="Tcp")
          DnsPermissionAttribute(SecurityAction.PermitOnly, Unrestricted=true)]
```

Unmanaged Code

Code that calls unmanaged Win32 APIs or COM components requires the unmanaged code permission. This should only be granted to highly trusted code. It is defined by the **SecurityPermission** type with its **Flags** property set to **SecurityPermissionFlag.UnmanagedCode**.

The following guidelines for calling unmanaged code build upon those introduced in Chapter 7, "Building Secure Assemblies."

- **Use naming conventions to indicate risk.**
- **Request the unmanaged code permission.**
- **Sandbox unmanaged API calls.**
- **Use SupressUnmanagedCodeSecurityAttribute with caution.**

Use Naming Conventions to Indicate Risk

Categorize your unmanaged code and prefix the types used to encapsulate the unmanaged APIs by using the following naming convention.

- **Safe**. This identifies code that poses no possible security threat. It is harmless for any code, malicious or otherwise, to call. An example is code that returns the current processor tick count. Safe classes can be annotated with the **SuppressUnmanagedCode** attribute which turns off the code access security permission demand for full trust.

```
[SuppressUnmanagedCode]
class SafeNativeMethods {
        [DllImport("user32")]
        internal static extern void MessageBox(string text);
}
```

- **Native.** This is potentially dangerous unmanaged code, but code that is protected with a full stack walking demand for the unmanaged code permission. These are implicitly made by the interop layer unless they have been suppressed with the **SupressUnmanagedCode** attribute.

```
class NativeMethods {
        [DllImport("user32")]
        internal static extern void FormatDrive(string driveLetter);
}
```

- **Unsafe.** This is potentially dangerous unmanaged code that has the security demand for the unmanaged code permission declaratively suppressed. These methods are potentially dangerous. Any caller of these methods must do a full security review to ensure that the usage is safe and protected because no stack walk is performed.

```
[SuppressUnmanagedCodeSecurity]
class UnsafeNativeMethods {
        [DllImport("user32")]
        internal static extern void CreateFile(string fileName);
}
```

Request the Unmanaged Code Permission

Strong-named

```
[assembly: SecurityPermission(SecurityAction.RequestMinimum,
                         UnmanagedCode=true)]
```

Sandbox Unmanaged API Calls

Isolate calls to unmanaged code in specific assemblies and keep the number of assemblies that call unmanaged code to a minimum. Then, use the sandboxing pattern to ensure that the unmanaged code permission is only granted to selected assemblies.

▶ **To sandbox your managed code that calls unmanaged code**

1. Place your code that calls unmanaged code in a separate (wrapper) assembly.

2. Add a strong name to the assembly.

   This allows custom code access security policy to be easily applied to the assembly. For more information, see the "Strong Names" section in Chapter 7, "Building Secure Assemblies."

3. Request the unmanaged code permission (as described in the preceding section.)

4. Authorize calling code with a full permission demand.

You typically need to use a custom permission that represents the unmanaged resource being exposed by your assembly. For example:

```
(new EncryptionPermission(EncryptionPermissionFlag.Encrypt,
                          storePermissionFlag.Machine)).Demand();
```

5. Assert the unmanaged code permission in your wrapper class:

```
(new SecurityPermission(SecurityPermissionFlag.UnmanagedCode)).Assert();
```

For a full example implementation that shows you how to call the unmanaged Win32 DPAPI functionality, see "How To: Create a Custom Encryption Permission," in the "How To" section of this guide.

Use SuppressUnmanagedCodeSecurity with Caution

If your assembly makes many calls to unmanaged code, the performance overhead associated with multiple unmanaged code permission demands can become an issue.

In this case, you can use the **SuppressUnmanagedCodeSecurity** attribute on the P/Invoke method declaration. This causes the full demand for the unmanaged permission to be replaced with a link demand which only occurs once at JIT compilation time.

In common with the use of link demands, your code is now vulnerable to luring attacks. To mitigate the risk, you should only suppress the unmanaged code permission demand if your assembly takes adequate precautions to ensure it cannot be coerced by malicious code to perform unwanted operations. An example of a suitable countermeasure is if your assembly demands a custom permission that more closely reflects the operation being performed by the unmanaged code

Using SuppressUnmanagedCodeSecurity with P/Invoke

The following code shows how to apply the **SuppressUnmanagedCodeSecurity** attribute to a Platform Invocation Services (P/Invoke) method declaration.

```
public NativeMethods
{
    // The use of SuppressUnmanagedCodeSecurity here applies only to FormatMessage
    [DllImport("kernel32.dll"), SuppressUnmanagedCodeSecurity]
    private unsafe static extern int FormatMessage(
                                int dwFlags,
                                ref IntPtr lpSource,
                                int dwMessageId,
                                int dwLanguageId,
                                ref String lpBuffer, int nSize,
                                IntPtr *Arguments);
}
```

Using SuppressUnmanagedCodeSecurity with COM Interop

For COM interop calls, the attribute must be used at the interface level, as shown in the following example.

```
[SuppressUnmanagedCodeSecurity]
public interface IComInterface
{
}
```

Delegates

There is no way of knowing in advance what a delegate method is going to do when you invoke it. If your assembly supports partial trust callers, you need to take extra precautions when you invoke a delegate. You can use code access security to further improve security.

- **Consider restricting permissions for the delegate.**
- **Do not assert a permission before calling a delegate.**

Consider Restricting Permissions for the Delegate

The permissions granted to the code that calls the delegate determine the capabilities of the delegate. If your code has more permissions than the code that gives you the delegate, this provides a way for the caller to execute code using elevated permissions. To address this issue, you can either authorize the external code at the point it passes you the delegate with an appropriate permission demand, or you can restrict the permissions of the delegate just prior to calling it by using a deny or permit only stack modifier. For example, the following code only grants the delegate code execution permission to constrain its capabilities.

```
// Delegate definition
public delegate void SomeDelegate();
. . .
// Permit only execution, prior to calling the delegate. This prevents the
// delegate code accessing resources or performing other privileged
// operations
new SecurityPermission(SecurityPermissionFlag.Execution).PermitOnly();
// Now call the "constrained" delegate
SomeDelegate();
// Revert the permit only stack modifier
CodeAccessPermission.RevertPermitOnly();
```

Do Not Assert a Permission Before Calling a Delegate

Asserting a permission before calling a delegate is dangerous to do because you have no knowledge about the nature or trust level of the code that will be executed when you invoke the delegate. The code that passes you the delegate is on the call stack and can therefore be checked with an appropriate security demand. However, there is no way of knowing the trust level or permissions granted to the delegate code itself.

For more guidelines about using delegates securely, see the "Delegates" section in Chapter 7, "Building Secure Assemblies."

Serialization

Code that supports serialization must be granted a **SecurityPermission** with its **Flag** attribute set to **SerializationFormatter**. If you develop classes that support serialization and your code supports partial trust callers, you should consider using additional permission demands to place restrictions on which code can serialize your object's state.

Restricting Serialization

If you create a class that implements the **ISerializable** interface, which allows your object to be serialized, you can add a permission demand to your **ISerializable.GetObjectData** implementation to authorize the code that is attempting to serialize your object. This is particularly important if your code supports partial trust callers.

For example, the following code fragment uses a **StrongNameIdentityPermission** demand to ensure that only code signed with a particular private key corresponding to the public key in the demand can serialize your object's state.

```
[StrongNameIdentityPermission(SecurityAction.Demand,
                    PublicKey="00240000048...97e85d098615")]
public override void GetObjectData(SerializationInfo info,
                              StreamingContext context)
```

For more guidelines about using serialization securely, see the "Serialization" section in Chapter 7, "Building Secure Assemblies."

Summary

Code access security allows you to restrict what your code can do, restrict which code can call your code, and identify code. In full trust environments where your code and the code that calls you have the unrestricted set of all permissions, code access security is of less significance.

If your code supports partial trust callers, the security risks are that much greater. In partial trust scenarios, code access security enables you to mitigate some of the additional risks and allows you to constrain privileged code.

Additional Resources

For more information, see the following resources:

- "Security in .NET: The Security Infrastructure of the CLR Provides Evidence, Policy, Permissions, and Enforcement Services" by Don Box, MSDN Magazine, September 2002, at *http://msdn.microsoft.com/msdnmag*.
- "Security in .NET: Enforce Code Access Rights with the Common Language Runtime" by Keith Brown, MSDN Magazine, February 2001, at *http://msdn.microsoft.com/msdnmag*.
- *.NET Framework Security* by LaMacchia, Lange, Lyons, Martin and Price, published by Addison Wesley.

9

Using Code Access Security
with ASP.NET

In This Chapter

- Configuring Web application trust levels and ASP.NET code access security policy
- Developing partial-trust Web applications
- Sandboxing privileged code
- Writing to the event log from medium-trust Web applications
- Calling OLE DB data sources from medium-trust Web applications
- Calling Web services from medium-trust Web applications

Overview

Code access security is a resource constraint model that allows administrators to determine if and how particular code is able to access specified resources and perform other privileged operations. For example, an administrator might decide that code downloaded from the Internet should not be given permission to access any resources, while Web application code developed by a particular company should be offered a higher degree of trust and, for example, be allowed to access the file system, the event log, and Microsoft SQL Server databases.

Traditional principal-based security, such as that provided by the operating system, authorizes access to resources based on user identity. For example, programs launched by a local administrator have no limitations on the local machine. Unfortunately, if the administrator's identity is spoofed and a malicious user is able to execute code using the administrator's security context, the malicious user also has no restrictions. This is where code access security is important because it can provide additional restrictions and security based on the code itself, rather than the user running the code.

With Microsoft .NET Framework version 1.1, administrators can configure policy for ASP.NET Web applications and Web services, which might consist of multiple assemblies. They can also grant code access security permissions to allow the application to access specific resource types and to perform specific privileged operations.

Note   Web applications and Web services built using .NET Framework version 1.0 always run with unrestricted code access permissions. This is not configurable.

Using code access security with Web applications helps you provide application isolation in hosted environments where multiple Web applications run on the same Web server. Internet service providers (ISPs) that run multiple applications from different companies can use code access security to:

- **Isolate applications from each other**.

  For example, code access security can be used to ensure that one Web application cannot write to another Web application's directories.

- **Isolate applications from system resources**.

  For example, code access security can restrict access to the file system, registry, event logs, and network resources, as well as other system resources.

Code access security is one mechanism that can be used to help provide application isolation. Microsoft Windows Server™ 2003 and Internet Information Services (IIS) 6.0 also provide process isolation for Web applications. Process isolation combined with code access security provides the recommended model for application isolation. For more information, see Chapter 20, "Hosting Multiple ASP.NET Applications."

How to Use This Chapter

This chapter does not cover the fundamentals of code access security. A certain amount of prerequisite knowledge is assumed, although key concepts are reiterated where appropriate. For more information about how code access security works, see Chapter 8, "Code Access Security in Practice."

The current chapter focuses on ASP.NET code access security policy configuration and shows you how to overcome some of the main hurdles that you might encounter when you develop partial-trust Web applications.

Resource Access

All resource access from ASP.NET applications and managed code in general is subject to the following two security layers:

- **Code access security**. This security layer verifies that all of the code in the current call stack, leading up to and including the resource access code, is authorized to access the resource. An administrator uses code access security policy to grant permissions to assemblies. The permissions determine precisely which resource types the assembly can access. Numerous permission types correspond to the different resource types that can be accessed. These types include the file system, registry, event log, directory services, SQL Server, OLE DB data sources, and network resources.

  For a full list of code access permissions, see Chapter 8, "Code Access Security in Practice."

- **Operating System/Platform Security**. This security layer verifies that the security context of the requesting thread can access the resource. If the thread is impersonating, then the thread impersonation token is used. If not, then the process token is used and is compared against the access control list (ACL) that is attached to the resource to determine whether or not the requested operation can be performed and the resource can be accessed.

Both checks must succeed for the resource to be successfully accessed. All of the resource types that are exposed by the .NET Framework classes are protected with code access permissions. Figure 9.1 shows a range of common resource types that are accessed by Web applications, as well as the associated code access permission that is required for the access attempt to succeed.

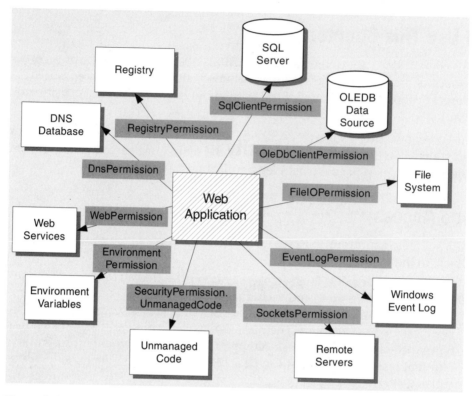

Figure 9.1

Common resource types accessed from ASP.NET Web applications and associated permission types

Full Trust and Partial Trust

By default, Web applications run with full trust. Full-trust applications are granted unrestricted code access permissions by code access security policy. These permissions include built-in system and custom permissions. This means that code access security will not prevent your application from accessing any of the secured resource types that Figure 9.1 shows. The success or failure of the resource access attempt is determined purely by operating system-level security. Web applications that run with full trust include all ASP.NET applications built using .NET Framework version 1.0. By default, .NET Framework version 1.1 applications run with full trust, but the trust level can be configured using the **<trust>** element, which is described later in this chapter.

If an application is configured with a trust level other than "Full," it is referred to as a partial-trust application. Partial-trust applications have restricted permissions, which limit their ability to access secured resources.

Important   Web applications built on .NET Framework version 1.0 always run with full trust because the types in **System.Web** demand full-trust callers.

Configuring Code Access Security in ASP.NET

By default, Web applications run with full trust and have unrestricted permissions. To modify code access security trust levels in ASP.NET, you have to set a switch in Machine.config or Web.config and configure the application as a partial-trust application.

Configuring Trust Levels

The **<trust>** element in Machine.config controls whether or not code access security is enabled for a Web application. Open Machine.config, search for "<trust>", and you will see the following.

```
<system.web>
  <!-- level="[Full|High|Medium|Low|Minimal]" -->
  <trust level="Full" originUrl=""/>
</system.web>
```

With the trust level set to "Full," code access security is effectively disabled because permission demands do not stand in the way of resource access attempts. This is the only option for ASP.NET Web applications built on .NET Framework version 1.0. As you go through the list from "Full" to "Minimal," each level takes away more permissions, which further restricts your application's ability to access secured resources and perform privileged operations. Each level gives greater degrees of application isolation. Table 9.1 shows the predefined trust levels and indicates the major restrictions in comparison to the previous level.

Table 9.1   Restrictions Imposed by the ASP.NET Trust Levels

ASP.NET Trust Level	Main Restrictions
Full	Unrestricted permissions. Applications can access any resource that is subject to operating system security. All privileged operations are supported.
High	Not able to call unmanaged code Not able to call serviced components Not able to write to the event log Not able to access Microsoft Message Queuing queues Not able to access OLE DB data sources
Medium	In addition to the above, file access is restricted to the current application directory and registry access is not permitted.
Low	In addition to the above, the application is not able to connect to SQL Server and code cannot call CodeAccessPermission.Assert (no assertion security permission).
Minimal	Only the execute permission is available.

Locking the Trust Level

If a Web server administrator wants to use code access security to ensure application isolation and restrict access to system level resources, the administrator must be able to define security policy at the machine level and prevent individual applications from overriding it.

Application service providers or anyone responsible for running multiple Web applications on the same server should lock the trust level for all Web applications. To do this, enclose the **<trust>** element in Machine.config within a **<location>** tag, and set the **allowOverride** attribute to **false**, as shown in the following example.

```
<location allowOverride="false">
  <system.web>
    <!-- level="[Full|High|Medium|Low|Minimal]" -->
    <trust level="Medium" originUrl=""/>
  </system.web>
</location>
```

You can also use a **path** attribute on the **<location>** element to apply a configuration to a specific site or Web application that cannot be overridden. For more information about the **<location>** element, see Chapter 19, "Securing Your ASP.NET Application and Web Services."

ASP.NET Policy Files

Each trust level is mapped to an individual XML policy file and the policy file lists the set of permissions granted by each trust level. Policy files are located in the following directory:

```
%windir%\Microsoft.NET\Framework\{version}\CONFIG
```

Trust levels are mapped to policy files by the **<trustLevel>** elements in Machine.config, which are located just above the **<trust>** element, as shown in the following example.

```
<location allowOverride="true">
  <system.web>
    <securityPolicy>
      <trustLevel name="Full" policyFile="internal"/>
      <trustLevel name="High" policyFile="web_hightrust.config"/>
      <trustLevel name="Medium" policyFile="web_mediumtrust.config"/>
      <trustLevel name="Low" policyFile="web_lowtrust.config"/>
      <trustLevel name="Minimal" policyFile="web_minimaltrust.config"/>
    </securityPolicy>
    <!-- level="[Full|High|Medium|Low|Minimal]" -->
    <trust level="Full" originUrl=""/>
  </system.web>
</location>
```

Note   No policy file exists for the full-trust level. This is a special case that simply indicates the unrestricted set of all permissions.

ASP.NET policy is fully configurable. In addition to the default policy levels, administrators can create custom permission files and configure them using the **<trust>** element, which is described later in this chapter. The policy file associated with the custom level must also be defined by a **<trustLevel>** element in Machine.config.

ASP.NET Policy

Code access security policy is hierarchical and is administered at multiple levels. Policy can be created for the enterprise, machine, user, and application domain levels. ASP.NET code access security policy is an example of application domain-level policy.

Settings in a separate XML configuration file define the policy for each level. Enterprise, machine, and user policy can be configured using the Microsoft .NET Framework configuration tool, but ASP.NET policy files must be edited manually using an XML or text editor.

The individual ASP.NET trust-level policy files say which permissions might be granted to applications configured at a particular trust level. The *actual* permissions that are granted to an ASP.NET application are determined by intersecting the permission grants from *all* policy levels, including enterprise, machine, user, and ASP.NET (application domain) level policy.

Because policy is evaluated from enterprise level down to ASP.NET application level, permissions can only be taken away. You cannot add a permission at the ASP.NET level without a higher level first granting the permission. This approach ensures that the enterprise administrator always has the final say and that malicious code that runs in an application domain cannot request and be granted more permissions than an administrator configures.

For more information about policy evaluation, see Chapter 8, "Code Access Security in Practice."

Inside an ASP.NET Policy File

To see which permissions are defined by a particular trust level, open the relevant policy file in Notepad or (preferably) an XML editor and locate the "ASP.NET" named permission set. This permission set lists the permissions that are configured for the application at the current trust level.

Note You will also see the "FullTrust" and "Nothing" permission sets. These sets contain no permission elements because "FullTrust" implies all permissions and "Nothing" contains no permissions.

The following fragment shows the major elements of an ASP.NET policy file:

```
<configuration>
    <mscorlib>
        <security>
            <policy>
                <PolicyLevel version="1">
                    <SecurityClasses>
                        ... list of security classes, permission types,
                        and code group types ...
                    </SecurityClasses>
                    <NamedPermissionSets>
                      <PermissionSet Name="FullTrust" ... />
                      <PermissionSet Name="Nothing" .../>
                      <PermissionSet Name="ASP.NET" ...
                        ... This is the interesting part ...
                        ... List of individual permissions...
```

(continued)

```
                    <IPermission
                            class="AspNetHostingPermission"
                            version="1"
                            Level="High" />
                    <IPermission
                            class="DnsPermission"
                            version="1"
                            Unrestricted="true" />
                ...Continued list of permissions...
                </PermissionSet>
            </PolicyLevel version="1">
        </policy>
      </security>
    </mscorlib>
</configuration>
```

Notice that each permission is defined by an **<IPermission>** element, which defines the permission type name, version, and whether or not it is in the unrestricted state.

Permission State and Unrestricted Permissions

Many permissions include state, which is used to fine-tune the access rights specified by the permission. The state determines precisely what the permission allows your application to do. For example, a **FileIOPermission** might specify a directory and an access type (read, write, and so on). The following permission demand requires that calling code is granted read permission to access the C:\SomeDir directory:

```
(new FileIOPermission(FileIOPermissionAccess.Read, @"C:\SomeDir")).Demand();
```

In its unrestricted state, the **FileIOPermission** allows any type of access to any area on the file system (of course, operating system security still applies). The following permission demand requires that the calling code be granted the unrestricted **FileIOPermission**:

```
(new FileIOPermission(PermissionState.Unrestricted)).Demand();
```

The ASP.NET Named Permission Set

ASP.NET policy files contain an "ASP.NET" named permission set. This defines the set of permissions that is granted by application domain policy to associated applications.

ASP.NET policy also introduces a custom **AspNetHostingPermission**, which has an associated **Level** attribute that corresponds to one of the default levels. All public types in the **System.Web** and **System.Web.Mobile** are protected with demands for the Minimum level of this permission. This risk mitigation strategy is designed to ensure that Web application code cannot be used in other partial-trust environments without specific policy configuration by an administrator.

Substitution Parameters

If you edit one of the ASP.NET policy files, you will notice that some of the permission elements contain substitution parameters ($AppDirUrl$, $CodeGen$, and Gac). These parameters allow you to configure permissions to assemblies that are part of your Web application, but are loaded from different locations. Each substitution parameter is replaced with an actual value at security policy evaluation time, which occurs when your Web application assembly is loaded for the first time. Your Web application might consist of the following three assembly types:

- Private assemblies that are compiled at build time and deployed in the application's bin directory

---

Important This type of assembly cannot be strong named. Strong named assemblies used by ASP.NET Web applications must be installed in the global assembly cache. This restriction is necessary because of the internal workings of the multi-application domain worker process.

- Dynamically compiled assemblies that are generated in response to a page request
- Shared assemblies that are loaded from the computer's global assembly cache

Each of these assembly types has an associated substitution parameter, which Table 9.2 summarizes.

Table 9.2   ASP.NET Code Access Security Policy Substitution Parameters

Parameter	Represents
$AppDirUrl$	The application's virtual root directory. This allows permissions to be applied to code that is located in the application's bin directory.
	For example, if a virtual directory is mapped to C:\YourWebApp, then $AppDirUrl$ would equate to C:\YourWebApp.
$CodeGen$	The directory that contains dynamically generated assemblies (for example, the result of .aspx page compiles). This can be configured on a per application basis and defaults to %windir%\Microsoft.NET\Framework\{version}\Temporary ASP.NET Files.
	$CodeGen$ allows permissions to be applied to dynamically generated assemblies.
Gac	Any assembly that is installed in the computer's global assembly cache (GAC) (%windir%\assembly). This allows permissions to be granted to strong named assemblies loaded from the GAC by the Web application.

Developing Partial Trust Web Applications

Partial trust Web applications are applications that do not have full trust and have a restricted set of code access permissions determined by code access security policy. As a result, partial-trust applications are limited in their ability to access secured resources and perform other privileged operations. Certain permissions are denied to partial-trust applications, so resources requiring those permissions cannot be directly accessed. Other permissions are granted in a restricted way, so resources that require those permissions might be accessible, but in a limited way. For example, a restricted **FileIOPermission** might specify that the application can access the file system, but only in directories beneath the application's virtual directory root.

Why Partial Trust?

By configuring a Web application or Web service for partial trust, you can restrict the application's ability to access crucial system resources or resources that belong to other Web applications. By granting only the permissions that the application requires and no more, you can build least privileged Web applications and limit damage potential should the Web application be compromised by a code injection attack.

Problems You Might Encounter

If you take an existing Web application and reconfigure it to run at a partial-trust level, you are likely to run into the following issues, unless the application is extremely limited in the resources it accesses:

- Your application is unable to call strong named assemblies that are not annotated with **AllowPartiallyTrustedCallersAttribute** (APTCA). Without APTCA, strong named assemblies issue a demand for full trust, which will fail when the demand reaches your partial-trust Web application. Many system assemblies only support full-trust callers. The following list shows which .NET Framework assemblies support partial-trust callers and can be called directly by partial-trust Web applications without necessitating sandboxed wrapper assemblies.

Note Sandboxing is discussed in detail later in this chapter.

The following system assemblies have APTCA applied, which means that they can be called by partial-trust Web applications or any partially trusted code:

- System.Windows.Forms.dll
- System.Drawing.dll
- System.dll
- Mscorlib.dll
- IEExecRemote.dll

- Accessibility.dll
- Microsoft.VisualBasic.dll
- System.XML.dll
- System.Web.dll
- System.Web.Services.dll
- System.Data.dll

If your partial-trust application fails because it calls a strong named assembly that is not marked with APTCA, a generic **SecurityException** is generated. In this circumstance, the exception contains no additional information to indicate that the call failed because of a failed demand for full trust.

- Permission demands might start to fail. The configured trust level might not grant the necessary permission for your application to access a specific resource type. The following are some common scenarios where this could prove problematic:

  - Your application uses the event log or registry. Partial trust Web applications do not have the necessary permissions to access these system resources. If your code does so, a **SecurityException** will be generated.

  - Your application uses the ADO.NET OLE DB data provider to access a data source. The OLE DB data provider requires full-trust callers.

  - Your application calls a Web service. Partial-trust Web applications have a restricted **WebPermission**, which affects the ability of the application to call Web services located on remote sites.

Trust Levels

If you plan to migrate an existing application to a partial-trust level, a good approach is to reduce permissions incrementally so that you can see what parts of your application break. For example, start by setting the trust **level** attribute to High, then Medium, and so on. Ultimately, the trust level you should target depends on the degree of restriction you want to place on the application. Use the following as guidance:

- Applications configured for high, medium, low, or minimal trust will be unable to call unmanaged code or serviced components, write to the event log, access Message Queuing queues, or access OLE DB data sources.

- Applications configured for high trust have unrestricted access to the file system.

- Applications configured for medium trust have restricted file system access. They can only access files in their own application directory hierarchy.

- Applications configured for low or minimal trust cannot access SQL Server databases.

- Minimal trust applications cannot access any resources.

Table 9.3 identifies the permissions that each ASP.NET trust level grants. The full level is omitted from the table because it grants all of the permissions in their unrestricted state.

Table 9.3 Default ASP.NET Policy Permissions and Trust Levels

Permission and State	High	Medium	Low	Minimal
AspNetHosting Level	High	Medium	Low	Minimal
DnsPermission Unrestricted	✓	✓		

EnvironmentPermission
  Unrestricted
  Read
  Write
	✓	TEMP; TMP;
		USERNAME; OS;
		COMPUTERNAME		

EventLogPermission				

FileIOPermission
  Unrestricted
  Read
  Write
  Append
  PathDiscovery
	✓	$AppDir$
		$AppDir$
		$AppDir$
		$AppDir$
			$AppDir$
			
			$AppDir$	

IsolatedStorageFilePermission
  Unrestricted
  AssemblyIsolationByUser-
  Unrestricted UserQuota
	✓	✓
		✓
			✓
			1MB
			(can vary
			with site)	

OleDbClientPermission Unrestricted				

PrintingPermission
  Unrestricted
  DefaultPrinting
	✓	✓		

ReflectionPermission
  Unrestricted
  ReflectionEmit
	✓			

RegistryPermission Unrestricted	✓			

(continued)

Table 9.3   Default ASP.NET Policy Permissions and Trust Levels *(continued)*

Permission and State	High	Medium	Low	Minimal

SecurityPermission
    Unrestricted
    Assertion
    Execution
    ControlThread
    ControlPrinicipal
    RemotingConfiguration
	
	✓
	✓
	✓
	✓
	✓
		
		✓
		✓
		✓
		✓
		✓
			
			✓
				
				✓

SocketPermission Unrestricted	✓			
SqlClientPermission Unrestricted	✓	✓		
WebPermission Unrestricted	✓	$OriginHost$		

Approaches for Partial Trust Web Applications

If you develop a partial-trust application or enable an existing application to run at a partial-trust level, and you run into problems because your application is trying to access resources for which the relevant permissions have not been granted, you can use two basic approaches:

- **Customize policy**

   Customize policy to grant the required permissions to your application. This might not be possible, for example in hosting environments, where policy restrictions are rigid.

- **Sandbox privileged code**

   Place resource access code in a wrapper assembly, grant the wrapper assembly full trust (not the Web application), and sandbox the permission requirements of privileged code.

The right approach depends on what the problem is. If the problem is related to the fact that you are trying to call a system assembly that does not contain **AllowPartiallyTrustedCallersAttribute,** the problem becomes how to give a piece of code full trust. In this scenario, you should use the sandboxing approach and grant the sandboxed wrapper assembly full trust.

Note   Customizing policy is the easier of the two approaches because it does not require any development effort.

Customize Policy

If your Web application contains code that requires more permissions than are granted by a particular ASP.NET trust level, the easiest option is customizing a policy file to grant the additional code access security permission to your Web application. You can either modify an existing policy file and grant additional permissions or create a new one based on an existing policy file.

Note   If you modify one of the built-in policy files, for example, the medium-trust Web_mediumtrust.config policy file, this affects all applications that are configured to run with medium trust.

▶ **To customize policy for a specific application**

1. Copy one of the existing policy files to create a new policy file. For example, copy the medium trust policy file and create a new policy file such as the following:

   ```
   %windir%\Microsoft.NET\Framework\{version}\CONFIG\web_yourtrust.config
   ```

2. Add the required permission to the ASP.NET permission set in the policy file or, alternatively, modify an existing permission to grant a less restrictive permission.

3. Add a new **<trustLevel>** mapping beneath **<securityPolicy>** in Machine.config for the new trust level file, as follows:

   ```
   <securityPolicy>
     <trustLevel name="Custom" policyFile="web_yourtrust.config"/>
     . . .
   </securityPolicy>
   ```

4. Configure your application to run with the new trust level by configuring the **<trust>** element in the application's Web.config file, as follows:

   ```
   <system.web>
     <trust level="Custom" originUrl=""/>
   </system.web>
   ```

Sandbox Privileged Code

Another approach that does not require an update to ASP.NET code access security policy is wrapping your resource access code in its own wrapper assembly and configuring machine-level code access security policy to grant the specific assembly the appropriate permission. Then you can sandbox the higher-privileged code using the **CodeAccessPermission.Assert** method so you do not have to change the overall permission grant of the Web application. The **Assert** method prevents the security demand issued by the resource access code from propagating back up the call stack beyond the boundaries of the wrapper assembly.

A Sandboxing Pattern

You can apply the following pattern to any privileged code that needs to access a restricted resource or perform another privileged operation for which the parent Web application does not have sufficient permissions:

1. **Encapsulate the resource access code in a wrapper assembly**.

   Make sure the assembly is strong named so that it can be installed in the GAC.

2. **Assert the relevant permission prior to accessing the resource**.

   This means that the caller must have the assertion security permission (**SecurityPermission** with **SecurityPermissionFlag.Assertion**). Applications configured for Medium or higher trust levels have this permission.

   Asserting permissions is a dangerous thing to do because it means that the code that calls your code can access the resource that is encapsulated by your assembly without requiring the relevant resource access permission. The **Assert** statement says that your code can vouch for the legitimacy of its callers. To do this, your code should demand an alternate permission so that it can authorize the calling code prior to calling **Assert**. In this way, you only allow code that has been granted the alternate permission to access the resource that your assembly exposes.

   The .NET Framework might not provide a suitable permission to demand. In this case, you can create and demand a custom permission. For more information about how to create a custom permission, see "How To: Create a Custom Encryption Permission" in the "How To" section of this guide.

3. **Annotate the wrapper assembly with APTCA**.

   This allows the partial-trust Web application to call the assembly.

4. Install the wrapper assembly in the GAC.

This gives full trust to the wrapper, but not the Web application. The ASP.NET policy files contain the following code group, which grants full trust to any assembly located in the GAC:

```
<CodeGroup
    class="UnionCodeGroup"
    version="1"
    PermissionSetName="FullTrust">
    <IMembershipCondition
        class="UrlMembershipCondition"
        Url="$Gac$/*"
        version="1"
    />
</CodeGroup>
```

> **Note**   Default enterprise and local machine policy also grant full trust to any code located in the My Computer zone, which includes code installed in the GAC. This is important because granted permissions are intersected across policy levels.

5. Configure the Web application trust level (for example, set it to "Medium").

Figure 9.2 shows the sandboxing approach.

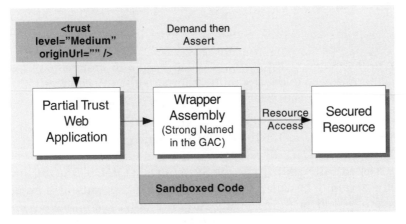

Figure 9.2
Sandboxing privileged code in its own assembly, which asserts the relevant permission

It is good practice to use separate assemblies to encapsulate resource access and avoid placing resource access code in .aspx files or code behind files. For example, create a separate data access assembly to encapsulate database access. This makes it easier to migrate applications to partial-trust environments.

Deciding Which Approach to Take

The right approach depends upon the problem you are trying to solve and whether or not you have the option of modifying security policy on the Web server.

Customizing Policy

This approach is the easier of the two and does not require any developer effort. However, you might not be permitted to modify policy on the Web server and, in certain scenarios, your code that calls the .NET Framework class library might require full trust. In these situations, you must use sandboxing. For example, the following resources demand full trust, and you must sandbox your resource access code when it accesses them:

- Event log (through the EventLog class)
- OLE DB data sources (through the ADO.NET OLE DB data provider)
- ODBC data sources (through the ADO.NET ODBC .NET data provider)
- Oracle databases (through the ADO.NET Oracle .NET data provider)

Note   This list is not exhaustive but it includes commonly used resource types that currently require full trust.

Sandboxing

If you sandbox your privileged application code in a separate assembly, you can grant additional permissions to the assembly. Alternatively, you can grant it full trust without requiring your entire application to run with extended permissions.

For example, consider code that uses the ADO.NET OLE DB data provider and interacts with the **System.Data.OleDb.OleDbCommand** class. This code requires full trust. Although the System.Data.dll assembly is marked with **AllowPartiallyTrustedCallersAttribute**, the **System.Data.OleDb.OleDbCommand** class, among others, cannot be called by partial-trust callers because it is protected with a link demand for full trust. To see this, run the following command using the permview utility from the %windir%\Microsoft.NET\Framework\{version} directory:

```
permview /DECL /OUTPUT System.Data.Perms.txt System.Data.dll
```

The output in System.Data.Perms.txt includes the following output:

```
class System.Data.OleDb.OleDbCommand LinktimeDemand permission set:
<PermissionSet class="System.Security.PermissionSet"
            version="1" Unrestricted="true"/>
```

This illustrates that an unrestricted permission set (full trust) is used in a link demand that protects the **System.Data.OleDb.OleDbCommand** class. In scenarios such as this, it is not sufficient to configure policy to grant specific unrestricted permissions, such as **OleDbPermission**, to your partial-trust code. Instead, you must sandbox your resource access code and grant it full trust, and the easiest way to do this is to install it in the GAC. Use Permview.exe to find out about the permission requirements of other classes, although this only shows declarative security attributes. If a class imperatively demands full trust, you cannot see this through Permview.exe. In this event, test the security requirements of the class by calling it from partial-trust code and diagnosing any security exceptions.

Note Just because an assembly is marked with APTCA, it does not mean all of the contained classes support partial-trust callers. Some classes may include explicit demands for full trust.

Medium Trust

If you host Web applications, you may choose to implement a medium trust security policy to restrict privileged operations. This section focuses on running medium trust applications, and shows you how to overcome the problems you are likely to encounter.

Running at medium trust has the following two main benefits:

- **Reduced attack surface**
- **Application isolation**

Reduced Attack Surface

Since medium trust does not grant the application unrestricted access to all permissions, your attack surface is reduced by granting the application a subset of the full permission set. Many of the permissions granted by medium trust policy are also in a restricted state. If an attacker is somehow able to take control of your application, the attacker is limited in what he or she can do.

Application Isolation

Application isolation with code access security restricts access to system resources and resources owned by other applications. For example, even though the process identity might be allowed to read and write files outside of the Web application directory, the **FileIOPermission** in medium trust applications is restricted. It only permits the application to read or write to its own application directory hierarchy.

Medium Trust Restrictions

If your application runs at medium trust, it faces a number of restrictions, the most significant of which are:

- It cannot directly access the event log.
- It has restricted file system access and can only access files in the application's virtual directory hierarchy.
- It cannot directly access OLE DB data sources (although medium trust applications are granted the **SqlClientPermission,** which allows them to access SQL Server).
- It has limited access to Web services.
- It cannot directly access the Windows registry.

This section shows you how to access the following resource types from a medium-trust Web application or Web service:

- **OLE DB**
- **Event log**
- **Web services**
- **Registry**

OLE DB

Medium-trust Web applications are not granted the **OleDbPermission.** Furthermore, the OLE DB .NET data provider currently demands full-trust callers. If you have an application that needs to access OLE DB data sources while running at medium trust, use the sandboxing approach. Place your data access code in a separate assembly, strong name it, and install it in the GAC, which gives it full trust.

Note Modifying policy does not work unless you set the trust level to "Full" because the OLE DB managed provider demands full trust.

Figure 9.3 shows the arrangement.

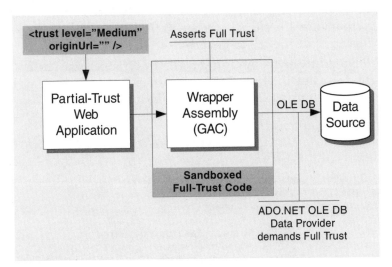

Figure 9.3
Sandboxing OLE DB resource access

Sandboxing

In this approach, you create a wrapper assembly to encapsulate OLE DB data source access. This assembly is granted full-trust permissions, which are required to use the ADO.NET OLE DB managed provider.

▶ **To build a sandboxed wrapper assembly to call OLE DB data sources**

1. Create an assembly for your data access code. Configure the assembly version, strong name the assembly, and mark it with the **AllowPartiallyTrustedCallersAttribute**, as follows:

```
[assembly: AssemblyVersion("1.0.0.0")]
[assembly: AssemblyKeyFile(@"..\..\oledbwrapper.snk")]
[assembly:AllowPartiallyTrustedCallersAttribute()]
```

You must annotate any strong named assembly with **AllowPartiallyTrustedCallersAttribute** if you want to support partial-trust callers. This suppresses an implicit link demand for full trust made by the .NET Framework whenever code from a strong named assembly is loaded and JIT-compiled.

2. **Request full trust**. Although not strictly necessary, requesting full trust is a good practice because it allows an administrator to view the assembly's permission requirements by using tools like Permview.exe. To request full trust, request the unrestricted permission set as follows:

```
[assembly: PermissionSet(SecurityAction.RequestMinimum, Unrestricted=true)]
```

3. Wrap database calls with an **Assert** statement to assert full trust. Wrap a matching **RevertAssert** call to reverse the effect of the assert. Although not strictly necessary, it is a good practice to place the call to **RevertAssert** in a **finally** block.

Because the OLE DB provider demands full trust, the wrapper must assert full-trust. Asserting an **OleDbPermission** is not sufficient. Step 7 explains how to improve the security of using **CodeAccessPermission.Assert**.

```
public OleDbDataReader GetProductList()
{
  try
  {
    // Assert full trust (the unrestricted permission set)
    new PermissionSet(PermissionState.Unrestricted).Assert();
    OleDbConnection conn = new OleDbConnection(
        "Provider=SQLOLEDB; Data Source=(local);" +
        "Integrated Security=SSPI; Initial Catalog=Northwind");
    OleDbCommand cmd = new OleDbCommand("spRetrieveProducts", conn);
    cmd.CommandType = CommandType.StoredProcedure;
    conn.Open();
    OleDbDataReader reader =
          cmd.ExecuteReader(CommandBehavior.CloseConnection);
    return reader;
  }
  catch(OleDbException dbex)
  {
    // Log and handle exception
  }
  catch(Exception ex)
  {
    //  Log and handle exception
  }
  finally
  {
    CodeAccessPermission.RevertAssert();
  }
  return null;
}
```

4. Build the assembly and install it in the GAC with the following command:

```
gacutil -i oledbwrapper.dll
```

To ensure that the assembly is added to the GAC after each subsequent rebuild, add the following post build event command line (available from the project's properties in Visual Studio.NET) to your wrapper assembly project:

```
"C:\Program Files\Microsoft Visual Studio .NET 2003\SDK\v1.1\Bin\gacutil.exe"
/i $(TargetPath)
```

Note Any strong named assembly that is called by an ASP.NET Web application or Web service must be installed in the GAC. In this instance, you should install the assembly in the GAC to ensure that it is granted full trust.

5. Configure your Web application for medium trust. Add the following code to Web.config or place it in Machine.config inside a **<location>** element that points to your application:

```
<trust level="Medium" originUrl=""/>
```

6. Reference the data access assembly from your ASP.NET Web application.

   Since a strong named assembly must be in the GAC and not the \bin directory of a Web application, you must add the assembly to the list of assemblies used in the application if you are not using code behind files. You can obtain the **PublicKeyToken** of your assembly by using the following command:

```
sn -Tp oledbwrapper.dll
```

Note Use a capital **–T** switch.

Then add the following to Machine.config or Web.config:

```
<compilation debug="false" >
  <assemblies>
    <add assembly="oledbwrapper, Version=1.0.0.0, Culture=neutral,
        PublicKeyToken=4b...06"/>
  </assemblies>
</compilation>
```

Note In between successive rebuilds of your wrapper assembly, you might need to recycle the ASP.NET worker process because your wrapper assembly, which is installed in the GAC is cached by the ASP.NET process. To recycle the ASP.NET worker process (Aspnet_wp.exe) you can run the IISreset.exe utility.

7. Protect the code that calls **Assert**.

   The **Assert** call means that any code that calls the data access wrapper can interact with the OLE DB data source. To prevent malicious code from calling the data access component and potentially using it to attack the database, you can issue a full demand for a custom permission prior to calling **Assert** and update the medium-trust policy file to grant your Web application the custom permission. This solution entails a reasonable amount of developer effort.

   For more information about developing a custom permission, see "How To: Create a Custom Encryption Permission" in the "How To" section of this guide.

Event Log

The **EventLogPermission** class is designed to encapsulate the rights of code to access the event log. Currently, however, code must be granted full trust to be able to access the event log. This means that a medium trust Web application cannot directly access the event log. To do so, you must sandbox your event logging code.

Accessing the Event Log

First, ensure that the process account that is used to run your Web application (or the thread identity if your application is impersonating) is able to create event sources. For this, the process or thread identity must be able to create registry keys beneath the following key:

```
HKEY_LOCAL_MACHINE\SYSTEM\CurrentControlSet\Services\Eventlog
```

At minimum, the ASP.NET process identity of any impersonated identity must have the following permissions on this registry key:

- Query key value
- Set key value
- Create subkey
- Enumerate subkeys
- Notify
- Read

These settings must be applied to the key shown above and subkeys. Alternatively, you can create event sources at installation time when administrative privileges are available. For more information about this approach, see "Auditing and Logging" in Chapter 10, "Building Secure ASP.NET Web Pages and Controls."

Sandboxing

To sandbox your event logging code, you create a wrapper assembly to encapsulate event log access. You then install the wrapper assembly in the global assembly cache so that is granted full trust by code access security policy.

▶ **To build a sandboxed wrapper assembly to write to the event log**

1. Create an assembly for your event log code. Configure the assembly version, strong name the assembly, and mark it with the **AllowPartiallyTrustedCallersAttribute**, as shown in the following example.

```
[[assembly: AssemblyVersion("1.0.0.0")]
[assembly: AssemblyKeyFile(@"..\..\eventlogwrapper.snk")]
[assembly:AllowPartiallyTrustedCallersAttribute()]
```

You must annotate any strong named assembly with **AllowPartiallyTrustedCallersAttribute** if you want to support partial-trust callers. This suppresses an implicit link demand for full trust made by the .NET Framework whenever code from a strong named assembly is loaded and JIT-compiled.

Note   **AllowPartiallyTrustedCallersAttribute** is defined in the **System.Security** namespace, so you must reference this namespace with a **using** statement.

---

2. Request appropriate permissions.

   Although not strictly necessary, requesting appropriate permissions is a good practice because it allows an administrator to view the assembly's permission requirements by using tools like Permview.exe. Since the event log assembly can be accessed from partial-trust callers, this assembly does not need to request a full trust permission set. The assembly in this example only writes to the event log on a specific machine and, therefore, only needs the following permission request:

```
[assembly:EventLogPermissionAttribute(SecurityAction.RequestMinimum,
MachineName="<machine name>",
PermissionAccess=EventLogPermissionAccess.Instrument)]
```

   However, if your assembly needs to request full trust, request the unrestricted permission set as follows:

```
[assembly: PermissionSet(SecurityAction.RequestMinimum, Unrestricted=true)]
```

3. Wrap event log calls with an **Assert** statement that asserts full trust and a matching **RevertAssert** that reverses the effect of the assert. Although not strictly necessary, it is a good practice to place the call to **RevertAssert** in a **finally** block. The following code writes an Information entry to the Application log with the text "Writing to the event log":

```
try
{
  string source = "Event Source";
  string log = "Application";
  string eventText = "Writing to the event log";
  EventLogEntryType eventType = EventLogEntryType.Information;

  //Assert permission
  EventLogPermission eventPerm;
  eventPerm = new EventLogPermission(EventLogPermissionAccess.Instrument,
"<machinename>");
  eventPerm.Assert();

  //Check to see if the source exists.
  if(!EventLog.SourceExists(source))
  {//The keys do not exist, so register your application as a source
      EventLog.CreateEventSource(source, log);
  }

  //Write to the log.
  EventLog.WriteEntry(source, eventText, eventType);
}
catch(Exception ex)
{/*Handle exception*/}
finally
{
  CodeAccessPermission.RevertAssert();
}
```

4. Build the assembly and install it in the GAC with the following command:

```
gacutil -i eventlogwrapper.dll
```

To ensure that the assembly is added to the GAC after each subsequent rebuild, add the following post build event command line (available from the project's properties in Visual Studio.NET) to your wrapper assembly project:

```
"C:\Program Files\Microsoft Visual Studio .NET 2003\SDK\v1.1\Bin\gacutil.exe"
/i $(TargetPath)
```

Note   Any strong named assembly called by an ASP.NET Web application or Web service must be installed in the GAC. Assemblies that are installed in the GAC are granted full trust by default code access security policy.

5. Configure your Web application for medium trust. Add the following to Web.config or place it in Machine.config inside a **<location>** element that points to your application:

```
<trust level="Medium" originUrl=""/>
```

6. Reference the event log assembly from your ASP.NET Web application.

   Since a strong named assembly must be in the GAC and not the \bin directory of a Web application, then you must add the assembly to the list of assemblies used in the application if you are not using code behind files. You can obtain the **PublicKeyToken** of your assembly by using the following command:

```
sn -Tp eventlogwapper.dll
```

Note Use a capital **–T** switch.

Then add the following code to Machine.config or Web.config:

```
<compilation debug="false" >
  <assemblies>
    <add assembly="eventlogwrapper, Version=1.0.0.0, Culture=neutral,
        PublicKeyToken=4b…06"/>
  </assemblies>
</compilation>
```

Note In between successive rebuilds of your wrapper assembly, you might need to recycle the ASP.NET worker process because your wrapper assembly, which is installed in the GAC is cached by the ASP.NET process. To recycle the ASP.NET worker process (Aspnet_wp.exe) you can run the iisreset.exe utility.

---

7. Protect the code that calls the **Assert** method. The **Assert** call means that any code that calls the event log wrapper is able to interact with the event log. To prevent malicious code from calling the event log wrapper and potentially using it to fill the event log, you can issue a full demand for a custom permission prior to calling **Assert** and update the medium trust policy file to grant your Web application the custom permission. This solution entails a reasonable amount of developer effort.

   For more information about how to develop a custom permission, see "How To: Create a Custom Encryption Permission" in the "How To" section of this guide.

Web Services

By default, medium-trust policy grants ASP.NET Web applications a restricted **WebPermission**. To be able to call Web services from your Web application, you must configure the **originUrl** attribute on your application's **<trust>** element.

▶ **To call a single Web service from a medium trust Web application**

1. Configure the application to run at medium trust.

2. Set the **originUrl** to point to the Web service you want to be able to call, as follows:

```
<trust level="Medium" originUrl="http://servername/.*"/>
```

The **originUrl** value is used in the constructor for a **System.Text.RegEx** regular expression class so that in can perform a match on the URLs that are accessible by the Web service. This **RegEx** class is used in conjunction with a **WebPermission** class. The ".*" matches any URL beginning with "http://*servername*/".

The **originUrl** attribute is used when ASP.NET policy is evaluated. It gives a value for the **$OriginHost$** substitution parameter. Here is the **WebPermission** definition from Web_mediumtrust.config:

```
<IPermission
   class="WebPermission"
   version="1">
   <ConnectAccess>
     <URI uri="$OriginHost$"/>
   </ConnectAccess>
</IPermission>
```

If you do not specify the Web servers accessed by your application, any Web service request will fail with a **SecurityException**. To call a Web service on the local Web server, use the following configuration:

```
<trust level="Medium" originUrl="http://localhost/.*" />
```

If your application needs to access multiple Web services on different servers, you need to customize ASP.NET policy because you can only specify one **originUrl** on the **<trust>** element in Web.config or Machine.config.

▶ To call multiple Web services from a medium-trust application

1. Copy the Web_mediumtrust.config file, which is in the following directory, to a file called Web_mediumtrust_WebService.config, which is located in the same directory.

```
%windir%\Microsoft.NET\Framework\{version}\CONFIG
```

2. Locate **WebPermission** and add a **<URI>** element for each server you will be accessing, as follows:

```
<IPermission class="WebPermission" version="1">
  <ConnectAccess>
    <URI uri="$OriginHost$"/>
    <URI uri="http://server1/.*"/>
    <URI uri="http://server2/.*"/>
    <URI uri="http://server3/.*"/>
  </ConnectAccess>
</IPermission>
```

If you call the Web service using its NetBIOS) name, DNS name, and/or IP address, you must have a separate **<URI>** element for each URI as shown in the following example.

```
<IPermission class="WebPermission" version="1">
  <ConnectAccess>
    <URI uri="$OriginHost$"/>
    <URI uri="http://servername.yourDomain.com/.*"/>
    <URI uri="http:// servername/.*"/>
    <URI uri="http://127.0.0.1/.*"/>
  </ConnectAccess>
</IPermission>
```

3. Save the file.

4. Update your application's Web.config file to point to the newly created policy file. This requires that you create a new trust level and map it to the new policy file. Next, configure the **<trust>** element of your application to use the new level.

   The following fragment shows the necessary additions to Web.config:

```
<system.web>
  <securityPolicy>
    <trustLevel name="MediumPlusWebPermission"
                policyFile="web_mediumtrust_WebService.config"/>
  </securityPolicy>
  <trust level=" MediumPlusWebPermission" originUrl=""/>
</system.web>
```

Using Default Credentials

You might need to call a Web service that uses Windows authentication and specify authentication credentials through the proxy credential cache. For example:

```
proxy.Credentials = System.Net.CredentialCache.DefaultCredentials;
```

In this case, the ASP.NET application requires the **EnvironmentPermission** with read access to the USERNAME environment variable. Default medium-trust policy grants this permission to Web applications.

In an ASP.NET server-side scenario, the credentials are obtained from the ASP.NET application's thread or process-level token. If **DefaultCredentials** are used from a desktop application, the current interactive user's token is used. The demand for **EnvironmentPermission** is a risk mitigation strategy designed to ensure that code cannot use the local user's credentials at will and expose them to the network.

Registry

By default, medium-trust Web applications are not granted the **RegistryPermission**. To configure your application to access the registry, you must either modify ASP.NET policy to grant this permission to your application or develop a sandboxed wrapper assembly that has the necessary permission.

The sandboxing approach is the same as described earlier for OLE DB data sources and the event log.

Customizing Policy

The easiest way to customize policy is to create a custom policy file based on the medium-trust policy file and configure your application to use the custom policy. The custom policy grants **RegistryPermission** to the application.

▶ To create a custom policy to allow registry access

1. Copy the Web_mediumtrust.config file, which is in the following directory, to a file called Web_mediumtrust_Registry.config, which is located in the same directory.

```
%windir%\Microsoft.NET\Framework\{version}\CONFIG
```

By making a copy and creating a custom policy file, you avoid making changes directly to the Web_mediumtrust.config file. Making changes directly to the default medium trust file affects every application on the machine that is configured for medium trust.

2. Locate the **<SecurityClasses>** element and add the following to register the **RegistryPermission** class:

```
<SecurityClass Name="RegistryPermission"
               Description="System.Security.Permissions.RegistryPermission,
               mscorlib, Version=1.0.5000.0, Culture=neutral,
               PublicKeyToken=b77a5c561934e089"/>
```

3. Locate the ASP.NET permission set and add the unrestricted **RegistryPermission** to the permission set as follows:

```
<IPermission class="RegistryPermission" version="1" Unrestricted="true" />
```

4. Save the file.

5. Update Machine.config to create a new trust level that is mapped to the new policy file.

```
<system.web>
  <securityPolicy>
    <trustLevel name="MediumPlusRegistry"
                policyFile="web_mediumtrust_Registry.config "/>
  </securityPolicy>
```

6. Update your application's Web.config to configure the application's **<trust>** level.

```
<system.web>
  <trust level="MediumPlusRegistry" originUrl=""/>
</system.web>
```

Summary

Code access security is a resource constraint security model that can be used to help provide application isolation. Applications can be configured to run at various partial-trust levels. The trust level determines the permissions that are granted to the ASP.NET Web application or Web service. This determines the resource types that can be accessed, and the other types of privileged operation that can be performed. Note that all resource access is ultimately subject to operating system security.

The recommended isolation model uses IIS 6.0 application pools on Windows Server 2003 and provides process level isolation in addition to code access security. On Windows 2000, isolation can only be achieved using code access security and separate thread identities.

Migrating an application to run with partial trust usually requires a certain amount of reengineering. You might need to reengineer if the application accesses resources that are not permitted by the partial trust level or if it calls strong named assemblies that do not contain APTCA. In these cases, you can sandbox privileged resource access in separate wrapper assemblies. In some scenarios, you might be able to create and use custom policy files, although this depends on your Web server's security policy.

It is a good design practice to place resource access code in separate assemblies and avoid placing this code in .aspx files and code behind files. The use of separate assemblies allows code access security policy to be applied to the assembly independently from the Web application and it allows you to develop sandboxed trusted code to perform resource access.

Additional Resources

For more information, see the following resources:

- "Security in .NET: The Security Infrastructure of the CLR Provides Evidence, Policy, Permissions, and Enforcement Services" in MSDN Magazine at *http://msdn.microsoft.com/msdnmag/issues/02/09/SecurityinNET/default.aspx*.
- "Security in .NET: Enforce Code Access Rights with the Common Language Runtime" in MSDN Magazine at *http://msdn.microsoft.com/msdnmag/issues/01/02/CAS/default.aspx*.
- LaMacchia, Lange, Lyons, Martin, and Price. *.NET Framework Security*. Addison Wesley Professional, 2002.
- "How To: Create a Custom Encryption Permission" in the "How To" section of this guide.

10

Building Secure ASP.NET Pages and Controls

In This Chapter

- Preventing cross-site scripting (XSS) attacks
- Partitioning sites into public and restricted areas
- Preventing session hijacking and cookie replay attacks
- Developing secure Forms authentication
- Preventing rich exception details from reaching the client
- Validating input in Web pages and controls

Overview

Web pages and controls are in your application's front line of defense and can be subject to intense probing by attackers who are intent on compromising your application's security. These attacks are often ultimately aimed at back-end systems and data stores.

Input data validation should be a top consideration when you build Web pages because the majority of top application-level attacks rely on vulnerabilities in this area. One of the most prevalent attacks today is cross-site scripting (XSS), which is more of an attack on your application's users than on the application itself, but it exploits server-side application vulnerabilities all the same. The results can be devastating and can lead to information disclosure, identity spoofing, and elevation of privilege.

How to Use This Chapter

To build secure Web pages and controls, you need to follow the correct programming practices that this chapter discusses. In addition to secure programming practices, use the corresponding chapters in this guide to help you build secure ASP.NET pages and controls.

- **Implement the steps in Chapter 19, "Securing Your ASP.NET Application and Web Services."** The chapter helps you configure ASP.NET appropriately with secure settings in Machine.config and Web.config.

- **Use the accompanying checklist in the checklist section of this guide.** "Checklist: Securing ASP.NET" ties the recommendations made in this chapter and in Chapter 19 together. Make sure you implement the guidance.

- **Understand the threats and attacks that are specific to ASP.NET pages and controls.** Apply countermeasures according to guidelines in this chapter.

- **Read Chapter 4, "Design Guidelines for Secure Web Applications."** Many of the recommendations in this chapter (Chapter 10) are based on the design guidelines discussed in Chapter 4.

- **Architects should use the "Design Considerations" section of this chapter.**

- **Developers should apply the guidance in this chapter to their development process.**

- **Learn the controls from a programmatic standpoint to fine-tune ASP.NET pages and controls security.**

- **Use the application vulnerability categories as a means to tackle common problems.** Application vulnerability categories provide a useful way to approach and group problems.

Threats and Countermeasures

Most Web application attacks require that malicious input is passed within HTTP requests. The general goal is either to coerce the application into performing unauthorized operations or to disrupt its normal operation. This is why thorough input validation is an essential countermeasure to many attacks and should be made a top priority when you develop ASP.NET Web pages and controls. Top threats include:

- **Code injection**
- **Session hijacking**
- **Identity spoofing**
- **Parameter manipulation**
- **Network eavesdropping**
- **Information disclosure**

Figure 10.1 highlights the most common threats to Web applications.

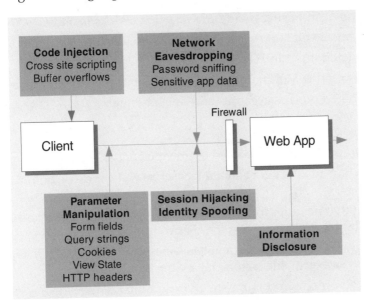

Figure 10.1
Common threats to ASP.NET Web pages and controls

Code Injection

Code injection occurs when an attacker causes arbitrary code to run using your application's security context. The risk increases if your application runs using a privileged account.

Attacks

There are various types of code injection attacks. These include:

- **Cross-site scripting**. Malicious script is sent to a Web application as input. It is echoed back to a user's browser, where it is executed.

- **Buffer overflows**. The type safe verification of managed code reduces the risk significantly, but your application is still vulnerable, especially where it calls unmanaged code. Buffer overflows can allow an attacker to execute arbitrary code inside your Web application process, using its security context.

- **SQL injection**. This attack targets vulnerable data access code. The attacker sends SQL input that alters the intended query or executes completely new queries in the database. Forms authentication logon pages are common targets because the username and password are used to query the user store.

Vulnerabilities

Vulnerabilities that can lead to successful code injection attacks include:

- Weak or missing input validation or reliance on client-side input validation
- Including unvalidated input in HTML output
- Dynamically constructing SQL statements that do not use typed parameters
- Use of over-privileged process accounts and database logins

Countermeasures

The following countermeasures can be used to prevent code injection:

- Validate input so that an attacker cannot inject script code or cause buffer overflows.
- Encode all output that includes input. This prevents potentially malicious script tags from being interpreted as code by the client's browser.
- Use stored procedures that accept parameters to prevent malicious SQL input from being treated as executable statements by the database.
- Use least privileged process and impersonation accounts. This mitigates risk and reduces the damage that can be done if an attacker manages to execute code using the application's security context.

Session Hijacking

Session hijacking occurs when the attacker captures an authentication token and takes control of another user's session. Authentication tokens are often stored in cookies or in URLs. If the attacker captures the authentication token, he can transmit it to the application along with a request. The application associates the request with the legitimate user's session, which allows the attacker to gain access to the restricted areas of the application that require authenticated access. The attacker then assumes the identity and privileges of the legitimate user.

Vulnerabilities

Common vulnerabilities that make your Web pages and controls susceptible to session hijacking include:

- Unprotected session identifiers in URLs
- Mixing personalization cookies with authentication cookies
- Authentication cookies passed over unencrypted links

Attacks

Session hijacking attacks include:

- **Cookie replay**. The attacker captures the authentication cookie either by using network monitoring software or by some other means, for example, by exploiting an XSS scripting vulnerability.
- **Query string manipulation**. A malicious user changes the session identifier that is clearly visible in the URL query string.

Countermeasures

You can employ the following countermeasures to prevent session hijacking:

- Separate personalization and authentication cookies.
- Only transmit authentication cookies over HTTPS connections.
- Do not pass session identifiers that represent authenticated users in query strings.
- Re-authenticate the user before critical operations, such as order placement, money transfers, and so on, are performed.

Identity Spoofing

Identity spoofing occurs when a malicious user assumes the identity of a legitimate user so that he can access the application.

Vulnerabilities

Common vulnerabilities that make your Web pages and controls susceptible to an identity spoofing attack include:

- Authentication credentials that are passed over unencrypted links
- Authentication cookies that are passed over unencrypted links
- Weak passwords and policies
- Weak credential storage in the user store

Attacks

Identity spoofing attacks include:

- **Cookie replay**. The attacker steals the authentication cookie either by using network monitoring software or by using an XSS attack. The attacker then sends the cookie to the application to gain spoofed access.
- **Brute force password attacks**. The attacker repeatedly tries username and password combinations.
- **Dictionary attacks**. In this automated form of a brute force password attack, every word in a dictionary is tried as a password.

Countermeasures

You can employ the following countermeasures to prevent identity spoofing:

- Only transmit authentication credentials and cookies over HTTPS connections.
- Enforce strong passwords. Regular expressions can be used to ensure that user-supplied passwords meet suitable complexity requirements.
- Store password verifiers in the database. Store non-reversible password hashes combined with a random salt value to mitigate the risk of dictionary attacks.

For more information about storing password hashes and other secrets in the database, see Chapter 14, "Building Secure Data Access."

Parameter Manipulation

Parameters are the items of data that are passed from the client to the server over the network. They include form fields, query strings, view state, cookies, and HTTP headers. If sensitive data or data that is used to make security decisions on the server are passed using unprotected parameters, your application is potentially vulnerable to information disclosure or unauthorized access.

Vulnerabilities

Vulnerabilities that can lead to parameter manipulation include:

- Using hidden form fields or query strings that contain sensitive data
- Passing cookies that contain security-sensitive data over unencrypted connections

Attacks

Parameter manipulation attacks include:

- **Cookie replay attacks**. The attacker captures and alters a cookie and then replays it to the application. This can easily lead to identity spoofing and elevation or privileges if the cookie contains data that is used for authentication or authorization on the server.
- **Manipulation of hidden form fields**. These fields contain data used for security decisions on the server.
- **Manipulation of query string parameters**.

Countermeasures

You can employ the following countermeasures to prevent parameter manipulation:

- Do not rely on client-side state management options. Avoid using any of the client-side state management options such as view state, cookies, query strings or hidden form fields to store sensitive data.

- Store sensitive data on the server. Use a session token to associate the user's session with sensitive data items that are maintained on the server.

- Use a message authentication code (MAC) to protect the session token. Pair this with authentication, authorization, and business logic on the server to ensure that the token is not being replayed.

Network Eavesdropping

Network eavesdropping involves using network monitoring software to trace packets of data sent between browser and Web server. This can lead to the disclosure of application-specific confidential data, the retrieval of logon credentials, or the capture of authentication cookies.

Vulnerabilities

Vulnerabilities that can lead to successful network eavesdropping include:

- Lack of encryption when sending sensitive data
- Sending authentication cookies over unencrypted channels

Attacks

Network eavesdropping attacks are performed by using packet sniffing tools that are placed on the network to capture traffic.

Countermeasures

To counter network eavesdropping, use Secure Sockets Layer (SSL) to provide an encrypted communication channel between browser and Web server. It is imperative that SSL is used whenever credentials, authentication tickets, or sensitive application data are sent over the network.

Information Disclosure

Information disclosure occurs when an attacker probes your Web pages looking for ways to cause exception conditions. This can be a fruitful exercise for the attacker because exception details, which often are returned as HTML and displayed in the browser, can divulge extremely useful information, such as stack traces that contain database connection strings, database names, database schema information, SQL statements, and operating system and platform versions.

Vulnerabilities

Vulnerabilities that lead to information disclosure include:

- Weak exception handling
- Letting raw exception details propagate to the client

Attacks

There are many attacks that can result in information disclosure. These include:

- Buffer overflows.
- Sending deliberately malformed input.

Countermeasures

To prevent information disclosure:

- Use structured exception handling.
- Return generic error pages to the client.
- Use default redirect pages that contain generic and harmless error messages.

Design Considerations

Before you develop Web pages and controls, there are a number of important issues that you should consider at design time. The following are the key considerations:

- **Use server-side input validation.**
- **Partition your Web site.**
- **Consider the identity that is used for resource access.**
- **Protect credentials and authentication tickets.**
- **Fail securely.**
- **Consider authorization granularity.**
- **Place Web controls and user controls in separate assemblies.**
- **Place resource access code in a separate assembly.**

Use Server-Side Input Validation

At design time, identify all the various sources of user input that your Web pages and controls process. This includes form fields, query strings, and cookies received from the Web user, as well as data from back-end data sources. The Web user clearly lives outside your application's trust boundary, so all of the input from that source must be validated at the server. Unless you can absolutely trust the data retrieved from back-end data sources, that data should also be validated and sanitized before it is sent to the client. Make sure your solution does not rely on client-side validation because this is easily bypassed.

Partition Your Web Site

Your Web site design should clearly differentiate between publicly accessible areas and restricted areas that require authenticated access. Use separate subdirectories beneath your application's virtual root directory to maintain restricted pages, such as checkout functionality in a classic e-commerce Web site that requires authenticated access and transmits sensitive data such as credit card numbers. Separate subdirectories allow you to apply additional security (for example, by requiring SSL) without incurring SSL performance overhead across the entire site. It also allows you to mitigate the risk of session hijacking by restricting the transmission of authentication cookies to HTTPS connections. Figure 10.2 shows a typical partitioning.

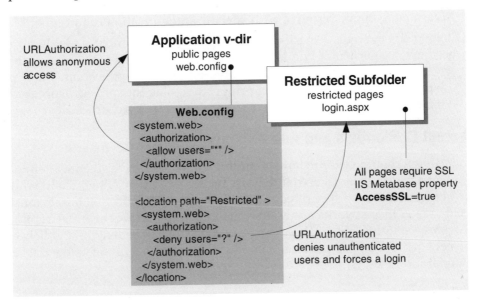

Figure 10.2
A Web site partitioned into public and secure areas

Note that in Figure 10.2, the restricted subfolder is configured in Internet Information Services (IIS) to require SSL access. The first **<authorization>** element in Web.config allows all users to access the public area, while the second element prevents unauthenticated users from accessing the contents of the secured subfolder and forces a login.

For more information about restricting authentication cookies so that they are passed only over HTTPS connections and about how to navigate between restricted and non-restricted pages, see "Use Absolute URLs for Navigation" in the "Authentication" section of this chapter.

Consider the Identity That Is Used for Resource Access

By default, ASP.NET applications do not impersonate, and the least privileged ASPNET process account is used to run ASP.NET Web applications and for resource access. The default is the recommended configuration. There are several situations in which you may want to use a different Windows security context for resource access. These include:

- **Hosting multiple applications on the same server**

    You can use IIS to configure each application to use a separate anonymous Internet user account and then enable impersonation. Each application then has a distinct identity for resource access. For more information about this approach, see Chapter 20, "Hosting Multiple Web Applications."

- **Accessing a remote resource with specific authentication requirements**

    If you need to access a specific remote resource (for example, a file share) and have been given a particular Windows account to use, you can use configure this account as the anonymous Web user account for your application. Then you can use programmatic impersonation prior to accessing the specific remote resource. For more information, see "Impersonation" later in this chapter.

Protect Credentials and Authentication Tickets

Your design should factor in how to protect credentials and authentication tickets. Credentials need to be secured if they are passed across the network and while they are in persistent stores such as configuration files. Authentication tickets must be secured over the network because they are vulnerable to hijacking. Encryption provides a solution. SSL or IPSec can be used to protect credentials and tickets over the network and DPAPI provides a good solution for encrypting credentials in configuration files.

Fail Securely

If your application fails with an unrecoverable exception condition, make sure that it fails securely and does not leave the system wide open. Make sure the exception details that are valuable to a malicious user are not allowed to propagate to the client and that generic error pages are returned instead. Plan to handle errors using structured exception handling, rather than relying on method error codes.

Consider Authorization Granularity

Consider the authorization granularity that you use in the authenticated parts of your site. If you have configured a directory to require authentication, should all users have equal access to the pages in that directory? If necessary, you can apply different authorization rules for separate pages based on the identity, or more commonly, the role membership of the caller, by using multiple **<authorization>** elements within separate **<location>** elements.

For example, two pages in the same directory can have different **<allow>** and **<deny>** elements in Web.config.

Place Web Controls and User Controls in Separate Assemblies

When Web controls and user controls are put in their own assemblies, you can configure security for each assembly independently by using code access security policy. This provides additional flexibility for the administrator and it means that you are not forced to grant extended permissions to all controls just to satisfy the requirements of a single control.

Place Resource Access Code in a Separate Assembly

Use separate assemblies and call them from your page classes rather than embedding resource access code in your page class event handlers. This provides greater flexibility for code access security policy and is particularly important for building partial-trust Web applications. For more information, see Chapter 9, "Using Code Access Security with ASP.NET."

Input Validation

If you make unfounded assumptions about the type, length, format, or range of input, your application is unlikely to be robust. Input validation can become a security issue if an attacker discovers that you have made unfounded assumptions. The attacker can then supply carefully crafted input that compromises your application. The misplaced trust of user input is one of the most common and devastating vulnerabilities in Web applications.

Constrain, Then Sanitize

Start by constraining input and check for known good data by validating for type, length, format, and range. Sometimes you also need to sanitize input and make potentially malicious input safe. For example, if your application supports free-format input fields, such as comment fields, you might want to permit certain "safe" HTML elements, such as <b> and <i>, and strip out any other HTML elements. The following table summarizes the options that are available for constraining and sanitizing data:

Table 10.1   Options for Constraining and Sanitizing Data

Requirement	Options
Type checks	.NET Framework type system. Parse string data, convert to a strong type, and then handle FormatExceptions.
	Regular expressions. Use ASP.NET **RegularExpressionValidator** control or **Regex** class.
Length checks	Regular expressions
	String.Length property
Format checks	Regular expressions for pattern matching
	.NET Framework type system
Range checks	ASP.NET **RangeValidator** control (supports currency, date, integer, double, and string data)
	Typed data comparisons

Regular Expressions

You can use regular expressions to restrict the range of valid characters, to strip unwanted characters, and to perform length and format checks. You can constrain input format by defining patterns that the input must match. ASP.NET provides the **RegularExpressionValidator** control and the **Regex** class is available from the **System.Text.RegularExpressions** namespace.

If you use the validator controls, validation succeeds if the control is empty. For mandatory fields, use a **RequiredFieldValidator**. Also, the regular expression validation implementation is slightly different on the client and server. On the client, the regular expression syntax of Microsoft JScript® development software is used. On the server, **System.Text.RegularExpressions.Regex** syntax is used. Since JScript regular expression syntax is a subset of **System.Text.RegularExpressions.Regex** syntax, it is recommended that JScript regular expression syntax be used to yield the same results on both the client and the server.

For more information about the full range of ASP.NET validator controls, refer to the .NET Framework documentation.

RegularExpressionValidator Control

To validate Web form field input, you can use the **RegularExpressionValidator** control. Drag the control onto a Web form and set its **ValidationExpression**, **ControlToValidate**, and **ErrorMessage** properties.

You can set the validation expression using the properties window in Microsoft Visual Studio .NET or you can set the property dynamically in the **Page_Load** event handler. The latter approach allows you to group together all of the regular expressions for all controls on the page.

Regex Class

If you use regular HTML controls with no **runat="server"** property (which rules out using the **RegularExpressionValidator** control), or you need to validate input from other sources such as query strings or cookies, you can use the **Regex** class either in your page class or in a validation helper method, possibly in a separate assembly. Some examples are shown later in this section.

Regular Expression Comments

Regular expressions are much easier to understand if you use the following syntax and comment each component of the expression using **#**. To enable comments, you must also specify **RegexOptions.IgnorePatternWhitespace**, which means that non-escaped white space is ignored.

```
Regex regex = new Regex(@"
            ^              # anchor at the start
            (?=.*\d)       # must contain at least one digit
            (?=.*[a-z])    # must contain one lowercase
            (?=.*[A-Z])    # must contain one uppercase
            .{8,10}        # From 8 to 10 characters in length
            $              # anchor at the end",
            RegexOptions.IgnorePatternWhitespace);
```

String Fields

To validate string fields, such as names, addresses, tax identification numbers, and so on, use regular expressions to do the following:

- Constrain the acceptable range of input characters.
- Apply formatting rules. For example, pattern-based fields, such as tax identification numbers, ZIP codes, or postal codes, require specific patterns of input characters.
- Check lengths.

Names

The following example shows a **RegularExpressionValidator** control that has been used to validate a name field.

```
<form id="WebForm" method="post" runat="server">
  <asp:TextBox id="txtName" runat="server"></asp:TextBox>
  <asp:RegularExpressionValidator id="nameRegex"runat="server"
      ControlToValidate="txtName"
      ValidationExpression="[a-zA-Z'.`-'\s]{1,40}"
      ErrorMessage="Invalid name">
  </asp:regularexpressionvalidator>
</form>
```

The preceding validation expression constrains the input name field to alphabetic characters (lowercase and uppercase), the single apostrophe for names such as O'Dell, and the dot character. In addition, the field length is constrained to 40 characters.

Social Security Numbers

The following example shows the HTML code that is generated for a **RegularExpressionValidator** control that has been used to validate a U.S. social security number form field:

```
<form id="WebForm" method="post" runat="server">
  <asp:TextBox id="txtSSN" runat="server"></asp:TextBox>
  <asp:RegularExpressionValidator id="ssnRegex" runat="server"
      ErrorMessage="Invalid social security number"
      ValidationExpression="\d{3}-\d{2}-\d{4}"
      ControlToValidate="txtSSN">
  </asp:RegularExpressionValidator>
</form>
```

The preceding validation expression is one of the standard expressions that Visual Studio .NET provides. It validates the format of the supplied input field as well as its type and length. The input must consist of three numeric digits followed by a dash, then two digits followed by a dash, and then four digits.

If you are not using server controls (which rule out the validator controls), or you need to validate input from sources other than form fields, you can use the **System.Text.RegularExpression.Regex** class in your method code. The following example shows how to validate the same field by using the static **Regex.IsMatch** method directly in the page class rather than using a validator control:

```
if (!Regex.IsMatch(txtSSN.Text, @"^\d{3}-\d{2}-\d{4}$"))
{
  // Invalid Social Security Number
}
```

Date Fields

Input fields that have an equivalent .NET Framework type can be type checked by the.NET Framework type system. For example, to validate a date, you can convert the input value to a variable of type **System.DateTime** and handle any resulting format exceptions if the input data is not compatible, as follows.

```
try
{
  DateTime dt = DateTime.Parse(txtDate.Text).Date;
}
// If the type conversion fails, a FormatException is thrown
catch( FormatException ex )
{
  // Return invalid date message to caller
}
```

In addition to format and type checks, you might need to perform a range check on a date field. This is easily performed using the **DateTime** variable, as follows.

```
// Exception handling is omitted for brevity
  DateTime dt = DateTime.Parse(txtDate.Text).Date;
  // The date must be today or earlier
  if ( dt > DateTime.Now.Date )
    throw new ArgumentException("Date must be in the past");
```

Numeric Fields

If you need to validate numeric data, for example, an age, perform type checks using the **int** type. To convert string input to integer form you can use **Int32.Parse** or **Convert.ToIn32**, and then handle any **FormatException** that occurs with an invalid data type, as follows:

```
try
{
  int i = Int32.Parse(txtAge.Text);
  . . .
}
catch( FormatException)
{
  . . .
}
```

Range Checks

Sometimes you need to validate that input data falls within a predetermined range. The following code uses an ASP.NET **RangeValidator** control to constrain input to whole numbers between 0 and 255. This example also uses the **RequiredFieldValidator**. Without the **RequiredFieldValidator**, the other validator controls accept blank input.

```
<form id="WebForm3" method="post" runat="server">
  <asp:TextBox id="txtNumber" runat="server"></asp:TextBox>
  <asp:RequiredFieldValidator
        id="rangeRegex"
        runat="server"
        ErrorMessage="Please enter a number between 0 and 255"
        ControlToValidate="txtNumber"
        style="LEFT: 10px; POSITION: absolute; TOP: 47px" >
  </asp:RequiredFieldValidator>
  <asp:RangeValidator
        id="RangeValidator1"
        runat="server"
        ErrorMessage="Please enter a number between 0 and 255"
        ControlToValidate="TextBox1"
        Type="Integer"
        MinimumValue="0"
        MaximumValue="255"
        style="LEFT: 10px; POSITION: absolute; TOP: 47px" >
  </asp:RangeValidator>
  <asp:Button id="Button1" style="LEFT: 10px; POSITION: absolute; TOP: 100px"
              runat="server" Text="Button"></asp:Button>
</form>
```

The following example shows how to validate range using the **Regex** class:

```
try
{
  // The conversion will raise an exception if not valid.
  int i = Convert.ToInt32(sInput);
  if ((0 <= i && i <= 255) == true)
  {
    // data is valid, use the number
  }
}
catch( FormatException )
{
  . . .
}
```

Sanitizing Input

Sanitizing is about making potentially malicious data safe. It can be helpful when the range of allowable input cannot guarantee that the input is safe. This might include stripping a null from the end of a user-supplied string or escaping values so they are treated as literals. If you need to sanitize input and convert or strip specific input characters, use **Regex.Replace**.

Note   Use this approach for defense in depth. Always start by constraining input to the set of known "good" values.

The following code strips out a range of potentially unsafe characters, including < > \ " ' % ; ( ) &.

```
private string SanitizeInput(string input)
{
  Regex badCharReplace = new Regex(@"^([<>""'%;()&])$");
  string goodChars = badCharReplace.Replace(input, "");
  return goodChars;
}
```

For more information about sanitizing free format input fields, such as comment fields, see "Sanitizing Free Format Input" under "Cross-Site Scripting," later in this chapter.

Validating HTML Controls

If you do not use server controls—that is, controls with the **runat="server"** attribute —and instead use regular HTML controls, you cannot use the ASP.NET validator controls. Instead, you can validate your Web pages' content by using regular expressions in the **Page_Load** event handler, as follows.

```
using System.Text.RegularExpressions;
. . .
private void Page_Load(object sender, System.EventArgs e)
{
  // Note that IsPostBack applies only for
  // server forms (with runat="server")
  if ( Request.RequestType == "POST" ) // non-server forms
  {
    // Validate the supplied email address
    if( !Regex.Match(Request.Form["email"],
        @"^\w+([-+.]\w+)*@\w+([-.]\w+)*\.\w+([-.]\w+)*$",
        RegexOptions.None).Success)
    {
      // Invalid email address
    }
```

(continued)

(continued)

```
  // Validate the supplied name
  if ( !RegEx.Match(Request.Form["name"],
      @"^[A-Za-z'\- ]$",
      RegexOptions.None).Success)
  {
    // Invalid name
  }
  }
}
```

Validating Input Used for Data Access

If you are generating dynamic SQL queries based on user input, a SQL injection attack can inject malicious SQL commands that can be executed by the database. In a typical Web-based data access scenario, the following defense in depth strategy can be used:

- Use regular expressions to constrain input within your page class.
- Sanitize or reject input. For defense in depth, you can choose to use a helper method to strip null characters or other known bad characters.
- Use parameterized stored procedures for data access to ensure that type and length checks are performed on the data used in SQL queries.

For more information about using parameters for data access and about writing secure data access code, see Chapter 14, "Building Secure Data Access."

Validating Input Used For File I/O

In general, you should avoid writing code that accepts file input or path input from the caller. Instead, use fixed file names and locations when reading and writing data. This ensures that your code cannot be coerced into accessing arbitrary files. It also ensures that your code is not vulnerable to canonicalization bugs.

If you do need to accept input file names, there are two main challenges. First, is the resulting file path and name a valid file system name? Second, is the path valid in the context of your application? For example, is it beneath the application's virtual directory root?

To canonicalize the file name, use **System.IO.Path.GetFullPath**. To check that the file path is valid in the context of your application, you can use .NET code access security to grant the precise **FileIOPermission** to your code so that is able to access only files from specific directories. For more information, see the "File I/O" sections in Chapter 7, "Building Secure Assemblies" and Chapter 8, "Code Access Security in Practice."

Using MapPath

If you use **MapPath** to map a supplied virtual path to a physical path on the server, use the overload of **Request.MapPath** that accepts a **bool** parameter so that you can prevent cross application mapping, as follows:

```
try
{
  string mappedPath = Request.MapPath( inputPath.Text,
                                 Request.ApplicationPath, false);

}
catch (HttpException)
{
  // Cross-application mapping attempted
}
```

The final **false** parameter prevents cross-application mapping. This means that a user cannot successfully supply a path that contains ".." to traverse outside of your application's virtual directory hierarchy. Any attempt to do so results in an exception of type **HttpException**.

Note Server controls can use the **Control.MapPathSecure** method to read files. This method requires that the calling code is granted full trust by code access security policy; otherwise an **HttpException** is thrown. For more information, see **Control.MapPathSecure** in the .NET Framework SDK documentation.

Common Regular Expressions

Visual Studio .NET provides a set of useful regular expressions. To access them, add a **RegularExpresssionValidator** control to a Web form and click the ellipsis button in the control's **Expression** property field. The following table shows several additional useful expressions for commonly used Web page fields.

Table 10.2 Useful Regular Expression Fields

Field	Expression	Format Samples	Description
Name	^[a-zA-Z'`-´\s]{1,40}$	John Doe O'Dell	Validates a name. Allows up to 40 uppercase and lowercase characters and a few special characters that are common to some names. This list can be tailored.
Numbers	^\D?(\d{3})\D?\D?(\d{3})\D?(\d{4})$	(425)-555-0123 425-555-0123 425 555 0123	Validates a U.S. phone number.

(continued)

Table 10.2   Useful Regular Expression Fields *(continued)*

Field	Expression	Format Samples	Description
E-mail	^\w+([-+.]\w+)*@\w+([-.]\w+)*\.\w+([-.]\w+)*$	*someone@ example.com*	Validates an e-mail address.
URL	^(http|https|ftp)\://[a-zA-Z 0-9\-\.]+\.[a-zA-Z]{2,3} (:[a-zA-Z0-9]*)?/?([a-zA-Z 0-9\-\._\?\,\'/\\\+&%\$# \=~])*$		Validates a URL.
Zip Code	^(\d{5}-\d{4}|\d{5}|\d{9}) $\|^([a-zA-Z]\d[a-zA-Z] \d[a-zA-Z]\d)$		Validates a U.S. ZIP code allowing 5 or 9 digits.
Password	^(?=.*\d)(?=.*[a-z])(?=.* [A-Z]).{8,10}$		Validates a strong password. Must be between 8 and 10 characters. Must contain a combination of uppercase, lowercase, and numeric digits, with no special characters.
Non- negative integers	\d+	0 986	Validates for integers greater than zero.
Currency (non- negative)	"\d+(\.\d\d)?"		Validates for a positive currency amount. Requires two digits after the decimal point.
Currency (positive or negative)	"(-)?\d+(\.\d\d)?"		Validates for a positive or negative currency amount. Requires two digits after the decimal point.

Cross-Site Scripting

XSS attacks exploit vulnerabilities in Web page validation by injecting client-side script code. This code is subsequently sent back to an unsuspecting user and executed by the browser. Because the browser downloads the script code from a trusted site, the browser has no way of identifying that the code is not legitimate, and Internet Explorer security zones provide no defense. XSS attacks also work over HTTP or HTTPS (SSL) connections. One of the most serious exploits occurs when an attacker writes script to retrieve the authentication cookie that provides access to the trusted site and posts it to a Web address known to the attacker. This allows the attacker to spoof the legitimate user's identity and gain illicit access to the Web site.

Use the following countermeasures to prevent XSS attacks:

● **Validate input**
● **Encode output**

Validate Input

Validate any input that is received from outside your application's trust boundary for type, length, format, and range using the various techniques described previously in this chapter.

Encode Output

If you write text output to a Web page and you do not know with absolute certainty that the text does not contain HTML special characters (such as <, >, and &), then make sure to pre-process it using the **HttpUtility.HtmlEncode** method. Do this even if the text came from user input, a database, or a local file. Similarly, use **HttpUtility.UrlEncode** to encode URL strings.

The **HtmlEncode** method replaces characters that have special meaning in HTML to HTML variables that represent those characters. For example, < is replaced with **&lt** and " is replaced with **&quot**. Encoded data does not cause the browser to execute code. Instead, the data is rendered as harmless HTML.

```
Response.Write(HttpUtility.HtmlEncode(Request.Form["name"]));
```

Data-Bound Controls

Data-bound Web controls do not encode output. The only control that encodes output is the **TextBox** control when its **TextMode** property is set to **MultiLine**. If you bind any other control to data that has malicious XSS code, the code will be executed on the client. As a result, if you retrieve data from a database and you cannot be certain that the data is valid (perhaps because it is a database that is shared with other applications), encode the data before you pass it back to the client.

Sanitizing Free Format Input

If your Web page includes a free-format text box, such as a "comments" field, in which you want to permit certain safe HTML elements such as <b> and <i>, you can handle this safely by first pre-processing with **HtmlEncode**, and then selectively removing the encoding on the permitted elements, as follows:

```
StringBuilder sb = new StringBuilder( HttpUtility.HtmlEncode(userInput) ) ;
sb.Replace("&lt;b&gt;", "<b>");
sb.Replace("&lt;/b&gt;", "</b>");
sb.Replace("&lt;i&gt;", "<i>");
sb.Replace("&lt;/i&gt;", "</i>");
Response.Write(sb.ToString());
```

Defense in Depth Countermeasures

In addition to the techniques discussed earlier, use the following countermeasures for defense in depth to prevent XSS:

- Set the correct character encoding.
- Use the ASP.NET version 1.1 validateRequest option.
- Install URLScan on your Web server.
- Use the HttpOnly cookie option.
- Use the <frame> security attribute.
- Use the innerText property.

Set the Correct Character Encoding

To successfully restrict what data is valid for your Web pages, it is important to limit the ways in which the input data can be represented. This prevents malicious users from using canonicalization and multi-byte escape sequences to trick your input validation routines.

ASP.NET allows you to specify the character set at the page level or at the application level by using the **<globalization>** element in Web.config. Both approaches are shown below using the ISO-8859-1 character encoding, which is the default in early versions of HTML and HTTP.

To set the character encoding at the page level, use the **<meta>** element or the **ResponseEncoding** page-level attribute as follows:

```
<meta http-equiv="Content Type"
      content="text/html; charset=ISO-8859-1" />
```

OR

```
<% @ Page ResponseEncoding="ISO-8859-1" %>
```

To set the character encoding in Web.config, use the following configuration:

```
<configuration>
   <system.web>
      <globalization
         requestEncoding="ISO-8859-1"
         responseEncoding="ISO-8859-1"/>
   </system.web>
</configuration>
```

Validating Unicode Characters

Use the following code to validate Unicode characters in a page:

```
using System.Text.RegularExpressions;
. . .
private void Page_Load(object sender, System.EventArgs e)
{
  // Name must contain between 1 and 40 alphanumeric characters
  // together with (optionally) special characters '`´ for names such
  // as D'Angelo
  if (!Regex.IsMatch(Request.Form["name"], @"^[\p{L}\p{Zs}\p{Lu}\p{Ll}]{1,40}$"))
    throw new ArgumentException("Invalid name parameter");
  // Use individual regular expressions to validate other parameters
  . . .
}
```

The following explains the regular expression shown in the preceding code:

- **{<name>}** specifies a named Unicode character class.
- **\p{<name>}** matches any character in the named character class specified by **{<name>}**.
- **{L}** performs a left-to-right match.
- **{Lu}** performs a match of uppercase.
- **{Ll}** performs a match of lowercase.
- **{Zs}** matches separator and space.
- **{1,40}** means no less that 1 and no more than 40 characters.
- **{Mn}** matches mark and non-spacing characters.
- **{Zs}** matches separator and space.
- ***** specifies zero or more matches.
- **$** means stop looking at this position.

Use the ASP.NET validateRequest Option

The **validateRequest** attribute is a .NET Framework version 1.1 feature. This attribute is set to true by default on the **<pages>** element in Machine.config. It instructs ASP.NET to examine all data received from the browser for potentially malicious input, for example, input that contains **<script>** elements. ASP.NET examines input received from HTML form fields, cookies, and query strings. .NET Framework version 1.0 does not provide any equivalent functionality, but the IIS URLScan Internet Server Application Programming Interface (ISAPI) filter can perform a similar job. You can also apply the setting to each page using the @ **Page** tag, as follows:

```
<% @ Page validateRequest="True" %>
```

Install URLScan on Your Web Server

URLScan is an ISAPI filter that is installed when you run the IISLockdown tool. This helps mitigate the threat of XSS attacks by rejecting potentially malicious input. For more information about IISLockdown and URLScan, see Chapter 16, "Securing Your Web Server."

Note   IIS 6.0 on Windows Server 2003 has functionality equivalent to URLScan built in.

Use the HttpOnly Cookie Option

Internet Explorer 6 Service Pack 1 supports a new **HttpOnly** cookie attribute, which prevents client-side script from accessing the cookie from the **document.cookie** property. Instead, an empty string is returned. The cookie is still sent to the server whenever the user browses to a Web site in the current domain.

Note   Web browsers that do not support the **HttpOnly** cookie attribute either ignore the cookie or ignore the attribute, which means it is still subject to XSS attacks.

The **System.Net.Cookie** class does not currently support an **HttpOnly** property. To add an **HttpOnly** attribute to the cookie, you need to use an ISAPI filter, or if you want a managed code solution, add the following code to your application's **Application_EndRequest** event handler in Global.asax:

```
protected void Application_EndRequest(Object sender, EventArgs e)
{
  string authCookie = FormsAuthentication.FormsCookieName;
  foreach (string sCookie in Response.Cookies)
  {
    // Just set the HttpOnly attribute on the Forms authentication cookie
    // Skip this check to set the attribute on all cookies in the collection
    if (sCookie.Equals(authCookie))
    {
      // Force HttpOnly to be added to the cookie header
      Response.Cookies[sCookie].Path += ";HttpOnly";
    }
  }
}
```

Note   A future version of the .NET Framework is likely to have an **HttpOnly** property on the **Cookie** class.

Use the <frame> Security Attribute

Internet Explorer 6 and later supports a new **security** attribute on the **<frame>** and **<iframe>** elements. You can use the **security** attribute to apply the user's Restricted Sites Internet Explorer security zone settings to an individual **frame** or **iframe**. By default, the Restricted Sites zone doesn't support script execution. If you use the **security** attribute, it must currently be set to "restricted" as shown below:

```
<frame security="restricted" src="http://www.somesite.com/somepage.htm"></frame>
```

Use the innerText Property

If you create a page with untrusted input, use the **innerText** property instead of **innerHTML**. The **innerText** property renders content safe and ensures that script is not executed.

Authentication

Weak authentication increases the identity spoofing threat. If a user's logon credentials fall into the wrong hands, an attacker can spoof the user's identity and gain access to the application. The attacker shares all of the user's privileges in the application. Credentials must be protected as they are passed over the network and while they are persistent, for example, in the application's user store. The authentication cookie that represents an authenticated identity to the application after the initial logon must also be protected to mitigate the risk of session hijacking and cookie replay attacks.

Forms Authentication

The threat of session hijacking and cookie replay attacks is particularly significant for applications that use Forms authentication. You must take particular care when querying the database using the user-supplied credentials to ensure that you are not vulnerable to SQL injection. Additionally, to prevent identity spoofing, you should make sure that the user store is secure and that strong passwords are enforced.

The following fragment shows a "secure" Forms authentication configuration in . Web.config:

```
<forms loginUrl="Restricted\login.aspx"    Login page in an SSL protected folder
       protection="All"                     Privacy and integrity
       requireSSL="true"                    Prevents cookie being sent over http
       timeout="10"                         Limited session lifetime
       name="AppNameCookie"                 Unique per-application name
       path="/FormsAuth"                       and path
       slidingExpiration="true" >           Sliding session lifetime
</forms>
```

The following recommendations help you build a secure Forms authentication solution:

- **Partition your Web site.**
- **Secure restricted pages with SSL.**
- **Use URL Authorization.**
- **Secure the authentication cookie.**
- **Use absolute URLs for navigation.**
- **Use secure credential management.**

Partition Your Web Site

In your site design, make sure that secure pages that require authenticated access are placed in a subdirectory that is separate from the anonymously accessible pages. Figure 10.3 shows a typical arrangement in the Visual Studio .NET Solution Explorer window. Notice how the Forms login page is placed along with other restricted pages in a separate subdirectory.

Figure 10.3

Subdirectory for restricted pages that require authenticated access

---

Note   If you are using **Server.Transfer** in your application to transfer from an anonymous page to a secure page, .NET Framework version 1.1 or earlier bypasses authentication checks, so code that uses **Server.Transfer** should be verified to ensure that it does not transfer to a secure directory.

Secure Restricted Pages with SSL

To ensure that SSL is used to protect the logon credentials that are posted from the login form, and that the authentication cookie passed on subsequent requests to restricted pages, configure the secure folders in IIS to require SSL. This sets the **AccessSSL=true** attribute for the folder in the IIS metabase. Requests for pages in the secured folders will only be successful if https is used on the request URL.

For SSL, you must have a server certificate installed on the Web server. For more information, see "How To: Setup SSL on a Web Server" in the "How To" section of "Microsoft *patterns & practices* Volume I, *Building Secure ASP.NET Applications: Authentication, Authorization, and Secure Communication*" at *http://msdn.microsoft.com/library/default.asp?url=/library/en-us/dnnetsec/html /secnetlpMSDN.asp*.

Use URL Authorization

To allow anonymous access to public pages, use the following **<authorization>** element.

```
<system.web>
    <!-- The virtual directory root folder contains general pages.
         Unauthenticated users can view them and they do not need
         to be secured with SSL. -->
    <authorization>
      <allow users="*" />
    </authorization>
</system.web>
```

Use the following **<authorization>** element inside a **<location>** element in Web.config to deny access to unauthenticated users and force a redirect to the login page that is specified on the **<forms>** element:

```
<!-- The restricted folder is for authenticated and SSL access only. -->
<location path="Secure" >
  <system.web>
    <authorization>
      <deny users="?" />
    </authorization>
  </system.web>
</location>
```

Secure the Authentication Cookie

To prevent session hijacking and cookie replay attacks, secure the cookie by making sure that it is only passed over SSL connections using the HTTPS protocol. For additional risk mitigation, encrypt the cookie before sending it to the client and limit the period for which the cookie is valid. To secure the authentication cookie:

- **Restrict the authentication cookie to HTTPS connections.**
- **Encrypt the cookie.**
- **Limit cookie lifetime.**
- **Consider using a fixed expiration period.**
- **Do not persist authentication cookies.**
- **Keep authentication and personalization cookies separate.**
- **Use distinct cookie names and paths.**

Restrict the Authentication Cookie-to-HTTPS Connections

Cookies support a "secure" property that determines whether or not browsers should send the cookie back to the server. With the secure property set, the cookie is sent by the browser only to a secure page that is requested using an HTTPS URL.

If you are using .NET Framework version 1.1, set the secure property by using **requireSSL="true"** on the **<forms>** element as follows:

```
<forms loginUrl="Secure\Login.aspx"
        requireSSL="true" . . . />
```

If you are using .NET Framework version 1.0, set the secure property manually in the **Application_EndRequest** event handler in Global.asax using the following code:

```
protected void Application_EndRequest(Object sender, EventArgs e)
{
  string authCookie = FormsAuthentication.FormsCookieName;

  foreach (string sCookie in Response.Cookies)
  {
    if (sCookie.Equals(authCookie))
    {
      // Set the cookie to be secure. Browsers will send the cookie
      // only to pages requested with https
      Response.Cookies[sCookie].Secure = true;
    }
  }
}
```

Encrypt the Cookie

Encrypt the cookie contents even if you are using SSL. This prevents an attacker from viewing or modifying the cookie if he or she manages to steal it through a XSS exploit. In this event, the attacker can still use the cookie to gain access to your application. The best way to mitigate this risk is to implement the appropriate countermeasures to prevent XSS attacks (described under "Cross-Site Scripting" earlier in this chapter), and limit the cookie lifetime as described in the next recommendation.

To provide privacy and integrity for the cookie, set the **protection** attribute on the **<forms>** element as follows:

```
<forms protection="All"    Privacy and integrity
```

Limit Cookie Lifetime

Limit the cookie lifetime to reduce the time window in which an attacker can use a captured cookie to gain spoofed access to your application.

```
<forms timeout="10"               Reduced cookie lifetime (10 minutes)
```

Consider Using a Fixed Expiration Period

Consider setting **slidingExpiration="false"** on the **<forms>** element to fix the cookie expiration, rather than resetting the expiration period after each Web request. This is particularly important if you are not using SSL to protect the cookie.

Note   This feature is available with .NET Framework version 1.1.

Do not Persist Authentication Cookies

Do not persist authentication cookies because they are stored in the user's profile and can be stolen if an attacker gets physical access to the user's computer. You can specify a non-persistent cookie when you create the **FormsAuthenticationTicket** as follows:

```
FormsAuthenticationTicket ticket =
          new FormsAuthenticationTicket(
              1,                             // version
              Context.User.Identity.Name,    // user name
              DateTime.Now,                  // issue time
              DateTime.Now.AddMinutes(15),   // expires every 15 mins
              false,                         // do not persist the cookie
              roleStr );                     // user roles
```

Keep Authentication and Personalization Cookies Separate

Keep personalization cookies that contain user-specific preferences and non-sensitive data separate from authentication cookies. A stolen personalization cookie might not represent a security threat, whereas an attacker can use a stolen authentication cookie to gain access to your application.

Use Distinct Cookie Names and Paths

Use unique **name** and **path** attribute values on the **<forms>** element. By ensuring unique names, you prevent possible problems that can occur when hosting multiple applications on the same server. For example, if you don't use distinct names, it is possible for a user who is authenticated in one application to make a request to another application without being redirected to that application's logon page.

For more information, see Microsoft Knowledge Base articles 313116, "PRB: Forms Authentication Requests Are Not Directed to loginUrl Page," and 310415, "PRB: Mobile Forms Authentication and Different Web Applications."

Use Absolute URLs for Navigation

Navigating between the public and restricted areas of your site (that is, between HTTP and HTTPS pages) is an issue because a redirect always uses the protocol (HTTPS or HTTP) of the current page, not the target page.

Once a user logs on and browses pages in a directory that is secured with SSL, relative links such as "..\publicpage.aspx" or redirects to HTTP pages result in the pages being served using the https protocol, which incurs an unnecessary performance overhead. To avoid this, use absolute links such as "http://servername /appname/publicpage.aspx" when redirecting from an HTTPS page to an HTTP page.

Similarly, when you redirect to a secure page (for example, the login page) from a public area of your site, you must use an absolute HTTPS path, such as "https://servername/appname/secure/login.aspx", rather than a relative path, such as restricted/login.aspx. For example, if your Web page provides a logon button, use the following code to redirect to the secure login page.

```
private void btnLogon_Click( object sender, System.EventArgs e )
{
    // Form an absolute path using the server name and v-dir name
    string serverName =
            HttpUtility.UrlEncode(Request.ServerVariables["SERVER_NAME"]);
    string vdirName = Request.ApplicationPath;
    Response.Redirect("https://" + serverName + vdirName +
                    "/Restricted/Login.aspx");
}
```

Use Secure Credential Management

Identity spoofing is one of the most common authentication-related threats to your application. Identity spoofing occurs when an attacker gains access to the application under the guise of another user. One way to do this is to hijack the session cookie, but if you have secured the authentication cookie as described earlier, the risk is significantly reduced. In addition, you must build secure credential management and a secure user store to mitigate the risk posed by brute force password attacks, dictionary attacks, and SQL injection attacks.

The following recommendations help you reduce risk:

- **Use one-way hashes for passwords.**
- **Use strong passwords.**
- **Prevent SQL injection.**

Use One-Way Hashes for Passwords

If your user store is SQL Server, store one-way password digests (hash values) with an added random salt value. The added salt value mitigates the risk of brute force password cracking attempts, for example, dictionary attacks. The digest approach means you never actually store passwords. Instead, you retrieve the password from the user and validate it by recalculating the digest and comparing it with the stored value.

Use Strong Passwords

Use regular expressions to ensure that user passwords conform to strong password guidelines. The following regular expression can be used to ensure that passwords are between 8 and 10 characters in length and contain a mixture of uppercase, lowercase, numeric, and special characters. This further mitigates the dictionary attack risk.

```
private bool IsStrongPassword( string password )
{
    return Regex.IsMatch(password, @"^(?=.*\d)(?=.*[a-z])(?=.*[A-Z]).{8,10}$");
}
```

Prevent SQL Injection

Forms authentication is especially prone to vulnerabilities that lead to SQL injection attacks because of the way that the user-supplied logon credentials are used to query the database. To mitigate the risk:

- Thoroughly validate the supplied credentials. Use regular expressions to make sure they do not include SQL characters.
- Use parameterized stored procedures to access the user store database.
- Use a login to the database that is restricted and least privileged.

For more information about preventing SQL injection, see Chapter 14, "Building Secure Data Access."

Authorization

You can use authorization to control access to directories, individual Web pages, page classes, and methods. If required, you can also include authorization logic in your method code. When you build authorization into your Web pages and controls, consider the following recommendations:

- Use URL authorization for page and directory access control.
- Use File authorization with Windows authentication.
- Use principal demands on classes and methods.
- Use explicit role checks for fine-grained authorization.

Use URL Authorization for Page and Directory Access Control

For page-level and directory-level access control, use URL authorization, which is configured by the **<authorization>** element. To restrict access to specific files or directories, place the **<authorization>** element inside a **<location>** element.

For more information, see "Authorization" in Chapter 19, "Securing Your ASP.NET Application and Web Services."

Use File Authorization with Windows Authentication

If ASP.NET is configured for Windows authentication, the **FileAuthorizationModule** checks all requests for ASP.NET file types. This includes ASP.NET page files (.aspx), user controls (.ascx), and any other file type mapped by IIS to the ASP.NET ISAPI filter.

To configure the **FileAuthorizationModule**, set the appropriate Windows access control lists (ACLs) on the ASP.NET files.

Use Principal Demands on Classes and Methods

Principal permission demands allow you to make authorization decisions based on the identity and role membership of the caller. The caller's identity and role membership is maintained by the principal object that is associated with the current Web request (accessed through **HttpContext.User**). Use declarative security attributes to provide access controls on classes and methods, as follows:

```
// Declarative syntax
[PrincipalPermission(SecurityAction.Demand,
        Role=@"DomainName\WindowsGroup")]
public void SomeRestrictedMethod()
{
}
```

Use Explicit Role Checks for Fine-Grained Authorization

Declarative security checks prevent a user from accessing a class or calling a specific method. If you need additional logic inside a method to make authorization decisions, either use imperative principal permission demands or explicit role checks using **IPrincipal.IsInRole**. These approaches allow you to use additional runtime variables to fine tune the authorization decision. The following example shows the use of an imperative principal permission demand:

```
// Imperative syntax
public void SomeRestrictedMethod()
{
  // Only callers that are members of the specified Windows group
  // are allowed access
  PrincipalPermission permCheck = new PrincipalPermission(
                                  null, @"DomainName\WindowsGroup");

  permCheck.Demand();
  // Some restricted operations (omitted)
}
```

The following example shows the use of **IPrincipal.IsInRole**:

```
public void TransferMoney( string fromAccount,
                           string toAccount, double amount)
{
  // Extract the authenticated user from the current HTTP context.
  // The User variable is equivalent to HttpContext.Current.User if you
  // are using an .aspx page (or .asmx)
  WindowsPrincipal authenticatedUser = User as WindowsPrincipal;
  if (null != authenticatedUser)
  {
    // Note:  To retrieve the authenticated user's username, use the
    // following line of code
    // string username = authenticatedUser.Identity.Name;
    // If the amount exceeds a threshold value, manager approval is required
    if (amount > thresholdValue) {
      // Perform a role check
      if (authenticatedUser.IsInRole(@"DomainName\Manager") )
      {
        // OK to proceed with transfer
      }
      else
      {
        throw new Exception("Unauthorized funds transfer");
      }
    }
    else
    {
      . . .
    }
  }
}
```

You may also have a method that allows callers from several different roles. However, you might want to subsequently call a different method, which is not possible with declarative security.

Impersonation

By default, ASP.NET applications usually do not impersonate the original caller for design, implementation, and scalability reasons. For example, impersonating prevents effective middle-tier connection pooling, which can have a severe impact on application scalability.

In certain scenarios, you might require impersonation (for example, if you require an alternate identity (non-process identity) for resource access). In hosting environments, multiple anonymous identities are often used as a form of application isolation. For example, if your application uses Forms or Passport authentication, you can impersonate the anonymous Internet user account associated by IIS with your application's virtual directory.

You can impersonate the original caller, which might be the anonymous Internet user account or a fixed identity. To impersonate the original caller (the IIS authenticated identity), use the following configuration:

```
<identity impersonate="true" />
```

To impersonate a fixed identity, use additional **userName** and **password** attributes on the <**identity**> element, but make sure you use Aspnet_setreg.exe to store encrypted credentials in the registry. For more information about encrypting credentials in configuration files and about Aspnet_setreg.exe, see Chapter 19, "Securing Your ASP.NET Application and Web Services."

Using Programmatic Impersonation

If you do not want to impersonate an account for the entire request, you can use programmatic impersonation to impersonate for a portion of the request. For example, you want to use the ASP.NET process account to access you application's primary resources and downstream database, but you need to access an alternate resource, such as another remote database or a remote file share, using an alternate identity.

To do this, use IIS to configure the anonymous user account as the trusted alternate identity. Then use the following code to create an impersonation token using the anonymous account only while you execute your remote resource access code:

```
HttpContext context = HttpContext.Current;
// Get the service provider from the context
IServiceProvider iServiceProvider = context as IServiceProvider;
//Get a Type which represents an HttpContext
Type httpWorkerRequestType = typeof(HttpWorkerRequest);
// Get the HttpWorkerRequest service from the service provider
// NOTE:  When trying to get a HttpWorkerRequest type from the HttpContext
// unmanaged code permission is demanded.
HttpWorkerRequest httpWorkerRequest =
      iServiceProvider.GetService(httpWorkerRequestType) as HttpWorkerRequest;
// Get the token passed by IIS
IntPtr ptrUserToken = httpWorkerRequest.GetUserToken();
// Create a WindowsIdentity from the token
WindowsIdentity winIdentity = new WindowsIdentity(ptrUserToken);
// Impersonate the user
Response.Write("Before impersonation: " +
              WindowsIdentity.GetCurrent().Name + "<br>");
WindowsImpersonationContext impContext = winIdentity.Impersonate();
Response.Write("Impersonating: " + WindowsIdentity.GetCurrent().Name + "<br>");
// Place resource access code here

// Stop impersonating
impContext.Undo();
Response.Write( "After Impersonating: " +
              WindowsIdentity.GetCurrent().Name + "<br>");
```

Note This approach assumes Forms or Passport authentication where your application's virtual directory is configured in IIS to support anonymous access.

If you use this code, use the following **<identity>** configuration:

```
<identity impersonate="false" />
```

Note The code demands the unmanaged code permission **SecurityPermission(SecurityPermissionFlag.UnmanagedCode)**, which is granted only to fully trusted Web applications.

Sensitive Data

Sensitive data includes application configuration details (for example, connection strings and service account credentials) and application-specific data (for example, customer credit card numbers). The following recommendations help to reduce risk when you handle sensitive data:

- **Do not pass sensitive data from page to page.**
- **Avoid plain text passwords in configuration files.**
- **Use DPAPI to avoid key management.**
- **Do not cache sensitive data.**

Do not Pass Sensitive Data from Page to Page

Avoid using any of the client-side state management options, such as view state, cookies, query strings, or hidden form-field variables, to store sensitive data. The data can be tampered with and viewed in clear text. Use server-side state management options, such as a SQL Server database for secure data exchange.

Avoid Plaintext Passwords in Configuration Files

The **<processModel>**, **<sessionState>**, and **<identity>** elements in Machine.config and Web.config have **userName** and **password** attributes. Do not store these in plaintext. Store encrypted credentials in the registry using the Aspnet_setreg.exe tool.

For more information about encrypting credentials in configuration files and about Aspnet_setreg.exe, see Chapter 19, "Securing Your ASP.NET Application and Web Services."

Use DPAPI to Avoid Key Management

DPAPI is ideally suited for encrypting secrets such as connection strings and service account credentials. If your pages need to use this type of configuration data, use DPAPI to avoid the key management problem.

For more information see "Cryptography" in Chapter 7, "Building Secure Assemblies."

Do Not Cache Sensitive Data

If your page contains data that is sensitive, such as a password, credit card number, or account status, the page should not be cached. Output caching is off by default.

Session Management

There are two main factors that you should consider to provide secure session management. First, ensure that the session token cannot be used to gain access to sensitive pages where secure operations are performed or to gain access to sensitive items of data. Second, if the session data contains sensitive items, you must secure the session data, including the session store.

The following two types of tokens are associated with session management:

- **The session token**. This token is generated automatically by ASP.NET if session state is enabled, for example, by setting the **mode** attribute of the **<sessionState>** element to **InProc**, **SQLServer**, or **StateServer**.

> **Note** You can override the **<sessionState>** configuration and disable or enable session state on a per-page basis using the **EnableSessionState** attribute on the **@Page** tag.

- **The authentication token**. This is generated by authentication mechanisms, such as Forms authentication, to track an authenticated user's session. With a valid authentication token, a user can gain access to the restricted parts of your Web site.

The following recommendations help you build secure session management:

- **Require authentication for sensitive pages**.
- **Do not rely on client-side state management options**.
- **Do not mix session tokens and authentication tokens**.
- **Use SSL effectively**.
- **Secure the session data**.

Require Authentication for Sensitive Pages

Make sure that you authenticate users before allowing them access to the sensitive and restricted parts of your site. If you use secure authentication and protect the authentication token with SSL, then a user's session is secure because an attacker cannot hijack and replay a session token. The attacker would need the authentication token to get past the authorization gates.

For more information about how to secure the authentication token for Forms authentication, see "Forms Authentication" earlier in this chapter.

Do Not Rely on Client-Side State Management Options

Avoid using any of the client-side state management options, such as view state, cookies, query strings, or hidden form fields, to store sensitive data. The information can be tampered with or seen in clear text. Use server-side state management options, for example, a database, to store sensitive data.

Do Not Mix Session Tokens and Authentication Tokens

Secure session management requires that you do not mix the two types of tokens. First, secure the authentication token to make sure an attacker cannot capture it and use it to gain access to the restricted areas of your application. Second, build your application in such a way that the session token alone cannot be used to gain access to sensitive pages or data. The session token should be used only for personalization purposes or to maintain the user state across multiple HTTP requests. Without authentication, do not maintain sensitive items of the user state.

Use SSL Effectively

If your site has secure areas and public access areas, you must protect the secure authenticated areas with SSL. When a user moves back and forth between secure and public areas, the ASP.NET-generated session cookie (or URL if you have enabled cookie-less session state) moves with them in plaintext, but the authentication cookie is never passed over unencrypted HTTP connections as long as the **Secure** cookie property is set.

Note   You can set the **Secure** property for a Forms authentication cookie by setting **requireSSL="true"** on the **<forms>** element.

An attacker is able to obtain a session cookie passed over an unencrypted HTTP session, but if you have designed your site correctly and place restricted pages and resources in a separate and secure directory, the attacker can use it to access only to the non-secure, public access pages. In this event, there is no security threat because these pages do not perform sensitive operations. Once the attacker tries to replay the session token to a secured page, because there is no authentication token, the attacker is redirected to the application's login page.

For more information about using the **Secure** cookie property and how to build secure Forms authentication solutions, see "Forms Authentication" earlier in this chapter.

Secure the Session Data

If the session data on the server contains sensitive items, the data and the store needs to be secured. ASP.NET supports several session state modes. For information about how to secure ASP.NET session state, see "Session State" in Chapter 19, "Securing Your ASP.NET Application and Web Services."

Parameter Manipulation

Parameters, such as those found in form fields, query strings, view state, and cookies, can be manipulated by attackers who usually intend to gain access to restricted pages or trick the application into performing an unauthorized operation.

For example, if an attacker knows that you are using a weak authentication token scheme such as a guessable number within a cookie, the attacker can construct a cookie with another number and make a request as a different (possibly privileged) user.

The following recommendations help you avoid parameter manipulation vulnerabilities:

- **Protect view state with MACs.**
- **Use Page.ViewStateUserKey to counter one-click attacks**.
- **Maintain sensitive data on the server.**
- **Validate input parameters**.

Protect View State with MACs

If your Web pages or controls use view state to maintain state across HTTP requests, ensure that the view state is encrypted and integrity checked through the use of MACs. By default, the **enableViewStateMac** attribute on the **<pages>** element in Machine.config ensures that view state is protected with a MAC.

```
<pages buffer="true" enableSessionState="true"
       enableViewState="true" enableViewStateMac="true"
       autoEventWireup="true" validateRequest="true"/>
```

Note The **@Page** directive also supports the preceding attributes, which allows you to customize settings on a per-page basis.

While you can override whether or not view state is enabled on a per-control, page, or application basis, make sure **enableViewStateMac** is set to true whenever you use view state.

Server.Transfer

If your application uses **Server.Transfer** as shown below and sets the optional second Boolean parameter to true so that the **QueryString** and **Form** collections are preserved, then the command will fail if **enableViewStateMac** is set to true.

```
Server.Transfer("page2.aspx", true);
```

If you omit the second parameter or set it to false, then an error will not occur. If you want to preserve the **QueryString** and **Form** collections instead of setting the **enableViewStateMac** to false, follow the workaround discussed in Microsoft Knowledge Base article 316920, "PRB: View State Is Invalid" Error Message When You Use Server.Transfer."

For information about configuring the **<machineKey>** element for view state encryption and integrity checks, see Chapter 19, "Securing Your ASP.NET Application and Web Services."

Use Page.ViewStateUserKey to Counter One-Click Attacks

If you authenticate your callers and use view state, set the **Page.ViewStateUserKey** property in the **Page_Init** event handler to prevent one-click attacks. A one-click attack occurs when an attacker creates a prefilled Web page (.htm or .aspx) with view state. The view state can be generated from a page that the attacker had previously created, for example, a shopping cart page with 100 items. The attacker lures an unsuspecting user into browsing to the page, then causes the page to be sent to the server where the view state is valid. The server has no way of knowing that the view state originated from the attacker. View state validation and MACs do not counter this attack because the view state is valid and the page is executed under the security context of the user.

Set the **Page.ViewStateUserKey** property to a suitably unique value as a countermeasure to the one-click attack. The value should be unique to each user and is typically a user name or identifier. When the attacker creates the view state, the **ViewStateUserKey** property is initialized to his or her name. When the user submits the page to the server, it is initialized with the attacker's name. As a result, the view state MAC check fails and an exception condition is generated.

Note   This attack is usually not an issue for anonymously browsed pages (where no user name is available) because this type of page should make no sensitive transactions.

Maintain Sensitive Data on the Server

Do not trust input parameters, especially when they are used to make security decisions at the server. Also, do not use clear text parameters for any form of sensitive data. Instead, store sensitive data on the server in a session store and use a session token to reference the items in the store. Make sure that the user is authenticated securely and that the authentication token is secured properly. For more information, see "Session Management" earlier in this chapter.

Validate Input Parameters

Validate all input parameters that come from form fields, query strings, cookies, and HTTP headers. The **System.Text.RegularExpressions.Regex** class helps validate input parameters. For example, the following code shows how to use this class to validate a name passed through a query string parameter. The same technique can be used to validate other forms of input parameter, for example, from cookies or form fields. For example, to validate a cookie parameter, use **Request.Cookies** instead of **Request.QueryString**.

```
using System.Text.RegularExpressions;
. . .
private void Page_Load(object sender, System.EventArgs e)
{
  // Name must contain between 1 and 40 alphanumeric characters
  // together with (optionally) special characters '`` for names such
  // as D'Angelo
  if (!Regex.IsMatch(Request.QueryString["name"],
                   @"^[\p{L}\p{Zs}\p{Lu}\p{Ll}]{1,40}$"))
    throw new Exception("Invalid name parameter");
  // Use individual regular expressions to validate all other
  // query string parameters
  . . .
}
```

For more information about using regular expressions and how to validate input data, see "Input Validation" earlier in this chapter.

Exception Management

Correct exception handling in your Web pages prevents sensitive exception details from being revealed to the user. The following recommendations apply to ASP.NET Web pages and controls.

- **Return generic error pages to the client**.
- **Implement page-level or application-level error handlers**.

For more information about exception management, see Chapter 7, "Building Secure Assemblies."

Return Generic Error Pages to the Client

In the event of an unhandled exception, that is, one that propagates to the application boundary, return a generic error page to the user. To do this, configure the **<customErrors>** element as follows:

```
<customErrors mode="On" defaultRedirect="YourErrorPage.htm" />
```

The error page should include a suitably generic error message, possibly with additional support details. The name of the page that generated the error is passed to the error page through the **aspxerrorpath** query parameter.

You can also use multiple error pages for different types of errors. For example:

```
<customErrors mode="On" defaultRedirect="YourErrorPage.htm">
    <error statusCode="404" redirect="YourNotFoundPage.htm"/>
    <error statusCode="500" redirect="YourInternalErrorPage.htm"/>
</customErrors>
```

For individual pages you can supply an error page using the following page-level attribute:

```
<% @ Page ErrorPage="YourErrorPage" %>
```

Implement Page-Level or Application-Level Error Handlers

If you need to trap and process unhandled exceptions at the page level, create a handler for the **Page_Error** event that is similar to the one shown below.

```
public void Page_Error(object sender,EventArgs e)
{
  // Get the source exception details
  Exception ex = Server.GetLastError();
  // Write the details to the event log for diagnostics
  . . .
  // Prevent the exception from propagating and generating an
  // application level event (Application.Error)
  Server.ClearError();
}
```

If exceptions are allowed to propagate from the page handler or there is no page handler, an application error event is raised. To trap application-level events, implement **Application_Error** in Global.asax, as follows:

```
protected void Application_Error(Object sender, EventArgs e)
{
  //  Write to the event log.
}
```

Auditing and Logging

The default ASP.NET process identity for Web applications can write new records to the event log, but it does not have sufficient permissions to create new event sources. To address this issue, you have two choices. You can create an installer class, which is invoked at installation time when administrator privileges are available, or you can configure the permissions on the **EventLog** registry key to allow the ASP.NET process identity (or impersonated identity) to create event sources at run time. The former approach is recommended.

▶ **To create an application event source at installation time**

1. Right-click your project in the Solution Explorer window in Visual Studio .NET, point to **Add,** and then click **Add Component**.

2. Select **Installer Class** from the list of templates and provide a suitable class file name.

   This creates a new installer class annotated with the **RunInstaller(true)** attribute.

   ```
   RunInstaller(true)
   public class EventSourceInstaller : System.Configuration.Install.Installer
   {
     . . .
   }
   ```

3. Display the new installer class in Design view, display the Toolbox, and then click **Components** in the Toolbox. Drag an **EventLogInstaller** component onto the Designer work surface.

   Note If **EventLogInstaller** does not appear in the Toolbox, right-click the Toolbox, and then click **Add/Remove Items**. Then select **EventLogInstaller** to add this component type.

4. Set the following **EventLogInstaller** properties:
   - **Log**. Set this property to **"Application"** which is the name of the event log you should use. You can use the default Application log or create an application-specific log.
   - **Source**. Set this property to the event source name. This is usually your application name.

5. Build your project and then create an instance of the installer class at installation time.

   Installer class instances are automatically created and invoked if you use a .NET Setup and Deployment project to create a Windows installer file (.msi). If you use **xcopy** or equivalent deployment, use the **InstallUtil.exe** utility to create an instance of the installer class and to execute it.

6. To confirm the successful generation of the event source, use a registry editor and navigate to:

```
HKLM\System\CurrentControlSet\Services\EventLog\Application\{source name}
```

Confirm that the key exists and that it contains an **EventMessageFile** string value that points to the default .NET Framework event message file:

```
\Windows\Microsoft.NET\Framework\{version}\EventLogMessages.dll
```

If you have an existing application and do not want to create an installer class, you must grant the ASP.NET process identity the correct access rights on the event log registry key. For registry key details and the precise access rights that are required, see "Event Log" in Chapter 19, "Securing Your ASP.NET Application and Web Services."

EventLogPermission

Code that writes to the event log must be granted the **EventLogPermission** by code access security policy. This becomes an issue if your Web application is configured to run at a partial-trust level. For information about how to write to the event log from a partial trust Web application, see Chapter 9, "Using Code Access Security with ASP.NET."

Summary

This chapter started by showing you the main threats that you need to address when you build Web pages and controls. Many application-level attacks rely on vulnerabilities in input validation. Take special care in this area to make sure that your validation strategy is sound and that all data that is processed from a non-trusted source is properly validated. Another common vulnerability is the failure to protect authentication cookies. The "Forms Authentication" section of this chapter showed you effective countermeasures to apply to prevent unauthorized access, session hijacking, and cookie replay attacks.

Additional Resources

For more information, see the following resources:

- For information about establishing a secure Machine.config and Web.config configuration, see Chapter 19, "Securing Your ASP.NET Application and Web Services."

- For a printable checklist, see "Checklist: Securing ASP.NET" in the "Checklists" section of this guide.

- For information on securing your developer workstation, see "How To: Secure Your Developer Workstation" in the "How To" section of this guide.

- For more information on authentication and authorization in ASP.NET, see Chapter 8, "ASP.NET Security," in "Microsoft *patterns & practices* Volume I, *Building Secure ASP.NET Applications: Authentication, Authorization, and Secure Communication*" at *http://msdn.microsoft.com/library/en-us/dnnetsec/html /SecNetch08.asp.*

- For walkthroughs of using Forms Authentication, see "How To: Use Forms Authentication with SQL Server 2000" and "How To: Use Forms Authentication with Active Directory", in the "How To" section of "Microsoft *patterns & practices* Volume I, *Building Secure ASP.NET Applications: Authentication, Authorization, and Secure Communication*" at *http://msdn.microsoft.com/library/en-us/dnnetsec/html /SecNetHT00.asp.*

- For more information about using regular expressions, see Microsoft Knowledge Base article 308252, "How To: Match a Pattern by Using Regular Expressions and Visual C# .NET."

- For more information about user input validation in ASP.NET, see MSDN article "User Input Validation in ASP.NET" at *http://msdn.microsoft.com/library /default.asp?url=/library/en-us/dnaspp/html/pdc_userinput.asp.*

- For more information about the **Secure** cookie property, see RFC2109 on the W3C Web site at *http://www.w3.org/Protocols/rfc2109/rfc2109.*

- For more information on security considerations from the Open Hack competition, see MSDN article "Building and Configuring More Secure Web Sites" at *http://msdn.microsoft.com/library/default.asp?url=/library/en-us/dnnetsec/html /openhack.asp.*

11

Building Secure Serviced Components

In This Chapter

- Preventing anonymous access to serviced components
- Protecting sensitive data
- Authorizing callers by using Enterprise Services (COM+) roles
- Using least privileged run-as accounts
- Securing secrets in object constructor strings
- Auditing from middle tier serviced components
- Deployment considerations for serviced components

Overview

COM+ infrastructure services, also known as Enterprise Services, can be accessed from managed code. Enterprise Services applications consist of one or more serviced components that are managed classes derived from **System.EnterpriseServices.ServicedComponent**.

Serviced components are typically used to encapsulate an application's business and data access logic and are used when infrastructure services such as distributed transactions, object pooling, queued components, and others are required in an application's middle tier. Enterprise Services applications often reside on middle-tier application servers as shown in Figure 11.1.

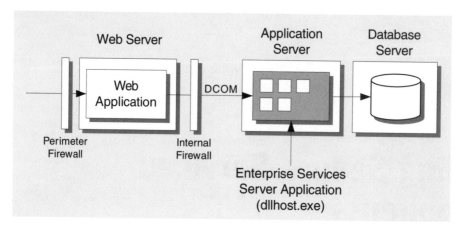

Figure 11.1
Serviced components in a middle-tier Enterprise Services application

How to Use This Chapter

This chapter is developer focused and shows how to build secure serviced components.

To get the most of this chapter:

- **Use this chapter in conjunction with the Enterprise Services section in Chapter 17, "Securing Your Application Server."** The section in Chapter 17 describes how to secure the Enterprise Services infrastructure and how to lock down your deployed Enterprise Services application.
- **Use the recommendations covered in Chapter 7, "Building Secure Assemblies."** The chapter teaches you secure coding practices that can be applied when you develop serviced component code.

Threats and Countermeasures

The top threats that you must address when building serviced components are:
- **Network eavesdropping**
- **Unauthorized access**
- **Unconstrained delegation**
- **Disclosure of configuration data**
- **Repudiation**

Figure 11.2 highlights these top threats together with common serviced component vulnerabilities.

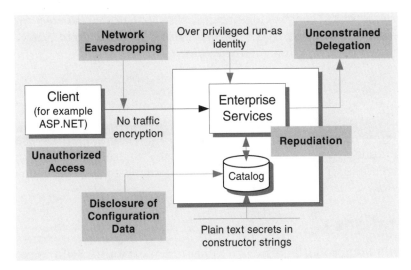

Figure 11.2
Enterprise Services threats

Network Eavesdropping

Enterprise Services applications often run on middle-tier application servers, remote from the Web server. As a result, sensitive application data must be protected from network eavesdroppers. You can use an Internet Protocol Security (IPSec) encrypted channel between Web and application server. This solution is commonly used in Internet data centers. Serviced components also support remote procedure call (RPC) packet level authentication, which provides packet-based encryption. This is most typically used to secure communication to and from desktop-based clients.

Unauthorized Access

By enabling COM+ role-based authorization (it is disabled by default on Microsoft Windows 2000), you can prevent anonymous access and provide role-based authorization to control access to the restricted operations exposed by your serviced components.

Unconstrained Delegation

If you enable delegation on Windows 2000 to allow a remote server to access network resources using the client's impersonated token, the delegation is unconstrained. This means that there is no limit to the number of network hops that can be made. Microsoft Windows Server 2003 introduces constrained delegation.

Disclosure of Configuration Data

Many applications store sensitive data such as database connection strings in the COM+ catalog using object constructor strings. These strings are retrieved and passed to an object by COM+ when the object is created. Sensitive configuration data should be encrypted prior to storage in the catalog.

Repudiation

The repudiation threat arises when a user denies performing an operation or transaction, and you have insufficient evidence to counter the claim. Auditing should be performed across all application tiers. Serviced components should log user activity in the middle tier. Serviced components usually have access to the original caller's identity because front-end Web applications usually enable impersonation in Enterprise Services scenarios.

Design Considerations

Before you start writing code, there are a number of important issues to consider at design time. The key considerations are:

- **Role-based authorization**
- **Sensitive data protection**
- **Audit requirements**
- **Application activation type**
- **Transactions**
- **Code access security**

Role-Based Authorization

For effective role-based authorization using COM+ roles, ensure that the original caller's security context is used for the call to the serviced component. This allows you to perform granular role-based authorization based on the caller's group membership. If an ASP.NET Web application calls your serviced components, this means that the Web application needs to impersonate its callers before calling your component.

Sensitive Data Protection

If your serviced components handle sensitive data, such as employee details, financial transactions, and health records, consider how to protect the data as it crosses the network. If your application does not run in a secure Internet Data Center (IDC) environment, where IPSec provides transport level encryption, an alternative option is to use RPC encryption. For this you must use the Packet Privacy authentication level. For more information, see the "Sensitive Data" section later in this chapter.

Audit Requirements

To address the repudiation threat, sensitive transactions performed by Enterprise Service components should be logged. At design time, consider the type of operations that should be audited and the details that should be logged. At a minimum, this should include the identity that initiated the transaction and the identity used to perform the transaction, which may or may not be the same.

Application Activation Type

At design time, decide how your serviced component will be activated. You can activate them using an instance of the Dllhost.exe process or you can run them inside the client process. Server applications run out of process in an instance of Dllhost.exe. Library applications run in the client's process address space. Library applications are more efficient due to the lack of inter-process communication. However, they are less configurable and are not protected with process level isolation. Many security settings, such as the authentication and impersonation levels, are inherited from the client process.

Transactions

If you plan to use distributed transactions, consider where the transaction is initiated and consider the implications of running transactions between components and resource managers separated by firewalls. In this scenario, the firewall must be configured to support the Microsoft Distributed Transaction Coordinator (DTC) traffic.

If your physical deployment architecture includes a middle-tier application server, it is generally preferable to initiate transactions from the Enterprise Services application on the application server and not from the front-end Web application.

Code Access Security

Typically, applications that use serviced components are fully trusted, and as a result code access security has limited use to authorize calling code. However, Enterprise Services demands that the calling code has the necessary permission to call unmanaged code. The main implication of this is that you will not be able to directly call into an Enterprise Services application from a partial trust Web application. The ASP.NET partial trust levels (High, Medium, Low, and Minimal) do not grant the unmanaged code permission. If you need to call a serviced component from a partial trust application, the privileged code that calls your component must be sandboxed. For more information, see "Code Access Security Considerations" later in this chapter.

Authentication

Enterprise Services applications use Windows authentication. This is either NTLM or Kerberos authentication depending on the client and server operating system. In Windows 2000 or Windows Server 2003 environments, Kerberos authentication is used.

The main issue for you to consider when building serviced components is to ensure that all calls are authenticated to prevent anonymous users from accessing your component's functionality.

Use (At Least) Call Level Authentication

To reject anonymous callers, use at least call level authentication. Configure this setting by adding the following attribute to your serviced component assembly:

```
[assembly: ApplicationAccessControl(
                Authentication = AuthenticationOption.Call)]
```

Note This is equivalent to setting **Authentication level for calls** to **Call** on the **Security** tab of the application's **Properties** dialog box in Component Services.

Authorization

Enterprise Services uses COM+ roles for authorization. You can control the granularity of authorization to applications, components, interfaces, and methods. To prevent users from performing restricted operations exposed by your application's serviced components:

- Enable role-based security.
- Enable component level access checks.
- Enforce component level access checks.

Enable Role-Based Security

Role-based security is disabled by default on Windows 2000. The reverse is true on Windows Server 2003. To ensure that role based security is automatically enabled when your component is registered (usually by using Regsvcs.exe), add the following attribute to your serviced component assembly.

```
[assembly: ApplicationAccessControl(true)]
```

Note Using this attribute is equivalent to selecting **Enforce access checks for this application** on the **Security** tab of the application's **Properties** dialog box in Component Services.

Enable Component Level Access Checks

Component level access checks must be enabled in order to support component, interface, or method level role checks. To ensure that component level access checks are automatically enabled when your component is registered, add the following attribute to your serviced component assembly.

```
[assembly: ApplicationAccessControl(AccessChecksLevel=
            AccessChecksLevelOption.ApplicationComponent)]
```

Note Using this attribute is equivalent to selecting **Perform access checks at the process and component level** on the **Security** tab of the application's **Properties** dialog box in Component Services.

Enforce Component Level Access Checks

To allow individual components to perform access checks, you must enforce component level access checks. This setting is only effective if the application-wide security level is set to the process and the component level as described above. To ensure that component level access checks are automatically enabled when your component is registered, add the following attribute to your serviced component classes.

```
[ComponentAccessControl(true)]
public class YourServicedComponent : ServicedComponent
{
}
```

Note Using this attribute is equivalent to selecting **Enforce component level access checks** on the **Security** tab of the component's **Properties** dialog box in Component Services.

Configuration Management

In addition to the configurable settings that COM+ provides to administrators through the Component Services tool, developers often perform configuration-related functions in code. For example, the functions might retrieve object construction strings stored in the COM+ catalog. Consider these main issues when you use configuration management with Enterprise Services:

- **Use least privileged run-as accounts**.
- **Avoid storing secrets in object constructor strings**.
- **Avoid unconstrained delegation**.

Use Least Privileged Run-As Accounts

During development, run and test your service components using a least privileged local account instead of the interactive user account. Configure the account as closely as possible to match the run-as account that the administrator is likely to use in the production environment.

Avoid Storing Secrets in Object Constructor Strings

If you store secrets such as database connection strings or passwords in object constructor strings in the COM+ catalog, any member of the local administrators group can view this plaintext data. Try to avoid storing secrets. If you have to store a secret, then encrypt the data. DPAPI is a good implementation option because it allows you to avoid problems associated with key management.

At runtime, retrieve the object construction string and use DPAPI to decrypt the data. For more information about using DPAPI from managed code, see "How to create a DPAPI library" in MSDN article, "Building Secure ASP.NET Applications," at *http://msdn.microsoft.com/library/en-us/dnnetsec/html/secnetlpMSDN.asp*.

```
[ConstructionEnabled(Default="")]
public class YourServicedComponent : ServicedComponent, ISomeInterface
{
  // The object constructor is called first.
  public YourServicedComponent() {}
  // Then the object construction string is passed to Construct method.
  protected override void Construct(string constructString)
  {
    // Use DPAPI to decrypt the configuration data.
  }
}
```

Avoid Unconstrained Delegation

Serviced component clients are authenticated with either NTLM or Kerberos authentication, depending on the environment. Kerberos in Windows 2000 supports delegation that is unconstrained; this means that the number of network hops that can be made with the client's credentials has no limit.

If ASP.NET is the client then you can set the **comImpersonation** attribute on the **<processModel>** element in Machine.config to configure the impersonation level:

```
comImpersonationLevel="[Default|Anonymous|Identify|Impersonate|Delegate]"
```

The impersonation level defined for an Enterprise Services server application determines the impersonation capabilities of any remote server that the serviced components communicate with. In this case, the serviced components are the clients.

You can specify the impersonation level for a serviced component, which applies when the service component is a client, using the following attribute:

```
[assembly: ApplicationAccessControl(
            ImpersonationLevel=ImpersonationLevelOption.Identify)]
```

Note Using this attribute is equivalent to setting the **Impersonation Level** value on the **Security** page of the application's **Properties** dialog within Component Services.

The following table describes the effect of each of these impersonation levels:

Table 11.1 Impersonation Levels

Impersonation Level	Description
Anonymous	The server cannot identify the client.
Identify	This allows the server to identify the client and perform access checks using the client's access token
Impersonate	This allows the server to gain access to local resources using the client's credentials
Delegate	This allows the server to access remote resources using the client's credentials (this requires Kerberos and specific account configuration)

For more information, see the "Impersonation" section in Chapter 17, "Securing Your Application Server" and "How to Enable Kerberos Delegation in Windows 2000" in the References section of MSDN article, "Building Secure ASP.NET Applications," at *http://msdn.microsoft.com/library/en-us/dnnetsec/html/secnetlpMSDN.asp.*

Sensitive Data

If your application transmits sensitive data to and from a serviced component across a network to address the network eavesdropping threat, the data should be encrypted to ensure it remains private and unaltered. You can use transport level protection with IPSec or you can use application level protection by configuring your Enterprise Services application to use the RPC packet privacy authentication level. This encrypts each packet of data sent to and from the serviced component to provide privacy and integrity.

You can configure packet privacy authentication using the Component Services tool or by adding the following attribute to your serviced component assembly:

```
[assembly: ApplicationAccessControl(
            Authentication = AuthenticationOption.Privacy)]
```

For more information about using IPSec to encrypt all of the data transmitted between two computers, see "How To: Use IPSec to Provide Secure Communication Between Two Servers" in the "How To" section of "Microsoft *patterns & practices* Volume I, *Building Secure ASP.NET Applications: Authentication, Authorization, and Secure Communication*" at *http://msdn.microsoft.com/library/default.asp?url=/library/en-us /dnnetsec/html/SecNetHT00.asp.*

Auditing and Logging

Auditing and logging should be performed across the tiers of your application to avoid potential repudiation threats where users deny performing certain transactions or key operations.

Audit User Transactions

If your Web application or Web service is configured for impersonation, the identity of the original caller automatically flows to an Enterprise Services application and is available using **SecurityCallContext.OriginalCaller**. This is useful for auditing in the middle tier. The following code shows how to access this information:

```
[ComponentAccessControl]
public class YourServicedComponent : ServicedComponent
{
  public void ShowCallers()
  {
    SecurityCallers callers = SecurityCallContext.CurrentCall.Callers;
    foreach(SecurityIdentity id in callers)
    {
      LogEvent(id.AccountName);
    }
  }
  private void LogEvent(string message)
  {
    try
    {
      if (!EventLog.SourceExists(appName))
      {
        EventLog.CreateEventSource(appName, eventLog);
      }
      EventLog.WriteEntry(appName, message, EventLogEntryType.Information );
    }
    catch (SecurityException secex)
    {
      throw new SecurityException(
          "Event source does not exist and cannot be created.", secex);
    }
  }
}
```

To successfully write to the event log, an event source must exist that associates the Enterprise Services application with a specific event log. The above code creates the event source at run time, which means that the serviced component process account must have the relevant permissions in the registry.

▶ **To enable the serviced component process identity to create event sources**

- Use regedit32.exe to update the permissions on the following registry key to grant access to the serviced component process account:

  ```
  HKLM\SYSTEM\CurrentControlSet\Services\Eventlog
  ```

  The account(s) must have the following minimum permissions:
  - Query key value
  - Set key value
  - Create subkey
  - Enumerate subkeys
  - Notify
  - Read

An alternate strategy is to use an **Installer** class and create the event source for the application at installation time, when administrator privileges are available. For more information about this approach, see "Auditing and Logging" in Chapter 10 "Building Secure ASP.NET Web Pages and Controls."

Building a Secure Serviced Component

Having covered the threats and countermeasures applicable to serviced components and Enterprise Services applications, the following code fragments illustrate the key characteristics of a secure serviced component for a simple **Customer** class implementation. Method implementation details have been omitted for the sake of clarity.

Assembly Implementation

The following code fragment from assemblyinfo.cs shows the assembly level metadata used to configure the COM+ catalog when the serviced component assembly is registered with Enterprise Services using regsvcs.exe.

```
// (1) Assembly has a strong name.
[assembly: AssemblyKeyFile(@"..\..\Customer.snk")]

// Enterprise Services configuration
[assembly: ApplicationName("CustomerService")]
[assembly: Description("Customer Services Application")]
// (2) Server application - runs in dllhost.exe process instance.
[assembly: ApplicationActivation(ActivationOption.Server)]
// (3) Enable component level access checks.
// (4) Specify call level authentication.
// (5) Specify Identify impersonation level for downstream calls.
[assembly: ApplicationAccessControl(
            AccessChecksLevel=AccessChecksLevelOption.ApplicationComponent,
            Authentication=AuthenticationOption.Call,
            ImpersonationLevel=ImpersonationLevelOption.Identify)]
```

The code shown above exhibits the following security characteristics (identified by the numbers in the comment lines).

1. The assembly is strong named. This is a mandatory requirement for serviced components. The added benefit from a security perspective is that the assembly is digitally signed. This means that any modification by an attacker will be detected and the assembly will fail to load.

2. The application is configured to run as a server application in a dedicated instance of dllhost.exe. This allows you to specify the least privileged run-as identity at deployment time.

3. The application is configured to support component level access checks. This allows you to authorize callers based on role membership at the class, interface, and method levels.

4. Call level authentication is specified. This means that each method call from a client is authenticated.

5. The impersonation level for outgoing calls from this serviced component to other components on remote servers is set to Identify. This means that the downstream component can identify the caller but cannot perform impersonation.

> **Note** The impersonation level for a calling ASP.NET Web application or Web service client is specified on the **<processModel>** element in Machine.config on the client Web server.

Serviced Component Class Implementation

The following code fragment highlights the security configuration of a partially implemented **Customer** class.

```
namespace busCustomer
{
  // (1) Explicit interface definition to support method level authorization
  public interface ICustomerAdmin
  {
    void CreditAccountBalance(string customerID, double amount);
  }
  // (2) Enforce component level access checks.
  [ComponentAccessControl]
  public sealed class Customer : ServicedComponent, ICustomerAdmin
  {
    private string appName = "Customer";
    private string eventLog = "Application";
    // ICustomer implementation
    // (3) Access to CreditAccountBalance is limited to members of the
    //     Manager and Senior Manager role.
    [SecurityRole("Manager")]
    [SecurityRole("Senior Manager")]
    public void CreditAccountBalance(string customerID, double amount)
    {
      // (4) Structured exception handling to protect implementation.
      try
      {
        // (5) Check that security is enabled.
        if (ContextUtil.IsSecurityEnabled)
        {
          // Only managers can credit accounts with sums of money
          // in excess of $1,000.
          if (amount > 1000) {
            // (6) Programmatic role check to authorize credit operation
            if (ContextUtil.IsCallerInRole("Senior Manager")) {
              // Call data access component to update database.
              . . .
              // (7) Audit the transaction.
              AuditTransaction(customerID, amount);
            }
            else {
              throw new SecurityException("Caller not authorized");
            }
          }
        }
        else {
          throw new SecurityException("Security is not enabled");
        }
      }
```

(continued)

(continued)

```
    catch( Exception ex)
    {
      // Log exception details.
      throw new Exception("Failed to credit account balance for customer: " +
                          customerID, ex);
    }
  }
  private void AuditTransaction(string customerID, double amount)
  {
    // (8) Original caller identity is obtained from call context for
    //     logging purposes.
    SecurityIdentity caller = SecurityCallContext.CurrentCall.OriginalCaller;
    try
    {
      if (!EventLog.SourceExists(appName))
      {
        EventLog.CreateEventSource(appName,eventLog);
      }
      StringBuilder logmessage = new StringBuilder();
      logmessage.AppendFormat("{0}User {1} performed the following transaction"
                     + "{2} Account balance for customer {3} "
                     + "credited by {4}",
                       Environment.NewLine, caller.AccountName,
                       Environment.NewLine, customerID, amount);
      EventLog.WriteEntry(appName, logmessage.ToString(),
                     EventLogEntryType.Information);
    }
    catch(SecurityException secex)
    {
      throw new SecurityException(
              "Event source does not exist and cannot be created", secex);
    }
  }
 }
}
```

The code shown above exhibits the following security characteristics (identified by the numbers in the comment lines):

1. An interface is defined and implemented explicitly to support interface and method level authorization with COM+ roles.

2. Component level access checks are enabled for the class by using the **[ComponentAccessControl]** attribute at the class level.

3. The **[SecurityRole]** attribute is used on the **CreditAccountBalance** method to restrict access to members of the Manager or Senior Managers role.

4. Structured exception handling is used to protect implementation. Exceptions are caught, logged, and an appropriate exception is propagated to the caller.

5. The code checks whether or not security is enabled prior to the explicit role check. This is a risk mitigation strategy to ensure that transactions cannot be performed if the application security configuration is inadvertently or deliberately disabled by an administrator.

Note   The **IsCallerInRole** method always returns "true" if security is disabled.

6. Callers must be members of either the Manager or Senior Manager role because of the declarative security used on the method. For fine-grained authorization, the role membership of the caller is explicitly checked in code.

7. The transaction is audited.

8. The audit implementation obtains the identity of the original caller by using the **SecurityCallContext** object.

Code Access Security Considerations

Applications that use serviced components are usually fully trusted and, as a result, code access security has limited use to authorize calling code. The calling code should consider the following points:

- Unmanaged code permission is required to activate and perform cross context calls on serviced components.

- If the client of a serviced component is an ASP.NET Web application, then its trust level must be set to "Full" as shown below.

```
<trust level="Full" />
```

  If your Web application is configured with a trust level other than "Full," it does not have the unmanaged code permission. In this instance, you must create a sandboxed wrapper assembly to encapsulate the communication with the serviced component. You must also configure code access security policy to grant the wrapper assembly the unmanaged code permission. For more information about the sandboxing technique used to encapsulate high privileged code, see Chapter 9, "Using Code Access Security with ASP.NET."

- If a reference to a serviced component is passed to untrusted code, methods defined on the serviced component cannot be called from the untrusted code. The exception to this rule is with methods than do not require context switching or interception services and do not call members of **System.EnterpriseServices**. Such methods can be called by untrusted code.

Deployment Considerations

Enterprise Services applications are typically installed on the Web server or on a remote application server. Figure 11.3 shows the two typical deployment scenarios for Enterprise Services. From a security perspective, the notable difference with the remote deployment scenario is that data passed to and from the serviced component is passed over the network, often through an internal firewall used to separate the internal and perimeter networks.

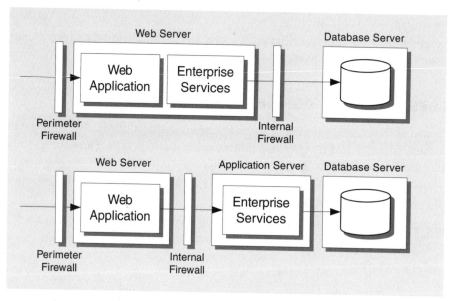

Figure 11.3
Enterprise Services typical deployment configurations

Developers and administrators need to be aware of the following deployment-related issues:

- Firewall restrictions, including port requirements for DCOM and DTC
- Run-as account configuration
- Storing secrets in object constructor strings

For more information about applying secure configuration at deployment time, see Chapter 17, "Securing Your Application Server."

Firewall Restrictions

If the client and Enterprise Services application are separated by an internal firewall, the relevant ports that support DCOM and possibly the DTC (if your application uses distributed transactions) must be open.

DCOM uses RPC dynamic port allocation that by default randomly selects port numbers above 1024. In addition, port 135 is used by the RPC endpoint mapper. You can restrict the ports required to support DCOM on the internal firewall in two ways:

- **Define port ranges**.

  This allows you to control the ports dynamically allocated by RPC.

- **Use static endpoint mapping**.

  Windows 2000 SP3 (or Quick Fix Engineering [QFE] 18.1 and greater) or Windows Server 2003 allow you to configure Enterprise Services applications to use a static endpoint. Static endpoint mapping means that you only need to open two ports in the firewall. Specifically, you must open port 135 for RPC and a nominated port for your Enterprise Services application.

For more information about defining port ranges and static endpoint mapping, see "Firewall Considerations" in Chapter 17, "Securing Your Application Server."

Using Web Services

If opening ports on the internal firewall is not an option, then you can introduce a Web services façade layer in front of the serviced components on the application server. This means that you only need to open port 80 for HTTP traffic and specifically for Simple Object Access Protocol (SOAP) messages to flow in both directions as shown in Figure 11.4.

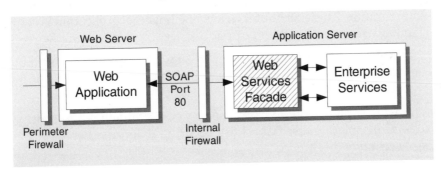

Figure 11.4
Using a Web services façade layer to communicate with Enterprise Services using HTTP

This approach does not allow you to flow transaction context from client to server, although in many cases where your deployment architecture includes a middle-tier application server, it is appropriate to initiate transactions in the remote serviced component on the application server.

For information about physical deployment requirements for service agents and service interfaces such as the Web services façade layer, see "Physical Deployment and Operational Requirements" in the Reference section of the MSDN article, *"Application Architecture for .NET: Designing Applications and Services."*

DTC Requirements

If your application uses COM+ distributed transactions and these are used across remote servers separated by an internal firewall, then the firewall must open the necessary ports to support DTC traffic.

If your deployment architecture includes a remote application tier, transactions are usually initiated within the Enterprise Services application and propagated to the database server. In the absence of an application server, the Enterprise Services application on the Web server initiates the transaction and propagates it to the SQL Server resource manager.

For information about configuring firewalls to support DTC traffic, see Chapter 18, "Securing Your Database Server."

Summary

Enterprise Services (COM+) security relies on Windows security to authenticate and authorize callers. Authorization is configured and controlled with COM+ roles that contain Windows group or user accounts. The majority of threats that relate to Enterprise Services applications and serviced components can be addressed with solid coding techniques, and appropriate catalog configuration.

The developer should use declarative attributes to set the serviced component security configuration. These attributes determine how the application is configured when it is initially registered with Enterprise Services (typically using Regsvcs.exe).

Not every security configuration setting can be set with attributes. An administrator must specify the run-as identity for a server application. The administrator must also populate roles with Windows group or user accounts at deployment time.

When you are developing serviced components or are evaluating the security of your Enterprise Security solution, use "Checklist: Securing Enterprise Services" in the "Checklists" section of this guide.

Additional Resources

For more information, see the following resources:

- For a printable checklist, see "Checklist: Securing Enterprise Services" in the "Checklists" section of this guide.

- For information on authentication, authorization and secure communication for Enterprise Services see "Enterprise Services Security" in "Microsoft *patterns & practices* Volume I, *Building Secure ASP.NET Applications: Authentication, Authorization, and Secure Communication*" at *http://msdn.microsoft.com/library /default.asp?url=/library/en-us/dnnetsec/html/SecNetch09.asp*.

- For frequently asked questions regarding Enterprise Services, see "Enterprise Services FAQ" at *http://www.gotdotnet.com/team/xmlentsvcs/esfaq.aspx*.

- For background on Enterprise Services, see MSDN article, "Understanding Enterprise Services (COM+) in .NET," at *http://msdn.microsoft.com/library /default.asp?url=/library/en-us/dndotnet/html/entserv.asp*.

12

Building Secure Web Services

In This Chapter

- Web service threats and countermeasures
- Strategies for Web service input validation
- Confidentiality and integrity for Web service messages
- Web Services Enhancements 1.0 for Microsoft .NET (WSE)

Overview

Web services are used by an increasing number of companies as they expose products and services to customers and business partners through the Internet and corporate extranets. The security requirements for these service providers are of paramount importance. In some cases, primarily intranet or extranet scenarios where you have a degree of control over both endpoints, the platform-based security services provided by the operating system and Internet Information Services (IIS) can be used to provide point-to-point security solutions. However, the message based architecture of Web services and the heterogeneous environments that span trust boundaries in which they are increasingly being used pose new challenges. These scenarios require security to be addressed at the message level to support cross-platform interoperability and routing through multiple intermediary nodes.

Web Services Security (WS-Security) is the emerging security standard designed to address these issues. Microsoft has released Web Services Enhancements 1.0 for Microsoft .NET (WSE), which supports WS-Security and a related family of emerging standards. WSE allows you to implement message level security solutions including authentication, encryption and digital signatures.

Note The specifications and standard supported by WSE are evolving and therefore the current WSE does not guarantee it will be compatible with future versions of the product. At the time of this writing, interoperability testing is under way with non-Microsoft toolkits provided by vendors including IBM and VeriSign.

How to Use This Chapter

This chapter discusses various practices and techniques to design and build secure Web services.

To get the most from this chapter:

- **Read Chapter 19, "Securing Your ASP.NET Application and Web Services."** It is geared toward an administrator so that an administrator can configure an ASP.NET Web Application or Web service, bringing a semi-secure application to a secure state.

- **Read Chapter 17, "Securing Your Application Server."** Read Chapter 17 to familiarize yourself with remote application server considerations.

- **Use the "Checklist: Securing Web Services"** in the "Checklists" section of this guide. The checklist is a summary of the security measures required to build and configure secure Web services.

- **Use this chapter to understand message level threats** and how to counter those threats.

- **Use the application categories as a means to tackle common problems.** The sections give you relevant information using these categories.

Threats and Countermeasures

To build secure Web services, know the associated threats. The top threats directed at Web services are:

- **Unauthorized access**
- **Parameter manipulation**
- **Network eavesdropping**
- **Disclosure of configuration data**
- **Message replay**

Figure 12.1 shows the top threats and attacks directed at Web services.

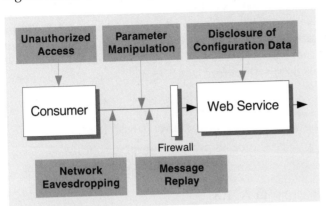

Figure 12.1
Main Web services threats

Unauthorized Access

Web services that provide sensitive or restricted information should authenticate and authorize their callers. Weak authentication and authorization can be exploited to gain unauthorized access to sensitive information and operations.

Vulnerabilities

Vulnerabilities that can lead to unauthorized access through a Web service include:

- No authentication used
- Passwords passed in plaintext in SOAP headers
- Basic authentication used over an unencrypted communication channel

Countermeasures

You can use the following countermeasures to prevent unauthorized access:

- Use password digests in SOAP headers for authentication.
- Use Kerberos tickets in SOAP headers for authentication.
- Use X.509 certificates in SOAP headers for authentication.
- Use Windows authentication.
- Use role-based authorization to restrict access to Web services. This can be done by using URL authorization to control access to the Web service file (.asmx) or at the Web method level by using principal-permission demands.

Parameter Manipulation

Parameter manipulation refers to the unauthorized modification of data sent between the Web service consumer and the Web service. For example, an attacker can intercept a Web service message, perhaps as it passes through an intermediate node en route to its destination; and can then modify it before sending it on to its intended endpoint.

Vulnerabilities

Vulnerabilities that can make parameter manipulation possible include:

- Messages that are not digitally signed to provide tamperproofing
- Messages that are not encrypted to provide privacy and tamperproofing

Countermeasures

You can use the following countermeasures to prevent parameter manipulation:

- Digitally sign the message. The digital signature is used at the recipient end to verify that the message has not been tampered with while it was in transit.
- Encrypt the message payload to provide privacy and tamperproofing.

Network Eavesdropping

With network eavesdropping, an attacker is able to view Web service messages as they flow across the network. For example, an attacker can use network monitoring software to retrieve sensitive data contained in a SOAP message. This might include sensitive application level data or credential information.

Vulnerabilities

Vulnerabilities that can enable successful network eavesdropping include:

- Credentials passed in plaintext in SOAP headers
- No message level encryption used
- No transport level encryption used

Countermeasures

You can use the following countermeasures to protect sensitive SOAP messages as they flow across the network:

- Use transport level encryption such as SSL or IPSec. This is applicable only if you control both endpoints.
- Encrypt the message payload to provide privacy. This approach works in scenarios where your message travels through intermediary nodes route to the final destination.

Disclosure of Configuration Data

There are two main ways in which a Web service can disclose configuration data. First, the Web service may support the dynamic generation of Web Service Description Language (WSDL) or it may provide WSDL information in downloadable files that are available on the Web server. This may not be desirable depending on your scenario.

Note WSDL describes the characteristics of a Web service, for example, its method signatures and supported protocols.

Second, with inadequate exception handling the Web service may disclose sensitive internal implementation details useful to an attacker.

Vulnerabilities

Vulnerabilities that can lead to the disclosure of configuration data include:

● Unrestricted WSDL files available for download from the Web server
● A restricted Web service supports the dynamic generation of WSDL and allows unauthorized consumers to obtain Web service characteristics
● Weak exception handling

Countermeasures

You can use the following countermeasures to prevent the unwanted disclosure of configuration data:

● Authorize access to WSDL files using NTFS permissions.
● Remove WSDL files from Web server.
● Disable the documentation protocols to prevent the dynamic generation of WSDL.
● Capture exceptions and throw a **SoapException** or **SoapHeaderExc**eption—that returns only minimal and harmless information—back to the client.

Message Replay

Web service messages can potentially travel through multiple intermediate servers. With a message replay attack, an attacker captures and copies a message and replays it to the Web service impersonating the client. The message may or may not be modified.

Vulnerabilities

Vulnerabilities that can enable message replay include:

- Messages are not encrypted
- Messages are not digitally signed to prevent tampering
- Duplicate messages are not detected because no unique message ID is used

Attacks

The most common types of message replay attacks include:

- **Basic replay attack**. The attacker captures and copies a message, and then replays the same message and impersonates the client. This replay attack does not require the malicious user to know the contents of the message.
- **Man in the middle attack**. The attacker captures the message and then changes some of its contents, for example, a shipping address, and then replays it to the Web service.

Countermeasures

You can use the following countermeasures to address the threat of message replay:

- Use an encrypted communication channel, for example, SSL.
- Encrypt the message payload to provide message privacy and tamperproofing. Although this does not prevent basic replay attacks, it does prevent man in the middle attacks where the message contents are modified before being replayed.
- Use a unique message ID or nonce with each request to detect duplicates, and digitally sign the message to provide tamperproofing.

Note A *nonce* is a cryptographically unique value used for the request.

When the server responds to the client it sends a unique ID and signs the message, including the ID. When the client makes another request, the client includes the ID with the message. The server ensures that the ID sent to the client in the previous message is included in the new request from the client. If it is different, the server rejects the request and assumes it is subject to a replay attack.

The attacker cannot spoof the message ID, because the message is signed. Note that this only protects the server from client-initiated replay attacks using the message request, and offers the client no protection against replayed responses.

Design Considerations

Before you start to develop Web services, there are a number of issues to consider at design time. The key security considerations are:

- **Authentication requirements**
- **Privacy and integrity requirements**
- **Resource access identities**
- **Code access security**

Authentication Requirements

If your Web service provides sensitive or restrictive information, it needs to authenticate callers to support authorization. In Windows environments, you can use Windows authentication. However, where you are not in control of both endpoints, WSE provides authentication solutions that conform to the emerging WS-Security standard. WSE provides a standard framework for using SOAP headers to pass authentication details in the form of user names and passwords, Kerberos tickets, X.509 certificates, or custom tokens. For more information, see the "Authentication" section later in this chapter.

Privacy and Integrity Requirements

If you pass sensitive application data in Web service requests or response messages, consider how you can ensure that they remain private and unaltered while in transit. WSE provides integrity checking through digital signatures, and it also supports XML encryption to encrypt sensitive elements of the entire message payload. The advantage of this approach is that it is based on the emerging WS-Security standard and that it provides a solution for messages that pass through multiple intermediate nodes.

The alternative is to use transport level encryption through SSL or IPSec channels. These solutions are only appropriate where you are in control of both endpoints.

Resource Access Identities

By default, ASP.NET Web services do not impersonate, and the least privileged ASPNET process account is used for local and remote resource access. You can use this ASPNET process account to access remote network resources such as SQL Servers that require Windows authentication, by creating a mirrored local account on the database server.

Note On Windows Server 2003, the Network Service account is used by default to run Web services.

For more information about using the ASP.NET process account for remote database access, see the "Data Access" section in Chapter 19, "Securing Your ASP.NET Application and Web Services."

If you use impersonation, the issues and considerations that apply to Web applications also apply to Web services. For more information, see the "Impersonation" sections in Chapter 10, "Building Secure ASP.NET Web Pages and Controls" and Chapter 19, "Securing Your ASP.NET Application and Web Services."

Code Access Security

Consider the trust level defined by security policy in your target deployment environment. Your Web service's trust level, defined by its **<trust>** element configuration, affects the types of resources that it can access and the other privileged operations it can perform.

Also, if you call a Web service from an ASP.NET Web application, the Web application's trust level determines the range of Web services it can call. For example, a Web application configured for Medium trust, by default, can only call Web services on the local computer.

For more information about calling Web services from Medium and other partial trust Web applications, see Chapter 9, "Using Code Access Security with ASP.NET."

Input Validation

Like any application that accepts input data, Web services must validate the data that is passed to them to enforce business rules and to prevent potential security issues. Web methods marked with the **WebMethod** attribute are the Web service entry points. Web methods can accept strongly typed input parameters or loosely typed parameters that are often passed as string data. This is usually determined by the range and type of consumers for which the Web service is designed.

Strongly Typed Parameters

If you use strongly typed parameters that are described by the .NET Framework type system, for example integers, doubles, dates, or other custom object types such as Address or Employee, the auto-generated XML Schema Definition (XSD) schema contains a typed description of the data. Consumers can use this typed description to construct appropriately formatted XML within the SOAP requests that are sent to Web methods. ASP.NET then uses the **System.Xml.Serialization.XmlSerializer** class to deserialize the incoming SOAP message into common language runtime (CLR) objects. The following example shows a Web method that accepts strongly typed input consisting of built-in data types.

```
[WebMethod]
public void CreateEmployee(string name, int age, decimal salary) {...}
```

In the preceding example, the .NET Framework type system performs type checks automatically. To validate the range of characters that are supplied through the **name** field, you can use a regular expression. For example, the following code shows how to use the **System.Text.RegularExpressions.Regex** class to constrain the possible range of input characters and also to validate the parameter length.

```
if (!Regex.IsMatch(name, @"^[a-zA-Z'.`-´\s]{1,40}$"))
{
  // Invalid name
}
```

For more information about regular expressions, see the "Input Validation " section in Chapter 10, "Building Secure ASP.NET Pages and Controls." The following example shows a Web method that accepts a custom Employee data type.

```
using Employees;  // Custom namespace
[WebMethod]

public void CreateEmployee(Employee emp) { ... }
```

The consumer needs to know the XSD schema to be able to call your Web service. If the consumer is a .NET Framework client application, the consumer can simply pass an Employee object as follows:

```
using Employees;
Employee emp = new Employee();
// Populate Employee fields
// Send Employee to the Web service
wsProxy.CreateEmployee(emp);
```

Consumer applications that are not based on the .NET Framework must construct the XML input manually, based on the schema definition provided by the organization responsible for the Web service.

The benefit of this strong typing approach is that the .NET Framework parses the input data for you and validates it based on the type definition. However, inside the Web method you might still need to constrain the input data. For example, while the type system confirms a valid Employee object, you might still need to perform further validation on the Employee fields. You might need to validate that an employee's date of birth is greater than 18 years ago. You might need to use regular expressions to constrain the range of characters that can be used in name fields, and so on.

For more information about constraining input, see the "Input Validation" section in Chapter 10, "Building Secure ASP.NET Pages and Controls."

Loosely Typed Parameters

If you use string parameters or byte arrays to pass arbitrary data, you lose many of the benefits of the .NET Framework type system. You must parse the input data manually to validate it because the auto-generated WSDL simply describes the parameters as string input of type xsd:string. You need to programmatically check for type, length, format, and range as shown in the following example.

```
[WebMethod]
public void SomeEmployeeFunction(string dateofBirth, string SSN)
{
    . . .
  // EXAMPLE 1: Type check the date
  try
  {
    DateTime dt = DateTime.Parse(dateofBirth).Date;
  }
  // If the type conversion fails, a FormatException is thrown
  catch( FormatException ex )
  {
    // Invalid date
  }

  // EXAMPLE 2: Check social security number for length, format, and range
  if( !Regex.IsMatch(empSSN,@"^\d{3}-\d{2}-\d{4}$",RegexOptions.None))
  {
      // Invalid social security number
  }
}
```

XML Data

In a classic business-to-business scenario, it is common for consumers to pass XML data that represents business documents such as purchase orders or sales invoices. The validity of the input data must be programmatically validated by the Web method before it is processed or passed to downstream components.

The client and the server have to establish and agree on a schema that describes the XML. The following code fragment shows how a Web method can use the **System.Xml.XmlValidatingReader** class to validate the input data, which, in this example, describes a simple book order. Notice that the XML data is passed through a simple string parameter.

```csharp
using System.Xml;
using System.Xml.Schema;

[WebMethod]
public void OrderBooks(string xmlBookData)
{
  try
  {
    // Create and load a validating reader
    XmlValidatingReader reader = new XmlValidatingReader(xmlBookData,
                                              XmlNodeType.Element,
                                              null);

    // Attach the XSD schema to the reader
    reader.Schemas.Add("urn:bookstore-schema",
                  @"http://localhost/WSBooks/bookschema.xsd");
    // Set the validation type for XSD schema.
    // XDR schemas and DTDs are also supported
    reader.ValidationType = ValidationType.Schema;
    // Create and register an event handler to handle validation errors
    reader.ValidationEventHandler += new ValidationEventHandler(
                                              ValidationErrors );

    // Process the input data
    while (reader.Read())
    {
      . . .
    }
    // Validation completed successfully
  }
  catch
  {
    . . .
  }
}

// Validation error event handler
private static void ValidationErrors(object sender, ValidationEventArgs args)
{
  // Error details available from args.Message
  . . .
}
```

The following fragment shows how the consumer calls the preceding Web method:

```csharp
string xmlBookData = "<book  xmlns='urn:bookstore-schema'
            xmlns:xsi='http://www.w3.org/2001/XMLSchema-instance'>" +
            "<title>Building Secure ASP.NET Applications</title>" +
            "<isbn>0735618909</isbn>" +
            "<orderQuantity>1</orderQuantity>" +
            "</book>";
BookStore.BookService bookService = new BookStore.BookService();
bookService.OrderBooks(xmlBookData));
```

The preceding example uses the following simple XSD schema to validate the input data.

```
<?xml version="1.0" encoding="utf-8" ?>
<xsd:schema xmlns:xsd="http://www.w3.org/2001/XMLSchema"
            xmlns="urn:bookstore-schema"
            elementFormDefault="qualified"
            targetNamespace="urn:bookstore-schema">
  <xsd:element name="book" type="bookData"/>
  <xsd:complexType name="bookData">
    <xsd:sequence>
      <xsd:element name="title" type="xsd:string" />
      <xsd:element name="isbn" type="xsd:integer" />
      <xsd:element name="orderQuantity" type="xsd:integer"/>
    </xsd:sequence>
  </xsd:complexType>
</xsd:schema>
```

The following table shows additional complex element definitions that can be used in an XSD schema to further constrain individual XML elements.

Table 12.1   XSD Schema Element Examples

Description	Example
Using regular expressions to constrain XML elements	```<xsd:element name="zip">
<xsd:simpleType>
<xsd:restriction base="xsd:string">
<xsd:pattern value="\d{5}(-\d{4})?" />
</xsd:restriction>
</xsd:simpleType>
</xsd:element>```
Constraining a decimal value to two digits after the decimal point	```<xsd:element name="Salary">
<xsd:simpleType>
<xsd:restriction base="xsd:decimal">
<xsd:fractionDigits value="2" />
</xsd:restriction>
</xsd:simpleType>
</xsd:element>```
Constraining the length of an input string	```<xsd:element name="FirstName">
<xsd:simpleType>
<xsd:restriction base="xsd:string">
<xsd:maxLength value="50" />
<xsd:minLength value="2" />
</xsd:restriction>
</xsd:simpleType>
</xsd:element>```

Table 12.1 XSD Schema Element Examples *(continued)*

Description	Example

Constraining input to values defined by an enumerated type	`<xsd:element name="Gender">`
	`  <xsd:simpleType>`
	`    <xsd:restriction base="xsd:string">`
	`      <xsd:enumeration value="Male" />`
	`      <xsd:enumeration value="Female" />`
	`    </xsd:restriction>`
	`  </xsd:simpleType>`
	`</xsd:element>`

For more information, see Microsoft Knowledge Base articles:

- 307379, "How To: Validate an XML Document by Using DTD, XDR, or XSD in Visual C# .NET."
- 318504, "How To: Validate XML Fragments Against an XML Schema in Visual C#.NET."

SQL Injection

SQL injection allows an attacker to execute arbitrary commands in the database using the Web service's database login. SQL injection is a potential issue for Web services if the services use input data to construct SQL queries. If your Web methods access the database, they should do so using SQL parameters and ideally, parameterized stored procedures. SQL parameters validate the input for type and length, and they ensure that the input is treated as literal text and not executable code. For more information about this and other SQL injection countermeasures, see the "Input Validation" section in Chapter 14, "Building Secure Data Access."

Cross-Site Scripting

With cross-site scripting (XSS), an attacker exploits your application to execute malicious script at the client. If you call a Web service from a Web application and send the output from the Web service back to the client in an HTML data stream, XSS is a potential issue. In this scenario, you should encode the output received from the Web service in the Web application before returning it to the client. This is particularly important if you do not own the Web service and it falls outside the Web application's trust boundary. For more information about XSS countermeasures, see the "Input Validation" section in Chapter 10, "Building Secure ASP.NET Pages and Controls."

Authentication

If your Web service outputs sensitive, restricted data or if it provides restricted services, it needs to authenticate callers. A number of authentication schemes are available and these can be broadly divided into three categories:

- Platform level authentication
- Message level authentication
- Application level authentication

Platform Level Authentication

If you are in control of both endpoints and both endpoints are in the same or trusting domains, you can use Windows authentication to authenticate callers.

Basic Authentication

You can use IIS to configure your Web service's virtual directory for Basic authentication. With this approach, the consumer must configure the proxy and provide credentials in the form of a user name and password. The proxy then transmits them with each Web service request through that proxy. The credentials are transmitted in plaintext and therefore you should only use Basic authentication with SSL.

The following code fragment shows how a Web application can extract Basic authentication credentials supplied by an end user and then use those to invoke a downstream Web service configured for Basic authentication in IIS.

```
// Retrieve client's credentials (available with Basic authentication)
string pwd = Request.ServerVariables["AUTH_PASSWORD"];
string uid = Request.ServerVariables["AUTH_USER"];
// Set the credentials
CredentialCache cache = new CredentialCache();
cache.Add( new Uri(proxy.Url), // Web service URL
          "Basic",
            new NetworkCredential(uid, pwd, domain) );
proxy.Credentials = cache;
```

Integrated Windows Authentication

You can use IIS to configure your Web service's virtual directory for Integrated Windows authentication, which results either in Kerberos or NTLM authentication depending on the client and server environment. The advantage of this approach in comparison to Basic authentication is that credentials are not sent over the network, which eliminates the network eavesdropping threat.

To call a Web service configured for Integrated Windows authentication, the consumer must explicitly configure the **Credentials** property on the proxy.

To flow the security context of the client's Windows security context (either from an impersonating thread token or process token) to a Web service you can set the **Credentials** property of the Web service proxy to **CredentialCache.DefaultCredentials** as follows.

```
proxy.Credentials = System.Net.CredentialCache.DefaultCredentials;
```

You can also use an explicit set of credentials as follows:

```
CredentialCache cache = new CredentialCache();
cache.Add( new Uri(proxy.Url), // Web service URL
          "Negotiate",          // Kerberos or NTLM
          new NetworkCredential(userName, password, domain));
proxy.Credentials = cache;
```

If you need to specify explicit credentials, do not hard code them or store them in plaintext. Encrypt account credentials by using DPAPI and store the encrypted data either in an **<appSettings>** element in Web.config or beneath a restricted registry key.

For more information about platform level authentication, see the "Web Services Security" section in "Microsoft *patterns & practices* Volume I, *Building Secure ASP.NET Applications: Authentication, Authorization, and Secure Communication*" at *http://msdn.microsoft.com/library/en-us/dnnetsec/html/secnetlpMSDN.asp?frame=true.*

Message Level Authentication

You can use WSE to implement a message level authentication solution that conforms to the emerging WS-Security standard. This approach allows you to pass authentication tokens in a standard way by using SOAP headers.

Note   When two parties agree to use WS-Security, the precise format of the authentication token must also be agreed upon.

The following types of authentication token can be used and are supported by WSE:

- **User name and password**
- **Kerberos ticket**
- **X.509 certificate**
- **Custom token**

User Name and Password

You can send user names and password credentials in the SOAP header. However, because these are sent in plaintext, this approach should only be used in conjunction with SSL due to the network eavesdropping threat. The credentials are sent as part of the **<Security>** element, in the SOAP header as follows.

```
<wsse:Security
        xmlns:wsse="http://schemas.xmlsoap.org/ws/2002/12/secext">
  <wsse:UsernameToken>
    <wsse:Username>Bob</wsse:Username>
    <wsse:Password>YourStr0ngPassWord</wsse:Password>
  </wsse:UsernameToken>
</wsse:Security>
```

User Name and Password Digest

Instead of sending a plaintext password, you can send a password digest. The digest is a Base64-encoded SHA1 hash value of the UTF8-encoded password. However, unless this approach is used over a secure channel, the data can still be intercepted by attackers armed with network monitoring software and reused to gain authenticated access to your Web service. To help address this replay attack threat, a nonce and a creation timestamp can be combined with the digest.

User Name and Password Digest with Nonce and Timestamp

With this approach the digest is a SHA1 hash of a nonce value, a creation timestamp, and the password as follows.

```
digest = SHA1(nonce + creation timestamp + password)
```

With this approach, the Web service must maintain a table of nonce values and reject any message that contains a duplicate nonce value. While the approach helps protect the password and offers a basis for preventing replay attacks, it suffers from clock synchronization issues between the consumer and provider when calculating an expiration time, and it does not prevent an attacker capturing a message, modifying the nonce value, and then replaying the message to the Web service. To address this threat, the message must be digitally signed. With the WSE, you can sign a message using a custom token or an X.509 certificate. This provides tamperproofing and authentication, based on a public, private key pair.

Kerberos Tickets

You can send a security token that contains a Kerberos ticket as follows.

```
<wsse:Security
        xmlns:wsse="http://schemas.xmlsoap.org/ws/2002/12/secext">
  <wsse:BinarySecurityToken
          ValueType="wsse:Kerberosv5ST"
          EncodingType="wsse:Base64Binary">
    U87GGH91TT ...
  </wsse:BinarySecurityToken>
</wsse:Security>
```

X.509 Certificates

You can also provide authentication by sending an X.509 certificate as an authentication token.

```
<wsse:Security
        xmlns:wsse="http://schemas.xmlsoap.org/ws/2002/12/secext">
  <wsse:BinarySecurityToken
          ValueType="wsse:X509v3"
          EncodingType="wsse:Base64Binary">
    Hg6GHjis1 ...
  </wsse:BinarySecurityToken>
</wsse:Security>
```

For more information about the above approaches, see the samples that ship with WSE.

Application Level Authentication

You can design and build your own custom authentication by using custom SOAP headers for your application. Before doing so, review the features provided by the platform and WSE to see if any of these features can be used. If you must use a custom authentication mechanism, and you need to use cryptography, then use standard encryption algorithms exposed by the **System.Security.Cryptography** namespace.

Authorization

After authentication, you can restrict callers to a subset of the functionality exposed by your Web service, based on the caller's identity or role membership. You can restrict access to service endpoints (at the .asmx file level), individual Web methods, or specific functionality inside Web methods.

Web Service Endpoint Authorization

If your Web service is configured for Integrated Windows authentication you can configure NTFS permissions on your Web service (.asmx) files to control access, based on the security context of the original caller. This authorization is performed by the ASP.NET **FileAuthorizationModule** and impersonation is not required.

Regardless of the authentication type, you can use the ASP.NET **UrlAuthorizationModule** to control access to Web service (.asmx) files. You configure this by adding **<allow>** and **<deny>** elements to the **<authorization>** element in Machine.config or Web.config.

For more information about both forms of authorization, see the "Authorization" section in Chapter 19, "Securing Your ASP.NET Application and Web Services."

Web Method Authorization

You can use declarative principal permission demands to control access to individual Web methods based on the identity or role membership of the caller. The caller's identity and role membership is maintained by the principal object associated with the current Web request (accessed through **HttpContext.User**.)

```
[PrincipalPermission(SecurityAction.Demand, Role=@"Manager")]
[WebMethod]
public string QueryEmployeeDetails(string empID)
{
}
```

For more information about principal permission demands, see the "Authorization" section in Chapter 10, "Building Secure ASP.NET Pages and Controls."

Programmatic Authorization

You can use imperative permission checks or explicit role checks by calling **IPrincipal.IsInRole** inside your Web methods for fine-grained authorization logic as follows.

```
// This assumes non-Windows authentication. With Windows authentication
// cast the User object to a WindowsPrincipal and use Windows groups as
// role names
GenericPrincipal user = User as GenericPrincipal;
if (null != user)
{
  if ( user.IsInRole(@"Manager") )
  {
    // User is authorized to perform manager functionality
  }
}
```

Sensitive Data

The threats of network eavesdropping or information disclosure at intermediate application nodes must be addressed if your Web service request or response messages convey sensitive application data, for example, credit card numbers, employee details, and so on.

In a closed environment where you are in control of both endpoints, you can use SSL or IPSec to provide transport layer encryption. In other environments and where messages are routed through intermediate application modes, a message level solution is required. The WS-Security standard defines a confidentiality service based on the World Wide Web Consortium (W3C) XML Encryption standard that allows you to encrypt some or all of a SOAP message before it is transmitted.

XML Encryption

You can encrypt all or part of a SOAP message in three different ways:

- **Asymmetric encryption using X.509 certificates**
- **Symmetric encryption using shared keys**
- **Symmetric encryption using custom binary tokens**

Asymmetric Encryption Using X.509 Certificates

With this approach, the consumer uses the public key portion of an X.509 certificate to encrypt the SOAP message. This can only be decrypted by the service that owns the corresponding private key.

The Web service must be able to access the associated private key. By default, WSE searches for X.509 certificates in the local machine store. You can use the **<x509>** configuration element in Web.config to set the store location to the current user store as follows.

```
<configuration>
  <microsoft.web.services>
    <security>
      <x509 storeLocation="CurrentUser" />
    </security>
  </microsoft.web.services>
</configuration>
```

If you use the user store, the user profile of the Web service's process account must be loaded. If you run your Web service using the default ASPNET least privileged local account, version 1.1 of the .NET Framework loads the user profile for this account, which makes the user key store accessible.

For Web services built using version 1.0 of the .NET Framework, the ASPNET user profile is not loaded. In this scenario, you have two options.

- Run your Web service using a custom least privileged account with which you have previously interactively logged on to the Web server to create a user profile.

- Store the key in the local machine store and grant access to your Web service process account. On Windows 2000, this is the ASPNET account by default. On Windows Server 2003, it is the Network Service account by default.

To grant access, use Windows Explorer to configure an ACL on the following folder that grants full control to the Web service process account.

```
\Documents and Settings\All Users\Application Data\
                                Microsoft\Crypto\RSA\MachineKeys
```

For more information, see the "Managing X.509 Certificates," "Encrypting a SOAP Message Using an X.509 Certificate," and "Decrypting a SOAP Message Using an X.509 Certificate" sections in the WSE documentation.

Symmetric Encryption Using Shared Keys

With symmetric encryption, the Web service and its consumer share a secret key to encrypt and decrypt the SOAP message. This encryption is faster than asymmetric encryption although the consumer and the service provider must use some out-of-band mechanism to share the key.

For more information, see the "Encrypting a SOAP Message Using a Shared Key" and "Decrypting a SOAP Message Using a Shared Key" sections in the WSE documentation.

Symmetric Encryption Using Custom Binary Tokens

You can also use WSE to define a custom binary token to encapsulate the custom security credentials used to encrypt and decrypt messages. Your code needs two classes. The sender class must be derived from the **BinarySecurityToken** class to encapsulate the custom security credentials and encrypt the message. The recipient class must be derived from **DecryptionkeyProvider** class to retrieve the key and decrypt the message.

For more information, see the "Encrypting a SOAP Message Using a Custom Binary Security Token" and "Decrypting a SOAP Message Using a Custom Binary Security Token" sections in the WSE documentation.

Encrypting Parts of a Message

By default, WSE encrypts the entire SOAP body and none of the SOAP header information. However, you can also use WSE to programmatically encrypt and decrypt portions of a message.

For more information, see the "Specifying the Parts of a SOAP Message that are Signed or Encrypted" section in the WSE documentation.

Parameter Manipulation

Parameter manipulation in relation to Web services refers to the threat of an attacker altering the message payload in some way while the message request or response is in transit between the consumer and service.

To address this threat, you can digitally sign a SOAP message to allow the message recipient to cryptographically verify that the message has not been altered since it was signed. For more information, see the "Digitally Signing a SOAP Message" section in the WSE documentation.

Exception Management

Exception details returned to the consumer should only contain minimal levels of information and not expose any internal implementation details. For example, consider the following system exception that has been allowed to propagate to the consumer.

```
System.Exception: User not in managers role
    at EmployeeService.employee.GiveBonus(Int32 empID, Int32 percentage) in
c:\inetpub\wwwroot\employeesystem\employee.asmx.cs:line 207
```

The exception details shown above reveal directory structure and other details to the service consumer. This information can be used by a malicious user to footprint the virtual directory path and can assist with further attacks.

Web Services can throw three types of exceptions:

- **SoapException** objects.

  These can be generated by the CLR or by your Web method implementation code.

- **SoapHeaderException** objects

  These are generated automatically when the consumer sends a SOAP request that the service fails to process correctly.

- **Exception** objects

  A Web service can throw a custom exception type that derives from **System.Exception**. The precise exception type is specific to the error condition. For example, it might be one of the standard .NET Framework exception types such as **DivideByZeroException**, or **ArgumentOutOfRangeException** and so on.

Regardless of the exception type, the exception details are propagated to the client using the standard SOAP **<Fault>** element. Clients and Web services built with ASP.NET do not parse the **<Fault>** element directly but instead deal consistently with **SoapException** objects. This allows the client to set up try blocks that catch **SoapException** objects.

Note If you throw a **SoapException** from a custom HTTP module, it is not automatically serialized as a SOAP **<Fault>**. In this case, you have to create the SOAP **<Fault>** manually.

Using SoapExceptions

The following code shows a simple WebMethod, where the validation of application logic fails and, as a result, an exception is generated. The error information sent to the client is minimal. In this sample, the client is provided with a help desk reference that can be used to call support. At the Web server, a detailed error description for the help desk reference is logged to aid problem diagnosis.

```
using System.Xml;
using System.Security.Principal;

[WebMethod]
public void GiveBonus(int empID, int percentage)
{
  // Only managers can give bonuses
  // This example uses Windows authentication
  WindowsPrincipal wp = (HttpContext.Current.User as WindowsPrincipal);
  if( wp.IsInRole(@"Domain\Managers"))
  {
    // User is authorized to give bonus
    . . .
  }
  else
  {
    // Log error details on the server. For example:
    //    "DOMAIN\Bob tried to give bonus to Employee Id 345667;
    //     Access denied because DOMAIN\Bob is not a manager."
    // Note: User name is available from wp.Identity.Name

    // Return minimal error information to client using a SoapException
    XmlDocument doc = new XmlDocument();
    XmlNode detail = doc.CreateNode(XmlNodeType.Element,
                            SoapException.DetailElementName.Name,
                            SoapException.DetailElementName.Namespace);
    // This is the detail part of the exception
    detail.InnerText = "User not authorized to perform requested operation";
    throw new SoapException("Message string from your Web service",
                        SoapException.ServerFaultCode,
                        Context.Request.Url.AbsoluteUri, detail, null );
  }
}
```

The consumer code that handles potential SoapExceptions follows:

```
try
{
  EmployeeService service = new EmployeeService();
  Service.GiveBonus(empID,percentage);
}
catch (System.Web.Services.Protocols.SoapException se)
{
    // Extract custom message from se.Detail.InnerText
    Console.WriteLine("Server threw a soap exception" + se.Detail.InnerText );
}
```

Application Level Error Handling in Global.asax

ASP.NET Web applications commonly handle application level exceptions that are allowed to propagate beyond a method boundary in the **Application_Error** event handler in Global.asax. This feature is not available to Web services, because the Web service's **HttpHandler** captures the exception before it reaches other handlers.

If you need application level exception handling, create a custom SOAP extension to handle it. For more information, see MSDN article, "Altering the SOAP Message using SOAP Extensions" in the "Building Applications" section of the .NET Framework SDK at *http://www.microsoft.com/downloads /details.aspx?FamilyID=9b3a2ca6-3647-4070-9f41-a333c6b9181d&DisplayLang=en.*

Auditing and Logging

With a Web service, you can audit and log activity details and transactions either by using platform-level features or by using custom code in your Web method implementations.

You can develop code that uses the **System.Diagnostics.EventLog** class to log actions to the Windows event log. The permission requirements and techniques for using this class from a Web service are the same as for a Web application. For more information, see the "Auditing and Logging" section in Chapter 10, "Building Secure ASP.NET Pages and Controls."

Proxy Considerations

If you use WSDL to automatically generate a proxy class to communicate with a Web service, you should verify the generated code and service endpoints to ensure that you communicate with the desired Web service and not a spoofed service. If the WSDL files on a remote server are inadequately secured, it is possible for a malicious user to tamper with the files and change endpoint addresses, which can impact the proxy code that you generate.

Specifically, examine the **<soap:address>** element in the .wsdl file and verify that it points to the expected location. If you use Visual Studio .NET to add a Web reference by using the **Add Web Reference** dialog box, scroll down and check the service endpoints.

Finally, whether you use Visual Studio.NET to add a Web reference or manually generate the proxy code using Wsdl.exe, closely inspect the proxy code and look for any suspicious code.

Note You can set the **URL Behavior** property of the Web service proxy to **Dynamic**, which allows you to specify endpoint addresses in Web.config.

Code Access Security Considerations

Code access security can limit the resources that can be accessed and the operations that can be performed by your Web service code. An ASP.NET Web service is subject to ASP.NET code access security policy, configured by the Web service's **<trust>** element.

.NET Framework consumer code that calls a Web service must be granted the **WebPermission** by code access security policy. The precise state of the **WebPermission** determines the range of Web services that can be called. For example, it can constrain your code so that it can only call local Web services or services on a specified server.

If the consumer code has full trust, it is granted the unrestricted **WebPermission** which allows it to call any Web service. Partial trust consumer code is subject to the following limitations:

- If you call a Web service from a Medium trust Web application, by default you can only access local Web services.

- Consumer code that uses the WSE classes must be granted full trust. For example, if your Web service proxy classes derive from **Microsoft.Web.Services.WebServicesClientProtocol**, which is provided by the WSE, full trust is required. To use WSE from a partial trust Web application, you must sandbox calls to the Web service.

For more information about calling Web services from partial trust Web applications, see Chapter 9, "Using Code Access Security with ASP.NET." For more information about **WebPermission**, see the "Web Services" section in Chapter 8, "Code Access Security in Practice."

Deployment Considerations

The range of security options available to you depends greatly on the specific deployment scenarios your Web services attempt to cover. If you build applications that consume Web services in an intranet, then you have the widest range of security options and techniques at your disposal. If, however, your Web service is publicly accessible over the Internet, your options are far more lijmited. This section describes the implications of different deployment scenarios on the applicability of the approaches to securing Web services discussed previously in this chapter.

Intranet Deployment

Because you control the consumer application, the service, and the platform, intranets usually provide the widest range of available options for securing Web services.

With an intranet scenario, you can usually choose from the full range of authentication and secure communication options. For example, you mgiht decide to use Windows authentication if the consumer and service are in the same or trusting domains. You can specify that client application developers set the credentials property on the client proxy to flow the user's Windows credentials to the Web service.

Intranet communication is often over a private network, with some degree of security. If this is insufficient, you might decide to encrypt traffic by using SSL. You can also use message level security and install WSE on both the client and server to handle security at both ends transparently to the application. WSE supports authentication, digital signatures, and encryption.

Extranet Deployment

In an extranet scenario, you may need to expose your Web service over the Internet to a limited number of partners. The user community is still known, predictable, and possibly uses managed client applications, although they come from separate, independent environments. In this situation, you need an authentication mechanism that is suitable for both parties and does not rely on trusted domains.

You can use Basic authentication if you make account information available to both parties. If you use Basic authentication, make sure that you secure the credentials by using SSL.

Note   SSL only protects credentials over the network. It does not protect them in situations where a malicious user successfully installs a proxy tool (such as sslproxy) local to the client machine to intercept the call before forwarding it to the Web service over SSL.

As an alternate option for use with an extranet, you can use IIS client certificate authentication instead of passing explicit credentials. In this case, the calling application must present a valid certificate with the call. The Web service uses the certificate to authenticate the caller and authorize the operation. For more information, see the "Extranet Security" section in MSDN article, "Building Secure ASP.NET Applications" at *http://msdn.microsoft.com/library/en-us/dnnetsec/html /SecNetch06.asp.*

Internet Deployment

If you expose your Web service to a large number of Internet consumers and require authentication, the options available to you are substantially constrained. Any form of platform level authentication is unikely to be suitable, since the consumers will not have proper domain accounts to which they can map their credentials. The use of IIS client certicate authentication and the transport (SSL) level is also problematic when a large number of client certificates must be made known to the target IIS Web server (or the ISA Server in front of it). This leaves message and application-level authentication and authorization the most likely choice. Credentials passed by the consumer of the service in the form of user name, password, certicate, Kerberos ticket, or custom token) can be validated transparently by the Web services infrastructure (WSE) or programmatically inside the target service. client certificates are difficult to manage scale. Key management (issuing and revoking) becomes an issue. Also, certificate-based authentication is resource intensive and therefore is subject to scalability issues with large number of clients.

SSL usually provides encryption of the network traffic (server-side certicate only), but can also be supplemented by message-level encryption.

Using client certicates, while advantageous from a seucrity point of view, often becomes problematic for large numbers of users. You must carefully manage the certicates and consider how they should be delivered to clients, renewed, revoked, and so on. Another pottential issue in Internet situaions Is the oveall scalability of the solution due to processing overhead or the encryption/decryption and certificate validation for a large-scale Web service with significant workload.

Summary

WS-Security is the emerging standard for Web services security. The specification defines options for authentication by passing security tokens in a standard way using SOAP headers. Tokens can include user name and password credentials, Kerberos tickets, X.509 certificates, or custom tokens. WS-Security also addresses message privacy and integrity issues. You can encrypt whole or partial messages to provide privacy, and digitally sign them to provide integrity.

In intranet scenarios, where you are in control of both endpoints, platform level security options such as Windows authentication, can be used. For more complex scenarios where you do not control both endpoints and where messages are routed through intermediate application nodes, message level solutions are required. The following section, "Additional References," lists the Web sites you can use to track the emerging WS-Security standard and the associated WSE tool kit that allows you to build solutions that conform to this and other emerging Web service standards.

Additional Resources

For more information, see the following resources:

- For a printable checklist, see "Checklist: Securing Web Services" in the "Checklists" section of this guide.
- You can download the WSE at the Microsoft Web Services Developer Center home page at *http://msdn.microsoft.com/webservices.*
- For information on authentication, authorization and secure communication for Web services see the "Web Services Security" section in "Microsoft *patterns & practices* Volume I, *Building Secure ASP.NET Applications: Authentication, Authorization, and Secure Communication*" at *http://msdn.microsoft.com/library /default.asp?url=/library/en-us/dnnetsec/html/SecNetch10.asp.*
- For articles specific to Web Services security, see the MSDN articles at *http://msdn.microsoft.com/webservices/building/security/default.aspx.*
- For articles specific to Web Services Enhancements, see the MSDN articles at *http://msdn.microsoft.com/webservices/building/wse/default.aspx.*
- For information on using SSL with Web Services, see "How to Call a Web Service Using SSL" in the "How To" section of "Microsoft *patterns & practices* Volume I, *Building Secure ASP.NET Applications: Authentication, Authorization, and Secure Communication*" at *http://msdn.microsoft.com/library/en-us/dnnetsec/html /SecNetHT14.asp.*

- For information on using client certificates with Web Services, see MSDN article, "How To: Call a Web Service Using Client Certificates from ASP.NET" in the "How To" section of "Microsoft *patterns & practices* Volume I, *Building Secure ASP.NET Applications: Authentication, Authorization, and Secure Communication*" at *http://msdn.microsoft.com/library/en-us/dnnetsec/html/SecNetHT13.asp*.

- For information on WS-Security, see MSDN article, "WS-Security: New Technologies Help You Make Your Web Services More Secure" at *http://msdn.microsoft.com/msdnmag/issues/03/04/WS-Security/default.aspx*.

- For information on XML Encryption, see the W3C XML Encryption Working Group at *http://www.w3.org/Encryption/2001/*.

13

Building Secure Remoted Components

In This Chapter

- Authenticating and authorizing callers
- Preventing denial of service attacks against remote components
- Implementing secure serialization
- Protecting sensitive data

Overview

The Microsoft .NET Framework Remoting infrastructure has no default authentication or authorization mechanisms. However, if you host remote components with ASP.NET and use the **HttpChannel** for communication, you can use ASP.NET and IIS authentication and authorization services.

If performance is an issue, you might decide to use a custom host with the **TcpChannel**. You should only do so in trusted subsystem scenarios, where the range of possible callers is carefully controlled through out-of-band techniques such as the use of IPSec policies, which only allow communication from specified Web servers. With the **TcpChannel**, you must build your own authentication and authorization mechanisms. This is contrary to the principle of using tried and tested platform level security services, and requires significant development effort.

This chapter gives recommendations and guidance to help you build secure remote components. This includes components that use ASP.NET and the **HttpChannel**, and those that use custom executables and the **TcpChannel**. The typical deployment pattern assumed by this chapter is shown in Figure 13.1, where remote objects are located on a middle-tier application server and process requests from ASP.NET Web application clients, and also Windows applications deployed inside the enterprise.

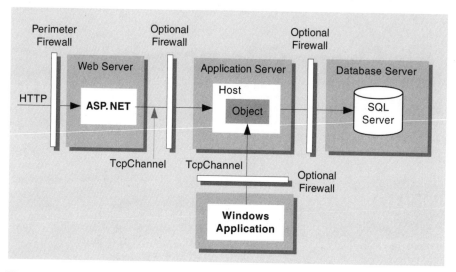

Figure 13.1
Typical remoting deployment

In this common scenario, the remote component services requests from front-end Web applications. In this case, ASP.NET on the Web server handles the authentication and authorization of callers. In addition, middle-tier remote components are often accessed by Enterprise Windows applications.

How to Use This Chapter

This chapter discusses various techniques to design and build secure components that you communicate with using the .NET Framework remoting technology.

To get the most from this chapter:

- **Use in conjunction with Chapter 17, "Securing Your Application Server."** Chapter 17 gives an administration perspective on securing a middle-tier remoting solution.

- **See "Checklist: Securing Remoting" in the Checklists section of this guide.** This gives a summary of the security measures required to build and configure secure .NET Framework remoting solutions.

Threats and Countermeasures

To build secure solutions that use remoting technology, you need to know the associated threats. The top threats to components that use remoting are:

- **Unauthorized access**
- **Network eavesdropping**
- **Parameter manipulation**
- **Serialization**

Figure 13.2 shows these threats.

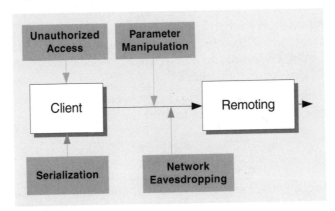

Figure 13.2
Main remoting threat

Unauthorized Access

Remote components that provide sensitive or restricted information should authenticate and authorize their callers to prevent unauthorized access. Weak authentication and authorization can be exploited to gain unauthorized access to sensitive information and operations.

Vulnerabilities

Vulnerabilities that make your remoting solution susceptible to unauthorized access include:

- No application level authentication because a custom Windows service host is used
- No IPSec policies to restrict which computers can communicate with the middle-tier application server that hosts the remote components
- No role-based authorization
- No file authorization to restrict access to remoting endpoints
- Trusting **IPrincipal** objects passed from the client

Countermeasures

Countermeasures that may be implemented to prevent unauthorized access include:

- Ensure that the front-end Web application authenticates and authorizes clients, and that communication to middle-tier application servers is restricted by using IPSec policies. These measures ensure that only the Web server can access the middle-tier application server directly.
- Use ASP.NET to host remote components and use Windows authentication to restrict access to remote components.
- Use the ASP.NET FileAuthorizationModule. This requires specific configuration and the creation of a physical file (.rem or .soap) to match the remoting endpoint.
- Use role-based authorization to restrict access to remote components, remote component classes, and methods. This can be done by using URL authorization to control access to the remoting endpoint (.rem or .soap) or, at the class or method level, by using principal-permission demands.
- Do not trust **IPrincipal** objects passed from the client unless the client is trusted. This is generally only the case if IPSec is used to limit the range of client computers.

Network Eavesdropping

With network eavesdropping, an attacker is able to view request and response messages as they flow across the network to and from the remote component. For example, an attacker can use network monitoring software to retrieve sensitive data. This might include sensitive application level data or credential information.

Vulnerabilities

Vulnerabilities that can lead to security compromises from network eavesdropping include:

- Basic authentication used over an unencrypted communication channel
- No transport level encryption
- No application level encryption

Countermeasures

Countermeasures that may be implemented to prevent successful network eavesdropping attacks include:

- Use transport level encryption such as SSL or IPSec. The use of SSL requires you to use an ASP.NET host and the **HttpChannel**. IPSec can be used with custom hosts and the **TcpChannel**.
- Encrypt the request at the application level to provide privacy. For example, you could create a custom encryption sink to encrypt part of the entire message payload.

Parameter Manipulation

Parameter manipulation refers to the unauthorized modification of data sent between the client and remote component. For example, an attacker can manipulate the request message destined for the remote component by intercepting the message while it is in transit.

Vulnerabilities

Vulnerabilities that can lead to parameter manipulation include:

- Messages that are not digitally signed to provide tamperproofing
- Message that are not encrypted to provide privacy and tamperproofing

Countermeasures

Countermeasures that may be implemented to prevent successful parameter manipulation include:

- Digitally sign the message. The digital signature is used at the recipient end to verify that the message has not been tampered with in transit.
- Encrypt the message payload to provide privacy and tamperproofing.

Serialization

Serialization is the process of converting an object's internal state to a flat stream of bytes. The remoting infrastructure uses the serialization services of the .NET Framework to pass objects between client and server. It is possible for malicious code to inject a serialized data stream to your server in order to coerce it into performing unintended actions. For example, malicious client-side code can initialize an object that, when de-serialized on the server, causes the server to consume server resources or execute malicious code.

Vulnerabilities

The main vulnerability that can lead to successful serialization attacks stems from the fact that the server trusts the serialized data stream and fails to validate the data retrieved from the stream.

Countermeasures

The countermeasure that prevents successful serialization attacks is to validate each item of data as it is deserialized on the server. Validate each field for type, length, format, and range.

Design Considerations

Before you begin to develop remote components, there are a number of issues to consider at design time. The key security considerations are:

- **Do not expose remoted objects to the Internet.**
- **Use the HttpChannel to take advantage of ASP.NET security.**
- **Use the TcpChannel only in trusted server scenarios.**

Do Not Expose Remoted Objects to the Internet

You should only host remoted objects on middle-tier application servers that are not directly accessible from the Internet, and that are only accessible from front-end Web applications and Web services. If you need to expose functionality provided by a remoted object to Internet clients, use a Web service to wrap the middle-tier object and expose the Web service to the Internet.

Use the HttpChannel to Take Advantage of ASP.NET Security

If security is your primary concern, use ASP.NET to host remoted objects. This allows you to take advantage of the authentication, authorization, and secure communication features provided by ASP.NET and IIS. For example, you can use Windows authentication and use SSL to provide privacy and for the integrity of requests and responses sent over the network.

Use the TcpChannel Only in Trusted Server Scenarios

If you use the **TcpChannel** with a custom host process for performance reasons, remember that no built-in authentication services exist.

For this reason, you should only use the **TcpChannel** in trusted server scenarios, where the upstream Web application or Web service authenticates and authorizes the original callers before it calls your middle-tier remoted components. To secure this scenario, use IPSec for machine-level authentication and secure communication. The IPSec policy should only permit traffic from the nominated Web server(s) to the middle-tier remote component host. This trusted server scenario is shown in Figure 13.3.

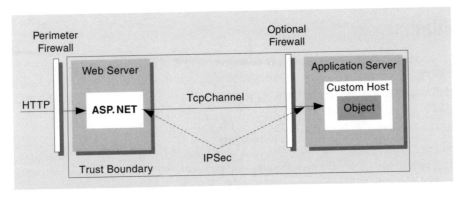

Figure 13.3
Remoting in a trusted server scenario

For more information about IPSec, see "How To: Use IPSec" in the "How To" section of this guide.

TcpChannel Considerations

If you use a custom executable host and the **TcpChannel**, and you cannot rely on an upstream Web application to perform client authentication and authorization, you have to develop your own authentication and authorization solutions.

As part of a custom solution you might decide to pass principal objects as method parameters or in the call context. You should only do so in a trusted environment to prevent malicious client-side code from creating an **IPrincipal** object with elevated roles and then sending it to your server. Your server implementation must be able to trust **IPrincipal** objects before using them for role-based authorization.

An alternative approach is to use the underlying services of the Security Support Provider Interface (SSPI). For more information about this approach, see MSDN article, ".NET Remoting Security Solution, Part 1: Microsoft.Samples.Security.SSPI Assembly," at *http://msdn.microsoft.com/library/en-us/dndotnet/html/remsspi.asp.*

To provide secure communication when you use the **TcpChannel**, use IPSec or a custom encryption channel sink to encrypt the request data.

Input Validation

In trusted server scenarios in which remoting solutions should be used, front-end Web applications generally perform input validation. The data is fully validated before it is passed to the remoted components. If you can guarantee that the data passed to a remoted component can only come from within the current trust boundary, you can let the upstream code perform the input validation.

If, however, your remoting solution can be accessed by arbitrary client applications running in the enterprise, your remote components should validate input and be wary of serialization attacks and **MarshalByRefObject** attacks.

Serialization Attacks

You can pass object parameters to remote components either by using the call context or by passing them through regular input parameters to the methods that are exposed by the remote component. It is possible for a malicious client to serialize an object and then pass it to a remote component with the explicit intention of tripping up the remote component or causing it to perform an unintended operation. Unless you can trust the client, you should carefully validate each field item in the deserialized object, because the object parameter is created on the server.

MarshalByRefObject Attacks

Objects that derive from **System.MarshalByRefObject** require a URL in order to make call backs to the client. It is possible for the callback URL to be spoofed so that the server connects to a different client computer, for example, a computer behind a firewall.

You can mitigate the risk of serialization and **MarshalByRefObject** attacks with version 1.1 of the .NET Framework by setting the **typeFilterLevel** attribute on the **<formatter>** element to **Low**. This instructs the .NET Framework remoting infrastructure to only serialize those objects it needs in order to perform the method invocation, and to reject any custom objects that support serialization that you create and put in the call context or pass as parameters. You can configure this setting in Web.config or programmatically as shown below.

```
<formatter ref="binary" typeFilterLevel="Low" />
```

or

```
BinaryServerFormatterSinkProvider provider = new
BinaryServerFormatterSinkProvider();
provider.TypeFilterLevel = TypeFilterLevel.Low;
```

Authentication

If your remote component exposes sensitive data or operations, it must authenticate its callers to support authorization. The .NET Framework remoting infrastructure does not define an authentication model. The host should handle authentication. For example, you can use ASP.NET to benefit from ASP.NET and IIS authentication features.

If you use a custom Windows service host, develop a custom authentication solution.

ASP.NET Hosting

The following guidelines apply if you use the ASP.NET host with the **HttpChannel**:

- **Turn off anonymous authentication in IIS.**
- **Configure ASP.NET for Windows authentication.**
- **Configure client credentials.**
- **Increase performance with authenticated connection sharing.**
- **Force clients to authenticate with each call.**
- **Control the use of authenticated connections.**

Turn off Anonymous Authentication in IIS

To ensure that callers are authenticated by IIS, make sure that your application's virtual directory does not support anonymous authentication. On Windows Server 2003, you should also ensure that .NET Passport authentication is disabled.

Since you have disabled IIS anonymous authentication, you can use any of the supported IIS authentication mechanisms to authenticate callers over the **HttpChannel**, for example Basic, Digest, and Integrated Windows. To avoid credentials being passed over the network and to take advantage of Windows 2000 security account and password policies, use Integrated Windows authentication.

Configure ASP.NET for Windows Authentication

Configure your application for Windows authentication with the following setting in Web.config:

```
<authentication mode="Windows" />
```

You cannot use Passport or Forms authentication because these require redirection to a login page.

Note When you use Windows authentication, you are recommended to enable File authorization. For more information, see "Authorization" later in this chapter.

Configure Client Credentials

To successfully communicate with a remote component that is configured for Windows authentication, the client must configure the remoting proxy with the credentials to use for authentication. Failure to do so results in an access denied error.

You can configure the use of default credentials to use the client's current thread or process token, or you can set explicit credentials.

Using Default Credentials

To use the client's process token (or thread token if the client thread is currently impersonating), set the **useDefaultCredentials** property of the client proxy to **true**. This results in the use of **CredentialsCache.DefaultCredentials** when the client receives an authentication challenge from the server. You can configure the proxy either by using the configuration file or programmatically in code. To configure the proxy externally, use the following element in the client configuration file:

```
<channel ref="http client" useDefaultCredentials="true" />
```

To set default credentials programmatically, use the following code:

```
IDictionary channelProperties;
channelProperties = ChannelServices.GetChannelSinkProperties(proxy);
channelProperties ["credentials"] = CredentialCache.DefaultCredentials;
```

If you use default credentials in an ASP.NET client application that is configured for impersonation, the thread level impersonation token is used. This requires Kerberos delegation.

Using Alternate Credentials

To use a specific set of credentials for authentication when you call a remote object, disable the use of default credentials within the configuration file by using the following setting.

```
<channel ref="http" useDefaultCredentials="false" />
```

Note   Programmatic settings always override the settings in the configuration file.

Then, use the following code to configure the proxy to use specific credentials:

```
IDictionary channelProperties =
                        ChannelServices.GetChannelSinkProperties(proxy);
NetworkCredential credentials;
credentials = new NetworkCredential("username", "password", "domain");
ObjRef objectReference = RemotingServices.Marshal(proxy);
Uri objectUri = new Uri(objectReference.URI);
CredentialCache credCache = new CredentialCache();
// Substitute "authenticationType" with "Negotiate", "Basic", "Digest",
// "Kerberos" or "NTLM"
credCache.Add(objectUri, "authenticationType", credentials);
channelProperties["credentials"] = credCache;
channelProperties["preauthenticate"] = true;
```

Increase Performance with Authenticated Connection Sharing

When you set **useDefaultCredentials="true"**, you should also set the **useAuthenticatedConnectionSharing** property on the client side to **true**. This enables the server to reuse authenticated connections, rather than authenticating each incoming call.

```
<channel ref="http client" useAuthenticatedConnectionSharing="true" >
```

This feature only works with the **HttpChannel** on version 1.1 of the .NET Framework.

Force Clients to Authenticate With Each Call

Set **unsafeAuthenticatedConnectionSharing** to **false** so that clients are not able to supply their own credentials and connection group name to the server.

If you set it to **true**, unauthenticated clients can possibly authenticate to the server using the credentials of a previously authenticated client. This setting is ignored if the **useAuthenticatedConnectionSharing** property is set to **true**. This setting has some performance implications since it closes each connection with the server, which means that clients must authenticate with each call. If you use this setting, you should also specify a **ConnectionGroupName** for each user that uses the connection.

```
<channel ref="http client" unsafeAuthenticatedConnectionSharing="false" >
```

This feature only works with the **HttpChannel** on version 1.1 of the .NET Framework.

Control the Use of Authenticated Connections

If you set **unsafeAuthenticationConnectionSharing** to **true**, you should provide a name to group together authenticated connections by setting the **connectionGroupName** property. If you use default credentials, the **connectionGroupName** is based on the user account used to run the thread.

```
<channel ref="http client" connectiongroupname="<name>" />
```

Custom Process Hosting

If you use a Windows service host and the **TcpChannel**, either use this approach only in a trusted server scenario, or provide a custom authentication scheme. The following guidelines apply if you use a custom host with the **TcpChannel**:

- **Do not pass plaintext credentials over the network.**
- **Do not trust IPrincipal objects passed from the client.**

Do Not Pass Plaintext Credentials over the Network

If your server requires the client's plaintext credentials, encrypt them before you send them over the network. If your server needs to validate the client credentials, use a challenge/response scheme to validate the credentials on the server. This could include sending a hash, keyed hash, a nonce encrypted with the hash, or a using a digital signature.

However, even in these scenarios, you should use an encrypted communication channel to prevent replay attacks.

Do Not Trust IPrincipal Objects Passed From the Client

Use caution if you pass **IPrincipal** objects from the client to the server. Untrusted code can create an **IPrincipal** object, initialize it with roles, and then send it to the server. If the server accepts the **IPrincipal** without validating it, the client can elevate the privileges of the caller on the server. For example, a malicious caller could create an **IPrincipal** object that contains common, highly privileged role names such as Administrators, Managers, ExpenseReportApprovers, and Supervisors. When the object is received on the server and placed in the **Thread.CurrentPrincipal** property, code that calls **IsInRole** on this object can be deceived into executing privileged code.

Authorization

Within the context of .NET Framework remoting, you can apply authorization to restrict the ability of computers and users to access functionality exposed by your remote objects. Use the following guidelines to ensure that you have an effective authorization approach:

- **Use IPSec for machine level access control.**
- **Enable file authorization for user access control.**
- **Authorize users with principal-based role checks.**
- **Consider limiting remote access.**

Use IPSec for Machine Level Access Control

You can define an IPSec policy to ensure that only a nominated Web server or cluster of servers can connect to the application server that hosts your remote objects. This significantly reduces the attack surface area.

Enable File Authorization for User Access Control

If your remote object is hosted by ASP.NET and uses Windows authentication, you can configure Windows access control lists (ACLs) on the remoting endpoints to authorize callers. ACLs are evaluated on a per-request basis by the ASP.NET **FileAuthorizationModule**. Under normal circumstances, a physical file representing your remoting endpoints to which your clients connect does not exist. The request for a file with a .rem or .soap extension is sufficient for IIS to be able to route the request based on application mappings defined in the IIS Metabase, to the remoting infrastructure in the appropriate ASP.NET application.

▶ **To configure the ASP.NET FileAuthorizationModule for .NET Framework remoting**

1. Create a file with the same name as the value specified in the **objectUri** property in Web.config, for example, RemoteMath.rem, in the root of the application's virtual directory.

   You can obtain the **objectUri** from the Web.config file used to configure the remote object on the server. Look for the **<wellknown>** element, as shown in the following example:

   ```
   <wellknown mode="SingleCall" objectUri="RemoteMath.rem"
   type="RemotingObjects.RemoteMath, RemotingObjects,
       Version=1.0.000.000 Culture=neutral, PublicKeyToken=4b5ae668c251b606"/>
   ```

2. Add the following line to the top of the file, and then save the file.

```
<%@ webservice class="YourNamespace.YourClass" ... %>
```

3. Add an appropriately configured ACL to the file using Windows Explorer to determine which users or user groups can and cannot access the object.

Authorize Users with Principal-Based Role Checks

The **FileAuthorizationModule** approach described above allows you to control who can and cannot access the remote object. For finer grained authorization that can be applied at the method level, you can perform authorization checks using the **IPrincipal** object attached to the current request.

If your remote object is hosed by ASP.NET and you use Windows authentication, an **IPrincipal** object based on the authenticated caller's Windows identity is automatically created and attached to **Thread.CurrentPrinicipal**.

If you use a custom host, create an **IPrincipal** object to represent the authenticated user. The mechanics depend on your authentication approach. For example if you use a named pipe transport, you can impersonate the caller to obtain their identity and construct an **IPrincipal** object.

With the **IPrincipal** object in place you can perform authorization using principal permission demands both declaratively and imperatively and you can call **IPrincipal.IsInRole**.

Consider Limiting Remote Access

In some scenarios, where you use remoting for inter process or cross application domain communication on a single computer, you can set **rejectRemoteRequests** to **true** to ensure that your object cannot be accessed from remote computers as shown below.

```
<channel ref="http server" rejectRemoteRequests="true" />
```

Sensitive Data

If you need to pass sensitive data over a remoting communication channel across a network, to address the network eavesdropping threat, consider the privacy and integrity of the data. You have three basic choices that are likely to be determined by your deployment environment and your choice of host. Your options include:

- Using IPSec
- Using SSL
- Using a custom encryption sink

Using IPSec

You can use IPSec policies to secure the communication channels to your remote objects, for example, the channel from a Web server. You can use IPSec to encrypt all of the TCP packets sent over a particular connection, which includes packets sent to and from your remote objects. This solution is generally used by secure Internet and intranet data center infrastructures and is beneficial because no additional coding effort is necessary.

The additional benefit of using IPSec is that it provides a secure communication solution irrespective of the remote object host and channel type. For example, the solution works when you use the **TcpChannel** and a custom host.

Using SSL

If you use the ASP.NET host, you can use IIS to configure the virtual directory of your application to require SSL. Clients must subsequently use an HTTPS connection to communicate with your remote objects.

Using a Custom Encryption Sink

If you do not have a secure data center with IPSec policies that secure the communication channels between your servers, an alternative strategy is to implement a custom encryption sink. You may also want to consider this option if you have a requirement to secure only the sensitive parts of the messages passed from client to server rather than the entire payload. This approach is shown in Figure 13.4.

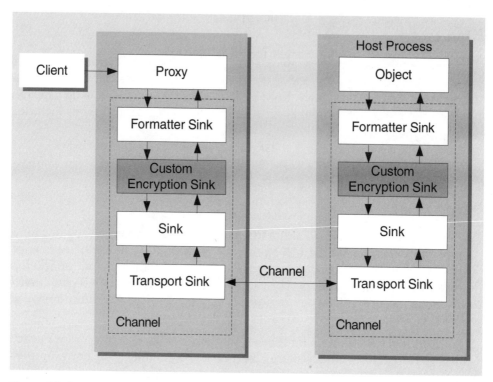

Figure 13.4

Using custom encryption sinks

An encryption sink is a custom channel sink that you can use when you use a custom host with the **TcpChannel**. On the client side, the sink encrypts request data before it is sent to the server and decrypts any encrypted response data received from the server. On the server side, the sink decrypts the request data and then encrypts response data.

Implementing a Custom Encryption Sink

The sink should use asymmetric encryption to exchange session level encryption keys. After exchanging a session key, the client and server maintain a copy of the key and either side may choose to create a new key at any time during the lifetime of the channel sink. The server should maintain a different key for each client it communicates with.

The following steps outline the basic approach to implement a custom encryption sink:

1. Create a public/private key pair for the solution.

```
const int AT_KEYEXCHANGE =  1;
CspParameters cspParams = new CspParameters();
cspParams.KeyContainerName = "<container name>";
cspParams.KeyNumber = AT_KEYEXCHANGE;
cspParams.ProviderName = "Microsoft Base Cryptographic Provider v1.0";
cspParams.ProviderType = PROV_RSA_FULL;
RSACryptoServiceProvider rsaServerSide = new
                              RSACryptoServiceProvider(cspParams);

rsaServerSide.PersistKeyInCsp = true;
Console.WriteLine(rsaServerSide.ToXmlString(true)); // Writes the public key
```

2. Expose the public key for clients to consume.

    The client maintains a copy of the public key in a file.

3. Initialize the client channel sink and create a random key for encryption.

```
byte[] randomKey = new byte[size];
RNGCryptoServiceProvider rng = new RNGCryptoServiceProvider();
rng.GetBytes(randomKey);
```

4. Encrypt the random key with the pubic key of your server. Use **IClientChannelSink.ProcessMessage** to send the encrypted key to the server.

```
RSACryptoServiceProvider rsa = new RSACryptoServiceProvider(csp);
rsa.FromXmlString("<server's public key>");
AsymmetricKeyExchangeFormatter formatter = new
                              RSAPKCS1KeyExchangeFormatter(rsa);
byte[] encryptedSessionKey =  formatter.CreateKeyExchange(_sessionKey);
```

5. Initialize the server channel sink and create an RSA object using the specific key container name.

```
const int AT_KEYEXCHANGE =  1;
CspParameters cspParams = new CspParameters();
cspParams.KeyContainerName = "<container name>";
cspParams.KeyNumber = AT_KEYEXCHANGE;
cspParams.ProviderName = "Microsoft Base Cryptographic Provider v1.0";
cspParams.ProviderType = PROV_RSA_FULL;
RSACryptoServiceProvider rsaServerSide = new
RSACryptoServiceProvider(cspParams);
```

6. Retrieve the encrypted key from the client. This key is normally sent in the request headers.

7. Decrypt the session encryption key using the private key of the server.

```
AsymmetricKeyExchangeDeformatter asymDeformatter = new
                                RSAPKCS1KeyExchangeDeformatter(_rsa);
byte[] decryptedSessionKey =  asymDeformatter.DecryptKeyExchange(
                                                    <encrypted key>);
```

8. Use a mechanism for mapping clients to encryption keys, for example, by using a hash table.

At this point, the client and server both share an encryption key, and can encrypt and decrypt method calls. Periodically during the object lifetime, new keys can and should be created.

Denial of Service

Denial of service attacks can occur when a malicious client creates multiple objects and continues to renew the lifetime lease to consume server resources. Server-side remote objects contain a default lease. In this state, a client can continue to renew the lease forever. However, you can implement the **ILease** interface on the server and explicitly control sponsors and renewals. To do this, override **InitializeLifetimeService** on your **MarshalByRefObject** object. The remoting infrastructure calls this method when the object is created. The lease can also be set programmatically by using the **<lifetime>** element.

Exception Management

Make sure you do not return full exception details to the caller. If you use an ASP.NET host, make sure ASP.NET is configured so that generic error messages are returned to the client, as shown below.

```
<configuration>
  <system.runtime.remoting>
   <!-- Valid values for mode attribute are
        on - callers receive default error messages
        remoteOnly - clients on the same computer as the remote component receive
                     detailed exception information. Remote calls receive a
                     default error message
        off - callers receive detailed exception information -->
     <customErrors mode="on"/>
  </system.runtime.remoting>
</configuration>
```

Use **mode="on"** or **mode="remoteOnly"**. Do not use **mode="off"** on production servers.

Using a Custom Channel Sink

You could implement a custom channel sink to perform client-side and/or server-side exception logging. You can log exception details in the **SyncProcessMessage**, **ProcessMessage**, or **SyncProcessMessage** methods if an exception occurs. The **IMessage** and **Exception** parameters provide exception details.

Auditing and Logging

If you use the ASP.NET host, you can use IIS auditing features. If you use a custom host, implement custom auditing. To do this, you could implement a custom channel sink.

Using a Custom Channel Sink

You could implement a custom channel sink to perform client-side and/or server-side auditing. You can get details from the **SyncProcessMessage**, **ProcessMessage**, or **SyncProcessMessage** methods.

Code Access Security (CAS) Considerations

Remoting clients require full trust on version 1.0 and 1.1 of the .NET Framework. The **System.Runtime.Remoting.dll** assembly is not marked with **AllowPartiallyTrustedCallersAttribute**.

To use remoting to call a remote component from partial trust code such as a partial trust Web application, you must create a full trust wrapper assembly and sandbox the remote object method calls. For more information about sandboxing code and using wrapper assemblies, see Chapter 9, "Using Code Access Security with ASP.NET."

Summary

The .NET Framework remoting infrastructure is designed for use in trusted server scenarios where you can limit callers to trusted clients, for example by using IPSec security policies. If you use an ASP.NET host and the **HttpChannel**, you benefit from being able to use the underlying security features provided by ASP.NET and IIS. If you use a custom host and the **TcpChannel**, perhaps for performance reasons, you must implement your own authentication and authorization solutions. IPSec can help in these scenarios by providing machine level authentication and secure communication.

Additional Resources

For more information, see the following resources:

- For a printable checklist, see "Checklist: Securing Remoting" in the "Checklists" section of this guide.

- For information on how to host a remoted component in a Windows service, see "How To: Host a Remote Object in a Windows Service" in the "How To" section of "Microsoft *patterns & practices* Volume I, *Building Secure ASP.NET Applications: Authentication, Authorization, and Secure Communication*" at *http://msdn.microsoft.com/library/en-us/dnnetsec/html/SecNetHT15.asp*.

- For more information about how to create a custom authentication solution that uses SSPI, see MSDN article, ".NET Remoting Security Solution, Part 1: Microsoft.Samples.Security.SSPI Assembly," at *http://msdn.microsoft.com/library /en-us/dndotnet/html/remsspi.asp*.

Note   The implementation in this article is a sample and not a product tested and supported by Microsoft.

14

Building Secure Data Access

In this Chapter

- Preventing SQL injection attacks
- Encrypting data in the database
- Securing data over the network
- Securing database connection strings
- Handling data access exceptions

Overview

The database is a prime target for application level attacks. Application level attacks are used to exploit vulnerabilities in your data access code to gain access to the database. If all other attack vectors are closed, then the application's front door, port 80, becomes the path of choice for an attacker to steal, manipulate, and destroy data.

This chapter shows you how to build secure data access code and avoid common vulnerabilities and pitfalls. The chapter presents a series of countermeasures and defensive techniques that you can use in your data access code to mitigate the top threats related to data access.

How to Use This Chapter

To get the most out of this chapter, read the following chapters before or in conjunction with this chapter:

- **Read Chapter 2, "Threats and Countermeasures."** This will give you a broader and deeper understanding of potential threats and countermeasures faced by Web applications.

- **Read Chapter 4, "Design Guidelines for Secure Web Applications."** In this chapter, you will learn the architecture and design challenges and guidelines for building a secure solution.

- **Read Chapter 18, "Securing Your Database Server."** Read Chapter 18 to understand how the database servers are secured.

- **Read Chapter 7, "Building Secure Assemblies."** The guidelines and recommendations in Chapter 7 for building secure assemblies and for developing secure managed code should also be applied to data access code.

- **Use the Assessing Chapters**. To review the security of your data access at different stages of the product cycle, refer to the Web services sections in the following chapters: Chapter 5, "Architecture and Design Review for Security," Chapter 21, "Code Review," and Chapter 22, "Deployment Review."

- **Use the Checklist**. "Checklist: Securing Data Access" in the Checklists section of this guide includes a checklist for easy reference. Use this task-based checklist as a summary of the recommendations in this chapter.

Threats and Countermeasures

To build secure data access code, know what the threats are, how common vulnerabilities arise in data access code, and how to use appropriate countermeasures to mitigate risk.

The top threats to data access code are:

- **SQL injection**
- **Disclosure of configuration data**
- **Disclosure of sensitive application data**
- **Disclosure of database schema and connection details**
- **Unauthorized access**
- **Network eavesdropping**

Figure 14.1 illustrates these top threats.

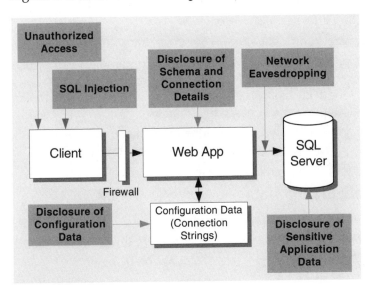

Figure 14.1
Threats and attacks to data access code

SQL Injection

SQL injection attacks exploit vulnerable data access code and allow an attacker to execute arbitrary commands in the database. The threat is greater if the application uses an unconstrained account in the database because this gives the attacker greater freedom to execute queries and commands.

Vulnerabilities

Common vulnerabilities that make your data access code susceptible to SQL injection attacks include:

- Weak input validation
- Dynamic construction of SQL statements without the use of type-safe parameters
- Use of over-privileged database logins

Countermeasures

To counter SQL injection attacks, be sure to:

- Constrain and sanitize input data.
- Use type safe SQL parameters for data access. These parameters can be used with stored procedures or dynamically constructed SQL command strings. Parameters perform type and length checks and also ensure that injected code is treated as literal data, not executable statements in the database.
- Use an account that has restricted permissions in the database. Ideally, you should only grant execute permissions to selected stored procedures in the database and provide no direct table access.

Disclosure of Configuration Data

The most sensitive configuration data used by data access code is the database connection string. If a compromised connection string includes a user name and password, the consequences can be greater still.

Vulnerabilities

The following vulnerabilities increase the security risk associated with compromised configuration data:

- Use of SQL authentication, which requires credentials to be specified in the connection string
- Embedded connection strings in code
- Clear text connection strings in configuration files
- Failure to encrypt a connection string

Countermeasures

To prevent disclosure of configuration data:

- Use Windows authentication so that connection strings do not contain credentials.
- Encrypt the connection strings and restrict access to the encrypted data.

Disclosure of Sensitive Application Data

Many applications store sensitive data, such as customer credit card numbers. It is essential to protect the privacy and integrity of this type of data.

Vulnerabilities

Coding practices that can lead to the disclosure of sensitive application data include:

- Storing data with no encryption
- Weak authorization
- Weak encryption

Countermeasures

To prevent disclosure of sensitive application data:

- Use strong encryption to secure the data.
- Authorize each caller prior to performing data access so that users are only able to see their own data.

Disclosure of Database Schema and Connection Details

If your code returns exception details to the client, a malicious user can use the information to attack the server. Exceptions in data access code can reveal sensitive information, such as database schema details, the nature of the data store, and SQL code fragments.

Vulnerabilities

The following vulnerabilities can result in information disclosure:

- Inadequate exception handling
- Weak ASP.NET configuration that allows unhandled exception details to be returned to the client

Countermeasures

To prevent such disclosure:

- Catch, log, and handle data access exceptions in your data access code.
- Return generic error messages to the caller. This requires appropriate configuration of the **<customErrors>** element in the Web.config or Machine.config configuration file.

Unauthorized Access

With inadequate authorization, users may be able to see another user's data and may be able to access other restricted data.

Vulnerabilities

Practices that can allow unauthorized access include:

- Lack of authorization in data access code providing unrestricted access
- Over-privileged database accounts

Countermeasures

To prevent unauthorized access:

- Use principal permission demands to authorize the calling user.
- Use code access security permission demands to authorize the calling code.
- Use limited permissions to restrict the application's login to the database and to prevent direct table access.

Network Eavesdropping

The deployment architecture of most applications includes a physical separation of the data access code from the database server. As a result, sensitive data such as application-specific data or database login credentials must be protected from network eavesdroppers.

Vulnerabilities

The following practices increase vulnerability to network eavesdropping:

- Clear text credentials passed over the network during SQL authentication
- Unencrypted sensitive application data sent to and from the database server

Countermeasures

To limit vulnerability to network eavesdropping:

- Use Windows authentication to avoid sending credentials over the network.
- Install a server certificate on the database server. This results in the automatic encryption of SQL credentials over the network.
- Use an SSL connection between the Web server and database server to protect sensitive application data. This requires a database server certificate.
- Use an IPSec encrypted channel between Web and database server.

Design Considerations

Before you start writing code, there are a number of important issues to consider at design time. The key considerations are:

- **Use Windows authentication.**
- **Use least privileged accounts.**
- **Use stored procedures.**
- **Protect sensitive data in storage.**
- **Use separate data access assemblies.**

Use Windows Authentication

Ideally, your design should use Windows authentication for the added security benefits. With Windows authentication, you do not have to store database connection strings with embedded credentials, credentials are not passed over the network, and you benefit from secure account and password management policies. You do however need to carefully consider which account you will use to connect to SQL Server using Windows authentication.

For more information, see "Authentication" later in this chapter.

Use Least Privileged Accounts

Your application should use a least privileged account that has limited permissions in the database. Be sure that the application login to the database is appropriately authorized and restricted. For details, see "Authorization" later in this chapter.

Using least privileged accounts reduces risk and limits the potential damage if your account is compromised or malicious code is injected. In the case of SQL injection, the command executes under the security context defined by the application login and is subject to the associated permissions that the login has in the database. If you connect using an overprivileged account—for example, as a member of the SQL Server **sysadmin** role—the attacker can perform any operation in any database on the server. This includes inserting, updating, and deleting data; dropping tables; and executing operating system commands.

Important   Do not connect to SQL Server using the **sa** account or any account that is a member of the SQL Server **sysadmin** or **db_owner** roles.

Use Stored Procedures

Stored procedures offer performance, maintenance, and security benefits. Use parameterized stored procedures for data access where possible. The security benefits include:

- You can restrict the application database login so that it only has permission to execute specified stored procedures. Granting direct table access is unnecessary. This helps mitigate the risk posed by SQL injection attacks.
- Length and type checks are performed on all input data passed to the stored procedure. Also, parameters cannot be treated as executable code. Again, this mitigates the SQL injection risk.

If you cannot use parameterized stored procedures for some reason and you need to construct SQL statements dynamically, do so using typed parameters and parameter placeholders to ensure that input data is length and type checked.

Protect Sensitive Data in Storage

Identify stored data that requires guaranteed privacy and integrity. If you store passwords in database solely for the purposes of verification, consider using a one-way hash. If the table of passwords is compromised, the hashes cannot be used to obtain the clear text password.

If you store sensitive user-supplied data such as credit card numbers, use a strong symmetric encryption algorithm such as Triple DES (3DES) to encrypt the data. Encrypt the 3DES encryption key using the Win32 Data Protection API (DPAPI), and store the encrypted key in a registry key with a restricted ACL that only administrators and your application process account can use.

Why not DPAPI?

While DPAPI is recommended for encrypting connection strings and other secrets such as account credentials that can be manually recovered and reconstructed in the event of machine failure, it is less suited to storing data like credit card numbers. This is because of recoverability issues (if the keys are lost, there is no way to recover the encrypted data) and Web farm issues. Instead, you should use a symmetric encryption algorithm such as 3DES and encrypt the encryption key using DPAPI.

The main issues that make DPAPI less suited for storing sensitive data in the database are summarized below:

- If DPAPI is used with the machine key and you pass **CRYPTPROTECT_LOCAL_MACHINE** to the **CryptProtectData** and **CryptUnprotectData** functions, the machine account generates the encryption keys. This means that each server in a Web farm has a different key, which prevents one server from being able to access data encrypted by another server. Also, if the Web server machine is destroyed, the key is lost, and the encrypted data cannot be recovered from the database.

- If you use the machine key approach, any user on that computer can decrypt the data (unless you use additional encryption mechanisms).

- If you use DPAPI with a user key and use local user accounts, each local account on each Web server has a different security identifier (SID) and a different key is generated, which prevents one server from being able to access data encrypted by another server.

- If you use DPAPI with a user key and you use a roaming user profile across the machines in the Web farm, all data will share the same encryption/decryption key. However, if the domain controller responsible for the roaming user profile account is damaged or destroyed, a user account with the same SID cannot be recreated, and you cannot recover the encrypted data from the database.

  Also, with a roaming user profile, if someone manages to retrieve the data, it can be decrypted on any machine in the network, provided that the attacker can run code under the specific user account. This increases the area for potential attack, and is not recommended.

Use Separate Data Access Assemblies

If you have a choice, avoid placing data access logic directly in ASP.NET pages or in code-behind files. There are security, reuse, and maintenance advantages to placing data access logic in a separate assembly and implementing a logical data access layer that is separate from your application business and presentation logic.

From a security perspective, you can:

- Use a strong name for the assembly, which provides tamperproofing.
- Use sandboxing to isolate your data access code, which is important if your code needs to support partial-trust callers — for example, partial-trust Web applications.
- Use data access methods and classes that authorize calling code using code identity permission demands.

For defense in depth, perform principal-based authorization using principal permission demands in your business components and use code identity permission demands to authorize the code that calls your data access logic, as shown in Figure 14.2.

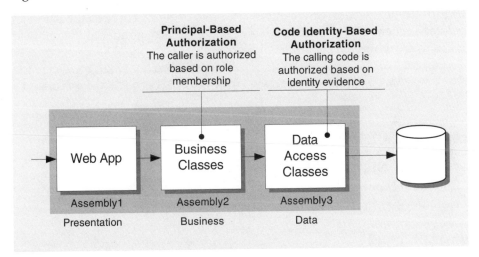

Figure 14.2
Separation of presentation, business, and data access layers

For more information about authorization for data access code, see the "Authorization" section, later in this chapter.

Input Validation

Aside from the business need to ensure that your databases maintain valid and consistent data, you must validate data prior to submitting it to the database to prevent SQL injection. If your data access code receives its input from other components inside the current trust boundary and you know the data has already been validated (for example, by an ASP.NET Web page or business component) then your data access code can omit extensive data validation. However, make sure you use SQL parameters in your data access code. These parameters validate input parameters for type and length. The next section discusses the use of SQL parameters.

SQL Injection

SQL injection attacks can occur when your application uses input to construct dynamic SQL statements to access the database. SQL injection attacks can also occur if your code uses stored procedures that are passed strings which contain unfiltered user input. SQL injection can result in attackers being able to execute commands in the database using the application login. The issue is magnified if the application uses an overprivileged account to connect to the database.

Note   Conventional security measures, such as the use of SSL and IPSec, do not protect you against SQL injection attacks.

Preventing SQL Injection

Use the following countermeasures to prevent SQL injection attacks:

- **Constrain input**.
- **Use type safe SQL parameters**.

Constrain Input

Validate input for type, length, format, and range. If you do not expect numeric values, then do not accept them. Consider where the input comes from. If it is from a trusted source that you know has performed thorough input validation, you may choose to omit data validation in your data access code. If the data is from an untrusted source or for defense in depth, your data access methods and components should validate input.

Use Type Safe SQL Parameters

The **Parameters** collection in SQL provides type checking and length validation. If you use the **Parameters** collection, input is treated as a literal value and SQL does not treat it as executable code. An additional benefit of using the **Parameters** collection is that you can enforce type and length checks. Values outside of the range trigger an exception. This is a healthy example of defense in depth.

Important   SSL does not protect you from SQL injection. Any application that accesses a database without proper input validation and appropriate data access techniques is susceptible to SQL injection attacks.

Use stored procedures where you can, and call them with the **Parameters** collection.

Using the Parameters Collection with Stored Procedures

The following code fragment illustrates the use of the **Parameters** collection:

```
SqlDataAdapter myCommand = new SqlDataAdapter("AuthorLogin", conn);
myCommand.SelectCommand.CommandType = CommandType.StoredProcedure;
SqlParameter parm = myCommand.SelectCommand.Parameters.Add(
                      "@au_id", SqlDbType.VarChar, 11);
parm.Value = Login.Text;
```

In this case, the **@au_id** parameter is treated as a literal value and not as executable code. Also, the parameter is type and length checked. In the sample above, the input value cannot be longer than 11 characters. If the data does not conform to the type or length defined by the parameter, an exception is generated.

Note that using stored procedures does not necessarily prevent SQL injection. The important thing to do is use parameters with stored procedures. If you do not use parameters, your stored procedures can be susceptible to SQL injection if they use unfiltered input. For example, the following code fragment is vulnerable:

```
SqlDataAdapter myCommand = new SqlDataAdapter("LoginStoredProcedure '" +
                      Login.Text + "'", conn);
```

Important   If you use stored procedures, make sure you use parameters.

Using the Parameters Collection with Dynamic SQL

If you cannot use stored procedures, you can still use parameters, as shown in the following code fragment:

```
SqlDataAdapter myCommand = new SqlDataAdapter(
"SELECT au_lname, au_fname FROM Authors WHERE au_id = @au_id", conn);
SqlParameter parm = myCommand.SelectCommand.Parameters.Add("@au_id",
                          SqlDbType.VarChar, 11);
parm.Value = Login.Text;
```

Using Parameter Batching

A common misconception is that if you concatenate several SQL statements to send a batch of statements to the server in a single round trip, then you cannot use parameters. However, you can use this technique if you make sure that parameter names are not repeated. You can easily do this by adding a number or some other unique value to each parameter name during SQL text concatenation.

Using Filter Routines

Another approach used to protect against SQL injection attacks is to develop filter routines that add escape characters to characters that have special meaning to SQL, such as the single apostrophe character. The following code fragment illustrates a filter routine that adds an escape character:

```
private string SafeSqlLiteral(string inputSQL)
{
   return inputSQL.Replace("'", "''");
}
```

The problem with routines such as this and the reason why you should not rely on them completely is that an attacker could use ASCII hexadecimal characters to bypass your checks. You should, however, filter input as part of your defense in depth strategy.

Note   Do not rely on filtering input.

Using LIKE Clauses

Note that if you are using a LIKE clause, wildcard characters still need escape characters. The following code fragment illustrates this technique:

```
s = s.Replace("[", "[[]");
s = s.Replace("%", "[%]");
s = s.Replace("_", "[_]");
```

Authentication

When your application connects to a SQL Server database, you have a choice of Windows authentication or SQL authentication. Windows authentication is more secure. If you must use SQL authentication, perhaps because you need to connect to the database using a number of different accounts and you want to avoid calling **LogonUser**, take additional steps to mitigate the additional risks as far as possible.

Note Using **LogonUser** to create an impersonation token requires the powerful "Act as part of the operating system" privilege on Microsoft Windows 2000 and so this approach should be avoided.

Consider the following recommendations:

- **Use Windows authentication.**
- **Protect the credentials for SQL authentication.**
- **Connect using a least privileged account.**

Use Windows Authentication

Windows authentication does not send credentials over the network. If you use Windows authentication for a Web application, in most cases, you use a service account or a process account, such as the ASPNET account, to connect to the database. Windows and SQL Server must both recognize the account you use on the database server. The account must be granted a login to SQL Server and the login needs to have associated permissions to access a database.

When you use Windows authentication, you use a trusted connection. The following code fragments show typical connection strings that use Windows authentication.

The example below uses the ADO.NET data provider for SQL Server:

```
SqlConnection pubsConn = new SqlConnection(
    "server=dbserver; database=pubs; Integrated Security=SSPI;");
```

The example below uses the ADO.NET data provider for OLE DB data sources:

```
OleDbConnection pubsConn = new OleDbConnection(
    "Provider=SQLOLEDB; Data Source=dbserver; Integrated Security=SSPI;" +
    "Initial Catalog=northwind");
```

Protect the Credentials for SQL Authentication

If you must use SQL authentication, be sure that the credentials are not sent over the network in clear text and encrypt the database connection string because it contains credentials.

To enable SQL Server to automatically encrypt credentials sent over the network, install a server certificate on the database server. Alternatively, use an IPSec encrypted channel between the Web and database servers to secure all traffic sent to and from the database server. To secure the connection string, use DPAPI. For more information, see "Secure Your Connection String" in the "Configuration Management" section, later in this chapter.

Connect Using a Least Privileged Account

Your application should connect to the database by using a least privileged account. If you use Windows authentication to connect, the Windows account should be least privileged from an operating system perspective and should have limited privileges and limited ability to access Windows resources. Additionally, whether or not you use Windows authentication or SQL authentication, the corresponding SQL Server login should be restricted by permissions in the database.

For more information about how to create a least privileged database account and the options for connecting an ASP.NET Web application to a remote database using Windows authentication, see "Data Access" in Chapter 19, "Securing Your ASP.NET Application and Web Services."

Authorization

The authorization process establishes if a user can retrieve and manipulate specific data. There are two approaches: your data access code can use authorization to determine whether or not to perform the requested operation, and the database can perform authorization to restrict the capabilities of the SQL login used by your application.

With inadequate authorization, a user may be able to see the data of another user and an unauthorized user may be able to access restricted data. To address these threats:

- **Restrict unauthorized callers.**
- **Restrict unauthorized code.**
- **Restrict the application in the database.**

Figure 14.3 summarizes the authorization points and techniques that should be used.

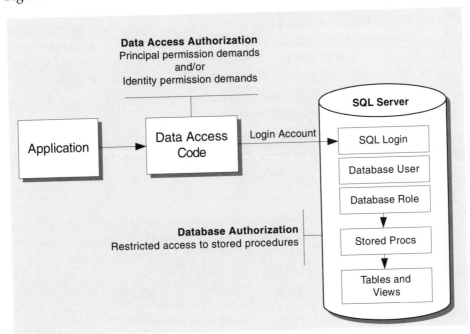

Figure 14.3
Data access authorization, assembly, and database

Notice how the data access code can use permission demands to authorize the calling user or the calling code. Code identity demands are a feature of .NET code access security.

To authorize the application in the database, use a least privileged SQL server login that only has permission to execute selected stored procedures. Unless there are specific reasons, the application should not be authorized to perform create, retrieve, update, destroy/delete (CRUD) operations directly on any table.

Note   Stored procedures run under the security context of the database system. Although you can constrain the logical operations of an application by assigning it permissions to particular stored procedures, you cannot constrain the consequences of the operations performed by the stored procedure. Stored procedures are trusted code. The interfaces to the stored procedures must be secured using database permissions.

Restrict Unauthorized Callers

You code should authorize users based on a role or identity before it connects to the database. Role checks are usually used in the business logic of your application, but if you do not have a clear distinction between business and data access logic, use principal permission demands on the methods that access the database.

The following attribute ensures that only users who are members of the **Manager** role can call the **DisplayCustomerInfo** method:

```
[PrincipalPermissionAttribute(SecurityAction.Demand, Role="Manager")]
public void DisplayCustomerInfo(int CustId)
{
}
```

If you need additional authorization granularity and need to perform role-based logic inside the data access method, use imperative principal permission demands or explicit role checks as shown in the following code fragment:

```
using System.Security;
using System.Security.Permissions;

public void DisplayCustomerInfo(int CustId)
{
  try
  {
    // Imperative principal permission role check to verify that the caller
    // is a manager
    PrincipalPermission principalPerm = new PrincipalPermission(
                                        null, "Manager");
    // Code that follows is only executed if the caller is a member
    // of the "Manager" role
  }
  catch( SecurityException ex )
  {
    . . .
  }
}
```

The following code fragment uses an explicit, programmatic role check to ensure that the caller is a member of the **Manager** role:

```
public void DisplayCustomerInfo(int CustId)
{
  if(!Thread.CurrentPrincipal.IsInRole("Manager"))
  {
    . . .
  }
}
```

Restrict Unauthorized Code

By using .NET Framework code access security—specifically, code identity demands —you can limit the assemblies that can access your data access classes and methods.

For example, if you only want code written by your company or a specific development organization to be able to use your data access components, use a **StrongNameIdentityPermission** and demand that calling assemblies have a strong name with a specified public key, as shown in the following code fragment:

```
using System.Security.Permissions;
. . .
[StrongNameIdentityPermission(SecurityAction.LinkDemand,
                             PublicKey="002...4c6")]
public void GetCustomerInfo(int CustId)
{
}
```

To extract a text representation of the public key for a given assembly, use the following command:

```
sn -Tp assembly.dll
```

Note   Use an uppercase "T" in the **–Tp** switch.

Because Web application assemblies are dynamically compiled, you cannot use strong names for these assemblies. This makes it difficult to restrict the use of a data access assembly to a specific Web application. The best approach is to develop a custom permission and demand that permission from the data access component. Full trust Web applications (or any fully trusted code) can call your component. Partial trust code, however, can call your data access component only if it has been granted the custom permission.

For an example implementation of a custom permission, see "How To: Create a Custom Encryption Permission" in the "How To" section of this guide.

Restrict the Application in the Database

The preferred approach is to create a SQL Server login for the Windows account that the application uses to connect to the database. Then map the SQL Server login to a database user in your database. Place the database user in a user-defined database role and grant permissions to that role. Ideally, you should only grant the role execute access to the stored procedures used by the application.

For details about how to configure this approach, see "Configuring Data Access for Your ASP.NET Application" in Chapter 19, "Securing Your ASP.NET Application and Web Services."

Configuration Management

Database connection strings are the main configuration management concern for data access code. Carefully consider where these strings are stored and how they are secured, particularly if they include credentials. To improve your encryption management security:

- **Use Windows authentication.**
- **Secure your connection strings.**
- **Secure UDL files with restricted ACLs.**

Use Window Authentication

When you use Windows authentication, the credentials are managed for you and the credentials are not transmitted over the network. You also avoid embedding user names and passwords in connection strings.

Secure Your Connection Strings

If you need to use SQL authentication, then your connection contains the user name and password. If an attacker exploits a source code disclosure vulnerability on the Web server or manages to log on to the server, the attacker can retrieve the connection strings. Similarly, anyone with a legitimate login to the server can view them. Secure connection strings using encryption.

Encrypt the Connection String

Encrypt connection strings by using DPAPI. With DPAPI encryption, you avoid encryption key management issues because the encryption key is managed by the platform and is tied to either a specific computer or a Windows user account. To use DPAPI, you must call the Win32 DPAPI functions through **P/Invoke.**

For details on how to build a managed wrapper class, see "How To: Create a DPAPI Library" in the "How To" section of "Microsoft *patterns & practices* Volume I, *Building Secure ASP.NET Applications: Authentication, Authorization, and Secure Communication*" at *http://msdn.microsoft.com/library/default.asp?url=/library/en-us/dnnetsec/html /secnetlpMSDN.asp.*

Store Encrypted Connection Strings Securely

The encrypted connection string can be placed in the registry or in the Web.config or Machine.config file. If you use a key beneath **HKEY_LOCAL_MACHINE**, apply the following ACL to the key:

```
Administrators: Full Control
Process Account: Read
```

Note The process account is determined by the process in which your data access assembly runs. This is usually the ASP.NET process or an Enterprise Services server process if your solution uses an Enterprise Services middle tier.

Alternatively you can consider using **HKEY_CURRENT_USER**, which provides restricted access. For more information, see the "Registry" section in Chapter 7, "Building Secure Assemblies."

Note If you use the Visual Studio.NET database connection Wizards, the connection strings are stored either as a clear text property value in the Web application code-behind file or in the Web.config file. Both of these approaches should be avoided.

Although it is potentially less secure than using a restricted registry key, you may want to store the encrypted string in the Web.config for easier deployment. In this case, use a custom **<appSettings>** name-value pair as shown below:

```xml
<?xml version="1.0" encoding="utf-8" ?>
<configuration>
 <appSettings>
    <add key="connectionString" value="AQA..bIE=" />
 </appSettings>
 <system.web>
   ...
 </system.web>
</configuration>
```

To access the cipher text from the **<appSettings>** element, use the **ConfigurationSettings** class as shown below:

```
using System.Configuration;
private static string GetConnectionString()
{
  return ConfigurationSettings.AppSettings["connectionString"];
}
```

Do Not Use Persist Security Info='True' or 'Yes'

When you include the **Persist Security Info** attribute in a connection string, it causes the **ConnectionString** property to strip out the password from the connection string before it is returned to the user. The default setting of **false** (equivalent to omitting the **Persist Security Info** attribute) discards the information once the connection is made to the database.

Secure UDL Files with Restricted ACLs

If your application uses external universal data link (UDL) files with the ADO.NET managed data provider for OLE DB, use NTFS permissions to restrict access. Use the following restricted ACL:

```
Administrators: Full Control
Process Account: Read
```

Note UDL files are not encrypted. A more secure approach is to encrypt the connection string using DPAPI and store it in a restricted registry key.

Sensitive Data

Many Web applications store sensitive data of one form or another in the database. If an attacker manages to execute a query against your database, it is imperative that any sensitive data items—such as credit card numbers—are suitably encrypted.

- **Encrypt sensitive data if you need to store it.**
- **Secure sensitive data over the network.**
- **Store password hashes with salt.**

Encrypt Sensitive Data if You Need to Store It

Avoid storing sensitive data if possible. If you must store sensitive data, encrypt the data.

Using 3DES Encryption

To store sensitive data, such as credit card numbers, in the database, use a strong symmetric encryption algorithm such as 3DES.

▶ **During development, to enable 3DES encryption**

1. Use the **RNGCryptoServiceProvider** class to generate a strong (192 bit, 24 byte) encryption key.
2. Back up the encryption key, and store the backup in a physically secure location.
3. Encrypt the key with DPAPI and store it in a registry key. Use the following ACL to secure the registry key:

```
Administrators: Full Control
Process Account (for example ASPNET): Read
```

▶ **At runtime, to store encrypted data in the database**

1. Obtain the data to be encrypted.
2. Retrieve the encrypted encryption key from the registry.
3. Use DPAPI to decrypt the encryption key.
4. Use the **TripleDESCryptoServiceProvider** class with the encryption key to encrypt the data.
5. Store the encrypted data in the database.

▶ **At runtime, to decrypt the encrypted secrets**

1. Retrieve the encrypted data from the database.
2. Retrieve the encrypted encryption key from the registry.
3. Use DPAPI to decrypt the encryption key.
4. Use the **TripleDESCryptoServiceProvider** class to decrypt the data.

With this process, if the DPAPI account used to encrypt the encryption key is damaged, the backup of the 3DES key can be retrieved from the backup location and be encrypted using DPAPI under a new account. The new encrypted key can be stored in the registry and the data in the database can still be decrypted.

For more information about creating a managed DPAPI library, see "How To: Create a DPAPI Library" in the "How To" section of "Microsoft *patterns & practices* Volume I, *Building Secure ASP.NET Applications: Authentication, Authorization, and Secure Communication*" at *http://msdn.microsoft.com/library/default.asp?url=/library/en-us/dnnetsec/html/secnetlpMSDN.asp*.

Secure Sensitive Data Over the Network

Sensitive data passed across the network to and from the database server may include application specific data or database login credentials. To ensure the privacy and integrity of data over the network, either use a platform-level solution (such as that provided by a secure datacenter where IPSec encrypted communication channels are used between servers) or configure your application to establish SSL connections to the database. The latter approach requires a server certificate installed on the database server.

For more information about using SSL and IPSec, see "How To: Use IPSec to Provide Secure Communication Between Two Servers" and "How To: Use SSL to Secure Communication to SQL Server 2000" in the "How To" section of "Microsoft *patterns & practices* Volume I, *Building Secure ASP.NET Applications: Authentication, Authorization, and Secure Communication*" at *http://msdn.microsoft.com/library/default.asp?url=/library/en-us/dnnetsec/html/secnetlpMSDN.asp*.

Store Password Hashes with Salt

If you need to implement a user store that contains user names and passwords, do not store the passwords either in clear text or in encrypted format. Instead of storing passwords, store non-reversible hash values with added salt to mitigate the risk of dictionary attacks.

Note   A salt value is a cryptographically strong random number.

Creating a Salt Value

The following code shows how to generate a salt value by using random number generation functionality provided by the **RNGCryptoServiceProvider** class within the **System.Security.Cryptography** namespace.

```
public static string CreateSalt(int size)
{
  RNGCryptoServiceProvider rng = new RNGCryptoServiceProvider();
  byte[] buff = new byte[size];
  rng.GetBytes(buff);
  return Convert.ToBase64String(buff);
}
```

Creating a Hash Value (with Salt)

The following code fragment shows how to generate a hash value from a supplied password and salt value.

```
public static string CreatePasswordHash(string pwd, string salt)
{
  string saltAndPwd = string.Concat(pwd, salt);
  string hashedPwd =
        FormsAuthentication.HashPasswordForStoringInConfigFile(
                                      saltAndPwd, "SHA1");
  return hashedPwd;
}
```

More Information

For more information about implementing a user store that stores password hashes with salt, see "How To: Use Forms Authentication with SQL Server 2000" in the "How To" section of "Microsoft *patterns & practices* Volume I, *Building Secure ASP.NET Applications: Authentication, Authorization, and Secure Communication*" at *http://msdn.microsoft.com/library/default.asp?url=/library/en-us/dnnetsec/html /secnetlpMSDN.asp.*

Exception Management

Exception conditions can be caused by configuration errors, bugs in your code, or malicious input. Without proper exception management, these conditions can reveal sensitive information about the location and nature of your data source in addition to valuable connection details. The following recommendations apply to data access code:

- **Trap and log ADO.NET exceptions.**
- **Ensure database connections are always closed.**
- **Use a generic error page in your ASP.NET applications.**

Trap and Log ADO.NET Exceptions

Place data access code within a **try / catch** block and handle exceptions. When you write ADO.NET data access code, the type of exception generated by ADO.NET depends on the data provider. For example:

- The SQL Server .NET Framework data provider generates **SqlExceptions**.
- The OLE DB .NET Framework data provider generates **OleDbExceptions**.
- The ODBC .NET Framework data provider generates **OdbcExceptions**.

Trapping Exceptions

The following code uses the SQL Server .NET Framework data provider and shows how you should catch exceptions of type **SqlException**.

```
try
{
  // Data access code
}
catch (SqlException sqlex) // more specific
{
}
catch (Exception ex) // less specific
{
}
```

Logging Exceptions

You should also log details from the **SqlException** class. This class exposes properties that contain details of the exception condition. These include a **Message** property that describes the error, a **Number** property that uniquely identifies the type of error, and a **State** property that contains additional information. The **State** property is usually used to indicate a particular occurrence of a specific error condition. For example, if a stored procedure generates the same error from more than one line, the **State** property indicates the specific occurrence. Finally, an **Errors** collection contains **SqlError** objects that provide detailed SQL server error information.

The following code fragment shows how to handle a SQL Server error condition by using the SQL Server .NET Framework data provider:

```csharp
using System.Data;
using System.Data.SqlClient;
using System.Diagnostics;

// Method exposed by a Data Access Layer (DAL) Component
public string GetProductName( int ProductID )
{
  SqlConnection conn = new SqlConnection(
        "server=(local);Integrated Security=SSPI;database=products");
  // Enclose all data access code within a try block
  try
  {
    conn.Open();
    SqlCommand cmd = new SqlCommand("LookupProductName", conn );
    cmd.CommandType = CommandType.StoredProcedure;

    cmd.Parameters.Add("@ProductID", ProductID );
    SqlParameter paramPN =
        cmd.Parameters.Add("@ProductName", SqlDbType.VarChar, 40 );
    paramPN.Direction = ParameterDirection.Output;

    cmd.ExecuteNonQuery();
    // The finally code is executed before the method returns
    return paramPN.Value.ToString();
  }
  catch (SqlException sqlex)
  {
    // Handle data access exception condition
    // Log specific exception details
    LogException(sqlex);
    // Wrap the current exception in a more relevant
    // outer exception and re-throw the new exception
    throw new Exception(
                "Failed to retrieve product details for product ID: " +
                ProductID.ToString(), sqlex );
  }
```

(continued)

```
  finally
  {
    conn.Close(); // Ensures connection is closed
  }
}

// Helper routine that logs SqlException details to the
// Application event log
private void LogException( SqlException sqlex )
{
  EventLog el = new EventLog();
  el.Source = "CustomAppLog";
  string strMessage;
  strMessage = "Exception Number : " + sqlex.Number +
               "(" + sqlex.Message + ") has occurred";
  el.WriteEntry( strMessage );

  foreach (SqlError sqle in sqlex.Errors)
  {
    strMessage = "Message: " + sqle.Message +
                 " Number: " + sqle.Number +
                 " Procedure: " + sqle.Procedure +
                 " Server: " + sqle.Server +
                 " Source: " + sqle.Source +
                 " State: " + sqle.State +
                 " Severity: " + sqle.Class +
                 " LineNumber: " + sqle.LineNumber;
    el.WriteEntry( strMessage );
  }
}
```

Ensure Database Connections Are Closed

If an exception occurs, it is essential that database connections are closed and any other limited resources are released. Use **finally** blocks, or the C# **using** statement to ensure that connections are closed whether an exception condition occurs or not. The above code illustrates the use of the **finally** block. You can also use the C# **using** statement, as shown below:

```
using ((SqlConnection conn = new SqlConnection(connString)))
{
  conn.Open();
  // Connection will be closed if an exception is generated or if control flow
  // leaves the scope of the using statement normally
}
```

Use a Generic Error Page in Your ASP.NET Applications

If your data access code is called by an ASP.NET Web application or Web service, you should configure the **<customErrors>** element to prevent exception details propagating back to the end user. You can also specify a generic error page by using this element, as shown below.

```
<customErrors mode="On" defaultRedirect="YourErrorPage.htm" />
```

Set **mode="On"** for production servers. Only use **mode="Off"** when you are developing and testing software prior to release. Failure to do so results in rich error information, such as that shown in Figure 14.4, being returned to the end user. This information can include the database server name, database name, and connection credentials.

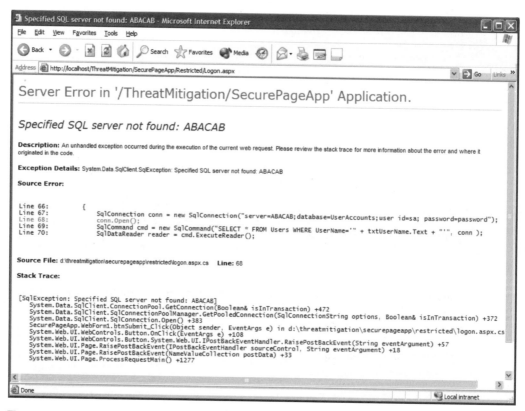

Figure 14.4
Detailed exception information revealing sensitive data

Figure 14.4 also shows a number of vulnerabilities in the data access code near the line that caused the exception. Specifically:

- The connection string is hard-coded.
- The highly privileged **sa** account is used to connect to the database.
- The **sa** account has a weak password.
- The SQL command construction is susceptible to SQL injection attack; the input is not validated, and the code does not use parameterized stored procedures.

Building a Secure Data Access Component

The following code shows a sample implementation of a **CheckProductStockLevel** method used to query a products database for stock quantity. The code illustrates a number of the important security features for data access code introduced earlier in this chapter.

```
using System;
using System.Data;
using System.Data.SqlClient;
using System.Text.RegularExpressions;
using System.Collections.Specialized;
using Microsoft.Win32;
using DataProtection;

public static int CheckProductStockLevel(string productCode)
{
  int quantity = 0;
  // (1) Code protected by try/catch block
  try
  {
    // (2) Input validated with regular expression
    //     Error messages should be retrieved from the resource assembly to help
    //     localization. The Localization code is omitted for the sake of brevity.
    if (Regex.IsMatch(productCode, "^[A-Za-z0-9]{12}$") == false)
      throw new ArgumentException("Invalid product code" );
    //(3) The using statement ensures that the connection is closed
    using (SqlConnection conn = new SqlConnection(GetConnectionString()))
    {
      // (4) Use of parameterized stored procedures is a countermeasure for
      //     SQL injection attacks
      SqlCommand cmd = new SqlCommand("spCheckProduct", conn);
      cmd.CommandType = CommandType.StoredProcedure;
```

(continued)

(continued)

```
            // Parameters are type checked
            SqlParameter parm =
                    cmd.Parameters.Add("@ProductCode",
                                        SqlDbType.VarChar,12);
            parm.Value = productCode;
            // Define the output parameter
            SqlParameter retparm = cmd.Parameters.Add("@quantity", SqlDbType.Int);
            retparm.Direction = ParameterDirection.Output;
            conn.Open();
            cmd.ExecuteNonQuery();
            quantity = (int)retparm.Value;
        }
    }
    catch (SqlException sqlex)
    {
        // (5) Full exception details are logged. Generic (safe) error message
        //     is thrown back to the caller based on the SQL error code
        //     Log and error identification code has been omitted for clarity
        throw new Exception("Error Processing Request");
    }
    catch (Exception ex)
    {
        // Log full exception details
        throw new Exception("Error Processing Request");
    }
    return quantity;
}


// (6) Encrypted database connection string is held in the registry
private static string GetConnectionString()
{
    // Retrieve the cipher text from the registry; the process account must be
    // granted Read access by the key's ACL
    string encryptedString = (string)Registry.LocalMachine.OpenSubKey(
                                    @"Software\OrderProcessing\")
                                    .GetValue("ConnectionString");
    // Use the managed DPAPI helper library to decrypt the string
    DataProtector dp = new DataProtector(DataProtector.Store.USE_MACHINE_STORE);
    byte[] dataToDecrypt = Convert.FromBase64String(encryptedString);
    return Encoding.ASCII.GetString(dp.Decrypt(dataToDecrypt,null));
}
```

The code shown above exhibits the following security characteristics (identified by the numbers in the comment lines).

1. **The data access code is placed inside a try/catch block.** This is essential to prevent the return of system level information to the caller in the event of an exception. The calling ASP.NET Web application or Web service might handle the exception and return a suitably generic error message to the client, but the data access code does not rely on this.

2. **Input is validated using a regular expression.** The supplied product ID is checked to verify that it contains characters in the range A–Z and 0–9 only, and does not exceed 12 characters. This is the first in a set of countermeasures designed to prevent SQL injection attacks.

3. **The SqlConnection object is created inside a C# using statement.** This ensures that the connection is closed inside the method regardless of whether an exception occurs. This mitigates the threat of denial of service attacks, which attempt to use all available connections to the database. You can achieve similar functionality by using a **finally** block.

4. **Parameterized stored procedures are used for data access.** This is another countermeasure to prevent SQL injection.

5. **Detailed error information is not returned to the client.** Exception details are logged to assist with problem diagnosis.

6. **The Encrypted database connection string is stored in the registry.** One of the most secure ways of storing database connection strings is to use DPAPI to encrypt the string and store the encrypted cipher text in a secured registry key that has a restricted ACL. (For example, use Administrators: Full Control and ASP.NET or Enterprise Services process account: Read, depending on which process hosts the component.)

   Other options are discussed in the "Database Connection Strings" section of this chapter.

Note   The code shows how to retrieve the connection string from the registry and then decrypt it using the managed DPAPI helper library. This library is provided in "How To: Create a DPAPI Library" in the "How To" section of "Microsoft *patterns & practices* Volume I, *Building Secure ASP.NET Applications: Authentication, Authorization, and Secure Communication*" at *http://msdn.microsoft.com/library/en-us/dnnetsec/html/SecNetHT07.asp*.

Code Access Security Considerations

All data access is subject to code access security permission demands. Your chosen ADO.NET managed data provider determines the precise requirements. The following table shows the permissions that must be granted to your data access assemblies for each ADO.NET data provider.

Table 14.1   Code Access Security Permissions Required by ADO.NET Data Providers

ADO.NET Data Provider	Required Code Access Security Permission
SQL Server	SqlClientPermission Supports partial trust callers including Medium trust Web applications.
OLE DB	OleDbPermission*
Oracle	OraclePermission*
ODBC	OdbcPermission*

*At the time of writing, the OLE DB, Oracle, and ODBC providers support only Full trust callers on versions 1.0 and 1.1 of the .NET Framework. To use these providers from partial trust Web applications, you must sandbox your data access code, which necessitates a dedicated data access assembly. For an example that shows how to sandbox data access code and use the OLE DB data provider from a Medium trust Web application see Chapter 9, "Using Code Access Security with ASP.NET."

If you use the ADO.NET SQL Server data provider, your code must be granted the **SqlClientPermission** by code access security policy. Full and Medium trust Web applications have this permission.

Whether or not code is granted the **SqlClientPermission** determines whether or not the code can connect to SQL Servers. You can also use the permission to place restrictions on the use of database connection strings. For example, you can force an application to use integrated security or you can ensure that if SQL Server security is used then blank passwords are not accepted. Violations of the rules you specify through the **SqlClientPermission** result in runtime security exceptions.

For more information about how to use **SqlClientPermission** to constrain data access, see "Data Access" in Chapter 8, "Code Access Security in Practice."

Deployment Considerations

A securely designed and developed data access component can still be vulnerable to attack if it is not deployed in a secure manner. A common deployment practice is for the data access code and database to reside on separate servers. The servers are often separated by an internal firewall, which introduces additional deployment considerations. Developers and administrators, be aware of the following issues:

- **Firewall restrictions**
- **Connection string management**
- **Login account configuration**
- **Logon auditing**
- **Data privacy and integrity on the network**

Firewall Restrictions

If you connect to SQL Server through a firewall, configure the firewall, client, and server. You configure the client by using the SQL Server Client Network Utility and you configure the database server by using the Server Network Utility. By default, SQL Server listens on TCP port 1433, although you can change this. You must open the chosen port at the firewall.

Depending on the SQL Server authentication mode you choose and your application's use of distributed transactions, you may need to open several additional ports at the firewall:

- If your application uses Windows authentication to connect to SQL Server, the necessary ports to support Kerberos or NTLM authentication must be open.

  For networks that do not use Active Directory, TCP port 139 is usually required for Windows authentication. For more information about port requirements, see TechNet articles, "TCP and UDP Port Assignments," at *http://www.microsoft.com /technet/prodtechnol/windows2000serv/reskit/tcpip/part4/tcpappc.asp*, and "Security Considerations for Administrative Authority," at *http://www.microsoft.com/technet /security/bestprac/bpent/sec2/seconaa.asp*

- If your application uses distributed transactions, for example automated COM+ transactions, you might also need to configure your firewall to allow DTC traffic to flow between separate DTC instances, and between the DTC and resource managers such as SQL Server.

For full configuration details, see the "Ports" section in Chapter 18, "Securing Your Database Server."

Connection String Management

Many applications store connection strings in code primarily for performance reasons. However, the performance benefit is negligible, and use of file system caching helps to ensure that storing connection strings in external files gives comparable performance. Using external files to store connection strings is superior for system administration.

For increased security, the recommended approach is to use DPAPI to encrypt the connection string. This is particularly important if your connection string contains user names and passwords. Then, decide where to store the encrypted string. The registry is a secure location particularly if you use **HKEY_CURRENT_USER**, because access is limited to processes that run under the associated user account. An alternative for easier deployment is to store the encrypted string in the Web.config file. Both approaches were discussed in the "Configuration Management" section earlier in this chapter.

Login Account Configuration

It is essential that your application uses a least privileged account to connect to the database. This is one of the primary threat mitigation techniques for SQL injection attacks.

As a developer you must communicate to the database administrator the precise stored procedures and (possibly) tables that the application's login needs to access. Ideally, you should only allow the application's login to have execute permissions on a restricted set of stored procedures that are deployed along with the application.

Use strong passwords for the SQL or Windows account or accounts used by the application to connect to the database.

See the "Authorization" section earlier in this chapter for the recommended authorization strategy for the application account in the database.

Logon Auditing

You should configure SQL Server to log failed login attempts and possibly successful login attempts. Auditing failed login attempts is helpful to detect an attacker who is attempting to discover account passwords.

For more information about how to configure SQL Server auditing, see Chapter 18, "Securing Your Database Server."

Data Privacy and Integrity on the Network

If you use SQL authentication to connect to SQL Server, ensure that login credentials are not exposed over the network. Either install a certificate on the database server (which causes SQL Server to encrypt the credentials) or use an IPSec encrypted channel to the database.

The use of IPSec or SSL to the database is recommended to protect sensitive application level data passed to and from the database. For more information, see Chapter 18, "Securing Your Database Server."

Summary

This chapter showed the top threats to data access code and highlighted the common vulnerabilities. SQL injection is one of the main threats to be aware of. Unless you use the correct countermeasures discussed in this chapter, an attacker could exploit your data access code to run arbitrary commands in the database. Conventional security measures such as firewalls and SSL provide no defense to SQL injection attacks. You should thoroughly validate your input and use parameterized stored procedures as a minimum defense.

Additional Resources

For more information, see the following resources:

- For a printable checklist, see "Checklist: Securing Data Access" in the "Checklists" section of this guide.
- For information on securing your developer workstation, see "How To: Secure Your Developer Workstation" in the "How To" section of this guide.
- For information on using SSL with SQL Server, see "How To: Use SSL to Secure Communication with SQL Server 2000," in the "How To" section of "Microsoft *patterns & practices* Volume I, *Building Secure ASP.NET Applications: Authentication, Authorization, and Secure Communication*" at *http://msdn.microsoft.com/library/en-us /dnnetsec/html/SecNetHT19.asp.*
- For information on using IPSec, see "How To: Use IPSec to Provide Secure Communication Between Two Servers" in the "How To" section of "Microsoft *patterns & practices* Volume I, *Building Secure ASP.NET Applications: Authentication, Authorization, and Secure Communication*" at *http://msdn.microsoft.com/library/en-us /dnnetsec/html/SecNetHT18.asp.*
- For information on using DPAPI, see "How To: Create a DPAPI Library" in the "How To" section of "Microsoft *patterns & practices* Volume I, *Building Secure ASP.NET Applications: Authentication, Authorization, and Secure Communication*" at *http://msdn.microsoft.com/library/en-us/dnnetsec/html/SecNetHT07.asp.*

Part IV

Securing Your Network, Host, and Application

In This Part:

- Securing Your Network
- Securing Your Web Server
- Securing Your Application Server
- Securing Your Database Server
- Securing Your ASP.NET Application and Web Services
- Hosting Multiple Web Applications

15

Securing Your Network

In This Chapter

- Securing your network
- Identifying network threats and describing countermeasures
- Showing secure router, firewall, and switch configurations
- Providing a snapshot of a secure network

Overview

The network is the entry point to your application. It provides the first gatekeepers that control access to the various servers in your environment. Servers are protected with their own operating system gatekeepers, but it is important not to allow them to be deluged with attacks from the network layer. It is equally important to ensure that network gatekeepers cannot be replaced or reconfigured by imposters. In a nutshell, network security involves protecting network devices and the data that they forward.

The basic components of a network, which act as the front-line gatekeepers, are the router, the firewall, and the switch. Figure 15.1 shows these core components.

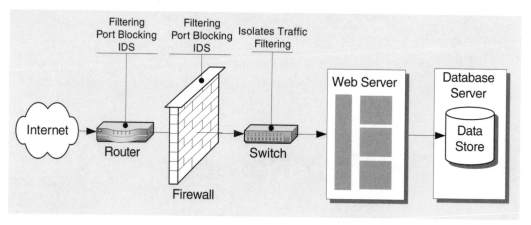

Figure 15.1

Network components: router, firewall, and switch

How to Use This Chapter

This chapter provides a methodology and steps for securing a network. The methodology can be adapted for your own scenario. The steps put the methodology into practice.

To get most out of this chapter:

- **Read Chapter 2, "Threats and Countermeasures."** This will give you a better understanding of potential threats to Web applications.

- **Use the snapshot.** Table 15.3, which is at the end of this chapter, provides a snapshot of a secure network. Use this table as a reference when configuring your network.

- **Use the Checklist.** Use "Checklist: Securing Your Network" in the "Checklist" section of this guide, to quickly evaluate and scope the required steps. The checklist will also help you complete the individual steps.

- **Use vendor details to implement the guidance**. The guidance in this chapter is not specific to specific network hardware or software vendors. Consult your vendor's documentation for specific instructions on how to implement the countermeasures given in this chapter.

Threats and Countermeasures

An attacker looks for poorly configured network devices to exploit. Common vulnerabilities include weak default installation settings, wide-open access controls, and unpatched devices. The following are high-level network threats:

- Information gathering
- Sniffing
- Spoofing
- Session hijacking
- Denial of service

With knowledge of the threats that can affect the network, you can apply effective countermeasures.

Information Gathering

Information gathering can reveal detailed information about network topology, system configuration, and network devices. An attacker uses this information to mount pointed attacks at the discovered vulnerabilities.

Vulnerabilities

Common vulnerabilities that make your network susceptible to an attack include:

- The inherently insecure nature of the TCP/IP protocol suite
- Configuration information provided by banners
- Exposed services that should be blocked

Attacks

Common information-gathering attacks include:

- Using **Tracert** to detect network topology
- Using **Telnet** to open ports for banner grabbing
- Using port scans to detect open ports
- Using broadcast requests to enumerate hosts on a subnet

Countermeasures

You can employ the following countermeasures:

- Use generic service banners that do not give away configuration information such as software versions or names.
- Use firewalls to mask services that should not be publicly exposed.

Sniffing

Sniffing, also called *eavesdropping*, is the act of monitoring network traffic for data, such as clear-text passwords or configuration information. With a simple packet sniffer, all plaintext traffic can be read easily. Also, lightweight hashing algorithms can be cracked and the payload that was thought to be safe can be deciphered.

Vulnerabilities

Common vulnerabilities that make your network susceptible to data sniffing include:
- Weak physical security
- Lack of encryption when sending sensitive data
- Services that communicate in plain text or weak encryption or hashing

Attacks

The attacker places packet sniffing tools on the network to capture all traffic.

Countermeasures

Countermeasures include the following:
- Strong physical security that prevents rogue devices from being placed on the network
- Encrypted credentials and application traffic over the network

Spoofing

Spoofing, also called *identity obfuscation*, is a means to hide one's true identity on the network. A fake source address is used that does not represent the actual packet originator's address. Spoofing can be used to hide the original source of an attack or to work around network access control lists (ACLs) that are in place to limit host access based on source address rules.

Vulnerabilities

Common vulnerabilities that make your network susceptible to spoofing include:
- The inherently insecure nature of the TCP/IP protocol suite
- Lack of ingress and egress filtering. Ingress filtering is the filtering of any IP packets with untrusted source addresses before they have a chance to enter and affect your system or network. Egress filtering is the process of filtering outbound traffic from your network.

Attacks

An attacker can use several tools to modify outgoing packets so that they appear to originate from an alternate network or host.

Countermeasures

You can use ingress and egress filtering on perimeter routers.

Session Hijacking

With session hijacking, also known as man in the middle attacks, the attacker uses an application that masquerades as either the client or the server. This results in either the server or the client being tricked into thinking that the upstream host is the legitimate host. However, the upstream host is actually an attacker's host that is manipulating the network so that it appears to be the desired destination. Session hijacking can be used to obtain logon information that can then be used to gain access to a system or to confidential information.

Vulnerabilities

Common vulnerabilities that make your network susceptible to session hijacking include:

- Weak physical security
- The inherent insecurity of the TCP/IP protocol suite
- Unencrypted communication

Attacks

An attacker can use several tools to combine spoofing, routing changes, and packet manipulation.

Countermeasures

Countermeasures include the following:

- Session encryption
- Stateful inspection at the firewall

Denial of Service

A denial of service attack is the act of denying legitimate users access to a server or services. Network-layer denial of service attacks usually try to deny service by flooding the network with traffic, which consumes the available bandwidth and resources.

Vulnerabilities

Vulnerabilities that increase the opportunities for denial of service include:

- The inherent insecurity of the TCP/IP protocol suite
- Weak router and switch configuration
- Unencrypted communication
- Service software bugs

Attacks

- Common denial of service attacks include:
- Brute force packet floods, such as cascading broadcast attacks
- SYN flood attacks
- Service exploits, such as buffer overflows

Countermeasures

Countermeasures include:

- Filtering broadcast requests
- Filtering Internet Control Message Protocol (ICMP) requests
- Patching and updating of service software

Methodology

Security begins with an understanding of how the system or network that needs to be secured works. This chapter breaks down network security by devices, which allows you to focus on single points of configuration.

In keeping with this guide's philosophy, this chapter uses the approach of analyzing potential threats; without these analyses, it's impossible to properly apply security.

The network infrastructure can be broken into the following three layers: access, distribution, and core. These layers contain all of the hardware necessary to control access to and from internal and external resources. The chapter focuses on the software that drives the network hardware that is responsible for delivering ASP.NET applications. The recommendations apply to an Internet or intranet-facing Web zone and therefore might not apply to your internal or corporate network.

The following are the core network components:

- Router
- Firewall
- Switch

Router

The router is the outermost security gate. It is responsible for forwarding IP packets to the networks to which it is connected. These packets can be inbound requests from Internet clients to your Web server, request responses, or outgoing requests from internal clients. The router should be used to block unauthorized or undesired traffic between networks. The router itself must also be secured against reconfiguration by using secure administration interfaces and ensuring that it has the latest software patches and updates applied.

Firewall

The role of the firewall is to block all unnecessary ports and to allow traffic only from known ports. The firewall must be capable of monitoring incoming requests to prevent known attacks from reaching the Web server. Coupled with intrusion detection, the firewall is a useful tool for preventing attacks and detecting intrusion attempts, or in worst-case scenarios, the source of an attack.

Like the router, the firewall runs on an operating system that must be patched regularly. Its administration interfaces must be secured and unused services must be disabled or removed.

Switch

The switch has a minimal role in a secure network environment. Switches are designed to improve network performance to ease administration. For this reason, you can easily configure a switch by sending specially formatted packets to it. For more information, see "Switch Considerations" later in this chapter.

Router Considerations

The router is the very first line of defense. It provides packet routing, and it can also be configured to block or filter the forwarding of packet types that are known to be vulnerable or used maliciously, such as ICMP or Simple Network Management Protocol (SNMP).

If you don't have control of the router, there is little you can do to protect your network beyond asking your ISP what defense mechanisms they have in place on their routers.

The configuration categories for the router are:

- Patches and updates
- Protocols
- Administrative access
- Services
- Auditing and logging
- Intrusion detection

Patches and Updates

Subscribe to alert services provided by the manufacturer of your networking hardware so that you can stay current with both security issues and service patches. As vulnerabilities are found—and they inevitably will be found—good vendors make patches available quickly and announce these updates through e-mail or on their Web sites. Always test the updates before implementing them in a production environment.

Protocols

Denial of service attacks often take advantage of protocol-level vulnerabilities, for example, by flooding the network. To counter this type of attack, you should:

- Use ingress and egress filtering.
- Screen ICMP traffic from the internal network.

Use Ingress and Egress Filtering

Spoofed packets are representative of probes, attacks, and a knowledgeable attacker. Incoming packets with an internal address can indicate an intrusion attempt or probe and should be denied entry to the perimeter network. Likewise, set up your router to route outgoing packets only if they have a valid internal IP address. Verifying outgoing packets does not protect you from a denial of service attack, but it does keep such attacks from originating from your network.

This type of filtering also enables the originator to be easily traced to its true source since the attacker would have to use a valid—and legitimately reachable—source address. For more information, see "Network Ingress Filtering: Defeating Denial of Service Attacks Which Employ IP Source Address Spoofing" at *http://www.rfc-editor.org/rfc/rfc2267.txt*.

Screen ICMP Traffic from the Internal Network

ICMP is a stateless protocol that sits on top of IP and allows host availability information to be verified from one host to another. Commonly used ICMP messages are shown in Table 15.1.

Table 15.1   Commonly Used ICMP Messages

Message	Description
Echo request	Determines whether an IP node (a host or a router) is available on the network
Echo reply	Replies to an ICMP echo request
Destination unreachable	Informs the host that a datagram cannot be delivered
Source quench	Informs the host to lower the rate at which it sends datagrams because of congestion
Redirect	Informs the host of a preferred route
Time exceeded	Indicates that the time to live (TTL) of an IP datagram has expired

Blocking ICMP traffic at the outer perimeter router protects you from attacks such as cascading ping floods. Other ICMP vulnerabilities exist that justify blocking this protocol. While ICMP can be used for troubleshooting, it can also be used for network discovery and mapping. Therefore, control the use of ICMP. If you must enable it, use it in echo-reply mode only.

Prevent TTL Expired Messages with Values of 1 or 0

Trace routing uses TTL values of 1 and 0 to count routing hops between a client and a server. Trace routing is a means to collect network topology information. By blocking packets of this type, you prevent an attacker from learning details about your network from trace routes.

Do Not Receive or Forward Directed Broadcast Traffic

Directed broadcast traffic can be used to enumerate hosts on a network and as a vehicle for a denial of service attack. For example, by blocking specific source addresses, you prevent malicious echo requests from causing cascading ping floods. Source addresses that should be filtered are shown in Table 15.2.

Table 15.2   Source Addresses That Should be Filtered

Source address	Description
0.0.0.0/8	Historical broadcast
10.0.0.0/8	RFC 1918 private network
127.0.0.0/8	Loopback
169.254.0.0/16	Link local networks
172.16.0.0/12	RFC 1918 private network
192.0.2.0/24	TEST-NET
192.168.0.0/16	RFC 1918 private network
224.0.0.0/4	Class D multicast
240.0.0.0/5	Class E reserved
248.0.0.0/5	Unallocated
255.255.255.255/32	Broadcast

For more information on broadcast suppression using Cisco routers, see "Configuring Broadcast Suppression" on the Cisco Web site at *http://www.cisco.com/en/US/products/hw/switches/ps708 /products_configuration_guide_chapter09186a00800eb778.html*.

Administrative Access

From where will the router be accessed for administration purposes? Decide over which interfaces and ports an administration connection is allowed and from which network or host the administration is to be performed. Restrict access to those specific locations. Do not leave an Internet-facing administration interface available without encryption and countermeasures to prevent hijacking. In addition:

- Disable unused interfaces.
- Apply strong password policies.
- Use static routing.
- Audit Web facing administration interfaces.

Disable Unused Interfaces

Only required interfaces should be enabled on the router. An unused interface is not monitored or controlled, and it is probably not updated. This might expose you to unknown attacks on those interfaces.

Apply Strong Password Policies

Brute force password software can launch more than just dictionary attacks. It can discover common passwords where a letter is replaced by a number. For example, if "p4ssw0rd" is used as a password, it can be cracked. Always use uppercase and lowercase, number, and symbol combinations when creating passwords.

Use Static Routing

Static routing prevents specially formed packets from changing routing tables on your router. An attacker might try to change routes to cause denial of service or to forward requests to a rogue server. By using static routes, an administrative interface must first be compromised to make routing changes.

Audit Web Facing Administration Interfaces

Also determine whether internal access can be configured. When possible, shut down the external administration interface and use internal access methods with ACLs.

Services

On a deployed router, every open port is associated with a listening service. To reduce the attack surface area, default services that are not required should be shut down. Examples include **bootps** and **Finger**, which are rarely required. You should also scan your router to detect which ports are open.

Auditing and Logging

By default, a router logs all deny actions; this default behavior should not be changed. Also secure log files in a central location. Modern routers have an array of logging features that include the ability to set severities based on the data logged. An auditing schedule should be established to routinely inspect logs for signs of intrusion and probing.

Intrusion Detection

With restrictions in place at the router to prevent TCP/IP attacks, the router should be able to identify when an attack is taking place and notify asystem administrator of the attack.

Attackers learn what your security priorities are and attempt to work around them. Intrusion Detection Systems (IDSs) can show where the perpetrator is attempting attacks.

Firewall Considerations

A firewall should exist anywhere you interact with an untrusted network, especially the Internet. It is also recommended that you separate your Web servers from downstream application and database servers with an internal firewall.

After the router, with its broad filters and gatekeepers, the firewall is the next point of attack. In many (if not most) cases, you do not have administrative access to the upstream router. Many of the filters and ACLs that apply to the router can also be implemented at the firewall. The configuration categories for the firewall include:

- Patches and updates
- Filters
- Auditing and logging
- Perimeter networks
- Intrusion detection

Patches and Updates

Subscribe to alert services provided by the manufacturer of your firewall and operating system to stay current with both security issues and service patches.

Filters

Filtering published ports on a firewall can be an effective and efficient method of blocking malicious packets and payloads. Filters range from simple packet filters that restrict traffic at the network layer based on source and destination IP addresses and port numbers, to complex application filters that inspect application-specific payloads. A defense in depth approach that uses layered filters is a very effective way to block attacks. There are six common types of firewall filters:

- **Packet filters**

  These can filter packets based on protocol, source or destination port number and source or destination address, or computer name. IP packet filters are static, and communication through a specific port is either allowed or blocked. Blocked packets are usually logged, and a secure packet filter denies by default.

  At the network layer, the payload is unknown and might be dangerous. More intelligent types of filtering must be configured to inspect the payload and make decisions based on access control rules.

- **Circuit-level filters**

  These inspect sessions rather than payload data. An inbound or outbound client makes a request directly against the firewall/gateway, and in turn the gateway initiates a connection to the server and acts as a broker between the two connections. With knowledge of application connection rules, circuit level filters ensure valid interactions. They do not inspect the actual payload, but they do count frames to ensure packet integrity and prevent session hijacking and replaying.

- **Application filters**

  Smart application filters can analyze a data stream for an application and provide application-specific processing, including inspecting, screening or blocking, redirecting, and even modifying the data as it passes through the firewall. Application filters protect against attacks such as the following:

  - Unsafe SMTP commands
  - Attacks against internal DNS servers.
  - HTTP-based attacks (for example, Code Red and Nimda, which use application-specific knowledge)

  For example, an application filter can block an HTTP DELETE, but allow an HTTP GET. The capabilities of content screening, including virus detection, lexical analysis, and site categorization, make application filters very effective in Web scenarios both as security measures and in enforcement of business rules.

- **Stateful inspection**

  Application filters are limited to knowledge of the payload of a packet and therefore make filtering decisions based only on the payload. Stateful inspection uses both the payload and its context to determine filtering rules. Using the payload and the packet contents allow stateful inspection rules to ensure session and communication integrity. The inspection of packets, their payload, and sequence limits the scalability of stateful inspection.

- **Custom application filters**

  These filters ensure the integrity of application server/client communication.

When you use filters at multiple levels of the network stack, it helps make your environment more secure. For example, a packet filter can be used to block IP traffic destined for any port other than port 80, and an application filter might further restrict traffic based on the nature of the HTTP verb. For example, it might block HTTP DELETE verbs.

Logging and Auditing

Logging all incoming and outgoing requests—regardless of firewall rules—allows you to detect intrusion attempts or, even worse, successful attacks that were previously undetected. Historically, network administrators sometimes had to analyze audit logs to determine how an attack succeeded. In those cases, administrators were able to apply solutions to the vulnerabilities, learn how they were compromised, and discover other vulnerabilities that existed.

Apply the following policies for logging and log auditing.

- Log all traffic that passes through the firewall.
- Maintain healthy log cycling that allows quick data analysis. The more data you have, the larger the log file size.
- Make sure the firewall clock is synchronized with the other network hardware.

Perimeter Networks

A firewall should exist anywhere your servers interact with an untrusted network. If your Web servers connect to a back-end network, such as a bank of database servers or corporate network, a screen should exist to isolate the two networks. While the Web zone has the greatest degree of exposure, a compromise in the Web zone should not result in the compromise of downstream networks.

By default, the perimeter network should block all outbound connections except those that are expected.

Advantages of a Perimeter Network

The perimeter network provides the following advantages:

- Hosts are not directly exposed to untrusted networks.
- Exposed or published services are the only point of external attack.
- Security rules can be enforced for access between networks.

Disadvantages of a Perimeter Network

The disadvantages of a perimeter network include:

- Network complexity
- IP address allocation and management
- Requirement that the application architecture accommodate the perimeter network design

Switch Considerations

A switch is responsible for forwarding packets directly to a host or network segment, rather than sharing the data with the entire network. Therefore, traffic is not shared between switched segments. This is a preventive measure against packet sniffing between networks. An attacker can circumvent this security by reconfiguring switching rules using easily accessed administrative interfaces, including known account names and passwords and SNMP packets.

The following configuration categories are used to ensure secure switch configuration:

- Patches and updates
- Virtual Local Area Networks (VLANs)
- Insecure defaults
- Services
- Encryption

Patches and Updates

Patches and updates must be tested and installed as soon as they are available.

VLANs

Virtual LANs allow you to separate network segments and apply access control based on security rules. However, a VLAN enhances network performance, but doesn't necessarily provide security. Limit the use of VLANs to the perimeter network (behind the firewall) since many insecure interfaces exist for ease of administration. For more information about VLANs, see the article "Configuring VLANS" on the Cisco Web site.

Insecure Defaults

To make sure that insecure defaults are secured, change all factory default passwords and SNMP community strings to prevent network enumeration or total control of the switch. Also investigate and identify potentially undocumented accounts and change the default names and passwords. These types of accounts are often found on well-known switch types and are well publicized and known by attackers.

Services

Make sure that all unused services are disabled. Also make sure that Trivial File Transfer Protocol (TFTP) is disabled, Internet-facing administration points are removed, and ACLs are configured to limit administrative access.

Encryption

Although it is not traditionally implemented at the switch, data encryption over the wire ensures that sniffed packets are useless in cases where a monitor is placed on the same switched segment or where the switch is compromised, allowing sniffing across segments.

Additional Considerations

The following considerations can further improve network security:

- Ensure that clocks are synchronized on all network devices. Set the network time and have all sources synchronized to a known, reliable time source.
- Use Terminal Access Controller Access Control System (TACACS) or Remote Authentication Dial-In User Service (RADIUS) authentication for highly secure environments as a means of limiting administrative access to the network.
- Define an IP network that can be easily secured using ACLs at subnets or network boundaries whenever possible.

Snapshot of a Secure Network

Table 15.3 provides a snapshot of the characteristics of a secure network. The security settings are abstracted from industry security experts and real-world applications in secure deployments. You can use the snapshot as a reference point when evaluating your own solution.

Table 15.3 Snapshot of a Secure Network

Component	Characteristic
Router	
Patches and Updates	Router operating system is patched with up-to-date software.
Protocols	Unused protocols and ports are blocked.
	Ingress and egress filtering is implemented.
	ICMP traffic is screened from the internal network.
	TTL expired messages with values of 1 or 0 are blocked (route tracing is disabled).
	Directed broadcast traffic is not forwarded.
	Large ping packets are screened.
	Routing Information Protocol (RIP) packets, if used, are blocked at the outermost router.
Administrative access	Unused management interfaces on the router are disabled.
	A strong administration password policy is enforced.
	Static routing is used.
	Web-facing administration is disabled.
Services	Unused services are disabled (for example **bootps** and **Finger**).
Auditing and logging	Logging is enabled for all denied traffic.
	Logs are centrally stored and secured.
	Auditing against the logs for unusual patterns is in place.
Intrusion detection	IDS is in place to identify and notify of an active attack.
Firewall	
Patches and updates	Firewall software and OS are patched with latest security updates.
Filters	Packet filtering policy blocks all but required traffic in both directions.
	Application-specific filters are in place to restrict unnecessary traffic.

Table 15.3   Snapshot of a Secure Network *(continued)*

Component	Characteristic
Logging and auditing	All permitted traffic is logged.
	Denied traffic is logged.
	Logs are cycled with a frequency that allows quick data analysis.
	All devices on the network are synchronized to a common time source.
Perimeter networks	Perimeter network is in place if multiple networks require access to servers.
	Firewall is placed between untrusted networks.
Switch	
Patches and updates	Latest security patches are tested and installed or the threat from known vulnerabilities is mitigated.
VLANs	Make sure VLANs are not overused or overly trusted.
Insecure defaults	All factory passwords are changed.
	Minimal administrative interfaces are available.
	Access controls are configured to secure SNMP community strings.
Services	Unused services are disabled.
Encryption	Switched traffic is encrypted.
Other	
Log synchronization	All clocks on devices with logging capabilities are synchronized.
Administrative access to the network	TACACS or RADIUS is used to authenticate administrative users.
Network ACLs	The network is structured so ACLs can be placed on hosts and networks.

Summary

Network security involves protecting network devices and the data that they forward to provide additional security for host servers. The primary network components that require secure configuration are the router, firewall, and switch.

This chapter has highlighted the top threats to your network infrastructure and has presented security recommendations and secure configurations that enable you to address these threats.

Additional Resources

For more information, see the following articles:

- "Network Ingress Filtering" at *http://www.rfc-editor.org/rfc/rfc2267.txt.*
- "Improving Security on Cisco Routers" at *http://www.cisco.com/en/US/tech/tk648 /tk361/technologies_tech_note09186a0080120f48.shtml.*
- "Configuring Broadcast Suppression" at *http://www.cisco.com/en/US/products/hw /switches/ps708/products_configuration_guide_chapter09186a00800eb778.html.*
- "Cisco IOS Intrusion Detection System Software App Overview" at *http://www.cisco.com/en/US/netsol/ns110/ns170/ns171/ns292 /networking_solutions_white_paper09186a008010e5c8.shtml.*
- "Configuring VLANs" at *http://www.cisco.com/en/US/products/hw/switches/ps663 /products_configuration_guide_chapter09186a00800e47e1.html#1020847.*

16

Securing Your Web Server

In This Chapter

- A proven methodology to secure Web servers
- An explanation of the most common Web server security threats
- Steps to secure your server
- A reference table that illustrates a secure Web server

Overview

A secure Web server provides a protected foundation for hosting your Web applications, and Web server configuration plays a critical role in your Web application's security. Badly configured virtual directories, a common mistake, can lead to unauthorized access. A forgotten share can provide a convenient back door, while an overlooked port can be an attacker's front door. Neglected user accounts can permit an attacker to slip by your defenses unnoticed.

What makes a Web server secure? Part of the challenge of securing your Web server is recognizing your goal. As soon as you know what a secure Web server is, you can learn how to apply the configuration settings to create one. This chapter provides a systematic, repeatable approach that you can use to successfully configure a secure Web server.

The chapter begins by reviewing the most common threats that affect Web servers. It then uses this perspective to create a methodology. The chapter then puts the methodology into practice, and takes a step-by-step approach that shows you how to improve your Web server's security. While the basic methodology is reusable across technologies, the chapter focuses on securing a Web server running the Microsoft Windows 2000 operating system and hosting the Microsoft .NET Framework.

How to Use This Chapter

This chapter provides a methodology and the steps required to secure your Web server. You can adapt the methodology for your own situation. The steps are modular and demonstrate how you can put the methodology in practice. You can use these procedures on existing Web servers or on new ones.

To gain the most from this chapter:

- **Read Chapter 2, "Threats and Countermeasures."** This will give you a broader understanding of potential threats to Web applications.

- **Use the Snapshot.** The section "Snapshot of a Secure Web Server" lists and explains the attributes of a secure Web server. It reflects input from a variety of sources including customers, industry experts, and internal Microsoft development and support teams. Use the snapshot table as a reference when configuring your server.

- **Use the Checklist.** "Checklist: Securing Your Web Server" in the "Checklist" section of this guide provides a printable job aid for quick reference. Use the task-based checklist to quickly evaluate the scope of the required steps and to help you work through the individual steps.

- **Use the "How To" Section.** The "How To" section in this guide includes the following instructional articles:
  - "How To: Use URLScan"
  - "How To: Use Microsoft Baseline Security Analyzer"
  - "How To: Use IISLockdown"

Threats and Countermeasures

The fact that an attacker can strike remotely makes a Web server an appealing target. Understanding threats to your Web server and being able to identify appropriate countermeasures permits you to anticipate many attacks and thwart the ever-growing numbers of attackers.

The main threats to a Web server are:

- **Profiling**
- **Denial of service**
- **Unauthorized access**
- **Arbitrary code execution**
- **Elevation of privileges**
- **Viruses, worms, and Trojan horses**

Figure 16.1 summarizes the more prevalent attacks and common vulnerabilities.

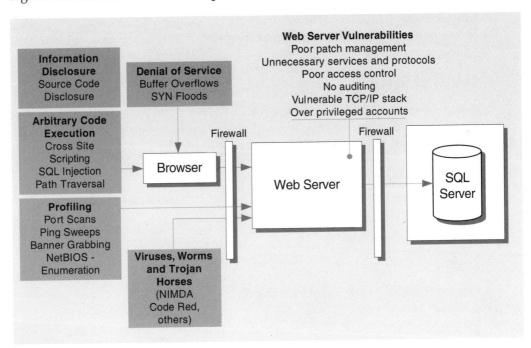

Figure 16.1
Prominent Web server threats and common vulnerabilities

Profiling

Profiling, or host enumeration, is an exploratory process used to gather information about your Web site. An attacker uses this information to attack known weak points.

Vulnerabilities

- Common vulnerabilities that make your server susceptible to profiling include:
- Unnecessary protocols
- Open ports
- Web servers providing configuration information in banners

Attacks

Common attacks used for profiling include:

- Port scans
- Ping sweeps
- NetBIOS and server message block (SMB) enumeration

Countermeasures

Countermeasures include blocking all unnecessary ports, blocking Internet Control Message Protocol (ICMP) traffic, and disabling unnecessary protocols such as NetBIOS and SMB.

Denial of Service

Denial of service attacks occur when your server is overwhelmed by service requests. The threat is that your Web server will be too overwhelmed to respond to legitimate client requests.

Vulnerabilities

Vulnerabilities that increase the opportunities for denial of service include:

- Weak TCP/IP stack configuration
- Unpatched servers

Attacks

Common denial of service attacks include:

- Network-level SYN floods
- Buffer overflows
- Flooding the Web server with requests from distributed locations

Countermeasures

Countermeasures include hardening the TCP/IP stack and consistently applying the latest software patches and updates to system software.

Unauthorized Access

Unauthorized access occurs when a user without correct permissions gains access to restricted information or performs a restricted operation.

Vulnerabilities

Common vulnerabilities that lead to unauthorized access include:

- Weak IIS Web access controls including Web permissions
- Weak NTFS permissions

Countermeasures

Countermeasures include using secure Web permissions, NTFS permissions, and .NET Framework access control mechanisms including URL authorization.

Arbitrary Code Execution

Code execution attacks occur when an attacker runs malicious code on your server either to compromise server resources or to mount additional attacks against downstream systems.

Vulnerabilities

Vulnerabilities that can lead to malicious code execution include:

- Weak IIS configuration
- Unpatched servers

Attacks

Common code execution attacks include:

- Path traversal
- Buffer overflow leading to code injection

Countermeasures

Countermeasures include configuring IIS to reject URLs with "../" to prevent path traversal, locking down system commands and utilities with restrictive access control lists (ACLs), and installing new patches and updates.

Elevation of Privileges

Elevation of privilege attacks occur when an attacker runs code by using a privileged process account.

Vulnerabilities

Common vulnerabilities that make your Web server susceptible to elevation of privilege attacks include:

- Over-privileged process accounts
- Over-privileged service accounts

Countermeasures

Countermeasures include running processes using least privileged accounts and using least privileged service and user accounts.

Viruses, Worms, and Trojan Horses

Malicious code comes in several varieties, including:

- **Viruses**. Programs that are designed to perform malicious acts and cause disruption to an operating system or applications.
- **Worms**. Programs that are self-replicating and self-sustaining.
- **Trojan horses**. Programs that appear to be useful but that actually do damage.

In many cases, malicious code is unnoticed until it consumes system resources and slows down or halts the execution of other programs. For example, the Code Red worm was one of the most notorious to afflict IIS, and it relied upon a buffer overflow vulnerability in an ISAPI filter.

Vulnerabilities

Common vulnerabilities that make you susceptible to viruses, worms, and Trojan horses include:

- Unpatched servers
- Running unnecessary services
- Unnecessary ISAPI filters and extensions

Countermeasures

Countermeasures include the prompt application of the latest software patches, disabling unused functionality such as unused ISAPI filters and extensions, and running processes with least privileged accounts to reduce the scope of damage in the event of a compromise.

Methodology for Securing Your Web Server

To secure a Web server, you must apply many configuration settings to reduce the server's vulnerability to attack. So, how do you know where to start, and when do you know that you are done? The best approach is to organize the precautions you must take and the settings you must configure, into categories. Using categories allows you to systematically walk through the securing process from top to bottom or pick a particular category and complete specific steps.

Configuration Categories

The security methodology in this chapter has been organized into the categories shown in Figure 16.2.

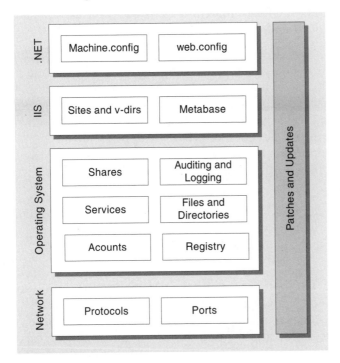

Figure 16.2
Web server configuration categories

The rationale behind the categories is as follows:

- **Patches and Updates**

  Many security threats are caused by vulnerabilities that are widely published and well known. In many cases, when a new vulnerability is discovered, the code to exploit it is posted on Internet bulletin boards within hours of the first successful attack. If you do not patch and update your server, you provide opportunities for attackers and malicious code. Patching and updating your server software is a critical first step towards securing your Web server.

- **Services**

  Services are prime vulnerability points for attackers who can exploit the privileges and capabilities of a service to access the local Web server or other downstream servers. If a service is not necessary for your Web server's operation, do not run it on your server. If the service is necessary, secure it and maintain it. Consider monitoring any service to ensure availability. If your service software is not secure, but you need the service, try to find a secure alternative.

- **Protocols**

  Avoid using protocols that are inherently insecure. If you cannot avoid using these protocols, take the appropriate measures to provide secure authentication and communication, for example, by using IPSec policies. Examples of insecure, clear text protocols are Telnet, Post Office Protocol (POP3), Simple Mail Transfer Protocol (SMTP), and File Transfer Protocol (FTP).

- **Accounts**

  Accounts grant authenticated access to your computer, and these accounts must be audited. What is the purpose of the user account? How much access does it have? Is it a common account that can be targeted for attack? Is it a service account that can be compromised and must therefore be contained? Configure accounts with least privilege to help prevent elevation of privilege. Remove any accounts that you do not need. Slow down brute force and dictionary attacks with strong password policies, and then audit and alert for logon failures.

- **Files and Directories**

  Secure all files and directories with restricted NTFS permissions that only allow access to necessary Windows services and user accounts. Use Windows auditing to allow you to detect when suspicious or unauthorized activity occurs.

- **Shares**

  Remove all unnecessary file shares including the default administration shares if they are not required. Secure any remaining shares with restricted NTFS permissions. Although shares may not be directly exposed to the Internet, a defense strategy—with limited and secured shares—reduces risk if a server is compromised.

- **Ports**

  Services that run on the server listen to specific ports so that they can respond to incoming requests. Audit the ports on your server regularly to ensure that an insecure or unnecessary service is not active on your Web server. If you detect an active port that was not opened by an administrator, this is a sure sign of unauthorized access and a security compromise.

- **Registry**

  Many security-related settings are stored in the registry and as a result, you must secure the registry. You can do this by applying restricted Windows ACLs and by blocking remote registry administration.

- **Auditing and Logging**

  Auditing is one of your most important tools for identifying intruders, attacks in progress, and evidence of attacks that have occurred. Use a combination of Windows and IIS auditing features to configure auditing on your Web server. Event and system logs also help you to troubleshoot security problems.

- **Sites and Virtual Directories**

  Sites and virtual directories are directly exposed to the Internet. Even though secure firewall configuration and defensive ISAPI filters such as URLScan (which ships with the IISLockdown tool) can block requests for restricted configuration files or program executables, a defense in depth strategy is recommended. Relocate sites and virtual directories to non-system partitions and use IIS Web permissions to further restrict access.

- **Script Mappings**

  Remove all unnecessary IIS script mappings for optional file extensions to prevent an attacker from exploiting any bugs in the ISAPI extensions that handle these types of files. Unused extension mappings are often overlooked and represent a major security vulnerability.

- **ISAPI Filters**

  Attackers have been successful in exploiting vulnerabilities in ISAPI filters. Remove unnecessary ISAPI filters from the Web server.

- **IIS Metabase**

  The IIS metabase maintains IIS configuration settings. You must be sure that the security related settings are appropriately configured, and that access to the metabase file is restricted with hardened NTFS permissions.

- **Machine.config**

  The Machine.config file stores machine-level configuration settings applied to .NET Framework applications including ASP.NET Web applications. Modify the settings in Machine.config to ensure that secure defaults are applied to any ASP.NET application installed on the server.

- **Code Access Security**

  Restrict code access security policy settings to ensure that code downloaded from the Internet or intranet have no permissions and as a result will not be allowed to execute.

IIS and .NET Framework Installation Considerations

Before you can secure your Web server, you need to know which components are present on a Windows 2000 server after IIS and the .NET Framework are installed. This section explains which components are installed.

What Does IIS Install?

IIS installs a number of services, accounts, folders, and Web sites. Some components that IIS installs may not be used by your Web applications, and if present on the server, could make the server vulnerable to attack. Table 16.1 lists the services, accounts, and folders that are created by a full installation of IIS on Windows 2000 Server with all components selected.

Table 16.1   IIS Installation Defaults

Item	Details	Default
Services	IIS Admin Service (for administration of Web and FTP services)	Installed
	World Wide Web Publishing Service	Installed
	FTP Publishing Service	Installed
	Simple Mail Transport Protocol (SMTP)	Installed
	Network News Transport Protocol (NNTP)	Installed
Accounts and Groups	IUSR_MACHINE (anonymous Internet users)	Added to Guest group
	IWAM_MACHINE (out-of-process ASP Web applications; not used for ASP.NET applications except those running on a domain controller; your Web server should not be a domain controller)	Added to Guest group
Folders	%windir%\system32\inetsrv (IIS program files)	
	%windir%\system32\inetsrv\iisadmin (Files used for remote IIS admin)	
	%windir%\help\iishelp (IIS help files)	
	%systemdrive%\inetpub (Web, FTP, and SMTP root folders)	
Web Sites	Default Web Site–port 80: %SystemDrive%\inetpub\wwwroot	Anonymous access allowed
	Administration Web Site–port 3693: %SystemDrive%\System32\inetsrv\iisadmin	Local machine and Administrators access only

What Does the .NET Framework Install?

When you install the .NET Framework on a server that hosts IIS, the .NET Framework registers ASP.NET. As part of this process, a local, least privileged account named ASPNET is created. This runs the ASP.NET worker process (aspnet_wp.exe) and the session state service (aspnet_state.exe), which can be used to manage user session state.

Note   On server computers running Windows 2000 and IIS 5.0, all ASP.NET Web applications run in a single instance of the ASP.NET worker process and application domains provide isolation. On Windows Server 2003, IIS 6.0 provides process-level isolation through the use of application pools.

Table 16.2 shows the services, accounts, and folders that are created by a default installation of version 1.1 of the .NET Framework.

Table 16.2   .NET Framework Installation Defaults

Item	Details	Default
Services	ASP.NET State Service: Provides support for out-of-process session state for ASP.NET.	Started manually
Accounts and Groups	ASPNET: Account used for running the ASP.NET worker process (Aspnet_wp.exe) and session state service (Aspnet_state.exe).	Added to **Users** group
Folders	%windir%\Microsoft.NET\Framework\{version} \1033 \ASP.NETClientFiles \CONFIG \MUI \Temporary ASP.NET Files	
ISAPI Extensions	Aspnet_isapi.dll: Handles requests for ASP.NET file types. Forwards requests to ASP.NET worker process (Aspnet_wp.exe).	
ISAPI Filters	Aspnet_filter.dll: Only used to support cookie-less session state. Runs inside Inetinfo.exe (IIS) process.	
Application Mappings	ASAX, ASCX, ASHX, ASPX, AXD, VDISCO, REM, SOAP, CONFIG, CS, CSPROJ, VB, VBPROJ, WEBINFO, LICX, RESX, RESOURCES	\WINNT\Microsoft.NET \Framework \{version} Aspnet_isapi.dll

Installation Recommendations

By default, the Windows 2000 Server setup installs IIS. However, the recommendation is that you do not install IIS as part of the operating system installation but install it later, after you have updated and patched the base operating system. After you install IIS, you must reapply IIS patches and harden the IIS configuration to ensure that it is fully secured. Only then is it safe to connect the server to the network.

IIS Installation Recommendations

If you are installing and configuring a new Web server, follow the procedure outlined below.

▶ **To build a new Web server**

1. Install Windows 2000 Server, but do not install IIS as part of the operating system installation.

2. Apply the latest service packs and patches to the operating system. (If you are configuring more than one server, see "Including Service Packs with a Base Installation," later in this section.)

3. Install IIS separately by using **Add/Remove Programs** in the Control Panel.

   If you do not need the following services, do not install them when you install IIS:

   - File Transfer Protocol (FTP) Server
   - Microsoft FrontPage® 2000 Server Extensions
   - Internet Service Manager (HTML)
   - NNTP Service
   - SMTP Service
   - Visual InterDev RAD Remote Deployment Support

Note By installing IIS on a fully patched and updated operating system, you can prevent attacks that take advantage of known vulnerabilities (such as NIMDA) that have now been patched.

.NET Framework Installation Recommendations

Do not install the .NET Framework Software Development Kit (SDK) on a production server. The SDK contains utilities that the server does not require. If an attacker gains access to your server, the attacker can use some of these tools to assist other attacks.

Instead, install the redistributable package, which you can obtain from the "Downloads" link at the .NET Framework site on Microsoft.com at *http://www.microsoft.com/net/*.

Including Service Packs with a Base Installation

If you need to build multiple servers, you can incorporate service packs directly into your Windows installations. Service packs include a program called Update.exe to combine a service pack with your Windows installation files.

▶ **To combine a service pack with a Windows installation**

1. Download the latest service pack.
2. Extract Update.exe from the service pack by launching the service pack setup with the **-x** option, as follows:

   w3ksp3.exe -x
3. Integrate the service pack with your Windows installation source, by running update.exe with the **-s** option, passing the folder path of your Windows installation as follows:

   update.exe -s c: YourWindowsInstallationSource

For more information, see the MSDN article, "Customizing Unattended Win2K Installations" at *http://msdn.microsoft.com/library/default.asp?url=/library/en-us /dnw2kmag01/html/custominstall.asp.*

Steps for Securing Your Web Server

The next sections guide you through the process of securing your Web server. These sections use the configuration categories introduced in the "Methodology for Securing Your Web Server" section of this chapter. Each high-level step contains one or more actions to secure a particular area or feature.

Step 1	Patches and Updates	**Step 10**	Auditing and Logging
Step 2	IISLockdown	**Step 11**	Sites and Virtual Directories
Step 3	Services	**Step 12**	Script Mappings
Step 4	Protocols	**Step 13**	ISAPI Filters
Step 5	Accounts	**Step 14**	IIS Metabase
Step 6	Files and Directories	**Step 15**	Server Certificates
Step 7	Shares	**Step 16**	Machine.config
Step 8	Ports	**Step 17**	Code Access Security
Step 9	Registry		

Step 1. Patches and Updates

Update your server with the latest service packs and patches. You must update and patch all of the Web server components including Windows 2000 (and IIS), the .NET Framework, and Microsoft Data Access Components (MDAC).

During this step, you:

- **Detect and install the required patches and updates.**
- **Update the .NET Framework.**

Detect and Install Patches and Updates

Use the Microsoft Baseline Security Analyzer (MBSA) to detect the patches and updates that may be missing from your current installation. MBSA compares your installation to a list of currently available updates maintained in an XML file. MBSA can download the XML file when it scans your server or you can manually download the file to the server or make it available on a network server.

▶ **To detect and install patches and updates**

1. Download and install MBSA.

   You can do this from the MBSA home page at *http://www.microsoft.com/technet/treeview/default.asp?url=/technet/security/tools/Tools/mbsahome.asp*.

   If you do not have Internet access when you run MBSA, MBSA cannot retrieve the XML file that contains the latest security settings from Microsoft. You can use another computer to download the XML file, however. Then you can copy it into the MBSA program directory. The XML file is available from *http://download.microsoft.com/download/xml/security/1.0/nt5/en-us/mssecure.cab*.

2. Run MBSA by double-clicking the desktop icon or selecting it from the **Programs** menu.

3. Click **Scan a computer**. MBSA defaults to the local computer.

4. Clear all check boxes apart from **Check for security updates**. This option detects which patches and updates are missing.

5. Click **Start scan**. Your server is now analyzed. When the scan is complete, MBSA displays a security report, which it also writes to the %userprofile%\SecurityScans directory.

6. Download and install the missing updates.

   Click the **Result details** link next to each failed check to view the list of security updates that are missing. The resulting dialog box displays the Microsoft security bulletin reference number. Click the reference to find out more about the bulletin and to download the update.

For more information on using MBSA, see "How To: Use Microsoft Baseline Security Analyzer" in the "How To" section of this guide.

Update the .NET Framework

At the time of this writing (May 2003), MBSA cannot detect .NET Framework updates and patches. Therefore, you must manually detect .NET Framework updates.

▶ **To manually update .NET Framework version 1.0**

1. Determine which .NET Framework service pack is installed on your Web server.

   To do this, see Microsoft Knowledge Base article 318785, "INFO: Determining Whether Service Packs Are Installed on .NET Framework."

2. Compare the installed version of the .NET Framework to the current service pack.

   To do this, use the .NET Framework versions listed in Microsoft Knowledge Base article 318836, "INFO: How to Obtain the Latest .NET Framework Service Pack."

Step 2. IISLockdown

The IISLockdown tool helps you to automate certain security steps. IISLockdown greatly reduces the vulnerability of a Windows 2000 Web server. It allows you to pick a specific type of server role, and then use custom templates to improve security for that particular server. The templates either disable or secure various features. In addition, IISLockdown installs the URLScan ISAPI filter. URLScan allows Web site administrators to restrict the kind of HTTP requests that the server can process, based on a set of rules that the administrator controls. By blocking specific HTTP requests, the URLScan filter prevents potentially harmful requests from reaching the server and causing damage.

During this step, you:

- **Install and run IISLockdown.**
- **Install and configure URLScan.**

Install and Run IISLockdown

IISLockdown is available as an Internet download from the Microsoft Web site at *http://download.microsoft.com/download/iis50/Utility/2.1/NT45XP/EN-US/iislockd.exe.*

Save IISlockd.exe in a local folder. IISlockd.exe is the IISLockdown wizard and not an installation program. You can reverse any changes made by IISLockdown by running IISlockd.exe a second time.

If you are locking down a Windows 2000-based computer that hosts ASP.NET pages, select the Dynamic Web server template when the IISLockdown tool prompts you. When you select Dynamic Web server, IISLockdown does the following:

- It disables the following insecure Internet services:
  - File Transfer Protocol (FTP)
  - E-mail service (SMTP)
  - News service (NNTP)
- It disables script mappings by mapping the following file extensions to the 404.dll:
  - Index Server
  - Web Interface (.idq, .htw, .ida)
  - Server-side include files (.shtml, .shtm, .stm)
  - Internet Data Connector (.idc)
  - .HTR scripting (.htr), Internet printing (.printer)
- It removes the following virtual directories: IIS Samples, MSADC, IISHelp, Scripts, and IISAdmin.
- It restricts anonymous access to system utilities as well as the ability to write to Web content directories using Web permissions.
- It disables Web Distributed Authoring and Versioning (WebDAV).
- It installs the URLScan ISAPI filter.

Note   If you are not using classic ASP, do not use the static Web server template. This template removes basic functionality that ASP.NET pages need, such as support for the **POST** command.

Log Files

IISLockdown creates two reports that list the changes it has applied:

- %windir%\system32\inetsrv\oblt-rep.log. This contains high-level information.
- %windir%\system32\inetsrv\oblt-log.log. This contains low-level details such as which program files are configured with a deny access control entry (ACE) to prevent anonymous Internet user accounts from accessing them. This log file is also used to support the IISLockdown Undo Changes feature.

Web Anonymous Users and Web Application Groups

IISLockdown creates the **Web Anonymous Users** group and the **Web Application** group. The **Web Anonymous Users** group contains the IUSR_MACHINE account. The **Web Application** group contains the IWAM_MACHINE account. Permissions are assigned to system tools and content directories based on these groups and not directly to the IUSR and IWAM accounts. You can review specific permissions by viewing the IISLockdown log, %windir%\system32\inetsrv\oblt-log.log.

The 404.dll

IISLockdown installs the 404.dll, to which you can map file extensions that must not be run by the client. For more information, see "Step 12. Script Mappings."

URLScan

If you install the URLScan ISAPI filter as part of IISLockdown, URLScan settings are integrated with the server role you select when running IISLockdown. For example, if you select a static Web server, URLScan blocks the **POST** command.

Reversing IISLockdown Changes

To reverse the changes that IISLockdown performs, run IISLockd.exe a second time. This does not remove the URLScan ISAPI filter. For more information, see "Removing URLScan" in the next topic.

More Information

See the following articles for more information about the IISLockdown tool:

- For more information on running IISLockdown, see "How To: Use IISLockdown.exe" in the "How To" section of this guide.
- For information on troubleshooting IISLockdown, see Microsoft Knowledge Base article 325864, "How To: Install and Use the IIS Lockdown Wizard." (The most common problem is receiving unexpected "404 File Not Found" error messages after running IISLockdown.)
- For information on automating IISLockdown, see Microsoft Knowledge Base article 310725, "How To: Run the IIS Lockdown Wizard Unattended in IIS."

Install and Configure URLScan

URLScan is installed when you run IISLockdown, although you can download it and install it separately.

▶ **To install URLScan without running IISLockdown**

1. Download IISLockd.exe from *http://download.microsoft.com/download/iis50/Utility/2.1/NT45XP/EN-US/iislockd.exe*.
2. Run the following command to extract the URLScan setup:

   iislockd.exe /q /c

URLScan blocks requests that contain unsafe characters (for example, characters that have been used to exploit vulnerabilities, such as ".." used for directory traversal). URLScan logs requests that contain these characters in the %windir%\system32\inetsrv\urlscan directory.

Part IV: Securing Your Network, Host, and Application

You configure URLScan using settings in the .ini file %windir%\system32\inetsrv \urlscan\urlscan.ini.

In addition to blocking malicious requests, you can use URLScan to defend your server against denial of service attacks before the requests reach ASP.NET. To do this, set limits in the **MaxAllowedContentLength**, **MaxUrl**, and **MaxQueryString** arguments in the URLScan.ini file. For more information, see "How To: Use URLScan" in the "How To" section of this guide.

Reversing URLScan Changes

There is no automatic operation to remove URLScan. If you have problems with URLScan, you can either remove it from IIS or you can analyze the problem by logging requests that are rejected. To do this, use the option **RejectResponseUrl=/~*** in the URLScan .ini file.

For more information about how to remove ISAPI filters, see "Step 13. ISAPI Filters," later in this chapter.

More Information

See the following articles for more information about the URLScan tool:

- For information on running URLScan, see "How To: Use URLScan" in the "How To" section of this guide.
- For information about URLScan configuration and the URLScan.ini file settings, see Microsoft Knowledge Base article 326444, "How To: Configure the URLScan Tool."

Step 3. Services

Services that do not authenticate clients, services that use insecure protocols, or services that run with too much privilege are risks. If you do not need them, do not run them. By disabling unnecessary services you quickly and easily reduce the attack surface .You also reduce your overhead in terms of maintenance (patches, service accounts, and so on.)

If you run a service, make sure that it is secure and maintained. To do so, run the service using a least privilege account, and keep the service current by applying patches.

During this step, you:

- **Disable unnecessary services.**
- **Disable FTP, SMTP, and NNTP unless you require them.**
- **Disable the ASP.NET State service unless you require it.**

Disable Unnecessary Services

Windows services are vulnerable to attackers who can exploit the service's privileges and capabilities and gain access to local and remote system resources. As a defensive measure, disable Windows services that your systems and applications do not require. You can disable Windows services by using the Services MMC snap-in located in the Administrative Tools programs group.

Note Before you disable a service, make sure that you first test the impact in a test or staging environment.

In most cases, the following default Windows services are not needed on a Web server: Alerter, Browser, Messenger, Netlogon (required only for domain controllers), Simple TCP/IP Services, and Spooler.

The Telnet service is installed with Windows, but it is not enabled by default. IIS administrators often enable Telnet. However, it is an insecure protocol susceptible to exploitation. Terminal Services provides a more secure remote administration option. For more information about remote administration, see "Remote Administration," later in this chapter.

Disable FTP, SMTP, and NNTP Unless You Require Them

FTP, SMTP, and NNTP are examples of insecure protocols that are susceptible to misuse. If you do not need them, do not run them. If you currently run them, try to find a secure alternative. If you must run them, secure them.

Note IIS Lockdown provides options for disabling FTP, SMTP, and NNTP.

To eliminate the possibility of FTP exploitation, disable the FTP service if you do not use it. If FTP is enabled and is available for outbound connections, an attacker can use FTP to upload files and tools to a Web server from the attacker's remote system. Once the tools and files are on your Web server, the attacker can attack the Web server or other connected systems.

If you use FTP protocol, neither the user name and password you use to access the FTP site nor the data you transfer is encoded or encrypted. IIS does not support SSL for FTP. If secure communications are important and you use FTP as your transfer protocol (rather than World Wide Web Distributed Authoring and Versioning (WebDAV) over SSL), consider using FTP over an encrypted channel such as a Virtual Private Network (VPN) that is secured with Point-to-Point Tunneling Protocol (PPTP) or Internet Protocol Security (IPSec).

Disable the ASP.NET State Service Unless You Require It

The .NET Framework installs the ASP.NET State service (aspnet_state.exe) to manage out-of-process user session state for ASP.NET Web applications and Web services. By default, this service is configured for manual startup and runs as the least privileged local ASPNET account. If none of your applications store state by using this service, disable it. For more information on securing ASP.NET session state, see the "Session State" section in Chapter 19, "Securing Your ASP.NET Application and Web Services."

Step 4. Protocols

By preventing the use of unnecessary protocols, you reduce the potential for attack. The .NET Framework provides granular control of protocols through settings in the Machine.config file. For example, you can control whether your Web Services can use HTTP GET, POST or SOAP. For more information about configuring protocols in Machine.config, see "Step 16. Machine.config."

During this step, you:

- **Disable or secure WebDav.**
- **Harden the TCP/IP stack.**
- **Disable NetBIOS and SMB.**

Disable or Secure WebDAV

IIS supports the WebDAV protocol, which is a standard extension to HTTP 1.1 for collaborative content publication. Disable this protocol on production servers if it is not used.

Note   IISLockdown provides an option to remove support for WebDAV.

WebDAV is preferable to FTP from a security perspective, but you need to secure WebDAV. For more information, see Microsoft Knowledge Base article 323470, "How To: Create a Secure WebDAV Publishing Directory."

If you do not need WebDAV, see Microsoft Knowledge Base article 241520, "How To: Disable WebDAV for IIS 5.0."

Harden the TCP/IP Stack

Windows 2000 supports the granular control of many parameters that configure its TCP/IP implementation. Some of the default settings are configured to provide server availability and other specific features.

For information about how to harden the TCP/IP stack see "How To: Harden the TCP/IP Stack" in the "How To" section of this guide.

Disable NetBIOS and SMB

Disable all unnecessary protocols, including NetBIOS and SMB. Web servers do not require NetBIOS or SMB on their Internet-facing network interface cards (NICs). Disable these protocols to counter the threat of host enumeration.

Note The SMB protocol can return rich information about a computer to unauthenticated users over a Null session. You can block null sessions by setting the **RestrictAnonymous** registry key as described in "Step 9. Registry."

Disabling NetBIOS

NetBIOS uses the following ports:

- TCP and User Datagram Protocol (UDP) port 137 (NetBIOS name service)
- TCP and UDP port 138 (NetBIOS datagram service)
- TCP and UDP port 139 (NetBIOS session service)

Disabling NetBIOS is not sufficient to prevent SMB communication because if a standard NetBIOS port is unavailable, SMB uses TCP port 445. (This port is referred to as the SMB Direct Host.) As a result, you must take steps to disable NetBIOS and SMB separately.

▶ **To disable NetBIOS over TCP/IP**

Note This procedure disables the Nbt.sys driver and requires that you restart the system.

1. Right-click **My Computer** on the desktop, and click **Manage**.
2. Expand **System Tools**, and select **Device Manager**.
3. Right-click **Device Manager**, point to **View**, and click **Show hidden devices**.
4. Expand **Non-Plug and Play Drivers**.
5. Right-click **NetBios over Tcpip**, and click **Disable**.

   This disables the NetBIOS direct host listener on TCP 445 and UDP 445.

Disabling SMB

SMB uses the following ports:

- TCP port 139
- TCP port 445

To disable SMB, use the TCP/IP properties dialog box in your **Local Area Connection** properties to unbind SMB from the Internet-facing port.

▶ **To unbind SMB from the Internet-facing port**

1. Click the Start menu, point to Settings, and click Network and Dial-up Connections.

2. Right-click your Internet-facing connection, and click **Properties**.

3. Clear the **Client for Microsoft Networks** box.

4. Clear the **File and Printer Sharing for Microsoft Networks** box.

Note The **WINS** tab of the **Advanced TCP/IP Settings** dialog box contains a **Disable NetBIOS over TCP/IP** radio button. Selecting this option disables the NetBIOS session service that uses TCP port 139. It does not disable SMB completely. To do so, use the procedure above.

Step 5. Accounts

You should remove accounts that are not used because an attacker might discover and use them. Require strong passwords. Weak passwords increase the likelihood of a successful brute force or dictionary attack. Use least privilege. An attacker can use accounts with too much privilege to gain access to unauthorized resources.

During this step, you:

- **Delete or disable unused accounts.**
- **Disable the Guest account.**
- **Rename the Administrator account.**
- **Disable the IUSR Account.**
- **Create a custom anonymous Web account.**
- **Enforce strong password policies.**
- **Restrict remote logons.**
- **Disable Null sessions (anonymous logons).**

Delete or Disable Unused Accounts

Unused accounts and their privileges can be used by an attacker to gain access to a server. Audit local accounts on the server and disable those that are unused. If disabling the account does not cause any problems, delete the account. (Deleted accounts cannot be recovered.) Disable accounts on a test server before you disable them on a production server. Make sure that disabling an account does not adversely affect your application operation.

Note The Administrator account and the Guest account cannot be deleted.

Disable the Guest Account

The Guest account is used when an anonymous connection is made to the computer. To restrict anonymous connections to the computer, keep this account disabled. The guest account is disabled by default on Windows 2000. To check whether or not it is enabled, display the **Users** folder in the Computer Management tool. The Guest account should be displayed with a cross icon. If it is not disabled, display its **Properties** dialog box and select **Account is disabled**.

Rename the Administrator Account

The default local Administrator account is a target for malicious use because of its elevated privileges on the computer. To improve security, rename the default Administrator account and assign it a strong password.

If you intend to perform local administration, configure the account to deny network logon rights and require the administrator to log on interactively. By doing so, you prevent users (well intentioned or otherwise) from using the Administrator account to log on to the server from a remote location. If a policy of local administration is too inflexible, implement a secure remote administration solution. For more information, see "Remote Administration" later in this chapter.

Disable the IUSR Account

Disable the default anonymous Internet user account, IUSR_MACHINE. This is created during IIS installation. MACHINE is the NetBIOS name of your server at IIS installation time.

Create a Custom Anonymous Web Account

If your applications support anonymous access (for example, because they use a custom authentication mechanism such as Forms authentication), create a custom least privileged anonymous account. If you run IISLockdown, add your custom user to the Web Anonymous Users group that is created. IISLockdown denies access to system utilities and the ability to write to Web content directories for the Web Anonymous Users group.

If your Web server hosts multiple Web applications, you may want to use multiple anonymous accounts, one per application, so that you can secure and audit the operations of each application independently.

For more information about hosting multiple Web applications see Chapter 20, "Hosting Multiple Web Applications."

Enforce Strong Password Policies

To counter password guessing and brute force dictionary attacks on your application, apply strong password policies. To enforce a strong password policy:

- **Set password length and complexity.** Require strong passwords to reduce the threat of password guessing attacks or dictionary attacks. Strong passwords are eight or more characters and must include both alphabetical and numeric characters.

- **Set password expiration.** Passwords that expire regularly reduce the likelihood that an old password can be used for unauthorized access. Frequency of expiration is usually guided by a company's security policy.

Table 16.3 shows the default and recommended password policy settings.

Table 16.3 Password Policy Default and Recommended Settings

Password Policy	Default Setting	Recommended Minimum Setting
Enforce password history	1 password remembered.	24 passwords remembered.
Maximum password age	42 days	42 days
Minimum password age	0 days	2 days
Minimum password length	0 characters	8 characters
Passwords must meet complexity requirement.	Disabled	Enabled
Store password using reversible encryption for all users in the domain.	Disabled	Disabled

In addition, record failed logon attempts so that you can detect and trace malicious behavior. For more information, see "Step 10. Auditing and Logging."

Restrict Remote Logons

Remove the **Access this computer from the network** privilege from the Everyone group to restrict who can log on to the server remotely.

Disable Null Sessions (Anonymous Logons)

To prevent anonymous access, disable null sessions. These are unauthenticated or anonymous sessions established between two computers. Unless null sessions are disabled, an attacker can connect to your server anonymously (without being authenticated).

Once an attacker establishes a null session, he or she can perform a variety of attacks, including enumeration techniques used to collect system-related information from the target computer—information that can greatly assist subsequent attacks. The type of information that can be returned over a null session includes domain and trust details, shares, user information (including groups and user rights), registry keys, and more.

Restrict Null sessions by setting **RestrictAnonymous** to **1** in the registry at the following subkey:

HKLM\System\CurrentControlSet\Control\LSA\RestrictAnonymous=1

For more information, see Microsoft Knowledge Base article 246261, "How To: Use the RestrictAnonymous Registry Value in Windows 2000."

Additional Considerations

The following is a list of additional steps you can consider to further improve security on your Web server:

- **Require approval for account delegation**.

  Do not mark domain accounts in Active Directory as trusted for delegation unless you first obtain special approval to do so.

- **Do not use shared accounts**.

  Do not create shared account for use by multiple individuals. Authorized individuals must have their own accounts. The activities of individuals can be audited separately and group membership and privileges appropriately assigned.

- **Restrict the Local Administrators Group Membership**.

  Try to limit administration accounts to two. This helps provide accountability. Also, passwords must not be shared, again to provide accountability.

- **Require the Administrator to log on interactively**.

  If you perform local administration only, you can require your Administrator account to log on interactively by removing the **Access this computer from the network** privilege.

Step 6. Files and Directories

Install Windows 2000 on partitions formatted with the NTFS file system so that you benefit from NTFS permissions to restrict access. Use strong access controls to protect sensitive files and directories. In most situations, an approach that allows access to specific accounts is more effective than one that denies access to specific accounts. Set access at the directory level whenever possible. As files are added to the folder they inherit permissions from the folder, so you need to take no further action.

During this step, you:

- **Restrict the Everyone group.**
- **Restrict the anonymous Web account(s).**
- **Secure or remove tools, utilities, and SDKs.**
- **Remove sample files.**

Restrict the Everyone Group

The default NTFS permissions for Windows 2000 grant members of the **Everyone** group full control access to a number of key locations, including the root directory, \inetpub, and \inetpub\scripts.

First grant FULL CONTROL to the Administrator account to the root (\), then remove access rights for the **Everyone** group from the following directories.

- Root (\)
- System directory (\WINNT\system32)
- Framework tools directory (\WINNT\Microsoft.NET\Framework\{version})
- Web site root directory and all content directories (the default is \inetpub*)

Restrict Access to the IIS Anonymous Account

The anonymous account is well known. Attackers target this well known account to perform malicious actions. To secure the anonymous account:

- **Deny write access to Web content directories.**

  Make sure that it is not possible for this account to write to content directories, for example, to deface Web sites.

- **Restrict access to System tools.**

  In particular, restrict access to command-line tools located in \WINNT\System32.

- **Assign permissions to groups instead of individual accounts.**

  Assigning users to groups and applying permissions to groups instead of individual accounts is good practice. For the anonymous account, create a group and add the anonymous account to it and then explicitly deny access to the group for key directories and files. Assigning permissions to a group allows you to more easily change the anonymous account or create additional anonymous accounts because you do not need to recreate the permissions.

  Note   IISLockdown denies write access to content directories for the anonymous account by applying a deny write access control entry (ACE) for the Web Anonymous Users and Web Applications groups. It also adds a deny execute ACL on command-line tools.

- **Use separate accounts for separate applications.**

  If your Web server hosts multiple applications, use a separate anonymous account for each application. Add the accounts to an anonymous Web users group, for example, the **Web Anonymous Users** group created by IISLockdown, and then configure NTFS permissions using this group.

  For more information about using multiple anonymous accounts and hosting multiple applications, see Chapter 20, "Hosting Multiple ASP.NET Applications."

Secure or Remove Tools, Utilities and SDKs

SDKs and resource kits should not be installed on a production Web server. Remove them if they are present.

- Ensure that only the .NET Framework Redistributable package is installed on the server and no SDK utilities are installed. Do not install Visual Studio .NET on production servers.
- Ensure that access to powerful system tools and utilities, such as those contained in the \Program Files directory, is restricted. IISLockdown does this for you.
- Debugging tools should not be available on the Web server. If production debugging is necessary, then you should create a CD that contains the necessary debugging tools.

Remove Sample Files

Sample applications are typically not configured with high degrees of security. It is possible that an attacker could exploit an inherent weakness in a sample application or in its configuration to attack your Web site. Remove sample applications to reduce the areas where your Web server can be attacked.

Additional Considerations

Also consider removing unnecessary Data Source Names (DSNs). These contain clear text connection details used by applications to connect to OLE DB data sources. Only those DSNs required by Web applications should be installed on the Web server.

Step 7. Shares

Remove any unused shares and harden the NTFS permissions on any essential shares. By default all users have full control on newly created file shares. Harden these default permissions to ensure that only authorized users can access files exposed by the share. In addition to explicit share permissions, use NTFS ACLs for files and folders exposed by the share.

During this step, you:

- **Remove unnecessary shares.**
- **Restrict access to required shares.**

Remove Unnecessary Shares

Remove all unnecessary shares. To review shares and associated permissions, run the Computer Management MMC snap-in, and select **Shares** from **Shared Folders** as shown in Figure 16.3.

Figure 16.3
Computer Management MMC snap-in Shares

Restrict Access to Required Shares

Remove the Everyone group and grant specific permissions instead. Everyone is used when you do not have restrictions on who should have access to the share.

Additional Considerations

If you do not allow remote administration of your server, remove unused administrative shares, for example **C$** and **Admin$**.

Note   Some applications may require administrative shares. Examples include Microsoft Systems Management Server (SMS) and Microsoft Operations Manager (MOM). For more information, see Microsoft Knowledge Base article 318751, "How To: Remove Administrative Shares in Windows 2000 or Windows NT 4.0."

Step 8. Ports

Services that run on the server use specific ports so that they can serve incoming requests. Close all unnecessary ports and perform regular audits to detect new ports in the listening state, which could indicate unauthorized access and a security compromise.

During this step, you:

- **Restrict Internet-facing ports to TCP 80 and 443.**
- **Encrypt or restrict intranet traffic.**

Restrict Internet-Facing Ports to TCP 80 and 443

Limit inbound traffic to port 80 for HTTP and port 443 for HTTPS (SSL).

For outbound (Internet-facing) NICs, use IPSec or TCP filtering. For more information, see "How To: Use IPSec" in the "How To" section of this guide.

Encrypt or Restrict Intranet Traffic

For inside (intranet-facing) NICs, if you do not have a secure data center and you have sensitive information passing between computers, you need to consider whether to encrypt the traffic and whether to restrict communications between the Web server and downstream servers (such as an application server or database server). Encrypting network traffic addresses the threat posed by network eavesdropping. If the risk is deemed sufficiently small you may choose not to encrypt the traffic.

The type of encryption used also affects the types of threats that it addresses. For example, SSL is application-level encryption, whereas IPSec is transport layer encryption. As a result, SSL counters the threat of data tampering or information disclosure from another process on the same machine, particularly one running under a different account in addition to the network eavesdropping threat.

Step 9. Registry

The registry is the repository for many vital server configuration settings. As such, you must ensure that only authorized administrators have access to it. If an attacker is able to edit the registry, he or she can reconfigure and compromise the security of your server.

During this step, you:

- **Restrict remote administration of the registry.**
- **Secure the SAM (stand-alone servers only).**

Restrict Remote Administration of the Registry

The Winreg key determines whether registry keys are available for remote access. By default, this key is configured to prevent users from remotely viewing most keys in the registry, and only highly privileged users can modify it. On Windows 2000, remote registry access is restricted by default to members of the **Administrators** and **Backup operators** group. Administrators have full control and backup operators have read-only access.

The associated permissions at the following registry location determine who can remotely access the registry.

HKLM\SYSTEM\CurrentControlSet\Control\SecurePipeServers\winreg

To view the permissions for this registry key, run Regedt32.exe, navigate to the key, and choose **Permissions** from the **Security** menu.

Note   Some services require remote access to the registry. Refer to Microsoft Knowledge Base article 153183, "How to Restrict Access to the Registry from a Remote Computer," to see if your situation demands limited remote registry access.

Secure the SAM (Stand-alone Servers Only)

Stand-alone servers store account names and one-way (non-reversible) password hashes (LMHash) in the local Security Account Manager (SAM) database. The SAM is part of the registry. Typically, only members of the Administrators group have access to the account information.

Although the passwords are not actually stored in the SAM and password hashes are not reversible, if an attacker obtains a copy of the SAM database, the attacker can use brute force password techniques to obtain valid user names and passwords.

Restrict LMHash storage in the SAM by creating the key (not value) **NoLMHash** in the registry as follows:

HKLM\System\CurrentControlSet\Control\LSA\NoLMHash

For more information, see Microsoft Knowledge Base article 299656, "New Registry Key to Remove LM Hashes from Active Directory and Security Account Manager."

Step 10. Auditing and Logging

Auditing does not prevent system attacks, although it is an important aid in identifying intruders and attacks in progress, and can assist you in diagnosing attack footprints. Enable a minimum level of auditing on your Web server and use NTFS permissions to protect the log files so that an attacker cannot cover his tracks by deleting or updating the log files in any way. Use IIS W3C Extended Log File Format Auditing.

During this step, you:

- **Log all failed Logon attempts.**
- **Log all failed actions across the file system.**
- **Relocate and secure the IIS log files.**
- **Archive log files for offline analysis.**
- **Audit access to the Metabase.bin file.**

Log All Failed Logon Attempts

You must log failed logon attempts to be able to detect and trace suspicious behavior.

▶ **To audit failed logon attempts**

1. Start the Local Security Policy tool from the Administrative Tools program group.
2. Expand **Local Policies** and then select **Audit Policy**
3. Double-click **Audit account logon events**.
4. Click **Failure** and then **OK**.

Logon failures are recorded as events in the Windows security event log. The following event IDs are suspicious:

- **531**. This means an attempt was made to log on using a disabled account.
- **529**. This means an attempt was made to log on using an unknown user account or using a valid user account but with an invalid password. An unexpected increase in the number of these audit events might indicate an attempt to guess passwords.

Log All Failed Actions Across the File System

Use NTFS auditing on the file system to detect potentially malicious attempts. This is a two-step process.

▶ **To enable logging**

1. Start the Local Security Policy tool from the Administrative Tools program group.
2. Expand **Local Policies** and then select **Audit Policy**
3. Double-click **Audit object access**.
4. Click **Failure** and then click **OK**.

▶ **To audit failed actions across the file system**

1. Start Windows Explorer and navigate to the root of the file system.
2. Right-click and then click **Properties**.
3. Click the **Security** tab.
4. Click **Advanced** and then click the **Auditing** tab.
5. Click **Add** and then enter Everyone in the **Name** field.
6. Click **OK** and then select all of the **Failed** check boxes to audit all failed events.

   By default, this applies to the current folder and all subfolders and files.
7. Click **OK** three times to close all open dialog boxes.

   Failed audit events are logged to the Windows security event log.

Relocate and Secure the IIS Log Files

By moving and renaming the IIS log files, you make it much more difficult for an attacker to cover his tracks. The attacker must locate the log files before he or she can alter them. To make an attacker's task more difficult still, use NTFS permissions to secure the log files.

Move and rename the IIS log file directory to a different volume than your Web site. Do not use the system volume. Then, apply the following NTFS permissions to the log files folder and subfolders.

- Administrators: Full Control
- System: Full Control
- Backup Operators: Read

Archive Log Files for Offline Analysis

To facilitate the offline analysis of IIS log files, you can use a script to automate secure removal of log files from an IIS server. Log files should be removed at least every 24 hours. An automated script can use FTP, SMTP, HTTP, or SMB to transfer log files from a server computer. However, if you enable one of these protocols, do so securely so that you do not open any additional attack opportunities. Use an IPSec policy to secure ports and channels.

Audit Access to the Metabase.bin File

Audit all failures by the Everyone group to the IIS metabase.bin file located in \WINNT\System32\inetsrv\. Do the same for the \Metabase backup folder for the backup copies of the metabase.

Additional Considerations

Additionally, you can configure IIS W3C Extended Log File Format Auditing. Select **W3C Extended Log File Format** on the **Web Site** tab of the Web site's properties dialog box. You can then choose **Extended Properties** such as URI Stem and URI Query.

Step 11. Sites and Virtual Directories

Relocate Web roots and virtual directories to a non-system partition to protect against directory traversal attacks. These attacks allow an attacker to execute operating system programs and utilities. It is not possible to traverse across drives. For example, this approach ensures that any future canonicalization worm that allows an attacker to access system files will fail. For example, if the attacker formulates a URL that contains the following path, the request fails:

/scripts/..%5c../winnt/system32/cmd.exe

During this step, you:

- **Move your Web site to a non-system volume.**
- **Disable the parent paths setting.**
- **Remove potentially dangerous virtual directories.**
- **Remove or secure RDS.**
- **Set Web permissions.**
- **Remove or secure FrontPage Server Extensions.**

Move Your Web site to a Non-System Volume

Do not use the default \inetpub\wwwroot directory. For example, if your system is installed on the C: drive, then move your site and content directory to the D: drive. This mitigates the risks associated with unforeseen canonicalization issues and directory traversal attacks.

Disable the Parent Paths Setting

This IIS metabase setting prevents the use of ".." in script and application calls to functions such as **MapPath**. This helps guard against directory traversal attacks.

► **To disable parent paths**

1. Start IIS.
2. Right-click the root of your Web site, and click **Properties**.
3. Click the **Home Directory** tab.
4. Click **Configuration**.
5. Click the **App Options** tab.
6. Clear **Enable parent paths**.

Note If you use the Application Center 2002 Administration Site, see Microsoft Knowledge Base article 288309, "PRB: Disabling Parent Paths Breaks User Interface."

Remove Potentially Dangerous Virtual Directories

Sample applications are not installed by default and should not be installed on production Web servers. Remove all sample applications, including the ones that can be accessed only from the local computer with http://localhost, or http://127.0.0.1.

Remove the following virtual directories from production servers: IISSamples, IISAdmin, IISHelp, and Scripts.

Note IISLockdown provides an option to remove the Scripts, IISSamples, IISAdmin, and IISHelp virtual directories.

Remove or Secure RDS

Remote Data Services (RDS) is a component that enables controlled Internet access to remote data resources through IIS. The RDS interface is provided by Msadcs.dll, which is located in the following directory: program files\common files\system \Msadc.

Removing RDS

If your applications do not use RDS, remove it.

► **To remove RDS support**

1. Remove the /MSADC virtual directory mapping from IIS.
2. Remove the RDS files and subdirectories at the following location:
   \Program Files\Common Files\System\Msadc
3. Remove the following registry key:
   HKLM\System\CurrentControlSet\Services\W3SVC\Parameters\ADCLaunch

Note IISLockdown provides an option to remove the MSADC virtual directory. Note that IISLockdown only removes the virtual directory, not the files or registry key.

Securing RDS

If your applications require RDS, secure it.

▶ **To secure RDS**

1. Delete the samples at the following location:

   \Progam Files\Common Files\System\Msadc\Samples

2. Remove the following registry key:

   **HKLM\System\CurrentControlSet\Services\W3SVC\Parameters
   \ADCLaunch\VbBusObj.VbBusObjCls**

3. Disable Anonymous access for the MSADC virtual directory in IIS.

4. Create a **HandlerRequired** registry key in the following location:

   HKLM\Software\Microsoft\DataFactory\HandlerInfo

5. Create a new DWORD value, and set it to **1** (1 indicates safe mode, while 0 indicates unsafe mode.

Note   You can use the registry script file Handsafe.reg to change the registry key. The script file is located in the msadc directory: \Program Files\Common Files\System\msadc

---

For more information about securing RDS, see the following:

- MS99-025 Microsoft Security Program: Unauthorized Access to IIS Servers through ODBC Data Access with RDS at *http://www.microsoft.com/technet/security/bulletin /ms99-025.asp.*

- MS98-004 Microsoft Security Program: Microsoft Security Bulletin: Unauthorized ODBC Data Access with RDS and IIS at *http://www.microsoft.com/technet/treeview /default.asp?url=/technet/security/bulletin/MS98-004.asp.*

- Microsoft Knowledge Base article 184375, "PRB: Security Implications of RDS 1.5, IIS 3.0 or 4.0, and ODBC."

Set Web Permissions

Web permissions are configured through the IIS snap-in and are maintained in the IIS metabase. They are not NTFS permissions.

Use the following Web permissions:

- **Read Permissions**. Restrict Read permissions on include directories.

- **Write and Execute Permissions**. Restrict Write and Execute permissions on virtual directories that allow anonymous access.

- **Script source access**. Configure Script source access permissions only on folders that allow content authoring.

- **Write**. Configure Write permissions only on folders that allow content authoring. Grant write access only to content authors.

Note   Folders that support content authoring should be configured to require authentication and SSL for encryption.

Remove or Secure FrontPage Server Extensions

If you do not use FrontPage Server Extensions (FPSE), disable it. If you use FPSE, take the following steps to improve security:

- **Upgrade server extensions**. See to the security issues covered in MSDN article, "Microsoft FrontPage Server Extensions 2002 for Windows" at *http://msdn.microsoft.com/library/default.asp?url=/library/en-us/dnservext/html /fpse02win.asp*.

- **Restrict access using FrontPage security**. FPSE installs groups that are granted permissions to those Web sites for which the server extensions are configured. These groups are used to restrict the access available based on the role of the user. For more information, see the Assistance Center at *http://office.microsoft.com /assistance/2002/articles/fp_colmanagesecurity.aspx*.

Step 12. Script Mappings

Script mappings associate a particular file extension, such as .asp, to the ISAPI extension that handles it, such as Asp.dll. IIS is configured to support a range of extensions including .asp, .shtm, .hdc, and so on. ASP.NET HTTP handlers are a rough equivalent of ISAPI extensions. In IIS, file extensions, such as .aspx, are first mapped in IIS to Aspnet_isapi.dll, which forwards the request to the ASP.NET worker process. The actual HTTP handler that processes the file extension is then determined by the **<HttpHandler>** mapping in Machine.config or Web.config.

The main security issues associated with script mappings are:

- **An attacker could exploit a vulnerability found in an extension**.

  This could occur if a vulnerability in an extension remains unpatched. Unused extensions increase the area of potential attack. For example, if you do not use a particular extension, you might not pay attention to relevant updates.

- **Server-side resources could be downloaded by the client**.

  This could occur when a file extension is not mapped correctly. Files that should not be directly accessible by the client should either be mapped to the appropriate handler, based on its extension, or should be removed.

During this step, you:

- **Map IIS file extensions**.
- **Map .NET Framework file extensions**.

Map IIS File Extensions

On Windows 2000, the IIS file extensions of interest include: .asp, .asa, .cer, .cdx, .htr, .idc, .shtm, .shtml, .stm, and .printer.

If you do not use any one of these extensions, map the extension to the 404.dll, which is provided by IISLockdown. For example, if you do not want to serve ASP pages to clients, map .asp to the 404.dll.

The mappings altered by IISLockdown depend on the server template that you choose:

- **Static Web Server**. If you run IISLockdown and choose the Static Web server option, then all of the above extensions are mapped to the 404.dll.
- **Dynamic Web Server**. If you choose the Dynamic Web server option, which is the preferred option when serving ASP.NET pages, then .htr, .idc, .shtm, .shtml, .stm, and .printer are mapped to the 404.dll, while .asp, .cer, .cdx, and .asa are not. In this case, you should manually map .cer, .cdx, and .asa to the 404.dll. If you are not serving .asp, then you can map that as well.

Why Map to the 404.dll?

By mapping file extensions to the 404.dll, you prevent files from being returned and downloaded over HTTP. If you request a file with an extension mapped to the 404.dll, a Web page with the message "HTTP 404 - File not found" is displayed. You are recommended to map unused extensions to the 404.dll rather than deleting the mapping. If you delete a mapping, and a file is mistakenly left on the server (or put there by mistake) it can be displayed in clear text when it is requested because IIS does not know how to process it.

▶ **To map a file extension to the 404.dll**

1. Start IIS.
2. Right-click your server name in the left window, and then click **Properties**.
3. Ensure that the **WWWService** is selected in the **Master Properties** drop-down list, and then click the adjacent **Edit** button.
4. Click the **Home Directory** tab.

5. Click **Configuration**. The tabbed page shown in Figure 16.4 is displayed.

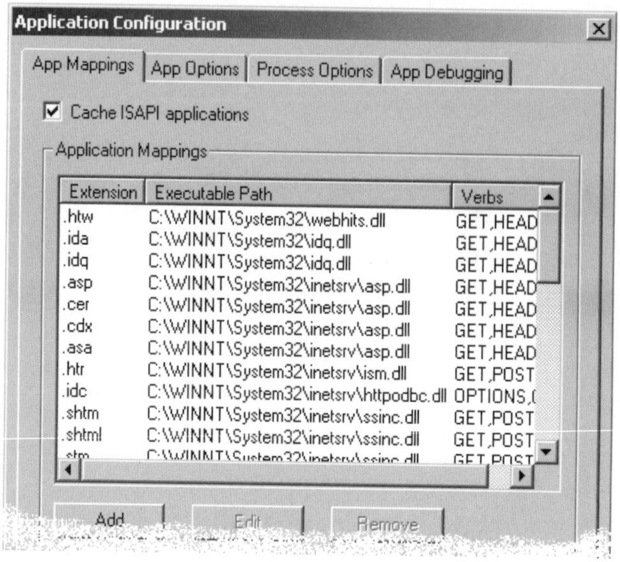

Figure 16.4
Mapping application extensions

6. Select one of the extensions from the list, and then click **Edit**.

7. Click **Browse** and navigate to \WINNT\system32\inetsrv\404.dll.

Note This step assumes that you have previously run IISlockd.exe, as the 404.dll is installed by the IISLockdown tool.

---

8. Click **Open**, and then click **OK**.

9. Repeat steps 6, 7 and 8 for all of the remaining file extensions.

Map .NET Framework File Extensions

The following .NET Framework file extensions are mapped to aspnet_isapi.dll: .asax, .ascx, .ashx, .asmx, .aspx, .axd, .vsdisco, .jsl, .java, .vjsproj, .rem, .soap, .config, .cs, .csproj, .vb, .vbproj, .webinfo, .licx, .resx, and .resources.

The .NET Framework protects file extensions that should not be directly called by clients by associating them with **System.Web.HttpForbiddenHandler** in Machine.config. The following file extensions are mapped to **System.Web.HttpForbiddenHandler** by default: .asax, .ascx, .config, .cs, .csproj, .vb, .vbproj, .webinfo, .asp, .licx, .resx, and .resources.

For more information on HTTP handlers, see "Step 16: Machine.config."

Additional Considerations

Because IIS processes a Web request first, you could map .NET Framework file extensions that you do not want clients to call, to the 404.dll directly. This does two tasks:

- The 404.dll handles and rejects requests before they are passed to ASP.NET and before they are processed by the ASP.NET worker process. This eliminates unnecessary processing by the ASP.NET worker process. Moreover, blocking requests early is a good security practice.
- The 404.dll returns the message "HTTP 404 - File not found" and **System.Web.HttpForbiddenHandler** returns the message "This type of page is not served." Arguably, the "File not found" message reveals less information and thus could be considered more secure.

Step 13. ISAPI Filters

In the past, vulnerabilities in ISAPI filters caused significant IIS exploitation. There are no unneeded ISAPI filters after a clean IIS installation, although the .NET Framework installs the ASP.NET ISAPI filter (Aspnet_filter.dll), which is loaded into the IIS process address space (Inetinfo.exe) and is used to support cookie-less session state management.

If your applications do not need to support cookie-less session state and they do not set the **cookieless** attribute to **true** on the **<sessionState>** element, this filter can be removed.

During this step, you remove unused ISAPI filters.

Remove Unused ISAPI Filters

Remove any unused ISAPI filters as explained in the following section.

▶ **To view ISAPI filters**

1. To start IIS, select **Internet Services Manager** from the Administrative Tools programs group.
2. Right-click the machine (not Web site, because filters are machine wide), and then click **Properties**.
3. Click **Edit**.

4. Click the **ISAPI Filters** tab.

The tabbed page shown in Figure 16.5 is displayed:

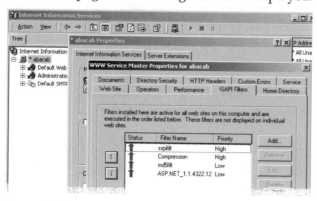

Figure 16.5
Removing unused ISAPI filters

Step 14. IIS Metabase

Security and other IIS configuration settings are maintained in the IIS metabase file. Harden the NTFS permissions on the IIS metabase (and the backup metabase file) to be sure that attackers cannot modify your IIS configuration in any way (for example, to disable authentication for a particular virtual directory.)

During this step, you:

● **Restrict access to the metabase using NTFS permissions.**
● **Restrict banner information returned by IIS.**

Restrict Access to the Metabase Using NTFS Permissions

Set the following NTFS permissions on the IIS metabase file (Metabase.bin) in the \WINNT\system32\inetsrv directory.

● Local System: Full Control
● Administrators: Full Control

Restrict Banner Information Returned by IIS

Banner information can reveal software versions and other information that may help an attacker. Banner information can reveal the software you run, allowing an attacker to exploit known software vulnerabilities.

When you retrieve a static page, for example, an .htm or a .gif file, a content location header is added to the response. By default, this content header references the IP address, and not the fully qualified domain name (FQDN). This means that your internal IP address is unwittingly exposed. For example, the following HTTP response header shows the IP address in bold font:

```
HTTP/1.1 200 OK
Server: Microsoft-IIS/5.0
Content-Location: http://10.1.1.1/Default.htm
Date: Thu, 18 Feb 1999 14:03:52 GMT
Content-Type: text/html
Accept-Ranges: bytes
Last-Modified: Wed, 06 Jan 1999 18:56:06 GMT
ETag: "067d136a639be1:15b6"
Content-Length: 4325
```

You can hide the content location returned in HTTP response headers by modifying a value in the IIS metabase to change the default behavior from exposing IP addresses, to sending the FQDN instead.

For more information about hiding the content location in HTTP responses, see Microsoft Knowledge Base article 218180, "Internet Information Server Returns IP Address in HTTP Header (Content-Location)."

Step 15. Server Certificates

If your Web application supports HTTPS (SSL) over port 443, you must install a server certificate. This is required as part of the session negotiation process that occurs when a client establishes a secure HTTPS session.

A valid certificate provides secure authentication so that a client can trust the server it is communicating with, and secure communication so that sensitive data remains confidential and tamperproof over the network.

During this step, you validate your server certificate.

Validate Your Server Certificate

Check the following four items to confirm the validity of your Web server certificate:
- Check that the valid from and valid to dates are in range.
- Check that the certificate is being used correctly. If it was issued as a server certificate it should not be used for e-mail.
- Check that the public keys in the certificate chain are all valid up to a trusted root.
- Check that it has not been revoked. It must not be on a Certificate Revocation List (CRL) from the server that issued the certificate.

Step 16. Machine.Config

This section covers hardening information about machine level settings that apply to all applications. For application specific hardening settings, see Chapter 19, "Securing Your ASP.NET Application."

The Machine.config file maintains numerous machine wide settings for the .NET Framework, many of which affect security. Machine.config is located in the following directory:

%windir%\Microsoft.NET\Framework\{version}\CONFIG

> **Note** You can use any text or XML editor (Notepad, for example) to edit XML configuration files. XML tags are case sensitive, so be sure to use the correct case.

During this step, you:

- **Map protected resources to HttpForbiddenHandler.**
- **Verify that tracing.is disabled.**
- **Verify that debug compiles are disabled.**
- **Verify that ASP.NET errors are not returned to the client.**
- **Verify session state settings.**

Map Protected Resources to HttpForbiddenHandler

HTTP handlers are located in Machine.config beneath the **<httpHandlers>** element. HTTP handlers are responsible for processing Web requests for specific file extensions. Remoting should not be enabled on front-end Web servers; enable remoting only on middle-tier application servers that are isolated from the Internet.

- The following file extensions are mapped in Machine.config to HTTP handlers:
- .aspx is used for ASP.NET pages
- .rem and .soap are used for Remoting.
- .asmx is used for Web Services.
- .asax, .ascx, .config, .cs, .csproj, .vb, .vbproj, .webinfo, .asp, .licx, .resx, and .resources are protected resources and are mapped to **System.Web.HttpForbiddenHandler**.

For .NET Framework resources, if you do not use a file extension, then map the extension to **System.Web.HttpForbiddenHandler** in Machine.config, as shown in the following example:

```
<add verb="*" path="*.vbproj" type="System.Web.HttpForbiddenHandler" />
```

In this case, the .vbproj file extension is mapped to
System.Web.HttpForbiddenHandler. If a client requests a path that ends with
.vbproj, then ASP.NET returns a message that states "This type of page is not served."

- The following guidelines apply to handling .NET Framework file extensions:
- **Map extensions you do not use to HttpForbiddenHandler**. If you do not serve
  ASP.NET pages, then map .aspx to **HttpForbiddenHandler**. If you do not use Web
  Services, then map .asmx to **HttpForbiddenHandler**.
- **Disable Remoting on Internet-facing Web servers**. Map remoting extensions
  (.soap and .rem) on Internet-facing Web servers to **HttpForbiddenHandler**.

Disable .NET Remoting

To disable .NET Remoting disable requests for .rem and .soap extensions, use the
following elements beneath **\<httpHandlers\>**:

```
<add verb="*" path="*.rem" type="System.Web.HttpForbiddenHandler"/>
<add verb="*" path="*.soap" type="System.Web.HttpForbiddenHandler"/>
```

Note This does not prevent a Web application on the Web server from connecting to a downstream
object by using the Remoting infrastructure. However, it prevents clients from connecting to objects
on the Web server.

Verify That Tracing Is Disabled

You configure tracing in Machine.config by using the **\<trace\>** element. While it is
useful on development and test servers, do not enable tracing on production servers,
because system-level trace information can greatly assist an attacker to profile an
application and probe for weak spots.

Use the following configuration on production servers:

```
<trace enabled="false" localOnly="true" pageOutput="false"
       requestLimit="10" traceMode="SortByTime"/>
```

Set **enabled="false"** on production servers. If you do need to trace problems with
live applications, simulate the problem in a test environment, or if necessary, enable
tracing and set **localOnly="true"** to prevent trace details from being returned to
remote clients.

Verify That Debug Compiles Are Disabled

You can control whether or not the compiler produces debug builds that include
debug symbols by using the **\<compilation\>** element. To turn off debug compiles, set
debug="false" as shown below:

```
<compilation debug="false" explicit="true" defaultLanguage="vb" />
```

Verify That ASP.NET Errors Are Not Returned to Clients

You can use the **<customErrors>** element to configure custom, generic error messages that should be returned to the client in the event of an application exception condition.

Make sure that the mode attribute is set to **"RemoteOnly"** as shown in the following example:

```
<customErrors mode="RemoteOnly" />
```

After installing an ASP.NET application, you can configure the setting to point to your custom error page as shown in the following example:

```
<customErrors mode="On" defaultRedirect="YourErrorPage.htm" />
```

Verify Session State Settings

If you do not use session state, verify that session state is disabled in Machine.config as shown in the following example:

```
<sessionState mode="Off" . . . />
```

Also, ensure that the ASP.NET State Service is disabled. The default session state mode is **"InProc"** and the ASP.NET State Service is set to manual. For more information about securing session state if you install an ASP.NET application that requires it, see "Session State," in Chapter 19, "Securing Your ASP.NET Application and Web Services."

Step 17. Code Access Security

Machine level code access security policy is determined by settings in the Security.config file located in the following directory: %windir%\Microsoft.NET\Framework\{version}\CONFIG

Run the following command to be sure that code access security is enabled on your server:

caspol -s On

For more information about configuring code access security for ASP.NET Web applications, see Chapter 9, "Using Code Access Security with ASP.NET."

During this step, you:

- **Remove all permissions for the local intranet zone.**
- **Remove all permissions for the Internet zone.**

Remove All Permissions for the Local Intranet Zone

The local intranet zone applies permissions to code running from UNC shares or internal Web sites. Reconfigure this zone to grant no permissions by associating it with the **Nothing** permission set.

▶ **To remove all permissions for the local intranet zone**

1. Start the Microsoft .NET Framework version 1.1 Configuration tool from the **Administrative Tools** program group.
2. Expand **Runtime Security Policy**, expand **Machine**, and then expand **Code Groups**.
3. Expand **All_Code** and then select **LocalIntranet_Zone**.
4. Click **Edit Code Group Properties**.
5. Click the **Permission Set** tab.
6. Select **Nothing** from the drop-down **Permission** list.
7. Click **OK**.

    The dialog box shown in Figure 16.6 is displayed.

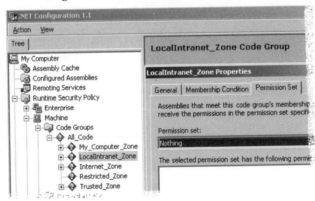

Figure 16.6
Setting LocalIntranet_Zone code permissions to Nothing

Remove All Permissions for the Internet Zone

The Internet zone applies code access permissions to code downloaded over the Internet. On Web servers, this zone should be reconfigured to grant no permissions by associating it with the **Nothing** permission set.

Repeat the steps shown in the preceding section, "Remove All Permissions for the Local Intranet Zone," except set the **Internet_Zone** to the **Nothing** permission set.

Snapshot of a Secure Web Server

A snapshot view that shows the attributes of a secure Web server allows you to quickly and easily compare settings with your own Web server. The settings shown in Table 16.4 are based on Web servers that host Web sites that have proven to be very resilient to attack and demonstrate sound security practices. By following the proceeding steps you can generate an identically configured server, with regard to security.

Table 16.4   Snapshot of a Secure Web Server

Component	Characteristics
Patches and Updates	Latest service packs and patches are applied for Windows, IIS, and the .NET Framework.
Services	Unnecessary services are disabled.
	NNTP, SMTP, and FTP are disabled unless you require them.
	WebDAV is disabled or secured if used.
	Service accounts run with least privilege.
	ASP.NET Session State service is disabled if not required.
Protocols	The NetBIOS and SMB protocols are not enabled on the server.
	The TCP stack has been hardened.
Accounts	Unused accounts are removed.
	Guest account is disabled.
	The default administrator account is renamed and has a strong password.
	Default anonymous account (IUSR_Machine) is disabled.
	Custom anonymous account is used for anonymous access.
	Strong password policies are enforced.
	Remote logons are restricted.
	Null sessions (anonymous logons) are disabled.
	Approval if required for account delegation.
	Shared accounts are not used.
	Membership of local **administrators** group is restricted (ideally to two members).
	Administrators are required to log on interactively (or a secure remote administration solution is implemented).

Table 16.4   Snapshot of a Secure Web Server *(continued)*

Component	Characteristics
Files and Directories	**Everyone** group has no rights to system, Web, or tools directories.
	Anonymous account has no access to Web site content directories and system utilities.
	Tools, utilities, and SDKs are removed or secured.
	Sample files are removed.
	Unnecessary DSNs are removed.
Shares	Unused shares are removed from the server.
	Access to required shares is secured (shares are not enabled to "Everyone" unless necessary.)
	Administration shares (C$ and Admin$) are removed if not required.
Ports	All ports except 80 and 443 (SSL) are blocked, especially vulnerable ports 135–139 and 445.
Registry	Remote administration of the registry is prevented.
	SAM has been secured (stand-alone servers only).
Auditing and Logging	Login failures are logged.
	Object access failures by the **Everyone** group are logged.
	Log files are relocated from %systemroot%\system32\LogFiles and secured with ACLs: Administrators and System have full control.
	IIS logging is enabled.
	Log files are regularly archived for offline analysis.
	Access to the metabase.bin file is audited.
	IIS is configured for W3C Extended Log File Format Auditing.
IIS	
Sites and Virtual Directories	Web roots and virtual directories are located on separate volumes from the system volume.
	Parent Paths setting is disabled.
	Dangerous virtual directories are removed (IIS Samples, MSADC, IISHelp, Scripts, and IISAdmin).
	RDS is removed or secured.
	Web permissions restrict inappropriate access.
	Include directories restrict Read Web permissions.

(continued)

Table 16.4 Snapshot of a Secure Web Server *(continued)*

Component	Characteristics
Sites and Virtual Directories *(continued)*	Folders with Anonymous access restrict Write and Execute Web permissions.
	Secured folders that allow content authoring allow Script Source Access Web permissions while all other folders do not.
	FPSE is removed if not required.
Script Mappings	Unused script-mappings are mapped to 404.dll: .idq, .htw , .ida , .shtml , .shtm , .stm , idc, .htr , .printer.
	Note The 404.dll is installed when you run the IIS Lockdown tool.
ISAPI Filters	Unused ISAPI filters are removed.
IIS Metabase	Access to IIS Metabase is restricted with NTFS permissions.
	Banner information is restricted; the content location in HTTP response headers is hidden.
Machine.config	
HttpForbiddenHandler	Protected resources are mapped to **System.Web.HttpForbiddenHandler**

Remoting	.NET Remoting is disabled.
	
	``
	<httpHandlers>
	  <add verb="*" path="*.rem"
	      type="System.Web.HttpForbiddenHandler"/>
	  <add verb="*" path="*.soap"
	      type="System.Web.HttpForbiddenHandler"/>
	</httpHandlers>
	``

trace	Trace information and detailed error information is not returned to the client: ``` <trace enabled="false"> ```
compilation	Debug compiles are disabled ``` <compilation debug="false"/> ```
customErrors	Error details are not returned to the client: ``` <customErrors mode="On" /> ``` A generic error page writes errors to the Event Log.
sessionState	Session State is disabled if not needed: ``` <sessionState mode="Off" /> ```

Table 16.4   Snapshot of a Secure Web Server *(continued)*

Component	Characteristics
Code Access Security	
Code Access Security	Code Access Security is enabled for the machine. **caspol -s On**
LocalIntranet_Zone	Local intranet zone has no permissions: PermissionSet=**Nothing**
Internet_Zone	Internet zone has no permissions: PermissionSet=**Nothing**

Staying Secure

You need to monitor the security state of your server and update it regularly to help prevent newly discovered vulnerabilities from being exploited. To help keep your server secure:

- **Audit group membership.**
- **Monitor audit logs.**
- **Stay current with service packs and patches.**
- **Perform security assessments.**
- **Use security notification services.**

Audit Group Membership

Keep track of user group membership, particularly for privileged groups such as Administrators. The following command lists the members of the **Administrators** group:

net localgroup administrators

Monitor Audit Logs

Monitor audit logs regularly and analyze the log files by manually viewing them or use the technique describe in Microsoft Knowledge Base article 296085, "How To: Use SQL Server to Analyze Web Logs."

Stay Current With Service Packs and Patches

Set up a schedule to analyze your server software and subscribe to security alerts. Use MBSA to regularly scan your server for missing patches. The following links provide the latest updates:

- **Windows 2000 service packs**. The latest service packs are listed at *http://www.microsoft.com/windows2000/downloads/servicepacks/default.asp*.

- **.NET Framework Service Pack**. For information about how to obtain the latest .NET Framework updates, see the MSDN article, "How to Get the Microsoft .NET Framework" at *http://msdn.microsoft.com/netframework/downloads/howtoget.asp*.

- **Critical Updates**. These updates help to resolve known issues and help protect your computer from known security vulnerabilities. For the latest critical updates, see "Critical Updates" at *http://www.microsoft.com/windows2000/downloads/critical /default.asp*

- **Advanced Security Updates**. For additional security updates, see "Advanced Security Updates" at *http://www.microsoft.com/windows2000/downloads/security /default.asp*.

   These also help protect your computer from known security vulnerabilities.

Perform Security Assessments

Use MBSA to regularly check for security vulnerabilities and to identify missing patches and updates. Schedule MBSA to run daily and analyze the results to take action as needed. For more information about automating MBSA, see "How To: Use MBSA" in the "How To" section of this guide.

Use Security Notification Services

Use the Microsoft services listed in Table 16.5 to obtain security bulletins with notifications of possible system vulnerabilities.

Table 16.5   Security Notification Services

Service	Location
TechNet Security Web site	*http://www.microsoft.com/technet/treeview/default.asp?url=/technet/security /current.asp* Use this Web page to view the security bulletins that are available for your system.
Microsoft Security Notification Service	*http://register.microsoft.com/subscription/subscribeme.asp?ID=135* Use this service to register for regular email bulletins that notify you of the availability of new fixes and updates.

Additionally, subscribe to the industry security alert services shown in Table 16.6. This allows you to assess the threat of a vulnerability where a patch is not yet available.

Table 16.6   Industry Security Notification Services

Service	Location
CERT Advisory Mailing List	*http://www.cert.org/contact_cert/certmaillist.html* Informative advisories are sent when vulnerabilities are reported.
Windows and .NET Magazine Security UPDATE	*http://email.winnetmag.com/winnetmag/winnetmag_prefctr.asp* Announces the latest security breaches and identifies fixes.
NTBugtraq	*http://www.ntbugtraq.com/default.asp?pid=31&sid=1 - 020* This is an open discussion of Windows security vulnerabilities and exploits. Vulnerabilities which currently have no patch are discussed.

Remote Administration

Administrators often need to be able to administer multiple servers. Make sure the requirements of your remote administration solution do not compromise security. If you need remote administration capabilities, then the following recommendations help improve security:

- **Restrict the number of administration accounts**. This includes restricting the number of administration accounts as well as restricting which accounts are allowed to log on remotely.
- **Restrict the tools**. The main options include Internet Services Manager and Terminal Services. Another option is Web administration (using the IISAdmin virtual directory), but this is not recommended and this option is removed by IISLockdown.exe. Both Internet Services Manager and Terminal Services use Windows security. The main considerations here are restricting the Windows accounts and the ports you use.
- **Restrict the computers that are allowed to administer the server**. IPSec can be used to restrict which computers can connect to your Web server.

Securing Terminal Services

It is possible to use Microsoft Terminal Services securely, to remotely administer your Web server.

Terminal Services is based on Microsoft's proprietary protocol known as Remote Desktop Protocol (RDP). RDP uses the TCP 3389 port and supports two concurrent users. The following sections describe how to install and configure Terminal Services for secure administration:

- **Install Terminal Services.**
- **Configure Terminal Services.**

Install Terminal Services

▶ To install Terminal Services:

1. Install Terminal Services by using **Add/Remove Programs** from the Control Panel. Use the **Add/Remove Windows Components** option. You do not need to install the Terminal Services Licensing service for remote administration.

2. Configure Terminal Services for remote administration mode.

3. Remove the **TsInternetUser** account, which is created during Terminal Services installation. This account is used to support anonymous Internet access to Terminal Services, which should not be enabled on the server.

Configure Terminal Services

Use the Terminal Services Configuration MMC snap-in available from the Administrative Tools program group to configure the following:

1. There are three levels (Low, Medium, and High) of encryption available for connections to Terminal Services. Set the encryption to 128-bit key. Note that the Windows high encryption pack should be installed on both the server and the client.

2. Configure the Terminal Services session to disconnect after idle connection time limit. Set it to end a disconnected session. A session is considered to be disconnected if the user closes the Terminal Services client application without logging off in a period of ten minutes.

3. Finally restrict permissions to access Terminal Services. Use the **RDP permissions** tab in the RDP dialog box. By default, all members of the Administrators group are allowed to access Terminal Services. If you don't want all members of the Administrators group to access Terminal Services, then remove the group and add individual accounts that need access. Note that the SYSTEM account must be in the list.

Use a secure VPN connection between the client and the server or an IPSec tunnel for enhanced security. This approach provides mutual authentication and the RDP payload is encrypted.

Copying Files over RDP

Terminal Services does not provide built-in support for file transfer. However, you can install the File Copy utility from the Windows 2000 Server Resource Kit to add file transfer functionality to the clipboard redirection feature in Terminal Services. For more information about the utility and installation instructions see Microsoft Knowledge Base article 244732, "How To: Install the File Copy Tool Included with the Windows 2000 Resource Kit."

Simplifying and Automating Security

This chapter has shown you how to manually configure security settings for an ASP.NET Web server. The manual process helps you to understand the configuration but can be time consuming Use the following resources to help automate the steps presented in this chapter:

- For information on how to automate IISLockdown, see Microsoft Knowledge Base article 310725 "How To: Run the IIS Lockdown Wizard Unattended in IIS."
- You can create and deploy security policies using security templates. For more information, see the following Microsoft Knowledge Base articles:
  - 313434, "How To: Define Security Templates in the Security Templates Snap-in in Windows 2000."
  - 309689, "How To: Apply Predefined Security Templates in Windows 2000."
  - 321679, "How To: Manage Security Templates in Windows 2000 Server."
- For detailed guidance about customizing and automating security templates, see the Microsoft *patterns & practices, Microsoft Solution for Securing Windows 2000 Server*, at *http://www.microsoft.com/technet/treeview/default.asp?url=/technet/security /prodtech/windows/secwin2k/default.asp*.

  The *Microsoft Solution for Securing Windows 2000 Server* addresses the most common server roles, including domain controllers, DNS servers, DHCP servers, IIS Web servers, and File and Print servers. The approach used in this guide allows you to take a default Windows 2000 installation and then create a secure server, the precise configuration of which varies depending upon its role. Administrators can then consciously weaken security to satisfy the needs of their particular environment. The guide provides a foundation of baseline security recommendations that covers services, accounts, group policies, and so on, that you can use as a starting point for the common types of server roles.

Summary

A secure Web server provides a protected foundation for hosting your Web applications. This chapter has shown you the main threats that have the potential to impact your ASP.NET Web server and has provided the security steps required for risk mitigation. By performing the hardening steps presented in this chapter, you can create a secure platform and host infrastructure to support ASP.NET Web applications and Web services.

The methodology used in this chapter allows you to build a secure Web server from scratch and also allows you to harden the security configuration of an existing Web server. The next step is to ensure that any deployed applications are correctly configured.

Additional Resources

For additional related reading, see the following resources:

- For information about securing your developer workstation, see "How To: Secure Your Developer Workstation" in the "How To" section of this guide.

- For more information about how to secure ASP.NET Web applications and Web services, see Chapter 19, "Securing Your ASP.NET Application."

- For information on how the Open Hack application was configured, see the MSDN article, "Building and Configuring More Secure Web Sites," at *http://msdn.microsoft.com/library/default.asp?url=/library/en-us/dnnetsec/html/openhack.asp*.

- For security-related resources on TechNet, see the TechNet Security page, *http://www.microsoft.com/technet/security/default.asp*.

- For a printable checklist, see "Checklist: Securing Your Web Server" in the "Checklists" section of this guide.

17

Securing Your Application Server

In This Chapter

- Identifying threats and countermeasures for middle-tier application servers
- Securing the communication channels between tiers
- Securing middle-tier Remoting and Web services applications
- Locking down an Enterprise Services application
- Configuring an internal firewall

Overview

Middle-tier application servers are most often used to host business logic and data access services. This functionality is usually packaged inside Enterprise Services applications or is exposed to front-end Web servers by using middle-tier Web services or Microsoft® .NET Remoting technology. This chapter addresses each technology separately and shows you how to secure your application server in each case.

Figure 17.1 shows the focus of this chapter, which includes configuring internal firewalls that are featured in many multitiered deployment models.

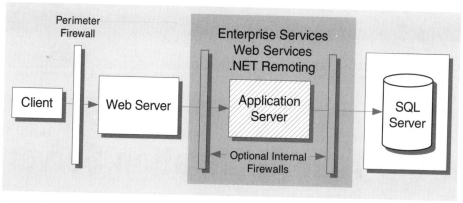

Figure 17.1
Remote application server deployment model

Before delving into technology-specific configuration, the chapter identifies the main threats to an application server. These threats are somewhat different from those that apply to an Internet-facing Web server because middle-tier application servers are (or should be) isolated from direct Internet access.

To secure the application server, you must apply an incremental security configuration after the underlying operating system and Internet Information Services (IIS) Web server (if installed) have been locked down.

How to Use This Chapter

This chapter focuses on the application server and the associated communication channels that connect the Web server to the application server and the application server to the database server.

To get the most out of this chapter:

- **Read Chapter 2, "Threats and Countermeasures."** This will give you a better understanding of potential threats to Web applications.
- **Use the companion securing chapters**. The current chapter is part of a securing solution that includes chapters that cover host (operating system) and network layer security. Use the following chapters in tandem with this one:
  - Chapter 15, "Securing Your Network"
  - Chapter 16, "Securing Your Web Server"
  - Chapter 18, "Securing Your Database Server"

Threats and Countermeasures

Many threats to an application server come from within an organization because application servers should be isolated from Internet access. The main threats to an application server are:

- Network eavesdropping
- Unauthorized access
- Viruses, Trojan horses, and worms

Figure 17.2 shows the main threats to an application server.

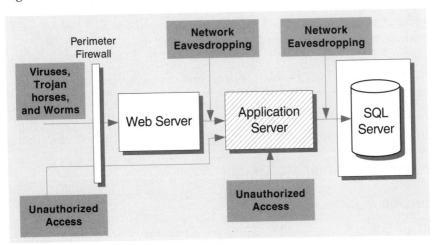

Figure 17.2
Top application server related threats and vulnerabilities

Network Eavesdropping

Attackers with network monitoring software can intercept data flowing from the Web server to the application server and from the application server to downstream systems and database servers. The attacker can view and potentially modify this data.

Vulnerabilities

Vulnerabilities that can make your application server vulnerable to network eavesdropping include:

- Sensitive data transmitted in clear text by the application
- Use of Microsoft SQL Server authentication to the database, resulting in clear text credentials

- Lack of transport or application layer encryption
- Insecure network-hardware administrative interfaces
- Use of the .NET Remoting TCP Channel to remote components

Attacks

The attacker places packet-sniffing tools on the network to capture traffic.

Countermeasures

Countermeasures to prevent packet sniffing include the following:

- Use secure authentication, such as Windows authentication, that does not send passwords over the network.
- Encrypt SQL Server authentication credentials. If you use SQL Server authentication, you can encrypt credentials automatically by installing a server certificate on the database server.
- Secure communication channels. Options include using Secure Sockets Layer (SSL) or Internet Protocol Security (IPSec).
- Use remote procedure call (RPC) encryption with Enterprise Services applications.
- Use a segmented network, which can isolate eavesdropping to compromised segments.
- Use the **HttpChannel** and SSL with .NET Remoting.

Unauthorized Access

If you fail to block the ports used by applications that run on the application server at the perimeter firewall, an external attacker can communicate directly with the application server. If you allow computers other than the front-end Web servers to connect to the application server, the attack profile for the application server increases.

Vulnerabilities

Vulnerabilities that can result in unauthorized access include:

- Weak perimeter network and firewall configurations
- Superfluous ports open on the internal firewall
- Lack of IPSec policies to restrict host connectivity
- Unnecessary active services
- Unnecessary protocols
- Weak account and password policies

Attacks

Common attacks to gain unauthorized access include:

- Port scanning that detects listening services
- Banner grabbing that gives away available services and possibly software versions
- Malicious application input
- Password attacks against default accounts with weak passwords

Countermeasures

Countermeasures to prevent unauthorized access include:

- Firewall policies that block all traffic except expected communication ports
- TCP/IP filtering or IPSec policies to prevent unauthorized hosts from establishing connections
- Disabling unused services
- Static DCOM endpoint mapping that allows access only to authorized hosts

Viruses, Worms, and Trojan Horses

These attacks are often not noticed until they begin to consume system resources, which slows down or halts the execution of other applications. Application servers that host IIS are susceptible to IIS attacks.

Vulnerabilities

- Unpatched servers
- Running unnecessary services
- Unnecessary ISAPI filters and ISAPI extensions

Countermeasures

Countermeasures that help mitigate the risk posed by viruses, Trojan horses, and worms include:

- Promptly applying the latest software patches
- Disabling unused functionality, such as unused ISAPI filters and extensions
- Running processes with least privileged accounts to reduce the scope of damage in the event of a compromise

Methodology

By securing the communication channels to the application server and preventing any hosts except authorized Web servers from accessing the application server, attackers are limited to application-layer attacks that exploit vulnerabilities in Web application design and development.

To mitigate this risk, developers must apply the secure design and development approaches described in Parts II and III of this guide.

The configuration solutions in this chapter are specific to the application server and they should not be applied in isolation. Apply them alongside the solutions presented in Chapter 15, "Securing Your Network," Chapter 16, "Securing Your Web Server," and Chapter 18, "Securing Your Database Server."

Communication Channel Considerations

Sensitive application data and authentication credentials that are sent to and from the application server should be encrypted to provide privacy and integrity. This mitigates the risk associated with eavesdropping and tampering.

Encrypting network traffic addresses the network eavesdropping and tampering threats. If you consider this threat to be negligible in your environment—for example, because your application is located in a closed and physically secured network—then you do not need to encrypt the traffic. If network eavesdropping is a concern, then you can use SSL, which provides a secure communication channel at the application layer, or IPSec, which provides a transport-level solution. IPSec encrypts all IP traffic that flows between two servers, while SSL allows each application to choose whether or not to provide an encrypted communication channel.

Enterprise Services

Enterprise Services (or COM+) applications communicate over the network using DCOM over RPC. RPC uses port 135, which provides endpoint mapping services to allow clients to negotiate parameters, including the communication port, which by default is dynamically assigned.

The Enterprise Service channel can be secured in one of two ways:

- **RPC Encryption**

  You can configure an Enterprise Services application for RPC Packet Privacy authentication. In addition to authentication, this provides encryption for every data packet sent to and from the Enterprise Services application.

- **IPSec**

  You can use an IPSec policy between the Web server and the application server to encrypt the communication channel.

.NET Remoting

Two possible implementation models exist for applications that use .NET Remoting:

- **HTTP channel over port 80**

  This model uses ASP.NET as the hosting service.

- **TCP channel over any port**

  In this model, the application is hosted inside a custom executable, usually a Windows service.

Depending on the performance and security requirements of the application, you can use one of two methods to secure the Remoting channel.

- **Use SSL with the HTTPChannel.**

  If you host in ASP.NET, you can take advantage of the built-in HTTPS functionality provided by IIS. HTTPS provides authentication and secure data communication.

- **Use IPSec with the TCPChannel.**

  With the TCP channel, you can use an IPSec policy to provide transport-layer encryption for all IP data. Note that if you use the TCP channel, you must provide your own authentication mechanism. For more information, see Chapter 13, "Building Secure Remoted Components."

Web Services

Web services are hosted by ASP.NET and IIS, and the services use the HTTP protocol for communication over the network.

SSL or IPSec can be used to secure the communication channel. Alternatively, encryption can be handled at the application layer by encrypting the message payload or the sensitive parts of the payload. To do this using open standards, use the Web Services Enhancements (WSE) download available for Web services. For more information, see Chapter 12, "Building Secure Web Services."

SQL Server

The application server communicates with SQL Server using TCP port 1433 by default. Unless otherwise configured, UDP port 1434 is also used for negotiation.

To secure the channel from the application server to SQL Server, use IPSec or SSL. SSL requires a server certificate to be installed on the database server.

For more information on using SSL with SQL Server, see Microsoft Knowledge Base article 276553, "How To: Enable SSL Encryption for SQL Server 2000 with Certificate Server."

Firewall Considerations

Your security infrastructure can include internal firewalls on either side of the application server. This section discusses the ports that you open on these firewalls to support the functionality of your application.

Enterprise Services

If you use middle-tier Enterprise Services, configure an internal firewall that separates the Web server and application server to allow DCOM and RPC traffic. Additionally, if you use Enterprise Services, your applications often use distributed transactions and the services of the Distributed Transaction Coordinator (DTC). In this event, open DTC ports on any firewall that separates the application server from remote resource managers, such as the database server. Figure 17.3 shows a typical Enterprise Services port configuration.

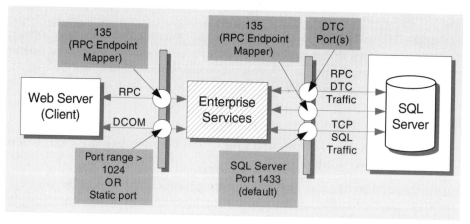

Figure 17.3

Typical Enterprise Services firewall port configuration

Note Figure 17.3 does not show the additional ports that are required for authentication mechanisms between a client and an Enterprise Services application and possibly between the Enterprise Services application and the database server. Commonly, for networks that do not use Active Directory, TCP port 139 is required for Windows authentication. For more information on port requirements, see the TechNet articles "TCP and UDP Port Assignments," at *http://www.microsoft.com/technet/prodtechnol/windows2000serv/reskit/tcpip/part4/tcpappc.asp*, and "Security Considerations for Administrative Authority," at *http://www.microsoft.com/technet /security/bestprac/bpent/sec2/seconaa.asp*.

By default, DCOM uses RPC dynamic port allocation, which randomly selects port numbers above 1024. In addition, port 135 is used by the RPC endpoint mapping service.

Restrict the ports required to support DCOM on the internal firewall in two ways:

- **Define port ranges**.

  This allows you to control the ports dynamically allocated by RPC. For more information about dynamic port restrictions, see Microsoft Knowledge Base article 300083, "How To: Restrict TCP/IP Ports on Windows 2000 and Windows XP."

- **Use static endpoint mapping**.

  Microsoft Windows 2000 SP3 (or QFE 18.1 and later) or Windows Server 2003 allows you to configure Enterprise Services applications to use a static endpoint. Static endpoint mapping means that you only need to open two ports in the firewall: port 135 for RPC and a nominated port for your Enterprise Services application.

  For more information about static endpoint mapping, see Microsoft Knowledge Base article 312960, "Cannot Set Fixed Endpoint for a COM+ Application."

Web Services

If you cannot open ports on the internal firewall, then you can introduce a Web-services façade layer in front of the serviced components on the application server. This means that you only need to open port 80 for HTTP traffic (specifically, SOAP messages) to flow in both directions.

This approach does not allow you to flow transaction context from client to server, although in many cases where your deployment architecture includes a middle-tier application server, it is appropriate to initiate transactions in the remote serviced component on the application server.

For information about physical deployment requirements for service agents and service interfaces, such as the Web-services façade layer, see "Physical Deployment and Operational Requirements" in the Reference section of MSDN article, "Application Architecture for .NET: Designing Applications and Services," at *http://msdn.microsoft.com/library/default.asp?url=/library/en-us/dnbda/html/distapp.asp*.

DTC Requirements

If your application uses COM+ distributed transactions and these are used across remote servers separated by an internal firewall, then the firewall must open the necessary ports to support DTC traffic. The DTC uses RPC dynamic port allocation. In addition to port 135 for RPC, DTC communication requires at least one additional port.

If your deployment architecture includes a remote application tier, transactions are normally initiated there within the Enterprise Services application and are propagated to the database server. In the absence of an application server, the Enterprise Services application on the Web server initiates the transaction and propagates it to the SQL Server resource manager.

For information about configuring firewalls to support DTC traffic, see:

- "DTC Security Considerations" in the COM+ platform SDK at *http://msdn.microsoft.com/library/default.asp?url=/library/en-us/cossdk/htm/pgdtc_admin_9dkj.asp*

- Microsoft Knowledge Base article 250367, "INFO: Configuring Microsoft Distributed Transaction Coordinator (DTC) to Work Through a Firewall."

- Microsoft Knowledge Base article 306843, "How To: Troubleshoot MS DTC Firewall Issues."

.NET Remoting

If you use the HTTP channel and host your remote components in ASP.NET, only open port 80 on the internal firewall to allow HTTP traffic. If your application also uses SSL, open port 443.

If you use the TCP channel and host in a Windows service, open the specific TCP port or ports that your Remoting application has been configured to use. The application might need an additional port to support callbacks.

Figure 17.4 shows a typical .NET Remoting firewall port configuration. Note that the port numbers shown for the TCP channel scenario (5555 and 5557) are illustrations. The actual port numbers are specified in web.config configuration files on the client and server machines. For more information, see Chapter 13, "Building Secure Remoted Components."

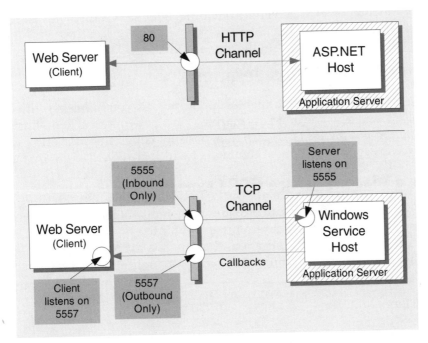

Figure 17.4
Typical Remoting firewall port configuration for HTTP and TCP channel scenarios

Web Services

Web services communicate using SOAP over HTTP; therefore, only open port 80 on the internal firewall.

SQL Server

If a firewall separates the application server from the database server, then connecting to SQL Server through a firewall requires that you configure the client using the SQL Server Client Network Utility and configure the database server using the Server Network Utility. By default, SQL Server listens on TCP port 1433, although this can be changed. The chosen port must be open at the firewall.

Depending on the chosen SQL Server authentication mode and use of distributed transactions by your application, you might also need to open several additional ports at the firewall:

- If your application uses Windows authentication to connect to SQL Server, open the necessary ports that support the Kerberos protocol or NTLM authentication.
- If your application uses distributed transactions, for example automated COM+ transactions, configure your firewall to allow DTC traffic to flow between separate DTC instances, and between the DTC and resource managers, such as SQL Server.

For more information on SQL Server port requirements, see Chapter 18, "Securing Your Database Server."

.NET Remoting Security Considerations

The .NET Remoting infrastructure enables applications to communicate with one another on the same machine or across machines in a network. The Remoting infrastructure can use the HTTP or TCP transports for communication and can send messages in many formats, the most common of which are SOAP or binary format.

Hosting in a Windows Service (TCP Channel)

Because the Remoting infrastructure provides no default authentication and authorization mechanisms, it is not recommended for use by Internet-facing applications. It is designed for applications that run in a trusted environment and is well suited for Web server communication to remote application servers, which is shown in Figure 17.5.

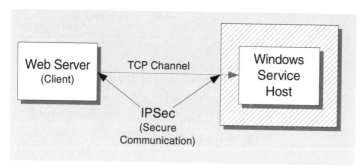

Figure 17.5
Remoting with the TCP channel and a Windows service host

In this scenario, a Windows service hosts the Remoting objects and communication occurs through a TCP channel. This approach offers good performance, but does not necessarily address security. For added security, use IPSec between the Web server and the application server and only allow the Web server to establish connections with the application server.

Hosting in IIS (HTTP Channel)

To benefit from the security features provided by ASP.NET and IIS, host your remote components in ASP.NET and use the HTTP channel for communication, as Figure 17.6 shows.

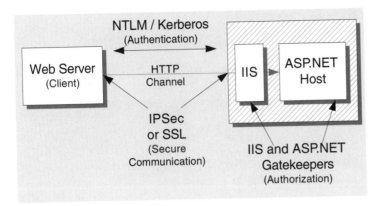

Figure 17.6
Remoting with the HTTP channel and an ASP.NET host

In this scenario, you can use Windows integrated authentication to authenticate the ASP.NET Web application process identity. You can also use SSL for secure communication and the gatekeepers provided by IIS and ASP.NET for authorization.

Enterprise Services (COM+) Security Considerations

COM+ provides the underlying infrastructure for Enterprise Services; therefore, secure COM+ if you use it on the middle-tier application server. Two main steps are involved in securing an application server that uses Enterprise Services:

- **Secure the Component Services Infrastructure**.

  You must secure the underlying operating system and Enterprise Services infrastructure. This includes base security measures, such as applying patches and updates, and disabling unused services, blocking unused ports, and so on.

- **Configure Enterprise Services application security**.

  You must secure the Enterprise Services application that is deployed on the server, taking into account application-specific security needs.

The developer can specify many of the application and component-level security configuration settings using metadata embedded in the deployed assemblies. These govern the initial catalog security settings that are applied to the application when it is registered with Enterprise Services. Then, the administrator can view and amend these if necessary by using the Component Services tool.

Secure the Component Services Infrastructure

Enterprise Services is not an optional component, and it is installed as an integral part of Windows 2000. From a security perspective, knowing what operating system components are installed to support Enterprise Services helps you take appropriate security measures.

What Does the Operating System Install?

The following table shows the core Component Services elements that are installed with a standard operating system installation.

Table 17.1   Enterprise Services Components

Item	Details
Administration	**Component Services Explorer** This provides configurable administration of COM+ applications, and is located at \WINNT\system32\Com\comexp.msc. **COM+ Catalog** The COM+ Catalog maintains configuration information for each COM+ application.
System Application (a COM+ server application)	**System Application** This application manages the configuration and tracking of COM+ components. It can be viewed from the Component Services Microsoft Management Console (MMC). It has two associated roles: *Administrator* and *Reader*. By default, the administrators are part of the Administrator role, which can modify the COM+ Catalog, while Everyone is part of the Reader role, which can read only COM+ Catalog values.
Services	**COM+ Event System** This service is required to support the COM+ loosely coupled event (LCE) system. The LCE system is used by operating system services such as the System Event Notification Services (SENS) service and optionally by your applications. **Distributed Transaction Coordinator (DTC)** This service is required if your Enterprise Services solution uses COM+ automatic transactions.
Accounts	Enterprise Services do not create any accounts. Library applications run as the identity of the process they run in. Server applications can be configured to run as the interactive user or a specific user. (You can configure the user account on the **Identity** tab of the COM+ application's **Properties** dialog box in Component Services).
Log Files	DTC log file: %windir%\system32\DTCLog CRM log file: %windir%\registration
Registry Keys	**HKEY_CLASSES_ROOT\CLSID** **HKEY_CLASSES_ROOT\AppID**

What Does the .NET Framework Install?

When you install the .NET Framework, the following components that relate to Enterprise Services are installed.

Table 17.2   .NET Framework Enterprise Services Tools and Configuration Settings

Item	Description
Regsvcs.exe	Command line tool used to register Enterprise Services components with COM+
Libraries	System.EnterpriseServices.dll System.EnterpriseServices.Thunk.dll System.EnterpriseServices.tlb
Machine.config Configuration Elements	If you call Enterprise Services from ASP.NET, the following entries in Machine.config are relevant: **\<assemblies\>** Loads the System.EnterpriseServices assembly for ASP.NET. **\<processModel\>** The **comAuthentication** attribute configures ASP.NET authentication levels. DCOM authentication levels are negotiated between the client (for example, the Web application) and the server (the Enterprise Services application). The higher of the two security settings is used. The **comImpersonationLevel** attribute configures ASP.NET impersonation levels (for all outgoing DCOM calls). The client determines the impersonation capabilities that are granted to the server.

To secure the component services infrastructure, consider the following items:

- Patches and updates
- Services
- Ports
- COM+ catalog

Patches and Updates

Update the application server with the latest service packs and patches to mitigate the risks posed by viruses, worms, and Trojan horses. The software that needs to be regularly updated includes the operating system, which includes IIS and the .NET Framework.

Updates to the COM+ runtime are sometimes released as QFE releases. Use the following resources to help manage patches and updates:

- **Windows updates and patches**

    Use the Microsoft Baseline Security Analyzer (MBSA) to detect missing security updates on application servers. For more information about how to use the MBSA on a single computer and to keep a group of servers up-to-date, see "How to: Use MBSA" in the "How To" section of this guide.

    For information about environments that require many servers to be updated from a centralized administration point, see "How To: Patch Management" in the "How To" section of this guide.

- **.NET Framework updates and patches**

At the time of this writing (May 2003), MBSA does not have the ability to detect the .NET Framework. Therefore, you must update the .NET Framework manually.

▶ **To manually update the .NET Framework**

1. Determine which .NET Framework service pack is installed on your Web server.

    To do this, see Microsoft Knowledge Base article 318785, "INFO: Determining Whether Service Packs Are Installed on .NET Framework."

2. Compare the installed version of the .NET Framework to the current service pack.

    To do this, use the .NET Framework versions listed in Microsoft Knowledge Base article 318836, "INFO: How to Obtain the Latest .NET Framework Service Pack."

- **COM+ updates and patches**

    The latest Windows service packs include the current fixes to COM+. However, updates to the COM+ runtime are sometimes released in the form of QFE releases. An automatic notification service for COM+ updates does not currently exist, so monitor the Microsoft Knowledge Base at *http://support.microsoft.com*. Use "kbQFE" as a search keyword to refine your search results.

Services

To reduce the attack surface profile, disable any services that are not required. Required services include the Microsoft DTC and the COM+ Event System service, which is required to support the LCE COM+ feature.

To secure the services on your application server, disable the MS DTC if it is not required.

Disable the Microsoft DTC If It Is Not Required

The DTC service is tightly integrated with COM+. It coordinates transactions that are distributed across two or more databases, message queues, file systems, or other resource managers. If your applications do not use the COM+ automated transaction services, then the DTC should be disabled by using the Services MMC snap-in.

Ports

Serviced components communicate using DCOM, which in turn communicates using the RPC transport.

By default, DCOM dynamically allocates ports, which is undesirable from a security and firewall configuration perspective. DCOM ports should be restricted to reduce the attack surface profile and to ensure that you do not need to open unnecessary ports on the internal firewall. Two options exist for restricting the ports used by DCOM:

● **Use port ranges**.
● **Use static endpoint mapping**.

Port Ranges

For incoming communication, you can configure RPC dynamic port allocation to select ports within a restricted range above 1024. Then configure your firewall to confine incoming external communication to only those ports and port 135, which is the RPC endpoint mapper port.

▶ **To control RPC dynamic port allocation**

1. Start the Component Services tool.
2. Click to expand the **Component Services** and **Computers** nodes, right-click **My Computer**, and then click **Properties**.
3. Click the **Default Protocols** tab, and then select **Connection-oriented TCP/IP** in the **DCOM Protocols** list box.
4. Click **Properties**.
5. In the **Properties for COM Internet Services** dialog box, click **Add**.
6. In the **Port range** text box, add a port range, for example 5000–5020, and then click **OK**.
7. Leave the **Port range assignment** and the **Default dynamic port allocation** options set to **Internet range**.
8. Click **OK** twice to close the dialog boxes.
9. Restart your computer so the changes can take effect.

Static Endpoint Mapping

Windows 2000 (SP3 or QFE 18.1) or Windows Server 2003 allows you to configure Enterprise Services applications to use a static endpoint. If a firewall separates the client from the server, you only need to open two ports in the firewall. Specifically, you must open port 135 for RPC and a port for your Enterprise Services application.

▶ To configure a static endpoint for DCOM

1. Obtain the application ID for your Enterprise Services application from the COM+ catalog. To do this:

    a. Start the Component Services tool.

    b. Display the **Properties** dialog box of the application, and retrieve the application ID from the **General** page.

2. Start the registry editor (Regedt32.exe).

3. Select the following registry key:

   ```
   HKEY_CLASSES_ROOT\AppID
   ```

4. From the **Edit** menu, click **Add Value**, and then add the following registry value, where {your AppID} is the Application ID of the COM+ application that you obtained in step 1:

   ```
   Key name: {Your AppID}
   Value name: Endpoints
   Data type: REG_MULTI_SZ
   Value data: ncacn_ip_tcp,0,<port number>
   ```

   The port number that you specify in the **Value data** text box must be greater than 1024 and must not conflict with well-known ports that other applications on the computer use. You cannot modify the ncacn_ip_tcp,0 portion of this key.

5. Close the registry editor.

COM+ Catalog

Enterprise Services application configuration settings are maintained in the COM+ catalog. The majority of configuration items are contained in the registration database (RegDB), which consists of files located in the following directory:

```
%windir%\registration
```

By default, the Everyone group has permission to read the database. Modify the access control list (ACL) for this directory to restrict read/write access to administrators and the local system account. Also grant read access to the accounts used to run Enterprise Services applications. Here is the required ACL:

```
Administrators: Read, Write
System: Read, Write
Enterprise Services Run-As Account(s): Read
```

Secure Enterprise Services Applications

Individual application configuration settings are maintained in the COM+ catalog and can be configured using the Component Services tool or by using script. Many of the settings discussed below can also be specified by application developers by using the correct assembly level metadata in the serviced component assembly. When you register the service component, for example by using Regsvcs.exe, the COM+ catalog is automatically configured using this metadata, although the application run-as identity must be configured administratively.

To secure an Enterprise Services application, you must configure the following items:

- **Identity (run as)**
- **Authentication level**
- **COM+ role based security**
- **Impersonation**
- **CRM log files**
- **Application assemblies**

Identity (Run As)

Configure Enterprise Services server applications to run with least privileged accounts. This reduces the potential damage that might occur if the server process is compromised by an attacker who manages to execute code using its security context.

If the serviced components within the Enterprise Services application are not impersonating the caller's security context, then the process-level identity specified through the run-as account is used for downstream local and remote resource access. To support network authentication to a remote database server, you can create a "mirrored" local account, which is a local account on the remote server that has a matching username and password.

Note When you set the run-as identity with Enterprise Services, the required "Logon as a batch job" privilege is automatically granted to the account.

Authentication Level

Enterprise Services applications authenticate callers using RPC, which in turn uses the underlying authentication services of the operating system provided through the Security Service Provider Interface (SSPI) layer. This means that applications authenticate callers using Windows authentication; either Kerberos or NTLM.

RPC defines authentication levels that determine when authentication occurs and whether the authenticated communication should be checked for integrity or encrypted. At minimum, you should use call-level authentication to ensure that every method call to a serviced component method is authenticated.

Note   Call-level authentication does not result in the encryption of message data. As a result, if network eavesdropping is a real concern, use the packet privacy authentication level, or use call-level authentication over a channel secured with IPSec.

Table 17.3 shows the various authentication levels:

Table 17.3   Enterprise Services Application Authentication Levels

Authentication Level	Description
Default	Choose authentication level using normal negotiation rules
None	No authentication
Connect	Only authenticates credentials when the client initially connects to the server
Call	Authenticates at the start of each remote procedure call
Packet	Authenticates all data received from the client
Packet integrity	Authenticates all data and verifies that none of the transferred data has been modified
Packet privacy	Authenticates all data and encrypts all packets transmitted using RPC encryption

► **To set call-level authentication**

1. Start Component Services and display the **Properties** dialog box of the application.
2. Click the **Security** tab.
3. Select **Call** from the **Authentication level for calls** drop-down list.

COM+ Role-Based Security

Authorization in Enterprise Services applications is provided by Enterprise Services (COM+) roles. COM+ roles contain Windows user and group accounts and are used to restrict access to the application, component, interfaces, and method. Ideally, your Enterprise Services applications should be configured for component level authorization, which allows you to authorize callers to individual serviced component methods.

To configure role-based security:

- **Enable role-based security**.
- **Enable component-level access checks**.
- **Enforce component-level access checks**.

Enable Role-Based Security

Role-based security is disabled by default on Windows 2000. The reverse is true for Windows Server 2003.

▶ **To enable role-based security**

1. Start the Component Services tool and display the **Properties** dialog box of the application.
2. Click the **Security** tab.
3. Select **Enforce access checks for this application**.

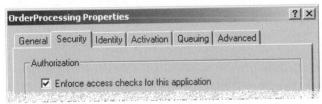

Figure 17.7
Enabling role-based security

Enable Component-Level Access Checks

Without component-level access checks, any account that is used to connect to any application component is granted access if it is a member of any role within the application. Component-level access checks allow individual components to apply their own authorization. This is the recommended level of granularity.

► **To enable component level access checks**

1. Start the Component Services tool and display the **Properties** dialog box of the application.
2. Click the **Security** tab.
3. Click **Perform access checks at the process and component level**.

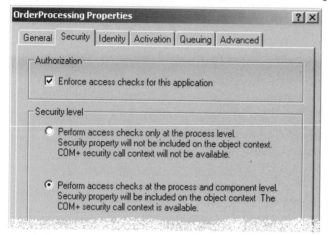

Figure 17.8
Enabling component-level access checks

Enforce Component-Level Access Checks

To allow individual components inside the Enterprise Services application to perform access checks and authorize callers, you must enable component-level access checks at the component level.

► **To enforce component-level access checks**

1. Start the Component Services tool and expand your application in the tree control.
2. Select the **Components** folder, right-click it, and then click **Properties**.
3. Click the **Security** tab.
4. Click **Enforce component level access checks**.

Note This setting is effective only if you have enabled application-level access checking and have configured process and component level access checks, as described earlier.

Impersonation

DCOM clients set the impersonation level to determine the impersonation capabilities of the server with which they are communicating. When an Enterprise Services application on a middle-tier application server is configured, the configured impersonation level affects any remote calls made to downstream components, including the database server. The impersonation level is set on the **Security** page of the **Properties** dialog box of the application in Component Services, as Figure 17.9 shows.

Figure 17.9
DCOM impersonation levels

The appropriate level depends on the desired application-level functionality, although you should use the following guidelines to determine an appropriate level:

- Avoid **Anonymous** impersonation. The downstream component will not be able to identify your application for authentication or authorization purposes.
- Use **Identify** to allow the downstream component to authenticate and authorize your application. It will not, however, be able to access local or remote resources using the impersonated security context of your application.
- Use **Impersonate** if you want to allow the downstream component to impersonate the identity of your application so that it can access local resources on the downstream server.
- Use **Delegate** if you want to allow the downstream component to impersonate the identity of your application so that it can access local or remote resources. This requires accounts configured for delegation in Active Directory

All downstream resource access that is performed by serviced components on your middle-tier application server normally uses the server application's identity. If, however, the serviced components perform programmatic impersonation, and the client application (usually an ASP.NET Web application or Web service on the Web server) has been configured to support Kerberos delegation, then the client's identity is used.

For more information, see "How To: Enable Kerberos Delegation in Windows 2000" in the "How To" section of "Microsoft *patterns & practices* Volume I, *Building Secure ASP.NET Applications: Authentication, Authorization, and Secure Communication*" at *http://msdn.microsoft.com/library/default.asp?url=/library/en-us/dnnetsec/html /secnetlpMSDN.asp*.

CRM Log Files

If your Enterprise Services application uses the CRM, you should ensure that the CRM log files are secured to prevent potential information disclosure. Depending on the nature of the application, the files can contain sensitive application data. The CRM log files are created in the following directory:

```
%windir%\system32\dtclog
```

CRM log file names are derived from the Enterprise Services application ID and have the file name extension .crmlog. CRM log files are secured when they are created by Enterprise Services and the file is configured with an ACL that grants Full Control to the run-as account of the application. No other account has access.

If you change the identity of the application after the log file is created, you must manually change the ACL on the file. Make sure that the new run-as identity of the application has Full Control permissions.

Application Assemblies

To protect the deployed application assemblies that contain the serviced components of the application, you should harden the ACL associated with the assembly .dll files to ensure they cannot be replaced or deleted by unauthorized users.

Apply the following ACL to the DLL folder of your application:

```
Users: Execute
Application Run as account: Execute
Administrators: Read, Write and Execute
```

The location of the assembly DLLs of an application is specified at deployment time and may therefore vary from installation to installation. The **Properties** dialog box in the Component Services tool does not show the assembly DLL location. Instead, it points to %windir%\System32\mscoree.dll, which provides the interception services for the component.

► **To check the location of application DLLs**

1. Start the Component Services tool and expand your application in the tree control.
2. Expand the **Components** folder, select a component, right-click it, and then click **Properties**.
3. In the **Properties** dialog box, retrieve the Class ID (CLSID) of the component.
4. Start Regedt32.exe and locate the retrieved CLSID beneath **HKEY_CLASSES_ROOT\CLSID**.
5. Click the **InprocServer32** key.

    The DLL location is indicated by the **CodeBase** named value.

Summary

When sufficient perimeter network defenses are in place, many of the threats that affect middle-tier application servers come from inside of an organization. A secure infrastructure that consists of IPSec policies that restrict access to the application server from selected Web servers only, and also provide secure communication channels, is an effective risk mitigation strategy.

This chapter has shown you additional security measures. These measures differ depending on the technology used on the application server.

Internal firewalls on either side of the application server present other issues. The ports that must be open depend on application implementation choices, such as transport protocols and the use of distributed transactions.

For a checklist that summarizes the steps in this chapter, see "Checklist: Securing Your Application Server" in the "Checklists" section of this guide.

Additional Resources

For more information about the issues addressed in this chapter, see the following articles in the Microsoft Knowledge Base at *http://support.microsoft.com*:

- Article 233256, "How to: Enable IPSec Traffic Through a Firewall"
- Article 312960, "Cannot Set Fixed Endpoint for a COM+ Application"
- Article 259011, "SAMPLE: A Simple DCOM Client Server Test Application"
- Article 248809, "PRB: DCOM Does Not Work over NAT-Based Firewall"
- Article 250367, "INFO: Configuring Microsoft Distributed Transaction Coordinator (DTC) to Work Through a Firewall"
- Article 154596, "How To: Configure RPC Dynamic Port Allocation to Work with a Firewall"

18

Securing Your Database Server

In This Chapter

- A proven methodology for securing database servers
- An explanation of the most common database server threats
- Steps to secure your server
- A reference table that illustrates a secure database server

Overview

There are many ways to attack a database. External attacks may exploit configuration weaknesses that expose the database server. An insecure Web application may also be used to exploit the database. For example, an application that is granted too much privilege in the database or one that does not validate its input can put your database at risk.

Internal threats should not be overlooked. Have you considered the rogue administrator with network access? What about the database user tricked into running malicious code? For that matter, could any malicious code on the network compromise your database?

This chapter begins by reviewing the most common threats that affect database servers. It then uses this perspective to create a methodology. This chapter then puts the methodology into practice and takes a step-by-step approach that shows you how to improve your database server's security.

How to Use This Chapter

This chapter provides a methodology and steps for securing a database server. The methodology can be adapted for your own scenario. The steps put the methodology into practice.

To gain the most from this chapter:

- **Read Chapter 2, "Threats and Countermeasures."** This chapter provides an explanation of potential threats faced by Web applications and downstream database servers.

- **Use the snapshot**. The section, "Snapshot of a Secure Database Server," later in this chapter lists the attributes of a secure database server. It reflects distilled input from a variety of sources including customers, industry experts, and internal Microsoft development and support teams. Use the snapshot table as a reference when configuring your database server.

- **Use the checklist**. The "Checklist: Securing Your Database Server" in the "Checklist" section of this guide provides a quick reference. Use the checklist to quickly evaluate the scope of the required steps and to help you work through the individual steps.

- **Use the "How To" section**. The "How To" section in this guide includes the following instructional articles that help you implement the guidance in this chapter:
  - "How To: Use Microsoft Security Baseline Analyzer"
  - "How To: Use IPSec"
  - "How To: Implement Patch Management"

Threats and Countermeasures

An attacker can target and compromise a database server in a number of ways by exploiting a variety of configuration and application level vulnerabilities.

The main threats to a database server are:

- **SQL injection**
- **Network eavesdropping**
- **Unauthorized server access**
- **Password cracking**

Figure 18.1 shows the major threats and vulnerabilities that can result in a compromised database server and the potential destruction or theft of sensitive data.

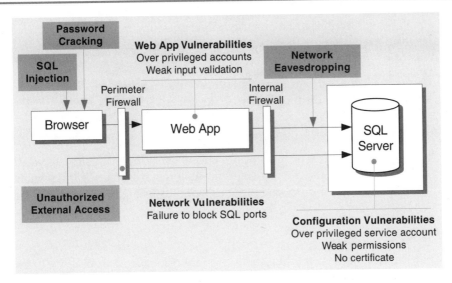

Figure 18.1
Top database server threats and vulnerabilities

The next sections describe each of these threats and vulnerabilities.

SQL Injection

With a SQL injection attack, the attacker exploits vulnerabilities in your application's input validation and data access code to run arbitrary commands in the database using the security context of the Web application.

Vulnerabilities

Vulnerabilities exploited by SQL injection include:

- Poor input validation in your Web applications
- Unsafe, dynamically constructed SQL commands
- Over-privileged application logins to the database
- Weak permissions that fail to restrict the application's login to the database

Countermeasures

To counter SQL injection attacks:

- Your application should constrain and sanitize input data before using it in SQL queries.
- Use type safe SQL parameters for data access. These can be used with stored procedures or dynamically constructed SQL command strings. Using SQL parameters ensures that input data is subject to type and length checks and also that injected code is treated as literal data, not as executable statements in the database.

- Use a SQL Server login that has restricted permissions in the database. Ideally, you should grant execute permissions only to selected stored procedures in the database and provide no direct table access.

For more information about application-level countermeasures to SQL injection attacks, see Chapter 14, "Building Secure Data Access."

Network Eavesdropping

The deployment architecture of most applications includes a physical separation of the data access code from the database server. As a result, sensitive data, such as application-specific data or database login credentials, must be protected from network eavesdroppers.

Vulnerabilities

Vulnerabilities that increase the likelihood of network eavesdropping include:
- Insecure communication channels
- Passing credentials in clear text to the database; for example:
  - Using SQL authentication instead of Windows authentication
  - Using SQL authentication without a server certificate

Countermeasures

To counter network eavesdropping:
- Use Windows authentication to connect to the database server to avoid sending credentials over the network.
- Install a server certificate on the database server. This results in the automatic encryption of SQL credentials over the network.
- Use an SSL connection between the Web server and database server to protect sensitive application data. This requires a database server certificate.
- Use an IPSec encrypted channel between Web and database server.

Unauthorized Server Access

Direct access to your database server should be restricted to specific client computers to prevent unauthorized server access.

Vulnerabilities

Vulnerabilities that make your database server susceptible to unauthorized server access include:
- Failure to block the SQL Server port at the perimeter firewall
- Lack of IPSec or TCP/IP filtering policies

Attacks

Direct connection attacks exist for both authenticated users and those without a user name and password; for example:

- Tools such as Query Analyzer (Isqlw.exe) or the command line equivalent (Osql.exe) are used to establish a direct connection to SQL Server and issue commands.
- Server information, such as software version, is revealed to an attacker who sends carefully constructed packets to listening ports.

Countermeasures

To counter these attacks:

- Make sure that SQL Server ports are not visible from outside of the perimeter network.
- Within the perimeter, restrict direct access by unauthorized hosts, for example, by using IPSec or TCP/IP filters.

Password Cracking

A common first line of attack is to try to crack the passwords of well known account names, such as **sa** (the SQL Server administrator account).

Vulnerabilities

Common vulnerabilities that lead to password cracking are:

- Weak or blank passwords
- Passwords that contain everyday words

Attacks

Common password cracking attacks include:

- Dictionary attacks
- Manual password guessing

Countermeasures

To counter these attacks:

- Create passwords for SQL Server login accounts that meet complexity requirements.
- Avoid passwords that contain common words found in the dictionary.

Note   If you use Windows authentication, password complexity can be enforced by Windows security policy.

Methodology for Securing Your Server

Securing SQL Server and Windows 2000 involves many configuration changes. The best approach is to separate the changes that must be made into specific configuration categories. Using categories allows you to systematically walk through the securing process from top to bottom or pick a particular category and apply specific steps.

Configuration Categories

The securing methodology has been organized into the categories shown in Figure 18.2.

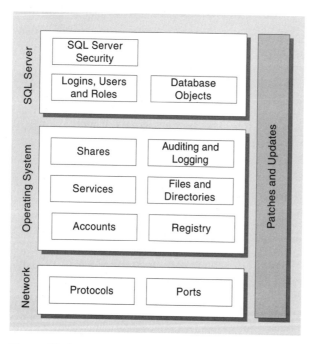

Figure 18.2

Database server security categories

The configuration categories shown in Figure 18.2 are based on best practices obtained from field experience, customer validation, and the study of secure deployments. The rationale behind the categories is as follows:

- **Patches and Updates**

  Many security threats exist because of vulnerabilities in operating systems, services, and applications that are widely published and well known. When new vulnerabilities are discovered, attack code is frequently posted on Internet bulletin boards within hours of the first successful attack. Patching and updating your server's software is the first step toward securing your database server. There may be cases where a vulnerability exists and no patch is available. In these cases, be aware of the details of the vulnerability to assess the risk of attack and take measures accordingly.

- **Services**

  Services are prime vulnerability points for attackers who can exploit the privileges and capabilities of the service to access the server and potentially other computers. Some services are designed to run with privileged accounts. If these services are compromised, the attacker can perform privileged operations. By default, database servers generally do not need all services enabled. By disabling unnecessary and unused services, you quickly and easily reduce the attack surface area.

- **Protocols**

  Limit the range of protocols that client computers can use to connect to the database server and make sure you can secure those protocols.

- **Accounts**

  Restrict the number of Windows accounts accessible from the database server to the necessary set of service and user accounts. Use least privileged accounts with strong passwords in all cases. A least privileged account used to run SQL Server limits the capabilities of an attacker who compromises SQL Server and manages to execute operating system commands.

- **Files and Directories**

  Use NTFS file system permissions to protect program, database, and log files from unauthorized access. When you use access control lists (ACLs) in conjunction with Windows auditing, you can detect when suspicious or unauthorized activity occurs.

- **Shares**

  Remove all unnecessary file shares, including the default administration shares if they are not required. Secure any remaining shares with restricted NTFS permissions. Although shares may not be directly exposed to the Internet, a defense in depth strategy with limited and secured shares reduces risk if a server is compromised.

- Ports

  Unused ports are closed at the firewall, but it is required that servers behind the firewall also block or restrict ports based on their usage. For a dedicated SQL Server, block all ports except for the necessary SQL Server port and the ports required for authentication.

- **Registry**

  SQL Server maintains a number of security-related settings, including the configured authentication mode in the registry. Restrict and control access to the registry to prevent the unauthorized update of configuration settings, for example, to loosen security on the database server.

- **Auditing and Logging**

  Auditing is a vital aid in identifying intruders, attacks in progress, and to diagnose attack footprints. Configure a minimum level of auditing for the database server using a combination of Windows and SQL Server auditing features.

- **SQL Server Security**

  A number of SQL Server security settings can be controlled through Enterprise Manager. These include the authentication mode, auditing level, and the accounts used to run the SQL Server service. For improved security, you should use Windows authentication. You should also enable SQL Server logon auditing and ensure that the SQL Server service runs using a least privileged account.

- **SQL Server Logins, Users, and Roles**

  SQL Server 2000 manages access control using logins, databases, users, and roles. Users (and applications) are granted access to SQL Server by way of a SQL server login. The login is associated with a database user and the database user is placed in one or more roles. The permissions granted to the role determine the tables the login can access and the types of operations the login can perform. This approach is used to create least privileged database accounts that have the minimum set of permissions necessary to allow them to perform their legitimate functionality.

- **SQL Server Database Objects**

  The ability to access SQL Server database objects, such as built-in stored procedures, extended stored procedures and **cmdExec** jobs, should be reviewed. Also, any sample databases should be deleted.

SQL Server Installation Considerations

Before taking steps to secure your database server, know the additional components that are present on a Windows 2000 Server after SQL Server is installed.

What Does SQL Server Install?

When you install SQL Server, a number of Windows services are installed in addition to program and data files. By default, program and data files are located in the \Program Files\Microsoft SQL Server\ directory. Table 18.1 shows the services and folders that are created.

Table 18.1 SQL Server Installation Defaults

Item	Details
Services	MSSQLSERVER MSSQLServerADHelper Microsoft Search SQLSERVERAGENT
Folders	\program files\Microsoft SQL Server\mssql\binn (program files) \program files\Microsoft SQL Server\mssql\data (data files including .mdf, .log, and .ndf) \program files\Microsoft SQL Server\80\tools (shared tools/books online) \program files\Microsoft SQL Server\mssql\logs (error logs) \program files\Microsoft SQL Server\mssql\backup (backup files) \program files\Microsoft SQL Server\mssql\jobs (temp job output files) For named instances, the instance name is used in the file path: \program files\Microsoft SQL Server\MSSQL$InstanceName\binn \program files\Microsoft SQL Server\MSSQL$InstanceName\data

SQL Server Installation Recommendations

If you are building a new database server from scratch, there are a number of considerations to take into account before installing SQL Server. Also, it is a good idea to perform a custom installation of SQL Server so you can select the most secure installation options.

Before Running SQL Server Setup

Before you run the SQL Server setup program, check the following items:

- Create a least privileged local account with which to run the SQL Server service. Use this account when you are prompted for service settings during setup. Do not use the local system account or an administrator account.
- Make sure you do not install SQL Server on a domain controller.
- Make sure you install SQL Server on a partition formatted with NTFS.
- Install SQL Server program and database files on a non-system volume, separate from the operating system.

Installing SQL Server

When installing SQL Server on a production server, choose the custom setup option. When you do this, you can selectively choose the items to install. You should not install the items listed in Table 18.2 on a production database server.

Table 18.2   Items Not to Install During Custom Installation

Tool	Purpose
Upgrade tools	Used to upgrade SQL Server 6.5 databases
Replication support	Script and binary files used for replication. (Do not install unless you need replication.)
Full text search	Full text search engine (Microsoft Search service). Do not install unless you require full text search.
Books online	SQL Server documentation
Development tools	Headers and library files used by C developers and Microsoft Data Access (MDAC), and XML software development kits (SDKs), and an interface for stored procedure debugging.
Code samples	Sample code used to educate developers.

Also, select Windows authentication mode unless SQL Server authentication is specifically required. Windows authentication offers the following advantages:

- Existing domain and local security policies can be used to enforce strong passwords and account management best practices.
- Credentials are not passed over the network.
- Application database connection strings do not require credentials.

If you select Mixed Mode, create a strong password for the sa account. The sa account is a prime target for password guessing and dictionary attacks.

Steps for Securing Your Database Server

This section guides you through the process of securing your database server using the configuration categories introduced earlier. The steps cover Windows 2000 and SQL Server 2000. Each step may contain one or more actions to secure a particular area or feature.

Step 1	Patches and Updates	**Step 7**	Ports
Step 2	Services	**Step 8**	Registry
Step 3	Protocols	**Step 9**	Auditing and Logging
Step 4	Accounts	**Step 10**	SQL Server Security
Step 5	Files and Directories	**Step 11**	SQL Server Logins, Users, and Roles
Step 6	Shares	**Step 12**	SQL Server Database Objects

Step 1. Patches and Updates

Failure to apply the latest patches and updates in a timely manner means that you are providing opportunities for attackers to exploit known vulnerabilities. You should verify that your database server is updated with the latest Windows 2000 and SQL Server service packs and updates.

Important Make sure to test patches and updates on test systems that mirror your production servers as closely as possible before applying them on production servers.

Detect Missing Service Packs and Updates

Use the Microsoft Baseline Security Analyzer (MBSA) to detect the necessary Windows and SQL Server updates that may be missing. MBSA uses an XML file as the reference of existing updates. This XML file is either downloaded by MBSA when a scan runs, or the file can be downloaded on the local server or from a network server.

▶ **To detect and install patches and updates**

1. Download and install MBSA.

   You can do this from the MBSA home page at *http://www.microsoft.com/technet /treeview/default.asp?url=/technet/security/tools/Tools/mbsahome.asp.*

   If you do not have Internet access when you run MBSA, it will not be able to retrieve the XML file containing the latest security settings from Microsoft. In this event, download the XML file manually and put it in the MBSA program directory. The XML file is available from *http://download.microsoft.com/download/xml/security /1.0/nt5/en-us/mssecure.cab.*

2. Run MBSA by double-clicking the desktop icon or selecting it from the **Programs** menu.

3. Click **Scan a computer**. MBSA defaults to the local computer.

4. Clear all check boxes apart from **Check for security updates**. This option detects which patches and updates are missing.

5. Click **Start scan**. Your server is now analyzed. When the scan is complete, MBSA displays a security report, which it also writes to the %userprofile%\SecurityScans directory.

6. Download and install the missing updates.

   Click the **Result details** link next to each failed check to view the list of security updates that are missing. The resulting dialog box displays the Microsoft security bulletin reference number. Click the reference to find out more about the bulletin and to download the update.

For more information about using MBSA, see "How To: Use the Microsoft Baseline Security Analyzer" in the "How To" section of this guide.

For more information about applying service packs, hot fixes, and security patches, see *http://www.microsoft.com/technet/treeview/default.asp?url=/technet/security/bestprac/bpsp.asp*.

Patching MSDE

The Microsoft Desktop Edition (MSDE) of SQL Server must be patched differently than the full version of SQL Server. For details about patching MSDE, see "How To: Secure Your Developer Workstation" in the "How To" section of this guide.

Step 2. Services

To reduce the attack surface area and to make sure you are not affected by undiscovered service vulnerabilities, disable any service that is not required. Run those services that remain using least privileged accounts.

In this step, you:

- **Disable unused SQL Server services.**
- **Disable the Microsoft DTC (if not required).**

Note   To disable a service, set its startup type to **Disabled** using the Services MMC snap-in in the Computer Management tool.

Disable Unused SQL Server Services

During a SQL Service installation, the following four Windows services are installed:

- **MSSQLSERVER** (or MSSQL$InstanceName for a named instance). This is the SQL Server database engine and is the only mandatory service.
- **SQLSERVERAGENT** (or SQLAgent$InstanceName for a named instance). With this support service, you can schedule commands and notify operators when errors occur.
- **MSSQLServerADHelper**. This provides Active Directory integration services, including database instance registration.
- **Microsoft Search**. This provides full text search capabilities. This service must always run under the local system account.

Only the MSSQLSERVER database engine is required. The remaining services provide additional functionality and are required only in specific scenarios. Disable these services if they are not required.

Note SQL Server should not be configured to run as the local System account or any account that is a member of the local Administrators group. For details about configuring the service account used to run MSSQLSERVER, see "Step 4: Accounts."

Disable the Microsoft DTC (if not required)

If you do not use distributed transactions through the Microsoft DTC, disable the service.

Step 3. Protocols

By preventing the use of unnecessary protocols, you reduce the surface area of attack. Configure SQL Server to support only clients that connect using the TCP/IP protocol. Disable all other protocols, unless required.

In this step, you:

- **Restrict SQL Server to TCP/IP.**
- **Harden the TCP/IP Stack.**

Restrict SQL Server to TCP/IP

By enforcing the use of TCP/IP you can control who connects to the server on specific ports using IPSec policies or TCP/IP filtering. To support IPSec or TCP/IP filtering, your SQL Server should support client connections over TCP/IP only.

▶ **To configure SQL Server network protocol support**

1. In the Microsoft SQL Server programs group, start the Server Network Utility.
2. Make sure that **TCP/IP** is the only SQL Server protocol that is enabled as shown in Figure 18.3. Disable all other protocols.

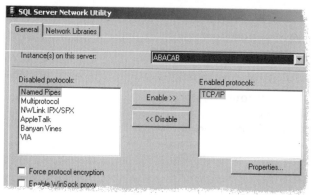

Figure 18.3
Disabling all protocols except TCP/IP in the SQL Server Network Utility

Harden the TCP/IP Stack

Windows 2000 allows you to control many parameters to configure its TCP/IP implementation. Some of the defaults are geared toward server availability and specific features.

For information about how to harden the TCP/IP stack, see "How To: Harden the TCP/IP Stack" in the "How To" section of this guide.

Additional Considerations

To further improve your database server security, disable NetBIOS and SMB. Both protocols can be used to glean host configuration information, so you should remove them when possible. For more information about removing NetBIOS and SMB, see "Protocols" in Chapter 16, "Securing Your Web Server."

Also consider using IPSec to restrict the ports on which your database server accepts incoming connections. For more information about how to do this, see "How To: Use IPSec for Filtering Ports and Authentication" in the "How To" section of this guide.

Step 4. Accounts

Follow the principle of least privilege for the accounts used to run and connect to SQL Server to restrict the capabilities of an attacker who manages to execute SQL commands on the database server. Also apply strong password policies to counter the threat of dictionary attacks.

In this step, you:

- **Secure the SQL Server service account.**
- **Delete or disable unused accounts.**
- **Disable the Windows guest account.**
- **Rename the administrator account.**
- **Enforce strong password policy.**
- **Restrict remote logins.**
- **Disable null sessions (anonymous logons).**

Secure the SQL Server Service Account

Run the SQL Server service using a least privileged account to minimize the damage that can be done by an attacker who manages to execute operating system commands from SQL Server. The SQL Server service account should not be granted elevated privileges such as membership to the Administrators group.

▶ **To create a new account to run the SQL Server service**

1. Start the Computer Management tool, and then expand **Local Users and Groups**.
2. Right-click the **Users** folder, and then click **New User**.
3. Create a new user making sure you use a strong password.

   In the **New User** dialog box, clear the **User must change password at next logon** check box, and then select the **User cannot change password** and **Password never expires** check boxes.
4. Remove the new account from the **Users** group because this group is granted liberal access across the computer.

You can now configure SQL Server to run using this new account. For more information, see "Step 10: SQL Server Security."

Accessing the Network from SQL Server

If you need to access network resources from SQL Server, for example to perform network backups, for replication or log shipping, the SQL Server service account must be capable of being authenticated across the network. You have two choices. Either create a duplicate local account with the same name and password on the remote server, or use a least privileged domain account.

Delete or Disable Unused Accounts

Unused accounts and their privileges may be a haven for an attacker who has gained access to a server. Audit local accounts on the server and delete those that are unused. The recommendation is to first disable an account to see if this causes any problems before deleting the account, because deleted accounts cannot be recovered. Note that the **administrator** account and **guest** account cannot be deleted.

Note   During SQL Server 200 SP3 installation, Sqldbreg2.exe creates the **SQL Debugger** account. Visual Studio .NET uses this account when debugging stored procedures from managed .NET code. Because this account is only used to support debugging, you can delete it from production database servers.

Disable the Windows Guest Account

The Windows **guest** account is the account used when an anonymous connection is made to the computer. To restrict anonymous connections to your database server, keep this account disabled. By default, the **guest** account in Windows 2000 is disabled. To see if it is enabled, display the **Users** folder in the Computer Management tool. It is represented by a cross icon. If it isn't disabled, display its **Properties** dialog box and select the **Account is disabled** check box.

Rename the Administrator Account

The default local **administrator** account is a target for malicious use because of its high privileges on the computer. To improve security, rename the default **administrator** account and assign it a strong password.

Enforce Strong Password Policy

To counter password guessing and brute force dictionary attacks, apply strong password policies by configuring security policy. The keys to strong account and password policies are:

- **Set password length and complexity.** Enforcing strong passwords reduces the chance of successful password guessing or dictionary attacks.
- **Set password expiration.** Regularly expiring passwords reduces the chance that an old password will be used for unauthorized access. The expiration period is typically guided by a company's security policy.

Table 18.3 shows the default and recommended password policy settings.

Table 18.3   Password Policy Default and Recommended Settings

Password Policy	Default Setting	Recommended Minimum Setting
Enforce password history	1 password remembered	24 passwords remembered
Maximum password age	42 days	42 days
Minimum password age	0 days	2 days
Minimum password length	0 characters	8 characters
Passwords must meet complexity requirement	Disabled	Enabled
Strong password using reversible encryption for all users in the domain	Disabled	Disabled

Additionally, log failed login attempts to detect and trace malicious behavior. For more information, see "Step 9: Auditing and Logging."

For more information about password policies, see password "Best Practices" on the Microsoft TechNet Web site at *http://www.microsoft.com/technet/treeview/default.asp?url= /technet/prodtechnol/windowsserver2003/proddocs/entserver/windows_password_protect.asp*.

Restrict Remote Logons

Use the Local Security Policy tool to remove the "Access this computer from the network" user right from the Everyone group to restrict who can log on to the server remotely.

Disable Null Sessions (Anonymous Logons)

To prevent anonymous access, disable null sessions. These are unauthenticated or anonymous sessions established between two computers. Unless null sessions are disabled, an attacker can connect to your server anonymously, that is, without requiring authentication.

As soon as an attacker establishes a null session, a variety of attacks can be performed, including enumeration used to obtain system-related information from the target computer. The type of information that can be returned over a null session includes domain and trust details, shares, user information including groups and user rights, registry keys, and more. Disable them because they represent a significant security threat.

Restrict null sessions by setting RestrictAnonymous=1 in the registry at the following location.

```
HKLM\System\CurrentControlSet\Control\LSA\RestrictAnonymous=1
```

For more information, see Microsoft Knowledge Base article 246261, "How To: Use the RestrictAnonymous Registry Value in Windows 2000."

Additional Considerations

Consider the following steps to improve security for your database server:

- **Require approval for account delegation**. Do not mark domain accounts as trusted for delegation in Active Directory without special approval.

- **Do not use shared accounts**. Do not create shared account for use by multiple individuals. Give authorized individuals their own accounts. The activities of individuals can be audited separately and group membership and privileges appropriately assigned.

- **Restrict the local Administrators group membership**. Ideally, have no more than two administration accounts. This helps provide accountability. Also, do not share passwords, again to provide accountability.

- **Limit the administrator account to interactive logins**. If you perform only local administration, you can restrict your **administrator** account to interactive logons by removing the "Access this computer from the network" user right to deny network logon rights. This prevents users (well intentioned or otherwise) from remotely logging on to the server using the administrator account. If a policy of local administration is too inflexible, implement secure remote administration.

  For more information about remote administration, see "Remote Administration" later in this chapter.

- **Enable NTLMv2 authentication**. If client computers connect to your database server by using Windows authentication, you should configure your database server to use the strongest version of Windows authentication, which is NTLMv2.

Note   To support NTLMV2, clients must be running Windows 2000, Windows Server 2003, or Windows NT® operating system version 4.0 with Service Pack 4.

▶ **To enable NTLMv2 authentication from the Local Security Policy Tool**

1. Expand Local Policies, select Security Options, and then double-click LAN Manager Authentication Level.

2. Select Send NTLMv2 response only\refuse LM & NTLM.

This is the most secure setting.

Note   This is equivalent to setting the HKLM\System\CurrentControlSet\Control\Lsa \LMCompatibilityLevel DWORD value to 5.

Step 5. Files and Directories

In addition to securing operating system files using ACLs, harden NTFS permissions to restrict access to SQL Server program files, data files, and log files together with system level tools. Additionally, the SQL Server service account should have access only to what it needs.

In this step, you:

- **Verify permissions on SQL Server install directories.**
- **Verify Everyone group does not have permissions to SQL Server files.**
- **Secure setup log files.**
- **Secure or remove tools, utilities, and SDKs.**

Verify Permissions on SQL Server Install Directories

Verify the permissions listed in Table 18.4 to the account the SQL Server service is running under. The location specified in parentheses is the default install location. This may vary for your installation.

Table 18.4   NTFS Permissions for SQL Server Service Account

Location	Permissions for SQL Service Account
Install location (\Program Files\Microsoft SQL Server\MSSQL\)	Read and Execute List Folder Contents Read
Database file directory (.mdf, .ndf, .ldf files) (\Program Files\Microsoft SQL Server\MSSQL\Data)	Full Control
Error log file directory (\Program Files\Microsoft SQL Server\MSSQL\LOG)	Full Control
Backup file directory (\Program Files\Microsoft SQL Server\MSSQL\Backup)	Full Control
Job temporary file output directory (\Program Files\Microsoft SQL Server\MSSQL\Jobs)	Full Control

If you use Enterprise Manager to set the SQL Server service account, it gives the account Full Control permissions on the SQL Server installation directory and all subfolders (\Program Files\Microsoft SQL Server\MSSQL*).

By removing write permissions on this folder and all subfolders, and then selectively granting full control to the data, error log, backup and job file directories, the new account cannot overwrite SQL Server binaries.

Verify Everyone Group Does Not Have Permissions for SQL Server Files

The Everyone group should not have access to the SQL Server file location (by default, \Program Files\Microsoft SQL Server\MSSQL) This is achieved by verifying the Everyone group is not granted access via an ACL and giving explicit full control to only the SQL Service account, the Administrators group, and the local system account.

Secure Setup Log Files

After installing SQL Server 2000 Service Pack 1 or 2, the system administrator or service account password may be left in the SQL installation directory. Use the Killpwd.exe utility to remove instances of passwords from the log files.

For information about obtaining and using this utility, see Microsoft Knowledge Base article 263968, "FIX: Service Pack Installation May Save Standard Security Password in File."

Secure or Remove Tools, Utilities, and SDKs

SDKs and resource kits should not be installed on a production database server. Remove them if they are. In addition:

- Ensure that access to powerful system tools and utilities, such as those contained in the \Program Files directory, is restricted.
- Debugging tools should not be available on the database server. If production debugging is necessary, you should create a CD that contains the necessary debugging tools.

Additional Considerations

To further improve your database server security:

- **Remove unused applications that may be installed on the server**. If you have applications on the server that you do not use, then remove them.
- **Encrypt your data files using Encrypting File System (EFS)**. You can use EFS to protect your data files. If your data files are stolen, encrypted files are more difficult to read. The use of EFS for SQL Server data files is supported.

  When using EFS, you should be aware of the following:

  - Encrypt the database files (.MDF) and not the log files (.LDF). If you encrypt the log files, then SQL Server cannot open your database.
  - Encrypt at the file level, not the directory level. While it is often a best practice to encrypt at the directory level when using EFS so that when new files are added they are automatically encrypted, you should encrypt your SQL Server data files at the file level only. This avoids encrypting your log files.

- Evaluate the performance cost. The use of EFS incurs a performance penalty. Test EFS before using it in your scenario to determine the actual performance impact. Usually the performance penalty is negligible because the data file is decrypted by SQL Server when the process starts.

To implement EFS, right-click the directory, click **Advanced**, and then click **Encrypt contents to be secure**. For more information about EFS, see the following resources:

- Microsoft Knowledge Base article 23050, "How To: Encrypt Data Using EFS in Windows 2000."
- TechNet article, "Step-by-Step Guide to Encrypting File System (EFS)" at *http://www.microsoft.com/technet/treeview/default.asp?url=/technet/prodtechnol/windows2000serv/deploy/walkthru/efsguide.asp.*

Step 6. Shares

Remove any unused shares and harden the NTFS permissions on any required shares. By default, all users have full control on newly created file shares. Harden these default permissions to make sure that only authorized users can access files exposed by the share. Also, use NTFS ACLs on files and folders exposed by the share in addition to explicit share permissions.

In this step, you:

- **Remove unnecessary shares**.
- **Restrict access to required shares**.

Remove Unnecessary Shares

Remove all unnecessary shares. To review shares, start the Computer Management MMC snap-in and select **Shares** under **Shared Folders**.

Restrict Access to Required Shares

Remove the Everyone group and grant specific permissions instead. Everyone is used when you do not have restrictions on who has access to the share.

Additional Considerations

If you are not allowing remote administration of the computer, remove unused administrative shares, for example, C$ and Admin$.

Note Some applications may require administrative shares such as Microsoft Management Server (SMS) or Microsoft Operations Manager (MOM). For more information, see Microsoft Knowledge Base article 318751, "How To: Remove Administrative Shares in Windows 2000 or Windows NT 4.0."

Step 7. Ports

By default, SQL Server listens on TCP port 1433 and uses UDP port 1434 for client-server negotiation. Use a combination of firewalls and IPSec policies to restrict access to these ports to minimize the avenues of attack open to an attacker.

In this step, you:

- **Restrict access to the SQL server port.**
- **Configure named instances to listen on the same port.**
- **Configure the firewall to support DTC traffic (if necessary).**

Restrict Access to the SQL Server Port

Use a perimeter firewall to prevent direct access from the Internet to the SQL Server ports—by default, TCP port 1433 and UDP port 1434. This does not protect your server against internal attacks. Configure IPSec policies to limit access, through TCP port 1433 and UDP port 1434, from Web or application servers that connect to the database by design.

For more information, see "How To: Use IPSec" in the "How To" section of this guide.

Configure Named Instances to Listen on the Same Port

By default, named instances of SQL Server dynamically allocate a port number and use UDP negotiation with the client to allow the client to locate the named instance. To avoid opening a range of port numbers on the internal firewall or having to create multiple IPSec policies, use the Server Network Utility to configure the instance to listen on a specific port number.

If you reconfigure the port number on the server, you must also reconfigure any clients to make sure they connect to the correct port number. You might be able to use the Client Network Utility, but this utility should not be installed on a Web server. Instead, applications can specify the port number in their connection strings by appending the port number to either the Server or Data Source attributes as shown in the following code.

```
"Server=YourServer|YourServerIPAddress,PortNumber"
```

Configure the Firewall to Support DTC Traffic (if necessary)

If your applications use Enterprise Services (COM+) transactions and require the services of the DTC, you may have to specifically configure the firewall that separates your Web application and database server to allow DTC traffic between separate DTC instances and between the DTC and SQL Server.

For more information about opening ports for the DTC, see Microsoft Knowledge Base article 250367, "INFO: Configuring Microsoft Distributed Transaction Coordinator (DTC) to Work Through a Firewall."

Additional Considerations

Consider using the **Hide Server** option from the Server Network Utility as shown in Figure 18.4. If you select this option in the TCP/IP properties dialog box in the SQL Network Utility, SQL Server is reconfigured to listen on port 2433. It also disables responses to broadcast requests from clients that try to enumerate SQL Server instances.

This measure cannot be relied upon to completely hide the SQL Server port. This is not possible because there are a variety of ways to enumerate ports to discover its location.

Note This option can be used only if you have a single instance of SQL Server. For more information, see Microsoft Knowledge Base article 308091, "BUG: Hide Server Option Cannot Be Used on Multiple Instances of SQL Server 2000."

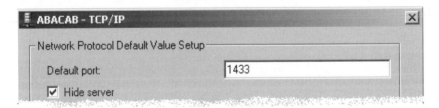

Figure 18.4
Setting the Hide Server option from the Server Network Utility

Step 8. Registry

When you install SQL Server, it creates a number of registry entries and subentries that maintain vital system configuration settings. It is important to secure these settings to prevent an attacker from changing them to compromise the security of your SQL Server installation.

When you install SQL Server, it creates the following registry entries and subentries:

- For a default instance:

```
HKEY_LOCAL_MACHINE\SOFTWARE\MICROSOFT\MSSQLSERVER
```

- For a named instance:

```
HKEY_LOCAL_MACHINE\SOFTWARE\MICROSOFT\MICROSOFT SQL SERVER\INSTANCENAME
```

- For the SQL service:

```
HKEY_LOCAL_MACHINE\SYSTEM\CurrentControlSet\Services\MSSQLSERVER
```

In this step, you:

- **Verify permissions for the SQL Server registry keys.**
- **Secure the SAM (stand-alone servers only).**

Verify Permissions for the SQL Server Registry Keys

Use Regedt32.exe to verify the Everyone group does not have permissions on the SQL Server registry keys, listed above. The following controls are in place by default:

```
Administrators: Full Control
SQL Server service account: Full Control
```

Note The Microsoft Baseline Security Analyzer will verify the registry permissions. Use the tool as an alternative to manually verifying the permissions with Regedt32.exe.

Secure the SAM (Stand-alone Servers Only)

Stand-alone servers store account names and one-way password hashes (LMHash) in the local SAM database, which is part of the registry. Generally, only members of the Administrators group have access to the account information.

Although the passwords are not actually stored in the SAM and password hashes are not reversible, if an attacker obtains a copy of the SAM database, he or she can use brute force password cracking techniques to obtain valid credentials.

Restrict LMHash storage in the SAM by creating the key (not value) NoLMHash in the registry as shown below.

```
HKLM\System\CurrentControlSet\Control\LSA\NoLMHash
```

For more information, see Microsoft Knowledge Base article 299656, "New Registry Key to Remove LM Hashes from Active Directory and Security Account Manager."

Step 9. Auditing and Logging

Auditing does not prevent system attacks, although it is a vital aid in identifying intruders, attacks in progress, and to diagnose attack footprints. It is important to enable all auditing mechanisms at your disposal, including Windows operating system level auditing and SQL Server login auditing. SQL Server also supports C2 level extended auditing. This may be required in specific application scenarios, where auditing requirements are stringent.

In this step, you:

- **Log all failed Windows login attempts.**
- **Log all failed actions across the file system.**
- **Enable SQL Server login auditing.**

Log All Failed Windows Logon Attempts

You must log failed Windows logon attempts to be able to detect and trace malicious behavior.

▶ **To audit failed logon attempts**

1. Start the Local Security Policy tool.
2. Expand **Local Policies** and then select **Audit Policy**.
3. Double-click **Audit account logon events**.
4. Click **Failure**, and then click **OK**.

Windows logon failures are recorded as events in the Windows security event log. The following event IDs are suspicious:

- **531.** This means an attempt was made to log on using a disabled account.
- **529.** This means an attempt was made to log on using an unknown user account or using a valid user account but with an invalid password. An unexpected increase in the number of these audit events might indicate an attempt to guess passwords.

Log All Failed Actions Across the File System

Use NTFS auditing on the file system to detect potentially malicious attempts. This is a two-step process:

▶ **To enable logging**

1. Start the Local Security Policy tool.
2. Expand **Local Policies**, and then select **Audit Policy**.
3. Double click **Audit object access**.
4. Click **Failure**, and then click **OK**.

▶ To audit failed actions across the file system

1. Start Windows Explorer and navigate to the root of the file system.
2. Right-click the root of the file system, and then click **Properties**.
3. Click the **Security** tab.
4. Click **Advanced**, and then click the **Auditing** tab.
5. Click **Add**, and then enter **Everyone** into the **object name to select** field.
6. Click **OK**, and then select the **Full Control** check box in the **Failed** column to audit all failed events.

   By default, this applies to the current folder and all subfolders and files.
7. Click **OK** three times to close all open dialog boxes.

Failed audit events are logged to the Windows security event log.

Enable SQL Server Login Auditing

By default, SQL Server login auditing is not enabled. Minimally, you should audit failed logins. Auditing failed login attempts is a useful way of detecting an attacker who is trying to crack account passwords. For more information, about how to enable SQL Server auditing, see "Step 10: SQL Server Security."

Additional Considerations

The following are additional measures to consider when auditing and logging:

- **Consider shutting down the system if unable to log security audits**. This policy option is set in the **Security Options** of the **Local Security Settings** management console. Consider this setting for highly secure servers.

- **Consider C2 level auditing**. SQL Server offers an auditing capability that complies with the U.S. Government C2 certification. C2 level auditing provides substantially more audit information at the expense of increased disk storage requirements.

  For more information about the configuration of a C2-compliant system, see the TechNet article "SQL Server 2000 C2 Administrator's and User's Security Guide" at *http://www.microsoft.com/technet/prodtechnol/sql/maintain/security /sqlc2.asp?frame=true#d.*

Step 10. SQL Server Security

The settings discussed in this section are configured using the **Security** tab of the **SQL Server Properties** dialog box in Enterprise Manager. The settings apply to all the databases in a single instance of SQL Server. The **SQL Server Properties** dialog box is shown in Figure 18.5.

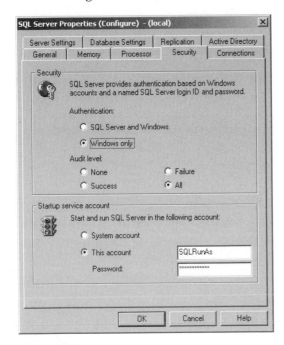

Figure 18.5
SQL Server security properties

In this step, you:

- **Set SQL Server authentication to Windows only.**
- **Set SQL Server audit level to Failure or All.**
- **Run SQL Server using a least privileged account.**

Set SQL Server Authentication to Windows Only

You should configure SQL Server to support Windows-only authentication because it provides a number of benefits. Credentials are not passed over the network, you avoid embedding usernames and passwords in database connection strings, security is easier to manage because you work with the single Windows security model instead of a separate SQL Server security model, and login security improves through password expiration periods, minimum lengths, and account lockout policies.

▶ **To configure Windows only authentication**

1. Start SQL Server Enterprise Manager, expand the **SQL Server Group**, and then expand your SQL Server.
2. Right-click your SQL Server, and then click **Properties**.
3. Click the **Security** tab.
4. Select **Windows only**, and then click **OK**.
5. Restart SQL Server for the changes to take effect.

Set SQL Server Audit Level to Failure or All

By default, SQL Server login auditing is not enabled. Minimally, you should audit failed logins.

Note   Log entries are written to SQL log files. By default, these are located in C:\Program Files\Microsoft SQL Server\MSSQL\LOG. You can use any text reader, such as Notepad, to view them.

▶ **To enable SQL Server auditing**

1. Start **SQL Server Enterprise Manager**, expand the **SQL Server Group**, and then expand your SQL Server.
2. Right-click your SQL Server, and then click **Properties**.
3. Click the **Security** tab.
4. Set the Audit level to either **All** or **Failure**.
5. Restart SQL Server for the changes to audit policy to take effect.

For more information about SQL Server audit logs, see the TechNet article and its section "Understanding the Audit Log" in the "SQL Server 2000 Auditing" article at *http://www.microsoft.com/technet/treeview/default.asp?url=/technet/security/prodtech/dbsql /sql2kaud.asp?frame=true*.

Run SQL Server Using a Least Privileged Account

Run the SQL Server service using a least privileged account to minimize the damage that can be done by an attacker who manages to execute operating system commands from SQL Server. The SQL Server service account should not be granted elevated privileges such as membership to the Administrators group.

▶ **To configure the SQL Server run as account**

This procedure uses Enterprise Manager instead of the Services MMC snap-in because Enterprise Manager automatically grants the user rights that a SQL Server service account requires.

1. Start **SQL Server Enterprise Manager**, expand the **SQL Server Group**, and then expand your SQL Server.

2. Right-click your SQL Server, and then click **Properties**.

3. Click the **Security** tab.

4. Click **This account** in the Startup service account group. Enter the user name and password of your least privileged account.

5. Restart SQL Server for the changes to take effect.

Note   If you use the SQLSERVERAGENT service, the run-as account must also be changed. Use the Services MMC snap-in to change this setting.

For more information about creating a least privileged account to run SQL Server, see "Step 4: Accounts."

Step 11. SQL Server Logins, Users, and Roles

To be able to access objects in a database you need to pass two layers of security checks. First, you need to present a valid set of login credentials to SQL Server. If you use Windows authentication, you need to connect using a Windows account that has been granted a SQL Server login. If you use SQL Server authentication, you need to supply a valid user name and password combination.

The login grants you access to SQL Server. To access a database, the login must be associated with a database user inside the database you want to connect to. If the login is associated with a database user, the capabilities of the login inside the database are determined by the permissions associated with that user. If a login is not associated with a specific database user, the capabilities of the login are determined by the permissions granted to the public role in the database. All valid logins are associated with the public role, which is present in every database and cannot be deleted. By default, the public role within any database that you create is not granted any permissions.

Use the following recommendations to improve authorization settings in the database:

- **Use a strong sa (system administrator) password**.
- **Remove the SQL guest user account**.
- **Remove the BUILTIN\Administrators server login**.
- **Do not grant permissions for the public role**.

Use a Strong sa (System Administrator) Password

The default system administrator (**sa**) account has been a subject of countless attacks. It is the default member of the SQL Server administration fixed server role **sysadmin**. Make sure you use a strong password with this account.

Important   The **sa** account is still active even when you change from SQL authentication to Windows authentication.

Apply strong passwords to all accounts, particularly privileged accounts such as members of the **sysadmin** and **db_owner** roles. If you are using replication, also apply a strong password to the **distributor_admin** account that is used to establish connections to remote distributor servers.

Remove the SQL Guest User Account

When you install SQL Server, a **guest** user account is created if the Windows 2000 **guest** account is enabled. A login assumes the identity of **guest** if the login has access to SQL Server but does not have access to a database through a database user account.

It is a good idea to disable the Windows **guest** account. Additionally, remove the **guest** account from all user-defined databases. Note that you cannot remove **guest** from the master, tempdb, and replication and distribution databases.

Remove the BUILTIN\Administrators Server Login

By default, the BUILTIN\Administrators local Windows group is added to the **sysadmin** fixed server role to administer SQL Server. This means that domain administrators who are members of BUILTIN\Administrators have unrestricted access to the SQL Server database. Most companies differentiate the role of domain administrator and database administrator. If you do this, remove the BUILTIN\Administrators SQL Server login. It is a good idea to create a specific Windows group containing specific database administrations in its place and added to SQL server as a server login as shown in the following procedure.

▶ **To add a new login for database administrators**

1. Start Enterprise Manager.
2. Expand **Microsoft SQL Server**, expand **SQL Server Group**, and then expand your SQL Server.
3. Expand the Security folder, select and right-click **Logins**, and then click **New Login**.
4. In the **Name** field, enter a custom Windows group that contains only database administrators.
5. Click the **Server Roles** tab, and then select **System Administrators**.

This adds the new login to the **sysadmin** server role.

▶ **To delete the BUILTIN\Administrators login**

1. Start Enterprise Manager.
2. Expand **Microsoft SQL Server**, expand **SQL Server Group**, and then expand your SQL Server.
3. Expand the **Security** folder, and select **Logins**. If BUILTIN\Administrators appears in the list of logins, right-click it, and then click **Delete** to remove the login.

For more information about reconfiguring the SQL service accounts after the installation, see the MSDN article, "Changing Passwords and User Accounts" at *http://msdn.microsoft.com/library/default.asp?url=/library/en-us/instsql /in_afterinstall_4p0z.asp*.

Do Not Grant Permissions for the Public Role

All databases contain a public database role. Every other user, group, and role is a member of the public role. You cannot remove members of the public role. Instead, do not grant the permissions for the public role that grant access to your application's database tables, stored procedures, and other objects. Otherwise, you cannot get the authorization that you want using user-defined database roles because the public role grants default permissions for users in a database.

Additional Considerations

Also consider the following recommendations when configuring SQL Server logins, users, and roles:

● **Limit the members of sysadmin**. To make sure there is individual accountability, restrict the number of accounts that are members of the **sysadmin** role. Ideally, no more than two users are members of this role.

● **Grant restricted database permissions**. Assign accounts only the absolute minimum permissions required to do a job. Avoid using the built-in roles, such as **db_datareader** and **db_datawriter**. These roles do not provide any authorization granularity and these roles have access to all of your custom database objects.

● **Do not change the default permissions that are applied to SQL Server objects**. In versions of SQL Server earlier than Service Pack 3, the public role does have access to various default SQL Server database objects. With Service Pack 3, the security design has been reviewed and security has been improved by removing the public role where it is unnecessary and by applying more granular role checks.

Step 12. SQL Server Database Objects

SQL Server provides two sample databases for development and education together with a series of built-in stored procedures and extended stored procedures. The sample databases should not be installed on production servers and powerful stored procedures and extended stored procedures should be secured.

In this step, you:

- Remove the sample databases.
- Secure stored procedures.
- Secure extended stored procedures.
- Restrict cmdExec access to the sysadmin role.

Remove the Sample Databases

Use SQL Server Enterprise Manager to remove any sample databases. By default SQL Server includes the Pubs and Northwind sample databases.

Secure Stored Procedures

Restrict access to your application's stored procedures. Do not grant the public role or the **guest** user access to any stored procedures that you create. Your main line of defense for securing stored procedures is to ensure that you use strong authentication, and then to provide granular authorization, allowing only the necessary users permission to run the stored procedures.

The recommended approach is to create a SQL Server login for your application, map the login to a database user, add the user to a user-defined database role, and then grant permissions to the role.

Secure Extended Stored Procedures

Deleting stored procedures is not tested and not supported.

Restrict cmdExec Access to the sysadmin Role

The **cmdExec** function is used by the SQL Server Agent to execute Windows command-line applications and scripts that are scheduled by the SQL Server Agent. Prior to SQL Server Service Pack 3, by default the SQL Server Agent allows users who are not in the **sysadmin** role to schedule jobs that may require privileged access to the system. You should change this setting to allow members only of the **sysadmin** role to schedule jobs.

▶ **To restrict cmdExec access to the sysadmin role**

1. Start **SQL Server Enterprise Manager**, expand the **SQL Server Group**, and then expand your **SQL Server**.
2. Expand the **Management** node, right-click **SQL Server Agent,** and then click **Properties**.
   The **SQL Server Agent Properties** dialog box is displayed.
3. Click the **Job System** tab.
4. At the bottom of the dialog, select the **Only users with SysAdmin privileges can execute CmdExec and ActiveScripting job steps** check box.
5. Click **OK**.

Note This change may require you to supply a user name and password. If the SQL Server service account is least privileged user (as advocated earlier in this chapter), you will be prompted for the user name and password of an administrator account that has privileges to modify the service.

Snapshot of a Secure Database Server

When you have a snapshot view that shows the attributes of a secured SQL Server database server, you can quickly and easily compare settings with your own server. The settings shown in Table 18.5 are based on an analysis of SQL Server database servers that have proven to be very resilient to attack and demonstrate sound security practices.

Table 18.5 Snapshot of a Secure Database Server

Component	Characteristics
Patches and Updates	Latest service packs and patches are applied for Windows 2000 and SQL Server
Services	Nonessential services are disabled.
	The MSDTC is disabled if not used.
	The MSSearch service is disabled if not required.
	The SQLServerAgent service is disabled if not required.
	The MSSQLServerADHelper service is disabled if not required.
Protocols	Unnecessary protocols are removed or disabled.
	The following protocols are not enabled on the server: NetBIOS and SMB.
	The TCP/IP stack is hardened.

(continued)

Table 18.5 Snapshot of a Secure Database Server *(continued)*

Component	Characteristics
Accounts	SQL Server service account is secured (least privileged).
	Unnecessary Windows accounts are deleted or disabled.
	The Windows **guest** account is disabled.
	A new administrator account is created.
	Strong password policy is enforced.
	Remote logons are restricted.
	Null sessions (anonymous logons) are disabled.
	Approval is required for account delegation.
	Shared accounts are not used.
	Membership of the local Administrators group is limited (ideally, no more than two members).
	The administrator account is limited to interactive logins (or a secure remote administration solution is provided).
	NTLMv2 authentication is enabled and enforced (LMCompatibilityLevel is set to 5).
Files and Directories	Volumes are formatted with NTFS.
	Everyone group has no rights to system or tools directories.
	Samples directories, Help directories, and unused admin directories are removed from the server.
	Permissions are hardened on SQL Server installation folder.
	Passwords removed from Service Pack 1 and Service Pack 2 setup log files.
	Tools, utilities and SDKs are removed.
	Unused applications are removed.
	Sensitive data files are encrypted using EFS. (This is optional for database files (.mdf), but not for log files (.ldf)).
Shares	Unnecessary shares are removed from the server.
	Access is restricted to required shares.
	Shares are not accessible by **Everyone**, unless necessary.
	Administration shares (C$, Admin$) are removed if they are not required.

Table 18.5   Snapshot of a Secure Database Server *(continued)*

Component	Characteristics
Ports	All ports except SQL Server listening port [Default 1433] are blocked
	Named instances are configured to listen on the same port.
	A non-standard SQL Server port (not TCP 1443) is used as an additional layer of defense.
	The hide server option is used as an additional layer of defense (optional).
	The firewall is configured to support DTC traffic (if necessary).
	A firewall is used to separate users from the SQL TCP/IP port.
Registry	**Everyone** group is removed from SQL Server registry keys.
	SAM is secured (stand-alone servers only).
Auditing and Logging	Failed Windows logon attempts are logged.
	Failed actions across the file system are logged.
	SQL Server login auditing is enabled.
SQL Server Settings	
SQL Server Security	Authentication setting for SQL Server is Windows Only if possible.
	SQL Server audit level set to Failure or All.
	The SQL Server Startup Service account is a least privileged account.
SQL Server Logins, Users and Roles	The **sa** account has a strong password.
	SQL Server **guest** accounts are removed from non-system databases.
	The BUILTIN\Administrators group is removed from the SQL Server logins.
	The sysadmin role does not contain the BUILTIN\Administrators group.
	Permissions are not granted for the public role.
	The sysadmin role contains no more than two users.
	Restricted (granular) database permissions are granted (Built-in, non-granular roles such as db_datareader and db_datawriter are avoided)
	Default permissions for SQL Server objects are not changed.
SQL Server Database Objects	All sample databases are removed from the server.
	Stored procedures are secured.
	Extended stored procedures are secured.
	cmdExec is restricted to the sysadmin role only.

Additional Considerations

In addition to the steps described in this chapter, consider the following guidelines:

- **Install a certificate on the database server**. If you use Windows authentication (NTLM or Kerberos), logon credentials are not passed over the network to SQL Server. If you use SQL authentication, it is a good idea to secure the credentials because they are passed to SQL Server in unencrypted format. Do this by installing a certificate on the database server. This automatically results in the encryption of SQL credentials over the wire. It is also a good idea to make sure that your application securely stores database connection strings. For more information, see Chapter 14, "Building Secure Data Access."

- **Restrict access to sensitive commands and stored procedures**. SQL Server provides powerful hooks into the operating system. For example, you can use the **xp_cmdshell** extended stored procedure to run any operating system command. If an attacker manages to run arbitrary commands in the database, for example through a SQL injection vulnerability, the ability to execute operating system commands is limited only by the security credentials of the account used to run SQL Server. This is the primary reason for running SQL Server with a least privileged local account.

- **Use a dedicated computer as a database server**. Also cluster it for failover.

- **Physically protect the database server**. Locate the server in a secure computer room.

- **Restrict local logons**. Do not allow anyone to locally log on to the server, apart from the administrator.

Staying Secure

You need to regularly monitor the security state of your database server and update it regularly to help prevent newly discovered vulnerabilities from being exploited. To help keep your database server secure:

- **Perform regular backups**.
- **Audit group membership**.
- **Monitor audit logs**.
- **Stay current with service packs and patches**.
- **Perform security assessments**.
- **Use security notification services**.

Perform Regular Backups

You must be able to restore data in the event of a compromise. If you have a recovery system in place, test it before you actually need it. The first time you need to recover data should not be the first time you test your backup and restore process. For more information on backing up and restoring SQL Server, see the following resources:

- SQL Server 2000 documentation, "Backing Up and Restoring Databases"
- "Backup and Restore Strategies with SQL Server 2000," by Rudy Lee Martinez, *http://www.dell.com/us/en/biz/topics/power_ps4q00-martin.htm*

Audit Group Membership

Keep track of user group membership, particularly for privileged groups such as Administrators. The following command lists the members of the Administrators group:

net localgroup administrators

Monitor Audit Logs

Monitor audit logs regularly and analyze the log files by manually viewing them or use the technique described in Microsoft Knowledge Base article 296085, "How To: Use SQL Server to Analyze Web Logs."

Stay Current with Service Packs and Patches

Set up a schedule to analyze your server's software and subscribe to security alerts. Use MBSA to regularly scan your server for missing patches. The following links provide the latest updates:

- **Windows 2000 service packs**. The latest service packs are listed at *http://www.microsoft.com/windows2000/downloads/servicepacks/default.asp*.
- **Critical updates**. These updates help to resolve known issues and help protect your computer from known security vulnerabilities. For the latest critical updates, see *http://www.microsoft.com/windows2000/downloads/critical/default.asp*.
- **Advanced security updates**. Also monitor the advanced security updates at *http://www.microsoft.com/windows2000/downloads/security/default.asp*.

  These also help protect your computer from known security vulnerabilities.

Perform Security Assessments

Use MBSA to regularly check for security vulnerabilities and to identify missing patches and updates. Schedule MBSA to run daily and analyze the results to take action as needed. For more information about automating MBSA, see "How To: Use MBSA" in the "How To" section of this guide.

Use Security Notification Services

Use the Microsoft services listed in Table 18.6 to obtain security bulletins with notifications of possible system vulnerabilities.

Table 18.6   Security Notification Services

Service	Location
TechNet security Web site	http://www.microsoft.com/technet/treeview/default.asp?url=/technet/security/current.asp
	Use this Web page to view the security bulletins that are available for your system.
Microsoft Security Notification Service	http://register.microsoft.com/subscription/subscribeme.asp?ID=135
	Use this service to register for regular email bulletins that notify you of the availability of new fixes and updates

Additionally, subscribe to the industry security alert services shown in Table 18.7. This allows you to assess the threat of a vulnerability where a patch is not yet available.

Table 18.7   Industry Security Notification Services

Service	Location
CERT Advisory Mailing List	http://www.cert.org/contact_cert/certmaillist.html
	Informative advisories are sent when vulnerabilities are reported.
Windows and .NET Magazine Security UPDATE	http://email.winnetmag.com/winnetmag/winnetmag_prefctr.asp
	Announces the latest security breaches and identifies fixes.
NTBugtraq	http://www.ntbugtraq.com/default.asp?pid=31&sid=1#020
	This is an open discussion of Windows security vulnerabilities and attacks. Vulnerabilities which currently have no patch are discussed.

Remote Administration

Administrators often need to be able to administer multiple servers. Make sure the requirements of your remote administration solution do not compromise security. If you need remote administration capabilities, the following recommendations help improve security:

- **Restrict the number of administration accounts**. This includes restricting the number of administration accounts as well as restricting which accounts are allowed to logon remotely.
- **Restrict the tools**. The main options include SQL Enterprise Manager and Terminal Services. Both SQL Enterprise Manager and Terminal Services use Windows security. As such, the main considerations here are restricting the Windows accounts and the ports you use.
- **Restrict the computers that are allowed to administer the server**. IPSec can be used to restrict which computers can connect to your SQL Server.

Securing Terminal Services

It is possible to use Microsoft Terminal Services securely to remotely administer your database server.

Terminal Services is based on Microsoft's proprietary protocol known as Remote Desktop Protocol (RDP). RDP uses the TCP 3389 port and supports two concurrent users. The following sections describe how to install and configure Terminal Services for secure administration:

- **Install Terminal Services**.
- **Configure Terminal Services**.

Install Terminal Services

▶ **To install terminal services, do the following**

1. Install Terminal Services by using **Add/Remove Programs** from the Control Panel. Use the **Add/Remove Windows Components** option. You do not need to install the Terminal Services Licensing service for remote administration.
2. Configure Terminal Services for remote administration mode.
3. Remove the **TsInternetUser** user account from the system, which is created during Terminal Services installation. This account is used to support anonymous Internet access to Terminal Services, which should not be enabled on the server.

Configure Terminal Services

▶ **Use the Terminal Services configuration MMC snap-in available from the Administrative Tools program group to configure the following**

1. There are three levels (Low, Medium, and High) of encryption available for connections to Terminal Services. Set the encryption to 128-bit key. Note that the Windows high encryption pack should be installed on both the server and the client.

2. Configure the Terminal Services session to disconnect after idle connection time limit. Set it to end a disconnected session. A session is considered to be disconnected if the user closes the Terminal Services client application without logging off in a period of 10 minutes.

3. Finally, restrict permissions to access Terminal Services. Use the RDP permissions tab in the RDP dialog box. By default, all members of the Administrators group are allowed to access Terminal Services. If you do not want all members of the Administrators group to access Terminal Services, remove the group and add individual accounts that need access. Note that the **SYSTEM** account must be in the list.

Use a secure VPN connection between the client and the server or an IPSec tunnel for enhanced security. This approach provides mutual authentication and the RDS payload is encrypted.

Copying Files over RDP

Terminal Services does not provide built-in support for file transfer. However, you can install the File Copy utility from the Windows 2000 Server Resource Kit to add file transfer functionality to the clipboard redirection feature in Terminal Services. For more information about the utility and installation instructions, see Microsoft Knowledge Base article 244732, "How To: Install the File Copy Tool Included with the Windows 2000 Resource Kit."

Summary

Database servers are a prime target for attackers. The database server must be secured against internal, external, network level, and application level attacks. A secure database server includes a hardened SQL Server 2000 installation on top of a hardened Windows 2000 installation, coupled with secure network defenses provided by routers and firewalls.

For a quick reference checklist, see "Checklist: Securing Your Database Server" in the "Checklists" section of this guide.

Additional Resources

For more information about SQL Server security, see the following resources:

- Microsoft SQL Server Security home page: *http://www.microsoft.com/sql/techinfo /administration/2000/security.asp*.

- SQL Server 2000 Resource Kit CD, Chapter 10—Implementing Security: *http://www.microsoft.com/technet/prodtechnol/sql/reskit/sql2000/part3/c1061.asp*.

- "SQL Server 2000 Security," by Richard Waymire and Ben Thomas: *http://www.microsoft.com/technet/treeview/default.asp?url=/technet/prodtechnol/sql /maintain/security/sql2ksec.asp*.

- For information about changing the SQL Server service account, see Microsoft Knowledge Base article 283811, "How To: Change the SQL Server Service Account Without Using SQL Enterprise Manager in SQL Server 2000."

- For information about SQL Server auditing, see the TechNet article, "SQL Server 2000 Auditing," by John Howie, at *http://www.microsoft.com/technet/treeview /default.asp?url=/technet/security/prodtech/dbsql/sql2kaud.asp?frame=true*.

19

Securing Your ASP.NET Application and Web Services

In This Chapter

- Locking down an ASP.NET application
- ASP.NET process identity security considerations
- Using Aspnet_setreg.exe to encrypt account credentials in configuration files
- Enforcing machine-wide and Web application security policy
- Accessing resources securely from ASP.NET
- Securing a Web service configuration
- Securing a Forms authentication configuration
- Securing ASP.NET session state and view state
- Securing a Web farm
- A reference table that illustrates a secure ASP.NET application
- Attributes of a secure ASP.NET application

Overview

Secure ASP.NET Web applications rely on a fully secured network, host, and platform infrastructure. When trust boundaries are set at each level to block the intruder, the attacker will attempt to exploit vulnerabilities in Web applications and Web services that are listening on port 80. If the Web application is configured defectively, attackers can gain access and exploit the system. As an administrator, you should review the default machine-level configuration and the individual application configurations to address and remove any vulnerable and insecure settings.

This chapter describes what is new with ASP.NET from a system administrator's standpoint and how to configure machine-wide and application-specific security settings.

How to Use This Chapter

This chapter focuses on the key security considerations for ASP.NET applications. To get the most out of this chapter:

- **Read Chapter 16, "Securing Your Web Server."** This shows you how to secure the Windows 2000 operating system and the Microsoft .NET Framework. A secure underlying platform is a prerequisite for securing an ASP.NET Web application or Web service.

- **Use the snapshot**. Table 19.4, which is at the end of this chapter, gives a snapshot of a secure ASP.NET application with secure configuration settings in Machine.config and Web.config. Use this table when configuring your server and application settings.

- **Use the checklist**. The "Checklist: Securing Your ASP.NET Application" in the "Checklist" section of this guide provides a printable job aid for quick reference. Use the task-based checklist to quickly evaluate the scope of the required steps and to help you work through individual steps.

For related guidance, read Chapter 20, "Hosting Multiple ASP.NET Applications," which shows you how to isolate multiple Web applications running on the same server from critical system resources and from one another. For more information about configuring code access security (CAS) policy for partial-trust Web applications and Web services, see Chapter 9, "Using Code Access Security with ASP.NET."

Methodology

To secure your ASP.NET application, start with a hardened operating system and .NET Framework installation base, and then apply secure application configuration settings to reduce the application's attack profile. The methodology that is applied in this chapter to secure ASP.NET Web applications and Web services is consistent with the methodology used to secure the underlying Web server host, and it shares common configuration categories. These include:

- Services. The .NET Framework installs the ASP.NET state service to manage out-of-process ASP.NET session state. Secure the ASP.NET state service if you install it. Disable the ASP.NET state service if you do not require it.

- Protocols. Restrict Web service protocols to reduce the attack surface area.

- Accounts. The default ASPNET account is created for running Web applications, Web services, and the ASP.NET state service. If you create custom accounts to run processes or services, they must be configured as least privileged accounts with the minimum set of required NTFS permissions and Windows privileges.

- Files and Directories. Application Bin directories that are used to hold private assemblies should be secured to mitigate the risk of an attacker downloading business logic.

- Configuration Store. Many security-related settings that control functional areas such as authentication, authorization, session state, and so on, are maintained in the Machine.config and Web.config XML configuration files. To secure ASP.NET applications, you must use secure configuration settings.

What You Must Know

Before you begin securing your Web applications and Web services, there are overarching considerations and details of which you should be aware.

ASP.NET Process Model

In Microsoft Windows 2000, Internet Information Services (IIS) 5.0 runs all Web applications and Web services in the ASP.NET worker process (Aspnet_wp.exe). The unit of isolation is the application domain and each virtual directory has its own application domain. Process-level configuration settings are maintained by the **<processModel>** element in Machine.config.

In Microsoft Windows Server 2003, IIS 6.0 application pools allow you to isolate applications using separate processes. For more information, see Chapter 20, "Hosting Multiple ASP.NET Applications."

ASP.NET Account

The ASPNET account is a least privileged, local account created when you install the .NET Framework. By default, it runs the ASP.NET worker process and the ASP.NET state service.

If you decide to run Web applications using a custom account, make sure you configure the account with minimum privileges. This reduces the risks associated with an attacker who manages to execute code using the application's security context. You must also specify the account's credentials on the **<processModel>** element. Make sure you do not store credentials in plaintext. Instead, use the Aspnet_setreg.exe tool to store encrypted credentials in the registry. The custom account must also be granted the appropriate NTFS permissions.

Aspnet_setreg.exe and Process, Session, and Identity

Aspnet_setreg.exe allows you to store credentials and connection strings in encrypted format in the registry. This tool allows you to encrypt the following attributes:

- <processModel userName = password= />
- <identity username = password= />
- <sessionState sqlConnectionString = stateConnectionString= />

The following example shows the **<processModel>** element with a custom account both before and after running Aspnet_setreg.exe to secure the credentials:

```
<!--Before-->
<processModel userName="CustomAccount" password="StrOngPassword" />
<!--After-->
<processModel
 userName="registry:HKLM\SOFTWARE\YourApp\process\ASPNET_SETREG,userName"
 password="registry:HKLM\SOFTWARE\YourApp\process\ASPNET_SETREG,password"/>
```

You can choose the registry location that stores the encrypted data, although it must be beneath HKEY_LOCAL_MACHINE. In addition to encrypting the data using the Data Protection API (DPAPI) and storing it in the registry, the tool applies a secure ACL to restrict access to the registry key. The ACL on the registry key grants Full Control to System, Administrators, and Creator Owner. If you use the tool to encrypt the credentials for the **<identity>** element or the connection string for the **<sessionState>** element, you must also grant read access to the ASP.NET process account.

To obtain the Aspnet_setreg.exe tool and for more information, see Microsoft Knowledge Base article 329290, "How To: Use the ASP.NET Utility to Encrypt Credentials and Session State Connection Strings."

Impersonation is Not the Default

By default, ASP.NET applications do not impersonate. As a result, resource access is performed using the ASP.NET worker process identity. You must grant the process identity read access (at minimum) to the Windows resources that your application requires access to by creating an appropriately configured ACL.

If you do enable impersonation, you can either impersonate the original caller—that is, the IIS authenticated identity—or a fixed identity specified on the **<identity>** element. For more information, see "Impersonation" later in this chapter.

Generally, ASP.NET applications do not use impersonation because it can negatively affect design, implementation, and scalability. For example, using impersonation prevents effective middle-tier connection pooling, which limits application scalability. Impersonation might make sense in specific scenarios, for example, when the application uses the anonymous user account's security context for resource access. This is a common technique often used when multiple applications are hosted on the same server. For more information, see Chapter 20, "Hosting Multiple Web Applications."

HttpForbiddenHandler, Urlscan, and the 404.dll

There are a number of techniques you can use to prevent access to restricted resources. ASP.NET provides the **HttpForbiddenHandler** to which you can map ASP.NET file types that should not be downloadable over HTTP. Mappings are applied using the **<httpHandlers>** element.

IISLockdown.exe provides the 404.dll. Using this, you can configure IIS to map unwanted file extensions to the 404.dll, which results in the "HTTP 404 - File not found" message when the file type is requested.

Finally, the URLScan ISAPI filter can be used to block requests for restricted file types and program executables. URLScan ships with the IISLockdown tool, although it can be obtained separately. For more information, see Microsoft Knowledge Base article 307608, "INFO: Availability of URLScan Version 2.5 Security Tool," and "How To: Use URLScan" in the "How To" section of this guide.

For more information about IISLockdown and URLScan, see Chapter 16, "Securing Your Web Server."

AppSettings

The **<appSettings>** element in Web.config allows applications to store configuration data, such as database connection strings or service account credentials. The advantage of this element is that it allows developers to centralize and standardize the storage and retrieval of configuration data. A single location in Web.config also eases administration and deployment.

Sensitive data, such as connection strings and credentials, should not be stored in plaintext format in configuration files. Instead, the developer should use DPAPI to encrypt secrets prior to storage.

For more information about AppSettings, see the "AppSettings in ASP.NET" show on MSDN® TV at *http://msdn.microsoft.com/msdntv*.

Machine.Config and Web.Config Explained

The configuration management provided by the .NET Framework encompasses a broad range of settings that allow an administrator to manage the Web application and its environment. These settings are stored in XML configuration files, some of which control machine-wide settings, while others control application-specific configuration.

XML configuration files can be edited with any text editor, such as Notepad, or with XML editors. XML tags are case sensitive, so ensure that the correct case is used.

Figure 19.1 shows the configuration files used to configure ASP.NET Web applications that are available to administrators.

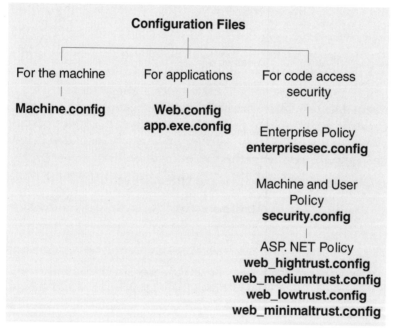

Figure 19.1
ASP.NET configuration files

The Machine.config and Web.config files share many of the same configuration sections and XML elements. Machine.config is used to apply machine-wide policy to all .NET Framework applications running on the local computer. Developers can also use application-specific Web.config files to customize settings for individual applications.

Note Windows executables, such as WinForm applications, are configured using configuration files. The names of these files are derived from the application executable name, for example, App.exe.config, where app is the application name.

Changes that you make to configuration files are applied dynamically and do not normally require that you restart the server or any service, except if changes are made to the **<processModel>** element in Machine.config, which is discussed later in this chapter.

Table 19.1 shows where the configuration files are located.

Table 19.1 Configuration File Locations

Configuration file	Location
Machine.config (one per machine per installed version of the .NET Framework)	%windir%\Microsoft.NET\Framework\{version}\CONFIG
Web.config (zero, one, or many per application)	\inetpub\wwwroot\web.config \inetpub\wwwroot\YourApplication\web.config \inetpub\wwwroot\YourApplication\SubDir\web.config
Enterprisesec.config (enterprise-level CAS) configuration)	%windir%\Microsoft.NET\Framework\{version}\CONFIG
Security.config (machine-level CAS configuration)	%windir%\Microsoft.NET\Framework\{version}\CONFIG
Security.config (user-level CAS configuration)	\Documents and Settings\{user}\Application Data\Microsoft\CLR Security Config\{version}
Web_hightrust.config Web_mediumtrust.config Web_lowtrust.config Web_minimaltrust.config (ASP.NET Web application CAS configuration)	%windir%\Microsoft.NET\Framework\{version}\CONFIG

For more information about ASP.NET Web application CAS configuration files, see Chapter 9, "Using Code Access Security with ASP.NET."

Hierarchical Policy Evaluation

For centralized administration, settings can be applied in Machine.config. The settings in Machine.config define machine-wide policy and can also be used to apply application-specific configuration using **<location>** elements. Developers can provide application-configuration files to override aspects of machine policy. For ASP.NET Web applications, a Web.config file is located in the application's virtual root directory and optionally in subdirectories beneath the virtual root. Consider the arrangement shown in Figure 19.2.

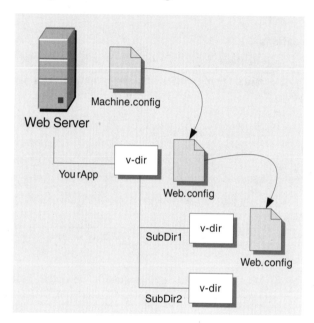

Figure 19.2

Hierarchical configuration

In Figure 19.2, the AppRoot Web application has a Web.config file in its virtual root directory. SubDir1 (not a virtual directory) also contains its own Web.config file, which gets applied when an HTTP request is directed at http://AppRoot/SubDir1. If a request is directed at SubDir2 (a virtual directory) through AppRoot, for example, http://Server/AppRoot/SubDir2, settings from Machine.config and the Web.config in the AppRoot directory are applied. If, however, a request is directed at SubDir2 bypassing AppRoot, for example, http://Server/SubDir2, then only the settings from Machine.config are applied.

In all cases, base settings are obtained from Machine.config. Next, overrides and additions are applied from any relevant Web.config files.

If the same configuration element is used in Machine.config and in one or more Web.config files, the setting from the file lowest in the hierarchy overrides the higher-level settings. New configuration settings that are not applied at the machine level can also be applied to Web.config files and certain elements can clear the parent-level settings using the **<clear>** element.

The following table shows where the combined configuration settings are obtained from for a combination of Web requests that apply to Figure 19.2.

Table 19.2   Applying Configuration Settings

HTTP Request	Combined Settings Obtained From
http://Server/AppRoot	Machine.config
	Web.config (AppRoot v-dir)
http://Server/AppRoot/SubDir1	Machine.config
	Web.config (AppRoot v-dir)
	Web.config (SubDir1)
http://Server/AppRoot/SubDir2	Machine.config
	Web.config (AppRoot v-dir)
http://Server/Subdir2	Machine.config

<location>

The **<location>** element is used for three main purposes:

- To apply configuration settings to specific application files.
- To centralize administration by applying application-specific settings in Machine.config.
- To lock configuration settings to prevent override at the application level.

The **<location>** tag can be used in Machine.config or Web.config. With Machine.config, if you specify the path, then it must be fully qualified and include the Web site name, virtual directory name, and optionally, a subdirectory and file name. For example:

```
<location path="Web Site Name/VDirName/SubDirName/PageName.aspx" >
  <system.web>
    . . .
  </system.web>
</location>
```

Note   You must include the Web site name when using the location tag from Machine.config.

With Web.config, the path is relative from the application's virtual directory. For example:

```
<location path="SubDirName/PageName.aspx" >
  <system.web>
  . . .
  </system.web>
</location>
```

Applying Configuration Settings to Specific Files

Use the **path** attribute to apply configuration settings for a specific file. For example, to apply authorization rules to the file Pagename.aspx from within Web.config, use the following **<location>** element:

```
<location path="SubDirName/PageName.aspx" >
  <system.web>
    <authorization>
      <deny roles="hackers" />
    </authorization>
    </system.web>
</location>
```

Applying Application Configuration Settings in Machine.config

You can also apply application-specific settings in Machine.config by using **<location>** statements that specify paths to application directories. This has the advantage of centralizing administration. For example, the following fragment shows how to enforce the use of Windows authentication and prevent the use of impersonation in a particular application.

```
<location path="Default Web Site/YourApp">
  <system.web>
    <authentication mode="Windows"/>
    <identity impersonate="false"/>
  </system.web>
</location>
```

Locking Configuration Settings

To prevent individual applications from overriding machine-level policy configuration, place settings within a **<location>** element in Machine.config and set the **allowOverride="false"** attribute.

For example, to apply machine-wide policy that cannot be overridden at the application level, use the following **<location>** element:

```
<location path="" allowOverride="false">
  <system.web>
    … machine-wide defaults
  </system.web>
</location>
```

By leaving the **path** attribute empty, you indicate that the settings apply to the machine, while **allowOverride="false"** ensures that Web.config settings do not override the specified values. Any attempt to add elements in Web.config will generate an exception, even if the elements in Machine.config match with those of Web.config.

Machine.Config and Web.Config Guidelines

Settings in Machine.config apply machine-level defaults for your server. Where you want to enforce a particular configuration for all applications on your server, use **allowOverride="false"** on the **<location>** element as described above. This is particularly appropriate for hosting scenarios, where you need to enforce aspects of security policy for all applications on the server.

For those settings that can be configured on an individual application basis, it is normal for the application to provide a Web.config file. While it is possible to configure individual applications from Machine.config using multiple **<location>** elements, separate Web.config files provide deployment advantages and lead to smaller Machine.config files.

The main item to consider is which settings should be enforced by machine policy. This depends on your specific scenario. Some common scenarios follow:

- **Windows authentication**. Consider a corporate intranet portal scenario where you want authentication to be abstracted away from the application and controlled by the organization through Active Directory. In this scenario, you can enforce Windows authentication, but allow individual applications to impersonate with the following configuration:

```
<location path="" allowOverride="false">
  <system.web>
    <authentication mode="Windows"/>
  </system.web>
</location>
```

- **Hosting scenario.** Hosting companies need to constrain applications so they cannot access each other's resources and so that they have limited access to critical system resources. To do so, you can configure all applications to run at a partial-trust level. For example, the medium-trust level constrains an application so that it can only access files within its own virtual directory hierarchy and restricts access to other types of resources. For more information, see Chapter 9, "Using Code Access Security with ASP.NET." To apply a medium-trust policy for all applications on your server, use the following configuration:

```
<location path="" allowOverride="false>
  <system.web>
    <trust level="Medium" />
  </system.web>
</location>
```

ACLs and Permissions

Configuration files contain sensitive data and therefore require appropriately configured ACLs to restrict access.

Machine.config

By default, Machine.config is configured with the following ACL:

```
Administrators: Full Control
System: Full Control
Power Users: Modify
Users: Read and Execute
LocalMachine\ASPNET (process identity): Read and Execute
```

Note On Windows Server 2003, the Local Service and Network Service accounts are also granted read access.

Members of the **Users** group are granted read access by default, since all managed code that runs on the computer must be able to read Machine.config.

The default ACL on Machine.config is a secure default. If, however, you only have a single Web application running on the server, or all of your Web applications use the same process identity, you can further restrict the ACL by removing the user's access control entry (ACE). If you do remove "users" from the DACL, you need to explicitly add the Web process identity.

Web.config

The .NET Framework does not install any Web.config files. If you install an application that supplies its own Web.config, it usually inherits its ACL from the inetpub directory, which by default grants read access to members of the **Everyone** group. To lock down an application-specific Web.config, use one the following ACLs.

For .NET Framework version 1.0:

```
Administrators: Full control
System: Full control
ASP.NET process identity: Read
UNC Identity: Read
Impersonated Identity (Fixed Identity): Read
Impersonated Identity (Original Caller): Read
```

For .NET Framework version 1.1:

```
Administrators: Full control
System: Full control
ASP.NET process identity: Read
UNC Identity: Read
Impersonated Identity (Fixed Identity): Read
```

If your applications use impersonation of an explicit account (that is, if they impersonate a a fixed identity), such as **<identity impersonate="true" username="WebUser" password="Y0urStr0ngPassw0rd$"/>**, then both that account (WebUser, in this case) and the process need Read access.

If your code base is on a Universal Naming Convention (UNC) share, you must grant read access to the IIS-provided UNC token identity.

If you are impersonating but not using explicit credentials, such as **<identity impersonate="true"/>**, and no UNC, then only the process should need access in the .NET Framework 1.1. For the .NET Framework 1.0, you must additionally configure the ACL to grant read access to any identity that will be impersonated (that is, you must grant read access to the original caller).

Trust Levels in ASP.NET

An application's trust level determines the permissions it is granted by CAS policy. This determines the extent to which the application can access secure resources and perform privileged operations.

<trust>

Use the **<trust>** element to configure the application's trust level. By default, the configuration level is set to Full, as shown below:

```
<!-- level="[Full|High|Medium|Low|Minimal]" -->
<trust level="Full" originUrl=""/>
```

This means that the application is granted full and unrestricted CAS permissions. With this configuration, the success or failure of any resource access performed by the application depends only on operating system security.

If you change the trust level to a level other than Full, you may break existing ASP.NET Web applications depending on the types of resources they access and the operations they perform. Applications should be thoroughly tested at each trust level.

For more information about building partial-trust Web applications that use CAS, see Chapter 9, "Using Code Access Security with ASP.NET." For more information about using trust levels to provide application isolation, see Chapter 20, "Hosting Multiple ASP.NET Web Applications."

Process Identity for ASP.NET

ASP.NET Web applications and Web services run in a shared instance of the ASP.NET worker process (Aspnet_wp.exe). Process-level settings, including the process identity, are configured using the **<processModel>** element in Machine.config.

<processModel>

The identity for the ASP.NET worker process is configured using the **userName** and **password** attributes on the **<processModel>** element. When you configure process identity:

- **Use the default ASPNET account.**
- **Use a least-privileged custom account.**
- **Encrypt <processModel> credentials.**
- **Do not run ASP.NET as SYSTEM.**

Use the Default ASPNET Account

The local ASPNET account is the default least privileged account specifically for running ASP.NET Web applications and Web services. Use this account if you can by using the following default configuration:

```
<processModel enable="true" userName="machine" password="AutoGenerate" ... />
```

Use a Least Privileged Custom Account

If you must use an alternate identity to run the ASP.NET worker process, make sure the account that you use is configured as a least privileged account. This limits the damage that can be done by an attacker who manages to execute code using the process security context.

You might decide to use an alternate account because you need to connect to a remote Microsoft SQL Server™ database or network resource using Windows authentication. Note that you can use the local ASPNET account for this purpose. For more information, see "Data Access" later in this chapter.

For more information about the NTFS permissions that the ASP.NET process account requires, see "NFTS Permission Requirements" later in this chapter.

You should also grant the following user rights to the ASP.NET process accounts:

- Access this computer from the network.
- Logon as a batch job.
- Logon as a service.
- Deny logon locally.
- Deny logon through terminal services.

Encrypt <processModel> Credentials

If you need to use a custom account, do not store plaintext credentials in Machine.config. Use the Aspnet_setreg.exe utility to store encrypted credentials in the registry.

▶ **To encrypt credentials for <processModel>**

1. Run the following command from the command prompt:

```
aspnet_setreg -k:Software\YourApp\process -u:CustomAccount :p:StrongPassword
```

This stores the encrypted credentials in the specified registry key and secures the registry key with a restricted ACL that grants Full Control to System, Administrators, and Creator Owner.

2. Reconfigure the **<processModel>** element and add the following **userName** and **password** attributes.

```
<processModel
userName="registry:HKLM\SOFTWARE\YourApp\process\ASPNET_SETREG,userName"
password="registry:HKLM\SOFTWARE\YourApp\process\ASPNET_SETREG,password"/>
```

For more information, see Microsoft Knowledge Base article 329290, "How To: Use the ASP.NET Utility to Encrypt Credentials and Session State Connection Strings."

Do Not Run ASP.NET as SYSTEM

Do not use the SYSTEM account to run ASP.NET and do not grant the ASP.NET process account the "Act as part of the operating system" user right. Doing so defeats the principle of least privilege and increases the damage that can be done by an attacker who is able to execute code using the Web application's process security context.

Impersonation

By default, ASP.NET applications do not impersonate. The security context of the ASP.NET worker process account (ASPNET by default) is used when your application accesses Windows resources.

<identity>

The **<identity>** element is used to enable impersonation. You can impersonate:
- The original caller (the IIS authenticated identity)
- A fixed identity

Impersonating the Original Caller

To impersonate the original caller, use the following configuration:

```
<identity impersonate="true" />
```

The impersonation uses the access token provided by IIS that represents the authenticated caller. This may be the anonymous Internet user account, for example, if your application uses Forms authentication, or it may be a Windows account that represents the original caller, if your application uses Windows authentication.

If you do enable original caller impersonation, note the following issues:
- Application scalability is reduced because database connections cannot be effectively pooled.
- Administration effort increases as ACLs on back-end resources need to be configured for individual users.
- Delegation requires Kerberos authentication and a suitably configured Windows 2000 environment.

For more information, see "How To: Implement Kerberos Delegation for Windows 2000" in the "How To" section of "Microsoft *patterns & practices* Volume I, *Building Secure ASP.NET Applications: Authentication, Authorization, and Secure Communication*" at *http://msdn.microsoft.com/library/default.asp?url=/library/en-us /dnnetsec/html/SecNetHT05.asp.*

Impersonating a Fixed Identity

To impersonate a fixed identity, specify the identity using the **userName** and password attributes on the **<identity>** element:

```
<identity impersonate="true" userName="MyServiceAccount"
                             password="Str0ng!Passw0rd"/>
```

Do not store credentials in plaintext as shown here. Instead, use the Aspnet_setreg.exe tool to encrypt the credentials and store them in the registry.

▶ To encrypt credentials for <identity>

1. Run the following command from the command prompt:

   ```
   aspnet_setreg -k:Software\YourApp\identity -u:CustomAccount :p:StrongPassword
   ```

   This stores the encrypted credentials in the specified registry key and secures the registry key with a restricted ACL that grants Full Control to System, Administrators, and Creator Owner.

2. Reconfigure the **<identity>** element and add the following **userName** and **password** attributes.

   ```
   <identity impersonate="true"
   userName="registry:HKLM\SOFTWARE\YourApp\identity\ASPNET_SETREG,userName"
   password="registry:HKLM\SOFTWARE\YourApp\identity\ASPNET_SETREG,password"/>
   ```

3. Use Regedt32.exe to create an ACL on the above registry key that grants read access to the ASP.NET process account.

For more information, see Microsoft Knowledge Base article 329290, "How To: Use the ASP.NET Utility to Encrypt Credentials and Session State Connection Strings."

Act as Part of the Operating System

The ASP.NET version 1.0 process account requires the "Act as part of the operating system" user right on Windows 2000 when you impersonate a fixed identity by specifying **userName** and **password** attributes. Because this effectively elevates the ASP.NET process account to a privilege level approaching the local System account, impersonating a fixed identity is not recommended with ASP.NET version 1.0.

Note   If you are running ASP.NET version 1.1 on Windows 2000 or Windows 2003 Server, this user right is not required.

NTFS Permission Requirements

NTFS permissions must be appropriately configured for impersonation identities. For more information, see "NTFS Permission Requirements" later in this chapter.

Authentication

The **<authentication>** element configures the authentication mode that your applications use.

<authentication>

The appropriate authentication mode depends on how your application or Web service has been designed. The default Machine.config setting applies a secure Windows authentication default as shown below.

```
<!-- authentication Attributes:
     mode="[Windows|Forms|Passport|None]" -->
<authentication mode="Windows" />
```

Forms Authentication Guidelines

To use Forms authentication, set **mode="Forms"** on the **<authentication>** element. Next, configure Forms authentication using the child **<forms>** element. The following fragment shows a secure **<forms>** authentication element configuration:

```
<authentication mode="Forms">
  <forms loginUrl="Restricted\login.aspx"    Login page in an SSL protected folder
         protection="All"                     Privacy and integrity
         requireSSL="true"                    Prevents cookie being sent over http
         timeout="10"                         Limited session lifetime
         name="AppNameCookie"                 Unique per-application name
         path="/FormsAuth"                        and path
         slidingExpiration="true" >           Sliding session lifetime
  </forms>
</authentication>
```

Use the following recommendations to improve Forms authentication security:

- **Partition your Web site.**
- **Set protection="All".**
- **Use small cookie time-out values.**
- **Consider using a fixed expiration period.**
- **Use SSL with Forms authentication.**
- **If you do not use SSL, set slidingExpiration = "false".**
- **Do not use the <credentials> element on production servers.**
- **Configure the <machineKey> element.**
- **Use unique cookie names and paths.**

Partition Your Web Site

Separate the public and restricted access areas of your Web site. Place your application's logon page and other pages and resources that should only be accessed by authentication users in a separate folder from the public access areas. Protect the restricted subfolders by configuring them in IIS to require SSL access, and then use **<authorization>** elements to restrict access and force a login. For example, the following Web.config configuration allows anyone to access the current directory (this provides public access), but prevents unauthenticated users from accessing the restricted sub folder. Any attempt to do so forces a Forms login.

```
<system.web>
  <!-- The virtual directory root folder contains general pages.
       Unauthenticated users can view them and they do not need
       to be secured with SSL. -->
  <authorization>
    <allow users="*" />
  </authorization>
</system.web>

<!-- The restricted folder is for authenticated and SSL access only. -->
<location path="Restricted" >
  <system.web>
    <authorization>
      <deny users="?" />
    </authorization>
  </system.web>
</location>
```

For additional programmatic considerations, such as how to navigate between restricted and non-restricted pages, see "Forms Authentication" in Chapter 10, "Building ASP.NET Web Pages and Controls."

Set Protection="All"

This setting ensures that the Forms authentication cookie is encrypted to provide privacy and integrity. The keys and algorithms used for cookie encryption are specified on the **<machineKey>** element.

Encryption and integrity checks prevent cookie tampering, although they do not mitigate the risk of cookie replay attacks if an attacker manages to capture the cookie. Also use SSL to prevent an attacker from capturing the cookie by using network monitoring software. Despite SSL, cookies can still be stolen with cross-site scripting (XSS) attacks. The application must take adequate precautions with an appropriate input validation strategy to mitigate this risk.

Use Small Cookie Time-out Values

Use small time-out values to limit the session lifetime and to reduce the window of opportunity for cookie replay attacks.

Consider Using a Fixed Expiration Period

Consider setting **slidingExpiration="false"** on the **<forms>** element to fix the cookie expiration, rather than resetting the expiration period after each Web request. This is important if you are not using SSL to protect the cookie.

Note   This feature is available with .NET Framework version 1.1.

Use SSL with Forms Authentication

Use SSL to protect credentials and the authentication cookie. SSL prevents an attacker from capturing credentials or the Forms authentication cookie that is used to identify you to the application. A stolen authentication cookie is a stolen logon.

Set **requireSSL="true"**. This sets the **Secure** attribute in the cookie, which ensures that the cookie is not transmitted from a browser to the server over an HTTP link. HTTPS (SSL) is required.

Note   This is a .NET Framework version 1.1 setting. It takes explicit programming to set the cookie **Secure** attribute in applications built on version 1.0. For more information and sample code, see Chapter 10, "Building Secure ASP.NET Web Pages and Controls."

If You Do Not Use SSL, Set slidingExpiration = "false"

With **slidingExpiration** set to false, you fix the cookie time-out period as a number of minutes from initial cookie creation. Otherwise, the time-out is renewed on each request to the Web server. If the cookie is captured, it gives an attacker as much time as he needs to access your application as an authenticated user.

Note   This feature is available in .NET Framework version 1.1.

Do Not Use the <credentials> Element on Production Servers

The ability to store user credentials in XML configuration files is provided to support rapid development and limited testing. Do not use actual end-user credentials. End-user credentials should not be stored in configuration files on production servers. Production applications should implement custom user credential stores, for example, in a SQL Server database.

Configure the MachineKey

The **<machineKey>** element defines the encryption algorithms that are used to encrypt the Forms authentication cookie. This element also maintains encryption keys. For more information, see the "MachineKey" section in this chapter.

Use Unique Cookie Names and Paths

Use unique **name** and **path** attribute values. By ensuring unique names, you prevent problems that can occur when you host multiple applications on the same server.

Authorization

Unless a user has explicit permission to access a resource, such as a particular Web page, a resource file, a directory, and so on, the configuration should deny access by default. ASP.NET provides two configurable gatekeepers that you can use to control access to restricted resources. These are:

- **File Authorization**. This gatekeeper is implemented by the ASP.NET **FileAuthorizationModule** HTTP module.
- **URL Authorization**. This gatekeeper is implemented by the ASP.NET **UrlAuthorizationModule** HTTP module.

File Authorization

Only applications that use Windows authentication and have the following configuration can use this gatekeeper:

```
<authentication mode="Windows"/>
```

This gatekeeper is automatically effective when you use Windows authentication, and there is no need to impersonate. To configure the gatekeeper, configure Windows ACLs on files and folders. Note that the gatekeeper only controls access to the file types mapped by IIS to the following ASP.NET ISAPI extension: Aspnet_isapi.dll.

URL Authorization

Any application can use this gatekeeper. It is configured using **<authorization>** elements that control which users and groups of users should have access to the application. The default element from Machine.config is shown below:

```
<authorization>
  <!-- allow/deny Attributes:
    users="[*|?|name]"
       * - All users
       ? - Anonymous users
       [name] - Named user
    roles="[name]" -->
 <allow users="*"/>
</authorization>
```

URL Authorization Notes

Use the following to help you successfully configure URL Authorization:

- Authorization settings in Web.config usually refer to all of the files in the current directory and all subdirectories, unless a subdirectory contains its own Web.config with an **<authorization>** element. In this case, the settings in the subdirectory override the parent directory settings.

- URL authorization only applies to file types that are mapped by IIS to the ASP.NET ISAPI extension: Aspnet_isapi.dll.

- When your application uses Windows authentication, you are authorizing access to Windows user and group accounts. User names take the form of "authority\WindowsUserName" and role names take the form of "authority\WindowsGroupName", where authority is either a domain name or the local machine name depending on the account type.

  A number of well known accounts are represented with "BUILTIN" strings. For example, the local administrators group is referred to as "BUILTIN\Administrators". The local users group is referred to as "BUILTIN\Users".

Note   With.NET Framework version 1.0, the authority and the group name are case sensitive. The group name must match the group name that appears in Windows exactly.

- When your application uses Forms authentication, you authorize the custom user and roles maintained in your custom user store. For example, if you use Forms to authenticate users against a database, you authorize against the roles retrieved from the database.

- You can use the **<location>** tag to apply authorization settings to an individual file or directory. The following example shows how you can apply authorization to a specific file (page.aspx):

```
<location path="page.aspx" />
  <authorization>
    <allow users="DomainName\Bob, DomainName\Mary" />
    <deny users="*" />
  </authorization>
</location>
```

Session State

Applications that rely on per user session state can store session state in the following locations:

- In the ASP.NET worker process
- In an out-of-process state service, which can run on the Web server, or on a remote server
- In a SQL Server data store

<sessionState>

The relevant location, combined with connection details, is stored in the **<sessionState>** element in Machine.config. This is the default setting:

```
<sessionState mode="InProc"
              stateConnectionString="tcpip=127.0.0.1:42424"
              stateNetworkTimeout="10" sqlConnectionString="data
              source=127.0.0.1;Integrated Security=SSPI"
              cookieless="false" timeout="20"/>
```

Note If you do not use the ASP.NET state service on the Web server, use the MMC Services snap-in to disable it.

Securing a SQL Server Session State Store

If you use a SQL Server session state store, use the following recommendations to help secure the session state:

- **Use Windows authentication to the database**
- **Encrypt sqlConnectionString**
- **Limit the application's login in the database**
- **Secure the channel**

For more information about setting up the SQL Server session state store database, see Microsoft Knowledge Base article 311209, "How To: Configure ASP.NET for Persistent SQL Server Session State Management."

Use Windows Authentication to the Database

If you use **mode="SQLServer"**, use Windows authentication to connect to the state database and use a least privileged account, such as a duplicate local ASPNET account. This means that you can use a trusted connection, you do not have credentials in the connection string, and credentials are not passed over the wire to the database.

Encrypt the sqlConnectionString

Encrypt the **sqlConnectionString** attribute value using the Aspnet_setreg.exe tool. This is particularly important if you use SQL authentication to connect to the state database because of the credentials in the connection string, but it is also recommended if you use Windows authentication.

▶ **To encrypt the sqlConnectionString**

1. Run the following command from the command prompt.

```
aspnet_setreg -k:Software\YourApp\sessionState -c:{your connection string}
```

This stores the encrypted connection string in the specified registry key and secures the registry key with a restricted ACL that grants Full Control to System, Administrators, and Creator Owner.

2. Reconfigure the **<sessionState>** element and add the following **sqlConnectionString** attribute.

```
<sessionState mode="SQLServer"
sqlConnectionString="registry:HKLM\SOFTWARE\YourApp\sessionState\ASPNET_SETREG,
sqlConnectionString" />
```

3. Use Regedt32.exe to create an ACL on the above registry key that grants read access to the ASP.NET process account.

Limit the Application's Login in the Database

The application's login in the database should be restricted so that it can only be used to access the necessary state tables and the stored procedures used by ASP.NET to query the database.

▶ To limit the application's login in the state database

1. Create a duplicate local account on the state database server with the same name and strong password of the account that runs your ASP.NET application.

   For more information about using the ASPNET account to access a remote database, see "Data Access" later in this chapter.

2. Create a local Windows group, for example ASPNETWebApps, on the database server and add the local ASPNET account to the group.

3. Grant the Windows group access to SQL Server by creating a new login.

   ```
   sp_grantlogin 'MACHINE\ASPNETWebApps'
   ```

Note   Replace MACHINE with your database server name.

---

4. Grant the SQL login access to the ASPState database. The following T-SQL creates a database user called WebAppUser, with which the login is associated.

   ```
   USE ASPState
   GO
   sp_grantdbaccess 'MACHINE\ASPNETWebApps', 'WebAppUser'
   ```

5. Create a user-defined database role.

   ```
   USE ASPState
   GO
   sp_addrole 'WebAppUserRole'
   ```

6. Add the database user to the new database role.

   ```
   USE ASPState
   GO
   sp_addrolemember 'WebAppUserRole', 'WebAppUser'
   ```

7. Configure permissions in the database for the database role. Grant execute permissions for the stored procedures that are provided with the ASPState database.

   ```
   grant execute on CreateTempTables to WebAppUserRole
   ```

   Repeat this command for all of the stored procedures that are provided with the ASPState database. Use SQL Server Enterprise Manager to see the full list.

Secure the Channel

To protect sensitive session state over the network between the Web server and remote state store, secure the channel to the two servers using IPSec or SSL. This provides privacy and integrity for the session state data across the network. If you use SSL, you must install a server certificate on the database server. For more information about using SSL with SQL Server, see Chapter 18, "Securing Your Database Server."

Securing the Out-of-Process State Service

If you use **mode=StateServer**, use the following recommendations to help secure session state:

- Use a least privileged account to run the state service
- Secure the channel
- Consider changing the default port
- Encrypt the state connection string

Use a Least Privileged Account to Run the State Service

The state service runs by default using the ASPNET local, least privileged account. You should not need to change this configuration.

Secure the Channel

If the state service is located on a remote server, secure the channel to the remote state store using IPSec to ensure the user state remains private and unaltered.

Consider Changing the Default Port

The ASP.NET state service listens on port 42424. To avoid using this default, well known port, you can change the port by editing the following registry key:

```
HKLM\SYSTEM\CurrentControlSet\Services\aspnet_state\Parameters
```

The port number is defined by the **Port** named value. If you change the port number in the registry, for example, to 45678, you must also change the connection string on the **<sessionState>** element, as follows:

```
stateConnectionString="tcpip=127.0.0.1:45678"
```

Encrypt the stateConnectionString

Encrypt the **stateConnectionString** attribute value to hide the IP address and port number of your state store. Use the Aspnet_setreg.exe tool.

▶ **To encrypt the stateConnectionString**

1. Run the following command from the command prompt.

```
aspnet_setreg -k:Software\YourApp\sessionState -d:{your connection string}
```

This stores the encrypted connection string in the specified registry key and secures the registry key with a restricted ACL that grants Full Control to System, Administrators, and Creator Owner.

2. Reconfigure the **<sessionState>** element and add the following **stateConnectionString** attribute:

```
<sessionState mode="StateServer"
sqlConnectionString="registry:HKLM\SOFTWARE\YourApp\sessionState\ASPNET_SETREG,
sqlConnectionString" ... />
```

3. Use Regedt32.exe to create an ACL on the above registry key that grants read access to the ASP.NET process account.

View State

If your applications use view state, make sure it is protected with message authentication codes (MACs) to ensure it is not modified at the client. View state and MAC protection can be enabled or disabled for all applications on the machine using the **<pages>** element in Machine.config.

<pages>

By default, the **enableViewStateMac** attribute on the **<pages>** element in Machine.config ensures that view state is protected with a MAC.

```
<pages buffer="true" enableSessionState="true"
       enableViewState="true" enableViewStateMac="true"
       autoEventWireup="true" validateRequest="true"/>
```

If you use view state, make sure that **enableViewStateMac** is set to true. The **<machineKey>** element defines the algorithms used to protect view state.

Machine Key

The **<machineKey>** element is used to specify encryption keys, validation keys, and algorithms that are used to protect Forms authentication cookies and page-level view state. The following code sample shows the default setting from Machine.config:

```
<machineKey validationKey="AutoGenerate,IsolateApps"
            decryptionKey="AutoGenerate,IsolateApps" validation="SHA1"/>
```

Consider the following recommendations when you configure the **<machineKey>**:

- **Use unique encryption keys with multiple applications**
- **Set validation="SHA1"**
- **Generate keys manually for Web farms**

Use Unique Encryption Keys with Multiple Applications

If you host multiple applications on a single Web server, use unique keys for each application on the machine instead of using a single key across all applications. This eliminates the likelihood that one application can spoof view state or encrypted Forms authentication cookies in hosting environments.

Also use the **IsolateApps** setting. This is a new .NET Framework version 1.1 setting that instructs ASP.NET to automatically generate encryption keys and to make them unique for each application.

Set validation="SHA1"

The **validation** attribute specifies the algorithm used for integrity-checking, page-level view state. Possible values are "SHA1", "MD5", and "3DES".

If you used **protection="All"** on the **<forms>** element, then the Forms authentication cookie is encrypted, which also ensures integrity. Regardless of the **validation** attribute setting, Forms authentication uses TripleDES (3DES) to encrypt the cookie.

> **Note** Forms-authentication cookie encryption is independent of the **validationkey** setting, and the key is based on the **decryptionKey** attribute.

If you set **validation="SHA1"** on the **<machineKey>**, then page-level view state is integrity checked using the SHA1 algorithm, assuming that the **<pages>** element is configured for view state MACs. For more information, see "View State" earlier in this chapter.

You can also set the validation attribute to MD5. You should use SHA1 because this produces a larger hash than MD5 and is therefore considered more secure.

If you set **validation="3DES"** on the **<machineKey>**, then page-level view state is encrypted (which also provides integrity checking) using the 3DES algorithm, even if the **<pages>** element is configured for view state MACs.

Generate Keys Manually For Web Farms

In Web farms, you must set explicit key values and use the same ones across all machines in the Web farm. See "Web Farm Considerations" later in this chapter.

Debugging

The **<compilation>** element controls compiler settings that are used for dynamic page compilation, which is initiated when a client requests a Web page (.aspx file) or Web service (.asmx file). It is important that debug builds are not used on the production server because debug information is valuable to attackers and can reveal source code details.

<compilation>

This element controls the compilation process. Make sure that debug compiles are disabled on production servers. Set **debug="false"** as follows:

```
<compilation debug="false" explicit="true" defaultLanguage="vb" />
```

By default, temporary files are created and compiled in the following directory:

```
%winnt%\Microsoft.NET\Framework\{version}\Temporary ASP.NET Files
```

You can specify the location on a per application basis using the **tempDirectory** attribute, although this provides no security benefit.

Note   The ASP.NET process identity specified on the **<processModel>** element requires Full Control access rights on the temporary compilation directory.

Make sure you do not store debug files (with .pdb extensions) on a production server with your assemblies.

Tracing

Tracing should not be enabled on production servers because system-level trace information can greatly help an attacker profile an application and probe for weak spots.

<trace>

Tracing is configured using the **<trace>** element. Set **enabled="false"** on production servers as follows:

```
<trace enabled="false" localOnly="true" pageOutput="false"
       requestLimit="10" traceMode="SortByTime"/>
```

If you do need to trace problems with live applications, it is preferable that you simulate the problem in a test environment, or if necessary, enable tracing and set **localOnly="true"** to prevent trace details from being returned to remote clients.

Exception Management

Do not allow exception details to propagate from your Web applications back to the client. A malicious user could use system-level diagnostic information to learn about your application and probe for weaknesses to exploit in future attacks.

<customErrors>

The **<customErrors>** element can be used to configure custom, generic error messages that should be returned to the client in the event of an application exception condition. The error page should include a suitably generic error message, optionally with additional support details. You can also use this element to return different error pages depending on the exception condition.

Make sure that the mode attribute is set to "**On**" and that you have specified a default redirect page as shown below:

```
<customErrors mode="On" defaultRedirect="YourErrorPage.htm" />
```

The **defaultRedirect** attribute allows you to use a custom error page for your application, which for example might include support contact details.

Note   Do not use **mode="Off"** because it causes detailed error pages that contain system-level information to be returned to the client.

If you want separate error pages for different types of error, use one or more **<error>** elements as shown below. In this example, "404 (not found)" errors are redirected to one page, "500 (internal system errors)" are directed to another page, and all other errors are directed to the page specified on the **defaultRedirect** attribute.

```
<customErrors mode="On" defaultRedirect="YourErrorPage.htm">
    <error statusCode="404" redirect="YourNotFoundPage.htm"/>
    <error statusCode="500" redirect="YourInternalErrorPage.htm"/>
</customErrors>
```

Remoting

Do not expose .NET Remoting endpoints on Internet-facing Web servers. To disable Remoting, disable requests for .rem and .soap extensions by mapping requests for these file extensions to the **HttpForbiddenHandler**. Use the following elements beneath **<httpHandlers>**:

```
<httpHandlers>
  <add verb="*" path="*.rem" type="System.Web.HttpForbiddenHandler"/>
  <add verb="*" path="*.soap" type="System.Web.HttpForbiddenHandler"/>
  . . .
</httpHandlers>
```

Note This does not prevent a Web application on the Web server from connecting to a downstream object by using the Remoting infrastructure. However, it prevents clients from being able to connect to objects on the Web server.

Web Services

Configure Web services using the **<webServices>** element. To establish a secure Web services configuration:

- **Disable Web services if they are not required**
- **Disable unused protocols**
- **Disable the automatic generation of WSDL**

Disable Web Services if They Are Not Required

If you do not use Web services, disable them by mapping requests for the .asmx (Web service) file extension to **HttpForbiddenHandler** in Machine.config as follows:

```
<httpHandlers>
  <add verb="*" path="*.asmx" type="System.Web.HttpForbiddenHandler"/>
  . . .
</httpHandlers>
```

Disable Unused Protocols

The **<protocols>** element defines the protocols that Web services support. By default, **HttpPost** and **HttpGet** are disabled on .NET Framework version 1.1 as follows:

```
<webServices>
  <protocols>
    <add name="HttpSoap1.2"/>
    <add name="HttpSoap"/>
    <!-- <add name="HttpPost"/> -->
    <!-- <add name="HttpGet"/> -->
    <add name="HttpPostLocalhost"/>
    <add name="Documentation"/>
  </protocols>
</webServices>
```

By disabling unnecessary protocols, including **HttpPost** and **HttpGet**, you reduce the attack surface area. For example, it is possible for an external attacker to embed a malicious link in an e-mail to execute an internal Web service using the end user's security context. Disabling the **HttpGet** protocol is an effective countermeasure. In many ways, this is similar to an XSS attack. A variation of this attack uses an **<img src="..." />** tag on a publicly accessible Web page to embed a GET call to an intranet Web service. Both attacks can allow an outsider to invoke an internal Web service. Disabling protocols mitigates the risk.

If your production server provides publicly discoverable Web services, you must enable **HttpGet** and **HttpPost** to allow the service to be discovered over these protocols.

Disable the Automatic Generation of WSDL

The Documentation protocol is used to dynamically generate Web Service Description Language (WSDL). WSDL describes the characteristics of a Web service, such as its method signatures and supported protocols. Clients use this information to construct appropriately formatted messages. By default, Web services publicly expose WSDL, which makes it available to anyone who can connect to the Web server over the Internet.

At times, you might want to distribute the WSDL files manually to your partners and prevent public access. With this approach, the development team can provide individual .wsdl files for each Web service to the operations team. The operations team can then distribute them to specified partners who want to use the Web services.

To disable the Documentation protocol, comment it out in Machine.config as follows:

```
<webServices>
  <protocols>
    <add name="HttpSoap"/>
    <!-- <add name="Documentation"/> -->
  </protocols>
</webServices>
```

Forbidden Resources

To prevent protected resources and files from being downloaded over HTTP, map them to the ASP.NET **HttpForbiddenHandler**.

Map Protected Resources to HttpForbiddenHandler

HTTP handlers are located in Machine.config beneath the **<httpHandlers>** element. HTTP handlers are responsible for processing Web requests for specific file extensions. Remoting should not be enabled on front-end Web servers; enable Remoting only on middle-tier application servers that are isolated from the Internet.

- The following file extensions are mapped in Machine.config to HTTP handlers:
- .aspx is used for ASP.NET pages.
- .rem and .soap are used for Remoting.
- .asmx is used for Web Services.
- .asax, .ascx, .config, .cs, .csproj, .vb, .vbproj, .webinfo, .asp, .licx, .resx, and .resources are protected resources and are mapped to **System.Web.HttpForbiddenHandler**.

For .NET Framework resources, if you do not use a file extension, then map the extension to **System.Web.HttpForbiddenHandler** in Machine.config, as shown in the following example:

```
<add verb="*" path="*.vbproj" type="System.Web.HttpForbiddenHandler" />
```

In this case, the .vbproj file extension is mapped to **System.Web.HttpForbiddenHandler**. If a client requests a path that ends with .vbproj, then ASP.NET returns a message that states "This type of page is not served."

The following guidelines apply to handling .NET Framework file extensions:

- **Map extensions you do not use to HttpForbiddenHandler**. If you do not serve ASP.NET pages, then map .aspx to **HttpForbiddenHandler**. If you do not use Web Services, then map .asmx to **HttpForbiddenHandler**.
- **Disable Remoting on Internet-facing Web servers**. Map remoting extensions (.soap and .rem) on Internet-facing Web servers to **HttpForbiddenHandler**.

Bin Directory

The bin directory beneath an ASP.NET application's virtual root directory contains the application's private assemblies, including the application's page-class implementations if code-behind files have been used during development.

Secure the Bin Directory

To secure the application's bin directory and protect your business logic against inadvertent download:

- **Remove Web permissions.**
- **Remove all authentication settings.**

Remove Web Permissions

Use the IIS snap-in and ensure that the bin directory does not have **Read**, **Write**, or **Directory** browsing permissions. Also ensure **Execute** permissions are set to **None**.

Remove All Authentication Settings

Use the IIS snap-in to remove authentication settings from the bin directory. This results in all access being denied.

Event Log

Least privileged accounts, such as ASPNET, have sufficient permissions to be able to write records to the event log using existing event sources. However, they do not have sufficient permissions to create new event sources. To do this, you must place a new entry beneath the following registry key:

```
HKEY_LOCAL_MACHINE\SYSTEM\CurrentControlSet\Services\Eventlog\<log>
```

To avoid this issue, you can create event sources at installation time when administrator privileges are available. You can use a .NET installer class, which can be instantiated by the Windows Installer (if you are using .msi deployment) or by the InstallUtil.exe system utility if you are not. For more information about using event log installers, see Chapter 10, "Building Secure ASP.NET Web Pages and Controls."

If you are unable to create event sources at installation time, you must add permission to the following registry key and grant access to the ASP.NET process account or to any impersonated account if your application uses impersonation.

```
HKEY_LOCAL_MACHINE\SYSTEM\CurrentControlSet\Services\Eventlog
```

At minimum, the account(s) must have the following permissions:

- Query key value
- Set key value
- Create subkey
- Enumerate subkeys
- Notify
- Read

File Access

Any file that your application accesses must have an access control entry (ACE) in the ACL that grants, at minimum, read access to the ASP.NET process account or impersonated identity. Normally, ACLs are configured on the directory and the file inherits the setting.

In addition to using NTFS permissions to restrict access to files and directories, you can also use ASP.NET trust levels to place constraints on Web applications and Web services to restrict which areas of the file system they can access. For example, Medium-trust Web applications can only access files within their own virtual directory hierarchy.

For more information about ASP.NET CAS policy, see Chapter 9, "Using Code Access Security with ASP.NET."

ACLs and Permissions

The ASP.NET process account and, for certain directories, any impersonation identities (if your applications use impersonation) require the following NTFS permissions. The permissions shown in Table 19.3 should be used in addition to any permissions your applications might require to access application-specific file system resources.

Table 19.3   Required NTFS Permissions for ASP.NET Process Accounts

Directory	Required permissions
Temporary ASP.NET Files %windir%\Microsoft.NET\Framework\ {version}Temporary ASP.NET Files	Process account and impersonated identities: Full Control
Temporary Directory (%temp%)	Process account: Full Control
.NET Framework directory %windir%\Microsoft.NET\Framework\ {version}	Process account and impersonated identities: Read and Execute List Folder Contents Read
.NET Framework configuration directory %windir%\Microsoft.NET\Framework\ {version}\CONFIG	Process account and impersonated Identities: Read and Execute List Folder Contents Read
Web site root C:\inetpub\wwwroot or the path that the default Web site points to	Process account: Read
System root directory %windir%\system32	Process account: Read
Global assembly cache %windir%\assembly	Process account and impersonated identities: Read
Content directory C:\inetpub\wwwroot\YourWebApp	Process account: Read and Execute List Folder Contents Read **Note** With .NET Framework version 1.0, all parent directories, back up to the file system root directory, also require the above permissions. Parent directories include: C:\ C:\inetpub\ C:\inetpub\wwwroot\

Registry

Any registry key that your application accesses must have an ACE in the ACL that grants, at minimum, read access to the ASP.NET process account or impersonated identity.

Data Access

To access a remote database using Windows authentication from your ASP.NET application, you have the following options:

- **Use the default ASP.NET process account**. Use the default ASP.NET process account by creating a mirrored account with the same user name and password on the database server. On Windows 2000, the default process account is ASPNET. On Windows Server 2003, the default process account is NetworkService.

   The disadvantage of using local accounts is that if you can dump the SAM database, which requires administration privileges, then you can access the credentials. The main advantage is that local accounts can be scoped to specific servers, which is difficult to achieve using domain accounts.

- **Use a least privileged domain account to run ASP.NET**. This approach simplifies administration, and it means that you do not need to synchronize the passwords of mirrored accounts. It will not work if the Web server and database server are in separate non-trusting domains, or if a firewall separates the two servers and the firewall does not permit the necessary ports for Windows authentication.

- **Impersonate the Anonymous Web account**. If you are using Forms or Passport authentication, you can impersonate the anonymous Web account (IUSR_MACHINE by default) and create a mirrored account on the database server. This approach is useful in scenarios where you host multiple Web applications on the same Web server. You can use IIS to configure each application's virtual directory with a different anonymous account.

   On Windows Server 2003, you can run multiple applications in separate worker processes, using IIS 6.0 application pools and configuring a separate identity for each one.

Configuring Data Access for Your ASP.NET Application

Whichever approach you use, restrict the application's account in the database. To do this, create a SQL Server login for the account, grant it access to the required database, and restrict its permissions so that it only has access to the minimum required database objects. Ideally, you should restrict permissions so that the login has access only to the stored procedures used by your application or Web service.

The following procedure assumes that you are using a mirrored local account, but you can use the same approach with a domain account to restrict the account's capabilities in the database.

► **To configure database access for your ASP.NET application**

1. Use the Computer Management tool to change the password of the local ASPNET account on the Web server to a known strong password.

   You need to do this so that you can create a mirrored account on the database server.

2. Change the **password** attribute on the **<processModel>** element in Machine.config so that the ASP.NET worker process continues to run using the ASPNET account. Use Aspnet_setreg.exe to store the encrypted credentials in the registry.

3. Create a local account on the database server with the same name (ASPNET) and strong password on the database server.

4. Create a local Windows group, such as ASPNETWebApp, on the database server, and then add the local ASPNET account to the group.

5. Grant the Windows group access to SQL Server by creating a new login, as follows:

```
sp_grantlogin 'MACHINE\ASPNETWebApp'
```

Note   Replace MACHINE with your database server name.

---

6. Grant the SQL login access to the database. The following T-SQL creates a database user called WebAppUser to which the login is associated.

```
USE YourDatabase
GO
sp_grantdbaccess 'MACHINE\ASPNETWebApp', 'WebAppUser'
```

7. Create a user-defined database role.

```
USE YourDatabase
GO
sp_addrole 'WebAppUserRole'
```

8. Add the database user to the new database role.

```
USE YourDatabase
GO
sp_addrolemember 'WebAppUserRole', 'WebAppUser'
```

9. Configure permissions in the database for the database role. Ideally, grant execute permissions only for the stored procedures that the application uses to query the database and do not provide direct table access.

```
grant execute on sprocname to WebAppUserRole
```

UNC Shares

There are two main ways that your ASP.NET application might use UNC shares:

- **Accessing files on UNC shares**

  For example, your application must access a remote file such as
  \\remoteserver\share\somefile.dat.

- **Hosting applications on UNC shares**

  Your application's IIS virtual directory is mapped to a remote share, for example,
  \\remoteserver\appname. In this scenario, HTTP requests are processed by your
  Web server, but the application's pages, resources, and private assemblies are
  located on the remote share.

Accessing Files on UNC Shares

If your application accesses files on a UNC share, the ASP.NET process account or
any impersonation identities must have the appropriate access rights defined by the
ACL on the share and on the underlying directory or file.

If you use the local ASPNET process account, this does not have a network identity,
so you must create a mirrored account on the remote server with a matching user
name and password, or you must use a least privileged domain account that has
access to both servers. On Windows Server 2003, the NetworkService account that is
used to run ASP.NET Web applications can be authenticated over the network, so all
you need to do is grant access rights to the machine account.

Hosting Applications on UNC Shares

You can use IIS to configure a virtual directory to point to a UNC share located on
another computer, for example \\remoteserver\appname. When you do so, IIS
prompts you to supply account credentials, which it uses to establish a connection to
the remote computer.

Note The account credentials are stored in encrypted format in the IIS metabase but are available
through an API. You should ensure that you use a least privileged account. For more information, see
Microsoft Knowledge Base article 280383, "IIS Security Recommendations When You Use a UNC
Share and Username and Password Credentials."

If your application resides on a UNC share, ASP.NET impersonates the IIS-provided
UNC token (created from the account credentials that you supplied to IIS) to access
that share, unless you have enabled impersonation and have used a fixed
impersonation identity, as shown with the following configuration:

```
<identity impersonate="true"
  userName="registry:HKLM\SOFTWARE\YourApp\identity\ASPNET_SETREG,userName"
  password="registry:HKLM\SOFTWARE\YourApp\identity\ASPNET_SETREG,password"/>
```

If a fixed impersonation account is provided through the **userName** and **password** attributes, ASP.NET uses that account instead of the IIS UNC token to access the share. Any resource access performed by your application also uses the fixed impersonation account.

Note   In the above example, Aspnet_setreg.exe has been used to store the encrypted account credentials in the registry.

If you enable impersonation of the original caller (IIS authenticated identity) by using the following configuration, ASP.NET still uses the UNC-provided token to access your application's files on the share, although any resource access performed by your application uses the impersonation token.

```
<identity impersonate="true" />
```

Note   The account used for the UNC share must also be able to read Machine.config.

Code Access Security Considerations

Applications on a UNC share are granted the intranet permission set by code access security policy. The intranet permission set does not contain **AspNetHostingPermission**, which ASP.NET Web applications require to run, so your application will not run without explicit policy modifications.

You have two options:

- Grant full trust to the UNC share on which your application is hosted.

  This is the simplest option to manage and if you run .NET Framework version 1.0, this is the only option because ASP.NET version 1.0 Web applications require full trust.

- Configure code access security policy to grant your code the **AspNetHostingPermission** and any other permission it might require based on the types of resources it accesses and the operations it performs.

  Because of the way in which ASP.NET dynamically creates code and compiles page classes, you must use a code group for the UNC and the Temporary ASP.NET Files directory when you configure policy. The default temporary directory is \WINNT\Microsoft.NET\Framework\{version}\Temporary ASP.NET Files, but the location is configurable on a per application basis by using the **tempDirectory** attribute of the **<compilation>** element.

  For more information about ASP.NET code access security policy and sandboxing privileged code, see Chapter 9, "Using Code Access Security with ASP.NET."

Note   When configuring policy, you should grant trust to the share (by using a file location) rather than to the zone. This provides finer granularity because you do not affect all the applications in a particular zone.

COM/DCOM Resources

Your application uses the process or impersonation identity when it calls COM-based resources, such as serviced components. Client-side authentication and impersonation levels are configured using the **comAuthenticationLevel** and **comImpersonation** level attributes on the **<processModel>** element in Machine.config.

For more information and recommendations, see "Enterprise Services Considerations" in Chapter 17, "Securing Your Application Server."

Denial of Service Considerations

ASP.NET has the following features to help counteract denial of service attacks aimed at your ASP.NET applications:

- POST requests are constrained by default to 4 megabytes (MB).
- Clients are checked to ensure that they are still connected before requests are queued for work. This is done in case an attacker sends multiple requests and then disconnects them.
- Request execution times out after a configurable limit.

<httpRuntime>

Configuration values are maintained on the **<httpRuntime>** element in Machine.config. The following code sample shows default settings from a version 1.1 Machine.config:

```
<httpRuntime executionTimeout="90"
             maxRequestLength="4096"
             useFullyQualifiedRedirectUrl="false"
             minFreeThreads="8"
             minLocalRequestFreeThreads="4"
             appRequestQueueLimit="100"
             enableVersionHeader="true"/>
```

You might want to reduce the **maxRequestLength** attribute to prevent users from uploading very large files. The maximum allowed value is 4 MB. In the Open Hack competition, the **maxRequestLength** was constrained to 1/2 MB as shown in the following example:

```
<system.web>
    <!-- 1/2 MB Max POST length -->
    <httpRuntime maxRequestLength="512"/>
</system.web>
```

Note ASP.NET does not address packet-level attacks. You must address this by hardening the TCP/IP stack. For more information about configuring the TCP/IP stack, see "How To: Harden the TCP/IP Stack" in the "How To" section of this guide.

Web Farm Considerations

If your ASP.NET Web application runs in a Web farm, there is no guarantee that successive requests from the same client will be serviced by the same Web server. This has implications for:

- **Session state**
- **Encryption and verification**
- **DPAPI**

Session State

To avoid server affinity, maintain ASP.NET session state out of process in the ASP.NET SQL Server state database or in the out-of-process state service that runs on a remote machine. For more information about securing session state in a remote state store, see the "Session State" section earlier in this document.

Encryption and Verification

The keys used to encrypt and verify Forms authentication cookies and view state must be the same across all servers in a Web farm. The **AutoGenerate** settings on the <**machineKey**> element must be replaced with common key values.

For more information on generating and configuring the keys, see Microsoft Knowledge Base article 312906, "How To: Create Keys by Using Visual C# .NET for Use in Forms."

DPAPI

To encrypt data, developers sometimes use DPAPI. If you use DPAPI with the machine key to store secrets, the encrypted string is specific to a given computer and you cannot copy the encrypted data across computers in a Web farm or cluster.

If you use DPAPI with a user key, you can decrypt the data on any computer with a roaming user profile. However, this is not recommended because the data can be decrypted by any machine on the network that can execute code using the account which encrypted the data.

DPAPI is ideally suited to storing configuration secrets, for example, database connection strings, that live on the Web server. Other encryption techniques should be used when the encrypted data is stored on a remote server, for example, in a database. For more information about storing encrypted data in the database, see Chapter 14, "Building Secure Data Access."

Snapshot of a Secure ASP.NET Application

The following snapshot view shows the attributes of a secure ASP.NET application and allows you to quickly and easily compare settings with your own configuration.

Table 19.4   Snapshot of a Secure ASP.NET Application Configuration

Component	Characteristics

Process identity	The ASP.NET worker process runs as ASPNET:
	
	`<processModel username="machine"`
	`              password="AutoGenerate" />`
	
	The custom account (if used) is least privileged.
	
	The custom account credentials are encrypted in the registry:
	
	`<processModel`
	`    userName="registry:HKLM\SOFTWARE\YourApp\`
	`process\ASPNET_SETREG,userName"`
	`    password="registry:HKLM\SOFTWARE\YourApp\`
	`process\ASPNET_SETREG,password"/>`

Impersonation	Impersonation identities are encrypted in the registry:
	
	`<identity impersonate="true"`
	`          userName="registry:HKLM\SOFTWARE\YourApp\`
	`identity\ASPNET_SETREG,userName"`
	`          password="registry:HKLM\SOFTWARE\YourApp\`
	`identity\ASPNET_SETREG,password"/>`

Authentication	The Web site is partitioned for public and restricted access.
	
	The Forms authentication configuration is secure:
	
	`<forms loginUrl="Restricted\login.aspx"`
	`       protection="All"`
	`       requireSSL="true"`
	`       timeout="10"`
	`       name="AppNameCookie"`
	`       path="/FormsAuth"`
	`       slidingExpiration="true" />`
	
	The authentication cookie is encrypted and integrity checked.
	
	SSL is required for authentication cookie.
	
	Sliding expiration is set to false, if SSL is it is not used.
	
	The session lifetime is restricted.
	
	Cookie names and paths are unique.
	
	The **<credentials>** element is not used.

(continued)

Table 19.4 Snapshot of a Secure ASP.NET Application Configuration *(continued)*

Component	Characteristics
Authorization	ACLs are configured on ASP.NET resources. **<authorization>** elements are configured.
Session state	The ASP.NET state service is disabled if it is not required. `<sessionState  mode="Off " />` The communication channel to the remote state store is encrypted if necessary. Windows authentication is used to connect to ASPState database. The application login has restricted access to ASPState database. The connection parameters (**sqlConnectionString** and **stateConnectionString**) are encrypted in the registry. The ASP.NET state service is configured for a non-default port.
View state	The view-state MAC is enabled on the **<pages>** element in Machine.config.

Machine key	The **validation** attribute set to SHA1.
	
	 Keys are unique for each application running on the Web server.
	
	 ViewState and Forms Authentication are protected:
	
	 `<machineKey validationKey="AutoGenerate,IsolateApps"`
	 `              decryptionKey="AutoGenerate,IsolateApps"`
	 `              validation="SHA1"/>`

Forbidden resources	Protected resources are mapped to **System.Web.HttpForbiddenHandler**.
Debugging	Debug builds are disabled: `<compilation debug="false" . . .`
Tracing	Tracing is disabled. `<trace enabled='false' localOnly='true . . .`

Exception management	Custom errors are enabled.
	
	 Default redirect page is used:
	
	 `<customErrors mode="On"`
	 `              defaultRedirect="YourErrorPage.htm" />`

Table 19.4   Snapshot of a Secure ASP.NET Application Configuration *(continued)*

Component	Characteristics
Remoting	Remoting is disabled on Internet-facing Web servers: ```<httpHandlers>\n <add verb="*" path="*.soap"\n type="System.Web.HttpForbiddenHandler"/>\n <add verb="*" path="*.rem"\n type="System.Web.HttpForbiddenHandler"/>\n\n . . .\n\n</httpHandlers>```

Web services	Web services are disabled if they are not required:
	
	```<httpHandlers>\n <add verb="*" path="*.asmx"\n type="System.Web.HttpForbiddenHandler"/>\n . . .\n</httpHandlers>```
	
	Unnecessary protocols are disabled:
	
	```<webServices>\n <protocols>\n <!-- <add name="HttpPost"/> -->\n <!-- <add name="HttpGet"/> -->\n . . .```
	
	The documentation protocol is disabled to prevent the automatic generation of WSDL:
	
	```<webServices>\n <protocols>\n <!--<add name="Documentation"/>-->\n . . .```

Bin directory	The bin directory is secured. (**Read**, **Write**, and **Directory** browsing permissions removed from bin. **Execute** permissions are set to **None**.) Authentication settings are removed from bin directory

Summary

This chapter has shown you how to secure an ASP.NET Web application or Web service by focusing on configuration categories that include accounts, services, protocols, files and directories, and configuration data that are maintained in Machine.config and Web.config files. This chapter has also shown you how to secure the various functional areas that are relied upon by ASP.NET Web applications and Web services, including authentication, authorization, session state, and data access.

For a related checklist, see "Checklist: Securing ASP.NET" in the "Checklist" section of this guide.

Additional Resources

For more information, see the following resources and articles:

- You can download Web Services Enhancements (WSE) 1.0 SP1 for Microsoft .NET at *http://microsoft.com/downloads/details.aspx?FamilyId=06255A94-2635-4D29-A90C-28B282993A41&displaylang=en.*

- Microsoft Knowledge Base article 329290, "How To: Use the ASP.NET Utility to Encrypt Credentials and Session State Connection Strings."

- Microsoft Knowledge Base article 311209, "How To: Configure ASP.NET for Persistent SQL Server Session State Management."

- Microsoft Knowledge Base article 312906, "How To: Create Keys by Using Visual C# .NET for Use in Forms."

- "How To: Implement Kerberos Delegation for Windows 2000" in the "How To" section of "Microsoft *patterns & practices* Volume I, *Building Secure ASP.NET Applications: Authentication, Authorization, and Secure Communication*" at *http://msdn.microsoft.com/library/default.asp?url=/library/en-us/dnnetsec/html/SecNetHT05.asp.*

- For more information on security considerations from the Open Hack competition, see MSDN article "Building and Configuring More Secure Web Sites" at *http://msdn.microsoft.com/library/default.asp?url=/library/en-us/dnnetsec/html/openhack.asp.*

20

Hosting Multiple Web Applications

In This Chapter

- Using multiple identities for application isolation
- Using Microsoft Windows Server 2003 application pools for application isolation
- Using code access security for application Isolation

Overview

If you host multiple ASP.NET Web applications on a shared Web server, you need to consider application isolation. For example, how can you ensure that individual applications will not affect one another at runtime? How can you prevent a single rogue or badly written application from consuming critical system level resources on the server that keeps other applications from running properly?

The issue is particularly significant for Internet Service Providers (ISPs) who host large numbers of applications from different companies. In a hosting scenario, it is essential to ensure that the installation of a new application cannot adversely impact the operation of existing applications.

There are a number of ways in which application isolation can be achieved. The available options vary depending on the version of the .NET Framework and the version of the operating system that you run on the Web server. If you are running version 1.1 of the .NET Framework, you can use the resource constraint model provided by code access security to provide one level of application isolation. This application isolation is achieved by restricting an application from to access different types of resources such as the file system, registry, event log, Active Directory, databases, network resources, and so on.

In addition, Windows Server 2003 provides process isolation through Internet Information Services 6.0 (IIS 6) application pools that enable multiple applications to run in separate IIS worker process instances. Process isolation is not possible on Windows 2000 because all Web applications run in a single instance of the ASP.NET worker process, with application domains providing isolation.

The Table 20.1 summarizes the various options for application isolation that are available on Windows 2000 and Windows Server 2003.

Table 20.1   Application Isolation Features for Windows 2000 and Windows Server 2003

Isolation Feature	Windows 2000	Windows Server 2003
Process isolation	No	Yes (IIS 6 App Pools)
Application domain isolation	Yes	Yes
Multiple thread identities	Yes	Yes
Code access security resource constraint	Yes (.NET Framework version 1.1)	Yes (.NET Framework version 1.1)

Windows Server 2003 running version 1.1 of the .NET Framework is the recommended platform for hosting multiple ASP.NET applications because it supports process isolation and provides the richest range of options for application isolation.

ASP.NET Architecture on Windows 2000

On Windows 2000, multiple Web applications run in a single instance of the ASP.NET worker process (Aspnet_wp.exe). Each application resides in its own application domain that provides a degree of isolation for managed code. The Windows 2000/IIS 5 architecture is shown in Figure 20.1.

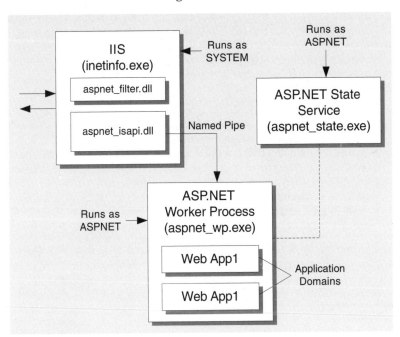

Figure 20.1
ASP.NET architecture on Windows 2000 with IIS 5

The components of the architecture depicted by Figure 20.1 are summarized in Table 20.2.

Table 20.2   Components of the Windows 2000 ASP.NET Architecture

Component	Description
Inetinfo.exe	The main IIS process. A Windows service that runs under the local SYSTEM account.
Aspnet_isapi.dll	IIS script mappings associate ASP.NET file types with this ASP.NET ISAPI extension that runs inside Inetinfo.exe. It is responsible for forwarding requests to the ASP.NET worker process through an asynchronous named pipe. It also starts the worker process and performs health monitoring. The ISAPI extension contains no managed code and performs no request processing itself.
Aspnet_filter.dll	A lightweight ISAPI filter used only to support cookie-less session state for ASP.NET applications. Runs inside Inetinfo.exe.
Aspnet_wp.exe	The ASP.NET worker process. Hosts multiple Web applications in separate application domains that are used to provide isolation. Generally one instance per server, although on multi-processor servers, a Web garden mode supports multiple identical processes with an affinity for a given processor. It is not possible to separate specific Web applications into different processes. This requires IIS 6 and Windows Server 2003. Aspnet_wp.exe runs under the local ASPNET account, although a custom account can be used.
Aspnet_state.exe	An optional Windows service used to store session state for ASP.NET applications. It can run on the Web server or on a remote machine (required for Web farm scenarios). It runs under the local ASPNET account, although a custom account can be used, configured via the Services snap-in.

ASP.NET Architecture on Windows Server 2003

On Windows Server 2003, the architecture changes because IIS 6 allows multiple processes to be used to host separate Web applications. This is shown in Figure 20.2.

Note   IIS 6 supports a backwards compatibility mode that, in turn, supports the IIS 5 ASP.NET worker process model.

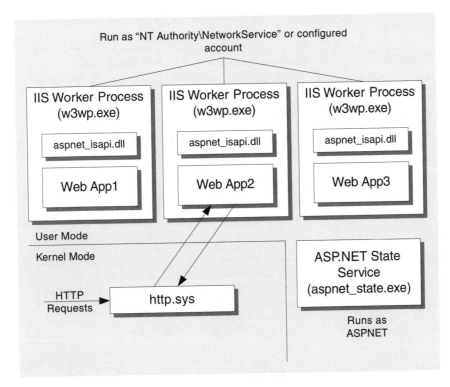

Figure 20.2
ASP.NET architecture on Windows Server 2003 with IIS 6

Compared to the ASP.NET architecture under Windows 2000, the primary difference in Windows Server 2003 is that separate IIS worker process instances (W3wp.exe) can be used to host Web applications. By default, these run using the **NT Authority\NetworkService** account, which is a least privileged local account that acts as the computer account over the network. A Web application that runs in the context of the Network Service account presents the computer's credentials to remote servers for authentication.

Configuring ACLs for Network Service

Configuring an access control list (ACL) for the Network Service account varies for local and remote machines. If you want to grant access to the Network Service account on the local machine, add the Network Service account to an ACL. If you want to grant access to the Network Service account on a remote machine, add the DomainName\MachineName$ account to an ACL.

Note Do not confuse the Network Service account with the Network built-in group, which includes users who were authenticated across the network.

The main components of the architecture depicted by Figure 20.2 are summarized in Table 20.3.

Table 20.3 Components of the Windows Server 2003 ASP.NET Architecture

Component	Description
Aspnet_isapi.dll	Queues requests for processing by the managed code ASP.NET engine and performs health monitoring.
Aspnet_filter.dll	A lightweight ISAPI filter used only to support cookie-less session state for ASP.NET applications. Runs inside W3wp.exe.
W3wp.exe	The IIS worker process that contains the managed code ASP.NET processing engine. The URL space can be arbitrarily divided among different W3wp.exe instances using IIS 6 application pools. A Web garden mode is also supported. Requests are routed to the W3wp.exe process instance directly from Http.sys which runs in kernel mode. By default, the process runs under the Network Service account but can be configured.
Aspnet_state.exe	An optional Windows service used to store session state for ASP.NET applications. It can run on the Web server or on a remote machine (required for Web farm scenarios). Runs under the Network Service account but can be configured using the Services snap-in.

Isolating Applications by Identity

You can isolate ASP.NET Web applications from an operating system identity standpoint by controlling the account identity used to run each application. If each application uses a separate fixed account identity, you can authorize and audit each application separately.

Note If you host an ASP.NET Web application built using the .NET Framework version 1.0, the process account needs appropriate permissions to the root of the current file system drive. For more information, see Microsoft Knowledge Base article 317955, "FIX: 'Failed to Start Monitoring Directory Changes' Error Message When You Browse to an ASP.NET Page."

There are two ways to use separate fixed identities for each application on a shared Web server:

- **Anonymous account impersonation**
- **Fixed identity impersonation**

Anonymous Account Impersonation

With anonymous account impersonation, your application impersonates the anonymous account specified by IIS and configured for your application's virtual directory. You can use this approach if your application authenticates users independently of IIS, for example, by using Forms or Microsoft Passport authentication. In these scenarios, you can isolate the application by using a fixed anonymous account. Once the caller is authenticated and roles are checked, the trusted server model can be used for downstream resource access, where the configured anonymous account provides the trusted identity.

To support this approach, the application's virtual directories in IIS must support anonymous access and a separate anonymous account must be configured for each application. The application must then be configured for impersonation. This approach is shown in Figure 20.3. Local and remote resource access assumes the security context of the impersonated anonymous account.

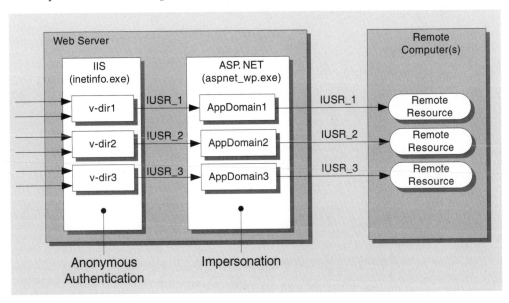

Figure 20.3

Multiple anonymous accounts used for each application

► **To use multiple anonymous accounts for resource access**

This procedure describes how to use multiple anonymous accounts, one per Web application, for resource access to support individual application authorization and auditing.

1. Create new anonymous user accounts, one per application.

   For more information about creating an anonymous user account, see the "Accounts" section in Chapter 16, "Securing Your Web Server."

   If you need to access remote resources using the anonymous account, either use a least privileged domain account, or use a local account and create a duplicated local account on the remote server with a matching user name and password.

2. Use **<location>** tags in Machine.config to configure each Web application for impersonation.

   ```
   <location path="Web Site Name/VDirName" allowOverride="false" >
     <system.web>
       <identity impersonate="true" />
     <system.web>
   <location>
   ```

   The **allowOverride="false"** setting prevents an individual application from overriding this setting in a Web.config file. For more information about the **<location>** element, see "Machine.config and Web.config Explained" in Chapter 19, "Securing Your ASP.NET Application and Web Services."

3. Use Internet Services Manager to configure each application's virtual directory to use a separate anonymous user account.

   a. Start Internet Services Manager from the Administrative Tools program group.

   b. Select the application's application directory, right-click and then click **Properties**.

   c. Click the **Security** tab and then click the **Edit** button.

   d. Ensure **Anonymous access** is selected and click **Edit**.

   e. Enter the user name for the anonymous account that you have created, or click **Browse** to select the user name from a list.

   f. If you want to use the account to access a remote resource, clear the **Allow IIS to Control Password** checkbox for the anonymous account.

   If you select **Allow IIS to Control Password**, the logon session created using the specified anonymous account has NULL network credentials and cannot be used to access network resources where authentication is required. If you clear this checkbox, the logon session is an interactive logon session with network credentials. However, if the account is local to the machine, no other machine on the network can authenticate the account. In this scenario, create a duplicate account on the target remote server.

> **Note**   The type of logon session created is controlled by the **LogonMethod** IIS Metabase
> setting. The default is an interactive logon session, which requires the account to have the
> "Allow Log on Locally" user privilege.
>
> The **Allow IIS to Control Password** option is not available on IIS 6. IIS 6 sets the default
> **LogonMethod** to **Network Cleartext**, which requires the account to have the "Access this
> computer from the network" user privilege. This allows the account to be authenticated by a
> network server.

4. Configure NTFS permissions for each account to ensure that each account has
   access only to the appropriate file system files and folders, and cannot access
   critical resources such as operating system tools.

   For more information about configuring NTFS permissions for the anonymous
   account, see Chapter 16, "Securing Your Web Server."

> **Note**   If you run the IISLockdown wizard, it creates a **Web Anonymous Users** group. Members of
> this group are denied access to system directories and tools.

Fixed Identity Impersonation

When you need IIS to authenticate users for your application, for example by using
Integrated Windows authentication or certificate authentication, you can use a fixed
impersonation identity to execute your ASP.NET application. This scenario is shown
in Figure 20.4.

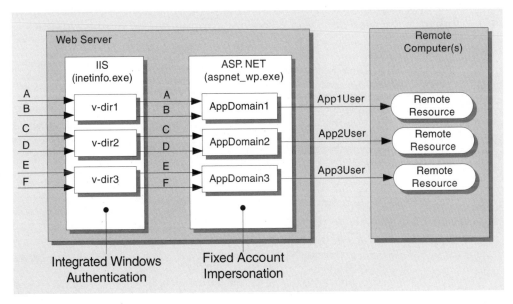

Figure 20.4
Applications impersonate a fixed account and use that to access resources

You can configure individual ASP.NET applications to impersonate a fixed account. The advantage of this configuration is that it can be used with any IIS authentication method, and does not require IIS anonymous authentication.

▶ **To use multiple fixed impersonation accounts for resource access**

This procedure describes how to use multiple fixed impersonation accounts, one per Web application, for resource access to support individual application authorization and auditing.

1. Create new anonymous user accounts, one per application.

   For more information about creating an anonymous user account, see the "Accounts" section in Chapter 16, "Securing Your Web Server."

   If you need access to remote resources using the anonymous account, either use a least privileged domain account, or use a local account and create a duplicated local account on the remote server with a matching user name and password.

2. Store the encrypted account credentials in the registry.

   Run Aspnet_setreg.exe to store the new account's encrypted credentials in the registry. For more information, see Microsoft Knowledge Base article 329290, "How To: Use the ASP.NET Utility to Encrypt Credentials and Session State Connection Strings."

3. Configure Web applications for impersonation.

   You can do this in Machine.config or Web.config. To configure multiple applications with different identities, use **<location>** tags in Machine.config. The output of Aspnet_setreg.exe run in the previous step shows you the required format of the **userName** and **password** attribute values for the **<identity>** element. Some examples are shown below.

```
<location path="Web Site Name/appvDir1" allowOverride="false" >
  <system.web>
    <identity impersonate="true"
            userName=
        "registry:HKLM\SOFTWARE\YourApp1\identity\ASPNET_SETREG,userName"
            password=
        "registry:HKLM\SOFTWARE\YourApp1\identity\ASPNET_SETREG,password"/>
  </system.web>
</location>

<location path="Web Site Name/appvDir2" allowOverride="false" >
  <system.web>
    <identity impersonate="true"
            userName=
        "registry:HKLM\SOFTWARE\YourApp2\identity\ASPNET_SETREG,userName"
            password=
        "registry:HKLM\SOFTWARE\YourApp2\identity\ASPNET_SETREG,password"/>
  </system.web>
</location>
```

To configure impersonation at the application level, use an **<identity>** element in the application's Web.config file as shown below.

```
<identity impersonate="true"
    userName="registry:HKLM\SOFTWARE\YourApp\identity\ASPNET_SETREG,userName"
    password="registry:HKLM\SOFTWARE\YourApp\identity\ASPNET_SETREG,password"/>
```

4. Configure NTFS permissions for each account to ensure that each account has access only to the appropriate file system files and folders, and no access to critical resources such as operating system tools.

   For more information about configuring NTFS permissions for the anonymous account, see Chapter 16, "Securing Your Web Server."

Note On Windows 2000 and the .NET Framework version 1.0, if you impersonate a fixed identity by using the above configuration, you must grant the "Act as part of the operating system" privilege to the ASP.NET process account used to run your Web applications. This is contrary to the principle of least privilege. You are recommended to upgrade to the .NET Framework version 1.1 where this is no longer a requirement.

Isolating Applications with Application Pools

If your applications run on Windows Server 2003, you can use application pools and configure each application to run in its own worker process that provides process-level isolation. By default, all applications run in a default application pool. With application pools, you can configure each process to run using a separate identity and, as a result, you do not need to use impersonation.

▶ **To provide process level isolation**

1. Create a set of new Windows accounts, one per application to run each worker process instance.

2. Configure NTFS permissions for each account to ensure that each account only has access to the appropriate file system files and folders, and cannot access critical resources such as operating system tools.

   For more information about configuring NTFS permissions for the anonymous account, see Chapter 16, "Securing Your Web Server."

3. Disable Web application impersonation.

   You can do this in Machine.config or Web.config. To disable impersonation for multiple applications in Machine.config, place **<identity>** elements inside **<location>** elements as shown below.

Use the following configuration. This configuration does not impersonate.

```
<location path="Web Site Name/appvDir1" allowOverride="false" >
  <system.web>
    <identity impersonate="false"
  </system.web>
</location>
```

Note   ASP.NET applications do not impersonate by default.

---

4. Create new application pools and configure them to run under the new accounts.

   Use IIS 6 to create new application pools with default settings, and use the accounts created in step 1 to configure the identity of each pool, so that each pool runs using a separate identity.

5. Configure each application to run in its own application pool.

   On the **Directory** tab of each IIS application, choose the application pool for the application to run in.

Isolating Applications with Code Access Security

With version 1.1 of the .NET Framework, you can configure applications to run at partial trust levels, using the **<trust>** element. The following configuration shows how to configure an application's trust level from Machine.config. In this example, the Medium trust level is used.

```
<location path="Web Site Name/appvDir1" allowOverride="false">
  <system.web>
    <trust level="Medium" originUrl="" />
  </system.web>
</location>
```

If you configure an application to run with a trust level other than "Full," the application has restricted code access security permissions to access specific types of resources. In this way, you can constrain applications to prevent them from interacting with one another and from gaining access to system level resources such as restricted areas of the file system, the registry, the event log, and so on.

For more information about the ASP.NET trust levels and how they can be used to provide application isolation and about application specific design and development considerations, see Chapter 9, "Using Code Access Security with ASP.NET."

Note   If you use code access security to provide application isolation, you should still consider the operating system identity of the application. The recommended isolation model is to use code access security together with process level isolation on Windows Server 2003.

Forms Authentication Issues

If you use Forms authentication with version 1.0 of the .NET Framework, you should use separate cookie paths and names. If you do not do so, it is possible for a user authenticated in one application to make a request to another application without being redirected to that application's logon page. The URL authorization rules within the second application may deny access to the user, without providing the opportunity to supply logon credentials using the logon form.

To avoid this issue, use unique cookie path and name attributes on the **<forms>** element for each application, and also use separate machine keys for each application.

Version 1.1 of the .NET Framework supports the **IsolateApps** setting shown below.

```
<machineKey validationKey="AutoGenerate,IsolateApps"
            decryptionKey="AutoGenerate,IsolateApps" validation="SHA1"/>
```

This ensures that each application on the machine uses a separate key for encryption and validation of Forms authentication cookies and view state.

With version 1.0 of the .NET Framework, you cannot use **IsolateApps** and you must manually generate **<machineKey>** elements. For more information about this issue, see the following articles in the Microsoft Knowledge Base.

- 313116, "PRB: Forms Authentication Requests Are Not Directed to loginUrl Page"
- 312906, "How To: Create Keys by Using Visual C# .NET for Use in Forms Authentication"

UNC Share Hosting

If you run an application with its content on a Universal Naming Convention (UNC) share, the credentials used to access the share are either the credentials of the application or of the authenticated client. This is configured in IIS by an administrator.

When an application is configured in this manner, ASP.NET impersonates the security context of the token it receives from IIS. This is not configurable with the **<identity>** tag unless explicit credentials are provided.

With version 1.0 of the .NET Framework, use Mscorcfg.msc to create a code group based on the URL and to grant it full trust.

When you use a virtual directory that points to a remote share to host an ASP.NET application, you may receive a security exception. For more information, see Microsoft Knowledge Base article 320268, "PRB: System.Security.SecurityException: Security error."

Summary

If you host multiple ASP.NET applications on a single Web server, you need to consider how applications are isolated from one another and from shared system resources such as the file system, registry, and event logs. Without adequate isolation, a rogue or badly developed application can adversely affect other applications on the server.

On Windows Server 2003, use the multiple worker process model supported by IIS 6 to provide operating system process isolation for applications. On Windows 2000, process isolation is not possible, although multiple applications can be configured to use separate anonymous user accounts. This provides separate application auditing and supports independent application authorization.

On both platforms you can use the resource constraint model provided by code access security as an additional control to restrict which applications have access to which resource types. The use of code access security with ASP.NET applications requires version 1.1 of the .NET Framework.

For more information about securing ASP.NET applications, see Chapter 19, "Securing Your ASP.NET Applications and Web Services."

Part V

Assessing Your Security

In This Part:

- Security Code Review
- Security Deployment Review

21

Code Review

In This Chapter

- Identifying cross-site scripting (XSS), SQL injection, buffer overflow, and other common vulnerabilities
- Identifying poor coding techniques that allow malicious users to launch attacks
- Security questions to ask so that you can locate problems quickly
- Evaluating security issues specific to individual .NET Framework technologies

Overview

Code reviews should be a regular part of your development process. Security code reviews focus on identifying insecure coding techniques and vulnerabilities that could lead to security issues. The review goal is to identify as many potential security vulnerabilities as possible before the code is deployed. The cost and effort of fixing security flaws at development time is far less than fixing them later in the product deployment cycle.

This chapter helps you review managed ASP.NET Web application code built using the Microsoft .NET Framework. In addition, it covers reviewing calls to unmanaged code. The chapter is organized by functional area, and includes sections that present general code review questions applicable to all types of managed code as well as sections that focus on specific types of code such as Web services, serviced components, data access components, and so on.

This chapter shows the questions to ask to expose potential security vulnerabilities. You can find solutions to these questions in the individual building chapters in Part III of this guide. You can also use the code review checklists in the "Checklists" section of the guide to help you during the review process.

FxCop

A good way to start the review process is to run your compiled assemblies through the FxCop analysis tool. The tool analyzes binary assemblies (not source code) to ensure that they conform to the .NET Framework Design Guidelines, available on MSDN. It also checks that your assemblies have strong names, which provide tamperproofing and other security benefits. The tool comes with a predefined set of rules, although you can customize and extend them.

For more information, see the following resources:

● To download the FxCop tool, see *http://www.gotdotnet.com/team/libraries/default.aspx.*

● To get help and support for the tool, see *http://www.gotdotnet.com/community /messageboard/MessageBoard.aspx?ID=234.*

● For the list of security rules that FxCop checks for, see *http://www.gotdotnet.com /team/libraries/FxCopRules/SecurityRules.aspx.*

● For the .NET Framework Design Guidelines, see *http://msdn.microsoft.com/library /default.asp?url=/library/en-us/cpgenref/html/cpconnetframeworkdesignguidelines.asp.*

Performing Text Searches

To assist the review process, check that you are familiar with a text search tool that you can use to locate strings in files. This type of tool allows you to quickly locate vulnerable code. Many of the review questions presented later in the chapter indicate the best strings to search for when looking for specific vulnerabilities.

You may already have a favorite search tool. If not, you can use the **Find in Files** facility in Visual Studio .NET or the **Findstr** command line tool, which is included with the Microsoft Windows operating system.

Note   If you use the Windows XP Search tool from Windows Explorer, and use the **A word or phrase in the file** option, check that you have the latest Windows XP service pack, or the search may fail. For more information, see Microsoft Knowledge Base article 309173, "Using the 'A Word or Phrase in the File' Search Criterion May Not Work."

Search for Hard-Coded Strings

Before you perform a detailed line-by-line analysis of your source code, start with a quick search through your entire code base to identify hard-coded passwords, account names, and database connection strings. Scan through your code and search for common string patterns such as the following: "key," "secret," "password," "pwd," and "connectionstring."

For example, to search for the string "password" in the Web directory of your application, use the **Findstr** tool from a command prompt as follows:

```
findstr /S /M /I /d:c:\projects\yourweb "password" *.*
```

Findstr uses the following command-line parameters:

- **/S**—include subdirectories.
- **/M**—list only the file names.
- **/I**—use a case insensitive search.
- **/D:**_dir_—search a semicolon-delimited list of directories. If the file path you want to search includes spaces, surround the path in double quotes.

Automating Findstr

You can create a text file with common search strings. **Findstr** can then read the search strings from the text file, as shown below. Run the following command from a directory that contains .aspx files.

```
findstr /N /G:SearchStrings.txt *.aspx
```

/N prints the corresponding line number when a match is found. **/G** indicates the file that contains the search strings. In this example, all ASP.NET pages (*.aspx) are searched for strings contained within SearchStrings.txt.

ILDASM

You can also use the **Findstr** command in conjunction with the ildasm.exe utility to search binary assemblies for hard-coded strings. The following command uses ildasm.exe to search for the **ldstr** intermediate language statement, which identifies string constants. Notice how the output shown below reveals a hard-coded database connection and the password of the well known **sa** account.

```
Ildasm.exe secureapp.dll /text | findstr ldstr
    IL_000c:  ldstr        "RegisterUser"
    IL_0027:  ldstr        "@userName"
    IL_0046:  ldstr        "@passwordHash"
    IL_0065:  ldstr        "@salt"
       IL_008b:  ldstr        "Exception adding account. "
    IL_000e:  ldstr        "LookupUser"
    IL_0027:  ldstr        "@userName"
       IL_007d:  ldstr         "SHA1"
       IL_0097:  ldstr         "Exeception verifying password. "
    IL_0009:  ldstr        "SHA1"
    IL_003e:  ldstr        "Logon successful: User is authenticated"
    IL_0050:  ldstr        "Invalid username or password"
    IL_0001:  ldstr        "Server=AppServer;database=users; username='sa'
                            password=password"
```

Note   Ildasm.exe is located in the \Program Files\Microsoft Visual Studio .NET 2003\SDK\v1.1 \bin folder. For more information about the supported command-line arguments, run **ildasm.exe /?**.

Cross-Site Scripting (XSS)

Your code is vulnerable to cross-site scripting (XSS, also referred to as CSS) attacks wherever it uses input parameters in the output HTML stream returned to the client. Even before you conduct a code review, you can run a simple test to check if your application is vulnerable to XSS. Search for pages where user input information is sent back to the browser.

XSS bugs are an example of maintaining too much trust in data entered by a user. For example, your application might expect the user to enter a price, but instead the attacker includes a price and some HTML and JavaScript. Therefore, you should always ensure that data that comes from untrusted sources is validated. When reviewing code, always ask the question, "Is this data validated?" Keep a list of all entry points into your ASP.NET application, such as HTTP headers, query strings, form data, and so on, and make sure that all input is checked for validity at some point. Do not test for incorrect input values because that approach assumes that you are aware of all potentially risky input. The most common way to check that data is valid in ASP.NET applications is to use regular expressions.

You can perform a simple test by typing text such as "XYZ" in form fields and testing the output. If the browser displays "XYZ" or if you see "XYZ" when you view the source of the HTML, then your Web application is vulnerable to XSS. If you want to see something more dynamic, inject **<script>alert('hello');</script>**. This technique might not work in all cases because it depends on how the input is used to generate the output.

The following process helps you to identify common XSS vulnerabilities:

- **Identify code that outputs input**.
- **Identify potentially dangerous HTML tags and attributes**.
- **Identify code that handles URLs**.
- **Check that output is encoded**.
- **Check for correct character encoding**.
- **Check the validateRequest attribute**.
- **Check the HttpOnly cookie option**.
- **Check the <frame> security attribute**.
- **Check the use of the innerText and innerHTML properties**.

Identify Code That Outputs Input

View the page output source from the browser to see if your code is placed inside an attribute. If it is, inject the following code and retest to view the output.

```
"onmouseover= alert('hello');"
```

A common technique used by developers is to filter for < and > characters. If the code that you review filters for these characters, then test using the following code instead:

```
&{alert('hello');}
```

If the code does not filter for those characters, then you can test the code by using the following script:

```
<script>alert(document.cookie);</script>;
```

You may have to close a tag before using this script, as shown below.

```
"></a><script>alert(document.cookie);</script>
```

Searching for ".Write"

Search for the ".Write" string across .aspx source code and code contained in any additional assembly you have developed for your application. This locates occurrences of **Response.Write**, and any internal routines that may generate output through a response object variable, such as the code shown below.

```
public void WriteOutput(Response respObj)
{
    respObj.Write(Request.Form["someField"]);
}
```

You should also search for the "<%=" string within .aspx source code, which can also be used to write output, as shown below:

```
<%=myVariable %>
```

The following table shows some common situations where **Response.Write** is used with input fields.

Table 21.1   Possible Sources of Input

Input Source	Examples
Form Fields	`Response.Write(name.Text);` `Response.Write(Request.Form["name"]);`
Query Strings	`Response.Write(Request.QueryString["name"]);`
Cookies	`Response.Write(` `        Request.Cookies["name"].Values["name"]);`
Session and Application variables	`Response.Write(Session["name"]);` `Response.Write(Application["name"]);`
Databases and data stores	`SqlDataReader reader = cmd.ExecuteReader();` `Response.Write(reader.GetString(1));`

Identify Potentially Dangerous HTML Tags and Attributes

While not exhaustive, the following commonly used HTML tags could allow a malicious user to inject script code:

- \<applet\>
- \<body\>
- \<embed\>
- \<frame\>
- \<script\>
- \<frameset\>
- \<html\>
- \<iframe\>
- \<img\>
- \<style\>
- \<layer\>
- \<ilayer\>
- \<meta\>
- \<object\>

HTML attributes such as **src**, **lowsrc**, **style**, and **href** can be used in conjunction with the tags above to cause XSS.

For example, the **src** attribute of the \<img\> tag can be a source of injection as shown in the following examples.

```
<IMG SRC="javascript:alert('hello');">
<IMG SRC="java&#010;script:alert('hello');">
<IMG SRC="java&#X0A;script:alert('hello');">
```

The \<style\> tag also can be a source of injection by changing the MIME type as shown below.

```
<style TYPE="text/javascript">
alert('hello');
</style>
```

Check to see if your code attempts to sanitize input by filtering out certain known risky characters. Do not rely upon this approach because malicious users can generally find an alternative representation to bypass your validation. Instead, your code should validate for known secure, safe input. The following table shows various ways to represent some common characters:

Table 21.2 Character Representation

Characters	Decimal	Hexadecimal	HTML Character Set	Unicode
" (double quotes)	&#34	&#x22;	&quot;	\u0022
' (single quotes)	&#39	&#x27;	&apos;	\u0027
& (ampersand)	&#38;	&#x26	&amp;	\u0026
< (lesser than)	&#60	&#x3C;	&lt;	\u003c
> (greater than)	&#62	&#x3E;	&gt;	\u003e

Identify Code That Handles URLs

Code that handles URLs can be vulnerable. Review your code to see if it is vulnerable to the following common attacks:

- If your Web server is not up-to-date with the latest security patches, it could be vulnerable to directory traversal and double slash attacks, such as:

```
http://www.YourWebServer.com/..%255%../winnt
http://www.YourWebServer.com/..%255%.//somedirectory
```

- If your code filters for "/", an attacker can easily bypass the filter by using an alternate representation for the same character. For example, the overlong UTF-8 representation of "/" is "%c0f%af" and this could be used in the following URL:

```
http://www.YourWebServer.com/..%c0f%af../winnt
```

- If your code processes query string input, check that it constrains the input data and performs bounds checks. Check that the code is not vulnerable if an attacker passes an extremely large amount of data through a query string parameter.

```
http://www.YourWebServer.com/test.aspx?var=InjectHugeAmountOfDataHere
```

Check That Output Is Encoded

While not a replacement for checking that input is well-formed and correct, you should check that **HtmlEncode** is used to encode HTML output that includes any type of input. Also check that **UrlEncode** is used to encode URL strings. Input data can come from query strings, form fields, cookies, HTTP headers, and input read from a database, particularly if the database is shared by other applications. By encoding the data, you prevent the browser from treating the HTML as executable script.

Check for Correct Character Encoding

To help prevent attackers using canonicalization and multi-byte escape sequences to trick your input validation routines, check that the character encoding is set correctly to limit the way in which input can be represented.

Check that the application Web.config file has set the **requestEncoding** and **responseEncoding** attributes configured by the **<globalization>** element as shown below.

```
<configuration>
   <system.web>
      <globalization
         requestEncoding="ISO-8859-1"
         responseEncoding="ISO-8859-1"/>
   </system.web>
</configuration>
```

Character encoding can also be set at the page level using a **<meta>** tag or **ResponseEncoding** page-level attribute as shown below.
```
<% @ Page ResponseEncoding="ISO-8859-1" %>
```

For more information, see Chapter 10, "Building Secure ASP.NET Pages and Controls."

Check the validateRequest Attribute

Web applications that are built using the .NET Framework version 1.1 perform input filtering to eliminate potentially malicious input, such as embedded script. Do not rely on this, but use it for defense in depth. Check the **<pages>** element in your configuration file to confirm that the **validateRequest** attribute is set to **true**. This can also be set as a page-level attribute. Scan your .aspx source files for **validateRequest**, and check that it is not set to **false** for any page.

Check the HttpOnly Cookie Option

Internet Explorer 6 SP 1 supports a new **HttpOnly** cookie attribute that prevents client-side script from accessing the cookie from the **document.cookie** property. Instead, an empty string is returned. The cookie is still sent to the server whenever the user browses to a Web site in the current domain. For more information, see the "Cross-Site Scripting" section in Chapter 10, "Building Secure ASP.NET Pages and Controls."

Check the <frame> Security Attribute

Internet Explorer 6 and later supports a new **security** attribute on the **<frame>** and **<iframe>** elements. You can use the **security** attribute to apply the user's Restricted Sites Internet Explorer security zone settings to an individual **frame** or **iframe**. For more information, see the "Cross-Site Scripting" section in Chapter 10, "Building Secure ASP.NET Pages and Controls."

Check the Use of the innerText and innerHTML Properties

If you create a page with untrusted input, verify that you use the **innerText** property instead of **innerHTML**. The **innerText** property renders content safe and ensures that script is not executed.

More Information

For more information about XSS, see the following articles:

- "CSS Quick Start: What Customers Can Do to Protect Themselves from Cross-Site Scripting," at *http://www.microsoft.com/technet/treeview/default.asp?url=/technet /security/news/crsstQS.asp*
- "CSS Overview," at *http://www.microsoft.com/technet/treeview/default.asp?url=/technet /security/news/csoverv.asp*.
- Microsoft Knowledge Base article 252985, "How To: Prevent Cross-Site Scripting Security Issues"
- "CERT Advisory CA-2000-02, Malicious HTML Tags Embedded in Client Web Requests," on the CERT/CC Web site at *http://www.cert.org/advisories /CA-2000-02.html*
- "Understanding Malicious Content Mitigation for Web Developers," on the CERT/CC Web site at *http://www.cert.org/tech_tips/malicious_code_mitigation.html/*

SQL Injection

Your code is vulnerable to SQL injection attacks wherever it uses input parameters to construct SQL statements. As with XSS bugs, SQL injection attacks are caused by placing too much trust in user input and not validating that the input is correct and well-formed.

The following process helps you locate SQL injection vulnerabilities:

1. Look for code that accesses the database.

   Scan for the strings "SqlCommand," "OleDbCommand," or "OdbcCommand."

2. Check whether the code uses parameterized stored procedures.

   Stored procedures alone cannot prevent SQL injection attacks. Check that your code uses parameterized stored procedures. Check that your code uses typed parameter objects such as **SqlParameter**, **OleDbParameter**, or **OdbcParameter**. The following example shows the use of a **SqlParameter**:

```
SqlDataAdapter myCommand = new SqlDataAdapter("spLogin", conn);
myCommand.SelectCommand.CommandType = CommandType.StoredProcedure;
SqlParameter parm = myCommand.SelectCommand.Parameters.Add(
                            "@userName", SqlDbType.VarChar,12);
parm.Value=txtUid.Text;
```

   The typed SQL parameter checks the type and length of the input and ensures that the *userName* input value is treated as a literal value and not as executable code in the database.

3. Check that your code uses parameters in SQL statements.

   If you do not use stored procedures, check that your code uses parameters in the SQL statements it constructs, as shown in the following example:

```
select status from Users where UserName=@userName
```

   Check that the following approach is *not* used, where the input is used directly to construct the executable SQL statement using string concatenation:

```
string sql = "select status from Users where UserName='"
        + txtUserName.Text + "'";
```

4. Check whether or not your code attempts to filter input.

   A common approach is to develop filter routines to add escape characters to characters that have special meaning to SQL. This is an unsafe approach, and you should not rely on it because of character representation issues.

Buffer Overflows

When you review code for buffer overflows, focus your review efforts on your code that calls unmanaged code through the P/Invoke or COM interop layers. Managed code itself is significantly less susceptible to buffer overflows because array bounds are automatically checked whenever an array is accessed. As soon as you call a Win32 DLL or a COM object, you should inspect the API calls closely.

The following process helps you to locate buffer overflow vulnerabilities:

1. Locate calls to unmanaged code.

   Scan your source files for "System.Runtime.InteropServices," which is the namespace name used when you call unmanaged code.

2. Check the string parameters passed to unmanaged APIs.

   These parameters are a primary source of buffer overflows. Check that your code checks the length of any input string to verify that it does not exceed the limit defined by the API. If the unmanaged API accepts a character pointer, you may not know the maximum allowable string length unless you have access to the unmanaged source. A common vulnerability is shown in the following code fragment:

   ```
   void SomeFunction( char *pszInput )
   {
     char szBuffer[10];
     // Look out, no length checks. Input is copied straight into the buffer
     // Should check length or use strncpy.
     strcpy(szBuffer, pszInput);
     . . .
   }
   ```

   Note Buffer overflows can still occur if you use **strncpy** because it does not check for sufficient space in the destination string and it only limits the number of characters copied.

   If you cannot inspect the unmanaged code because you do not own it, rigorously test the API by passing in deliberately long input strings and invalid arguments.

3. Check file path lengths.

   If the unmanaged API accepts a file name and path, check that your wrapper method checks that the file name and path do not exceed 260 characters. This is defined by the Win32 **MAX_PATH** constant. Also note that directory names and registry keys can be 248 characters maximum.

4. Check output strings.

   Check if your code uses a **StringBuilder** to receive a string passed back from an unmanaged API. Check that the capacity of the **StringBuilder** is long enough to hold the longest string the unmanaged API can hand back, because the string coming back from unmanaged code could be of arbitrary length.

5. Check array bounds.

   If you use an array to pass input to an unmanaged API, check that the managed wrapper verifies that the array capacity is not exceeded.

6. Check that your unmanaged code is compiled with the /GS switch.

   If you own the unmanaged code, use the **/GS** switch to enable stack probes to detect some kinds of buffer overflows.

Managed Code

Use the review questions in this section to analyze your entire managed source code base. The review questions apply regardless of the type of assembly. This section helps you identify common managed code vulnerabilities. For more information about the issues raised in this section and for code samples that illustrate vulnerabilities, see Chapter 7, "Building Secure Assemblies."

If your managed code uses explicit code access security features, see "Code Access Security" later in this chapter for additional review points. The following review questions help you to identify managed code vulnerabilities:

- **Is your class design secure?**
- **Do you create threads?**
- **Do you use serialization?**
- **Do you use reflection?**
- **Do you handle exceptions?**
- **Do you use cryptography?**
- **Do you store secrets?**
- **Do you use delegates?**

Is Your Class Design Secure?

An assembly is only as secure as the classes and other types it contains. The following questions help you to review the security of your class designs:

- **Do you limit type and member visibility?**

  Review any type or member marked as **public** and check that it is an intended part of the public interface of your assembly.

- **Are non-base classes sealed?**

  If you do not intend a class to be derived from, use the **sealed** keyword to prevent your code from being misused by potentially malicious subclasses.

  For public base classes, you can use code access security inheritance demands to limit the code that can inherit from the class. This is a good defense in depth measure.

- **Do you use properties to expose fields?**

  Check that your classes do not directly expose fields. Use properties to expose non-private fields. This allows you to validate input values and apply additional security checks.

- **Do you use read-only properties?**

  Verify that you have made effective use of read-only properties. If a field is not designed to be set, implement a read-only property by providing a **get** accessor only.

- **Do you use virtual internal methods?**

  These methods can be overridden from other assemblies that have access to your class. Use declarative checks or remove the **virtual** keyword if it is not a requirement.

- **Do you implement IDisposable?**

  If so, check that you call the **Dispose** method when you are finished with the object instance to ensure that all resources are freed.

Do You Create Threads?

Multithreaded code is prone to subtle timing-related bugs or race conditions that can result in security vulnerabilities. To locate multithreaded code, search source code for the text "Thread" to identify where new **Thread** objects are created, as shown in the following code fragment:

```
Thread t = new Thread(new ThreadStart(someObject.SomeThreadStartMethod));
```

The following review questions help you to identify potential threading vulnerabilities:

- **Does your code cache the results of a security check?**

    Your code is particularly vulnerable to race conditions if it caches the results of a security check, for example in a static or global variable, and then uses the flag to make subsequent security decisions.

- **Does your code impersonate?**

    Is the thread that creates a new thread currently impersonating? The new thread always assumes the process-level security context and not the security context of the existing thread.

- **Does your code contain static class constructors?**

    Check static class constructors to check that they are not vulnerable if two or more threads access them simultaneously. If necessary, synchronize the threads to prevent this condition.

- **Do you synchronize Dispose methods?**

    If an object's **Dispose** method is not synchronized, it is possible for two threads to execute **Dispose** on the same object. This can present security issues, particularly if the cleanup code releases unmanaged resource handlers such as file, process, or thread handles.

Do You Use Serialization?

Classes that support serialization are either marked with the **SerializableAttribute** or derive from **ISerializable**. To locate classes that support serialization, perform a text search for the "Serializable" string. Then, review your code for the following issues:

- **Does the class contain sensitive data?**

    If so, check that the code prevents sensitive data from being serialized by marking the sensitive data with the [**NonSerialized**] attribute by or implementing **ISerializable** and then controlling which fields are serialized.

    If your classes need to serialize sensitive data, review how that data is protected. Consider encrypting the data first.

- **Does the class implement ISerializable?**

    If so, does your class support only full trust callers, for example because it is installed in a strong named assembly that does not include **AllowPartiallyTrustedCallersAttribute**? If your class supports partial-trust callers, check that the **GetObjectData** method implementation authorizes the calling code by using an appropriate permission demand. A good technique is to use a **StrongNameIdentityPermission** demand to restrict which assemblies can serialize your object.

- **Does your class validate data streams?**

  If your code includes a method that receives a serialized data stream, check that every field is validated as it is read from the data stream.

Do You Use Reflection?

To help locate code that uses reflection, search for "System.Reflection" — this is the namespace that contains the reflection types. If you do use reflection, review the following questions to help identify potential vulnerabilities:

- **Do you dynamically load assemblies?**

  If your code loads assemblies to create object instances and invoke types, does it obtain the assembly or type name from input data? If so, check that the code is protected with a permission demand to ensure all calling code is authorized. For example, use a **StrongNameIdentity** permission demand or demand full trust.

- **Do you create code dynamically at runtime?**

  If your assemblies dynamically generate code to perform operations for a caller, check that the caller is in no way able to influence the code that is generated. For example, does your code generation rely on caller-supplied input parameters? This should be avoided, or if it is absolutely necessary, make sure that the input is validated and that it cannot be used to adversely affect code generation.

- **Do you use reflection on other types?**

  If so, check that only trusted code can call you. Use code access security permission demands to authorize calling code.

Do You Handle Exceptions?

Secure exception handling is required for robust code, to ensure that sufficient exception details are logged to aid problem diagnosis and to help prevent internal system details being revealed to the client. Review the following questions to help identify potential exception handling vulnerabilities:

- **Do you fail early?**

  Check that your code fails early to avoid unnecessary processing that consumes resources. If your code does fail, check that the resulting error does not allow a user to bypass security checks to run privileged code.

- **How do you handle exceptions?**

  Avoid revealing system or application details to the caller. For example, do not return a call stack to the end user. Wrap resource access or operations that could generate exceptions with try/catch blocks. Only handle the exceptions you know how to handle and avoid wrapping specific exceptions with generic wrappers.

- **Do you log exception details?**

    Check that exception details are logged at the source of the exception to assist problem diagnosis.

- **Do you use exception filters?**

    If so, be aware that the code in a filter higher in the call stack can run before code in a **finally** block. Check that you do not rely on state changes in the **finally** block, because the state change will not occur before the exception filter executes.

    For an example of an exception filter vulnerability, see "Exception Management" in Chapter 7, "Building Secure Assemblies."

Do You Use Cryptography?

If so, check that your code does not implement its own cryptographic routines. Instead, code should use the **System.Security.Cryptography** namespace or use Win32 encryption such as Data Protection Application Programming Interface (DPAPI). Review the following questions to help identify potential cryptography related vulnerabilities:

- **Do you use symmetric encryption?**

    If so, check that you use Rijndael (now referred to as Advanced Encryption Standard [AES]) or Triple Data Encryption Standard (3DES) when encrypted data needs to be persisted for long periods of time. Use the weaker (but quicker) RC2 and DES algorithms only to encrypt data that has a short lifespan, such as session data.

- **Do you use the largest key sizes possible?**

    Use the largest key size possible for the algorithm you are using. Larger key sizes make attacks against the key much more difficult, but can degrade performance.

- **Do you use hashing?**

    If so, check that you use MD5 and SHA1 when you need a principal to prove it knows a secret that it shares with you. For example, challenge-response authentication systems use a hash to prove that the client knows a password without having the client pass the password to the server. Use HMACSHA1 with Message Authentication Codes (MAC), which require you and the client to share a key. This can provide integrity checking and a degree of authentication.

- **Do you generate random numbers for cryptographic purposes?**

    If so, check that your code uses the **System.Security.Cryptography.RNGCryptoServiceProvider** class to generate random numbers, and not the **Random** class. The **Random** class does not generate truly random numbers that are not repeatable or predictable.

Do You Store Secrets?

If your assembly stores secrets, review the design to check that it is absolutely necessary to store the secret. If you have to store a secret, review the following questions to do so as securely as possible:

- **Do you store secrets in memory?**

  Do not store secrets in plaintext in memory for prolonged periods. Retrieve the secret from a store, decrypt it, use it, and then substitute zeros in the space where the secret is stored.

- **Do you store plaintext passwords or SQL connection strings in Web.config or Machine.config?**

  Do not do this. Use aspnet_setreg.exe to store encrypted credentials in the registry on the **<identity>**, **<processModel>**, and **<sessionState>** elements. For information on obtaining and using Aspnet_setreg.exe, see Microsoft Knowledge Base article 329290, "How To: Use the ASP.NET Utility to Encrypt Credentials and Session State."

- **How do you encrypt secrets?**

  Check that the code uses DPAPI to encrypt connection strings and credentials. Do not store secrets in the Local Security Authority (LSA), as the account used to access the LSA requires extended privileges. For information on using DPAPI, see "How To: Create a DPAPI Library" in the "How To" section of "Microsoft *patterns & practices* Volume I, *Building Secure ASP.NET Applications: Authentication, Authorization, and Secure Communication*" at *http://msdn.microsoft.com/library /default.asp?url=/library/en-us/dnnetsec/html/SecNetHT07.asp*.

- **Do you store secrets in the registry?**

  If so, check that they are first encrypted and then secured with a restricted ACL if they are stored in **HKEY_LOCAL_MACHINE**. An ACL is not required if the code uses **HKEY_CURRENT_USER** because this is automatically restricted to processes running under the associated user account.

- **Are you concerned about reverse engineering?**

  If so, consider an obfuscation tool. For more information, see the list of obfuscator tools listed at *http://www.gotdotnet.com/team/csharp/tools/default.aspx*.

Note Do not rely on an obfuscation tool to hide secret data. Obfuscation tools make identifying secret data more difficult but do not solve the problem.

Do You Use Delegates?

Any code can associate a method with a delegate. This includes potentially malicious code running at a lower trust level than your code.

- **Do you accept delegates from untrusted sources?**

  If so, check that you restrict the code access permissions available to the delegate methods by using security permissions with **SecurityAction.PermitOnly**.

- **Do you use assert before calling a delegate?**

  Avoid this because you do not know what the delegate code is going to do in advance of calling it.

Code Access Security

All managed code is subject to code access security permission demands. Many of the issues are only apparent when your code is used in a partial trust environment, when either your code or the calling code is not granted full trust by code access security policy.

For more information about the issues raised in this section, see Chapter 8, "Code Access Security in Practice."

Use the following review points to check that you are using code access security appropriately and safely:

- **Do you support partial-trust callers?**
- **Do you restrict access to public types and members?**
- **Do you use declarative security?**
- **Do you call Assert?**
- **Do you use permission demands when you should?**
- **Do you use link demands?**
- **Do you use Deny or PermitOnly?**
- **Do you use particularly dangerous permissions?**
- **Do you compile with the /unsafe option?**

Do You Support Partial-Trust Callers?

If your code supports partial-trust callers, it has even greater potential to be attacked and as a result it is particularly important to perform extensive and thorough code reviews. Review the **<trust>** level configuration setting in your Web application to see if it runs at a partial-trust level. If it does, the assemblies you develop for the application need to support partial-trust callers.

The following questions help you to identify potentially vulnerable areas:

- **Is your assembly strong named?**

    If it is, then default security policy ensures that it cannot be called by partially trusted callers. The Common Language Runtime (CLR) issues an implicit link demand for full trust. If your assembly is not strong named, it can be called by any code unless you take explicit steps to limit the callers, for example by explicitly demanding full trust.

    Note Strong named assemblies called by ASP.NET applications must be installed in the Global Assembly Cache.

- **Do you use APTCA?**

    If your strong named assembly contains **AllowPartiallyTrustedCallersAttribute**, partially trusted callers can call your code. In this situation, check that any resource access or other privileged operation performed by your assembly is authorized and protected with other code access security demands. If you use the .NET Framework class library to access resources, full stack walking demands are automatically issued and will authorize calling code unless your code has used an **Assert** call to prevent the stack walk.

- **Do you hand out object references?**

    Check method returns and **ref** parameters to see where your code returns object references. Check that your partial-trust code does not hand out references to objects obtained from assemblies that require full-trust callers.

Do You Restrict Access to Public Types and Members?

You can use code access security identity demands to limit access to public types and members. This is a useful way of reducing the attack surface of your assembly.

- **Do you restrict callers by using identity demands?**

    If you have classes or structures that you only intend to be used within a specific application by specific assemblies, you can use an identity demand to limit the range of callers. For example, you can use a demand with a **StrongNameIdentityPermission** to restrict the caller to a specific set of assemblies that have a have been signed with a private key that corresponds to the public key in the demand.

- **Do you use inheritance demands to restrict subclasses?**

    If you know that only specific code should inherit from a base class, check that the class uses an inheritance demand with a **StrongNameIdentityPermission**.

Do You Use Declarative Security Attributes?

Declarative security attributes can be displayed with tools such as Permview.exe. This greatly helps the consumers and administrators of your assemblies to understand the security requirements of your code.

- **Do you request minimum permissions?**

  Search for ".RequestMinimum" strings to see if your code uses permission requests to specify its minimum permission requirements. You should do this to clearly document the permission requirements of your assembly.

- **Do you request optional or refuse permissions?**

  Search for ".RequestOptional" and ".RequestRefuse" strings. If you use either of these two actions to develop least privileged code, be aware that your code can no longer call strong named assemblies unless they are marked with the **AllowPartiallyTrustedCallersAttribute**.

- **Do you use imperative security instead of declarative security?**

  Sometime imperative checks in code are necessary because you need to apply logic to determine which permission to demand or because you need a runtime variable in the demand. If you do not need specific logic, consider using declarative security to document the permission requirements of your assembly.

- **Do you mix class and member level attributes?**

  Do not do this. Member attributes, for example on methods or properties, replace class-level attributes with the same security action and do not combine with them.

Do You Call Assert?

Scan your code for **Assert** calls. This may turn up instances of **Debug.Assert**. Look for where your code calls **Assert** on a **CodeAccessPermission** object. When you assert a code access permission, you short-circuit the code access security permission demand stack walk, which is a risky practice. What steps does your code take to ensure that malicious callers do not take advantage of the assertion to access a secured resource or privileged operation? Review the following questions:

- **Do you use the demand, assert pattern?**

  Check that your code issues a **Demand** prior to the **Assert**. Code should demand a more granular permission to authorize callers prior to asserting a broader permission such as the unmanaged code permission.

- **Do you match Assert calls with RevertAssert?**

  Check that each call to **Assert** is matched with a call to **RevertAssert**. The **Assert** is implicitly removed when the method that calls **Assert** returns, but it is good practice to explicitly call **RevertAssert**, as soon as possible after the **Assert** call.

- **Do you reduce the assert duration?**

  Check that you only assert a permission for the minimum required length of time. For example, if you need to use an **Assert** call just while you call another method, check that you make a call to **RevertAssert** immediately after the method call.

Do You Use Permission Demands When You Should?

Your code is always subject to permission demand checks from the .NET Framework class library, but if your code uses explicit permission demands, check that this is done appropriately. Search your code for the ".Demand" string to identity declarative and imperative permission demands, and then review the following questions:

- **Do you cache data?**

  If so, check whether or not the code issues an appropriate permission demand prior to accessing the cached data. For example, if the data is obtained from a file, and you want to ensure that the calling code is authorized to access the file from where you populated the cache, demand a **FileIOPermission** prior to accessing the cached data.

- **Do you expose custom resources or privileged operations?**

  If your code exposes a custom resource or privileged operation through unmanaged code, check that it issues an appropriate permission demand, which might be a built-in permission type or a custom permission type depending on the nature of the resource.

- **Do you demand soon enough?**

  Check that you issue a permission demand prior to accessing the resource or performing the privileged operation. Do not access the resource and then authorize the caller.

- **Do you issue redundant demands?**

  Code that uses the .NET Framework class libraries is subject to permission demands. Your code does not need to issue the same demand. This results in a duplicated and wasteful stack walk.

Do You Use Link Demands?

Link demands, unlike regular demands, only check the immediate caller. They do not perform a full stack walk, and as a result, code that uses link demands is subject to luring attacks. For information on Luring Attacks, see "Link Demands" in Chapter 8, "Code Access Security in Practice."

Search your code for the ".LinkDemand" string to identify where link demands are used. They can only be used declaratively. An example is shown in the following code fragment:

```
[StrongNameIdentityPermission(SecurityAction.LinkDemand,
                             PublicKey="00240000048...97e85d098615")]
public static void SomeOperation() {}
```

For more information about the issues raised in this section, see "Link Demands" in Chapter 8, "Code Access Security in Practice." The following questions help you to review the use of link demands in your code:

- **Why are you using a link demand?**

  A defensive approach is to avoid link demands as far as possible. Do not use them just to improve performance and to eliminate full stack walks. Compared to the costs of other Web application performance issues such as network latency and database access, the cost of the stack walk is small. Link demands are only safe if you know and can limit which code can call your code.

- **Do you trust your callers?**

  When you use a link demand, you rely on the caller to prevent a luring attack. Link demands are safe only if you know and can limit the exact set of direct callers into your code, and you can trust those callers to authorize their callers.

- **Do you call code that is protected with link demands?**

  If so, does your code provide authorization by demanding a security permission from the callers of your code? Can the arguments passed to your methods pass through to the code that you call? If so, can they maliciously influence the code you call?

- **Have you used link demands at the method and class level?**

  When you add link demands to a method, it overrides the link demand on the class. Check that the method also includes class-level link demands.

- **Do you use link demands on classes that are not sealed?**

  Link demands are not inherited by derived types and are not used when an overridden method is called on the derived type. If you override a method that needs to be protected with a link demand, apply the link demand to the overridden method.

- **Do you use a link demand to protect a structure?**

  Link demands do not prevent the construction of a structure by an untrusted caller. This is because default constructors are not automatically generated for structures, and therefore the structure level link demand only applies if you use an explicit constructor.

- **Do you use explicit interfaces?**

    Search for the **Interface** keyword to find out. If so, check if the method implementations are marked with link demands. If they are, check that the interface definitions contain the same link demands. Otherwise, it is possible for a caller to bypass the link demand.

Do You Use Potentially Dangerous Permissions?

Check that the following permission types are only granted to highly trusted code. Most of them do not have their own dedicated permission type, but use the generic **SecurityPermission** type. You should closely scrutinize code that uses these types to ensure that the risk is minimized. Also, you must have a very good reason to use these permissions.

Table 21.3 Dangerous Permissions

Permission	Description
SecurityPermission.UnmanagedCode	Code can call unmanaged code.
SecurityPermission.SkipVerification	The code in the assembly no longer has to be verified as type safe.
SecurityPermission.ControlEvidence	The code can provide its own evidence for use by security policy evaluation.
SecurityPermission.ControlPolicy	Code can view and alter policy.
SecurityPermission.SerializationFormatter	Code can use serialization.
SecurityPermission.ControlPrincipal	Code can manipulate the principal object used for authorization.
ReflectionPermission.MemberAccess	Code can invoke private members of a type through reflection.
SecurityPermission.ControlAppDomain	Code can create new application domains.
SecurityPermission.ControlDomainPolicy	Code can change domain policy.

Do You Compile With the /unsafe Option?

Use Visual Studio .NET to check the project properties to see whether **Allow Unsafe Code Blocks** is set to **true**. This sets the **/unsafe** compiler flag, which tells the compiler that the code contains unsafe blocks and requests that a minimum **SkipVerification** permission is placed in the assembly.

If you compiled with **/unsafe**, review why you need to do so. If the reason is legitimate, take extra care to review the source code for potential vulnerabilities.

Unmanaged Code

Give special attention to code that calls unmanaged code, including Win32 DLLs and COM objects, due to the increased security risk. Unmanaged code is not verifiably type safe and introduces the potential for buffer overflows. Resource access from unmanaged code is not subject to code access security checks. This is the responsibility of the managed wrapper class.

Generally, you should not directly expose unmanaged code to partially trusted callers. For more information about the issues raised in this section, see the "Unmanaged Code" sections in Chapter 7, "Building Secure Assemblies," and Chapter 8, "Code Access Security in Practice."

Use the following review questions to validate your use of unmanaged code:

- **Do you assert the unmanaged code permission?**

  If so, check that your code demands an appropriate permission prior to calling the **Assert** method to ensure that all callers are authorized to access the resource or operation exposed by the unmanaged code. For example, the following code fragment shows how to demand a custom Encryption permission and then assert the unmanaged code permission:

  ```
  // Demand custom EncryptionPermission.
  (new EncryptionPermission(
          EncryptionPermissionFlag.Encrypt, storeFlag)).Demand();
  // Assert the unmanaged code permission.
  (new SecurityPermission(SecurityPermissionFlag.UnmanagedCode)).Assert();
  // Now use P/Invoke to call the unmanaged DPAPI functions.
  ```

  For more information see "Assert and RevertAssert" in Chapter 8, "Code Access Security in Practice."

- **Do you use SuppressUnmanagedCodeAttribute?**

  This attribute suppresses the demand for the unmanaged code permission issued automatically when managed code calls unmanaged code. If **P/Invoke** methods or COM interop interfaces are annotated with this attribute, ensure that all code paths leading to the unmanaged code calls are protected with security permission demands to authorize callers. Also check that this attribute is used at the method level and not at the class level.

Note   Adding a **SuppressUnmanagedCodeSecurityAttribute** turns the implicit demand for the **UnmanagedCode** permission issued by the interop layer into a **LinkDemand**. Your code is vulnerable to luring attacks.

- **Is the unmanaged entry point publicly visible?**

  Check that your unmanaged code entry point is marked as **private** or **internal**. Callers should be forced to call the managed wrapper method that encapsulates the unmanaged code.

- **Do you guard against buffer overflows?**

  Unmanaged code is susceptible to input attacks such as buffer overflows. Unmanaged code APIs should check the type and length of supplied parameters. However, you cannot rely on this because you might not own the unmanaged source. Therefore, the managed wrapper code must rigorously inspect input and output parameters. For more information, see "Buffer Overflows" in this chapter.

Note   All code review rules and disciplines that apply to C and C++ apply to unmanaged code.

- **Do you range check enumerated types?**

  Verify that all enumerated values are in range before you pass them to a native method.

- **Do you use naming conventions for unmanaged code methods?**

  All unmanaged code should be inside wrapper classes that have the following names: **NativeMethods**, **UnsafeNativeMethods**, and **SafeNativeMethods**. You must thoroughly review all code inside **UnsafeNativeMethods** and parameters that are passed to native APIs for security vulnerabilities.

- **Do you call potentially dangerous APIs?**

  You should be able to justify the use of all Win32 API calls. Dangerous APIs include:

  - Threading functions that switch security context
  - Access token functions, which can make changes to or disclose information about a security token
  - Credential management functions, including functions that creates tokens
  - Crypto API functions that can decrypt and access private keys
  - Memory Management functions that can read and write memory
  - LSA functions that can access system secrets

ASP.NET Pages and Controls

Use the review questions in this section to review your ASP.NET pages and controls. For more information about the issues raised in this section, see Chapter 10, "Building Secure ASP.NET Pages and Controls."

- Do you disable detailed error messages?
- Do you disable tracing?
- Do you validate form field input?
- Are you vulnerable to XSS attacks?
- Do you validate query string and cookie input?
- Do you rely on HTTP headers for security?
- Do you secure view state?
- Do you prevent XSS?
- Are your global.asax event handlers secure?
- Do you provide adequate authorization?

Do You Disable Detailed Error Messages?

If you let an exception propagate beyond the application boundary, ASP.NET can return detailed information to the caller. This includes full stack traces and other information that is useful to an attacker. Check the **<customErrors>** element and ensure that the mode attribute is set to **"On"** or **"RemoteOnly"**.

```
<customErrors mode="On" defaultRedirect="YourErrorPage.htm" />
```

Do You Disable Tracing?

Trace information is also extremely useful to attackers. Check the **<trace>** element to ensure that tracing is disabled.

```
<trace enabled="false" localOnly="true" pageOutput="false"
       requestLimit="10" traceMode="SortByTime"/>
```

Do You Validate Form Field Input?

Attackers can pass malicious input to your Web pages and controls through posted form fields. Check that you validate all form field input including hidden form fields. Validate them for type, range, format, and length. Use the following questions to review your ASP.NET input processing:

- **Does your input include a file name or file path?**

  You should generally avoid this because it is a high risk operation. Why do you need the user to specify a file name or path, rather than the application choosing the location based on the user identity?

  If you accept file names and paths as input, your code is vulnerable to canonicalization bugs. If you must accept path input from the user, then check that it is validated as a safe path and canonicalized. Check that the code uses **System.IO.Path.GetFullPath**.

- **Do you call MapPath?**

  If you call **MapPath** with a user supplied file name, check that your code uses the override of **HttpRequest.MapPath** that accepts a **bool** parameter, which prevents cross-application mapping.

```
try
{
  string mappedPath = Request.MapPath( inputPath.Text,
                                  Request.ApplicationPath, false);
}
catch (HttpException)
{
  // Cross application mapping attempted.
}
```

  For more information see, section "Using MapPath" in Chapter 10, "Building Secure ASP.NET Pages and Controls."

- **How do you validate data types?**

  Check that your code validates the data type of the data received from posted form fields and other forms of Web input such as query strings. For non-string data, check that your code uses the .NET Framework type system to perform the type checks. You can convert the string input to a strongly typed object, and capture any type conversion exceptions. For example, if a field contains a date, use it to construct a **System.DateTime** object. If it contains an age in years, convert it to a **System.Int32** object by using **Int32.Parse** and capture format exceptions.

- **How do you validate string types?**

  Check that input strings are validated for length and an acceptable set of characters and patterns by using regular expressions. You can use a **RegularExpressionValidator** validation control or use the **RegEx** class directly. Do not search for invalid data; only search for the information format you know is correct.

- **Do you use validation controls?**

  If you use a validation control such as **RegularExpressionValidator**, **RequiredFieldValidator**, **CompareValidator**, **RangeValidator**, or **CustomValidator,** check that you have not disabled the server side validation and are not relying purely on client-side validation.

- **Do you rely on client side validation?**

  Do not do this. Use client-side validation only to improve the user experience. Check that all input is validated at the server.

Are You Vulnerable to XSS Attacks?

Be sure to review your Web pages for XSS vulnerabilities. For more information, see "Cross-Site Scripting (XSS)" earlier in this chapter.

Do You Validate Query String and Cookie Input?

Check that your code validates input fields passed by URL query strings and input fields extracted from cookies. To locate vulnerable code search for the following text strings:

- "Request.QueryString"
- "Request.Cookies"

Check that input is validated for type, range, format, and length using typed objects, and regular expressions as you would for form fields (see the previous section, "Do You Validate Form Field Input?"). Also consider HTML or URL encoding any output derived from user input, as this will negate any invalid constructs that could lead to XSS bugs.

Do You Secure View State?

If your application uses view state, is it tamperproof? Review the following questions:

- **Is view state protection enabled at the application level?**

    Check the **enableViewState** attribute of the **<pages>** element in the application Machine.config or Web.config file to see if view state is enabled at the application level. Then check that **enableViewStateMac** is set to **"true"** to ensure it is tamperproof.

    ```
    <pages enableViewState="true" enableViewStateMac="true" />
    ```

- **Do you override view state protection on a per page basis?**

    Check the page-level directive at the top of your Web pages to verify that view state is enabled for the page. Look for the **enableViewStateMac** setting and if present check that it is set to **"true"**. If **enableViewStateMac** is not present and set to **true**, the page assumes the application-level default setting specified in the Web.config file. If you have disabled view state for the page by setting **enableViewState** to **"false"** the protection setting is irrelevant.

- **Do you override view state protection in code?**

    Check that your code does not disable view state protection by setting **Page.EnableViewStateMac** property to **false**. This is a safe setting only if the page does not use view state.

Are Your Global.asax Event Handlers Secure?

The global.asax file contains event handling code for application-level events generated by ASP.NET and by HTTP modules. Review the following event handlers to ensure that the code does not contain vulnerabilities:

- **Application_Start**. Code placed here runs under the security context of the ASP.NET process account, not the impersonated user.

- **Application_BeginRequest**. Code placed here runs under the security context of the ASP.NET process account, or the impersonated user.

- **Application_EndRequest**. If you need to modify the properties of outgoing cookies, for example to set the "Secure" bit or the domain, **Application_EndRequest** is the right place to do it.

- **Application_AuthenticateRequest**. This performs user authentication.

- **Application_Error**. The security context when this event handler is called can have an impact on writing the Windows event log. The security context might be the process account or the impersonated account.

- **protected void Session_End**. This event is fired non-deterministically and only for in-process session state modes.

Do You Provide Adequate Authorization?

Review the following questions to verify your authorization approach:

- **Do you partition your Web site between restricted and public access areas?**
  If your Web application requires users to complete authentication before they can access specific pages, check that the restricted pages are placed in a separate directory from publicly accessible pages. This allows you to configure the restricted directory to require SSL. It also helps you to ensure that authentication cookies are not passed over unencrypted sessions using HTTP.

- **How do you protect access to restricted pages?**
  If you use Windows authentication, have you configured NTFS permissions on the page (or the folder that contains the restricted pages) to allow access only to authorized users?

  Have you configured the **<authorization>** element to specify which users and groups of users can access specific pages?

- **How do you protect access to page classes?**
  Have you use added principal permission demands to your classes to determine which users and groups of users can access the classes?

- **Do you use Server.Transfer?**
  If you use **Server.Transfer** to transfer a user to another page, ensure that the currently authenticated user is authorized to access the target page. If you use **Server.Transfer** to a page that the user is not authorized to view, the page is still processed.

  Server.Transfer uses a different module to process the page rather than making another request from the server, which would force authorization. Do not use **Server.Transfer** if security is a concern on the target Web page. Use **HttpResponse.Redirect** instead.

Web Services

ASP.NET Web services share many of the same features as ASP.NET Web applications. Review your Web service against the questions in the "ASP.NET Pages and Controls" section before you address the following questions that are specific to Web services. For more information about the issues raised in this section, see Chapter 12, "Building Secure Web Services."

- **Do you expose restricted operations or data?**
- **How do you authorize callers?**
- **Do you constrain privileged operations?**
- **Do you use custom authentication?**
- **Do you validate all input?**
- **Do you validate SOAP Headers?**

Do You Expose Restricted Operations or Data?

If your Web service exposes restricted operations or data, check that the service authenticates callers. You can use platform authentication mechanisms such as NTLM, Kerberos, Basic authentication or Client X.509 Certificates, or you can pass authentication tokens in SOAP headers.

If you pass authentication tokens, you can use the Web Services Enhancements (WSE) to use SOAP headers in a way that conforms to the emerging WS-Security standard.

How Do You Authorize Callers?

Choose appropriate authorization schemes provided by either .NET Framework (such as URL authorization, File authorization, .NET Roles) or platform options such as File ACLs.

Do You Constrain Privileged Operations?

The trust level of the code access security policy determines the type of resource the Web service can access. Check the **<trust>** element configuration in Machine.config or Web.config.

Do You Use Custom Authentication?

Use features provided by Web Service Enhancements (WSE) instead of creating your own authentication schemes.

Do You Validate All Input?

Check that all publicly exposed Web methods validate their input parameters if the input is received from sources outside the current trust boundary, before using them or passing them to a downstream component or database.

Do You Validate SOAP Headers?

If you use custom SOAP headers in your application, check that the information is not tampered or replayed. Digitally sign the header information to ensure that it has not been tampered. You can use the WSE to help sign Web service messages in a standard manner.

Check that **SoapException** and **SoapHeaderException** objects are used to handle errors gracefully and to provide minimal required information to the client. Verify that exceptions are logged appropriately for troubleshooting purposes.

Serviced Components

This section identifies the key review points that you should consider when you review the serviced components used inside Enterprise Services applications. For more information about the issues raised in this section, see Chapter 11, "Building Secure Serviced Components."

- Do you use assembly level metadata?
- Do you prevent anonymous access?
- Do you use a restricted impersonation level?
- Do you use role-based security?
- Do you use method level authorization?
- Do you use object constructor strings?
- Do you audit in the middle tier?

Do You Use Assembly Level Metadata?

Check that you use assembly level metadata to define Enterprise Services security settings. Use the assemblyinfo.cs file and use attributes to define authentication and authorization configuration. This helps to ensure that the settings are established correctly at administration time. Although the administrator can override these settings, it provides the administrator with a clear definition of how you expect the settings to be configured.

Do You Prevent Anonymous Access?

Check that your code specifies an authentication level using the **ApplicationAccessControl** attribute. Search for the "AuthenticationOption" string to locate the relevant attribute. Check that you use at least call-level authentication to ensure that each call to your component is authenticated.

```
[assembly: ApplicationAccessControl(
              Authentication = AuthenticationOption.Call)]
```

Do You Use a Restricted Impersonation Level?

The impersonation level you define for your serviced components determines the impersonation capabilities of any remote server that you communicate with. Search for the "ImpersonationLevel" string to check that your code sets the level.

```
[assembly: ApplicationAccessControl(
              ImpersonationLevel=ImpersonationLevelOption.Identify)]
```

Check that you set the most restricted level necessary for the remote server. For example, if the server needs to identify you for authentication purposes, but does not need to impersonate you, use the identify level as shown above. Use delegation-level impersonation with caution on Windows 2000 because there is no limit to the number of times that your security context can be passed from computer to computer. Windows Server 2003 introduces constrained delegation.

Note In Windows Server 2003 and Windows 2000 Service Pack 4 and later, the impersonation privilege is not granted to all users.

If your components are in a server application, the assembly level attribute shown above controls the initial configuration for the component when it is registered with Enterprise Services.

If your components are in a library application, the client process determines the impersonation level. If the client is an ASP.NET Web application, check the **comImpersonationLevel** setting on the **<processModel>** element in the Machine.config file.

Do You Use Role-Based Security?

Check that your code uses role-based security correctly to prevent unauthorized access by reviewing the following questions:

- **Is role-based security enabled?**

  Check that role-based security is enabled. It is disabled by default on Windows 2000. Check that your code includes the following attribute:

  ```
  [assembly: ApplicationAccessControl(true)]
  ```

- **Do you use component level access checks?**

  COM+ roles are most effective if they are used at the interface, component, or method levels and are not just used to restrict access to the application. Check that your code includes the following attribute:

  ```
  [assembly: ApplicationAccessControl(AccessChecksLevel=
              AccessChecksLevelOption.ApplicationComponent)]
  ```

  Also check that each class is annotated with **ComponentAccessControl** attribute as follows:

  ```
  [ComponentAccessControl(true)]
  public class YourServicedComponent : ServicedComponent
  {
  }
  ```

- **Do you perform role checks in code?**

  If your method code calls **ContextUtil.IsCallerInRole**, check that these calls are preceded with calls to **ContextUtil.IsSecurityEnabled**. If security is not enabled, **IsCallerInRole** always returns **true**. Check that your code returns a security exception if security is not enabled.

Do You Use Object Constructor Strings?

Search your code for "ConstructionEnabled" to locate classes that use object construction strings.

```
[ConstructionEnabled(Default="")]
public class YourServicedComponent : ServicedComponent, ISomeInterface
```

If you use object constructor strings, review the following questions:

- **Do you store sensitive data in constructor strings?**

  If you store data such as connection strings, check that the data is encrypted prior to storage in the COM+ catalog. Your code should then decrypt the data when it is passed to your component through the **Construct** method.

- **Do you provide default construction strings?**

  Do not do this if the data is in any way sensitive.

Do You Audit in the Middle Tier

You should audit across the tiers of your distributed application. Check that your service components log operations and transactions. The original caller identity is available through the **SecurityCallContext** object. This is only available if the security level for your application is configured for process and component-level checks by using the following attribute:

```
[assembly: ApplicationAccessControl(AccessChecksLevel=
            AccessChecksLevelOption.ApplicationComponent)]
```

Remoting

This section identifies the key review points that you should consider when you review code that uses .NET Remoting. For more information about the issues raised in this section, see Chapter 13, "Building Secure Remoted Components."

- **Do you pass objects as parameters?**
- **Do you use custom authentication and principal objects?**
- **How do you configure proxy credentials?**

Do You Pass Objects as Parameters?

If you use the **TcpChannel** and your component API accepts custom object parameters, or if custom objects are passed through the call context, your code has two security vulnerabilities.

- If the object passed as a parameter derives from **System.MarshalByRefObject**, it is passed by reference. In this case, the object requires a URL to support call backs to the client. It is possible for the client URL to be spoofed, which can result in a call back to an alternate computer.

- If the object passed as a parameter supports serialization, the object is passed by value. In this instance, check that your code validates each field item as it is deserialized on the server to prevent the injection of malicious data.

To prevent custom objects being passed to your remote component either by reference or by value, set the **TypeFilterLevel** property on your server-side formatter channel sink to **TypeFilterLevel.Low**.

To locate objects that are passed in the call context, search for the "ILogicalThreadAffinative" string. Only objects that implement this interface can be passed in the call context.

Do You Use Custom Authentication and Principal Objects?

If you use custom authentication, do you rely on principal objects passed from the client? This is potentially dangerous because malicious code could create a principal object that contains extended roles to elevate privileges. If you use this approach, check that you only use it with out-of-band mechanisms such as IPSec policies that restrict the client computers that can connect to your component.

How Do You Configure Proxy Credentials?

Review how your client code configures credentials on the remoting proxy. If explicit credentials are used, where are those credentials maintained? They should be encrypted and stored in a secure location such as a restricted registry key. They should not be hard-coded in plain text. Ideally, your client code should use the client process token and use default credentials.

Data Access Code

This section identifies the key review points that you should consider when you review your data access code. For more information about the issues raised in this section, see Chapter 14, "Building Secure Data Access."

- Do you prevent SQL injection?
- Do you use Windows authentication?
- Do you secure database connection strings?
- How do you restrict unauthorized code?
- How do you secure sensitive data in the database?
- Do you handle ADO .NET exceptions?
- Do you close database connections?

Do You Prevent SQL Injection?

Check that your code prevents SQL injection attacks by validating input, using least privileged accounts to connect to the database, and using parameterized stored procedures or parameterized SQL commands. For more information, see "SQL Injection" earlier in this chapter.

Do You Use Windows Authentication?

By using Windows authentication, you do not pass credentials across the network to the database server, and your connection strings do not contain user names and passwords. Windows authentication connection strings either use Trusted_Connection='Yes' or Integrated Security='SSPI' as shown in the following examples.

```
"server='YourServer'; database='YourDatabase' Trusted_Connection='Yes'"
"server='YourServer'; database='YourDatabase' Integrated Security='SSPI'"
```

Do You Secure Database Connection Strings?

Review your code for the correct and secure use of database connection strings. These strings should not be hard coded or stored in plaintext in configuration files, particularly if the connection strings include user names and passwords.

Search for the "Connection" string to locate instances of ADO .NET connection objects and review how the **ConnectionString** property is set.

- **Do you encrypt the connection string?**

    Check that the code retrieves and then decrypts an encrypted connection string. The code should use DPAPI for encryption to avoid key management issues.

- **Do you use a blank password?**

    Do not. Check that all SQL accounts have strong passwords.

- **Do you use the sa account or other highly privileged accounts?**

    Do not use the **sa** account or any highly privileged account, such as members of **sysadmin** or **db_owner** roles. This is a common mistake. Check that you use a least privileged account with restricted permissions in the database.

- **Do you use Persist Security Info?**

    Check that the **Persist Security Info** attribute is not set to **true** or **yes** because this allows sensitive information, including the user name and password, to be obtained from the connection after the connection has been opened.

How Do You Restrict Unauthorized Code?

If you have written a data access class library, how do you prevent unauthorized code from accessing your library to access the database? One approach is to use **StrongNameIdentityPermission** demands to restrict the calling code to only that code that has been signed with specific strong name private keys.

How Do You Secure Sensitive Data in the Database?

If you store sensitive data, such as credit card numbers, in the database, how do you secure the data? You should check that it is encrypted by using a strong symmetric encryption algorithm such as 3DES.

If you use this approach, how do you secure the 3DES encryption key? Your code should use DPAPI to encrypt the 3DES encryption key and store the encrypted key in a restricted location such as the registry.

Do You Handle ADO .NET Exceptions?

Check that all data access code is placed inside **try/catch** blocks and that the code handles the **SqlExceptions**, **OleDbExceptions** or **OdbcExceptions**, depending on the ADO .NET data provider that you use.

Do You Close Database Connections?

Check that your code is not vulnerable to leaving open database connections if, for example, exceptions occur. Check that the code closes connections inside a **finally** block or that the connection object is constructed inside a C# **using** statement as shown below. This automatically ensures that it is closed.

```
using ((SqlConnection conn = new SqlConnection(connString)))
{
  conn.Open();
  // Connection will be closed if an exception is generated or if control flow
  // leaves the scope of the using statement normally.
}
```

Summary

Security code reviews are similar to regular code reviews or inspections except that the focus is on the identification of coding flaws that can lead to security vulnerabilities. The added benefit is that the elimination of security flaws often makes your code more robust.

This chapter has shown you how to review managed code for top security issues including XSS, SQL injection, and buffer overflows. It has also shown you how to identify other more subtle flaws that can lead to security vulnerabilities and successful attacks.

Security code reviews are not a panacea. However, they can be very effective and should feature as a regular milestone in the development life cycle.

Additional Resource

For more information, see MSDN article, "Securing Coding Guidelines for the .NET Framework," at *http://msdn.microsoft.com/library/default.asp?url=/library/en-us/dnnetsec/html/seccodeguide.asp*.

22

Deployment Review

In This Chapter

- Reviewing network and host configuration
- Reviewing base Windows 2000 configuration
- Reviewing IIS and .NET Framework configuration
- Reviewing Web application and Web service configuration
- Reviewing Enterprise Services configuration
- Reviewing Remoting configuration
- Reviewing SQL Server configuration

Overview

Web application security is dependent upon the security of the underlying infrastructure on which the application is deployed. Weak network or host configuration settings result in vulnerabilities that can and will be exploited. The deployment review covered in this chapter inspects the configuration of the network and host. The host includes Windows 2000 Server and, depending on the server role, it can also include IIS, the Microsoft .NET Framework, Enterprise Services, and SQL Server.

The main configuration elements that are subject to the deployment review process are shown in Figure 22.1.

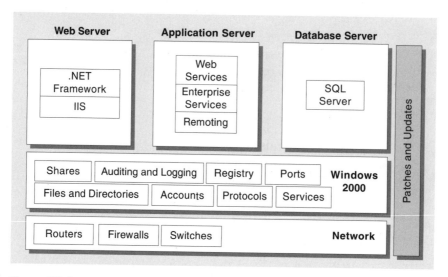

Figure 22.1
Core elements of a deployment review

Web Server Configuration

The goal for this phase of the review is to identify vulnerabilities in the configuration of the base operating system on your Web server. This does not include IIS configuration, which is dealt with separately. For further background information about the issues raised by the review questions in this section, see Chapter 16, "Securing Your Web Server."

To help focus and structure the review process, the review questions have been divided into the following configuration categories:

- **Patches and updates**
- **Services**
- **Protocols**
- **Accounts**
- **Files and directories**
- **Shares**
- **Ports**
- **Registry**
- **Auditing and logging**

Patches and Updates

Verify that your server is updated with the latest service packs and software patches. You need to separately check operating system components and the .NET Framework. Review the following questions:

- **Have you run MBSA?**

  Make sure you have run the MBSA tool to identify common Windows and IIS vulnerabilities, and to identify missing service packs and patches.

  Respond to the MBSA output by fixing identified vulnerabilities and by installing the latest patches and updates. For more information, see "Step 1. Patches and Updates" in Chapter 16, "Securing Your Web Server."

- **Have you installed .NET Framework updates?**

  To determine the current version of the .NET Framework, see Microsoft Knowledge Base article 318785, "INFO: Determining Whether Service Packs Are Installed on .NET Framework." Then compare the installed version of the .NET Framework against the current service pack. To do this, use the .NET Framework versions listed in article 318836, "INFO: How to Obtain the Latest .NET Framework Service Pack."

Services

Make sure that only the services that you require are enabled. Check that all others are disabled to reduce your server's attack profile. To see which services are running and enabled, use the Services and Applications Microsoft Management Console (MMC) snap-in available from Computer Management. To disable a service, make sure it is stopped and set its startup type to manual.

Review the following questions to verify your services configuration:

- **Do you run unnecessary services?**

  Review each service that is running by using the Services snap-in and confirm that each service is required. Identify why it is required and which solutions rely on it. Make sure all unnecessary services are disabled.

- **Have you disabled the Telnet service?**

  Telnet is often used for remote IIS administration. However, it is an insecure protocol susceptible to many attacks. Check that the Telnet service is disabled. For a more secure administration solution, use Terminal Services.

- **Have you disabled FTP, SMTP, and NNTP services?**

  These services are not secure protocols and have known vulnerabilities. If you do not need them, disable them. If you use them, find secure alternatives. These services are listed in the Services MMC snap-in as FTP Publishing Service, Simple Mail Transport Protocol (SMTP) and Network News Transport Protocol (NNTP).

  Note   IISLockdown disables these services.

- **Do you use the ASP.NET session state service?**

  To see whether your applications use this service, review the **<sessionState>** element in your application's Web.config file. If Web.config does not contain this element, check its setting in Machine.config. You use the session state service on your Web server if the **mode** attribute is set to "StateServer" and the **stateConnectionString** points to the local machine, for example with a localhost address as shown below:

  ```
  <sessionState mode="StateServer"
          stateConnectionString="tcpip=127.0.0.1:42424" />
  ```

  If you do not use the service on the Web server, disable it. It is listed as "ASP.NET State Service" in the Services MMC snap-in.

  For more information on how to secure ASP.NET session state, refer to "Session State" in Chapter 19, "Securing Your ASP.NET Application and Web Services."

Protocols

Review which protocols are enabled on your server and make sure that no unnecessary protocol is enabled. Use the following questions to help review protocols on your server:

- **Do you use WebDAV?**

  If you use the Web Distributed Authoring and Versioning protocol (WebDAV) to publish content then make sure it is secure. If you do not use it, disable the protocol.

  For information on how to secure WebDAV, see Microsoft Knowledge Base article 323470, "How To: Create a Secure WebDAV Publishing Directory." For information about disabling WebDAV, see article 241520, "How To Disable WebDAV for IIS 5.0."

- **Have you hardened the TCP/IP stack?**

  Make sure the TCP/IP stack is hardened to prevent network level denial of service attacks including SYN flood attacks. To check whether the stack is hardened on your server, use Regedt32.exe and examine the following registry key:

  ```
  HKLM\SYSTEM\CurrentControlSet\Services\Tcpip\Parameters
  ```

  The presence of the following child keys indicates a hardened TCP/IP stack: **SynAttackProtect, EnableICMPRedirect,** and **EnableDeadGWDetect.**

  For a full list of the required keys and the appropriate key values for a fully hardened stack, see "How To: Harden the TCP/IP Stack" in the "How To" section of this guide.

- **Have you disabled NetBIOS and SMB for internet facing network cards?**

  Check that NetBIOS over TCP/IP is disabled and that SMB is disabled to prevent host enumeration attacks. For more information, see "Protocols" in Chapter 16, "Securing Your Web Server."

Accounts

Review the use of all the Windows accounts on the server to make sure that no unnecessary accounts exist, and that all of the necessary accounts are configured with the minimum privileges and the required access rights. The following questions help you identify account vulnerabilities:

- **Have you deleted or disabled all unused accounts?**

  Perform an audit to verify that all your accounts are used and required. Delete or disable any unnecessary accounts. The local administrator account and **Guest** account cannot be deleted. You should disable the **Guest** account and rename the **Administrator** account, making sure it has a strong password.

- **Have you disabled the Guest account?**

  To check if the **Guest** account is disabled, display the **Users** folder in the Computer Management tool and check that the **Guest** account appears with a cross icon next to it. If it is not disabled, display its **Properties** dialog box and select **Account is disabled**.

- **Have you renamed the default administrator account?**

  The default local **administrator** account is a prime target for attack. Verify that you have renamed the **administrator** account and given it a strong password.

- **Have you created a custom anonymous Web account?**

  Check that the default **IUSR_MACHINE** account is disabled and that you have configured an alternate **anonymous user** account for use by your Web applications.

- **Do you use strong password policies?**

  Use the Local Security Policy tool to review password policy. For information about the recommended password policy, see "Step 5. Accounts" in Chapter 16, "Securing Your Web Server."

- **Do you restrict remote logons?**

  Check the user rights assignments within the Local Security Policy tool to ensure that the Everyone group is not granted the "Access this computer from the network" user right.

- **Have you disabled null sessions?**

  Check that null sessions are disabled to prevent anonymous (unauthenticated) sessions from being created with your server. To check this, run Regedt32.exe and confirm that the **RestrictAnonymous** key is set to 1 as shown below.

  ```
  HKLM\System\CurrentControlSet\Control\LSA\RestrictAnonymous=1
  ```

Files and Directories

The following review questions enable you to verify that you have used NTFS permissions appropriately to lock down accounts such as the anonymous Web user account.

- **Is IIS installed on an NTFS volume?**

  This allows you to use NTFS to configure ACLs on resources to restrict access. Do not build a server that uses FAT partitions.

- **Have you restricted the Everyone group?**

  Use Windows Explorer to ensure that the Everyone group does not have access to the following directories:

  - Root (:\)
  - System directory (\WINNT\system32)
  - Framework tools directory (\WINNT\Microsoft.NET\Framework\{version})
  - Web site root directory and all content directories (default is \inetpub*)

- **Have you restricted the anonymous Web user account?**

  Make sure that the anonymous Internet user account does not have the ability to write to Web content directories. Use Windows Explorer to view the ACL on each content directory. Also check the ACL on the %windir%\system32 directory to make sure that it cannot access system tools and utilities.

Note If you ran IISLockdown, the Web Anonymous Users group and the Web Applications group can be used to restrict access. By default, the Web Anonymous Users group contains the IUSR account and the Web Applications group contains Internet Web Application Manager (IWAM). From an administrative perspective, restricting access to a group is preferred to individual account restriction.

- **Have you secured or removed utilities and SDKs?**

  Verify that you have no utilities or software development kits (SDKs) on your server. Make sure that neither Visual Studio.NET nor any .NET Framework SDKs are installed. Also make sure that you have restricted access with NTFS permissions to powerful system tools such as At.exe, Cmd.exe, Net.exe, Pathping.exe, Regedit.exe, Regedt32.exe, Runonce.exe, Runas.exe, Telnet.exe, and Tracert.exe. Finally, make sure that no debugging tools are installed on the server. IISLockdown automatically restricts access to system tools by the Web Anonymous Users group and the Web Applications group.

- **Have you removed unused DSNs?**

  Verify that all unused data source names (DSNs) have been removed from the server because they can contain clear text database connection details.

Shares

Review the following questions to ensure that your server is not unnecessarily exposed by the presence of file shares:

- **What shares are available on your server?**

  To review shares and associated permissions, run the Computer Management MMC snap-in and select **Shares** beneath **Shared Folders**. Check that all the shares are required. Remove any unnecessary shares.

- **Can the Everyone group access shares?**

  Verify that the Everyone group is not granted access to your shares unless intended, and that specific permissions are configured instead.

- **Have you removed the administration shares?**

  If you do not allow remote administration of your server, then check that the administration shares, for example, C$ and IPC$ have been removed.

Ports

Review the ports that are active on your server to make sure that no unnecessary ports are available. To verify which ports are listening, run the following **netstat** command.

```
netstat -n -a
```

This command generates the following output:

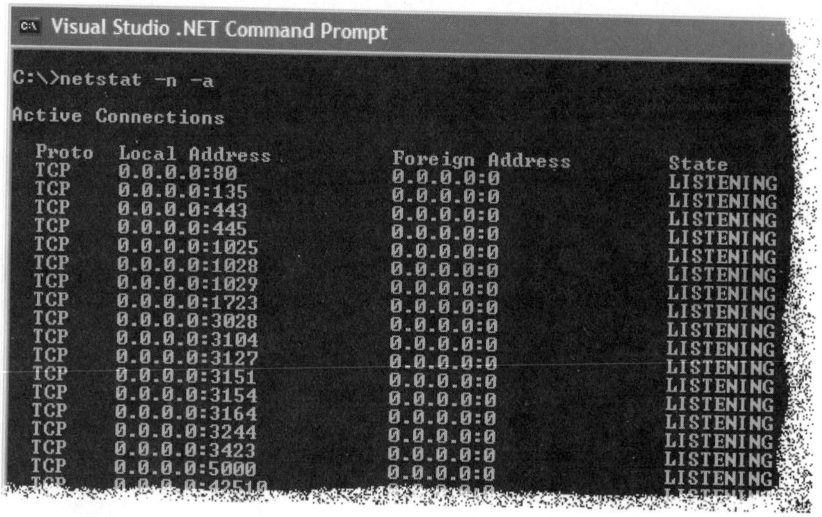

Figure 22.2
Netstat output

This output lists all the ports together with their addresses and current state. Make sure you know which services are exposed by each listening port and verify that each service is required. Disable any unused service.

To filter out specific string patterns from netstat output, use it in conjunction with the operating system findstr tool. The following example filters the output for ports in the "LISTENING" state.

```
netstat -n -a | findstr LISTENING
```

You can also use the Portqry.exe command line utility to verify the status of TCP/IP ports. For more information about the tool and how to download it, see Microsoft Knowledge Base article 310099, "Description of the Portqry.exe Command Line Utility."

Also review the following:

- **Internet-facing ports are restricted to TCP 80 and 443**.
- **Intranet traffic is restricted or encrypted**.

Registry

Review the security of your registry configuration with the following questions:

- **Have you restricted remote registry administration?**

  Use Regedt32.exe to review the ACL on the WinReg registry key, which controls whether or not the registry can be remotely accessed.

  ```
  HKEY_LOCAL_MACHINE\SYSTEM\CurrentControlSet\Control\SecurePipeServers\winreg
  ```

  By default in Windows 2000, remote registry access is restricted to members of the **Administrators** and **Backup operators** group. For maximum security, restrict all remote access to the registry by using an empty Discretionary Access Control List (DACL).

  Note Some services require remote access to the registry. See Microsoft Knowledge Base article 153183, "How to Restrict Access to the Registry from a Remote Computer," to see if your scenario demands limited remote registry access.

- **Have you secured the SAM?**

  This only applies to stand-alone servers. Check that you have restricted LMHash storage in the Security Account Manager (SAM) database by creating the key (not value) **NoLMHash** in the registry as follows:

  ```
  HKLM\System\CurrentControlSet\Control\LSA\NoLMHash
  ```

Auditing and Logging

Review your use of Windows auditing with the following questions.

- **Do you log all failed logon attempts?**

  Use the Local Security Policy tool to check that you have enabled the auditing of failed logon attempts.

- **Do you log all failed actions across the file system?**

  Use the Local Security Policy tool to check that you have enabled object access auditing. Then check that auditing has been enabled across the file system.

IIS Configuration

By reviewing and improving the security of IIS configuration settings, you are in effect reducing the attack surface of your Web server. For more information about the review points covered in this section, see Chapter 16, "Securing Your Web Server."

The review questions in this section have been organized by the following configuration categories.

- **IISLockdown**
- **URLScan**
- **Sites and virtual directories**
- **ISAPI filters**
- **IIS Metabase**
- **Server certificates**

IISLockdown

The IISLockdown tool identifies and turns off features to reduce the IIS attack surface area. To see if it has been run on your server, check for the following report generated by IISLockdown:

```
\WINNT\system32\inetsrv\oblt-rep.log
```

For more information about IISLockdown, see "How To: Use IISLockdown" in the "How To" section of this guide.

URLScan

URLScan is an ISAPI filter that is installed with IISLockdown. It helps prevent potentially harmful requests from reaching the server and causing damage. Check that it is installed and that it is configured appropriately.

▶ **To see if URLScan is installed**

1. Start **Internet Information Services**.
2. Right-click your server (not Web site) and then click **Properties**.
3. Click the **Edit** button next to **Master Properties**.
4. Click the **ISAPI Filters** tab and see if URLScan is listed.

To check the URLScan configuration, use Notepad to edit the following URLScan configuration file.

```
%WINDIR%\System32\Inetsrv\URLscan\Urlscan.ini
```

For more information about URLScan, see "How To: Use URLScan" in the "How To" section of this guide.

Sites and Virtual Directories

The review questions in this section relate to the specific configuration of your Web sites and the virtual directories of your applications. In this section, you review the following categories:

- Web site location
- Script mappings
- Anonymous Internet user accounts
- Auditing and logging
- Web permissions
- IP address and domain name restrictions
- Authentication
- Parent path setting
- Microsoft FrontPage Server extensions

Web Site Location

Check that your Web site root directory is installed on a non-system volume. By relocating your Web site root to a non-system volume, you prevent attackers who use directory traversal attacks from accessing the system tools and executables such as Cmd.exe.

Script Mappings

Check that you have mapped all unnecessary file extensions to the 404.dll, which is installed when you run IISLockdown.

▶ **To review script mappings**

1. Start **Internet Information Manager**.
2. Right-click your Web site and click **Properties**.
3. Click the **Home Directory** tab and then click the **Configuration** button within the **Application Settings** group.

Anonymous Internet User Accounts

Verify that your application is configured to use a non-default anonymous Internet user account. If you have multiple Web applications on your server, check that each application is configured to use a separate anonymous account. This allows you to configure permissions and to track activity on a per Web application basis.

Auditing and Logging

Check that you have configured IIS auditing to help detect attacks in progress and to diagnose attack footprints. The following review questions help identify vulnerabilities in IIS auditing:

- **Are log files located on a separate non-system volume?**

  Right click your Web site in IIS and click the **Web Site** tab. Click the **Properties** button to check the log file location. Check that the log files are located in a non-default location using a non-default name, preferably on a non-system volume.

- **Do you restrict access to the log files?**

  Use Windows Explorer to view the ACL on the log files directory. Check that the ACL grants Administrators and System full control but grants access to no other user.

Web Permissions

Review the default Web permissions configured for your Web site and for each virtual directory. Check that the following conditions are met:

- Include directories restrict Read permissions.
- Virtual directories for which anonymous access is allowed are configured to restrict Write and Execute permissions.
- Write permissions and script source access permissions are only granted to content folders that allow content authoring. Also check that folders that allow content authoring require authentication and Secure Sockets Layer (SSL) encryption.

IP Address and Domain Name Restrictions

Do you use IP and domain name restrictions to restrict access to your Web server? If so, have you considered the risks of IP spoofing?

Authentication

Check the authentication settings for your Web sites and virtual directories. Ensure that anonymous access is only supported for publicly accessible areas of your site. If you are selecting multiple authentication options, thoroughly test the effects and authentication-precedence on your application.

If Basic authentication is selected, check that SSL is used across the site to protect credentials.

Parent Path Setting

Check that you have disabled the parent path setting to prevent the use of ".."
in script and application calls to functions such as **MapPath**. This helps prevent
directory traversal attacks.

▶ **To review the parent paths setting**

1. Start **Internet Services Manager**.
2. Right-click your Web site, and click **Properties**.
3. Click the **Home Directory** tab.
4. Click **Configuration**.
5. Click the **App Options** tab.
6. Check that the **Enable parent paths** check box is clear.

FrontPage Server Extensions (FPSE)

FrontPage Server Extensions are used for accessing, authoring, and administering
the FrontPage-based Web site. Use the latest versions of these extensions to avoid
security vulnerabilities. If you do not use FPSE, disable them to reduce the attack
surface.

For more information, see "Step 11. Sites and Virtual Directories" in Chapter 16,
"Securing Your Web Server."

ISAPI Filters

Make sure that no unused ISAPI filters are installed to prevent any potential
vulnerabilities in these filters from being exploited.

▶ **To review ISAPI filters**

1. Start **Internet Information Manager**.
2. Right click your **server** (not Web site) and then click **Properties**.
3. Click the **Edit** button next to **Master Properties**.
4. Click the **ISAPI Filters** tab to view the installed filters.

IIS Metabase

The IIS Metabase contains IIS configuration settings, many but not all of which are configured through the IIS administration tool. The file itself must be protected and specific settings that cannot be maintained using the IIS configuration tool should be checked. Review the following questions to ensure appropriate metabase configuration:

- **Have you restricted access to the metabase?**

  Check that the ACL on the metabase file allows full control access to the system account and administrators. No other account should have access. The metabase file and location is:

  ```
  %windir%\system32\inetsrv\metabase.bin
  ```

- **Do you reveal internal IP addresses?**

  By default, IIS returns the internal IP address of your server in the Content-Location section of the HTTP response header. You should prevent this by setting the **UseHostName** metabase property to **true**. To check if it has been set, run the following command from the \inetpub\adminscripts directory:

  ```
  adsutil GET w3svc/UseHostName
  ```

  Confirm that the property value has been set to **true**. If the property is not set, this command returns the message "The parameter 'UseHostName' is not set at this node." For more information, see "Step 14. IIS Metabase" in Chapter 16, "Securing Your Web Server."

Server Certificates

If your applications use SSL, make sure that you have a valid certificate installed on your Web server. To view the properties of your server's certificate, click **View Certificate** on the **Directory Security** page of the **Properties** dialog of your Web site in IIS. Review the following questions:

- **Has your server certificate expired?**
- **Are all public keys in the certificate chain valid up to the trusted root?**
- **Has your certificate been revoked?**

  Check that it is not on a Certificate Revocation List (CRL) from the server that issued the certificate.

Machine.Config

The .NET Framework configuration for all applications on your server is maintained in Machine.config. For the purposes of the security review, this section examines the settings in Machine.config from top to bottom and considers only those settings that relate to security.

The majority of security settings are contained beneath the **<system.web>** element, with the notable exception of Web service configuration and .NET Remoting configuration. The review process for Web services and .NET Remoting configuration is presented later in this chapter.

For more information and background about the issues raised by the following review questions, see Chapter 19, "Securing Your ASP.NET Application and Web Services." The following elements are reviewed in this section:

- <trace>
- <httpRunTime>
- <compilation>
- <pages>
- <customErrors>

- <authentication>
- <identity>
- <authorization>
- <machineKey>
- <trust>

- <sessionState>
- <httpHandlers>
- <processModel>

<trace>

Make sure tracing is disabled with the following setting.

```
<trace enabled="false" ... />
```

<httpRunTime>

Verify the value of the **maxRequestLength** attribute on the **<httpRunTime>** element. You can use this value to prevent users from uploading very large files. The maximum allowed value is 4 MB.

<compilation>

Check that you do not compile debug binaries. Make sure the **debug** attribute is set to **false**.

```
<compilation debug="false" ... />
```

\<pages\>

The **\<pages\>** element controls default page level configuration settings. From a security perspective, review the view state and session state settings.

- **Do you use view state?**

    If **enableViewState** is set to **true**, make sure that **enableViewStateMac** is also set to **true** to protect the view state over the network. Also make sure that you review the **\<machineKey\>** configuration because this specifies the encryption and hashing algorithms to use together with the associated keys.

- **Do you use session state?**

    If **enableSessionState** is set to **true**, make sure you review the **\<sessionState\>** element configuration.

\<customErrors\>

Make sure that the **mode** attribute is set to **On** to ensure that detailed exception information is not disclosed to the client. Also check that a default error page is specified via the **defaultRedirect** attribute.

```
<customErrors mode="On" defaultRedirect="/apperrorpage.htm" />
```

\<authentication\>

This element governs your application's authentication mechanism. Check the **mode** attribute to see which authentication mechanism is configured and then use the specific review questions for your configured authentication mode.

```
<authentication mode="[Windows|Forms|Passport|None"] />
```

Forms Authentication

Review the following questions to verify your Forms authentication configuration.

- **Do you encrypt the authentication cookie?**

    Cookies should be encrypted and checked for integrity to detect tampering even over an SSL channel because cookies can be stolen through cross-site scripting (XSS) attacks. Check that the **protection** attribute of the **\<forms\>** element is set to **All**.

```
<forms protection="All" .../>   All indicates encryption and verification
```

- **Do you use SSL with Forms authentication?**

  SSL prevents session hijacking and cookie replay attacks. Check the **requireSSL** attribute of the **<forms>** element.

  ```
  <forms requireSSL="true" ... />
  ```

- **Do you limit authentication cookie lifetime?**

  Minimize the cookie timeout to limit the amount of time an attacker can use the cookie to access your application. Check the **timeout** attribute on the **<forms>** element.

  ```
  <forms timeout="10" ... />
  ```

- **Do you use sliding expiration?**

  Check the **slidingExpiration** attribute. **slidingExpiration="true"** means that the cookie expires at a fixed duration after its initial duration. The timeout clock is not reset after each request. Use of a sliding expiration is particularly recommended for applications that do not use SSL on all pages to protect the cookie.

- **Do you use unique cookie paths and names?**

  Check that you use a separate cookie name and path for each Web application. This ensures that users who are authenticated against one application are not treated as authenticated when using a second application hosted by the same Web server. Check the **path** and **name** attributes on the **<forms>** element.

  ```
  <forms name=".ASPXAUTH" path="/" ... />
  ```

- **Do you use the <credentials> element?**

  You should not use the **<credentials>** element on production servers. This element is intended for development and testing purposes only. Credentials should instead be stored in Microsoft Active Directory® directory service or SQL Server.

- **How do you store credentials?**

  If your application uses Windows authentication, credentials are stored in Active Directory, which passes the credential management issue to the operating environment. If your application uses Forms authentication, make sure you use a SQL Server or Active Directory credential store.

- **Do you store password hashes?**

  Make sure passwords are not stored in the database. Instead, store password hashes with added salt to foil dictionary attacks.

- **Do you use strong passwords?**

  Your application should enforce the use of strong passwords. A good way to do this is to use a regular expression in the Forms logon page.

<identity>

The following questions help verify your impersonation configuration specified on the <identity> element:

- **Do you impersonate the original caller?**

  If the **impersonate** attribute is set to **true** and you do not specify **userName** or **password** attributes, you impersonate the IIS authenticated identity, which may be the anonymous Internet user account.

  Make sure that ACLs are configured to allow the impersonated identity access only to those resources that it needs to gain access to.

- **Do you impersonate a fixed identity?**

  If you impersonate and set the **userName** and **password** attributes, you impersonate a fixed identity and this identity is used for resource access.

  Make sure you do not specify plaintext credentials on the <identity> element. Instead, use Aspnet_setreg.exe to store encrypted credentials in the registry.

  On Windows 2000 this approach forces you to grant the "Act as part of the operating system" user right to the ASP.NET process account, which is not recommended. For alternative approaches, see Chapter 19, "Securing Your ASP.NET Application and Web Services."

<authorization>

This element controls ASP.NET URL authorization and specifically the ability of Web clients to gain access to specific folders, pages, and resources.

- **Have you used the correct format for user and role names?**

  When you have **<authentication mode="Windows" />**, you are authorizing access to Windows user and group accounts.

  User names take the form "DomainName\WindowsUserName". Role names take the form "DomainName\WindowsGroupName".

Note The local administrators group is referred to as "BUILTIN\Administrators". The local users group is referred to as "BUILTIN\Users".

When you have **<authentication mode="Forms" />**, you are authorizing against the identity that is authenticated by the application. Normally, you authorize against the roles that are retrieved from the database. Role names are application specific.

\<machineKey>

This element is used to specify encryption and validation keys, and the algorithms used to protect Forms authentication cookies and page level view state.

- **Do you run multiple applications on the same server?**

  If so, use the **IsolateApps** setting to ensure a separate key is generated for each Web application.

  ```
  <machineKey validationKey="AutoGenerate,IsolateApps"
              decryptionKey="AutoGenerate,IsolateApps" validation="SHA1"/>
  ```

- **Do you run in a Web farm?**

  If so, make sure that you use specific machine keys and copy them across all servers in the farm.

- **Do you protect view state?**

  If you protect view state, for example, by setting **enableViewSetMac="true"** on the **\<pages>** element, set validation="SHA1" (Secure Hash Algorithm) or "3DES" on the **\<machineKey>** element. The Triple Data Encryption Standard (3DES) setting is required if you also encrypt the Forms authentication cookie by setting **protection="All"** on the **\<forms>** element.

\<trust>

The **\<trust>** element determines the code access security trust level used to run ASP.NET Web applications and Web services.

- **What version of the .NET Framework do you run?**

  If you run .NET Framework 1.0 then the trust level must be set to **Full**. For versions equal to or greater than 1.1, you can change it to one of the following:

  ```
  <!-- level="[Full|High|Medium|Low|Minimal]" -->
  <trust level="Full" originUrl=""/>
  ```

- **What trust level do you use?**

  Based on security policy and the agreement with the development team; set an appropriate trust level for the application either in Web.config or in Machine.config.

<sessionState>

The **sessionState** element configures user session state management for your application. Review the following questions:

- **Do you use a remote state store?**

  Check the state store by examining the **mode** attribute.

  ```
  <sessionState mode="Off|Inproc|stateServer|SQLServer" ... />
  ```

  If you use a remote state store and the **mode** attribute is set to **stateServer** or **SQLServer**, check the **stateConnectionString** and **sqlConnectionString** attributes respectively. So that credentials are not included in the database connection string, make sure the connection strings are secured in encrypted format in the registry using the Aspnet_setreg.exe tool, or that Windows authentication is used to connect to the SQL Server state store.

  The following configuration shows what the **stateConnectionString** looks like when Aspnet_setreg.exe has been used to encrypt the string in the registry.

  ```
  <!-- aspnet_setreg.exe has been used to store encrypted details -->
  <!-- in the registry. -->
  <sessionState mode="StateServer"
          stateConnectionString="registry:HKLM\SOFTWARE\YourSecureApp\
          identity\ASPNET_SETREG,stateConnectionString" />
  ```

- **Do you use Windows authentication to the state database?**

  If you use the SQL Server state store, check to see if you use Windows authentication to connect to the state database. This means that credentials are not stored in the connection string and that credentials are not transmitted over the wire.

  If you must use SQL authentication, make sure the connection string is encrypted in the registry and that a server certificate is installed on the database server to ensure that credentials are encrypted over the wire.

<httpHandlers>

This element lists the HTTP handlers that process requests for specific file types. Check to ensure that you have disabled all unused file types.

Map unused file types to **System.Web.HttpForbiddenHandler** to prevent their HTTP retrieval. For example, if your application does not use Web services, map the .asmx extension as follows:

```
<httpHandlers>
  <add verb="*" path="*.asmx" type="System.Web.HttpForbiddenHandler"/>
</httpHandlers>
```

<processModel>

The identity under which the ASP.NET worker process runs is controlled by settings on the **<processModel>** element in Machine.config. The following review questions help verify your process identity settings:

- **What identity do you use to run ASP.NET?**

  Check the **userName** and **password** attributes. Ideally, you use the following configuration that results in the ASP.NET process running under the least privileged ASPNET account.

  ```
  <processModel userName="Machine" password="AutoGenerate" . . ./>
  ```

- **Do you encrypt the <processModel> credentials?**

  If you use a custom account, make sure that the account credentials are not specified in plaintext in Machine.config. Make sure the Aspnet_setreg.exe utility has been used to store encrypted credentials in the registry. If this has been used, the **userName** and **password** attributes look similar to the settings shown below:

  ```
  <processModel
          userName="registry:HKLM\SOFTWARE\YourSecureApp\processModel\
                  ASPNET_SETREG,userName"
          password="registry:HKLM\SOFTWARE\YourSecureApp\processModel\
                  ASPNET_SETREG,password" . . ./>
  ```

- **Do you use a least privileged account?**

  The default ASPNET account is a least privileged local account designed to run ASP.NET. To use it for remote resource access, you need to create a duplicate account on the remote server. Alternatively, you can create a least privileged domain account.

  Check that the account is not a member of the Users group, and view the user rights assignment in the Local Security Policy tool to confirm it is not granted any extended or unnecessary user rights. Make sure it is not granted the "Act as part of the operating system" user right.

Web Services

The goal for this phase of the review is to identify vulnerabilities in the configuration of your Web services. For further background information about the issues raised by the review questions in this section, see Chapter 17, "Securing Your Application Server," and Chapter 19, "Securing Your ASP.NET Applications and Web Services."

Use the following questions to help review the security configuration of your Web service:

- **Have you disabled the Documentation protocol?**

  If you do not want to expose your Web services endpoints, then you can remove the **Documentation** protocol from the **<protocols>** element in Machine.config and manually distribute the .Web Services Description Language (WSDL) file to specific Web service consumers.

- **Have you disabled the HTTP Get and Post protocols?**

  By disabling (commenting) **HttpGet** and **HttpPost** protocols from **<protocols>** element in Machine.config file, you help to reduce the attack profile for your Web services.

- **Do you restrict access to WSDL?**

  If you store the generated .WSDL files on the Web server to distribute them to the consumers, make sure that the files are protected by an appropriate ACL. This prevents a malicious user from updating or replacing the WSDL so that it points to endpoints that differ from the intended URL.

- **Do you pass sensitive data in SOAP requests or responses?**

  If your Web service handles sensitive data, how do you protect the data over the network and address the network eavesdropping threat? Do you use SSL or IPSec encrypted channels, or do you encrypt parts of the message by using XML encryption?

- **How do you authenticate callers?**

  If your Web service exposes restricted operations or data, it needs to authenticate callers to support authorization. Review how the Web service authenticates its clients.

- **Do you pass credentials in SOAP headers?**

  If you pass credentials in SOAP headers, are they passed in plaintext? If they are, make sure an encrypted channel is used.

Enterprise Services

This section identifies the key review points that should be considered when you review your Enterprise Services applications and components. For more information about the issues raised in this section, see Chapter 17, "Securing Your Application Server."

When you review Enterprise Services applications consider the following issues:

- **Accounts**
- **Files and directories**
- **Authentication**
- **Authorization**
- **Remote serviced component**

Accounts

If you use an Enterprise Services server application, check which account you use to run the application. This is displayed on the **Identity** page of the application's **Properties** dialog box in Component Services. Review the following questions:

- **Do you use a least privileged account?**

  Check the account that you use to run your Enterprise Services server applications to ensure they are configured as least privileged accounts with restricted user rights and access rights. If you use the process account to access a downstream database, make sure that the database login is restricted in the database.

- **Do you use the Interactive account?**

  Do not use the Interactive account on production servers. This is only intended to be used during development and testing.

Files and Directories

Review the following questions to ensure that you are using NTFS permissions appropriately to secure the various files associated with an Enterprise Services application:

- **Is the COM+ catalog secured?**

  The COM+ catalog maintains configuration data for COM+ applications. Make sure that the following folder that maintains the catalog files is configured with a restricted ACL.

  ```
  %windir%\registration
  ```

  Configure the following ACL:

  ```
  Administrators: Read, Write
  System: Read, Write
  Enterprise Services Run-As Account(s): Read
  ```

- **Are the CRM log files secured?**

  If your application uses the Compensating Resource Manager, the CRM log files (.crmlog) should be secured with NTFS permissions because the log files may contain sensitive application data.

- **Are your application DLLs secured?**

  Make sure that the folder used to hold the DLLs of your application is configured with the following restricted ACL.

  ```
  Users: Execute
  Application Run as account: Execute
  Administrators: Read, Write and Execute
  ```

For more information, see Chapter 17, "Securing Your Application Server."

Authentication

Serviced components can be hosted in a library application that runs in the client's process address space or in a server application that runs in a separate instance of Dllhost.exe. This is determined by the activation type specified on the **Activation** page of the application's **Properties** dialog box in Component Services. The client process for an Enterprise Services library application is usually the ASP.NET Web application process.

The settings discussed below are specified on the **Security** page of the application's **Properties** dialog box in Component Services.

Server Applications

If the Activation type is set to Server application, review the following questions:

- **Do you prevent anonymous access?**

  Check that your application uses at least call level authentication to ensure that clients are authenticated each time they make a method call. This prevents anonymous access.

- **What impersonation level do you use?**

  Check to make sure that you use at least identify level impersonation to allow downstream systems to identify your serviced component. By default, this is the process identity determined by the run-as account of the application. If your serviced components use programmatic impersonation, this may be an impersonated identity. Use delegate level only if you want the downstream system to be able to access remote resources using your serviced component's identity.

Library Applications

If the activation type is set to Library application, the authentication and impersonation settings are inherited from the host process. The review questions in this section assume the ASP.NET process is the host process.

- **Have you disabled authentication?**

  To check, view the **Enable authentication** check box setting on the **Security** page of the application's **Properties** dialog box. You should not disable authentication unless you have a specific requirement such as handling unauthenticated callbacks from a remote serviced component.

- **What authentication level do you use?**

  The authentication level specified on the **<processModel>** element in Machine.config governs the authentication level used for outgoing calls to remote serviced components or DCOM components. The higher of this value and the value configured at the remote server is used. Check the **comAuthenticationLevel** setting on the **<processModel>** element:

- **What impersonation level do you use?**

  This affects outgoing calls from the library component to other remote components. Check the **comImpersonationLevel** attribute on the **<processModel>** element in Machine.config.

```
<processModel comImpersonationLevel=
              "Default|Anonymous|Identify|Impersonate|Delegate" .../>
```

Authorization

Serviced components in Enterprise Services applications use COM+ role based security to authorize callers. Review the following issues to ensure appropriate authorization:

- **Are access checks enabled?**

  This controls whether or not COM+ authorization is enabled or not. Check that **Enforce access checks for this application** is selected on the **Security** page of the application's **Properties** dialog box in Component Services.

- **What security level do you use?**

  Check the **Security level** specified on the **Security** page of the application's **Properties** dialog box in Component Services. Applications should use process and component level access checks to support granular authorization. This allows the application to use roles to control access to specific classes, interfaces, and methods.

Note Process and component level access checks must be enabled for library applications or you will not be able to use role-based authorization.

- **Do you enforce component level access checks?**

  To support authorization checks at the component, interface, and method levels, each component must be appropriately configured in the COM+ catalog. Check each component in your application to ensure that **Enforce component level access checks** is selected on the **Security** page of the component's **Properties** dialog box.

Remote Serviced Components

The following issues apply if you use remote serviced components, and communication is across a network. A typical scenario is an ASP.NET client communicating with an Enterprise Services application on a remote application server.

- **Do you pass sensitive data?**

  If so, what mechanism is in place to address the network eavesdropping threat? Make sure the link between client and server is encrypted at the transport level, for example, by IPSec. Alternatively, make sure your Enterprise Services application is configured for Packet Privacy level authentication, which forces the use of RPC encryption for all data packets sent to and from the application.

- **Do you communicate through a firewall?**

  Enterprise Services uses DCOM, which in turn uses RPC communication. RPC communication requires port 135 to be open on the firewall. Review your firewall and Enterprise Services configuration to ensure that only the minimal additional ports is open.

  The range of ports dynamically allocated by DCOM can be restricted or static endpoint mapping can be used to specify individual ports. For more information, see Chapter 17, "Securing Your Application Server."

Remoting

This section identifies the key review points that should be considered when you review your application's use of .NET Remoting. For more information about the issues raised in this section see Chapter 17, "Securing Your Application Server."

When you review your .NET Remoting solution, start by identifying which host is used to run your remote components. If you use the ASP.NET host with the **HttpChannel**, you need to check that IIS and ASP.NET security is appropriately configured to provide authentication, authorization, and secure communication services to your remote components. If you use a custom host and the **TcpChannel**, you need to review how your components are secured, because this host and channel combination requires custom authentication and authorization solutions.

Port Considerations

Remoting is not designed to be used with Internet clients. Check that the ports that your components listen on are not directly accessible by Internet clients. The port or ports are usually specified on the **<channel>** element in the server side configuration file.

Hosting in ASP.NET with the HttpChannel

If you use the ASP.NET host, review the following items:

- **How do you protect sensitive data over the network?**

  Do you use SSL or IPSec? Without SSL or IPSec, data passed to and from the remote component is subject to information disclosure and tampering. Review what measures are in place to address the network eavesdropping threat.

- **How do you authenticate callers?**

  Make sure that anonymous access is disabled in IIS for your application's virtual directory. Also check that you use Windows authentication. The Web.config of your application should contain the following configuration.

  ```
  <authentication mode="Windows" />
  ```

- **Do you use ASP.NET file authorization?**

  If not, why? You can use ASP.NET file authorization to control access to the endpoints of your remoting application by creating a .rem or .soap file and configuring the NTFS permissions on the file. The ASP.NET FileAuthorizationModule will then authorize access to the component. For more information, see "Authorization" in Chapter 13, "Building Secure Remoted Components."

- **Do you use URL authorization?**

  Check your application's use of the **<authorization>** element. Use the ASP.NET **UrlAuthorizationModule** by applying **<allow>** and **<deny>** tags.

- **Do you prevent detailed errors from being returned to the client?**

  Check the configuration of your application to make sure that you have correctly configured the **<customErrors>** element to prevent detailed errors from being returned to the client. Make sure the **mode** attribute is set to **On** as shown below.

  ```
  <customErrors mode="On" />
  ```

- **What identity do you use to run ASP.NET?**

  Check that you use a least privileged account to run ASP.NET, such as the default ASPNET account, or Network Service account on Windows Server 2003.

Hosting in a Custom Process with the TcpChannel

If you use a custom host process such as a Windows service, review the following items.

- **How do you protect sensitive data over the network?**

  Have you secured the channel from client to server? You may use transport level IPSec encryption or your application may use a custom encryption sink to encrypt request and response data.

- **How do you authenticate callers?**

  The **TcpChannel** provides no authentication mechanism, so you must develop your own. Review how your application authenticates its callers.

- **Do you restrict your clients?**

  Remoting with the **TcpChannel** is designed to be used in trusted server scenarios, where the remote components trust their clients. Do you restrict the range of clients that can connect to your remote components, for example, by using IPSec policies?

- **Do you use a least privileged process identity?**

  Review which account you use to run your custom host process and ensure it is configured as a least privileged account.

Database Server Configuration

The goal for this phase of the review is to identify vulnerabilities in the configuration of your SQL Server database server. For further background information about the issues raised by the review questions in this section, see Chapter 18, "Securing Your Database Server."

To help focus and structure the review process, the review questions have been divided into the following configuration categories:

- **Patches and updates**
- **Services**
- **Protocols**
- **Accounts**
- **Files and directories**
- **Shares**
- **Ports**
- **Registry**
- **Auditing and logging**
- **SQL Server security**
- **SQL Server logins, users, and roles**

Patches and Updates

Check that your server is updated with the latest service packs and software patches. This includes service packs and patches for the operating system and SQL Server.

Make sure you have run the Microsoft Baseline Security Analyzer (MBSA) tool to identify common Windows and SQL Server vulnerabilities, and to identify missing service packs and patches.

Respond to the MBSA output by fixing identified vulnerabilities and by installing the latest patches and updates. For more information, see "Step 1. Patches and Updates" in Chapter 18, "Securing Your Database Server."

Services

Make sure that only those services that you require are enabled. Check that all others are disabled to reduce the attack surface of your server.

- **Which SQL Server services do you run?**

  SQL Server installs four services. If you require just the base functionality, then disable Microsoft Search Service, MSSQLServerADHelper, and SQLServerAgent to reduce the attack surface of your server.

- **Do you use distributed transactions?**

  If your applications use the transactional services of COM+ to manage transactions with SQL Server, then the Microsoft Distributed Transaction Coordinator (DTC) service is required on the database server.

  If you do not use distributed transactions, ensure that the DTC service is disabled.

Protocols

By preventing the use of unnecessary protocols, you reduce the attack surface area. Review the following questions:

- **For which protocols is SQL Server configured?**

  SQL Server supports multiple protocols. Use the Server Network Utility to check that only TCP/IP protocol support is enabled.

- **Have you hardened the TCP/IP stack?**

  To check whether the stack is hardened on your server, use Regedt32.exe and examine the following registry key:

```
HKLM\SYSTEM\CurrentControlSet\Services\Tcpip\Parameters
```

  The presence of the following child keys indicates a hardened TCP/IP stack: **SynAttackProtect, EnableICMPRedirect,** and **EnableReadGWDetect**.

  For a full list of the required keys and appropriate key values for a fully hardened stack, see "How To: Harden the TCP/IP Stack" in the How To section of this guide.

Accounts

Review the accounts used on your database server by answering the following questions:

- **Do you use a least privileged account to run SQL Server?**

  Review which account you use to run SQL Server and make sure it is a least privileged account. It should not be an administrative account or the powerful local system account. Also make sure that the account is not a member of the Users group on the local computer.

- **Have you deleted or disabled unused accounts?**

  Audit local accounts on the server and check that all unused accounts are disabled.

- **Have you disabled the Guest account?**

  Check that the Windows **Guest** account is disabled to restrict anonymous connections to your database server.

- **Have you created a new administrator account?**

  The default local administrator account is a prime target for attack. To improve security, check that you have created a new custom account for administration and that the default Administrator account has been disabled.

- **Do you use strong password policies?**

  Use the Local Security Policy tool to review password policy. For information about the recommended password policy, see "Step 4. Accounts" in Chapter 18, "Securing Your Database Server."

- **Do you restrict remote logons?**

  Check the user rights assignments within the Local Security Policy tool to ensure that the **Everyone** group is not granted the "Access this computer from the network" user right.

- **Have you disabled null sessions?**

  Check that null sessions are disabled to prevent anonymous (unauthenticated) sessions from being created with your server. To check this, run Regedt32.exe and confirm that the **RestrictAnonymous** key is set to **1**, as shown below.

  ```
  HKLM\System\CurrentControlSet\Control\LSA\RestrictAnonymous=1
  ```

- **Do clients connect by using Windows authentication?**

  If so, check that the strongest version of NTLM authentication (NTLMv2) is enabled and enforced. To check that NTLMv2 authentication is enforced, use the Local Security Policy Tool. Expand **Local Policies** and select **Security Options** and then double-click **LAN Manager Authentication Level**. Verify that **Send NTLMv2 response only\refuse LM & NTLM** is selected.

Files and Directories

The following review questions enable you to verify that you have used NTFS permissions appropriately on your database server.

- **Have you configured permissions on the SQL Server install directories?**

  Review the permissions on the SQL Server installation directories and make sure that the permissions grant limited access. For detailed permissions, see "Step 5. Files and Directories" in Chapter 18, "Securing Your Database Server."

- **Have you removed Everyone permissions for SQL Server files?**

  Review the permissions on the SQL Server file location (by default, \Program Files\Microsoft SQL Server\MSSQL) and check that the **Everyone** group has been removed from the directory ACL. At the same time, make sure that full control has been granted to only the SQL Service account, the **Administrators** group, and the local system account.

- **Have you secured setup log files?**

  If you have installed SQL Server 2000 Service Pack 1 or 2, the system administrator or service account password may be left in the SQL installation directory. Make sure that you have used the Killpwd.exe utility to remove instances of passwords from the log files.

  For information about obtaining and using this utility, see Microsoft Knowledge Base article 263968, "FIX: Service Pack Installation May Save Standard Security Password in File."

Shares

Review the following questions to ensure that your server is not unnecessarily exposed by the presence of file shares:

- **What shares are available on your server?**

  To review shares and associated permissions, run the Computer Management MMC snap-in and select **Shares** beneath **Shared Folders**. Check that all the shares are required. Remove any unnecessary shares.

- **Can the Everyone group access shares?**

  Check that the **Everyone** group is not granted access to your shares unless intended, and that specific permissions are configured instead.

- **Have you removed the administration shares?**

  If you do not allow remote administration of your server, then check that the administration shares, for example, C$ and IPC$, have been removed.

Note   Some applications may require administrative shares. Examples include Microsoft Systems Management Server (SMS) and Microsoft Operations Manager (MOM). For more information, see Microsoft Knowledge Base article 318751, "How To: Remove Administrative Shares in Windows 2000 or Windows NT4."

Ports

Review the ports that are active on your server to make sure that no unnecessary ports are available. For more information about using the netstat command to do this, see the "Ports" subsection in "Web Server Configuration," earlier in this chapter. Then review the following questions:

- **Have you restricted access to the SQL Server port?**

  Review how you restrict access to the SQL Server port. Check that your perimeter firewall prevents direct access from the Internet. To protect against internal attacks, review your IPSec policies to ensure they limit access to the SQL Server ports.

- **Have you configured named instances to listen on the same port?**

  If you use named instances, check with the Network Server Utility to verify that you have configured the instance to listen on a specific port. This avoids UDP negotiation between the client and server, and means you do not need to open additional ports.

Registry

Review the security of your registry configuration with the following questions:

- **Have you secured the SQL Server registry keys?**

  Use Regedt32.exe to check that the Everyone group has been removed from the ACL attached to the following registry key.

  ```
  Administrators: Full Control
  SQL Server service account: Full Control
  ```

- **Have you secured the SAM?**

  Check that you have restricted LMHash storage in the Security Account Manager (SAM) by creating the key (not value) **NoLMHash** in the registry as shown below.

  ```
  HKLM\System\CurrentControlSet\Control\LSA\NoLMHash
  ```

  For more information, see Microsoft Knowledge Base article 299656, "New Registry Key to Remove LM Hashes from Active Directory and Security Account Manager".

Auditing and Logging

Review the following questions to check whether or not you have used appropriate auditing and logging on your database server.

- **Have you enabled SQL Server auditing?**

  Check that SQL Server auditing is enabled. Make sure that the **Audit level** setting on the **Security** page of the SQL Server **Properties** dialog box in Enterprise Manager is set to either **All** or **Failure**.

- **Do you log all failed logon attempts?**

  Use the Local Security Policy tool to check that you have enabled the auditing of failed logon attempts.

- **Do you log all failed actions across the file system?**

  Use the Local Security Policy tool to check that you have enabled object access auditing. Then check that auditing has been enabled across the file system.

SQL Server Security

Review which authentication mode your SQL Server is configured to use. You can see this by viewing the **Security** page of your server's **Properties** dialog box in Enterprise Manager. If your server is configured to support **SQL Server and Windows** authentication, check that your applications do require SQL authentication. If possible, use **Windows only** authentication.

If your applications do require SQL authentication, review how they manage database connection strings. This is important if they use SQL authentication because they contain user name and passwords. Also ensure that a server certificate is installed on the database server to ensure that credentials are encrypted when they are passed over the network to the database server, or that transport level encryption is used.

SQL Server Logins, Users, and Roles

Authorization in SQL Server is managed through SQL Server logins, database users, and a variety of different types of roles. Review the following questions to ensure these roles are configured appropriately:

- **Do you have a strong sa (system administrator) password?**

  Make sure the **sa** account has a strong password.

  > **Important**   The **sa** account is still active even when you change from SQL authentication to Windows authentication.

  Also make sure you have applied strong passwords to all database accounts, particularly privileged accounts, for example, members of **sysadmin** and **db_owner**. If you use replication, check that the **distributer_admin** account has a strong password.

- **Have you removed the SQL Server guest account?**

  If when you installed SQL Server the Windows **Guest** account was enabled, a SQL Server **guest** account is created. Check each database and ensure that the SQL Server **guest** account is not present. If it is, remove it.

  > **Note**   You cannot remove **guest** from the master, tempdb, and replication and distribution databases.

- **Have you removed the BUILTIN\Administrators server login?**

  If your company differentiates the role of domain administrator and database administrator, remove the BUILTIN\Administrators SQL Server login. It is a good idea to create a specific Windows group containing specific database administrations in its place.

- **Have you removed permissions for the public role?**

  Review the permissions granted to the public role in each database. Make sure it has no permissions to access any database objects.

- **How many members are there that belong to the sysadmin role?**

  Check how many logins belong to the **sysadmin** role. Ideally, no more than two users should be system administrators.

- **Do you grant restricted database permissions to logins?**

  Review the permissions granted to each database user account and make sure that each account (including application accounts) only has the minimum required permissions.

SQL Server Database Objects

Review the following questions to ensure that you have removed unnecessary database objects, including the sample databases, and that stored procedures are appropriately secured.

- **Have you removed sample databases?**

  Use SQL Server Enterprise Manager to check that all sample databases, including Pubs and Northwind, have been removed.

- **Have you secured stored procedures?**

  Check to make sure that neither the public role nor the guest user has access to any of your stored procedures. To authorize access to stored procedures, you should map the SQL Server login of your server to a database user, place the database user in a user-defined database role, and then apply permissions to this role to provide execute access to the stored procedures of your application.

- **Have you restricted access to cmdExec?**

  The **cmdExec** function is used by the SQL Server Agent to execute Windows command-line applications and scripts that are scheduled by the SQL Server Agent. Check that access to **cmdExec** is restricted to members of the **sysadmin** role.

  To check this, use SQL Server Enterprise Manager to expand the **Management** node. Right-click **SQL Server Agent** and display the **SQL Server Agent Properties** dialog box. Click the Job System tab and check that **Only users with SysAdmin privileges can execute CmdExec and ActiveScripting job steps** is selected.

Network Configuration

The goal for this phase of the review is to identify vulnerabilities in the configuration of your network. For further background information about the issues raised by the review questions in this section, see Chapter 15, "Securing Your Network."

To help focus and structure the review process, the review questions have been divided into the following configuration categories:

- **Router**
- **Firewall**
- **Switch**

Router

Use the following questions to review your router configuration:

- **Have you applied the latest patches and updates?**

  Check with the networking hardware manufacturer to ensure you have the latest patches.

- **Do you use Ingress and Egress filtering?**

  For more information, see "Network Ingress Filtering: Defeating Denial of Service Attacks which employ IP Source Address Spoofing," at *http://www.rfc-editor.org /rfc/rfc2267.txt*.

- **Do you block ICMP traffic?**

  Make sure you block Internet Control Message Protocol (ICMP) traffic at the outer perimeter router to prevent attacks such as cascading ping floods and other potential ICMP vulnerabilities.

- **Do you prevent time-to-live (TTL) expired messages with values of 0 or 1?**

  This prevents information disclosure caused by route tracing.

- **Do you receive or forward broadcast traffic?**

  Source addresses that should be filtered are shown in Table 22.1.

Table 22.1 Source Addresses that Should Be Filtered

Source Address	Description
0.0.0.0/8	Historical broadcast
10.0.0.0/8	RFC 1918 private network
127.0.0.0/8	Loopback
169.254.0.0/16	Link local networks
172.16.0.0/12	RFC 1918 private network
192.0.2.0/24	TEST-NET
192.168.0.0/16	RFC 1918 private network
224.0.0.0/4	Class D multicast
240.0.0.0/5	Class E reserved
248.0.0.0/5	Unallocated
255.255.255.255/32	Broadcast

- **Have you disabled unused interfaces?**

  Make sure that only the required interfaces are enabled on the router.

- **Do you use strong password policies?**

  You should use strong password policies to mitigate the risks posed by brute force and dictionary attacks.

- **Do you use static routing?**

  By using static routes, an administrative interface must first be compromised to make routing changes.

- **Do you audit Web facing administrative interfaces?**

  When possible, shut down the external administration interface and use internal access methods with ACLs.

- **Do you use the logging features of your router?**

  Check that your routers log all deny actions.

- **Do you use an Intrusion Detection System?**

  Intrusion Detection Systems (IDSs) can show where the perpetrator is attempting attacks.

Firewall

Use the following questions to review your router configuration:

- **Have you applied the latest patches and updates?**

  Check with the networking hardware manufacturer to ensure you have the latest patches.

- **Do you log all traffic that flows though the firewall?**

- **How often do you cycle logs?**

  Ensure that you maintain healthy log cycling that allows quick data analysis.

- **Is the firewall clock synchronized with the other network hardware?**

Switch

Use the following questions to review your router configuration:

- **Have you applied the latest patches and updates?**

  Check with the networking hardware manufacturer to ensure that you have the latest patches.

- **Have you disabled factory default settings?**

  To make sure that insecure defaults are secured, check that you have changed all factory default passwords and Simple Network Management Protocol (SNMP) community strings to prevent network enumeration or total control of the switch.

- **Have you disabled unused services?**

  Make sure that all unused services are disabled. Also, make sure that Trivial File Transfer Protocol (TFTP) is disabled, Internet-facing administration points are removed, and ACLs are configured to limit administrative access.

Summary

When you perform a deployment review, make sure that you review the configuration of the underlying infrastructure on which the application is deployed and the configuration of the application itself. Review the network, host, and application configuration and, where possible, involve members of the various teams including infrastructure specialists, administrators and developers.

Use the configuration categories identified in this chapter to help focus the review. These categories include patches and updates, services, protocols, accounts, files and directories, shares, ports, registry, and auditing and logging.

Related Security Resources

Related Microsoft patterns & practices Guidance

- *Building Secure ASP.NET Applications: Authentication, Authorization, and Secure Communication* on the MSDN® Web site at *http://msdn.microsoft.com/library /default.asp?url=/library/en-us/dnnetsec/html/secnetlpMSDN.asp.*

  This guide focuses on the key elements of authentication, authorization, and secure communication within and across the tiers of distributed .NET Web applications. It is written for architects and developers.

- *Designing Application-Managed Authorization* on the MSDN Web site at *http://msdn.microsoft.com/library/?url=/library/en-us/dnbda/html/damaz.asp.*

  This guide focuses on common authorization tasks and scenarios, and it provides information that helps you choose the best approaches and techniques. It is written for architects and developers.

- *Microsoft Solution for Securing Windows 2000 Server* on the Microsoft Technet Web site at *http://www.microsoft.com/technet/treeview/default.asp?url=/technet/security /prodtech/windows/secwin2k/default.asp.*

  This guide delivers procedures and best practices for system administrators to lock down their Windows 2000-based servers and maintain secure operations once they're up and running. It is written for IT Pros.

More Information

For more information on *patterns and practices*, refer to the Microsoft patterns & practices home page at *http://msdn.microsoft.com/practices/.*

Security-Related Web Sites

Microsoft Security-Related Web Sites

- Microsoft Security & Privacy home page at *http://www.microsoft.com/security/.*
- Microsoft Security Update subscription at *http://register.microsoft.com/subscription /subscribeme.asp?id=166.*
- Technet Security home page at *http://www.microsoft.com/technet/security/.*
- MSDN Security home page at *http://msdn.microsoft.com/security/.*
- .NET Framework Security home page at *http://msdn.microsoft.com/net/security/.*

- Security and Trustworthy Computing at *http://www.microsoft.com/enterprise /security/*.
- Microsoft Training & Certification Security Product and Technology Resources at *http://www.microsoft.com/traincert/centers/security.asp*.

Third-Party, Security-Related Web Sites

- CERT (Computer Emergency Response Team) at *http://www.cert.org/*.
- SANS Institute Web site at *http://www.sans.org/*.
- Computer Security Resource Center at *http://csrc.nist.gov/*.

Microsoft Security Services

- Awareness and educational services
  - Enterprise Security Strategy Seminar
  - Securing the Enterprise Platforms Workshop
- Security assessment services
  - Vulnerability assessment
- Security solutions services
  - Security design reviews
  - Incident response service

For information on these services, contact Microsoft Consulting Services:

- Microsoft Consulting Services (MCS) home page at *http://www.microsoft.com /business/services/mcs.asp*.
- U.S. sales offices at *http://www.microsoft.com/usa/*.
- Worldwide at *http://www.microsoft.com/worldwide/*.

For free support on virus issues:

- The Microsoft 1-866-PCSAFETY line (U.S. and Canada)
- Microsoft local support resources (all other locations) at *http://support.microsoft.com /common/international.aspx*.

Partners and Service Providers

- Microsoft USA Partner site at *http://www.microsoft.com/usa/partner/default.asp*.
- Microsoft Service Providers at *http://www.microsoft.com/serviceproviders/default.asp*.

Communities and Newsgroups

Newsgroup Home Pages

- Microsoft Product Support Newsgroups at *http://support.microsoft.com/newsgroups /default.aspx*.
- MSDN Newsgroups at *http://msdn.microsoft.com/newsgroups/*.
- Technet Newsgroups at *http://www.microsoft.com/technet/newsgroups/*.

For security issues within specific .NET Framework technologies, refer to the appropriate newsgroup:

- Microsoft Security Newsgroups at *http://www.microsoft.com/technet/newsgroups /default.asp?url=/technet/newsgroups/NodePages/security.asp*.
- Virus Newsgroup at *http://www.microsoft.com/technet/newsgroups/default.asp?url= /technet/newsgroups/NodePages/security.asp*.
- .NET Framework Security Newsgroup at *http://msdn.microsoft.com/newsgroups /loadframes.asp?icp=msdn&slcid=us&newsgroup=microsoft.public.dotnet.security*.
- ASP.NET Security Newsgroup at *http://msdn.microsoft.com/newsgroups /loadframes.asp?icp=msdn&slcid=us&newsgroup=microsoft.public.dotnet.framework .aspnet.security*.

Patches and Updates

- Hotfix and Security Bulletin Service at *http://www.microsoft.com/technet/treeview /default.asp?url=/technet/security/current.asp*.

  View the security bulletins that are available for your system.

Service Packs

- Microsoft Service Packs at *http://support.microsoft.com /default.aspx?scid=FH;[LN];sp&*.
- .NET Framework Service Packs:
    - Article 318836, "INFO: How to Obtain the Latest .NET Framework Service Pack" in the Microsoft Knowledge Base at *http://support.microsoft.com /default.aspx?scid=kb;en-us;318836*.
    - Article 318785, "INFO: Determining Whether Service Packs Are Installed on .NET Framework" in the Microsoft Knowledge Base at *http://support.microsoft.com/default.aspx?scid=kb;en-us;318785*.

Alerts and Notification

Microsoft Security Notification Services

- Virus alerts for Microsoft products at *http://www.microsoft.com/technet/treeview/?url= /technet/security/virus/alerts/*.

- Security Notification Service at *http://register.microsoft.com/subscription /subscribeme.asp?ID=135*.

  Use this service to register for regular e-mail bulletins that notify you of the availability of new fixes and updates.

Third Party Security Notification Services

- CERT Advisory Mailing List at *http://www.cert.org/contact_cert/certmaillist.html*.

  Informative advisories are sent when vulnerabilities are reported.

- Windows and .NET Magazine Security UPDATE at *http://email.winnetmag.com /winnetmag/winnetmag_prefctr.asp#Security*.

  This announces the latest security breaches and corresponding fixes. It also gives advice on reacting to vulnerabilities.

- NTBugtraq at *http://www.ntbugtraq.com/default.asp?pid=31&sid=1#020*.

  This is an open discussion of Windows security bugs and exploits. Vulnerablities that do not have patches are discussed.

- Internet Storm Center at *http://isc.incidents.org*.

  This site tracks the frequency of worms, denial of service attacks, as well as other kinds of attacks.

- Security Focus Web site at *www.securityfocus.com*.

Additional Resources

Checklists and Assessment Guidelines

- IIS 5.0 Security Checklist at *http://www.microsoft.com/technet/treeview /default.asp?url=/technet/security/tools/chklist/iis5chk.asp*.

- Security Tools and Checklists at *http://www.microsoft.com/technet/treeview /default.asp?url=/technet/security/tools/tools.asp*.

Common Criteria

- Windows 2000 Common Criteria Guide (see Chapter 4) at *http://www.microsoft.com /technet/treeview/default.asp?url=/technet/security/issues/W2kCCSCG/default.asp*.

  The Windows 2000 Common Criteria Security Target (ST) provides a set of security requirements taken from the Common Criteria (CC) for Information Technology Security Evaluation. The Windows 2000 product was evaluated against the Windows 2000 ST and satisfies the ST requirements.

  This document is written for those who are responsible for ensuring that the installation and configuration process results in a secure configuration. A secure configuration is one that enforces the requirements presented in the Windows 2000 ST, referred to as the Evaluated Configuration.

Reference Hub

- Reference hub from *Building Secure ASP.NET Applications* at *http://msdn.microsoft.com/library/default.asp?url=/library/en-us/dnnetsec/html /SecNetAP03.asp?frame=true*.

Security Knowledge in Practice

- CERT Security Improvement Modules at *http://www.cert.org/security-improvement /skip.html*.

Vulnerabilities

- SANs TOP 20 List at *http://www.sans.org/top20/*.
- CERT (Computer Emergency Response Team) at *http://www.cert.org*.

World Wide Web Security FAQ

- *http://www.w3.org/Security/faq/www-security-faq.html*.

Index of Checklists

Overview

Improving Web Application Security: Threats and Countermeasures provides a series of checklists that help you turn the information and details that you learned in the individual chapters into action. The following checklists are included:

- Checklist: Architecture and Design Review
- Checklist: Securing ASP.NET
- Checklist: Securing Web Services
- Checklist: Securing Enterprise Services
- Checklist: Securing Remoting
- Checklist: Securing Data Access
- Checklist: Securing Your Network
- Checklist: Securing Your Web Server
- Checklist: Securing Your Database Server
- Checklist: Security Review for Managed Code

Designing Checklist

Checklist: Architecture and Design Review covers aspects of the architecture and design stages of the project life cycle, including: input validation, authentication, authorization, configuration management, sensitive data, session management, cryptography, parameter manipulation, exception management, and auditing and logging.

Building Checklists

Each checklist in the building series covers the following application categories: input validation, authentication, authorization, configuration management, sensitive data, session management, cryptography, parameter manipulation, exception management, and auditing and logging. These checklists are:

- **Checklist: Securing ASP.NET**
- **Checklist: Securing Web Services**
- **Checklist: Securing Enterprise Services**
- **Checklist: Securing Remoting**
- **Checklist: Securing Data Access**

Securing Checklists

Each checklist in the securing series covers aspects of securing the servers based on roles. The checklists cover the following: patches and updates, services, protocols, accounts, files and directories, shares, ports, registry, and auditing and logging. These checklists are:

- **Checklist: Securing Web Server**. In addition to the common checklist information cited previously, this checklist covers the following points that are specific to a Web server: sites and virtual directories, script mappings, ISAPI filters, metabase, Machine.config, and code access security.

- **Checklist: Securing Database Server**. In addition to the common checklist information cited previously, this checklist covers following points that are specific to a database server: SQL Server security; and SQL Server logins, users, and roles.

Assessing Checklist

Checklist: Security Review for Managed Code helps you to uncover security vulnerabilities in your managed code. This checklist covers the following: assembly-level checks, class-level checks, cryptography, secrets, exception management, delegates, serialization, threading, reflection, unmanaged code access, file I/O, event log, registry, environment variables and code access security considerations.

Checklist:
Architecture and Design Review

How to Use This Checklist

This checklist is a companion to Chapter 4, "Design Guidelines for Secure Web Applications," and Chapter 5, "Architecture and Design Review for Security." Use it to help you perform architecture and design reviews to evaluate the security of your Web applications and to implement the design guidelines in Chapter 4.

This checklist should evolve based on the experience you gain from performing reviews. You might also want to perform custom checks that are based on a specific aspect of your architecture or design to ensure that your deployment environment the design.

Deployment and Infrastructure Considerations

Check	Description
☐	The design identifies, understands, and accommodates the company security policy.
☐	Restrictions imposed by infrastructure security (including available services, protocols, and firewall restrictions) are identified.
☐	The design recognizes and accomodates restrictions imposed by hosting environments (including application isolation requirements).
☐	The target environment code-access-security trust level is known.
☐	The design identifies the deployment infrastructure requirements and the deployment configuration of the application.
☐	Domain structures, remote application servers, and database servers are identified.
☐	The design identifies clustering requirements.
☐	The design identifies the application configuration maintenance points (such as what needs to be configured and what tools are available for an IDC admin).
☐	Secure communication features provided by the platform and the application are known.
☐	The design addresses Web farm considerations (including session state management, machine specific encryption keys, Secure Sockets Layer (SSL), certificate deployment issues, and roaming profiles).
☐	The design identifies the certificate authority (CA) to be used by the site to support SSL.
☐	The design addresses the required scalability and performance criteria.

Application Architecture and Design Considerations

Input Validation

Check	Description
☐	All entry points and trust boundaries are identified by the design.
☐	Input validation is applied whenever input is received from outside the current trust boundary.
☐	The design assumes that user input is malicious.
☐	Centralized input validation is used where appropriate.
☐	The input validation strategy that the application adopted is modular and consistent.
☐	The validation approach is to constrain, reject, and then sanitize input. (Looking for known, valid, and safe input is much easier than looking for known malicious or dangerous input.)
☐	Data is validated for type, length, format, and range.
☐	The design addresses potential canonicalization issues.
☐	Input file names and file paths are avoided where possible.
☐	The design addresses potential SQL injection issues.
☐	The design addresses potential cross-site scripting issues.
☐	The design does not rely on client-side validation.
☐	The design applies defense in depth to the input validation strategy by providing input validation across tiers.
☐	Output that contains input is encoded using HtmlEncode and UrltEncode.

Authentication

Check	Description
☐	Application trust boundaries are identified by the design.
☐	The design identifies the identities that are used to access resources across the trust boundaries.
☐	The design partitions the Web site into public and restricted areas using separate folders.
☐	The design identifies service account requirements.
☐	The design identifies secure storage of credentials that are accepted from users.

Authentication *(continued)*

Check	Description
☐	The design identifies the mechanisms to protect the credentials over the wire (SSL, IPSec, encryption and so on).
☐	Account management policies are taken into consideration by the design.
☐	The design ensure that minimum error information is returned in the event of authentication failure.
☐	The identity that is used to authenticate with the database is identified by the design.
☐	If SQL authentication is used, credentials are adequately secured over the wire (SSL or IPSec) and in storage (DPAPI).
☐	The design adopts a policy of using least-privileged accounts.
☐	Password digests (with salt) are stored in the user store for verification.
☐	Strong passwords are used.
☐	Authentication tickets (cookies) are not transmitted over non-encrypted connections.

Authorization

Check	Description
☐	The role design offers sufficient separation of privileges (the design considers authorization granularity).
☐	Multiple gatekeepers are used for defense in depth.
☐	The application's login is restricted in the database to access-specific stored procedures.
☐	The application's login does not have permissions to access tables directly.
☐	Access to system level resources is restricted.
☐	The design identifies code access security requirements. Privileged resources and privileged operations are identified.
☐	All identities that are used by the application are identified and the resources accessed by each identity are known.

Configuration Management

Check	Description
☐	Administration interfaces are secured (strong authentication and authorization is used).
☐	Remote administration channels are secured.
☐	Configuration stores are secured.
☐	Configuration secrets are not held in plain text in configuration files.
☐	Administrator privileges are separated based on roles (for example, site content developer or system administrator).
☐	Least-privileged process accounts and service accounts are used.

Sensitive Data

Check	Description
☐	Secrets are not stored unless necessary. (Alternate methods have been explored at design time.)
☐	Secrets are not stored in code.
☐	Database connections, passwords, keys, or other secrets are not stored in plain text.
☐	The design identifies the methodology to store secrets securely. (Appropriate algorithms and key sizes are used for encryption. It is preferable that DPAPI is used to store configuration data to avoid key management.)
☐	Sensitive data is not logged in clear text by the application.
☐	The design identifies protection mechanisms for sensitive data that is sent over the network.
☐	Sensitive data is not stored in persistent cookies.
☐	Sensitive data is not transmitted with the GET protocol.

Session Management

Check	Description
☐	SSL is used to protect authentication cookies.
☐	The contents of authentication cookies are encrypted.
☐	Session lifetime is limited.
☐	Session state is protected from unauthorized access.
☐	Session identifiers are not passed in query strings.

Cryptography

Check	Description
☐	Platform-level cryptography is used and it has no custom implementations.
☐	The design identifies the correct cryptographic algorithm (and key size) for the application's data encryption requirements.
☐	The methodology to secure the encryption keys is identified.
☐	The design identifies the key recycle policy for the application.
☐	Encryption keys are secured.
☐	DPAPI is used where possible to avoid key management issues.
☐	Keys are periodically recycled.

Parameter Manipulation

Check	Description
☐	All input parameters are validated (including form fields, query strings, cookies, and HTTP headers).
☐	Cookies with sensitive data are encrypted.
☐	Sensitive data is not passed in query strings or form fields.
☐	HTTP header information is not relied on to make security decisions.
☐	View state is protected using MACs.

Exception Management

Check	Description
☐	The design outlines a standardized approach to structured exception handling across the application.
☐	Application exception handling minimizes the information disclosure in case of an exception.
☐	The design identifies generic error messages that are returned to the client.
☐	Application errors are logged to the error log.
☐	Private data (for example, passwords) is not logged.

Auditing and Logging

Check	Description
☐	The design identifies the level of auditing and logging necessary for the application and identifies the key parameters to be logged and audited.
☐	The design considers how to flow caller identity across multiple tiers (at the operating system or application level) for auditing.
☐	The design identifies the storage, security, and analysis of the application log files.

Checklist: Securing ASP.NET

How to Use This Checklist

This checklist is a companion to Chapter 10, "Building Secure ASP.NET Pages and Controls," Chapter 19, "Securing Your ASP.NET Application and Web Services," and Chapter 20, "Hosting Multiple Web Applications." Use it to help you secure an ASP.NET application and also as a snapshot of the corresponding chapters.

Design Considerations

Check	Description
☐	Security decisions should not rely on client-side validations; they are made on the server side.
☐	The Web site is partitioned into public access areas and restricted areas that require authentication access. Navigation between these areas should not flow sensitive credentials information.
☐	The identities used to access remote resources from ASP.NET Web applications are clearly identified.
☐	Mechanisms have been identified to secure credentials, authentication tickets, and other sensitive information over network and in persistent stores.
☐	A secure approach to exception management is identified. The application fails securely in the event of exceptions.
☐	The site has granular authorization checks for pages and directories.
☐	Web controls, user controls, and resource access code are all partitioned in their own assemblies for granular security.

Application Categories Considerations

Input Validation

Check	Description
☐	User input is validated for type, length, format, and range. Input is checked for known valid and safe data and then for malicious, dangerous data.
☐	String form field input is validated using regular expressions (for example, by the **RegularExpressionValidator** control.)
☐	Regular HTML controls, query strings, cookies, and other forms of input are validated using the **Regex** class and/or your custom validation code.
☐	The **RequiredFieldValidator** control is used where data must be entered.
☐	Range checks in server controls are checked by **RangeValidator** controls.
☐	Free form input is sanitized to clean malicious data.
☐	Input file names are well formed and are verifiably valid within the application context.
☐	Output that includes input is encoded with HtmlEncode and UrlEncode.
☐	MapPath restricts cross-application mapping where appropriate.
☐	Character encoding is set by the server (ISO-8859-1 is recommended).
☐	The ASP.NET version 1.1 **validateRequest** option is enabled.
☐	URLScan is installed on the Web server.
☐	The HttpOnly cookie option is used for defense in depth to help prevent cross-site scripting. (This applies to Internet Explorer 6.1 or later.)
☐	SQL parameters are used in data access code to validate length and type of data and to help prevent SQL injection.

Authentication

Check	Description
☐	Site is partitioned to restricted areas and public areas.
☐	Absolute URLs are used for navigation where the site is partitioned with secure and non-secure folders.
☐	Secure Sockets Layer (SSL) is used to protect credentials and authentication cookies.
☐	The **slidingExpiration** attribute is set to "false" and limited authentication cookie time-outs are used where the cookie is not protected by using SSL.

Authentication *(continued)*

Check	Description
☐	The forms authentication cookie is restricted to HTTPS connections by using the **requireSSL** attribute or the **Secure** cookie property.
☐	The authentication cookie is encrypted and integrity checked (protection="All").
☐	Authentication cookies are not persisted.
☐	Application cookies have unique path/name combinations.
☐	Personalization cookies are separate from authentication cookies.
☐	Passwords are not stored directly in the user store; password digests with salt are stored instead.
☐	The impersonation credentials (if using a fixed identity) are encrypted in the configuration file by using Aspnet_setreg.exe.
☐	Strong password policies are implemented for authentication.
☐	The **<credentials>** element is not used inside **<forms>** element for Forms authentication (use it for testing only).

Authorization

Check	Description
☐	URL authorization is used for page and directory access control.
☐	File authorization is used with Windows authentication.
☐	Principal permission demands are used to secure access to classes and members.
☐	Explicit role checks are used if fine-grained authorization is required.

Configuration Management

Check	Description
☐	Configuration file retrieval is blocked by using **HttpForbiddenHandler**.
☐	A least-privileged account is used to run ASP.NET.
☐	Custom account credentials (if used) are encrypted on the **<processModel>** element by using Aspnet_setreg.exe.
☐	To enforce machine-wide policy, Web.config settings are locked by using **allowOveride="false"** in Machine.config.

Sensitive Data

Check	Description
☐	SSL is used to protect sensitive data on the wire.
☐	Sensitive data is not passed across pages; it is maintained using server-side state management.
☐	Sensitive data is not stored in cookies, hidden form fields, or query strings.
☐	Do not cache sensitive data. Output caching is off by default.
☐	Plain text passwords are avoided in Web.config and Machine.config files. (Aspnet_setreg.exe is used to encrypt credentials.)

Session Management

Check	Description
☐	The session cookie is protected using SSL on all pages that require authenticated access.
☐	The session state service is disabled if not used.
☐	The session state service (if used) runs using a least-privileged account.
☐	Windows authentication is used to connect to Microsoft® SQL Server™ state database.
☐	Access to state data in the SQL Server is restricted.
☐	Connection strings are encrypted by using Aspnet_setreg.exe.
☐	The communication channel to state store is encrypted (IPSec or SSL).

Parameter Manipulation

Check	Description
☐	View state is protected using message authentication codes (MACs).
☐	Query strings with server secrets are hashed.
☐	All input parameters are validated.
☐	**Page.ViewStateUserKey** is used to counter one-click attacks.

Exception Management

Check	Description
☐	Structured exception handling is used.
☐	Exception details are logged on the server.
☐	Generic error pages with harmless messages are returned to the client.
☐	Page-level or application-level error handlers are implemented.
☐	The application distinguishes between errors and exception conditions.

Auditing and Logging

Check	Description
☐	The ASP.NET process is configured to allow new event sources to be created at runtime, or application event sources to be created at installation time.

Configuration File Settings

Check	Description
☐	**<trace/>** Tracing is not enabled on the production servers. `<trace enabled="false">`
☐	**<globalization>** Request and response encoding is appropriately configured.
☐	**<httpRuntime>** **maxRequestLength** is configured to prevent users from uploading very large files (optional).
☐	**<compilation>** Debug compiles are not enabled on the production servers by setting **debug="false"** `<compilation debug="false" . . ./>`

☐	**<pages>**
	
	 If the application does not use view state, **enableViewState** is set to "false".
	
	 `<pages enableViewState="false" . . ./>`
	
	 If the application uses view state, **enableViewState** is set to "true" and **enableViewStateMac** is set to "true" to detect view state tampering.
	
	 `<pages enableViewState="true" enableViewStateMac="true" />`

(continued)

Configuration File Settings *(continued)*

Check	Description

☐	**<customErrors>**
	
	Custom error pages are returned to the client and detailed exception details are prevented from being returned by setting **mode="On"**.
	
	`<customErrors mode="On" />`
	
	A generic error page is specified by the **defaultRedirect** attribute.
	
	`<customErrors mode="On" defaultRedirect="/apperrorpage.htm" />`

☐	**<authentication>**
	
	The authentication mode is appropriately configured to support application requirements. To enforce the use of a specific authentication type, a **<location>** element with **allowOverride="false"** is used.
	
	`<location path="" allowOverride="false">`
	`  <system.web>`
	`    <authentication mode="Windows" />`
	`  </system.web>`
	`</location>`

☐	**<forms>**
	
	The Web site is partitioned for public and restricted access.
	
	The Forms authentication configuration is secure:
	
	`<forms loginUrl="Restricted\login.aspx"`
	`       protection="All"`
	`       requireSSL="true"`
	`       timeout="10"`
	`       name="AppNameCookie"`
	`       path="/FormsAuth"`
	`       slidingExpiration="true" />`
	
	The authentication cookie is encrypted and integrity checked (**protection**).
	
	SSL is required for authentication cookie (**requireSSL**).
	
	Sliding expiration is set to false if SSL is not used (**slidingExpiration**).
	
	The session lifetime is restricted (**timeout**).
	
	Cookie names and paths are unique (**name** and **path**).
	
	The **<credentials>** element is not used.

Configuration File Settings *(continued)*

Check	Description
☐	**<identity>** Impersonation identities (if used) are encrypted in the registry by using Aspnet_setreg.exe: ```<identity impersonate="true"
userName="registry:HKLM\SOFTWARE\YourApp\
identity\ASPNET_SETREG,userName"
password="registry:HKLM\SOFTWARE\YourApp\
identity\ASPNET_SETREG,password"/>```
☐	**<authorization>** Correct format of role names is verified.
☐	**<machineKey>** If multiple ASP.NET Web applications are deployed on the same Web server, the "IsolateApps" setting is used to ensure that a separate key is generated for each Web application. ```<machineKey validationKey="AutoGenerate,IsolateApps"
decryptionKey="AutoGenerate,IsolateApps"
validation="SHA1" />``` If the ASP. NET Web application is running in a Web farm, specific machine keys are used, and these keys are copied across all servers in the farm. If the view state is enabled, the **validation** attribute is set to "SHA1". The **validation** attribute is set to "3DES" if the Forms authentication cookie is to be encrypted for the application.
☐	**<sessionState>** If **mode="StateServer"**, then credentials are stored in an encrypted form in the registry by using Aspnet_setreg.exe. If **mode="SQLServer"**, then Windows authentication is used to connect to the state store database and credentials are stored in an encrypted form in the registry by using Aspnet_setreg.exe.
☐	**<httpHandlers>** Unused file types are mapped to HttpForbiddenHandler to prevent files from being retrieved over HTTP. For example: ```<add verb="*" path="*.rem"
type="System.Web.HttpForbiddenHandler"/>```

(continued)

Configuration File Settings *(continued)*

Check	Description

☐	**<processModel>**
	
	A least-privileged account like ASPNET is used to run the ASP.NET process.
	
	`<processModel userName="Machine" password="AutoGenerate"`
	
	The system account is not used to run the ASP.NET process.
	
	The **Act as part of the operating system** privilege is not granted to the process account.
	
	Credentials for custom accounts are encrypted by using Aspnet_setreg.exe.
	
	`<processModel`
	`  userName="registry:HKLM\SOFTWARE\MY_SECURE_APP\`
	`  processmodel\ASPNET_SETREG,userName"`
	`  password="registry:HKLM\SOFTWARE\MY_SECURE_APP\`
	`  processmodel\ASPNET_SETREG,password" . . ./>`
	
	If the application uses Enterprise Services, **comAuthenticationLevel** and **comImpersonationLevel** are configured appropriately.
	
	Call level authentication is set at minimum to ensure that all method calls can be authenticated by the remote application.
	
	PktPrivacy is used to encrypt and tamper proof the data across the wire in the absence of infrastructure channel security (IPSec).
	
	PktIntegrity is used for tamper proofing with no encryption (Eavesdroppers with network monitors can see your data.)

☐	**<webServices>** Unused protocols are disabled. Automatic generation of Web Services Description Language (WSDL) is disabled (optional).

Web Farm Considerations

Check	Description
☐	**Session state**. To avoid server affinity, the ASP.NET session state is maintained out of process in the ASP.NET SQL Server state database or in the out-of-process state service that runs on a remote machine.
☐	**Encryption and verification**. The keys used to encrypt and verify Forms authentication cookies and view state are the same across all servers in a Web farm.
☐	**DPAPI**. DPAPI cannot be used with the machine key to encrypt common data that needs to be accessed by all servers in the farm. To encrypt shared data on a remote server, use an alternate implementation, such as 3DES.

Hosting Multiple Applications

Check	Description

☐	Applications have distinct machine keys.
	
	 Use **IsolateApps** on **<machineKey>** or use per application **<machineKey>** elements.
	
	 `<machineKey validationKey="AutoGenerate,IsolateApps"`
	               `decryptionKey="AutoGenerate,IsolateApps" . . . />`

☐	Unique path/name combinations for Forms authentication cookies are enabled for each application.
☐	Multiple processes (IIS 6.0 application pools) are used for application isolation on Microsoft Windows® Server 2003.
☐	Multiple anonymous user accounts (and impersonation) are used for application isolation on Windows 2000.
☐	Common machine keys are enabled on all servers in a Web farm.
☐	Separate machine keys for each application are used when hosting multiple applications on a single server.
☐	Code access security trust levels are used for process isolation and to restrict access to system resources (requires .NET Framework version 1.1).

ACLs and Permissions

Check	Description
☐	Temporary ASP.NET files `%windir%\Microsoft.NET\Framework\{version}Temporary ASP.NET Files` ASP.NET process account and impersonated identities: Full Control
☐	Temporary directory `(%temp%)` ASP.NET process account: Full Control
☐	.NET Framework directory `%windir%\Microsoft.NET\Framework\{version}` ASP.NET process account and impersonated identities: Read and Execute List Folder Contents

(continued)

ACLs and Permissions *(continued)*

Check	Description
☐	.NET Framework configuration directory `%windir%\Microsoft.NET\Framework\{version}\CONFIG` ASP.NET process account and impersonated Identities: Read and Execute List Folder Contents Read
☐	Web site root `C:\inetpub\wwwroot` or the path that the default Web site points to ASP.NET process account: Full Control
☐	System root directory `%windir%\system32` ASP.NET process account: Read
☐	Global assembly cache `%windir%\assembly` Process account and impersonated identities: Read

☐	Content directory
	
	`C:\inetpub\wwwroot\YourWebApp`
	Process account:
	Read and Execute
	List Folder Contents
	Read
	
	Note With .NET Framework version 1.0, all parent directories from the content directory to the file system root directory also require the above permissions. Parent directories include:
	`C:\`
	`C:\inetpub\`
	`C:\inetpub\wwwroot\`

Application Bin Directory

Check	Description
☐	IIS Web permissions are configured. Bin directory does not have Read, Write, or Directory browsing permissions. Execute permissions are set to None.
☐	Authentication settings are removed (so that all access is denied).

Checklist:
Securing Web Services

How to Use This Checklist

This checklist is a companion to Chapter 12, "Building Secure Web Services." Use it to help you build and secure your Web services and also as a snapshot of the corresponding chapter.

Design Considerations

Check	Description
☐	The authentication strategy has been identified.
☐	Privacy and integrity requirements of SOAP messages have been considered.
☐	Identities that are used for resource access have been identified.
☐	Implications of code access security trust levels have been considered.

Development Considerations

Input Validation

Check	Description
☐	Input to Web methods is constrained and validated for type, length, format, and range.
☐	Input data sanitization is only performed in addition to constraining input data.
☐	XML input data is validated based on an agreed schema.

Authentication

Check	Description
☐	Web services that support restricted operations or provide sensitive data support authentication.
☐	If plain text credentials are passed in SOAP headers, SOAP messages are only passed over encrypted communication channels, for example, using SSL.
☐	Basic authentication is only used over an encrypted communication channel.
☐	Authentication mechanisms that use SOAP headers are based on Web Services Security (WS Security) using the Web Services Enhancements WSE).

Authorization

Check	Description
☐	Web services that support restricted operations or provide sensitive data support authorization.
☐	Where appropriate, access to Web service is restricted using URL authorization or file authorization if Windows authentication is used.
☐	Where appropriate, access to publicly accessible Web methods is restricted using declarative principle permission demands.

Sensitive Data

Check	Description
☐	Sensitive data in Web service SOAP messages is encrypted using XML encryption OR messages are only passed over encrypted communication channels (for example, using SSL.)

Parameter Manipulation

Check	Description
☐	If parameter manipulation is a concern (particularly where messages are routed through multiple intermediary nodes across multiple network links). Messages are digitally signed to ensure that they cannot be tampered with.

Exception Management

Check	Description
☐	Structured exception handling is used when implementing Web services.
☐	Exception details are logged (except for private data, such as passwords).
☐	**SoapExceptions** are thrown and returned to the client using the standard **\<Fault>** SOAP element.
☐	If application-level exception handling is required a custom SOAP extension is used.

Auditing and Logging

Check	Description
☐	The Web service logs transactions and key operations.

Proxy Considerations

Check	Description
☐	The endpoint address in Web Services Description Language (WSDL) is checked for validity.
☐	The URL Behavior property of the Web reference is set to dynamic for added flexibility.

Administration Considerations

Check	Description
☐	Unnecessary Web service protocols, including HTTP GET and HTTP POST, are disabled.
☐	The documentation protocol is disabled if you do not want to support the dynamic generation of WSDL.
☐	The Web service runs using a least-privileged process account (configured through the **\<processModel>** element in Machine.config.) Custom accounts are encrypted by using Aspnet_setref.exe.
☐	Tracing is disabled with: `<trace enabled="false" />`
☐	Debug compilations are disabled with: `<compilation debug="false" explicit="true" defaultLanguage="vb">`

Checklist:
Securing Enterprise Services

How to Use This Checklist

This checklist is a companion to Chapter 11, "Building Secure Serviced Components" and Chapter 17, "Securing Your Application Server." Use it to help you secure Enterprise Services and the server it runs on, or as a quick evaluation snapshot of the corresponding chapters.

This checklist should evolve with steps that you discover to secure Enterprise Services.

Developer Checks

Use the following checks if you build serviced components.

Authentication

Check	Description

☐	Call-level authentication is used at minimum to prevent anonymous access. Serviced component assemblies include:
	
	`[assembly: ApplicationAccessControl(`
	`           Authentication = AuthenticationOption.Call)]`

Authorization

Check	Description
☐	Role-based security is enabled. Serviced component assemblies include: [assembly: ApplicationAccessControl(true)]

☐	Component-level access checks are enabled to support component-level, interface-level, and method-level role checks. Serviced component assemblies include:
	
	`[assembly: ApplicationAccessControl(AccessChecksLevel=`
	`              AccessChecksLevelOption.ApplicationComponent)]`

(continued)

Authorization *(continued)*

Check	Description
☐	Component-level access checks are enforced for all serviced components. Classes are annotated with: `[ComponentAccessControl(true)]`
☐	To support method-level security, the **[SecurityMethod]** attribute is used on classes or method implementations, or the **[SecurityRole]** attribute is used on method implementations.

Configuration Management

Check	Description
☐	Server applications are configured to run with least-privileged accounts.
☐	Server applications only run using the interactive user account during development.
☐	Object constructor strings do not contain plain text secrets.

Sensitive Data

Check	Description

☐	In the absence of IPSec encryption, RPC encryption is used to secure sensitive data over the network in the absence of an IPSec infrastructure. Serviced component assemblies that use RPC encryption include:
	
	`[assembly: ApplicationAccessControl(`
	`            Authentication = AuthenticationOption.Privacy)]`

Auditing and Logging

Check	Description
☐	User transactions are logged to an event log. The audit record includes original caller identity from **SecurityCallContext.OriginalCaller**.

Deployment Considerations

Check	Description
☐	Port ranges are defined if you use dynamic port range allocation OR static endpoint mapping is configured.
☐	Secrets are not stored in object constructor strings. Secrets such as database connection strings are encrypted prior to storage.
☐	The server application run-as account is configured as a least-privileged account.

Impersonation

Check	Description
☐	The impersonation level is configured correctly. For ASP.NET clients, the impersonation level is configured in Machine.config on the **<processModel>** element. For Enterprise Services client applications, the level is configured in the COM+ catalog.
☐	Serviced component assemblies define the required impersonation level by using the ApplicationAccessControl attribute as shown below: `[assembly: ApplicationAccessControl( ImpersonationLevel=ImpersonationLevelOption.Identify)]`

Administrator Checklist

Check	Description
☐	Latest COM+ updates and patches are installed.
☐	Object constructor strings do not contain plain text secrets.
☐	COM+ administration components are restricted.
☐	Impersonation level that is set for the application is correct.
☐	Server applications are configured to run with a least-privileged account. Server applications do not run using the identity of the interactively logged on user.
☐	DTC service is disabled if it is not required.

Checklist:
Securing Remoting

How to Use This Checklist

This checklist is a companion to Chapter 13, "Building Secure Remoted Components." Use it to help you build secure components that use the Microsoft ® .NET remoting technology and as a snapshot of the corresponding chapter.

Design Considerations

Check	Description
☐	Remote components are not exposed to the Internet.
☐	The ASP.NET host and HttpChannel are used to take advantage of Internet Information Services (IIS) and ASP.NET security features.
☐	TcpChannel (if used) is only used in trusted server scenarios.
☐	TcpChannel (if used) is used in conjunction with custom authentication and authorization solutions.

Input Validation

Check	Description
☐	**MarshalByRefObj** objects from clients are not accepted without validating the source of the object.
☐	The risk of serialization attacks are mitigated by setting the **typeFilterLevel** attribute programmatically or in the application's Web.config file.
☐	All field items that are retrieved from serialized data streams are validated as they are created on the server side.

Authentication

Check	Description
☐	Anonymous authentication is disabled in IIS.
☐	ASP.NET is configured for Windows authentication.
☐	Client credentials are configured at the client through the proxy object.
☐	Authentication connection sharing is used to improve performance.
☐	Clients are forced to authenticate on each call (**unsafeAuthenticatedConnectionSharing** is set to "false").
☐	**connectionGroupName** is specified to prevent unwanted reuse of authentication connections.
☐	Plain text credentials are not passed over the network.
☐	**IPrincipal** objects passed from the client are not trusted.

Authorization

Check	Description
☐	IPSec is used for machine-level access control.
☐	File authorization is enabled for user access control.
☐	Users are authorized with principal-based role checks.
☐	Where appropriate, access to remote resources is restricted by setting **rejectRemoteRequest** attribute to "true".

Configuration Management

Check	Description
☐	Configuration files are locked down and secured for both the client and the server.
☐	Generic error messages are sent to the client by setting the **mode** attribute of the **<customErrors>** element to "On".

Sensitive Data

Check	Description
☐	Exchange of sensitive application data is secured by using SSL, IPSec, or a custom encryption sink.

Exception Management

Check	Description
☐	Structured exception handling is used.
☐	Exception details are logged (not including private data, such as passwords).
☐	Generic error pages with standard, user friendly messages are returned to the client.

Auditing and Logging

Check	Description
☐	If ASP.NET is used as the host, IIS auditing features are enabled.
☐	If required, a custom channel sink is used to perform logging on the client and the server.

Checklist:
Securing Data Access

How to Use This Checklist

This checklist is a companion to Chapter 14, "Building Secure Data Access" and Chapter 16, "Securing Your Database Server." Use it to help you build secure data access, or as a quick evaluation snapshot of the corresponding chapters.

This checklist should evolve with secure data access practices that you discover during software development.

SQL Injection Checks

Check	Description
☐	Input passed to data access methods that originates outside the current trust boundary is constrained. Sanitization of input is only used as a defense in depth measure.
☐	Stored procedures that accept parameters are used by data access code. If stored procedures are not used, type safe SQL parameters are used to construct SQL commands.
☐	Least-privileged accounts are used to connect to the database.

Authentication

Check	Description
☐	Windows authentication is used to connect to the database.
☐	Strong passwords are used and enforced.
☐	If SQL Server authentication is used, the credentials are secured over the network by using IPSec or SSL, or by installing a database server certificate.
☐	If SQL Server authentication is used, connection strings are encrypted by using DPAPI and are stored in a secure location.
☐	Application connects using a least-privileged account. The **sa** account or other privileged accounts that are members of the **sysadmin** or **db_owner** roles are not used for application logins.

Authorization

Check	Description
☐	Calling users are restricted using declarative or imperative principal permission checks (normally performed by business logic).
☐	Calling code is restricted using identity permission demands in scenarios where you know and want to limit the calling code.
☐	Application login is restricted in the database and can only execute selected stored procedures. Application's login has no direct table access.

Configuration Management

Check	Description
☐	Windows authentication is used to avoid credential management.
☐	Connection strings are encrypted and encrypted data is stored securely, for example, in a restricted registry key.
☐	OLE DB connection strings do not contain Persist Security Info="true" or "yes".
☐	UDL files are secured with restricted ACLs.

Sensitive Data

Check	Description
☐	Sensitive data is encrypted in the database using strong symmetric encryption (for example, 3DES).
☐	Symmetric encryption keys are backed up and encrypted with DPAPI and stored in a restricted registry key.
☐	Sensitive data is secured over the network by using SSL or IPSec.
☐	Passwords are not stored in custom user store databases. Password hashes are stored with salt values instead.

Exception Management

Check	Description
☐	ADO.NET exceptions are trapped and logged.
☐	Database connections and other limited resources are released in case of exception or completion of operation.
☐	ASP.NET is configured with a generic error page using the **<customErrors>** element.

Deployment Considerations

Check	Description
☐	Firewall restrictions ensure that only the SQL Server listening port is available on the database server.
☐	A method for maintaining encrypted database connection strings is defined.
☐	The application is configured to use a least-privileged database login.
☐	SQL server auditing is configured. Failed login attempts are logged at minimum.
☐	Data privacy and integrity over the network is provided with IPSec or SSL.

Checklist:
Securing Your Network

How to Use This Checklist

This checklist is a companion to Chapter 15, "Securing Your Network." Use it to help secure your network, or as a quick evaluation snapshot of the corresponding chapters.

This checklist should evolve as you discover steps that help implement your secure network.

Router Considerations

Check	Description
☐	Latest patches and updates are installed.
☐	You subscribed to router vendor's security notification service.
☐	Known vulnerable ports are blocked.
☐	Ingress and egress filtering is enabled. Incoming and outgoing packets are confirmed as coming from public or internal networks.
☐	ICMP traffic is screened from the internal network.
☐	Administration interfaces to the router are enumerated and secured.
☐	Web-facing administration is disabled.
☐	Directed broadcast traffic is not received or forwarded.
☐	Unused services are disabled (for example, TFTP).
☐	Strong passwords are used.
☐	Logging is enabled and audited for unusual traffic or patterns.
☐	Large ping packets are screened.
☐	Routing Information Protocol (RIP) packets, if used, are blocked at the outermost router.

Firewall Considerations

Check	Description
☐	Latest patches and updates are installed.
☐	Effective filters are in place to prevent malicious traffic from entering the perimeter
☐	Unused ports are blocked by default.
☐	Unused protocols are blocked by default.
☐	IPsec is configured for encrypted communication within the perimeter network.
☐	Intrusion detection is enabled at the firewall.

Switch Considerations

Check	Description
☐	Latest patches and updates are installed.
☐	Administrative interfaces are enumerated and secured.
☐	Unused administrative interfaces are disabled.
☐	Unused services are disabled.
☐	Available services are secured.

Checklist:
Securing Your Web Server

How to Use This Checklist

This checklist is a companion to Chapter 16, "Securing Your Web Server." Use it to help implement a secure Web server, or as a quick evaluation snapshot of the corresponding chapter.

This checklist should evolve with steps that you discover to secure your Web server.

Patches and Updates

Check	Description
☐	MBSA is run on a regular interval to check for latest operating system and components updates. For more information, see *http://www.microsoft.com/technet/treeview /default.asp?url=/technet/security/tools/Tools/mbsahome.asp*.
☐	The latest updates and patches are applied for Windows, IIS server, and the .NET Framework. (These are tested on development servers prior to deployment on the production servers.)
☐	Subscribe to the Microsoft Security Notification Service at *http://www.microsoft.com /technet/treeview/default.asp?url=/technet/security/bulletin/notify.asp*.

IISLockdown

Check	Description
☐	IISLockdown has been run on the server.
☐	URLScan is installed and configured.

Services

Check	Description
☐	Unnecessary Windows services are disabled.
☐	Services are running with least-privileged accounts.
☐	FTP, SMTP, and NNTP services are disabled if they are not required.
☐	Telnet service is disabled.
☐	ASP .NET state service is disabled and is not used by your applications.

Protocols

Check	Description
☐	WebDAV is disabled if not used by the application OR it is secured if it is required. For more information, see Microsoft Knowledge Base article 323470, "How To: Create a Secure WebDAV Publishing Directory."
☐	TCP/IP stack is hardened.
☐	NetBIOS and SMB are disabled (closes ports 137, 138, 139, and 445).

Accounts

Check	Description
☐	Unused accounts are removed from the server.
☐	Windows Guest account is disabled.
☐	Administrator account is renamed and has a strong password..
☐	IUSR_MACHINE account is disabled if it is not used by the application.
☐	If your applications require anonymous access, a custom least-privileged anonymous account is created.
☐	The anonymous account does not have write access to Web content directories and cannot execute command-line tools.
☐	ASP.NET process account is configured for least privilege. (This only applies if you are not using the default ASPNET account, which is a least-privileged account.)
☐	Strong account and password policies are enforced for the server.
☐	Remote logons are restricted. (The "Access this computer from the network" user-right is removed from the Everyone group.)
☐	Accounts are not shared among administrators.
☐	Null sessions (anonymous logons) are disabled.
☐	Approval is required for account delegation.
☐	Users and administrators do not share accounts.
☐	No more than two accounts exist in the Administrators group.
☐	Administrators are required to log on locally OR the remote administration solution is secure.

Files and Directories

Check	Description
☐	Files and directories are contained on NTFS volumes.
☐	Web site content is located on a non-system NTFS volume.
☐	Log files are located on a non-system NTFS volume and not on the same volume where the Web site content resides.
☐	The Everyone group is restricted (no access to \WINNT\system32 or Web directories).
☐	Web site root directory has deny write ACE for anonymous Internet accounts.
☐	Content directories have deny write ACE for anonymous Internet accounts.
☐	Remote IIS administration application is removed (\WINNT\System32\Inetsrv\IISAdmin).
☐	Resource kit tools, utilities, and SDKs are removed.
☐	Sample applications are removed (\WINNT\Help\IISHelp, \Inetpub\IISSamples).

Shares

Check	Description
☐	All unnecessary shares are removed (including default administration shares).
☐	Access to required shares is restricted (the Everyone group does not have access).
☐	Administrative shares (C$ and Admin$) are removed if they are not required (Microsoft Management Server (SMS) and Microsoft Operations Manager (MOM) require these shares).

Ports

Check	Description
☐	Internet-facing interfaces are restricted to port 80 (and 443 if SSL is used).
☐	Intranet traffic is encrypted (for example, with SSL) or restricted if you do not have a secure data center infrastructure.

Registry

Check	Description
☐	Remote registry access is restricted.
☐	SAM is secured (HKLM\System\CurrentControlSet\Control\LSA\NoLMHash). This applies only to standalone servers.

Auditing and Logging

Check	Description
☐	Failed logon attempts are audited.
☐	IIS log files are relocated and secured.
☐	Log files are configured with an appropriate size depending on the application security requirement.
☐	Log files are regularly archived and analyzed.
☐	Access to the Metabase.bin file is audited.
☐	IIS is configured for W3C Extended log file format auditing.

Sites and Virtual Directories

Check	Description
☐	Web sites are located on a non-system partition.
☐	"Parent paths" setting is disabled.
☐	Potentially dangerous virtual directories, including IISSamples, IISAdmin, IISHelp, and Scripts virtual directories, are removed.
☐	MSADC virtual directory (RDS) is removed or secured.
☐	Include directories do not have Read Web permission.
☐	Virtual directories that allow anonymous access restrict Write and Execute Web permissions for the anonymous account.
☐	There is script source access only on folders that support content authoring.
☐	There is write access only on folders that support content authoring and these folder are configured for authentication (and SSL encryption, if required).
☐	FrontPage Server Extensions (FPSE) are removed if not used. If they are used, they are updated and access to FPSE is restricted.

Script Mappings

Check	Description
☐	Extensions not used by the application are mapped to 404.dll (.idq, .htw, .ida, .shtml, .shtm, .stm, idc, .htr, .printer).
☐	Unnecessary ASP.NET file type extensions are mapped to "HttpForbiddenHandler" in Machine.config.

ISAPI Filters

Check	Description
☐	Unnecessary or unused ISAPI filters are removed from the server.

IIS Metabase

Check	Description
☐	Access to the metabase is restricted by using NTFS permissions (%systemroot%\system32\inetsrv\metabase.bin).
☐	IIS banner information is restricted (IP address in content location disabled).

Server Certificates

Check	Description
☐	Certificate date ranges are valid.
☐	Certificates are used for their intended purpose (for example, the server certificate is not used for e-mail).
☐	The certificate's public key is valid, all the way to a trusted root authority.
☐	The certificate has not been revoked.

Machine.config

Check	Description
☐	Protected resources are mapped to HttpForbiddenHandler.
☐	Unused HttpModules are removed.
☐	Tracing is disabled <trace enable="false"/>
☐	Debug compiles are turned off. `<compilation debug="false" explicit="true" defaultLanguage="vb">`

Code Access Security

Check	Description
☐	Code access security is enabled on the server.
☐	All permissions have been removed from the local intranet zone.
☐	All permissions have been removed from the Internet zone.

Other Check Points

Check	Description
☐	IISLockdown tool has been run on the server.
☐	HTTP requests are filtered. URLScan is installed and configured.
☐	Remote administration of the server is secured and configured for encryption, low session time-outs, and account lockouts.

Dos and Don'ts

- Do use a dedicated machine as a Web server.
- Do physically protect the Web server machine in a secure machine room.
- Do configure a separate anonymous user account for each application, if you host multiple Web applications,
- Do not install the IIS server on a domain controller.
- Do not connect an IIS Server to the Internet until it is fully hardened.
- Do not allow anyone to locally log on to the machine except for the administrator.

Checklist:
Securing Your Database Server

How to Use This Checklist

This checklist is a companion to Chapter 18, "Securing Your Database Server." Use it to help you secure a database server and also as a snapshot of the corresponding chapter.

Installation Considerations for Production Servers

Check	Description
☐	Upgrade tools, debug symbols, replication support, books online, and development tools are not installed on the production server.
☐	Microsoft ® SQL Server™ is not installed on a domain controller.
☐	SQL Server Agent is not installed if it is not being used by any application.
☐	SQL Server is installed on a dedicated database server.
☐	SQL Server is installed on an NTFS partition.
☐	Windows Authentication mode is selected unless SQL Server Authentication is specifically required, in which case Mixed Mode is selected.
☐	A strong password is applied for the **sa** account or any other member of the **sysadmin** role. (Use strong passwords for all accounts.)
☐	The database server is physically secured.

Patches and Updates

Check	Description
☐	The latest service packs and patches have been applied for SQL Server. (See *http://support.microsoft.com/default.aspx?scid=kb;EN-US;290211.*)
☐	Post service-pack patches have been applied for SQL server. (See *http://www.microsoft.com/technet/treeview/default.asp?url=/technet/security /current.asp?productid=30&servicepackid=0.*)

Services

Check	Description
☐	Unnecessary Microsoft Windows˚ services are disabled on the database server.
☐	All optional services, including Microsoft Search Service, MSSQLServerADHelper, and SQLServerAgent, are disabled if not used by any applications.
☐	The Microsoft Distributed Transaction Coordinator (MS DTC) is disabled if it is not being used by any applications.
☐	A least-privileged local/domain account is used to run the various SQL Server services, for example, back up and replication.

Protocols

Check	Description
☐	All protocols except TCP/IP are disabled within SQL Server. Check this using the Server Network Utility.
☐	The TCP/IP stack is hardened on the database server.

Accounts

Check	Description
☐	SQL Server is running using a least-privileged local account (or optionally, a least-privileged domain account if network services are required).
☐	Unused accounts are removed from Windows and SQL Server.
☐	The Windows guest account is disabled.
☐	The administrator account is renamed and has a strong password.
☐	Strong password policy is enforced.
☐	Remote logons are restricted.
☐	Null sessions (anonymous logons) are restricted.
☐	Approval is required for account delegation.
☐	Shared accounts are not used.
☐	Membership of the local administrators group is restricted (ideally, no more than two administration accounts).

Files and Directories

Check	Description
☐	Restrictive permissions are configured on SQL Server installation directories (per the guide).
☐	The Everyone group does not have permission to access SQL Server installation directories.
☐	Setup log files are secured.
☐	Tools, utilities, and SDKs are removed or secured.
☐	Sensitive data files are encrypted using EFS (This is an optional step. If implemented, use EFS only to encrypt MDF files, not LDF log files).

Shares

Check	Description
☐	All unnecessary shares are removed from the server.
☐	Access to required shares is restricted (the Everyone group doesn't have access).
☐	Administrative shares (C$ and Admin$) are removed if they are not required (Microsoft Management Server (SMS) and Microsoft Operations Manager (MOM) require these shares).

Ports

Check	Description
☐	Restrict access to all ports on the server except the ports configured for SQL Server and database instances (TCP 1433 and UDP 1434 by default).
☐	Named instances are configured to listen on the same port.
☐	Port 3389 is secured using IPSec if it is left open for remote Terminal Services administration
☐	The firewall is configured to support DTC traffic (if required by the application).
☐	The **Hide server** option is selected in the Server Network Utility (optional).

Registry

Check	Description
☐	SQL Server registry keys are secured with restricted permissions.
☐	The SAM is secured (standalone servers only).

Auditing and Logging

Check	Description
☐	All failed Windows login attempts are logged.
☐	All failed actions are logged across the file system.
☐	SQL Server login auditing is enabled.
☐	Log files are relocated from the default location and secured with access control lists.
☐	Log files are configured with an appropriate size depending on the application security requirement.
☐	Where the database contents are highly sensitive or vital, Windows is set to Shut Down mode on overflow of the security logs.

SQL Server Security

Check	Description
☐	SQL Server authentication is set to **Windows only** (if supported by the application).
☐	The SQL Server audit level is set to **Failure** or **All**.
☐	SQL Server runs using a least-privileged account.

SQL Server Logins, Users, and Roles

Check	Description
☐	A strong **sa** password is used (for all accounts).
☐	SQL Server guest user accounts are removed.
☐	BUILTIN\Administrators server login is removed.
☐	Permissions are not granted for the public role.
☐	Members of **sysadmin** fixed server role are limited (ideally, no more than two users).
☐	Restricted database permissions are granted. Use of built-in roles, such as db_datareader and db_datawriter, are avoided because they provide limited authorization granularity.
☐	Default permissions that are applied to SQL Server objects are not altered.

SQL Server Database Objects

Check	Description
☐	Sample databases (including Pubs and Northwind) are removed.
☐	Stored procedures and extended stored procedures are secured.
☐	Access to cmdExec is restricted to members of the sysadmin role.

Additional Considerations

Check	Description
☐	A certificate is installed on the database server to support SSL communication and the automatic encryption of SQL account credentials (optional).
☐	NTLM version 2 is enabled by setting **LMCompatibilityLevel** to 5.

Staying Secure

Check	Description
☐	Regular backups are performed.
☐	Group membership is audited.
☐	Audit logs are regularly monitored.
☐	Security assessments are regularly performed.
☐	You subscribe to SQL security bulletins at *http://www.microsoft.com/technet/treeview /default.asp?url=/technet/security/current.asp?productid=30&servicepackid=0.*
☐	You subscribe to the Microsoft Security Notification Service at *http://www.microsoft.com /technet/treeview/default.asp?url=/technet/security/bulletin/notify.asp.*

Checklist:
Security Review for Managed Code

How to Use This Checklist

This checklist is a companion to Chapter 7, "Building Secure Assemblies", and Chapter 8, "Code Access Security in Practice." Use it to help you implement a security review for managed code in your Web application, or as a quick evaluation snapshot of the corresponding chapters.

This checklist should evolve so that you can repeat a successful security review of managed code.

General Code Review Guidelines

Check	Description
☐	Potential threats are clearly documented. (Threats are dependent upon the specific scenario and assembly type.)
☐	Code is developed based on .NET framework coding guidelines and secure coding guidelines at *http://msdn.microsoft.com/library/default.asp?url=/library/en-us/cpgenref/html/cpconnetframeworkdesignguidelines.asp*.
☐	The FXCop analysis tool is run on assemblies and security warnings are addressed.

Managed Code Review Guidelines

Assembly-Level Checks

Check	Description
☐	Assemblies have a strong name. (Dynamically generated ASP.NET Web page assemblies cannot currently have a strong name.)
☐	You have considered delay signing as a way to protect and restrict the private key that is used in the strong name and signing process.
☐	Assemblies include declarative security attributes (with **SecurityAction.RequestMinimum**) to specify minimum permission requirements.
☐	Highly privileged assemblies are separated from lower privileged assemblies. If the assembly is to be used in a partial-trust environment (for example, it is called from a partial-trust Web application), then privileged code is sandboxed in a separate assembly.

Class-Level Checks

Check	Description
☐	Class and member visibility is restricted. The most restrictive access modifier is used (private where possible).
☐	Non-base classes are sealed.
☐	Input from outside the current trust boundary is validated. Input data is constrained and validated for type, length, format, and range.
☐	Code implements declarative checks where virtual internal methods are used.
☐	Access to public classes and methods are restricted with principal permission demands (where appropriate).
☐	Fields are private. When necessary, field values are exposed by using read/write or read-only public properties.
☐	Read-only properties are used where possible.
☐	Types returned from methods that are not designed to be created independently contain private default constructors.
☐	Unsealed public types do not have internal virtual members.
☐	Use of event handlers is thoroughly reviewed.
☐	Static constructors are private.

Cryptography

Check	Description
☐	Code uses platform-provided cryptography and does not use custom implementations.
☐	Random keys are generated by using RNGCryptoServiceProvider (and not the Random class).
☐	PasswordDeriveBytes is used for password-based encryption.
☐	DPAPI is used to encrypt configuration secrets to avoid the key management issue.
☐	The appropriate key sizes are used for the chosen algorithm, or if they are not, the reasons are identified and understood.
☐	Keys are not held in code.
☐	Access to persisted keys is restricted.
☐	Keys are cycled periodically.
☐	Exported private keys are protected.

Secrets

Check	Description
☐	Secrets are not hard coded.
☐	Plain text secrets are not stored in configuration files.
☐	Plain text secrets are not stored in memory for extended periods of time.

Exception Management

Check	Description
☐	Code uses exception handling. You catch only the exceptions that you know about.
☐	Exception details are logged on the server to assist in diagnosing problems.
☐	The information that is returned to the end user is limited and safe.
☐	Code that uses exception filters is not sensitive to filter execution sequence (filter runs before finally block).
☐	Code fails early to avoid unnecessary processing that consumes resources.
☐	Exception conditions do not allow a user to bypass security checks to run privileged code.

Delegates

Check	Description
☐	Delegates are not accepted from untrusted sources.
☐	If code does accept a delegate from untrusted code, it constrains the delegate before calling it by using security permissions with SecurityAction.PermitOnly.
☐	Permissions are not asserted before calling a delegate.

Serialization

Check	Description
☐	Serialization is restricted to privileged code.
☐	Sensitive data is not serialized.
☐	Field data from serialized data streams is validated.
☐	ISerializable.GetObjectData implementation is protected with an identity permission demand in scenarios where you want to restrict which code can serialize the object.

Threading

Check	Description
☐	Results of security checks are not cached.
☐	Impersonation tokens are considered when new threads are created (any existing thread token is not passed to the new thread).
☐	Threads are synchronized in static class constructors for multithreaded application code.
☐	Object implementation code is designed and built to be thread safe.
☐	Threads are synchronized in static class constructors.

Reflection

Check	Description
☐	Caller cannot influence dynamically generated code (for example, by passing assembly and type names as input arguments).
☐	Code demands permission for user authorization where assemblies are loaded dynamically.

Unmanaged Code Access

Check	Description
☐	Input and output strings that are passed between managed and unmanaged code are constrained and validated.
☐	Array bounds are checked.
☐	File path lengths are checked and do not exceed MAX_PATH.
☐	Unmanaged code is compiled with the /GS switch.
☐	Use of "dangerous" APIs by unmanaged code is closely inspected. These include **LogonUser**, **RevertToSelf**, **CreateThread**, Network APIs, and Sockets APIs.
☐	Naming conventions (safe, native, unsafe) are applied to unmanaged APIs.
☐	Assemblies that call unmanaged code specify unmanaged permission requirements using declarative security (**SecurityAction.RequestMinimum**).
☐	Unmanaged API calls are sandboxed and isolated in a wrapper assembly.
☐	Use of **SuppressUnmanagedCodeSecurityAttribute** is thoroughly reviewed and additional security checks are implemented.
☐	Types are not annotated with **SuppressUnmanagedCodeSecurityAttribute**. (This attribute is used on specific P/Invoke method declarations instead.)
☐	Calling code is appropriately authorized using a full stack walk Demand (using either a .NET Framework permission or custom permission).

Unmanaged Code Access *(continued)*

Check	Description
☐	Unmanaged types or handles are never exposed to partially trusted code.
☐	Pointers are private fields.
☐	Methods that use **IntPtr** fields in a type that has a finalizer call **GC.KeepAlive(object)**.

Resource Access Considerations

File I/O

Check	Description
☐	No security decisions are made based on filenames.
☐	Input file paths and file names are well formed.
☐	Environment variables are not used to construct file paths.
☐	File access is constrained to the context of the application (by using a restricted **FileIOPermission**).
☐	Assembly file I/O requirements are specified using declarative security attributes (with **SecurityAction.RequestMinimum**).

Event Log

Check	Description
☐	Event log access code is constrained using **EventLogPermission**. This particularly applies if your event logging code could be called by untrusted callers.
☐	Event sources are created at installation time (or the account used to run the code that writes to the event log must be allowed to create event sources by configuring an appropriate ACL in the registry).
☐	Security-sensitive data, such as passwords, is not written to the event log.

Registry

Check	Description
☐	Sensitive data, such as database connection strings or credentials, is encrypted prior to storage in the registry.
☐	Keys are restricted. If a key beneath HKEY_CURRENT_MACHINE is used, the key is configured with a restricted ACL. Alternatively, HKEY_CURRENT_USER is used.
☐	Registry access is constrained by using **RegistryPermission**. This applies especially if your registry access code could be called by untrusted callers.

Environment Variables

Check	Description
☐	Code that accesses environment variables is restricted with **EnvironmentPermission**. This applies especially if your code can be called by untrusted code.
☐	Environment permission requirements are declared by using declarative security attributes with **SecurityAction.RequestMinimum**.

Code Access Security Considerations

If an entry is preceded by a star (*), it indicates that the checks are performed by the FXCop analysis tool. For more information about FXCop security checks, see *http://www.gotdotnet.com/team/libraries/FxCopRules/SecurityRules.aspx.*

Check	Description
☐	Assemblies marked with AllowPartiallyTrustedCallersAttribute (APTCA) do not expose objects from non-APTCA assemblies.
☐	Code that only supports full-trust callers is strong named or explicitly demands the full-trust permission set.
☐	All uses of **Assert** are thoroughly reviewed.
☐	All calls to **Assert** are matched with a corresponding call to **RevertAssert**.
☐	*The Assert window is as small as possible.
☐	*Asserts are proceeded with a full permission demand.
☐	*Use of Deny or PermitOnly is thoroughly reviewed.
☐	All uses of LinkDemand are thoroughly reviewed. (Why is a LinkDemand and not a full Demand used?)
☐	LinkDemands within Interface declarations are matched by LinkDemands on the method implementation.
☐	*Unsecured members do not call members protected by a LinkDemand.
☐	Permissions are not demanded for resources accessed through the .NET Framework classes.
☐	Access to custom resources (through unmanaged code) is protected with custom code access permissions.
☐	Access to cached data is protected with appropriate permission demands.
☐	If LinkDemands are used on structures, the structures contain explicitly defined constructors.

Code Access Security Considerations *(continued)*

Check	Description
☐	*Methods that override other methods that are protected with LinkDemands also issue the same LinkDemand.
☐	*LinkDemands on types are not used to protect access to fields inside those types.
☐	*Partially trusted methods call only other partially trusted methods.
☐	*Partially trusted types extend only other partially trusted types.
☐	*Members that call late bound members have declarative security checks.
☐	*Method-level declarative security does not mistakenly override class-level security checks.
☐	Use of the following "potentially dangerous" permissions is thoroughly reviewed: SecurityPermission Unmanaged Code SkipVerification ControlEvidence ControlPolicy SerializationFormatter ControlPrincipal ControlThread ReflectionPermission MemberAccess
☐	Code identity permission demands are used to authorize calling code in scenarios where you know in advance the range of possible callers (for example, you want to limit calling code to a specific application).
☐	Permission demands of the .NET Framework are not duplicated.
☐	Inheritance is restricted with SecurityAction.InheritanceDemand in scenarios where you want to limit which code can derive from your code.

How To:
Index

Improving Web Application Security: Threats and Countermeasures includes the following
How Tos, each of which shows you the steps to complete a specific security task:

- How To: Implement Patch Management
- How To: Harden the TCP Stack
- How To: Secure Your Developer Workstation
- How To: Use IPSec for Filtering Ports and Authentication
- How To: Use the Microsoft Baseline Security Analyzer
- How To: Use IISLockdown.exe
- How To: Use URLScan
- How To: Create a Custom Encryption Permission
- How To: Use Code Access Security Policy to Constrain an Assembly

How To:
Implement Patch Management

Applies To

This information applies to server or workstation computers that run the following:

- Microsoft® Windows® 2000

Summary

This How To explains patch management, including how to keep single or multiple servers up to date. Additional software is not required, except for the tools available for download from Microsoft.

Operations and security policy should adopt a patch management process. This How To defines the processes required to create a sound patch management system. The patch management process can be automated using the guidance in this How To.

What You Must Know

Before using this How To, you should be aware of the following issues and considerations.

The Patch Management Process

Patch management is a circular process and must be ongoing. The unfortunate reality about software vulnerabilities is that, after you apply a patch today, a new vulnerability must be addressed tomorrow.

Develop and automate a patch management process that includes each of the following:

- **Detect**. Use tools to scan your systems for missing security patches. The detection should be automated and will trigger the patch management process.
- **Assess**. If necessary updates are not installed, determine the severity of the issue(s) addressed by the patch and the mitigating factors that may influence your decision. By balancing the severity of the issue and mitigating factors, you can determine if the vulnerabilities are a threat to your current environment.

- **Acquire**. If the vulnerability is not addressed by the security measures already in place, download the patch for testing.
- **Test**. Install the patch on a test system to verify the ramifications of the update against your production configuration.
- **Deploy**. Deploy the patch to production computers. Make sure your applications are not affected. Employ your rollback or backup restore plan if needed.
- **Maintain**. Subscribe to notifications that alert you to vulnerabilities as they are reported. Begin the patch management process again.

The Role of MBSA in Patch Management

The Microsoft Baseline Security Analyzer (MBSA) is a tool that is designed for two purposes: first, to scan a computer against vulnerable configurations; and second, to detect the availability of security updates that are released by Microsoft.

In this How To, you use MBSA without scanning for vulnerable configurations. When using the graphical user interface (GUI), specify this by unchecking the options in Figure 1 and only choosing **Check for security updates**.

☐ Check for Windows vulnerabilities
☐ Check for weak passwords
☐ Check for IIS vulnerabilities
☐ Check for SQL vulnerabilities
☑ Check for security updates

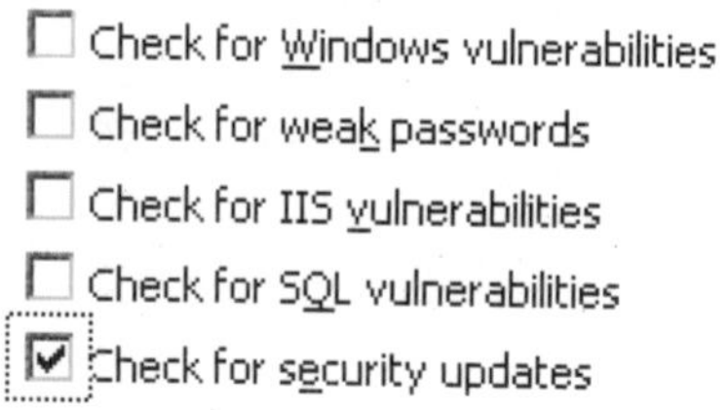

Figure 1
MBSA scan options

When using the command line interface (Mbsacli.exe), you can use the following command to scan only missing security updates.

```
Mbsacli.exe /n OS+IIS+SQL+PASSWORD
```

The option **/n** specifies the checks to skip. The selection (**OS+IIS+SQL+PASSWORD**) skips the checks for vulnerabilities and weak passwords.

For more details about using MBSA, including the security configuration scan, see "How To: Use MBSA" in the How To section of this guide.

Backups and Patch Management

You should perform backups prior to deploying an update on production servers. Regularly test backups as well as your backup process. Discovering that your backup process is broken during restoration can be devastating.

Before You Begin

This section provides information about downloads and documentation that are needed before you walk through the steps in this How To.

Tools You Will Need

You need the following tools in order to be able to perform the steps in this How To:

- **Microsoft Baseline Security Analyzer (MBSA)**

  Download MBSA from the MBSA Home Page: *http://www.microsoft.com/technet /treeview/default.asp?url=/technet/security/tools/Tools/mbsahome.asp*

- **Latest Mssecure.cab**

  By default, MBSA downloads the latest update list (Mssecure.cab) from Microsoft.com. If you do not have Internet access from the computer running MBSA, you must download the file and copy it to the MBSA installation directory. You can download the update file from: *http://download.microsoft.com/download /xml/security/1.0/NT5/EN-US/mssecure.cab*

- Microsoft **Software Update Service (SUS)**

  Microsoft Software Update Services (SUS) Server 1.0 enables administrators to deploy critical updates to Windows 2000-based, Windows XP, and Windows Server 2003 computers. You can download it from: *http://www.microsoft.com /downloads/details.aspx?FamilyId=A7AA96E4-6E41-4F54-972C-AE66A4E4BF6C &displaylang=en*

Contents

This How To shows you how to implement each phase of the patch management process. These phases include:

- **Detecting**
- **Assessing**
- **Acquiring**
- **Testing**
- **Deploying**
- **Maintaining**

Detecting

Use MBSA to detect missing security patches for Windows NT 4.0, Windows 2000, and Windows XP. You can use MBSA in two modes; GUI and command line. Both modes are used to scan single or multiple computers. The command line can be scripted to run on a schedule.

Note   The login used to run MBSA must be a member of the Administrators group on the target computer(s). To verify adequate access and privilege, use the command **net use** **\\computername\c$** where computername is the network name of a machine which you are going to scan for missing patches. Resolve any issues accessing the administrative share before using MBSA to scan the remote computer.

▶ **To manually detect missing updates using the MBSA graphical interface**

1. Run MBSA by double-clicking the desktop icon or by selecting it from the Programs menu.

2. Click **Scan a computer**. MBSA defaults to the local computer. To scan multiple computers, select **Scan more than one computer** and select either a range of computers to scan or an IP address range.

3. Clear all check boxes except **Check for security updates**. This option detects uninstalled patches and updates.

4. Click **Start scan**. Your server is now analyzed. When the scan is complete, MBSA displays a security report and also writes the report to the %userprofile%\SecurityScans directory.

5. Download and install the missing updates.

   Click the Result details link next to each failed check to view the list of uninstalled security updates. A dialog box displays the Microsoft security bulletin reference number. Click the reference to find out more about the bulletin and to download the update.

▶ **To detect missing updates using the MBSA command line interface**

- From a command window, change directory to the MBSA installation directory, and type the following command:

```
mbsacli /i 127.0.0.1 /n OS+IIS+SQL+PASSWORD
```

You can also specify a computer name. For example:

```
mbsacli /c domain\machinename /n OS+IIS+SQL+PASSWORD
```

You can also specify a range of computers by using the /r option. For example:

```
mbsacli /r 192.168.0.1-192.168.0.254 /n OS+IIS+SQL+PASSWORD
```

Finally, you can scan a domain by using the **/d** option. For example:

```
mbsacli /d NameOfMyDomain /n OS+IIS+SQL+PASSWORD
```

► **To analyze the generated report**

1. Run MBSA by double-clicking the desktop icon or by selecting it from the Programs menu.
2. Click **Pick a security report to view** and open the report or reports, if you scanned multiple computers.
3. To view the results of a scan against the target machine, mouse over the computer name listed. Individual reports are sorted by the timestamp of the report.

As previously described, the advantage of the command line method is that it may be scripted and scheduled to execute. This schedule is determined by the exposure of your systems to hostile networks, and by your security policy.

MBSA Output Explained

The following example was taken using the MBSA version 1.1.

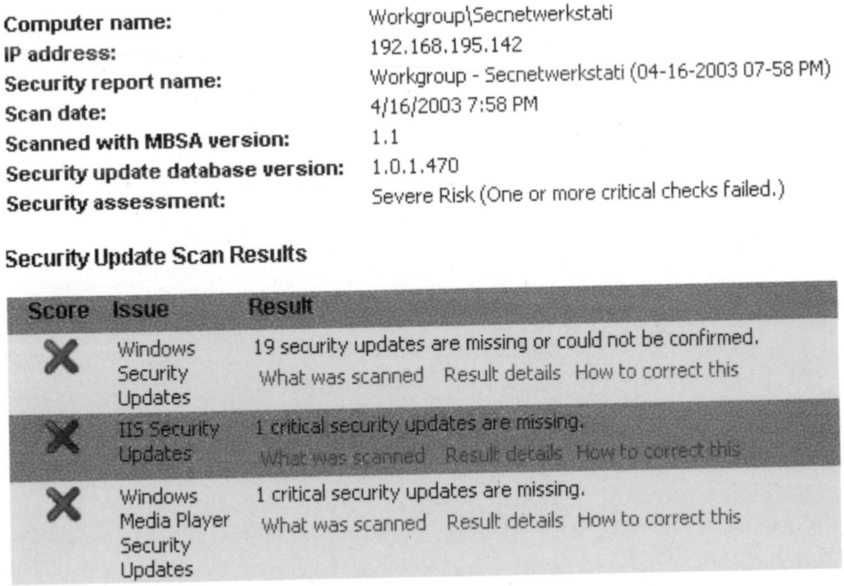

Computer name:	Workgroup\Secnetwerkstati
IP address:	192.168.195.142
Security report name:	Workgroup - Secnetwerkstati (04-16-2003 07-58 PM)
Scan date:	4/16/2003 7:58 PM
Scanned with MBSA version:	1.1
Security update database version:	1.0.1.470
Security assessment:	Severe Risk (One or more critical checks failed.)

Security Update Scan Results

Score	Issue	Result
✗	Windows Security Updates	19 security updates are missing or could not be confirmed. What was scanned Result details How to correct this
✗	IIS Security Updates	1 critical security updates are missing. What was scanned Result details How to correct this
✗	Windows Media Player Security Updates	1 critical security updates are missing. What was scanned Result details How to correct this

Figure 2

Screenshot of the report details for a scanned machine

The top portion of the MBSA screenshot shown in Figure 2 is self explanatory.

Red crosses indicate that a critical issue has been found. To view the list of missing patches, click the associated **Result details** link.

The results of a security update scan might show two types of issues:

- Missing patches
- Patch cannot be confirmed

Both types include links to the relevant Hotfix and security bulletin pages that provide details about the patch together with download instructions.

Missing patches are indicated by a red cross. An example is shown in Figure 3.

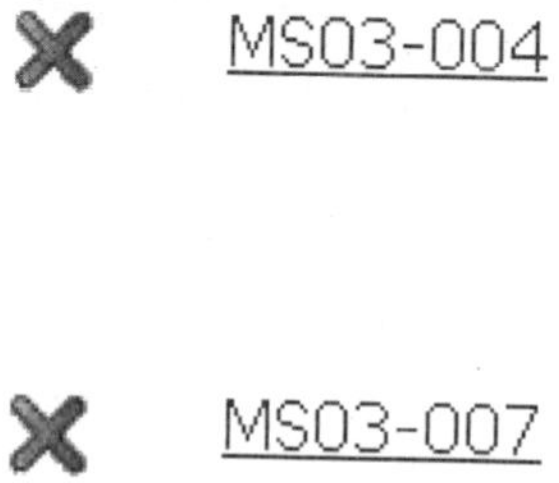

 MS03-004

 MS03-007

Figure 3
Missing patch indication

When a patch cannot be confirmed, it is indicated by a blue asterisk. This occurs when your system has a file that is newer than the file provided with a security bulletin. This might occur if you install a new version of a product that updates a common file.

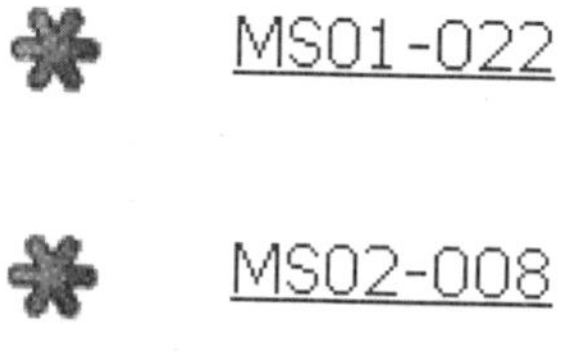

 MS01-022

 MS02-008

Figure 4
Patch cannot be confirmed indication

For updates that cannot be confirmed, review the information in the bulletin and follow the instructions. This may include installing a patch or making configuration changes. For more information on patches that cannot be verified by MBSA, see Microsoft Knowledge Base article, 306460, "HFNetChk Returns Note Messages for Installed Patches."

Assessing

With the list of missing patches identified by MBSA, you must determine if the vulnerabilities pose a significant risk. Microsoft Security Bulletins provide technical details to help you determine the level of threat the vulnerability poses to your systems.

The details from security bulletins that help you assess the risk of attack are:

- **Technical details of requirements an attacker needs to exploit the vulnerability addressed by the bulletin**. For example, an attack may require physical access or the user must open a malicious email attachment.

- **Mitigating factors that you need to compare against your security policy to determine your level of exposure to the vulnerability**. It may be that your security policy mitigates the need to apply a patch. For example, if you do not have the Indexing Service running on your server, you do not need to install patches to address vulnerabilities in the service.

- **Severity rating that assists in determining priority**. The severity rating is based on multiple factors including the role of the machines that may be vulnerable, and the level of exposure to the vulnerability.

  For more information about the severity rating system used by the security bulletins, see the TechNet article, "Microsoft Security Response Center Security Bulletin Severity Rating System" at *http://www.microsoft.com/technet/treeview /default.asp?url=/technet/security/policy/rating.asp*

> **Note** If you use an affected product, you should almost always apply patches that address vulnerabilities rated **critical** or **important**. Patches rated **critical** should be applied as soon as possible.

Acquiring

There are several ways you can obtain patches, including:

- **Using MBSA report details**. MBSA links to the security bulletin that contains the patch, or instructions about obtaining the patch. You can use the link to download the patch and save it on your local network. You can then apply the patch to multiple computers.

- **Windows Update**. With a list of the updates you want to install, use Internet Explorer on the server that requires the patch, and access *http://windowsupdate.microsoft.com/*. Then select the required updates for installation. The updates are installed from the site and cannot be downloaded for installation on another computer. Windows Update requires that an ActiveX control is installed on the server (you will be prompted when you visit the site if the control is not found.) This method works well for standalone workstations or where a small number of servers are involved.

- **HotFix & Security Bulletin Search**. MBSA includes the Microsoft Knowledge Base article ID of the corresponding article for a given security bulletin. You can use the article ID at the HotFix and Security Bulletin Search site to reach the matching security bulletin. The search page is located at *http://www.microsoft.com/technet /treeview/default.asp?url=/technet/security/current.asp*. The bulletin contains the details to acquire the patch.

Testing

If the results of your assessment determine that a patch must be installed, you should test that patch against your system to ensure that no breaking changes are introduced or, if a breaking change is expected, how to work around the change.

Methods for Testing Security Patches

Methods used to test the installation of security patches against your systems include:

- **Testing security patches against a test mirror of your live server configuration and scenario**. This method allows you to both test the installation offline, without disrupting service, and the freedom to test workarounds if a breaking change is introduced, again without disrupting service.
- **Testing the patch on a few select production systems prior to fully deploying the update**. If a test network that matches your live configuration is not available, this is the safest method to introduce the security patch. If this method is employed, you must perform a backup prior to installing the update.

Confirming the Installation of a Patch

Before deploying a patch to production servers, confirm that the tested patch has made the appropriate changes on the test servers. Each security bulletin includes the information you need to confirm that the patch has been installed. In each bulletin, the **Additional information about this patch** section contains the entry **Verifying patch installation**. It includes registry values, file versions, or similar configuration changes that you can use to verify that the patch is installed.

Uninstalling a Security Patch

If you need to uninstall a patch, use Add/Remove Programs in the Control Panel. If an uninstall routine is not an option for the patch and its installation introduces breaking changes, you must restore your system from backup. Make sure that your testing process also covers the patch uninstall routine.

The security bulletin lists the availability of an uninstall routine in the **Additonal information about this patch** section.

Deploying

If you decide that the patch is safe to install, you must deploy the update to your production servers in a reliable and efficient way. You have a number of options for deploying patches throughout the enterprise. These include:

- **Using Software Updates Services (SUS)**
- **Using Systems Management Server (SMS)**

Using Software Update Services (SUS)

SUS provides a way to automatically deploy crucial updates and security rollups to computers throughout a network, without requiring you to visit each computer or write script. For more information about using SUS, see "Software Update Services, Part 1" at *http://www.microsoft.com/technet/security/tools/tools/sadsus1.asp*.

Using Systems Management Server (SMS)

SMS is an enterprise management tool for delivering configuration and change management of Microsoft Windows server and workstation operating systems. For more information about using SMS to deploy updates, see TechNet article, "Patch Management Using Microsoft Systems Management Server" at *http://www.microsoft.com/technet/treeview/default.asp?url=/technet/itsolutions /MSM/swdist/pmsmsog.asp*.

Maintaining

Bringing your servers up to date with the latest patches is part of the patch management cycle. The patch management cycle begins again by knowing when new security vulnerabilities are found and missing security updates become available.

Keeping your servers up to date with the latest security patches involves this entire cycle. You start the cycle again by:

- **Performing security assessments**
- **Using security notification services**

Performing Security Assessments

Use MBSA to regularly check for security vulnerabilities and to identify missing patches and updates. Schedule MBSA to run daily and analyze the results to take action as needed. For more information about automating MBSA, see "How To: Use MBSA" in the How To section of this guide.

Using Security Notification Services

Register to receive notifications of security bulletins released by Microsoft. Use the following services:

- Microsoft Security Notification Service at *http://register.microsoft.com/subscription /subscribeme.asp?ID=135*.

- TechNet security Web site at *http://www.microsoft.com/technet/treeview /default.asp?url=/technet/security/current.asp*

Additional Considerations

When bringing a new service online on an existing server, run MBSA to verify the patches for the service have been applied prior to having the server and service listening on the network. For example, disconnect the network cable or apply network based rules that block the newly added service's ports.

Additional Resources

For related information, see the following resources:

- For more information about Software Update Services, see:
  - The SUS homepage at *http://www.microsoft.com/windows2000/windowsupdate /sus/default.asp*.
  - TechNet article, "Patch Management Using Microsoft Software Update Services" at *http://www.microsoft.com/technet/treeview/default.asp?url=/technet /itsolutions/msm/swdist/pmsusog.asp*.
  - Software Update Services Deployment white paper at *http://www.microsoft.com /windows2000/windowsupdate/sus/susdeployment.asp*.
  - SUS Server with SP1 release notes and installation instructions at *http://www.microsoft.com/windows2000/windowsupdate/sus/sp1relnotes.asp*.
  - SUS Server with SP1 download page at *http://www.microsoft.com/downloads /details.aspx?FamilyId=A7AA96E4-6E41-4F54-972C-AE66A4E4BF6C&displaylang=en*.
- TechNet article, "Managing Security Hotfixes" at *http://www.microsoft.com/technet /treeview/default.asp?url=/technet/security/tips/sechotfx.asp*.
- TechNet article, "Enterprise Software Update Management using Systems Management Server 2.0 Software Update Services Feature Pack" at *http://www.microsoft.com/technet/treeview/default.asp?url=/technet/prodtechnol /sms/deploy/confeat/SMSFPDEP.asp*.
- TechNet article, "Best Practices for Applying Service Packs, Hotfixes and Security Patches" at *http://www.microsoft.com/technet/treeview/default.asp?url=/technet/security /bestprac/bpsp.asp*.

How To:
Harden the TCP/IP Stack

Applies To

This information applies to server computers that run the following:

- Microsoft® Windows® 2000 Server and Advanced Server

Summary

You can configure various TCP/IP parameters in the Windows registry in order to protect against network-level denial of service attacks including SYN flood attacks, ICMP attacks and SNMP attacks. You can configure registry keys to:

- Enable SYN flood protection when an attack is detected.
- Set threshold values that are used to determine what constitutes an attack.

This How To shows an administrator which registry keys and which registry values must be configured to protect against network-based denial of service attacks.

Note   These settings modify the way TCP/IP works on your server. The characteristics of your Web server will determine the best thresholds to trigger denial of service countermeasures. Some values may be too restrictive for your client connections. Test this document's recommendations before you deploy to a production server.

What You Must Know

TCP/IP is an inherently insecure protocol. However, the Windows 2000 implementation allows you to configure its operation to counter network denial of service attacks. Some of the keys and values referred to in this How To may not exist by default. In those cases, create the key, value, and value data.

For more details about the TCP/IP network settings that the registry for Windows 2000 controls, see the white paper "Microsoft Windows 2000 TCP/IP Implementation Details," at *http://www.microsoft.com/technet/treeview/default.asp?url=/technet/itsolutions /network/deploy/depovg/tcpip2k.asp*.

Contents

This How To is divided into sections that address specific types of denial of service protections that apply to the network. Those sections are:

- Protect Against SYN Attack
- Protect Against ICMP Attacks
- Protect Against SNMP Attacks
- AFD.SYS Protections
- Additional Protections
- Pitfalls
- Additional Resources

Protect Against SYN Attacks

A SYN attack exploits a vulnerability in the TCP/IP connection establishment mechanism. To mount a SYN flood attack, an attacker uses a program to send a flood of TCP SYN requests to fill the pending connection queue on the server. This prevents other users from establishing network connections.

To protect the network against SYN attacks, follow these generalized steps, explained later in this document:

- **Enable SYN attack protection**
- **Set SYN protection thresholds**
- **Set additional protections**

Enable SYN Attack Protection

The named value to enable SYN attack protection is located beneath the registry key: **HKEY_LOCAL_MACHINE\SYSTEM\CurrentControlSet\Services**.

Value name: SynAttackProtect

Recommended value: 2

Valid values: 0–2

Description: Causes TCP to adjust retransmission of SYN-ACKS. When you configure this value the connection responses timeout more quickly in the event of a SYN attack. A SYN attack is triggered when the values of **TcpMaxHalfOpen** or **TcpMaxHalfOpenRetried** are exceeded.

Set SYN Protection Thresholds

The following values determine the thresholds for which SYN protection is triggered. All of the keys and values in this section are under the registry key **HKEY_LOCAL_MACHINE\SYSTEM\CurrentControlSet\Services**. These keys and values are:

- **Value name:** TcpMaxPortsExhausted

  Recommended value: 5

  Valid values: 0–65535

  Description: Specifies the threshold of TCP connection requests that must be exceeded before SYN flood protection is triggered.

- **Value name:** TcpMaxHalfOpen

  Recommended value data: 500

  Valid values: 100–65535

  Description: When **SynAttackProtect** is enabled, this value specifies the threshold of TCP connections in the SYN_RCVD state. When **SynAttackProtect** is exceeded, SYN flood protection is triggered.

- **Value name:** TcpMaxHalfOpenRetried

  Recommended value data: 400

  Valid values: 80–65535

  Description: When **SynAttackProtect** is enabled, this value specifies the threshold of TCP connections in the SYN_RCVD state for which at least one retransmission has been sent. When **SynAttackProtect** is exceeded, SYN flood protection is triggered.

Set Additional Protections

All the keys and values in this section are located under the registry key **HKEY_LOCAL_MACHINE\SYSTEM\CurrentControlSet\Services**. These keys and values are:

- **Value name:** TcpMaxConnectResponseRetransmissions

  Recommended value data: 2

  Valid values: 0–255

  Description: Controls how many times a SYN-ACK is retransmitted before canceling the attempt when responding to a SYN request.

- **Value name:** TcpMaxDataRetransmissions

  Recommended value data: 2

  Valid values: 0–65535

  Description: Specifies the number of times that TCP retransmits an individual data segment (not connection request segments) before aborting the connection.

- **Value name:** EnablePMTUDiscovery

  Recommended value data: 0

  Valid values: 0, 1

  Description: Setting this value to 1 (the default) forces TCP to discover the maximum transmission unit or largest packet size over the path to a remote host. An attacker can force packet fragmentation, which overworks the stack. Specifying 0 forces the MTU of 576 bytes for connections from hosts not on the local subnet.

- **Value name:** KeepAliveTime

  Recommended value data: 300000

  Valid values: 80–4294967295

  Description: Specifies how often TCP attempts to verify that an idle connection is still intact by sending a keep-alive packet.

- **Value name:** NoNameReleaseOnDemand

  Recommended value data: 1

  Valid values: 0, 1

  Description: Specifies to not release the NetBIOS name of a computer when it receives a name-release request.

Use the values that are summarized in Table 1 for maximum protection.

Table 1   Recommended Values

Value Name	Value (REG_DWORD)
SynAttackProtect	2
TcpMaxPortsExhausted	1
TcpMaxHalfOpen	500
TcpMaxHalfOpenRetried	400
TcpMaxConnectResponseRetransmissions	2
TcpMaxDataRetransmissions	2
EnablePMTUDiscovery	0
KeepAliveTime	300000 (5 minutes)
NoNameReleaseOnDemand	1

Protect Against ICMP Attacks

The named value in this section is under the registry key
HKLM\System\CurrentControlSet\Services\AFD\Parameters

Value: EnableICMPRedirect

Recommended value data: 0

Valid values: 0 (disabled), 1 (enabled)

Description: Modifying this registry value to 0 prevents the creation of expensive host routes when an ICMP redirect packet is received.

Use the value summarized in Table 2 for maximum protection:

Table 2 Recommended Values

Value Name	Value (REG_DWORD)
EnableICMPRedirect	0

Protect Against SNMP Attacks

The named value in this section is located under the registry key
HKLM\System\CurrentControlSet\Services\Tcpip\Parameters.

Value: EnableDeadGWDetect

Recommended value data: 0

Valid values: 0 (disabled), 1, (enabled)

Description: Prevents an attacker from forcing the switching to a secondary gateway

Use the value summarized in Table 3 for maximum protection.

Table 3 Recommended Values

Value Name	Value (REG_DWORD)
EnableDeadGWDetect	0

AFD.SYS Protections

The following keys specify parameters for the kernel mode driver Afd.sys. Afd.sys is used to support Windows sockets applications. All of the keys and values in this section are located under the registry key **HKLM\System\CurrentControlSet\Services\AFD\Parameters**. These keys and values are:

- **Value:** EnableDynamicBacklog

  Recommended value data: 1

  Valid values: 0 (disabled), 1 (enabled)

  Description: Specifies AFD.SYS functionality to withstand large numbers of SYN_RCVD connections efficiently. For more information, see "Internet Server Unavailable Because of Malicious SYN Attacks," at *http://support.microsoft.com/default.aspx?scid=kb;en-us;142641.*

- **Value name:** MinimumDynamicBacklog

  Recommended value data: 20

  Valid values: 0–4294967295

  Description: Specifies the minimum number of free connections allowed on a listening endpoint. If the number of free connections drops below this value, a thread is queued to create additional free connections

- **Value name:** MaximumDynamicBacklog

  Recommended value data: 20000

  Valid values: 0–4294967295

  Description: Specifies the maximum total amount of both free connections plus those in the SYN_RCVD state.

- **Value name:** DynamicBacklogGrowthDelta

  Recommended value data: 10

  Valid values: 0–4294967295

  Present by default: No

  Description: Specifies the number of free connections to create when additional connections are necessary.

Use the values summarized in Table 4 for maximum protection.

Table 4   Recommended Values

Value Name	Value (REG_DWORD)
EnableDynamicBacklog	1
MinimumDynamicBacklog	20
MaximumDynamicBacklog	20000
DynamicBacklogGrowthDelta	10

Additional Protections

All of the keys and values in this section are located under the registry key **HKLM\System\CurrentControlSet\Services\Tcpip\Parameters**.

Protect Screened Network Details

Network Address Translation (NAT) is used to screen a network from incoming connections. An attacker can circumvent this screen to determine the network topology using IP source routing.

Value: DisableIPSourceRouting

Recommended value data: 1

Valid values: 0 (forward all packets), 1 (do not forward Source Routed packets), 2 (drop all incoming source routed packets).

Description: Disables IP source routing, which allows a sender to determine the route a datagram should take through the network.

Avoid Accepting Fragmented Packets

Processing fragmented packets can be expensive. Although it is rare for a denial of service to originate from within the perimeter network, this setting prevents the processing of fragmented packets.

Value: EnableFragmentChecking

Recommended value data: 1

Valid values: 0 (disabled), 1 (enabled)

Description: Prevents the IP stack from accepting fragmented packets.

Do Not Forward Packets Destined for Multiple Hosts

Multicast packets may be responded to by multiple hosts, resulting in responses that can flood a network.

Value: EnableMulticastForwarding

Recommended value data: 0

Valid range: 0 (false), 1 (true)

Description: The routing service uses this parameter to control whether or not IP multicasts are forwarded. This parameter is created by the Routing and Remote Access Service.

Only Firewalls Forward Packets Between Networks

A multi-homed server must not forward packets between the networks it is connected to. The obvious exception is the firewall.

Value: IPEnableRouter

Recommended value data: 0

Valid range: 0 (false), 1 (true)

Description: Setting this parameter to 1 (true) causes the system to route IP packets between the networks to which it is connected.

Mask Network Topology Details

The subnet mask of a host can be requested using ICMP packets. This disclosure of information by itself is harmless; however, the responses of multiple hosts can be used to build knowledge of the internal network.

Value: EnableAddrMaskReply

Recommended value data: 0

Valid range: 0 (false), 1 (true)

Description: This parameter controls whether the computer responds to an ICMP address mask request.

Use the values summarized in Table 5 for maximum protection

Table 5   Recommended Values

Value Name	Value (REG_DWORD)
DisableIPSourceRouting	1
EnableFragmentChecking	1
EnableMulticastForwarding	0
IPEnableRouter	0
EnableAddrMaskReply	0

Pitfalls

When testing the changes of these values, test against the network volumes you expect in production. These settings modify the thresholds of what is considered normal and are deviating from the tested defaults. Some may be too narrow to support clients reliably if the connection speed from clients varies greatly.

Additional Resources

For additional reading about TCP/IP, refer to the following resources:

- For more information on hardening the TCP/IP stack, see Microsoft Knowledge Base article, 315669, "How To: Harden the TCP/IP Stack Against Denial of Service Attacks in Windows 2000."

- For more details on the Windows 2000 TCP/IP implementation, see the Microsoft Press book, "Windows 2000 TCP/IP Protocols and Services," by Lee Davies.

- For more information about the Windows 2000 TCP/IP implementation, see "Microsoft Windows 2000 TCP/IP Implementation Details," at *http://www.microsoft.com/technet/treeview/default.asp?url=/technet /itsolutions/network/deploy/depovg/tcpip2k.asp*, on the TechNet Web site.

How To:
Secure Your Developer Workstation

Applies To

This information applies to developer workstations that run the following:

- Microsoft® Windows® 2000 Server and Professional, Windows XP Professional
- Internet Information Services (IIS)
- .NET Framework versions 1.0 and 1.1
- Microsoft SQL Server™ 2000 and the Desktop Edition

Summary

This How To helps you improve your development workstation security. Developers often have computers running software such as IIS, Microsoft SQL Server, or the Microsoft SQL Server Desktop Engine (MSDE.) For example, Microsoft Visual Studio® .NET is designed for local development with IIS, so it is common for a developer to run IIS locally. As a developer, you need to be able to secure these services against attack, even if your computer is in a protected local area network.

This How To provides quick tips to help you improve the security of your developer workstation, along with tips about how to keep it secure. It also helps you avoid common problems that you are likely to encounter when you secure your workstation. Finally, it provides tips about how to determine problems and to revert security settings if they prove too restrictive.

Note   This How To is not exhaustive, but it highlights many of the key issues.

Before You Begin

Before you begin securing your workstation, you need the following tools:

- **Microsoft Baseline Security Analyzer (MBSA)**. Microsoft provides the MBSA tool to help analyze the security configuration of your computers and to identify missing patches and updates. You can download the MBSA tool from *http://download.microsoft.com/download/e/5/7/e57f498f-2468-4905-aa5f-369252f8b15c /mbsasetup.msi*.

- **IISLockdown**. The IISLockdown tool reduces your computer's attack surface by hardening default IIS and Windows configuration settings and by removing unnecessary IIS extensions. IISLockown also installs the "404.dll" ISAPI filter, which is used to report "404 File Not Found" messages when disabled extensions are requested.

  You can download the IISLockdown tool from *http://download.microsoft.com /download/iis50/Utility/2.1/NT45XP/EN-US/iislockd.exe*.

- **URLScan**. URLScan is an ISAPI filter that rejects or allows HTTP requests based on a configurable set of rules. It is integrated with IISLockdown, although you can also download it separately. It comes with customizable templates for each supported server role.

  To install URLScan without IISLockdown, see Microsoft Knowledge Base article 307608, "INFO: Availability of URLScan Version 2.5 Security Tool," at *http://support.microsoft.com/default.aspx?scid=kb;en-us;307608*, in the Microsoft Knowledge Base.

Steps to Secure Your Developer Workstation

To secure your developer workstation, perform the following tasks:

- **Run using a least privileged account**
- **Patch and update**
- **Secure IIS**
- **Secure SQL Server and MSDE**
- **Evaluate your configuration categories**
- **Stay secure**

Run Using a Least-Privileged Account

You should develop applications using a non administrator account. Doing so is important primarily to limit the exposure of the logged on user and to help you to design more secure software. For example, if you design, develop, and test an application while you are interactively logged in as an administrator, you are much more likely to end up with software that requires administrative privileges to run.

You should not generally log on using the local administrator account. The account that you use on a daily basis should not be a member of the local Administrators group. Sometimes you might still need an account that has administrative privileges —for example, when you install software or edit the registry. Because the default local administrator account is well known, however, and it is the target of many attacks, create a non-standard administrator account and use this only when it is required.

► **To create accounts for development**

1. Remove your current user account from the Administrators group if it is a member.
2. Create a new custom administration account using a nonstandard name and strong password.
3. Use your non-administrator account to logon interactively on a daily basis. When you need to run a command with administrative privileges, use your custom administration account with the Runas.exe command line utility.

Running Privileged Commands

To run a privileged command, you can use one of the following techniques to temporarily change your security context:

- **Use the Runas.exe utility from a command line**. The following command shows you how to use the Runas.exe utility to launch a command console that runs under your custom administration account.

```
runas.exe /user:mymachine\mycustomadmin cmd.exe
```

  By executing Cmd.exe, you start a new command window that runs under the security context of the user you specify with the **/user** switch. Any program you launch from this command window also runs under this context.

- **Use Run As from Windows Explorer**. You can right-click an executable file in Windows Explorer and click **Run As**. To display this item on Windows 2000, hold the shift key down and then right-click an executable file. When you click **Run As**, you are prompted for the credentials of the account you want to use to run the executable file.

- **Use Run As shortcuts**. You can create quick launch and desktop shortcuts to easily run applications using a privileged user account. The following example shows a shortcut that you can use to run Windows Explorer (Explorer.exe) using the administrator account:

```
%windir%\System32\runas.exe /user:administrator explorer
```

Note If using a non-administrator account proves impractical for your environment, still test your application or component while running as a least privileged user to catch and correct problems before deploying. For example, your application might incorrectly require administrator privileges without your realizing it, which would cause the application to fail when it is deployed in a production environment.

More Information

For more information about developing with a non-administrative account, see the following articles:

- "Essential .NET Security," at *http://www.develop.com/kbrown/book/html/lifestyle.html*
- "Developing Software in Visual Studio .NET with Non-Administrative Privileges," at *http://msdn.microsoft.com/library/default.asp?url=/library/en-us /dv_vstechart/html/tchDevelopingSoftwareInVisualStudioNETWithNon-Administrative Privileges.asp*

Patch and Update

Ensure that your workstation has the latest service packs and patches. Check the operating system, IIS, SQL Server, MSDE, Microsoft Data Access Components (MDAC), and the .NET Framework. Microsoft offers several tools and methods to help you scan and update your system. These include the Windows Update site, the Microsoft Baseline Security Analyzer (MBSA) tool, and the Automatic Updates feature.

Using Windows Update

You can use Windows Update (available from the Start menu) to scan for updates and patches for Windows. Alternatively, you can directly scan for updates at *http://windowsupdate.microsoft.com*.

Note   After you update your system using the Windows Update site, use MBSA to detect missing updates for SQL Server, MSDE, and MDAC.

Using MBSA

You can use MBSA to assess security and to verify patches. If you used automatic updates or Windows Update to update your operating system and components, MBSA verifies those updates and additionally checks the status of updates for SQL Server and Microsoft Exchange Server. MBSA lets you create a script to check multiple computers.

▶ To detect and install patches and updates

1. Download MBSA from the MBSA home page at *http://www.microsoft.com/technet /treeview/default.asp?url=/technet/security/tools/Tools/mbsahome.asp*.

   If you do not have Internet access when you run MBSA, MBSA cannot retrieve the XML file that contains the latest security settings from Microsoft. You can use another computer to download the XML file, however. Then you can copy it into the MBSA program directory. The XML file is available at *http://download.microsoft.com/download/xml/security/1.0/nt5/en-us/mssecure.cab*.

2. Run MBSA by double-clicking the desktop icon or selecting it from the **Programs** menu.

3. Click **Scan a computer**. MBSA defaults to the local computer.

4. Clear all check boxes except for **Check for security updates**. This option detects which patches and updates are missing.

5. Click **Start scan**. Your server is now analyzed. When the scan completes, MBSA displays a security report, which it also writes to the %Userprofile%\SecurityScans directory.

6. Download and install the missing updates. Click **Result details** next to each failed check to view the list of missing security updates.

   The resulting dialog box displays the Microsoft security bulletin reference number. Click the reference to find out more about the bulletin and to download the update.

For more information about using MBSA, see "How To: Use Microsoft Baseline Security Analyzer (MBSA)," in the How To section of this guide.

Note   MBSA will not indicate required .NET Framework updates and patches. Browse the .NET Framework downloads page at *http://msdn.microsoft.com/netframework/downloads/default.asp*.

Using Automatic Updates

The Automatic Updates feature offers the easiest method to update your operating system with the latest critical security patches. The feature is built into Windows XP and is installed with Windows 2000 Service Pack 3.

To configure Automatic Updates with Windows 2000, click **Automatic Updates** in the Control Panel. For more information about Automatic Updates and Windows 2000, see Microsoft Knowledge Base article 327850, "How To: Configure and Use Automatic Updates in Windows 2000."

► To configure Automatic Updates with Windows XP

1. Right-click the **My Computer** icon on the desktop or the **System** icon in Control Panel.

2. Click **System Properties**.

For more information about Automatic Updates and Windows XP, see Microsoft Knowledge Base article, 306525, "How To: Configure and Use Automatic Updates in Windows XP."

Automatic Updates scans and installs updates for the following operating systems (including the .NET Framework and IIS where applicable):

- Microsoft Windows 2000 Professional
- Microsoft Windows 2000 Server
- Microsoft Windows XP Professional

In addition to using Automatic Updates, use MBSA to detect missing updates for SQL Server, MSDE and MDAC.

Secure IIS

You often need to run IIS locally for Web development. If you run IIS, secure it. IISLockdown and URLScan significantly reduce your Web server's attack profile. IISLockdown points unused or forbidden script mappings to 404.dll and helps secure access to system directories and system tools. URLScan blocks known dangerous requests.

Although IISLockdown improves IIS security, if you choose the wrong installation options or do not modify the URLScan configuration file, URLScan.ini, you could encounter the following issues:

- **You cannot create new ASP.NET Web applications**. NTFS file system permissions are configured to strengthen default access to Web locations. This may prevent the logged on user from creating new ASP.NET Web applications.
- **Cannot debug existing ASP.NET Web applications**. URLScan blocks the DEBUG verb, which is used when you debug ASP.NET Web applications.

The following steps show you how to improve IIS security on your development workstation and avoid the issues listed above:

- **Install and run IISLockdown**
- **Configure URLScan**
- **Restrict access to the local Web server**

Install and Run IISLockdown

▶ **To install and run IISLockdown**

1. Run the **IISLockdown** installation program (Iislockd.exe) from
   http://download.microsoft.com/download/iis50/Utility/2.1/NT45XP/EN-US/iislockd.exe.

   Note   If you run iislockd.exe a second time, it removes all changes based on the log file
   \WINNT\System32\Inetsrv\oblt-log.log.

2. During setup, choose the **Dynamic Web Site** option, and choose the option to install URLScan. ASP.NET Web Forms use the HTTP POST verb. Choosing the static option and installing URLScan blocks the POST verb in URLScan.ini.

The **Dynamic Web Site** option does the following:

- Adds POST to the [AllowVerbs] section as shown below.

```
[AllowVerbs]
GET
HEAD
POST
```

- Disables the following Internet Services: Web service (HTTP), File Transfer Protocol (FTP), the Simple Mail Transport Protocol (SMTP) e-mail service, and the Network News Transport Protocol (NNTP) news service.
- Maps the following script maps to 404.dll: Index Server, Web Interface (.idq, .htw, .ida), server side includes (.shtml, .shtm, .stm), Internet Data Connector (.idc), HTR scripting (.htr), Internet printing (.printer)
- Removes the following virtual directories: IIS Samples, MSADC, IISHelp, Scripts, and IISAdmin.
- Restricts anonymous access to system utilities and the ability to write to Web content directories.
- Disables Web Distributed Authoring and Versioning (WebDAV).
- Installs the URLScan ISAPI filter.

Pitfalls

If you use IISLockdown, note the following pitfalls:

- **IIS metabase updates can be lost**. If you undo IISLockdown changes by running Iislockd.exe a second time, you lose any changes made to the IIS metabase since the last time IISLockdown was run. For example, if you configure a virtual directory as an application root after running IIS lockdown, that change is lost when you run IISLockdown again.
- **Resources are blocked by 404.dll**. If you receive a 404 error for a previously available resource, it might be because the resource type is blocked by 404.dll. To confirm whether or not this is the case, check the script mapping for the requested resource type in IIS.

Configure URLScan

The URLScan ISAPI filter installs when you run IISLockdown. If you do not explicitly allow the DEBUG verb, URLScan prevents debugging. Also, URLScan blocks requests that contain unsafe characters such as the period (.) used for directory traversal.

To configure URLScan, edit URLScan.ini in %Windir%\System32\inetsrv\urlscan\. To allow debugging with URLScan, add DEBUG to the [AllowVerbs] section in URLScan.ini as shown below.

```
[AllowVerbs]
GET
HEAD
POST
DEBUG
```

Pitfalls

If you install URLScan, note the following pitfalls:

- When you debug an application by using Visual Studio.NET, you may see the following error:

```
Microsoft Development Environment:
Error while trying to run project: Unable to start debugging on the Web server.
Could not start ASP.NET or ATL Server debugging.
Verify that ASP.NET or ATL Server is correctly installed on the server. Would
you like to disable future attempts to debug ASP.NET pages for this project?
```

  You should see a log entry similar to the one shown below in URLScan<date>.log in the \WINNT\system32\inetsrv\urlscan folder.

```
[01-18-2003 - 22:25:26] Client at 127.0.0.1: Sent verb 'DEBUG', which is not
specifically allowed. Request will be rejected.
```

- Requests that you expect to work might get blocked.
- You may not be able to create new Web projects in Visual Studio .NET because you use characters in the project name that URLScan rejects. For example, the comma (,) and the pound sign (#) will be blocked.

If you experience errors during debugging, see Microsoft Knowledge Base article 306172, "INFO: Common Errors When You Debug ASP.NET Applications in Visual Studio .NET," at *http://support.microsoft.com/default.aspx?scid=kb;EN-US;306172*.

Secure SQL Server and MSDE

To update SQL Server and MSDE, you must:

- **Apply patches for each instance of SQL Server and MSDE**
- **Analyze SQL Server and MSDE security configuration**

Apply Patches for Each Instance of SQL Server and MSDE

MSDE shares common technology with SQL Server, and it enables developers, partners, and IT professionals to build database applications without requiring the full SQL Server product. MSDE can be packaged with applications that require database support. To apply patches to MSDE, you must know which application installed it on your system. This is important because you must obtain the patch for MSDE from the product vendor.

For more information on applications that include MSDE, refer to the following resources:

- "Microsoft Products That Include MSDE," at *http://www.microsoft.com/technet /treeview/default.asp?url=/technet/security/MSDEapps.asp*
- "SQL Server/MSDE-Based Applications," at *http://www.sqlsecurity.com/forum /applicationslistgridall.aspx*

If your third-party vendor does not supply a patch for MSDE, and if it becomes critical to have the latest patches, you can only do the following:

- Uninstall the instance of SQL Server using Add/Remove Programs. If you do not see an uninstall option for your instance, you might need to uninstall your application.
- Stop the instance of SQL Server using the Services MMC snap-in in Computer Management. You can also stop the instance from the command line by running the following command:

```
net stop mssqlserver (default instance), mssql$instancename (for instances)
```

- Use IPSec to limit which hosts can connect to the abandoned (unpatched) instances of SQL Server. Restrict access to localhost clients.

Analyze SQL Server and MSDE Security Configuration

Use MBSA to analyze your Microsoft SQL Server or MSDE configuration on your workstation.

▶ **To analyze SQL Server and MSDE security configuration**

1. Run MBSA by double-clicking the desktop icon or selecting it from the **Programs** menu.
2. Click **Scan a computer**. MBSA defaults to the local computer.
3. Clear all check boxes except for **Check for SQL vulnerabilities**.

   This option scans for security vulnerabilities in the configurations of SQL Server 7.0, SQL Server 2000, and MSDE. For example, it checks the authentication mode, the sa account password, and the SQL Server service account, among other checks.

   A number of the checks require that your instance of SQL Server is running. If it is not running, start it.

4. Click **Start scan**. Your configuration is now analyzed. When the scan completes, MBSA displays a security report, which it also writes to the %Userprofile%\SecurityScans directory.

5. Review the failed checks, and fix vulnerable configuration settings.

    Click **Result details** next to each failed check for more information about why the check failed. Click **How to correct this**, for information about how to fix the vulnerability.

For more information about using MBSA, see "How To: Use Microsoft Baseline Security Analyzer (MBSA)," in the How To section of this guide.

Evaluate Your Configuration Categories

To evaluate the security of your workstation configuration, review the configuration categories shown in Table 6. Start by using the categories to evaluate the security configuration of the base operating system. Then apply the same configuration categories to review your IIS, SQL Server, and .NET Framework installation.

Table 6   Configuration Categories

Configuration Category	Methodology
Patches and updates	Setup Automatic Updates. Use MBSA or Windows Updates to verify that the latest updates are installed
Services	Disable unused services.
Protocols	Check that SMB and NetBIOS over TCP are removed if your workstation is not a member of a domain.
Accounts	Check that all local accounts use strong passwords.
Files and directories	Be sure your workstation uses only NTFS partitions.
Shares	Enumerate shares, remove unnecessary ones, and secure the remaining ones with restricted permissions.
Ports	Ensure that unused ports are closed by disabling the service that has the port open. To verify which ports are listening use the **netstat −n −a** command.
Registry	Disable null sessions.
Auditing and logging	Audit failed Windows attempts to log on and log failed actions across the file system.

Stay Secure

Monitor the security state of your workstation, and update it regularly to help prevent newly discovered vulnerabilities from being exploited. In addition to using Windows Update, subscribe to the Microsoft Security Notification Service, at *http://register.microsoft.com/subscription/subscribeme.asp?ID=135*, to register for regular e-mail bulletins that notify you of new fixes and updates.

You can also use the "Hotfix & Security Bulletin Service," at *http://www.microsoft.com /technet/treeview/default.asp?url=/technet/security/current.asp*, on the TechNet Web site. This allows you to view the security bulletins that are available for your system.

How To:
Use IPSec for Filtering Ports and Authentication

Applies To

This information applies to server computers that run the following:
- Microsoft® Windows® 2000 Server or Windows Server 2003 operating system
- SQL Server™ 2000

Summary

Internet Protocol security (IPSec) is a protocol, not a service, that provides encryption, integrity, and authentication services for IP-based network traffic. Because IPSec provides server-to-server protection, you can use IPSec to counter internal threats to the network, including eavesdropping, tampering, man in the middle attacks, IP spoofing, and other password-based attacks. IPSec is completely transparent to applications because encryption, integrity, and authentication services are implemented at the transport level. Applications continue to communicate normally with one another using TCP and UDP ports.

Contents

This How To contains the following sections:
- What you must know
- Restricting Web server communication
- Restricting database server communication
- Restricting server-to-server communication
- Using IPSec tools

What You Must Know

Before you start to configure IPSec, you should be aware of the following.

Identify Your Protocol and Port Requirements

Before you create and apply IPSec policies to block ports and protocols, make sure you know which communication you need to secure including the ports and protocols used by day-to-day operations. Consider the protocol and port requirements for remote administration, application communication, and authentication.

IPSec Does Not Secure All Communication

Several types of IP traffic are exempt from filtering. For more information, see Microsoft Knowledge Base article 253169, "Traffic That Can and Cannot Be Secured by IPSec."

Firewalls and IPSec

If a firewall separates two hosts that use IPSec to secure the communication channel, the firewall must open the following ports:

- TCP port 50 for IPSec Encapsulating Security Protocol (ESP) traffic
- TCP port 51 for IPSec Authentication Header (AH) traffic
- UDP port 500 for Internet Key Exchange (IKE) negotiation traffic

Filters, Filter Actions, and Rules

An IPSec policy consists of a set of filters, filter actions, and rules.

- **Filters**

  A *filter* is used to match traffic. It consists of:

  - A source IP address or range of addresses
  - A destination IP address or range of addresses
  - An IP protocol, such as TCP, UDP, or "any"
  - Source and destination ports (for TCP or UDP only)

Note An IP filter list is used to group multiple filters together so that multiple IP addresses and protocols can be combined into a single filter.

- **Filter Actions**

  A *filter action* specifies which actions to take when a given filter is invoked. It can be one of the following:

  - **Permit**. The traffic is not secured; it is allowed to be sent and received without intervention.
  - **Block**. The traffic is not permitted.
  - **Negotiate security**. The endpoints must agree on and then use a secure method to communicate. If they cannot agree on a method, the communication does not take place. If negotiation fails, you can specify whether to allow unsecured communication or to whether all communication should be blocked.

- **Rules**

  A *rule* associates a filter with a filter action and is defined by the IPSec policy.

Restricting Web Server Communication

The following example shows you how to use IPSec to limit communication with a Web server to port 80 (for HTTP traffic) and port 443 (for HTTPS traffic that uses SSL.) This is a common requirement for Internet-facing Web servers.

Note After applying the steps below, communication will be limited to port 80 and 443. In a real world environment, you will require additional communication such as that required for remote administration, database access and authentication. A complete IPSec policy, in a production environment, will include all authorized communication.

▶ **Create filter actions**

1. Start the Local Security Policy Microsoft Management Console (MMC) snap-in.
2. Right-click **IPSec Security Policies on Local Machine**, and then click **Manage IP filter lists and filter actions**.
3. Click the **Manage Filter Actions** tab.
4. Click **Add** to create a new filter action, and then click **Next** to move past the introductory Wizard dialog box.
5. Type **MyPermit** as the name for the new filter action. This filter action is used to permit traffic.
6. Click **Next**.
7. Select **Permit**, click **Next**, and then click **Finish**.
8. Create a second filter action called "MyBlock" by repeating steps 4 to 8. This time, select **Block** when you are prompted by the **Filter Action** dialog box.
9. Click **Close** to close the **Manage IP filter lists and filter actions** dialog box.

▶ **Create IP filters and filter lists**

1. Right-click **IPSec Security Policies on Local Machine**, and then click **Manage IP filter lists and filter actions**.

2. Click **Add** to add a new IP filter list., and then type **MatchAllTraffic** for the filter list name.

3. Click **Add** to create a new filter and proceed through the IP Filter Wizard dialogs boxes by selecting the default options.

   This creates a filter that matches all traffic.

4. Click **Close** to close the **IP Filter List** dialog box.

5. Click **Add** to create a new IP filter list, and then type **MatchHTTPAndHTTPS** for the filter list name.

6. Click **Add**, and then click **Next** to move past the introductory Wizard dialog box.

7. Select **Any IP Address** from the **Source address** drop-down list, and then click **Next**.

8. Select **My IP Address** from the **Destination** address drop-down list, and then click **Next**.

9. Select **TCP** from the **Select a protocol type** drop-down list, and then click **Next**.

10. Select **To this port** and then specify **port 80**.

11. Click **Next** and then **Finish**.

12. Click **Add**, and then repeat steps 9 to 14 to create another filter that allows traffic through port 443.

    Use the following values to create a filter that allows TCP over port 443:

    • Source Address: Any IP address

    • Destination Address: My IP Address

    • Protocol: TCP

    • From Port: Any

    • To Port: 443

After finishing these steps, your IP Filter List should look like the one that Figure 5 shows.

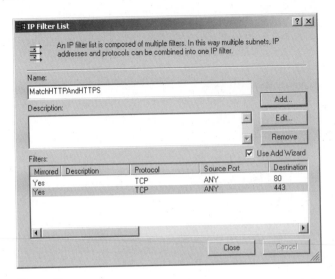

Figure 5
IP Filter List dialog box

After creating the filter actions and filter lists, you need to create a policy and two rules to associate the filters with the filter actions.

▶ **Create and apply IPSec policy**

1. In the main window of the Local Security Policy snap-in, right-click **IPSec Security policies on Local Machine**, and then click **Create IPSecurity Policy**.

2. Click **Next** to move past the initial Wizard dialog box.

3. Type **MyPolicy** for the IPSec policy name and **IPSec policy for a Web server that accepts traffic to TCP/80 and TCP/443 from anyone** for the description, and then click **Next**.

4. Clear the **Activate the default response rule** check box, click **Next**, and then click **Finish**.

   The **MyPolicy Properties** dialog box is displayed so that you can edit the policy properties.

5. Click **Add** to start the Security Rule Wizard, and then click **Next** to move past the introductory dialog box.

6. Select **This rule does not specify a tunnel**, and then click **Next**.

7. Select **All network connections**, and then click **Next**.

8. Select **Windows 2000 default (Kerberos V5 protocol)**, and then click **Next**.

9. Select the **MatchHTTPAndHTTPS** filter list, and then click **Next**.

10. Select the **MyPermit** filter action, click **Next**, and then click **Finish**.

11. Create a second rule by repeating steps 5 to 10. Instead of selecting **MatchHTTPAndHTTPS** and **MyPermit**, select **MatchAllTraffic** and **MyBlock**.

After creating the second rule, the **MyPolicy Properties** dialog box should look like the one in Figure 6.

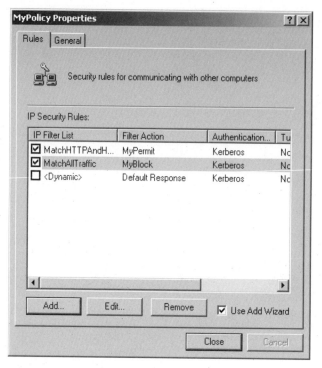

Figure 6
MyPolicy Properties dialog box

Your IPSec policy is now ready to use. To activate the policy, right-click **MyPolicy** and then click **Assign**.

Summary of What You Just Did

In the previous three procedures, you performed these actions:

- You started by creating two filter actions: one to allow traffic and one to block traffic.

- Next, you created two IP filter lists. The one called **MatchAllTraffic** matches on all traffic, regardless of port. The one called **MatchHTTPAndHTTPS** contains two filters that match TCP traffic from any source address to TCP ports 80 and 443.

- Then you created an IPSec policy by creating a rule that associated the **MyBlock** filter action with the **MatchAllTraffic** filter list and the **MyPermit** filter action with the **MatchHTTPAndHTTPS** filter list. The result of this is that the Web server only allows TCP traffic destined for port 80 or 443. All other traffic is rejected.

Restricting Database Server Communication

On a dedicated SQL Server database server, you often want to restrict communication to a specific SQL Server port over a particular protocol. By default, SQL Server listens on TCP port 1433, and UDP port 1434 is used for negotiation purposes.

The following steps restrict a database server so that it only accepts incoming connections on TCP port 1433 and UDP port 1434:

- Create two filter actions: one to permit traffic and the other to block traffic. For details, see the Create filter actions procedure under "Restricting Web Server Communication" earlier in this How To.
- Create two filter lists: one that matches all traffic and one that contains two filters that match TCP traffic destined for port 1433 and UDP traffic destined for port 1433. For details, see "Create IP filter lists and filters" under "Restricting Web Server Communication" earlier in this How To. The required filters are summarized below.
  - Enter the following values to create a filter that allows TCP over port 1433:
    - Source Address: Any IP address
    - Destination Address: My IP Address
    - Protocol: TCP
    - From Port: Any
    - To Port: 1433
  - Enter the following values to create a filter that allows UDP over port 1434:
    - Source Address: Any IP address
    - Destination Address: My IP Address
    - Protocol: UDP
    - From Port: Any
    - To Port: 1434
- Create and apply IPSec policy by repeating the procedure under "Restricting Web Server Communication" earlier in this How To.

Restricting Server-to-Server Communication

You can also use IPSec to provide server authentication. This is useful when restricting the range of computers that can connect to middle-tier application servers or database servers. IPSec provides three authentication options:

- **Kerberos**

  To use Kerberos, the computers must:

  - Be part of the same domain and forest
  - Be within a specific source address range
  - Be within the same subnet
  - Use static IP addresses

- **Pre-shared secret key**

  To use pre-shared secret-key-based authentication, the two computers must share an encryption key.

- **Certificate-based authentication**

  To use certificate authentication, the two computers must trust a common certificate authority (CA), and the server that performs the authentication must request and install a certificate from the CA.

In this section, you set up IPSec authentication between two servers by using a pre-shared secret key.

▶ **To perform server-to-server authentication**

1. Start the Local Security Policy MMC snap-in.
2. Right-click **IPSec Security policies on the local machine**, and then click **Create IP Security Policy**.
3. Type "MyAuthPolicy" [SSJ2]for the name, and then click **Next**.
4. Clear the **Activate the default response rule** check box.
5. Click **Next** and then **Finish**.

   The **MyAuthPolicy Properties** dialog box is displayed so that you can edit the policy properties.
6. Click **Add**, and then click **Next** three times.
7. In the **Authentication Method** dialog box, select **Use this string to protect the key exchange (preshared key)**.
8. Enter a long, random set of characters in the text box, and then click **Next**.

   You should copy the key to a floppy disk or CD. You need it to configure the communicating server.

9. In the **IP Filter List** dialog box, select **All IP Traffic**, and then click **Next**.

10. In the **Filter Action** dialog box, select **Request Security (Optional)**, and then click **Next**.

11. Click **Finish**.

12. Test your application to verify the configured policy.

Using IPSec Tools

This section describes two useful IPSec diagnostic tools that are available as part of the Windows 2000 resource kit:

- Netdiag.exe
- IPSecpol.exe

Netdiag.exe

Before creating a new policy, determine if your system already has an existing policy. You can do this by performing the following steps:

▶ **To check for existing IPSec policy**

1. To install Netdiag.exe, run the Setup.exe program from the \Support\Tools folder on the Windows 2000 Server CD.

   The tools are installed in C:\Program Files\Resource kit.

2. Run the following command from the command line:

   ```
   netdiag /test:ipsec
   ```

   If there are no existing filters, then the output looks like the following:

   ```
   IP Security test . . . . . . . . . : Passed IPSec policy service is active, but
   no policy is assigned.
   ```

IPSecpol.exe

The Internet Protocol Security Policies tool helps you automate the creation of policies in local and remote registries. The tool supports the same settings that you can configure by using the MMC snap-in.

Download the tool from the Microsoft Windows 2000 Web site at *http://www.microsoft.com/windows2000/techinfo/reskit/tools/existing/ipsecpol-o.asp*.

For detailed examples of using Ipsecpol.exe to create and manipulate IPSec rules, see Microsoft Knowledge Base article 813878, "How to Block Specific Network Protocols and Ports by Using IPSec."

Additional Resources

For more information, see the following resources:

- Step-by-Step guide to IPSec at *http://www.microsoft.com/windows2000/techinfo /planning/security/ipsecsteps.asp*.
- IP Security for Windows 2000 Server at *http://www.microsoft.com/windows2000 /techinfo/howitworks/security/ip_security.asp*.
- "How To: Use IPSec to Provide Secure Communication Between Two Servers" in the How To section of "Building Secure ASP.NET Applications" on MSDN.
- Article 313190, "How To: Use IPSec IP Filter Lists in Windows 2000" in the Microsoft Knowledge Base.
- Article 813878, "How to Block Specific Network Protocols and Ports by Using IPSec" in the Microsoft Knowledge Base.
- Article 313195, "How To: Use IPSec Monitor in Windows 2000" in the Microsoft Knowledge Base.
- IPSec considerations at *http://www.microsoft.com/technet/treeview/default.asp?url= /technet/prodtechnol/winxppro/proddocs/sag_IPSECsec_con.asp?frame=true*.

How To:
Use the Microsoft Baseline
Security Analyzer

Applies To

This information applies to computers that run the following:

- Servers running Microsoft® Windows 2000 Server or Windows 2003 Server
- Developer workstations running Windows 2000 (all flavors), Windows XP Professional or Windows 2003 Server
- SQL Server 2000, including the Desktop Edition (MSDE)

Summary

Microsoft Baseline Security Analyzer (MBSA) checks for operating system and SQL Server updates. MBSA also scans a computer for insecure configuration. When checking for Windows service packs and patches, it includes Windows components such as Internet Information Service (IIS) and COM+. MBSA uses an XML file as the manifest of existing updates. This XML file, contained in the archive Mssecure.cab, is either downloaded by MBSA when a scan is run, or the file can be downloaded on the local computer, or made available from a network server.

In this chapter, you will learn how to use MBSA to perform two processes:

- A security updates scan
- A check for default settings that are not secure

This How To reviews each mode separately, although both modes can be performed in the same pass.

Contents

- Before You Begin
- What You Must Know
- Scanning for Security Updates and Patches
- Scanning Multiple Systems for Updates and Patches
- SQL Server and MSDE Specifics
- Scanning for Secure defaults
- Pitfalls
- Additional Resources

Before You Begin

Install MBSA, using Mbsasetup.msi, to a tools directory. Copy the file Mssecure.cab to the MBSA installation directory.

- **Download MBSA**. Download MBSA from the MBSA Home Page:
  http://www.microsoft.com/technet/treeview/default.asp?url=/technet/security/tools/Tools/mbsahome.asp

- **Updates for MBSA**. If the machine you use has Internet access, the latest security XML file will be downloaded automatically, if needed. If your computer does not have Internet access, you need to download the latest XML file using the signed CAB at the following location: *http://download.microsoft.com/download/xml/security/1.0/NT5/EN-US/mssecure.cab*

  The CAB file is signed to ensure it has not been modified. You must uncompress it and store it in the same folder where MBSA is stored.

  Note   To view the latest XML file without downloading it, use the following location: *https://www.microsoft.com/technet/security/search/mssecure.xml*

- **Default installation directory:** \Program Files\Microsoft Baseline Security Analyzer\

  Note   You need to run commands from this directory. MBSA does not create an environment variable for you.

What You Must Know

Before using this How To, you should be aware of the following:

- You can use MBSA by using the graphical user interface (GUI) or from the command line. The GUI executable is Mbsa.exe and the command line executable is Mbsacli.exe.
- MBSA uses ports 138 and 139 to perform its scans.
- MBSA requires administrator privileges on the computer that you scan. The options /u (username) and /p (password) can be used to specify the username to run the scan. Do not store user names and passwords in text files such as command files or scripts.
- MBSA requires the following software:
  - Windows NT 4.0 SP4 and above, Windows 2000, or Windows XP (local scans only on Windows XP computers that use simple file sharing).
  - IIS 4.0, 5.0 (required for IIS vulnerability checks).
  - SQL 7.0, 2000 (required for SQL vulnerability checks).
  - Microsoft Office 2000, XP (required for Office vulnerability checks).
  - The following services must be installed/enabled: Server service, Remote Registry service, File & Print Sharing.
  - The section Additional Information later in this How To includes tips on working with MBSA.

Scanning for Security Updates and Patches

You can run Mbsa.exe and Mbsacli.exe with options to verify the presence of security patches.

Using the Graphical Interface

Use the MBSA GUI tool as described next.

▶ **To use the MBSA GUI to scan for updates and patches**

1. Click **Microsoft Baseline Security Analyzer** from the **Programs** menu.
2. Click **Scan a computer**.
3. Make sure that the following options are not selected, and then click **Start scan**.
   - Check for Windows vulnerabilities
   - Check for weak passwords
   - Check for IIS vulnerabilities
   - Check for SQL vulnerabilities

The advantage of the GUI is that the report is opened immediately after scanning the local computer. More details on interpreting the report are explained later in this section.

Using the Command Line (Mbsacli.exe)

To use the command line tool (Mbsacli.exe) to check for security updates and patches, run the following command from a command window. This scans the specified computer with the supplied IP address and checks for missing updates:

```
mbsacli /i 192.168.195.137 /n OS+IIS+SQL+PASSWORD
```

A successful scan produces results similar to those shown below:

```
Scanning...
[      ] 0 o[.........] 1 of 1 computer scan(s) complete.
Scan Complete.
Computer Name, IP Address, Assessment, Report Name
----------------------------------------------------
Workgroup\SECNETSQL, 192.168.195.137, Severe Risk, Workgroup - SECNETSQL (04-07-
2003 03-01 PM)
```

You can view the report by using Mbsacli.exe, but is not recommended since it is easier to extract patch details using the GUI. The command below allows you to view a scan report using Mbsacli.exe:

```
mbsacli /ld "SecurityReportFile.xml"
```

Analyzing the Output

A report file is generated in the profile directory of the logged in user (%userprofile%), on the computer from where you ran the Mbsacli.exe command. The easiest way to view the results of those reports is by using the GUI mode of MBSA.

Scanning Multiple Systems for Updates and Patches

You can also use MBSA to scan a range of computers. To do so, use the /r command line switch as shown below.

```
mbsacli /r 192.168.195.130-192.168.195.254 /n OS+IIS+SQL+PASSWORD
```

```
The above command scans all computers in the range 192.168.195.130 to
192.168.195.254.
```

To scan all computers in a domain, use the /d option as show below:

```
mbsacli /d DOMAINNAME /n OS+IIS+SQL+PASSWORD
```

SQL Server and MSDE Specifics

SQL Server, including MSDE, instances are each scanned and reported separately. Instances are noted with Instance Name as shown in Figure 7.

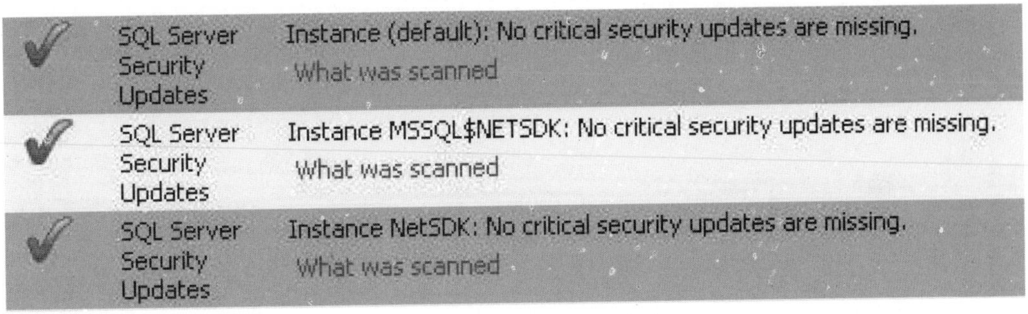

Figure 7
SQL Server and MSDE specifics

For more details on installing patches and service packs for SQL Server 2000, including the Desktop Edition (MSDE), see "How To: Patch Management" in the How To section of this guide.

Scanning for Secure Configuration

In addition to scanning for missing security updates, MBSA scans for system configurations that are not secure. For a detailed list of what is checked by this scan, see the MBSA documentation at: *http://www.microsoft.com/technet/treeview /default.asp?url=/technet/security/tools/tools/mbsawp.asp*

The secure configuration scan can be done in the following phases

- Perform the scan.
- Analyze the scan.
- Correct any issues that you find.

These phases are described below.

Performing the Scan

Run MBSA and deselect **Check for security updates** when performing the scan.

Analyzing the Scan

The resulting report will appear similar to the patch scan you performed earlier. The only difference is the link **How to correct this** will be available when issues are found. When you click the link, a page will appear with the details of the issue found, the solution to the issue, and instructions to correct the issue.

Compare the issue details against your security policy and follow the instructions if the issue is not addressed by your policy.

Correcting Issues Found

Choose the link **How to correct this**. In the resulting page, the solution and instructions explain the steps that you need to take to correct the issue.

Additional Information

The following information will help you troubleshoot scanning errors or explain inconsistencies between scans.

False Positives From Security Update Checks

There may be cases where MBSA reports that an update is not installed, even after you complete an update or take the steps documented in a security bulletin. There are two reasons for these false reports:

1. **Files scanned were updated by an installation that is unrelated to a security bulletin.** For example, a file shared by different versions of the same program may be updated by the newer version. MBSA is unaware of the new versions and, because it is not what is expected, it reports the update is missing.

2. **Some security bulletins are not addressed by a file update but a configuration change that cannot be verified.** These types of flags will appear as **Note** or **Warning** messages, marked with yellow Xs.

Both must be noted and ignored for future scans.

Requirements for Performing Remote Scans

MBSA makes use of the following network services to scan a computer:

- Windows NT 4.0 SP4 and above, Windows 2000, or Windows XP (local scans only on Windows XP computers that use simple file sharing)
- IIS 4.0, 5.0 (required for IIS vulnerability checks)
- SQL 7.0, 2000 (required for SQL vulnerability checks)
- Services must be installed or enabled: Server service, Remote Registry service, File & Print Sharing

f any of the services are unavailable or administrative shares (C$) are not accessible, errors will result during the scan.

Password Scans

Password check performed by MBSA can take a long time, depending on the number of user accounts on the machine. The password check enumerates all user accounts and performs several password change attempts using common password pitfalls such as a password that is the same as the username. Users may want to disable this check before scanning Domain Controllers on their network. For details on the MBSA password check, see the topic "Local Accounts Passwords" in the MBSA whitepaper on TechNet *http://www.microsoft.com/technet/treeview/default.asp?url=/technet/security /tools/tools/mbsawp.asp.*

Differences Between Mbsa.exe and Mbsacli.exe

It is important to know the differences between the default options of the two MBSA clients: the GUI tool, Mbsa.exe, and the command-line tool, Mbsacli.exe. The examples shown previously in this How To take these defaults into account.

The MBSA GUI calls **/nosum**, **/v**, and **/baseline** by default. The details for those options are:

/nosum   Security update checks will not test file checksums.

/v   Displays security update reason codes.

/baseline Checks only for baseline security updates.

The MBSA command line calls no options and runs a default scan.

Additional Resources

The MBSA home is the best resources for the latest on the Microsoft Baseline Security Analyzer. *http://www.microsoft.com/technet/treeview/default.asp?url=/technet/security/tools /Tools/MBSAhome.asp*

How To:
Use IISLockdown.exe

Applies To

This information applies to server computers that run the following:

- Microsoft® Windows® 2000 Server

Summary

You can largely automate the process of securing your Web server by running the IISLockdown tool. It allows you to pick a specific type of server role and then improve security for that server with customized templates that either disable or secure various features. In addition, the URLScan ISAPI filter is installed when you run IISLockdown. The URLScan ISAPI filter rejects potentially malicious requests and accepts or rejects client requests based on a configurable set of rules.

What Does IISLockdown Do?

For a Windows 2000 computer that serves ASP.NET pages, select the **Dynamic Web server (ASP enabled)** template when you run IISLockdown. When you use this template, IIS Lockdown performs the following actions:

- It disables the following Internet Services:
  - File Transfer Protocol (FTP)
  - E-mail service (SMTP)
  - News service (NNTP)
- It maps the following script maps to 404.dll:
  - Index Server Web Interface (.idq, .htw, .ida)
  - Server-side includes (.shtml, .shtm, .stm)
  - Internet Data Connector (.idc)
  - .HTR scripting (.htr)
  - Internet printing (.printer)

- It removes the following virtual directories:
  - IIS Samples
  - MSADC
  - IISHelp
  - Scripts
  - IISAdmin
- It restricts anonymous access to system utilities as well as the ability to write to Web content directories. To do this, IISLockdown creates two new local groups called **Web Anonymous Users** and **Web Applications** and then it adds deny access control entries (ACEs) for these groups to the access control list (ACL) on key utilities and directories.

  Next, IISLockdown adds the default anonymous Internet user account (IUSR_MACHINE) to **Web Anonymous Users** and the IWAM_MACHINE account to **Web Applications**.

Note If you create custom, anonymous Internet user accounts, add them to the **Web Anonymous Users** group.

- It disables Web Distributed Authoring and Versioning (WebDAV).
- It installs the URLScan ISAPI filter.

Installing IISLockdown

To install IISlockdown, download it from the Microsoft Web site at *http://download.microsoft.com/download/iis50/Utility/2.1/NT45XP/EN-US/iislockd.exe*.

You can save it locally or run it directly by clicking **Open** when you are prompted. If you save IISLockd.exe, you can unpack helpful files by running the following command:

```
iislockd.exe /q /c
```

This command unpacks the following files:

- **IISLockd.chm.** This is the compiled help file for the IISLockdown tool.
- **RunLockdUnattended.doc.** This file includes instructions for unattended IISLockdown execution.
- **URLScan.exe and associated files.** These files install URLScan without running IISLockdown.exe.

Running IISLockdown

IISLockdown detects the Microsoft .NET Framework and takes steps to secure .NET Framework files. Install the .NET Framework on your Web server before you run IISLockdown.

IISLockd.exe is not an installation program. When you launch IISLockd.exe, it runs the IIS Lockdown Wizard.

▶ To run IISLockdown

1. Run IISlockd.exe on your IIS Web server, click **Next**, and then read and accept the license agreement.
2. For Web servers that host ASP.NET Web applications, select **Dynamic Web server (ASP enabled)** from the **Server templates** list.
3. Select **View template settings** and then click **Next**.

   This allows you to specify the changes that the IIS Lockdown tool should perform.
4. Select **Web service (HTTP)** and make sure that no other services are selected.
5. Select **Remove unselected services**, click **Yes** in response to the warning message box, and then click **Next**.
6. On the **Script Maps** page, disable support for the following script maps, and then click **Next**.
   - Index Server Web Interface (.idq, .htw, .ida)
   - Server side includes (.shtml, .shtm, .stm)
   - Internet Data Connector (.idc)
   - .HTR scripting (.htr)
   - Internet printing (.printer)
7. On the **Additional Security** page, select all of the available options.

   This causes IISLockdown to remove all of the listed virtual directories, configure NTFS permissions for the anonymous Internet account, and disable WebDAV.
8. Click **Next**.
9. On the **URLScan** page, select **Install URLScan** filter on the server.
10. Click **Next** twice.

    IISLockdown updates your server configuration using the selected options.
11. Click **Next** and then **Finish** to exit the tool.

Log Files

A log file detailing the changes made by IISLockdown is written to \WINNT\System32\inetsrv\oblt-log.log. When you run IISLockdown a second time, it undoes any changes it made based on this log. You can view the log file by using any text editor to see the exact changes made by IISLockdown.

Undoing IISLockdown Changes

To undo the changes made by IISLockdown, run IISlockd.exe a second time and choose to undo the changes. The undo operation restores the system settings that were in effect immediately before you previously ran IISLockdown. These details are contained in the log file \WINNT\System32\inetsrv\0blt-log. Therefore, it is important that you test the system promptly after you run IISLockdown. If an undo is required, perform it immediately.

> **Note**   The URLScan ISAPI filter that is installed as part of IIS Lockdown is not removed as part of the undo process. You can remove URLScan manually by using the **ISAPI filters** tab at the server level in Internet Services Manager.

Unattended Execution

The following steps are from RunLockdUnattended.doc, which is available if you unpack files by running IISLockd.exe with the /q and /c arguments.

▶ **To configure IISLockdown for unattended execution**

1. Open IISlockd.ini in a text editor.

2. Under the **[Info]** section, configure the **UnattendedServerType** setting by entering the name that matches the server template you want to use. For example, if you want to apply the dynamicweb template, the setting would look like this:

   ```
   UnattendedServerType=dynamicweb
   ```

3. Change the **Unattended** setting to **TRUE**, as follows:

   ```
   Unattended=TRUE
   ```

> **Note**   If you want to run IISlockd.exe unattended to undo a previous set of changes, ensure that both the **Unattended** and **Undo** settings are set to **TRUE**.

4. Configure the server template that you chose in step 2. The template configuration is denoted with square brackets around the server template name, for example, **[dynamicweb]**. The template configuration contains the various feature settings for that specific server template. These feature settings can be toggled on or off by setting them to **TRUE** or **FALSE**.

> **Note**   The **AdvancedSetup** setting is ignored during an unattended installation, and the **UninstallServices** setting applies only to Windows 2000.

5. Save IISlockd.ini.
6. Run IISlockd.exe using the command line or scripting.

Pitfalls

Be aware of the following potential pitfalls when working with IISLockdown:

- IISLockdown configures NTFS permissions using the new group **Web Anonymous Users**. By default, this contains the IUSR_MACHINE account. If you create new anonymous accounts, you must manually add these accounts to the **Web Anonymous Users** group.
- If you debug ASP.NET pages using Microsoft Visual Studio® .NET, debugging stops working. This is because IISLockdown installs URLScan and URLScan blocks the DEBUG verb. For more information about using IISLockdown on developer workstations, see "How To: Secure Your Developer Workstation" in this guide.

How To:
Use URLScan

Applies To

This information applies to server computers that run the following:

- Microsoft® Windows® 2000 Server operating system

Summary

URLScan is an ISAPI filter that allows Web site administrators to restrict the kind of HTTP requests that the server will process. By blocking specific HTTP requests, the URLScan filter prevents potentially harmful requests from reaching the server and causing damage.

Contents

This How To contains the following items:

- Installing URLScan
- Log files
- Removing URLScan
- Configuring URLScan
- Throttling request sizes with URLScan
- Debugging Microsoft ® Visual Studio .NET with URLScan installed
- Masking content headers (banners)
- Pitfalls
- References

Installing URLScan

At the time of writing (April 2003), URLScan 2.0 is installed when you run IISLockdown (IISLockd.exe,) or you can install it independently.

- **Installing URLScan 2.0 with IISLockdown:** You can install URLScan 2.0 as part of the IIS Lockdown Wizard (IISLockd.exe). IISLockd.exe is available as an Internet download from Microsoft's Web site at: *http://download.microsoft.com/download/iis50 /Utility/2.1/NT45XP/EN-US/iislockd.exe*.

- **Installing URLScan 2.0 without running IISLockdown:** To install URLScan without running IISLockdown, you need to manually extract it from the IIS Lockdown Tool. First you need to save IISLockd.exe to a directory. Then to extract the URLScan setup files, run the following command at the command line from the directory where you installed IISLockd.exe:

```
iislockd.exe /q /c
```

  This unpacks URLScan.exe which is the URLScan installation program.

  For more information, refer to Microsoft Knowledge Base article 315522, "How To: Extract the URLScan Tool and Lockdown Template Files from the IIS Lockdown Tool."

- **Installing URLScan 2.5:** URLScan 2.5 is currently the latest version of URLScan. If you want to install URLScan 2.5, you first need URLScan 1.0 or URLScan 2.0.

  For more information, refer to Microsoft Knowledge Base article 307608, "INFO: Availability of URLScan Version 2.5 Security Tool."

- **Default installation directory:** The URLScan files including Urlscan.dll, URLScan.ini and URLScan logs are stored in %windir%\system32\inetsrv\urlscan. URLScan.dll is the filter. You use URLScan.ini to configure the way it works.

Log Files

URLScan creates log files that record rejected requests. Log files are located in the following folder:

```
%windir%\system32\inetsrv\urlscan
```

Log files are named using the following convention: URLScan<date>.log.

Removing URLScan

You remove URLScan manually by using the ISAPI filters page of the Web server properties dialog in Internet Services Manager

Configuring URLScan

To configure URLScan to determine which requests should be rejected, you use URLScan.ini. This is located in the following folder:

```
%windir%\system32\inetsrv\urlscan
```

For more information on how to modify the various sections in URLScan.ini, refer to Microsoft Knowledge Base article 815155 "How To: Configure URLScan to Protect ASP.NET Web Applications."

Throttling Request Sizes with URLScan

You can use URLScan as another line of defense against denial of service attacks even before requests reach ASP.NET. You do this by setting limits on the **MaxAllowedContentLength**, **MaxUrl** and **MaxQueryString** attributes.

To throttle the request sizes, add the following configuration to URLScan.ini:

```
[RequestLimits]
; The entries in this section impose limits on the length
; of allowed parts of requests reaching the server.
;MaxAllowedContentLength=2000000000
;MaxUrl=16384
;MaxQueryString=4096
```

Debugging VS .NET with URLScan Installed

By default, URLScan does not allow the DEBUG verb. Therefore, when you use VS.NET to debug a Web application on a server where URLScan is installed, you may see the following error:

```
Microsoft Development Environment:
Error while trying to run project: Unable to start debugging on the web server.
Could not start ASP.NET or ATL Server debugging.

Verify that ASP.NET or ATL Server is correctly installed on the server. Would you
like to disable future attempts to debug ASP.NET pages for this project? Yes    No
Help
```

Your URLScan log file will also contain an entry similar to the following:

```
[01-18-2003 - 22:25:26] Client at 127.0.0.1: Sent verb 'DEBUG', which is not
specifically allowed. Request will be rejected.
```

To support debugging, add DEBUG to the **AllowVerbs** section in URLScan.ini as shown below:

```
[AllowVerbs]
GET
HEAD
POST
DEBUG
```

Note   You need to restart IIS for changes to take effect.

Masking Content Headers (Banners)

To prevent banner information that reveals the type and version of your Web server, locate the RemoveServerHeader attribute in URLScan.ini, and set its value to 1 as shown below.

```
RemoveServerHeader=1
```

For more information, see Microsoft Knowledge Base article, 317741, "How To: Mask IIS Version Information from Network Trace and Telnet."

Pitfalls

If you use URLScan, you might run into the following issues:

- URLScan blocks the DEBUG verb which breaks application debugging. If you need to support debugging, add the DEBUG verb to the [**AllowVerbs**] section in URLScan.ini.

- You need to recycle IIS for changes to take effect. URLScan is an ISAPI filter that runs inside the IIS process (Inetinfo.exe) and URLScan's options are loaded from URLScan.ini when IIS starts up. You can run the IISReset command from a command prompt to recycle IIS.

- URLScan blocks requests that contain potentially harmful characters, for example, characters that have been used to exploit vulnerabilities in the past such as "." used for directory traversal. It is not recommended that project paths contain the "." character. If you must allow this, you need to set AllowDotInPath=1 in URLScan.ini.

  If your Web application directories include dots in the path, for example, a directory containing the name "Asp.Net", then URLScan will reject the request and a "404 not found" message will be returned to the client.

  Other characters to avoid in project names because they will be rejected by URLScan include comma (,) and the pound sign (#).

References

For additional information, refer to the following resources:

- For more information about how to modify the various sections in Urlscan.ini, refer to Microsoft Knowledge Base article 815155 "How To: Configure URLScan to Protect ASP.NET Web Applications."

- For more information about using URLScan, see *http://www.nardware.co.uk/Security /Docs/Nmsurlscan.html*.

- For more information about URLScan 2.5, refer to Microsoft Knowledge Base article 307608, "INFO: Availability of URLScan Version 2.5 Security Tool."

How To: Create a Custom Encryption Permission

Applies To

This information applies to server or workstation computers that run the following:

- Microsoft® Windows® 2000 Server and Windows 2000 Professional, Windows Server 2003, Windows XP Professional
- Internet Information Server (IIS)
- .NET Framework 1.1

Summary

This How To describes how to create a custom code access security permission to control programmatic access to unmanaged encryption functionality that Win32® Data Protection API (DPAPI) provides. Use this custom permission with the managed DPAPI wrapper code described in "How To: Create a DPAPI Library," in "Building Secure ASP.NET Applications," in the MSDN Library.

Before You Begin

Code access security permissions must derive from **System.Security.CodeAccessPermission**, which provides an implementation of the **Demand** method defined by the **IPermission** interface, together with others such as **Assert**, **Deny**, and **PermitOnly**, which are defined by the **IStackWalk** interface.

Code access permissions (not identity permissions) also implement the **IUnrestrictedPermission** interface, to indicate that the permission is part of the unrestricted permission set. This means that the permission is automatically granted to any code that has full trust. The inheritance hierarchy for the custom **EncryptionPermission** implemented in this How To is shown in Figure 8.

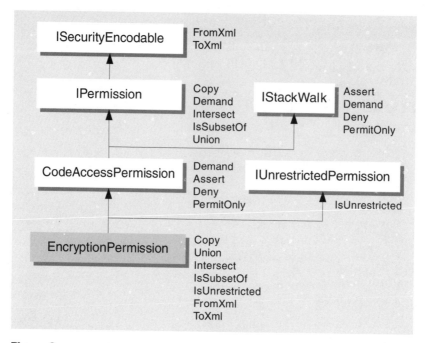

Figure 8
Custom EncryptionPermission inheritance hierarchy

The custom **EncryptionPermission** class maintains the following states:

- **EncryptionPermissionFlag**. Determines whether code that is granted this permission is able to encrypt data, decrypt data, or both.
- **StorePermissionFlag**. Determines whether code that is granted this permission is able to use DPAPI with the machine store, current user store, or both.

Summary of Steps

This How To includes the following steps:

Step 1. Create the **EncryptionPermission** class.

Step 2. Create the **EncryptionPermissionAttribute** class.

Step 3. Install the **Permission** assembly in the global assembly cache (GAC).

Step 4. Update the DPAPI managed wrapper code.

Step 5. Call DPAPI from a medium trust Web application.

Step 1. Create the EncryptionPermission Class

The **EncryptionPermission** class is the custom permission implementation used to authorize access to the unmanaged DPAPI functionality.

▶ **To create the CustomPermission class**

1. Create a new Visual C#™ development tool Class Library project **CustomPermission**, and rename **class1.cs** to **EncryptionPermission.cs**.

2. Add a strong name to the assembly so that you can install it in the GAC. Use the following attribute in **assemblyinfo.cs**:

   ```
   [assembly: AssemblyKeyFile(@"..\..\CustomPermissions.snk")]
   ```

3. Use a fixed assembly version.

   ```
   [assembly: AssemblyVersion("1.0.0.1")]
   ```

4. Add the following **using** statements to the top of EncryptionPermission.cs.

   ```
   using System.Security;
   using System.Security.Permissions;
   ```

5. Add the following enumerated types to the **CustomPermissions** namespace.

   ```
   [Flags, Serializable]
   public enum EncryptionPermissionFlag
   {Encrypt = 0x01, Decrypt = 0x02}

   [Flags, Serializable]
   public enum StorePermissionFlag
   {User = 0x01, Machine = 0x02}
   ```

6. Add serialization support to the **EncryptionPermission** class with the **[Serializable]** attribute, and derive it from **CodeAccessSecurity** and **IUnrestrictedPermission**. Also, seal the class, as the following shows.

   ```
   [Serializable]
   public sealed class EncryptionPermission : CodeAccessPermission,
                                              IUnrestrictedPermission
   ```

7. Add two private member variables to maintain the permission state.

   ```
   private EncryptionPermissionFlag _permFlag;
   private StorePermissionFlag _storePermFlag;
   ```

8. Replace the default constructor with the following constructors.

```
// It is convention for permission types to provide a constructor
// that accepts the PermissionState enumeration.
public EncryptionPermission(PermissionState state)
{
  if (state.Equals(PermissionState.Unrestricted))
  {
    _permFlag = EncryptionPermissionFlag.Encrypt |
                EncryptionPermissionFlag.Decrypt;
    _storePermFlag = StorePermissionFlag.User | StorePermissionFlag.Machine;
  }
  else
  {
    _permFlag &= ~(EncryptionPermissionFlag.Encrypt |
                   EncryptionPermissionFlag.Decrypt);
    _storePermFlag &= ~(StorePermissionFlag.User |
                        StorePermissionFlag.Machine);
  }
}
// This constructor allows you to specify the encryption type (encrypt
// or decrypt) by using the EncryptionPermissionFlag enumeration and the DPAPI
// key store to use (user or machine) as defined by the StorePermissionFlag
// enumeration.
public EncryptionPermission(EncryptionPermissionFlag cipher,
                            StorePermissionFlag store)
{
  _permFlag = cipher;
  _storePermFlag = store;
}
public EncryptionPermission()
{
  _permFlag &= ~EncryptionPermissionFlag.Encrypt |
               EncryptionPermissionFlag.Decrypt;
  _storePermFlag &= ~(StorePermissionFlag.User | StorePermissionFlag.Machine);
}
```

9. Add the following public properties to allow a consumer application to set the permission class state.

```
// Set this property to true to allow encryption.
public bool Encrypt
{
  set {
    if(true == value)
    {
      _permFlag |= EncryptionPermissionFlag.Encrypt;
    }
    else
    {
      _permFlag &= ~EncryptionPermissionFlag.Encrypt;
    }
  }
```

(continued)

```
      get {
        return (_permFlag & EncryptionPermissionFlag.Encrypt).Equals(
                         EncryptionPermissionFlag.Encrypt);
      }
    }

    // Set this property to true to allow decryption.
    public bool Decrypt
    {
      set {
        if(true == value)
        {
          _permFlag |= EncryptionPermissionFlag.Decrypt;
        }
        else
        {
          _permFlag &= ~EncryptionPermissionFlag.Decrypt;
        }
      }
      get {
        return (_permFlag & EncryptionPermissionFlag.Decrypt).Equals(
                         EncryptionPermissionFlag.Decrypt);
      }
    }
    // Set this property to true to use the DPAPI machine key.
    public bool MachineStore
    {
      set {
        if(true == value)
        {
          _storePermFlag |= StorePermissionFlag.Machine;
        }
        else
        {
          _storePermFlag &= ~StorePermissionFlag.Machine;
        }
      }
      get {
        return (_storePermFlag & StorePermissionFlag.Machine).Equals(
                            StorePermissionFlag.Machine);
      }
    }
    // Set this property to true to use the DPAPI user key.
    public bool UserStore
    {
      set {
        if(true == value)
        {
          _storePermFlag |= StorePermissionFlag.User;
        }
```

(continued)

(continued)

```
      else
      {
        _storePermFlag &= ~StorePermissionFlag.User;
      }
    }
    get {
      return (_storePermFlag & StorePermissionFlag.User).Equals(
                          StorePermissionFlag.User);
    }
  }
```

10. Implement **IPermission.Copy**. This creates an identical copy of the current permission instance and returns it to the caller.

```
public override IPermission Copy()
{
  return  new EncryptionPermission(_permFlag, _storePermFlag);
}
```

11. Implement **IPermission.Intersect**. This returns a permission object that is the result of the set intersection between the current permission and the supplied permission.

```
public override IPermission Intersect(IPermission target)
{
  // An input of null indicates a permission with no state.
  // There can be no common state, so the method returns null.
  if (target == null)
    return null;

  if (!(target.GetType().Equals(this.GetType())))
    throw new ArgumentException(
                "Argument must be of type EncryptionPermission.");

  // Cast target to an EncryptionPermission.
  EncryptionPermission targetPerm = (EncryptionPermission)target;

  EncryptionPermissionFlag intersectEncryption = this._permFlag &
                                    targetPerm._permFlag;
  StorePermissionFlag intersectStore = this._storePermFlag &
                                    targetPerm._storePermFlag;

  return new EncryptionPermission(intersectEncryption, intersectStore);
}
```

12. Implement **IPermission.Union**. This returns a permission object that is the result of the set union between the current permission and the supplied permission.

```
public override IPermission Union(IPermission target)
{
  if (target == null)
    return Copy();

  if (!(target.GetType().Equals(this.GetType())))
    throw new ArgumentException(
                   "Argument must be of type EncryptionPermission.");

  // Cast the target to an EncryptionPermission.
  EncryptionPermission targetPerm = (EncryptionPermission)target;

  EncryptionPermissionFlag unionEncryption = this._permFlag |
                                  targetPerm._permFlag;
  StorePermissionFlag unionStore = this._storePermFlag |
                             targetPerm._storePermFlag;

  return new EncryptionPermission(unionEncryption, unionStore);
}
```

13. Implement the **IPermission.IsSubsetOf**. This method returns a bool to indicate whether or not the current permission is a subset of the supplied permission. To be a subset, every item of state in the current permission must also be in the target permission.

```
public override bool IsSubsetOf(IPermission target)
{
  // An input of null indicates a permission with no state.
  // The permission can only be a subset if it's in a similar empty state.
  bool canEncrypt, canDecrypt;
  bool canUseMachineStore, canUseUserStore;

  bool canTargetEncrypt, canTargetDecrypt;
  bool canTargetUseMachineStore, canTargetUseUserStore;

  canEncrypt = (this._permFlag &
             EncryptionPermissionFlag.Encrypt).
             Equals(EncryptionPermissionFlag.Encrypt);
  canDecrypt = (this._permFlag &
             EncryptionPermissionFlag.Decrypt).
             Equals(EncryptionPermissionFlag.Decrypt);
  canUseMachineStore = (this._storePermFlag &
                  StorePermissionFlag.Machine).
                  Equals(StorePermissionFlag.Machine);
  canUseUserStore = (this._storePermFlag &
                StorePermissionFlag.User).
                Equals(StorePermissionFlag.User);
```

(continued)

(continued)

```
if (target == null)
{
  if ((canEncrypt == false && canDecrypt == false) && (canUseMachineStore ==
      false  && canUseUserStore == false))
    return true;
  else
    return false;
}

if (!(target.GetType().Equals(this.GetType())))
  throw new ArgumentException(
                        "Argument must be of type EncryptionPermission.");

// Cast the target to an EncryptionPermission.
EncryptionPermission targetPerm = (EncryptionPermission)target;

canTargetEncrypt = (targetPerm._permFlag &
                   EncryptionPermissionFlag.Encrypt).
                   Equals(EncryptionPermissionFlag.Encrypt);
canTargetDecrypt = (targetPerm._permFlag &
                   EncryptionPermissionFlag.Decrypt).
                   Equals(EncryptionPermissionFlag.Decrypt);

canTargetUseMachineStore = (targetPerm._storePermFlag &
                           StorePermissionFlag.Machine).
                           Equals(StorePermissionFlag.Machine);
canTargetUseUserStore = (targetPerm._storePermFlag &
                        StorePermissionFlag.User).
                        Equals(StorePermissionFlag.User);

// Every value set (true) in this permission must be in the target.
// The following code checks to see if the current permission is a subset
// of the target. If the current permission has something that the target
// does not have, it cannot be a subset.
if(canEncrypt == true && canTargetEncrypt == false)
  return false;
if(canDecrypt == true && canTargetDecrypt == false)
  return false;
if(canUseMachineStore == true && canTargetUseMachineStore == false)
  return false;
if(canUseUserStore == true && canTargetUseUserStore == false)
  return false;

return true;
}
```

14. Implement **ISecurityEncodable.ToXml** and **FromXml**. These methods convert instances of a permission object into an XML format and vice-versa. These methods are used to support serialization. This is used, for example, when the security attribute is stored in assembly metadata.

```
public override SecurityElement ToXml()
{
  // Create a new element. The tag name must always be IPermission.
  SecurityElement elem = new SecurityElement("IPermission");

  // Determine the fully qualified type name (including the assembly name) of
  // the EncryptionPermission class. (The security system uses this name to
  // locate and load the class.)
  string name = typeof(EncryptionPermission).AssemblyQualifiedName;

  // Add attributes for the class name and protocol version.
  // The version must currently be 1.
  elem.AddAttribute("class", name);
  elem.AddAttribute("version", "1" );

  if (IsUnrestricted())
  {
    // Using the Unrestricted attribute is consistent with the
    // built-in .NET Framework permission types and helps keep
    // the encoding compact.
    elem.AddAttribute("Unrestricted", Boolean.TrueString);
  }
  else
  {
    // Encode each state field as an attribute of the Permission element.
    // To compact, encode only nondefault state parameters.
    elem.AddAttribute("Flags", this._permFlag.ToString());
    elem.AddAttribute("Stores", this._storePermFlag.ToString());
  }
  // Return the completed element.
  return elem;
}

// Converts a SecurityElement (or tree of elements) to a permission
// instance.
public override void FromXml(SecurityElement elem)
{
  string attrVal = "";
  // Check for an unrestricted instance.
  attrVal = elem.Attribute("Unrestricted");
  if (attrVal != null)
  {
    if(attrVal.ToLower().Equals("true"))
    {
      this._permFlag = EncryptionPermissionFlag.Encrypt |
                       EncryptionPermissionFlag.Decrypt;
      this._storePermFlag = StorePermissionFlag.Machine |
                            StorePermissionFlag.User;
    }
    return;
  }
```

(continued)

(continued)

```
//Turn off the permission and store flags.
this._permFlag &= ~(EncryptionPermissionFlag.Encrypt |
                    EncryptionPermissionFlag.Decrypt);
this._storePermFlag &= ~(StorePermissionFlag.Machine |
                         StorePermissionFlag.User);

attrVal = elem.Attribute("Flags");
if (attrVal != null)
{
  if(!attrVal.Trim().Equals(""))
  {
    this._permFlag =
      (EncryptionPermissionFlag)Enum.Parse(typeof(EncryptionPermissionFlag),
                                           attrVal);
  }
}

attrVal = elem.Attribute("Stores");
if (attrVal != null)
{
  if(!attrVal.Trim().Equals(""))
  {
    this._storePermFlag =
               (StorePermissionFlag)Enum.Parse(typeof(StorePermissionFlag),
                                               attrVal);
  }
}
}
```

15. Implement **IUnrestrictedPermission.IsUnrestricted**. This method returns **true** if the permission instance is in the unrestricted state. In this case, an unrestricted **EncryptionPermission** instance allows code to encrypt and decrypt data using both the DPAPI machine and user stores.

```
public bool IsUnrestricted()
{
  bool canEncrypt, canDecrypt, canUseUserStore, canUseMachineStore;
  canEncrypt = (this._permFlag &
                EncryptionPermissionFlag.Encrypt).
                Equals(EncryptionPermissionFlag.Encrypt);
  canDecrypt = (this._permFlag &
                EncryptionPermissionFlag.Decrypt).
                Equals(EncryptionPermissionFlag.Decrypt);
  canUseUserStore = (this._storePermFlag &
                     StorePermissionFlag.User).
                     Equals(StorePermissionFlag.User);
  canUseMachineStore = (this._storePermFlag &
                        StorePermissionFlag.Machine).
                        Equals(StorePermissionFlag.Machine);
  return ((canEncrypt && canDecrypt) &&
          (canUseUserStore && canUseMachineStore));
}
```

Step 2. Create the EncryptionPermissionAttribute Class

The .NET Framework uses attribute classes that are associated with their partner permission classes to encode permission instances. You need permission attributes to support declarative security syntax.

▶ **To create the EncryptionPermissionAttribute class**

1. Add a new class file to the current project, **EncryptionPermissionAttribute.cs**.
2. Add the following **using** statements to the top of the new file.

```
using System.Security;
using System.Diagnostics;
using System.Security.Permissions;
```

3. Derive the attribute class from **CodeAccessSecurityAttribute**, and seal it.

```
public sealed class EncryptionPermissionAttribute :
                                CodeAccessSecurityAttribute
```

4. Add serialization support to the class, and use the **AttributeUsage** attribute to indicate where the custom permission attribute can be used.

```
[Serializable,
AttributeUsage(AttributeTargets.Method |      // Can use on methods
            AttributeTargets.Constructor |    // Can use on constructors
            AttributeTargets.Class |          // Can use on classes
            AttributeTargets.Struct |         // Can use on structures
            AttributeTargets.Assembly,        // Can use at the assembly level
            AllowMultiple = true,             // Can use multiple attribute
                                              // instances per program element
                                              // (class, method and so on)

            Inherited = false)]               // Can not be inherited
```

5. Add private member variables to the class to mirror the state maintained by the associated permission class.

```
// The following state fields mirror those used in the associated
// permission type.
private bool _encrypt = false;
private bool _decrypt = false;
private bool _machineStore = false;
private bool _userStore = false;
```

6. Replace the default constructor with the following constructor.

```
// Pass the action code back to the base class.
public EncryptionPermissionAttribute(SecurityAction action) : base(action)
{
}
```

7. Add the following public properties to mirror those provided by the associated permission class.

```
public bool Encrypt
{
  get {
    return _encrypt;
  }
  set {
    _encrypt = value;
  }
}
public bool Decrypt
{
  get {
    return _decrypt;
  }
  set {
    _decrypt = value;
  }
}
public bool UserStore
{
  get {
    return _userStore;
  }
  set {
    _userStore = value;
  }
}
public bool MachineStore
{
  get {
    return _machineStore;
  }
  set {
    _machineStore = value;
  }
}
```

8. Implement **SecurityPermissionAttribute.CreatePermission**. This method creates a permission object that can then be serialized and persisted with the specified **SecurityAction** enumeration in an assembly's metadata.

```
public override IPermission CreatePermission()
{
  // The runtime automatically provides a property to indicate
  // whether or not an unrestricted instance is required.
  if((Unrestricted) || ((_encrypt && _decrypt) &&
                        (_userStore && _machineStore)))
  {
    return new EncryptionPermission(PermissionState.Unrestricted);
  }
```

(continued)

```
      // Copy the state from the attribute to the permission object
      EncryptionPermissionFlag cipher = 0x0;
      StorePermissionFlag store = 0x0;

      if(_encrypt)
        cipher |= EncryptionPermissionFlag.Encrypt;

      if(_decrypt)
        cipher |= EncryptionPermissionFlag.Decrypt;

      if(_userStore)
        store |= StorePermissionFlag.User;

      if(_machineStore)
        store |= StorePermissionFlag.Machine;

      // Return the final permission.
      return new EncryptionPermission(cipher, store);
    }
```

9. Build the solution.

Step 3. Install the Permission Assembly in the GAC

You must grant full trust to any assembly that implements a custom security permission. In practice, this means that you need to install the assembly on the computer where it is used, to ensure that it is granted full trust by default security policy. Code within the **My_Computer_Zone** is granted full trust by default policy.

Installing an assembly in the GAC is one way to be sure it is granted full trust by code access security policy. The GAC is an appropriate location for the permission assembly because the assembly is used by code access security policy on the local computer and is available for any .NET Framework application that is installed on the local computer.

To install the custom permission assembly in the local computer's GAC, run the following command.

```
gacutil.exe /i custompermission.dll
```

Step 4. Update the DPAPI Managed Wrapper Code

DPAPI functionality is not currently exposed by the .NET Framework class library. To call DPAPI from a .NET Framework application, you must use **P/Invoke**. For code that demonstrates how to create a managed DPAPI wrapper assembly, see "How To: Create a DPAPI Library," in "Building Secure ASP.NET Applications: Authentication, Authorization, and Secure Communication," in the MSDN Library.

Without further modification, you can only call the managed DPAPI wrapper in the referenced How To article from full trust code. To be able to call the DPAPI wrapper from partial trust code, such as a medium trust ASP.NET Web application, you must sandbox the calls to the unmanaged DPAPI functions. To do this, make the following modifications:

- Assert the unmanaged code permission in the DPAPI wrapper code. This means that any calling code does not require the unmanaged code permission.

- Authorize the calling code inside the wrapper by demanding the custom **EncryptionPermission**. The **Demand** call occurs before the **Assert** call to, in accordance with the Demand/Assert usage pattern. For more information about using **Assert** safely, see "Assert and RevertAssert," in Chapter 8, "Code Access Security in Practice."

▶ **To modify the DPAPI managed wrapper**

1. Build the DPAPI managed wrapper by following the instructions in "How To: Create a DPAPI Library."

2. Add a reference to the **CustomPermission** assembly.

3. Open **dataprotection.cs** from the managed wrapper library, and add the following **using** statements beneath the existing **using** statements at the top of the file.

```
using System.Security;
using System.Security.Permissions;
using CustomPermissions;
```

4. Locate the **Encrypt** method in **dataprotection.cs**, and add the following code at the top of the outer **try** block in the **Encrypt** method.

```
// Set the storeFlag depending on how the caller uses
// the managed DPAPI wrapper.
StorePermissionFlag storeFlag;
if(Store.USE_MACHINE_STORE == store)
{
  storeFlag = StorePermissionFlag.Machine;
}
else
{
  storeFlag = StorePermissionFlag.User;
}
// Demand custom EncryptionPermission.
(new EncryptionPermission(EncryptionPermissionFlag.Encrypt, storeFlag)).
                                                          Demand();

// Assert the unmanaged code permission.
(new SecurityPermission(SecurityPermissionFlag.UnmanagedCode)).Assert();
// Now use P/Invoke to call the unmanaged DPAPI functions.
```

5. Add the following **finally** block to the outer try block in the **Encrypt** method.

```
finally
{
  CodeAccessPermission.RevertAssert();
}
```

6. Locate the **Decrypt** method in **dataprotection.cs,** and add the following code at the top of the outer try block.

```
StorePermissionFlag storeFlag;
if(Store.USE_MACHINE_STORE == store)
{
  storeFlag = StorePermissionFlag.Machine;
}
else
{
  storeFlag = StorePermissionFlag.User;
}
  // Demand custom EncryptionPermission.
  (new EncryptionPermission(EncryptionPermissionFlag.Decrypt, storeFlag)).
                                                  Demand();

  // Assert the unmanaged code permission.
  (new SecurityPermission(SecurityPermissionFlag.UnmanagedCode)).Assert();
```

7. Add the following **finally** block to the outer try block in the **Decrypt** method.

```
finally
{
  CodeAccessPermission.RevertAssert();
}
```

Step 5. Call DPAPI from a Medium Trust Web Application

To use the DPAPI managed wrapper from a medium trust Web application or any partial trust code, you must configure code access security policy to grant the code the custom **EncryptionPermission.**

In this step, you create a test Web application and then modify ASP.NET code access security policy for a medium trust Web application to grant it the **EncryptionPermission.**

▶ To create a test Web application

1. Add a new C# ASP.NET Web application project to your current solution.
2. Add a reference to the Dataprotection.dll assembly.
3. Add the following fields to Webform1.aspx.
   - An input field for the data to encrypt. Use the ID **txtDataToEncrypt**.
   - A field for the encrypted data. Use the ID **txtEncryptedData**.
   - A field for the decrypted data. Use the ID **txtDecryptedData**.
   - An **Encrypt** button. Use the ID **btnEncrypt**.
   - A **Decrypt** button. Use the ID **btnDecrypt**.
   - A label for an error message. Use the ID **lblError**.
4. Add the following **using** statement to the top of WebForm1.aspx.cs beneath the existing **using** statements.

   ```
   using DataProtection;
   ```

5. Add the following code for the **Encrypt** button-click event handler.

   ```
   private void btnEncrypt_Click(object sender, System.EventArgs e)
   {
     DataProtector dp = new DataProtector(
                         DataProtector.Store.USE_MACHINE_STORE );
     try
     {
       byte[] dataToEncrypt = Encoding.ASCII.GetBytes(txtDataToEncrypt.Text);
       // Not passing optional entropy in this example
       // Could pass random value (stored by the application) for added security
       // when using DPAPI with the machine store.
       txtEncryptedData.Text =
               Convert.ToBase64String(dp.Encrypt(dataToEncrypt,null));
     }
     catch(Exception ex)
     {
       lblError.ForeColor = Color.Red;
       lblError.Text = "Exception.<br>" + ex.Message;
       return;
     }
     lblError.Text = "";
   }
   ```

6. Add the following code for the **Decrypt** button-click event handler.

```
private void btnDecrypt_Click(object sender, System.EventArgs e)
{
  DataProtector dp = new DataProtector(DataProtector.Store.USE_MACHINE_STORE);
  try
  {
    byte[] dataToDecrypt = Convert.FromBase64String(txtEncryptedData.Text);
    // Optional entropy parameter is null.
    // If entropy was used within the Encrypt method, the same entropy
    // parameter must be supplied here.
    txtDecryptedData.Text =
        Encoding.ASCII.GetString(dp.Decrypt(dataToDecrypt,null));
  }
  catch(Exception ex)
  {
    lblError.ForeColor = Color.Red;
    lblError.Text = "Exception.<br>" + ex.Message;
    return;
  }
  lblError.Text = "";
}
```

7. Configure the Web application for medium trust by adding the following element to the application's Web.config file inside the **<system.web>** section.

```
<trust level="Medium" />
```

8. Build the solution.

▶ To modify medium trust policy

1. Open the medium trust policy file using Visual Studio® .NET or Notepad. The policy file is in the following location.

```
%windir%\Microsoft.NET\Framework\{version}\CONFIG\web_mediumtrust.config
```

2. Declare the **EncryptionPermission** by adding the following **<SecurityClass>** element to the **<SecurityClasses>** element.

```
<SecurityClass Name="EncryptionPermission"
            Description="CustomPermission.EncryptionPermission,
                     CustomPermission, Version=1.0.0.1,
                     Culture=neutral,
                     PublicKeyToken=951cd7d57a536a94"/>
```

Set the **PublicKeyToken** attribute value to the specific public key token for your assembly. To extract the public key token for your custom permission assembly, use the following command.

```
sn -T custompermission.dll
```

Note Use a capital **-T** switch.

3. Locate the ASP.NET named permission set in the medium trust policy file, and add the following permission element.

```
<IPermission class="EncryptionPermission"
              version="1" Flags="Encrypt,Decrypt"
              Stores="Machine,User">
</IPermission>
```

This permission grants medium trust Web applications the unrestricted **EncryptionPermission** because it allows code to encrypt and decrypt data and to use the DPAPI machine and user store. The above element demonstrates the supported syntax. It is equivalent to the following:

```
<IPermission class="EncryptionPermission"
              version="1" Unrestricted="true" >
</IPermission>
```

You can grant code a restricted permission by using only the relevant attributes. For example, to limit code to decrypt data using only the machine key in the machine store, use the following element.

```
<IPermission class="EncryptionPermission"
              version="1" Flags="Decrypt"
              Stores="Machine">
</IPermission>
```

4. Save the policy file.

You can now run the test Web application and verify that you can encrypt and decrypt data by using DPAPI from a partial trust Web application.

For more information about sandboxing highly privileged code and about working with ASP.NET code access security policy, see Chapter 9, "Using Code Access Security with ASP.NET."

How To:
Use Code Access Security Policy to Constrain an Assembly

Applies To

This information applies to server or workstation computers that run the following:

- Microsoft® Windows® 2000 Server and the Windows 2000 Professional, Windows Server 2003, Windows XP Professional operating systems
- Microsoft .NET Framework version 1.1

Summary

An administrator can configure code access security policy to constrain the operations of .NET Framework code (assemblies.) In this How To, you configure code access security policy to constrain the ability of an assembly to perform file I/O and restrict file I/O to a specific directory.

You use the.NET Framework 1.1 Configuration tool to create a new permission set and a new code group. The permission set defines what the code can and cannot do, and the code group associates the permission set with particular code, for example a specific assembly or set of assemblies.

In addition to constraining file I/O, you can use code access security policy to impose other constraints on code. For example, you can restrict the ability of code to access other types of resources protected by code access security, including databases, directory services, event log, registry, Domain Name System (DNS) servers, unmanaged code, and environment variables.

Note   This list is not exhaustive but represents many of the common resource types accessed by Web applications.

Before You Begin

Before you begin to use code access security policy to constrain an assembly, you should be aware of the following:

- To constrain a Web application so that it is only able to access files within its own virtual directory hierarchy, you can configure the application to run with medium trust by placing the following in Web.config:

```
<system.web>
  <trust level="Medium" />
</system.web>
```

  This uses ASP.NET code access security policy to constrain the ability of the Web application to perform file I/O and it also imposes other constraints. For example, a medium trust application cannot directly access the event log, registry, or OLE DB data sources.

- ASP.NET code access security policy is configured independently from enterprise-level, machine-level, and user-level code access security policy. The .NET Framework version 1.1 Configuration tool only supports enterprise-level, machine-level, and user-level policy.

  You must maintain ASP.NET policy by using a text or XML editor. For more information about running Web applications using medium trust, see Chapter 9, "Using Code Access Security with ASP.NET."

- When you build an assembly, you can impose constraints programmatically using code access security. For more information about how to do this, see Chapter 8, "Code Access Security in Practice."

- You should generally avoid building Web applications that accept file names and paths from the user because of the security risks posed by canonicalization issues. On occasion, you might need to accept a file name as input. This How To shows you how you can constrain an assembly to ensure that it cannot access arbitrary parts of the file system. For more information about performing file I/O, see "File I/O" sections in Chapter 7, "Building Secure Assemblies" and Chapter 8, "Using Code Access Security in Practice," of *Improving Web Application Security*.

- For more information about code access security fundamentals, see Chapter 8, "Code Access Security in Practice," of *Improving Web Application Security*.

Summary of Steps

This How To includes the following steps:

1. Create an assembly that performs file I/O.
2. Create a Web application.
3. Test file I/O with no code access security constraints.
4. Configure code access security policy to constrain file I/O.
5. Test file I/O with code access security constraints.

Step 1. Create an Assembly That Performs File I/O

In this step, you create an assembly that performs file I/O using a supplied filename.

▶ **To create a new assembly that performs file I/O**

1. Create a new Microsoft Visual C#™ development tool class library project called **FileIO** and rename **class1.cs** to **FileIO.cs**.

2. Add a strong name to the assembly.

   By adding a strong name, you make the assembly tamper proof by digitally signing it. The public key component of the strong name also provides cryptographically strong evidence for code access security policy. An administrator can apply policy by using the strong name to uniquely identify the assembly.

3. Use a fixed assembly version. Open Assemblyinfo.cs and set the **AssemblyVersion** attribute as shown below:

   ```
   [assembly: AssemblyVersion("1.0.0.1")]
   ```

4. Add the following **using** statements to the top of FileIO.cs:

   ```
   using System.IO;
   using System.Text;
   ```

5. Rename **Class1** to **FileWrapper** and seal the class to prevent inheritance.

   ```
   public sealed class FileWrapper
   ```

6. Rename the default constructor to match the class name and change it to **private**, which prevents instances of the **FileWrapper** class from being created. This class provides static methods only.

7. Add the following public method so that it reads from a specified file.

```
public static string ReadFile(string filename)
{
  byte[] fileBytes = null;
  long fileSize = -1;
  Stream fileStream = null;

  try
  {
    if(null == filename)
    {
      throw new ArgumentException("Missing filename");
    }
    // Canonicalize and validate the supplied filename
    // GetFullPath:
    // - Checks for invalid characters (defined by Path.InvalidPathChars)
    // - Checks for Win32 non file-type device names including
    //   physical drives, parallel and serial ports, pipes, mail slots,
    //   and so on
    // - Normalizes the file path

    filename = Path.GetFullPath(filename);
    fileStream = File.OpenRead(filename);
    if(!fileStream.CanRead)
    {
      throw new Exception("Unable to read from file.");
    }
    fileSize = fileStream.Length;
    fileBytes = new byte[fileSize];
    fileStream.Read(fileBytes, 0, Convert.ToInt32(fileSize));
    return Encoding.ASCII.GetString(fileBytes);
  }
  catch (Exception ex)
  {
    throw ex;
  }
  finally
  {
    if (null != fileStream)
      fileStream.Close();
  }
}
```

Step 2. Create a Web Application

In this step, you create a Web application assembly that calls the file I/O assembly.

▶ To create a Web application

1. Add a new C# ASP.NET Web application project called **FileIOWeb** to the current solution.
2. Add a project reference in the new project that references the **FileIO** project.
3. Add a text box to WebForm1.aspx to allow the user to supply a path and filename. Set its **Text** property to **c:\temp\somefile.txt** and set its **ID** to **txtFileName**.
4. Add a button to WebForm1.aspx and set its **Text** property to **Read File** and its **ID** to **btnReadFile**.
5. Double-click the **Read File** button and add the following code to the event handler:

```
string s = FileIO.FileWrapper.ReadFile( txtFileName.Text );
Response.Write(s);
```

6. Build the solution.

Step 3. Test File I/O with No Code Access Security Constraints

By default, Web applications and any assemblies they call on the local computer are granted full trust by code access security policy. The default **<trust>** configuration in Machine.config assigns the full trust level to all Web applications, as follows:

```
<trust level="Full" originUrl="" />
```

With full trust, Web applications are not constrained in any way by code access security policy. The success or failure of resource access is determined purely by operating system security.

▶ To test file I/O with no code access security constraints

1. Use Notepad to create a text file called Somefile.txt that contains a simple text string, and then place the file in the C:\temp directory. Also place a copy in the root C:\ directory.
2. Run the Web application and click **Read File**.
   The contents of the text file are displayed.
3. Enter c:\somefile.txt in the text box and click **Read File**.
   The contents of the text file are displayed.

Step 4. Configure Code Access Security Policy to Constrain File I/O

In this step, you configure code access security policy for the **FileIO** assembly and grant it a restricted **FileIOPermission** so that it is only able to access files from beneath C:\Temp. You start by creating a new permission set that includes a restricted **FileIOPermission**. You then create a new code group to associate the new permission set with the **FileIO** assembly by using strong name evidence.

▶ **To create a new permission set**

1. Start the .NET Framework version 1.1 Configuration tool from the Administrative Tools program folder.

2. Expand the **Runtime Security Policy** node.

   Three levels of code access security policy are displayed: Enterprise, Machine, and User. The fourth level at which you can configure code access security policy is the application domain level. ASP.NET implements application domain level policy, but this is not maintained using the .NET Framework version 1.1 Configuration tool. To edit ASP.NET policy, you must use a text editor.

   For more information about ASP.NET policy and how to use it, see Chapter 9, "Using Code Access Security with ASP.NET."

3. Expand the **Machine** node.

   The **Code Groups** and **Permission Sets** folders are displayed. Each policy file contains a hierarchical collection of code groups. Code groups are used to assign permissions to assemblies. A code group consists of two elements:

   - A membership condition—This is based on evidence, for example an assembly's strong name.

   - A permission set—The permissions that the permission set contains are granted to assemblies whose evidence matches the membership condition.

   A *permission set* is a grouping that contains a collection of individual code access security permissions. Individual permissions represent the rights for code to access specific resource types or perform specific types of privileged operations.

4. Right-click **Permission Sets**, and then click **New**.

5. Enter **RestictedFileIO** in the **Name** field, and then click **Next**.

6. Select **FileIO** from the **Available Permissions** list, and then click **Add**.

7. Enter **c:\temp** in the **File Path** column and select **Read** and **Path Disc** (path discovery.)

   Path discovery permissions are required by the **Path.GetFullPath** function that is used by the **FileIO** assembly to canonicalize and validate the supplied filename.

   Read permissions are required by the **File.OpenRead** method, which is used by the **FileIO** assembly to open the text file.

8. Click **OK**.

9. Select **Security** from the **Available Permissions** list and click **Add**.

   The **FileIO** assembly also needs the permission to execute in addition to the **FileIOPermission**. The permission to execute is represented by **SecurityPermission** with its **Flags** property set to **SecurityPermissionFlag.Execution**.

10. Click **Enable assembly execution**, and then click **OK**.

11. Click **Finish** to complete the creation of the permission set.

    You have now created a new permission set called **RestrictedFileIO** that contains a restricted **FileIOPermission**, which allows read and path discovery to the C:\Temp directory, and a restricted **SecurityPermission**, which allows assembly execution.

▶ **To create a new code group**

1. Expand **Code Groups**, and then expand **All_Code**.

2. Right-click **All_Code**, and then click **New**.

3. Enter **FileIOAssembly** as the code group name, and then click **Next**.

4. Select **StrongName** from the **Choose the condition type for this code group** drop-down list.

   You use this code group to apply specific permissions as defined by the **RestrictedFileIO** permission set to the **FileIO** assembly. A strong name provides cryptographically strong evidence to uniquely identify an assembly.

5. To specify the **FileIO** assembly's public key, (which it has because it contains a strong name), click **Import**, and then browse to the project output folder that contains FileIO.dll. Click **Open** to extract the public key from the assembly.

6. Click **Next**, and then select **RestrictedFileIO** from the **Use existing permission set** drop-down list.

7. Click **Next** and then **Finish** to complete the creation of the code group.

   You have now created a new code group that applies the permissions defined by the **RestrictedFileIO** permission set to the **FileIO** assembly.

8. In the right window, select the **FileIOAssembly** code group, and then click **Edit Code Group Properties**.

9. Select **This policy level will only have the permissions from the permission set associated with this code group and Policy levels below this level will not be evaluated**.

   By selecting these attributes for the code group, you ensure that no other code group, either at the current machine level or from the ASP.NET application domain level, affects the permission set that is granted to the **FileIO** assembly. This ensures that the assembly is only granted the permissions defined by the **RestrictedFileIO** permission set that you created earlier.

   Note   If you do not select these options, default machine policy grants the assembly full trust because the assembly is installed on the local computer and falls within the **My_Computer_Zone** setting.

10. Click **OK** to close the Properties dialog box.

Step 5. Test File I/O With Code Access Security Constraints

In this procedure, you install the **FileIO** assembly in the global assembly cache (GAC). You then run the Web application and try to access files inside and outside of C:\Temp. The code access security policy that you configured in Step 4 constrains the code so that it is only allowed to access files from beneath C:\Temp.

The assembly should be installed in the GAC because of the ASP.NET loads strong named assemblies as domain neutral assemblies. All strong named assemblies that ASP.NET Web applications call should be installed in the GAC. For more information about this issue, see "Strong Names" in Chapter 7, "Building Secure Assemblies."

Note   Normally, default machine policy and ASP.NET policy grant full trust to assemblies that are installed in the GAC. The **This policy level will only have the permissions from the permission set associated with this code group and Policy levels below this level will not be evaluated** attributes that you assigned to the code group created in Step 4 ensure that the assembly is not granted full trust, and is only granted the permissions defined by the **RestrictedFileIO** permission set that you created earlier.

▶ **To test file I/O with code access security constraints**

1. Install the **FileIO** assembly into the GAC using the Gacutil.exe utility.

   You can call Gacutil.exe as a post-build step to ensure that it is placed in the GAC when it has been successfully built inside Microsoft Visual Studio® .NET.

   a. Display the **FileIO** project's **Properties** dialog box in Visual Studio .NET.

   b. In **Common Properties**, select **Build Events**.

   c. Type "C:\Program Files\Microsoft Visual Studio .NET 2003\SDK\v1.1 \Bin\gacutil" -i $(TargetPath) in the **Post-build Event Command Line** field.

   d. Click **OK** to close the project Properties dialog box.

2. Rebuild the solution.

3. Run Iisreset.exe from a command line to force the ASP.NET process to be recycled.

   This forces the permission grant for the **FileIO** assembly to be recomputed. If the ASP.NET application domain is still active from the last time you ran the Web application, the assembly could still be cached by ASP.NET.

4. Run the Web application, and then click **Read File**.

   The contents of the text file should be successfully displayed. The policy that you created allows the **FileIO** assembly to read files from C:\Temp and below.

5. Enter C:\somefile.txt in the text box, and then click **Read File**.

   A **SecurityException** should be generated because the code access security policy that you configured does not allow file I/O outside of the C:\Temp directory.

   The exception details indicate that a request for the FileIOPermission has failed, as shown below:

```
System.Security.SecurityException: Request for the permission of type
System.Security.Permissions.FileIOPermission, mscorlib, Version=1.0.5000.0,
Culture=neutral, PublicKeyToken=b77a5c561934e089 failed.
```

Index

G